AMISH
Cooking

AMISH
Cooking

· Deluxe Edition ·

Compiled by a Committee of Amish Women

HERALD PRESS
Scottdale, Pennsylvania
Kitchener, Ontario

AMISH COOKING (Deluxe Edition)
Copyright © 1980 by Pathway Publishing Corporation
Published by Herald Press, Scottdale, Pa. 15683 and
    simultaneously in Canada by Herald Press,
    Kitchener, Ont. N2G 4M5. All rights reserved.
Library of Congress Catalog Card Number: 81-80123
International Standard Book Number: 0-8361-1958-4
Editor: Mark Eric Miller. *Illustrations:* Donald V. Sands.
Food Consultant: Dorothy Ferguson. *Design:* First Image.
Printed in the United States of America

90 89 88 87 86 85 84 10 9 8 7 6 5 4 3 2

TABLE OF CONTENTS

USING METRIC MEASUREMENTS

As foods and kitchen implements are increasingly sold in metric sizes, it may be a good idea to try to accustom yourself to using metric measures. It is easy to do and requires a minimum of new equipment.

Liquid measuring cups already have liter markings on the right side. For dry food measuring (where you can level off the top for accurate measuring) you will need a set of three milliliter measures: 250, 125 and 50. As well, a set of five small milliliter measures will be handy: 25, 15, 5, 2 and 1. As we are already accustomed to measuring by weight in the case of meats, butter, cheese, chocolate etc., we have only to adjust from pounds and ounces to kilograms, grams and milligrams. Otherwise, measuring is still done by volume.

If you wish to convert the recipes in this book to metric, the following tables may be helpful. It is important to note that baking recipes may not work by doing an exact conversion from Imperial to metric. Measure as closely as you can, and learn through trial and error.

Metric		Imperial
Measurements		
1 kilogram	*replaces*	2 pounds
500 grams	*replace*	1 pound
1 liter	*replaces*	1 quart
250 milliliters	*replace*	1 cup
125 milliliters	*replace*	½ cup
50 milliliters	*replace*	⅓ to ¼ cup
15 milliliters	*replace*	1 tablespoon
5 milliliters	*replace*	1 teaspoon
Baking Dishes		
2-liter square baking pan	*replaces*	8-inch square baking pan
2.5-liter square baking pan	*replaces*	9-inch square baking pan
1.3-liter round cake pan	*replaces*	8-inch round cake pan
1.5-liter round cake pan	*replaces*	9-inch round cake pan
1.5-liter loaf pan	*replaces*	8 x 4-inch loaf pan
2-liter loaf pan	*replaces*	9 x 5-inch loaf pan
3.5-liter rectangular pan	*replaces*	9 x 13-inch rectangular pan
22.5-centimeter pie plate	*replaces*	9-inch pie plate

Oven Conversion Temperatures

100°C	=	200°F	(warming)
140°C	=	275°F	(fruitcake)
150°C	=	300°F	(soufflé)
160°C	=	325°F	(roasting)
180°C	=	350°F	(cakes)
190°C	=	375°F	(quickbread)
200°C	=	400°F	(muffins)
220°C	=	425°F	(tea biscuits)
230°C	=	450°F	(fish)

TABLE OF EQUIVALENT MEASURES

1 stick (¼ pound) butter or margarine = ½ cup
1 square chocolate = 3 tablespoons cocoa
2 large eggs = 3 small eggs
1 cup macaroni = 2¼ cups cooked
1 cup buttermilk = 1 or 2 tablespoons vinegar with sweet milk to fill cup (let stand 5 minutes)
1 tablespoon quick-cooking tapioca = 1 tablespoon cornstarch or 1⅓ to 1½ tablespoons flour
1 package active dry yeast = 1 tablespoon
1 package plain gelatin = 1 tablespoon
1 pound granulated sugar = 2 cups
1 pound brown sugar = 2¼ to 2½ cups (packed)
1 pound confectioner's or icing sugar = 4 to 4½ cups (sifted)
1 pound all-purpose flour = 4 cups
1 pound butter = 2 cups
1 can soup = 1¼ cups

AMISH BEGINNINGS

The Amish are one of the few minority groups which have escaped the great "melting pot" of North America. Because they have been able to retain a group identity, they have become very visible to the general public. As a result, many books, magazine features, newspaper accounts and sociological studies of the Amish have been published. However, not all that has been written is accurate, leaving the question in many people's minds, "Who really are the Amish?"

The Amish (pronounced "Ah-mish") are the direct descendants of the Swiss Brethren who in 1525 left both the Catholic Church and the Protestant Reformed Church. The Swiss Brethren, or "Anabaptists" as they were often called, did not believe in infant baptism, taking oaths, fighting wars or dressing in stylish clothing. Another of their main tenets was complete separation of church and state, a principle taken for granted in many nations today but unheard of in sixteenth-century Europe.

Because of their religious views, many of the Amish forbears were martyred. To escape this persecution they migrated across the Swiss border into Alsace, today a part of France. There, between 1693 and 1700, the Swiss Brethren experienced a division among themselves. Bishop Jacob Ammann, from whom the Amish derive their name, felt the congregations were becoming lax and called for a stricter observance. His followers became known as "Amish" and the others as "Mennonites" after Menno Simons, a Dutch Anabaptist bishop of the sixteenth century. Today many people confuse these two groups which in fact are separate and distinct denominations even though they share a common historical connection.

When King Louis XIV expelled the Amish from France in 1712, they were forced to migrate to Germany, which at the time was composed of several independent states. Over the following 100 years, the Amish settled in various areas of Germany where they were tolerated by local rulers. But as early as 1720 some Amish immigrated to America where they settled in the present area of Pennsylvania. Most, however, made the journey after 1800, and by 1824 some Amish began to immigrate to Canada, settling in Ontario. Eventually so many Amish left Europe that congregations there became extinct. Of the 80,000 Amish in North America today, 98 per cent live in the United States, primarily in Pennsylvania, Ohio and Indiana and in 18 other states, while the remainder live in Ontario.

The Amish are a rural people who have retained many older customs, such as the horse and buggy as their means of transportation, and their distinctive cooking and eating habits. All Amish farmhouses have vegetable gardens and truck patches beside them which provide the families with a year-round supply of vegetables. The result is cellars lined with shelves of canned goods—not the kind from the supermarket but glass ones containing the produce from their own land and labor.

As homecooked meals are the center of each Amish family's day, it is an infrequent event for them to eat in restaurants. Thus it is only natural that recipes would be shared among the Amish to provide wholesome yet varied meals, and that these recipes would eventually be collected in book form.

Amish Cooking did not originate from any one Amish person or Amish region. It contains recipes from areas throughout the United States and Canada. Originally the book appeared in 1965 as *Favorite Amish Family Recipes* and contained recipes mainly from the Amish settlement in Mifflin County, Pennsylvania. Then, in 1977, it appeared with its new title, *Amish Cooking,* containing about half the recipes from the former book. Other recipes were selected from the Amish monthly magazine, *Family Life,* which has a section of recipes from a wide range of regions and generations in each issue. Some of these recipes have been handed down from grandmother to granddaughter, while others were taken from farm magazines over the years. None would be selected for gourmet cooking, but all are simple and hearty. These recipes are time-tested by a people who know about delicious yet practical cooking. You will enjoy them too.

David Luthy
PATHWAY PUBLISHING CORPORATION
Aylmer, Ontario
July, 1980

BREADS

HINTS FOR BREADS

- Some recipes call for cake yeast and others for dried yeast—they are interchangeable. One package of yeast is the same as one cake of yeast. If bulk yeast is used, 1 tablespoon is the equivalent of 1 package.

- Adding a little sugar to the liquid used to dissolve the yeast will make it more active.

- All milk used in bread recipes should be scalded then cooled to lukewarm before using.

- For many bread and roll recipes, the steps may be simplified if all the liquid, sugar, salt and even the shortening is put into a bowl and the yeast sprinkled or crumbled in to dissolve it. When the yeast is dissolved or becomes bubbly, add the rest of the ingredients that the various recipes call for.

- When making bread or rolls, always have the flour at room temperature before mixing. This will help keep the dough at a warm temperature and encourage it to rise.

- Always use all-purpose flour with any recipe that calls for yeast. To many people this is simply known as bread flour. It is made from hard wheat. Some common brands are Maple Leaf, Five Roses, Pillsbury, Gold Medal and Robin Hood. Use any brand you prefer.

- If your bread loaves get flat instead of nice and round, try making a stiffer dough.

- For a finer textured bread, try letting the dough rise in a place where it is a little cooler.

- Using milk instead of another liquid usually gives a softer crust which becomes a richer brown when baked.

- People who bake regularly will not need to grease their bread pans before baking if:
  –they do not wash the pans between bakings
  –they work out the loaves with greased hands
  –new or cleaned pans are seasoned by greasing them well for a few bakings and setting them aside without washing.

- Bread will then slip easily out of the pans, leaving them clean and ready for the next time.

- For best results with bread, have the water very warm, but not hot, about 115°.

- For extra flavor in your homemade bread, use cooking oil instead of lard.

- Bread is better when worked down twice or more.

- If bread is baked before it rises to double size, it will not crumble so easily.

  Replace ⅛ of the water with vinegar in your bread recipe if you do not make the dough too stiff. The dough should be sticky so that you have to use shortening on your hands to work it.

  You can add whole wheat flour to any bread recipe if you do not make the dough too stiff. Again, the dough should be sticky so that you have to use shortening on your hands to work it.

- When taking bread from the oven, grease the top to make the crust softer.

11

GENERAL BREAD MAKING DIRECTIONS

After mixing the ingredients as directed in the recipe, grease your hands and knead the dough vigorously for about five to ten minutes, or until the dough squeaks. You may wish to turn the dough out on a floured table top for kneading. Place the dough in a greased bowl and grease the top of it. Cover it and set it in a warm place, out of drafts, and let it rise until double in size. Knead it lightly. Again grease the bowl and the top of the dough and let it rise until double. Repeat this procedure until the dough has risen two or three times (or whatever the recipe calls for).

Divide the dough into the required portions and form them into loaves. Bang each loaf hard with the palm of your hand to get rid of air bubbles. Place the loaves, smooth side up, into greased loaf pans, brush the top of each loaf with grease and prick them deeply with a fork to release any further air bubbles. Let them rise until double in size, and bake as directed. Grease the top of each loaf again immediately after removing it from the oven. Remove the loaves from the pans and cool them on racks.

Sealing bread in plastic bags before it has completely cooled will keep the crust nice and soft.

AYLMER BREAD

For each loaf use:
1 cup very warm water
1 teaspoon melted lard or cooking oil
1 teaspoon salt (scant)
(milk may be used as part of liquid, if
    desired)

1 tablespoon sugar
1 teaspoon dry yeast
3 cups all-purpose flour

Combine the first 5 ingredients in the order given. Let the mixture stand until the yeast dissolves. Stir in ½ of the flour, beat it until smooth, then add the remaining flour. Work the dough on a greased board or in a bowl, kneading it vigorously with both hands for 5 to 10 minutes, or until the dough squeaks. Grease your hands lightly if the dough sticks to them while working. Cover the dough and set it in a warm place (out of any draft) to rise until double in size. Knead the dough lightly, then let it rise again until double in size. Knead once again. After you have let the dough rise again, punch it down and divide it into loaves. Brush grease over each loaf and prick it deeply with a fork. This will release air bubbles. Let the loaves rise until they are double in size. Bake them for 30 minutes or until done: 15 minutes at 400°, and the remaining 15 minutes at 350°.

Grease the top of the loaves when you remove them from the oven. Take them out of their pans, and cool them on racks.

For 8 loaves, use 2 rounded tablespoons of yeast.

BROWN BREAD

3 cups lukewarm water
2 tablespoons sugar
6 tablespoons cake yeast
1⅓ cups milk
1¼ cups honey (or brown sugar)

2 tablespoons salt
⅔ cup butter or corn oil
5 to 6 cups whole wheat flour
White (unbleached) flour

Pour the water into a large bowl, adding the sugar and yeast, then let it stand for 10 minutes without stirring.

Scald the milk and add to it the honey, salt and melted butter. Set it aside to cool, then add it to the yeast mixture and mix well. Stir in 5 to 6 cups of whole wheat flour. Then add enough white flour to make a soft dough. Knead it for 15 minutes or until the dough is smooth and elastic. Divide the dough into loaves, and bake them at 350° for 45 minutes. This recipe makes 6 medium-sized loaves.

HEALTH-CONSCIOUS HOUSEWIFE BREAD

2 cups stone ground whole wheat flour
2 cups rye flour
2 cups unbleached white flour
1 pint buttermilk, whey, or sweet milk
2 tablespoons brown sugar

1 tablespoon dark molasses
½ teaspoon salt
2 rounded tablespoons dry yeast
1 cup warm water
1 teaspoon brown or white sugar
¾ cup lard

Mix all 3 flours in a large bowl and have the mixture ready to use. Heat the 1 quart of liquid to more than lukewarm, but not hot, before pouring it into a large bowl. Then add the 2 tablespoons of brown sugar, the molasses and salt, stirring well until they are dissolved. Melt the yeast in the 1 cup of warm water, adding to it 1 teaspoon of brown or white sugar. (This makes it rise faster). When the yeast is dissolved and beginning to rise, add it to the liquid mixture.

With a large spoon, stir in enough of the previously mixed flours to make a stiff batter. Then add the melted lard and beat the dough until it is smooth. Let the dough rise for 12 minutes, a step which is very important if you want a soft brown bread. After this time has elapsed, add more flour to form a bread dough the same as for white bread—if this is not enough, add more unbleached or white flour to finish. This recipe makes 3 medium-sized loaves.

If flour is left over, you can always store it for use in the next batch. Bread made by this method never gets stiff or hard with age. Never bake it in a too hot oven—350° is about right, for 1 hour (although oven thermometers tend to vary).

POTATO BREAD

1 medium-sized potato	2 packages dry yeast
1 quart water	1 teaspoon sugar
2 tablespoons butter	1 cup warm water
3 teaspoons salt	11 to 12 cups sifted all-purpose flour

Cook the diced, peeled potato in the quart of water until it is tender. Drain the potato, reserving the water, and mash it until no lumps remain. Add the mashed potato to the reserved water, and stir in the butter and salt. Let this mixture cool until it is lukewarm. Dissolve the yeast and sugar in the 1 cup of warm water, and let it stand for 5 to 10 minutes. Gradually add 6 cups of the flour to the potato water, beating it until it is smooth. Mix in the dissolved yeast/sugar mixture, and beat it thoroughly. Cover and let the dough rise in a warm place for about 2 hours. Then work in enough of the remaining flour to make a soft dough.

On a floured surface, knead the dough until it is smooth and satiny. Put it into a greased bowl, greasing the top of the dough. Cover, then let it rise until it is double in size, which should take about 1½ hours. Punch down the dough and divide it into 3 portions. Form each portion into a loaf and place each loaf in a greased pan. Cover and let the loaves rise until they are double in size, for about 30 to 40 minutes. Bake them at 375° for 40 minutes, then allow the loaves to cool.

Variations: For Raisin Bread add 1 pound of dark seedless raisins, ½ teaspoon of cloves, and 2 teaspoons of cinnamon after all the flour has been worked in. Also add ½ cup more of sugar. Frost the bread with confectioner's (icing) sugar.

OATMEAL BREAD

4 cups boiling water	4 tablespoons butter or margarine
2 cups instant oatmeal	2 packages dry yeast
1 cup whole wheat flour	1 cup warm water
½ cup brown sugar	10 cups all-purpose or bread flour
2 tablespoons salt	(approximate)

Mix the oatmeal, whole wheat flour, sugar, salt and butter with the boiling water, then cool the batter until it is lukewarm. Dissolve the yeast in the warm water and add it to the batter. Add enough white flour to make an elastic dough. Place it in a bowl and let it rise before punching it down and letting it rise again until double in size. Shape the dough into 4 loaves, and let them rise again until they are about double. Bake them at 350° for 30 minutes or longer, until done.

RAISIN OATMEAL BATTER BREAD

1 package active dry yeast
2 cups warm water
1½ teaspoons salt
3 tablespoons sugar
2 tablespoons soft shortening

2 cups all-purpose flour
1 cup rolled oats
2 cups whole wheat flour
½ cup seedless raisins

In a large mixing bowl, dissolve the yeast in the warm water. Stir in the salt, sugar and shortening, plus 2 cups of the flour, and the rolled oats. Beat this mixture for 3 minutes, then stir in the rest of the flour and the raisins, mixing it until the batter is smooth and satiny. Cover it with a cloth and let it rise in a warm place until it is double in size. Stir it down while counting slowly to 15, then spoon the batter into a greased loaf pan. Cover it with a cloth and let it rise before baking it in 2 greased loaf pans at 350° for 50 minutes.

HONEY OATMEAL BREAD

2 packages dry yeast
1 cup warm water
2½ cups boiling water
2 cups instant oatmeal
1 cup honey (or part corn syrup)

¾ cup cooking oil
4 beaten eggs
2 tablespoons salt
2 cups or more whole wheat flour
White unbleached flour

Dissolve the yeast in the cup of warm water. Pour the boiling water over the oatmeal and set it aside to cool until it is lukewarm. Then, being sure that everything is just warm before adding, mix together with the oatmeal the rest of the ingredients except the yeast and flour, and beat the mixture well. Add the yeast, and work in enough white flour (preferably unbleached) to make a nice spongy dough that is not sticky. Grease the top of the dough before letting it rise, then knead it and let it rise again. Divide it into 3 loaves, and bake them at 400° for 10 minutes, then at 350° for 25 to 30 minutes.

This is a delicious, nourishing bread.

BEST WHOLE WHEAT BREAD

2 cups milk
⅓ cup, plus 2 tablespoons shortening
⅓ cup sugar
1 tablespoon salt
2 cups whole wheat flour

3 tablespoons yeast
1 cup very warm water
1 cup cold water
White unbleached flour

Scald the milk, then add the shortening, sugar and salt, stirring until it is dissolved. Add the whole wheat flour and beat it rapidly with a spoon. Dissolve the yeast in the warm water, then add it, with the cold water, to the mixture. Mix it well, then add enough white flour to mike a nice, soft dough. Knead it for 10 minutes. Let it rise until it is double in size, then punch it down and turn it over in a greased bowl. Let it rise again until double, then shape the dough into 3 loaves and spank them quite hard to remove all the air bubbles. Cover them for 15 minutes, letting the dough rise until double, then bake them at 350° for 50 to 60 minutes.

WHOLE WHEAT BREAD

1 cake yeast
¼ cup lukewarm water
2 tablespoons sugar
2 cups milk, scalded

1 tablespoon salt
3¼ cups sifted whole wheat flour
2 tablespoons cooking oil
2¼ cups all-purpose flour

Crumble the yeast into the lukewarm water and add 1 teaspoon of sugar. Stir it well, then let it stand in a warm place until foamy. Pour the milk into a mixing bowl, adding the remaining sugar, and salt. Cool this mixture until it is lukewarm, then add the yeast. Add 3 cups of the whole wheat flour, beating it thoroughly, then add the cooking oil. Stir in enough of the all-purpose flour to make a soft dough. Let it stand for 10 minutes before turning it onto a floured board. Knead the dough for 10 minutes while working in the remaining whole wheat flour, until it is soft but not sticky. Place it in a bowl and let the dough rise. Knead it again, then shape it into 2 loaves. Let them rise until double in bulk. Bake them at 400° (a hot oven) for 10 minutes, then reduce the heat to 375° and bake them for 40 minutes more.

QUICK YEAST ROLLS

2 tablespoons sugar
2 tablespoons shortening, melted and
    cooled
1½ teaspoons salt

1 cake yeast or 1 package granules
1 cup lukewarm water
3¼ cups sifted bread flour

Add the sugar, shortening, salt and crumbled yeast to the lukewarm water before adding 1 cup of the flour and beating it with a rotary beater until smooth. Then mix in the remaining flour. Place the dough on a slightly floured board and let it rest for about 5 minutes. Knead the dough until it is smooth, then place it in a greased bowl, cover it and allow it to rise for about 1 hour. Follow the directions for Chelsea Buns (see page 18) to roll the dough into buns. Bake them in a hot oven (450°) for 12 to 15 minutes. This recipe makes 18 medium-sized rolls.

CORNMEAL ROLLS

⅓ cup cornmeal
½ cup sugar
1 teaspoon salt
½ cup melted shortening
2 cups milk

2 eggs, beaten
1 package yeast
¼ cup lukewarm water
4 cups all-purpose flour

Combine the cornmeal, sugar, salt, shortening and milk in a double boiler, cooking the mixture until it is thick, stirring it often. Cool it to lukewarm, adding the eggs, and the yeast dissolved in water. Beat the mixture well. Let it rise in a greased bowl for 2 hours, then add the flour to form a soft dough. Knead it lightly, letting it rise in a greased bowl for 1 hour. Knead the dough again before rolling it out and cutting it with a biscuit cutter. Brush the dough pieces with fat, crease them, and fold them like Parkerhouse rolls. Place them on an oiled sheet to rise for 1 hour, then bake them at 375° for 15 minutes. This recipe makes a very soft dough. It yields 3 dozen rolls, which may be made in different shapes—use flour generously when handling and shaping them.

PULL BUNS ("PLUCKETS")

⅓ cup sugar
⅓ cup melted butter
½ teaspoon salt
1 cup scalded milk

1 yeast cake
¼ cup lukewarm water
3 eggs, well-beaten
3¾ cups all-purpose flour
(approximate)

Add the sugar, butter and salt to the scalded milk. When it becomes lukewarm, add the yeast (which has been dissolved in the ¼ cup lukewarm water), the eggs and just enough flour to make a stiff batter. Cover and let it rise until the mixture doubles in bulk, then knead it down and let it rise again. Roll the dough into small balls, about the size of walnuts, and dip them into melted butter. Then roll each ball in a mixture of the following:

¾ cup sugar
½ cup ground nut meats
3 teaspoons cinnamon

Pile the balls loosely in an ungreased angel food cake pan and let them rise again for 30 minutes. (Do not use a pan with a removable bottom.) Bake the buns until they are brown, about 40 minutes, beginning at 400° and decreasing the heat after 10 minutes to 350°. Turn the pan upside down and remove them immediately, serving them while still warm.

The buns will be stuck together and that's the way you serve them. Everyone plucks his bun right from the central supply. (If you want these for dinner, start the recipe in the morning.)

CHELSEA BUNS

½ cup cooled mashed potatoes
½ cup lukewarm water
1 teaspoon sugar
1 package dry yeast
⅓ cup melted shortening

2 well-beaten eggs
⅓ cup sugar
½ teaspoon salt
2½ cups all-purpose flour
  (approximate)

Combine the potatoes, water and 1 teaspoon of sugar, then sprinkle the yeast on top. Let it stand until the yeast is dissolved. Add the rest of the ingredients, stirring in enough flour to make a soft dough (less stiff than bread dough). Knead it until it is smooth, then let it rise until double in bulk before rolling the dough out to a 9 x 15-inch rectangle.

2 tablespoons soft butter
¾ cup brown sugar
¼ cup corn syrup

½ teaspoon vanilla
½ cup chopped nuts

Mix together the above ingredients except the nuts, and spread the mixture in a greased 9 x 13-inch pan. Then sprinkle the nuts over this mixture and set it aside. This is equally good if you substitute raisins for the nuts, or even if you don't use either ingredient.

¼ cup soft butter
¾ cup brown sugar

1 tablespoon cinnamon
1 cup washed raisins

(See Illustration 1–.) Spread the butter on the rolled rectangle of dough and sprinkle it with the sugar, cinnamon and raisins. (See Illustration 2–.) Roll it up like a jelly roll and cut it into 15 one-inch slices (–see Illustrations 3 and 4). (See Illustration 5–.) Place the slices cut-side down in the previously prepared pan. Cover and let them rise until they fill the pan, then bake them at 375° for about 40 minutes. Cool the buns for 3 minutes before inverting the pan to remove them.

1. Roll a portion of the dough into a 9 x 15-inch rectangle about ¼ inch thick. Spread with the soft butter and sprinkle with sugar, cinnamon and raisins.

2. Roll up as you would for a jelly roll.

3. To slice, slip a length of regular sewing thread under the roll, placing the thread to make slices about 1 inch thick.

4. Cross the two ends above the roll and pull. You will have a perfect, clean-cut slice.

5. Place the slices, cut side down, in the previously prepared 9 x 13-inch cake pan, about ½ inch apart.

SWEET BUNS

3 cups lukewarm water
1½ cups sugar
1 cake yeast

1 tablespoon lard
1 tablespoon salt
All-purpose flour

Mix together the first 5 ingredients until the yeast is dissolved. Then stir in enough flour (about 8 cups) to make a fairly stiff dough. Let it rise in a warm place for 2 hours. Punch down the dough and form it into balls the size of a small egg. Place them on a greased baking pan and let them rise until double in size. Bake them at 400° for 10 to 15 minutes, or until they are golden brown.

For sandwich buns, make the dough balls slightly larger and flatten them with your hands.

COFFEE BUNS

Dissolve 1 package of dry yeast in ¼ cup of lukewarm water. Mix the following like pie crumbs;

4 cups bread flour
1 cup shortening
¼ cup sugar

Then add and mix thoroughly along with the dissolved yeast;

2 eggs
1 cup milk, scalded and cooled
1 teaspoon salt
½ teaspoon lemon extract

Let the dough rise in the refrigerator overnight. Then divide it into 3 parts, rolling them out and spreading them with melted butter and sprinkling them with brown sugar and cinnamon. Roll the dough up like a jelly roll and slice it very thinly (it is not necessary to let it rise again) before baking it at 350° for 15 minutes or until brown.

Top it with powdered sugar icing if preferred: Dissolve 1 cup of powdered sugar in a very small amount of hot water, then dribble it over the hot buns.

BUTTERHORNS

1 cake yeast
½ cup sugar
3 eggs, beaten
1 cup lukewarm water

½ cup melted margarine
1 teaspoon salt
4½ to 5 cups sifted all-purpose flour

Blend the yeast with 1 tablespoon of the sugar, then add the beaten eggs and the rest of the sugar. Add the rest of the ingredients, the flour last, and put it into the refrigerator overnight. The next morning, roll out the dough like a pie dough, cut it into pie-wedge shapes and roll them up before dipping them into melted margarine. Let them rise for 3 hours before baking them at 325° for 15 to 20 minutes.

If you leave the dough in the refrigerator for awhile, punch it down each day.

NO-KNEAD ROLLS

4 cups milk
11 tablespoons margarine
2 or 3 packages cake yeast, OR
2 heaping tablespoons dry yeast
⅓ cup sugar
1 cup warm water

1½ cups sugar
5 eggs, beaten
2 teaspoons salt
All-purpose flour
Butter
Cinnamon

Scald the milk, then add the margarine. While this mixture cools to lukewarm, mix the yeast with the ⅓ cup of sugar in the cup of warm water. When the milk mixture has cooled to about 115° (lukewarm), add the 1½ cups of sugar, the eggs, salt and the yeast and water mixture. Add the flour, 1½ cups or more for each cup of liquid—it should make a dough soft enough to stir with a spoon. Let it rise, then stir it down and let it rise again before rolling the dough out on a floured board. Butter it well and sprinkle it with cinnamon. Roll up the dough and cut slices about 1-inch thick. Place them on buttered cookie sheets or baking pans, and let them rise until they are light and fluffy before baking them in a 350° oven for 15 to 20 minutes or until golden brown. Frost the rolls when they have cooled.

The rolls may be dipped in melted margarine and rolled in the following mixture:

1½ cups white sugar
1½ cups brown sugar
2 tablespoons cinnamon
½ cup nuts

Place the coated rolls on buttered pans and let them rise. Bake them as above, removing them from the pans while still warm.

RAISIN CINNAMON ROLLS

½ cup milk
1½ teaspoons salt
½ cup sugar
¼ cup shortening
2 tablespoons dry yeast

½ cup lukewarm water
2 teaspoons sugar
2 eggs, beaten
4 cups all-purpose flour
Melted butter

Scald the milk, then add the salt, sugar and shortening. Cool it to lukewarm. Sprinkle the yeast over the ½ cup of lukewarm water to which the 2 teaspoons of sugar have been added. Let this mixture stand for 10 to 15 minutes before stirring it and adding it to the milk. Add the beaten eggs, then work in about 4 cups of flour. Cover the batter and let it rise until double in bulk. Divide the dough in 2 and roll each half into a 9 x 12-inch rectangle. Brush each half with melted butter and sprinkle it with the following mixture:

1 cup brown sugar
2 tablespoons cinnamon
⅔ cup raisins

Roll up the rectangles as you would for jelly rolls. Cut them into 1-inch slices and place them on greased pans. Cover and let them rise until double in bulk, then bake them at 350° for about 35 minutes. Frost the rolls while they are warm with the following icing:

1 cup icing sugar
¼ teaspoon vanilla
Enough milk to make a stiff icing

IDA MAE DOUGHNUTS

Add 1½ packages of yeast to 2 cups of warm water and 1 cup of scalded milk (lukewarm) to which ½ cup of sugar has been added. Let the mixture stand for 15 minutes, then add:

¾ cup cream
5 eggs, beaten
¾ cup raisins, if desired

½ cup margarine or butter
1 cup sugar
½ teaspoon salt

Also add 9 to 10 cups of flour—enough to make a moderately stiff dough. Let it rise, then roll it out, cutting out doughnuts before letting it rise again. Deep fry the doughnuts in lard or cooking oil, first adding several tablespoons of vinegar to keep the grease from soaking into them. This recipe makes about 50 medium-sized doughnuts.

NO-FRY DOUGHNUTS

2 packages active dry yeast
¼ cup warm water
1½ cups lukewarm milk (scalded, then
    cooled)
½ cup sugar
1 teaspoon salt
1 teaspoon nutmeg

¼ teaspoon cinnamon
2 eggs
⅓ cup shortening
4½ cups all-purpose flour
¼ cup butter or margarine, melted
Cinnamon sugar or sugar

In a large mixing bowl, dissolve the yeast in the warm water. Add the milk, sugar, salt, nutmeg, cinnamon, eggs, shortening and 2 cups of the flour. Blend these ingredients for ½ minute with an egg beater, scraping the bowl constantly, then beat the mixture hard for 2 minutes more, scraping the bowl only occasionally. Stir in the remaining flour until the batter is smooth, scraping the side of the bowl. Cover it and let it rise in a warm place until double in size (50 to 60 minutes).

Turn the dough out onto a well-floured cloth-covered board, and roll it around lightly to coat it with flour. (The dough should be soft to handle.) With a flour-covered rolling pin, gently roll the dough to ½-inch thickness. With a floured 2½-inch doughnut cutter, cut out doughnuts and lift them carefully with a spatula to a greased baking sheet, placing them 2 inches apart. Brush them with melted butter, then cover and let them rise until double in size, for about 20 minutes.

Preheat the oven to 425°, then bake the doughnuts 8 to 10 minutes or until they are golden in color. Immediately brush them with melted butter and shake on cinnamon sugar or sugar. This recipe makes 1½ to 2 dozen doughnuts.

YEAST DOUGHNUTS

6 cups all-purpose flour (or more)
1 cup lukewarm water
2 cakes yeast
1 tablespoon sugar
1 cup scalded milk

2 teaspoons salt
3 tablespoons sugar
¼ pound shortening
3 eggs, beaten

Sift the flour. Pour the water over the yeast, adding the tablespoon of sugar; stir it and let it stand. Meanwhile, pour the scalded milk into a bowl and add the salt, 3 tablespoons of sugar and the shortening. When it cools to lukewarm, add the water/yeast mixture and 3 cups of the flour. Beat the mixture until it is smooth, then add the eggs and the rest of the flour. Let the dough rise in a warm place until it is double in size. Roll it out, cutting out the doughnuts and letting it rise again. Fry the doughnuts in hot grease. This recipe makes about 75 doughnuts.

CREAM STICKS

2 packages yeast
1 cup warm water
6 cups all-purpose flour
1 cup scalded milk
½ cup margarine

⅔ cup sugar
2 eggs
½ teaspoon salt
1 teaspoon vanilla

Dissolve the yeast in the water, then mix it with the rest of the ingredients to form a dough. Let the dough rise until it is double in size; knead and form it into sticks 3½ x 1½-inches. Let it rise again before frying it in deep fat.

Cream Filling;

3 tablespoons flour
1 cup milk
1 cup sugar

1 cup Crisco
1 teaspoon vanilla
2½ cups confectioner's or icing sugar

To make the filling, cook together the flour and milk. Cream the sugar and Crisco, then add the flour/milk mixture and the vanilla. Cream it well and add the powdered sugar. Slit open the top of the cream sticks to fill them. If desired, frost them with the following frosting.

Frosting;

½ cup brown sugar
4 tablespoons butter
2 tablespoons milk

1 teaspoon vanilla
Icing sugar

Mix the first three ingredients and let them come to a boil before allowing them to cool. Add the vanilla and enough icing sugar to make the frosting the right spreading consistency.

PUFFY STICKS

1 cup boiling water
¼ cup shortening
½ cup sugar
1 teaspoon salt
1 cup milk

1 cake yeast
½ cup lukewarm water
2 eggs, beaten
8 cups flour

Pour the boiling water onto the shortening, sugar and salt, then add the milk. When the mixture is lukewarm, add the yeast which has been dissolved in the lukewarm water, then the eggs and about half of the flour. Beat it vigorously, then add the remaining flour to make a soft dough. Place it in a greased bowl and keep it covered in the refrigerator until it is ready to use. Then take part of the dough and roll it out to about ¼-inch thickness. With a knife, cut it into oblong pieces and fry them in deep fat (400° to 425°). Put the rest of the dough into the refrigerator to keep for another day.

RUBY'S LONG JOHNS

1½ packages dry yeast
¼ cup warm water
½ cup boiling water
½ cup shortening
⅓ cup sugar

1 teaspoon salt
½ cup milk
2 eggs, beaten
5 to 6 cups sifted all-purpose flour

Dissolve the yeast in the warm water. Combine the boiling water and the shortening, add the sugar and salt, and stir the mixture until it is lukewarm. Blend in the dissolved yeast, the milk and eggs. Gradually stir in enough flour for easy handling, kneading the dough until it is smooth. Place it in a greased bowl, turning the dough to grease the top. Cover it and let it rise in a warm place until double in size (about 1 hour). Turn the dough onto a floured surface, and roll it to ½-inch thickness. Cut it into strips, any size, before covering it and letting it rise to double in size (about 30 minutes). Deep fry the strips at 375°, drain them on absorbent paper, then dip them into a thin glaze.

DATE AND NUT BREAD

Pour 1½ cups of boiling water over 1 cup of chopped pitted dates or raisins. Let them stand for 10 minutes, then add the following and beat the mixture well:

1½ cups sugar
2¼ cups sifted flour
½ teaspoon salt
2 teaspoons soda
1 tablespoon melted shortening

1 beaten egg
½ teaspoon baking powder
½ teaspoon vanilla
1 cup chopped nuts

Bake it in a greased 9 x 5 x 3-inch loaf pan at 350° for 1¼ hours or until done.

You may like it best after it "ages" for a day or two, or after you take it from the freezer later on.

ORANGE NUT BREAD

Grated rind of 1 orange
½ cup water
1 teaspoon salt
½ cup sugar
Milk
Juice of 1 orange
1 egg, beaten

1 cup sifted all-purpose flour
1 cup whole wheat flour
2 teaspoons baking powder
¼ teaspoon soda
¼ cup shortening
½ cup chopped nuts

Combine the orange rind, water, salt and sugar and boil the mixture for 10 minutes. Allow it to cool. Add milk to the orange juice to make 1 cup, before adding it with the beaten egg to the cooled mixture. Blend the flours with the baking powder and soda, and cut in the shortening until the mixture is of meal-like consistency. Pour the liquids into the dry ingredients and stir vigorously until they are well mixed, then add the nuts and blend the mixture. Bake it in a loaf pan in a moderate oven (350°) for 50 to 60 minutes.

DELICIOUS PUMPKIN BREAD

1⅔ cups sifted all-purpose flour
¼ teaspoon baking powder
1 teaspoon soda
¾ teaspoon salt
½ teaspoon cinnamon
½ teaspoon nutmeg
⅓ cup shortening

1⅓ cups sugar
½ teaspoon vanilla
2 eggs
1 cup mashed pumpkin
⅓ cup water
½ cup chopped walnuts or pecans

Grease a regular (9 x 5 x 3-inch) loaf pan. Sift together the flour, baking powder, soda, salt and spices. Cream the shortening, sugar and vanilla before adding the eggs, one at a time, and beating thoroughly after each addition. Stir in the pumpkin. Then add the previously sifted dry ingredients alternately with the water, beating just until the mixture is smooth. Be careful not to overbeat. Fold in the nuts.

Turn the batter into the prepared pan and bake it at 350° for about 45 to 55 minutes or until done. Turn the bread out onto a wire rack and allow it to cool before storing it in a tight container. Slice and serve this bread with butter.

CREAM PUFFS

½ cup butter
1 cup boiling water
1 cup sifted all-purpose flour

¼ teaspoon salt
4 eggs

Melt the butter in the boiling water and add the flour and salt together, stirring vigorously. Cool the mixture, stirring it constantly until it forms a ball that doesn't separate. Add the eggs, one at a time, beating hard after each addition until the mixture is smooth. Form cream puffs 2½ inches in diameter and place them 2 inches apart on greased cookie sheets. Bake them at 450° for 15 minutes or 325° for 25 minutes. Remove them from the cookie sheets to cool on a wire rack. When the cream puffs are cold, cut a hole in the side of each one, and fill them with sweetened whipped cream or vanilla sauce. This recipe makes 12 cream puffs.

CORNMEAL MUFFINS

1 cup cornmeal
1 cup all-purpose flour
¼ cup sugar
1 teaspoon salt
4 teaspoons baking powder

1 cup milk
2 eggs, beaten
4 tablespoons melted butter or other
    shortening

Sift together the dry ingredients, then add the milk, eggs and melted shortening. Stir the mixture quickly until the dry ingredients are just moistened. Bake the batter in greased muffin tins for about 20 minutes at 400°.

SIX-WEEK MUFFINS

2 cups boiling water
6 cups bran (or all-bran cereal)
1 cup shortening
3 cups sugar (scant)
4 eggs, beaten

1 quart buttermilk
5 cups all-purpose flour
5 teaspoons soda
2 teaspoons salt

Pour the boiling water over 2 cups of the bran and let it stand. Mix in the melted shortening. Mix the rest of the bran with the sugar, eggs and buttermilk. Sift the flour with the soda and salt. Then combine all the ingredients and bake the batter as needed at 400° for 20 minutes. Dates, raisins or chopped apples may be added at baking time.

This batter will keep for up to 6 weeks in the refrigerator.

BLUEBERRY MUFFINS

2 tablespoons shortening
2 tablespoons sugar
1 egg
2 cups all-purpose flour

3 teaspoons baking powder
¼ teaspoon salt
1 cup milk
1¼ cups floured blueberries

Cream together the shortening and sugar before adding the egg, flour, baking powder, salt and milk. Mix it thoroughly, then fold in the blueberries. Bake the batter in greased muffin tins at 400° for 20 minutes.

WHOLE WHEAT MUFFINS

2 cups whole wheat flour
4 teaspoons baking powder
1 teaspoon salt

2 tablespoons sugar
1 cup milk
2 tablespoons lard

Mix together the flour, baking powder, salt and sugar, then stir in the milk. Mix in the melted lard and beat the batter well. Bake it in greased muffin pans in a moderate oven (425°) for 20 to 25 minutes. This recipe makes 18 muffins.

Chopped figs or dates may be added if desired.

BISCUITS SUPREME

2 cups all-purpose flour
½ teaspoon salt
2 teaspoons sugar
4 teaspoons baking powder

½ teaspoon cream of tartar
½ cup shortening
⅔ cup milk

Sift together the dry ingredients, then cut in the shortening until the mixture resembles coarse crumbs. Add the milk all at once and stir it just until the dough follows the fork around the bowl. Roll out the dough to ½-inch thickness. Cut it with a biscuit cutter and place the dough pieces on an ungreased cookie sheet. Bake them in a hot oven (450°) for 10 to 12 minutes.

SOUTHERN BISCUITS

2 cups all-purpose flour
¾ teaspoon salt
3 teaspoons baking powder

1 teaspoon soda
4 tablespoons shortening
1 cup buttermilk

Sift together all the dry ingredients, and work in the shortening. Add the liquid to make a soft dough, then roll it out on a slightly floured board to a thickness of ½-inch. With a biscuit cutter, cut the dough before putting it into a greased pan and baking it in a hot oven (425°) for 15 minutes.

For cheese biscuits, add 1 cup of grated cheese to the mixture.

SOUPS

AMISH BEAN SOUP

2 to 3 tablespoons butter
1 cup cooked navy beans
¼ cup water
3 quarts milk (approximate)

Salt
Pepper
Allspice
2 quarts (approximate) stale bread,
thinly sliced

Brown the butter in a saucepan, then add the beans and water. Bring them to the boiling point before adding the milk, salt and pepper to taste, and allspice if desired. Boil the mixture then remove it from the stove, and add enough of the bread to thicken it. Cover it and let it stand for about ½ hour before serving. Serve the soup with pickled red beets or pickles.

Variations: Instead of beans, try diced potatoes.

For Egg Soup, add about 6 or 8 diced hardcooked eggs with the bread, omitting the beans.

BACON BEAN SOUP

1 pound bacon ends, cut into small
   pieces (do not fry)
1 pound navy beans
1 chopped onion
4 quarts water (approximate)
Salt and pepper to taste

Boil the ingredients slowly for about 2 hours. Serve the soup with crackers.

Bacon ends are inexpensive and have lots of smoke flavor and meat. This soup is excellent for those very cold winter evenings.

DELICIOUS BEAN SOUP

1 pound (2 cups) navy beans, dried
2½ quarts water
1 meaty ham bone (1½ pounds)
1 clove garlic, minced
1 small bay leaf
1 cup cubed potatoes

1 cup celery, thinly sliced
1 cup onion, finely chopped
1 cup carrots, cubed
Salt
Pepper

Boil the beans in the water for 2 minutes before removing them from the heat to let stand for 1 hour. Then add the ham bone, garlic and bay leaf to the beans, and cover and simmer them for 2 hours or until the ingredients are almost tender. Add the vegetables and salt and pepper to taste, and simmer them for 1 hour longer. Remove the ham bone, cut off the meat and dice it to add to the beans. Reheat the soup almost to boiling, then remove the bay leaf.

OLD-FASHIONED BEAN SOUP AND HAM

1 pound navy beans
1 ham bone (or bacon)
3 quarts water
½ cup chopped green pepper
1 cup celery, chopped
2 cups diced potatoes

1 medium onion, chopped
3 carrots, sliced
1 tablespoon salt
¼ teaspoon pepper
1 cup tomato juice

Simmer the beans and the ham bone in the water for 2 hours. Add the rest of the ingredients and simmer them for 2 hours longer, or until the beans are tender. (Cut down the cooking time of the beans by soaking them before boiling.)

YANKEE BEAN SOUP

1¼ cups dried navy beans
5 cups water
½ teaspoon salt
1 teaspoon molasses
½ cup salt pork, cut into ¼-inch cubes
⅓ cup onion rings
3 slices bacon, cut into pieces

¼ cup chopped onion
½ cup diced cooked carrots
⅓ cup finely chopped celery leaves
1 teaspoon molasses
2 cups milk
Salt to taste

Place the beans in a 3 to 4 quart sauce pan and add the water. Bring them to a boil before removing them from the heat to stand for 2 hours or overnight. Add the salt, 1 teaspoon of molasses, pork and onions, then cover and simmer them for 2 hours or until the beans are tender. Shake the pan occasionally to prevent sticking. Cook the bacon and chopped onion until the bacon is lightly browned. Mash the beans mixture slightly then add the bacon and the remaining ingredients. Simmer them for 10 minutes.

CABBAGE CHOWDER

3 cups water
4 cups coarsely shredded cabbage
2 cups sliced carrots
3 cups diced potatoes
1 tablespoon salt

½ teaspoon sugar
¼ teaspoon pepper
4 cups scalded milk
2 tablespoons butter

Cook the vegetables and the seasonings in water until they are tender. Add the scalded milk and butter. Serve it with crackers.

CHILLY DAY STEW

1 large carrot, chopped
3 onions
1 quart potatoes, peeled and diced
2 tablespoons rice

2 tablespoons macaroni
1 teaspoon salt
1 pint cream

In a kettle of rapidly boiling water, cook the carrot while you are cleaning and chopping the onions. Add them to the stew kettle, along with the potatoes, rice, macaroni, salt and enough water to cover the ingredients. Cook them slowly until they are tender. When ready to serve, add the cream, or substitute butter and milk. Let it mix thoroughly, but do not boil the stew again. Serve it with crackers or hot toast.

CORN SOUP

3 pints milk
1½ cups creamed corn
1 teaspoon salt

1 tablespoon sugar
2 eggs, well-beaten
2 tablespoons butter

Combine the milk, corn, salt and sugar, and boil the mixture for a few minutes. Add the eggs but do not stir them in. Boil the soup a little longer, then beat it lightly before adding the butter. Serve it with crackers.

CREAM OF CORN SOUP

2 cups boiling water
2 cups canned corn
½ cup celery, chopped
1 tablespoon onion, chopped
½ cup parsley, chopped

2 cups milk
2 tablespoons butter
2 tablespoons flour
1 teaspoon salt
⅛ teaspoon pepper

Add the corn, celery, onion and parsley to the boiling water, cover and simmer for 20 minutes, then strain. Scald the milk and add it to the strained corn stock. Melt the butter and add it to the flour before adding this to the combined liquids. Season and heat the mixture to the boiling point.

FRENCH ONION SOUP

¼ cup butter or margarine
3 large onions, sliced
1 quart beef broth

1 quart water
1 teaspoon Worcestershire sauce
Salt and pepper

Melt the butter or margarine in a large pan. Add the onions and fry them slowly, stirring occasionally until they are soft and golden. Then add the beef broth, water and Worcestershire sauce, and season with salt and pepper. This recipe serves 6 to 8.

Variations: *Just before serving, slice in a couple of wieners.*

Serve it with cheese crackers.

For a richer soup, add a couple of beef bouillon cubes.

ONION TOMATO SOUP

½ medium-sized onion, cut up
Celery leaves, dried or fresh
4 tablespoons margarine
½ cup flour (approximate)
Tomato juice (about 4 cups)

Water
Sugar
Salt
Red pepper or paprika
Cream or milk

Sauté in the margarine the onion and some celery leaves. When the onion is tender, stir in the flour until it is slightly browned, then slowly add tomato juice. Stir the mixture to smooth the lumps until it becomes the thickness of gravy. Add some water, sugar, salt and red pepper or paprika to suit your taste. Before serving this soup add some cream or milk.

CREAM OF PEA SOUP

1 quart fresh peas	3 cups milk
1 cup cubed ham	1 teaspoon salt
½ cup ham broth	1 tablespoon sugar

Cook the peas and put them through a strainer, reserving the water in which they were cooked. Brown and cook the ham until it is tender. Combine all the ingredients with the reserved water and bring it to a boil. If desired, add ½ cup of cream before serving. Serve this soup with crackers.

SPLIT PEA SOUP

1 cup dried split peas	3 tablespoons flour
3 quarts water	1 teaspoon salt
1 ham bone	Pepper
1 tablespoon minced onion	2 cups milk
3 tablespoons butter	

Soak the peas overnight in water, drain them in the morning and cover them with 3 quarts of water. Add the ham bone and onion and cook them until they are soft. Melt the butter and stir in the flour until they are well blended and smooth. Add the salt, some pepper and the milk and cook, stirring constantly until the mixture thickens. Combine it with the peas and ham bone and cook it until the soup is rather thick.

WINTER VEGETABLE SOUP

1 pint celery	2 tablespoons salt
1 pint carrots	1 pint corn
1 pint cabbage	1 cup soup beans
1 pint green beans	1 pint lima beans
1 quart beef broth, OR	1 pint tomatoes
1 soup bone	Water
1 pint peas	½ cup rice

Chop finely the celery, carrots, cabbage and green beans. Combine them with the rest of the ingredients in water to cover (except the rice), and cook them for 2½ to 3 hours. Add the rice 15 minutes before serving.

POTATO CREAM SOUP

2 cups raw potatoes, diced	1 tablespoon butter
2 onions, minced	3½ tablespoons flour
2 stalks celery, diced, OR	2 cups milk
2 tablespoons dried celery leaves	1½ teaspoons salt
2½ cups boiling water	¼ teaspoon pepper

Cook the potatoes, onions and celery in the boiling water. Melt the butter in a double boiler, then add the flour, milk and seasoning to make a basic white sauce (see page 49). Cook it until it is thick and smooth. Rub the potato mixture through a sieve, add the white sauce and garnish it with parsley before serving. Serve the soup with crackers.

Variations: *This soup may also be made with milk instead of white sauce.*

One cup of noodles may be used instead of the potatoes and white sauce. Bring the milk to a boil and cook the noodles until they are soft. Combine all the ingredients, and let the soup stand a short while before serving.

Chopped hardboiled eggs may also be added.

POTATO RIVVEL SOUP

1 medium-sized onion, chopped	Flour
5 medium potatoes, diced	½ cup butter
Salt and pepper	⅛ teaspoon celery seed
2 eggs, beaten	1 to 1½ quarts milk
1 teaspoon salt	Parsley

Cook the first 3 ingredients in water until the potatoes are soft. To make rivvels, add flour to the eggs and salt, and toss and stir them until the mixture is lumpy and almost dry. Sift out the excess flour, then dump the rivvels into the potato mixture and boil them for 15 minutes. Add the butter, celery seed, milk and a pinch of parsley. Heat the soup and serve it.

This is another dish great for those cold winter evenings.

RIVVEL SOUP

½ teaspoon salt
1 cup flour
1 egg
1 quart whole milk

Mix the salt with the flour, then toss the egg lightly through it with a fork until small crumbs form. Stir this into the scalding milk, bring it to a boil, and serve it at once.

When making a small amount of this soup, use only the yolk of the egg to make extra fine rivvels.

VEGETABLE SOUP

1 large soup bone, OR
Ribs of beef
2 cups diced potatoes
2 large onions
1 cup shredded cabbage
4 ripe tomatoes
3 large carrots
½ stalk celery
½ can whole corn, OR

4 ears of corn
½ pint string beans, cut finely
1 green pepper, diced
1 red pepper, diced
1 cup lima beans
⅛ cup rice
¼ cup barley
Parsley leaves

Cook the soup bone or meat in water to cover until it is half done. Add the raw vegetables and cook them for ½ hour, then add the cooked vegetables and cook them until all the ingredients are well done. Cook the rice and barley separately or put it into the kettle with the meat when it is placed on the stove. Add chili powder to make the soup more tasty.

SUCCOTASH CHOWDER

1 large onion, chopped
3 tablespoons butter
1 cup fresh or canned corn
1 cup fresh or canned lima beans
2 cups potatoes, diced
1 cup water

1 teaspoon salt
¼ teaspoon pepper
1 teaspoon parsley, chopped
3 cups milk
2 tablespoons flour
¼ cup water

Sauté the onion in the butter in a pressure cooker until the onion is slightly browned. Add the vegetables, 1 cup of water, and the salt and pepper, cover, and set the control. After the control jiggles, cook the mixture for 2 minutes, then reduce the pressure immediately. Add the milk and heat it to boiling. Blend the flour with the water to make a smooth paste, and add it to the soup, cooking it for 1 minute while stirring constantly. Garnish the servings with chopped parsley.

VEGETABLE OYSTER SOUP (SALSIFY)

Scrape the salsify clean and slice it thinly (about 1 or 2 cups, according to family size). Cook it in water until it is tender, then add milk, salt and pepper to taste, and a chunk of butter. Bring the soup to the boiling point, then serve it over crackers. A few dried parsley or celery leaves may be added.

OYSTER STEW

3 pints milk
1 pint water
1 tablespoon salt (scant)

10-ounce can oysters (or amount
desired)
3 tablespoons butter

Bring the milk, water and salt to a boil, letting it boil for a few minutes. Add the oysters and keep it over the heat for a few minutes but do not let it boil. Reduce the heat and let the mixture stand until the oysters come to the surface. Then use low heat for 5 to 10 minutes longer, or until the oysters disappear from the top. Add the butter. Serve the stew with crackers.

SALMON SOUP

2 to 3 tablespoons butter
3 quarts milk (approximate)

Salt and pepper
1 can salmon, chopped

Brown the butter in a saucepan, then add the milk, and salt and pepper to taste. When it begins to boil, add the salmon, and heat it. Serve this soup with crackers or toasted bread cubes.

CREAM OF CHICKEN SOUP

Make a medium white sauce. Add a little bit of chopped onion, some peas, diced, cooked carrots, diced cooked potatoes, chopped chicken meat, a pinch of sugar, and salt and pepper to taste.

This recipe may be used as a casserole. Just add more vegetables, a thicker sauce and top it with biscuits. Then bake it.

HAM SOUP

4 cups cubed ham
¾ cup chopped onion
4 medium-sized potatoes

Large handful of noodles
3 quarts milk

Combine the ham and onions and cook them until the ham is soft and brown. Cut the potatoes into small cubes, add a little salt and cook them until they are soft, before adding them to the ham. Cook the noodles in salt water until they are soft, drain, and add them to the ham too, along with the milk. Bring the mixture to a boil, add salt and pepper, and it's ready to serve with crackers.

CHILI SOUP

1 pound ground beef
2 tablespoons shortening
2 onions, minced
½ green pepper, diced
1 quart tomato juice or soup (diluted if
  desired)

1 small can kidney beans plus liquid
2 teaspoons salt
1 teaspoon chili powder

Brown the beef in the shortening and add the onions and pepper. Brown them lightly. Stir in the tomatoes, kidney beans, salt and chili powder, and simmer the soup for 1 hour.

WIENER SOUP

Noodles, a handful
1½ quarts milk
½ pound wieners, sliced

1 teaspoon salt
2 tablespoons butter

Cook the noodles until they are tender. Heat the milk, add the wieners, salt and noodles, and boil them together. Then add the butter. Serve the soup with crackers.

HEARTY HAMBURGER SOUP

2 tablespoons butter
1 pound ground beef
1 cup chopped onions
1 cup sliced carrots
½ cup chopped green peppers
2 cups tomato juice

1 cup diced potatoes
1½ teaspoons salt
1 teaspoon seasoned salt
⅛ teaspoon pepper
⅓ cup flour
4 cups milk

Melt the butter in a saucepan and brown the meat. Then add the onions and cook them until they are transparent. Stir in the remaining ingredients except the flour and milk. Cover and cook the mixture over low heat until the vegetables are tender, about 20 to 25 minutes. Combine the flour with 1 cup of the milk, and stir it into the soup mixture. Boil it, add the remaining milk, and heat it, stirring frequently. Do not boil the soup after the remaining milk has been added. This recipe makes quite a large amount.

Hearty Hamburger Soup can be adapted to your family's taste; for example, you can substitute celery for the green pepper, and instead of the 4 cups of milk, use 1 to 1½ cups of skim milk powder and less flour.

VEGETABLES AND SAUCES

HINTS FOR VEGETABLES AND SAUCES

For more economical, nutritious and tasteful mashed potatoes, cook the potatoes with the skins on. When they are soft, push them through a ricer or Foley mill. Immediately stir in hot milk and add salt. They are also good without the milk.

In grandmother's day lard was often used on vegetables instead of butter. It is surprisingly good on cooked cabbage and on cooked navy or snap beans.

To get youngsters to eat more of the healthful salads, give them a serving when they are hungry and impatiently waiting for dinner to be ready.

Vegetables retain their flavor and value more when cooked with very little water, in a pan with a tight-fitting lid. When they begin to boil, lower the heat and allow them to simmer.

Add butter to your red beets and they will not be so apt to boil over.

For something different, put the potatoes through the cole slaw cutter. Add a finely cut red pepper, then fry them.

New potatoes are delicious when washed (unpeeled), grated, then fried in oil, with or without onions. Add salt and pepper.

Add herbs, Italian seasoning, fried chicken seasoning or other seasonings to string beans for a delightful new flavor.

Cut all asparagus tops off beneath the ground, not above. When the stalk is cut, the stump bleeds, and bleeding takes the strength out of the roots. When loose dirt covers the stump it can't bleed.

Put extra value into your cooking by adding herbs. Add parsley to creamed potatoes, chives to cottage cheese, mint to meats, sage and thyme to dressings, dill to pickles, and caraway seeds to rye bread. Herbs are easily grown and make nice shrubs or can be raised in flower boxes.

ASPARAGUS AND KNEPP

6 eggs
2 cups all-purpose flour
1 teaspoon baking powder
¾ teaspoon salt

Boiling water
Asparagus
Butter

Mix together the first four ingredients. Bring some water to a boil. To make the knepp, dip a spoon into the boiling water each time, then put the mixture by spoonfuls into the water. Cook it for 15 to 20 minutes, then drain off the water and put the knepp in a dish. Top it with cooked, well-buttered asparagus.

The knepp are also good topped with peas.

CREAMED ASPARAGUS

Cook asparagus until it is soft, then remove it from the water. Make a gravy from the asparagus water—it is also good when made with whole wheat flour. Butter, salt and pepper it to taste. Put the asparagus with large broken pieces of toast into a dish. Pour the hot sauce over them and serve. Diced hardboiled eggs may be added.

BAKED BEANS

2 pounds navy beans
1 pound bacon, cut into pieces
Salt and pepper to taste

1 cup brown sugar
1 quart tomato juice

Soak the beans in water overnight. Cook them until they are almost soft, drain them, and add the rest of the ingredients. If more liquid is needed, add some water. Bake the beans at 325° for 3 or 4 hours.

BOSTON BAKED BEANS

2 cups small dried beans
2 teaspoons salt
⅛ teaspoon pepper
½ cup brown sugar
½ cup minced onion

3 tablespoons good brown bacon
   drippings
1 teaspoon prepared mustard
2 cups tomato juice
2 cups water, OR
2 cups juice from cooking beans

Soak the beans overnight, then cook them until tender. Cubed ham may be added if desired. Combine the beans with the rest of the ingredients. Bake them in a slow oven (325°) for 6 to 8 hours or longer until the beans have colored and become tender. Add more water as necessary.

Variations: Try ¼ cup brown sugar and ½ cup molasses instead of the ½ cup brown sugar.

INDIANA BAKED BEANS

2½ quarts dried navy beans (4 pounds)
4 quarts water
¾ cup brown sugar
2 tablespoons salt

2 cups ketchup
1 cup molasses
3½ teaspoons prepared mustard
1 large onion (2½ to 3-inch diameter)

Soak the beans overnight in a large kettle of water. Simmer them for about 1 hour in the water in which they were soaked. Mix together the sugar, salt, ketchup, molasses and mustard, and add this mixture to the beans. Lay the onion on top and bake them, covered, in a slow oven (300°) for 5 hours. Add boiling water during cooking if necessary to keep the beans from becoming dry. Remove the onion before serving or canning the beans.

CANNED STRING BEAN DISHES

Make layers of string beans and onion rings. Add mushroom soup (which may be diluted with a little milk). Top them with bread crumbs and bake. (Toasted bread crumbs may be substituted for onion rings.)

Put the string beans in layers in a baking dish with 5 or 6 cut up wieners. Add 1 can of mushroom soup, and bake them at 350° until the soup bubbles.

Add fried or cooked cut up raw onions to the beans, and sprinkle the top with bacon chips.

Dried bread crumbs browned in butter may be added to cooked green beans just before serving. This adds a delicious touch to an ordinary dish.

Fry the beans with flour, minus the liquid. Before serving add a bit of celery seasoning and fried chicken seasoning, or any other seasoning with herbs. Adding leftover meat, finely cut, is also a good idea.

HARVARD BEETS

4 cups cooked diced beets	¼ cup vinegar
½ cup sugar	¼ cup water
1 teaspoon salt	2 tablespoons butter
1 tablespoon cornstarch	

Mix the sugar, salt and cornstarch. Add the vinegar and water and stir the mixture until it is smooth. Cook it for 5 minutes, then add the beets and let it stand for 30 minutes. Just before serving, bring the beets to a boil and add the butter. (Omit the salt when using canned beets which have been salted.)

Variations: Harvard Beets can also be made with canned pickled red beets by omitting the vinegar, sugar and salt. Use the beet water to make the sauce.

BROCCOLI WITH SAUCE

Broccoli	1 teaspoon salt
2 cups chopped onions	2 cups milk
4 tablespoons flour	¼ pound mild Cheddar cheese

Cook broccoli in a small amount of water, then drain it. Put half of the broccoli in a buttered casserole, and add the onions. Make a cheese sauce by cooking the flour, salt and milk until it is thick, then adding the cheese and stirring until it melts. Pour ½ of the sauce on top of the broccoli in the casserole. Add the remainder of the broccoli, then the rest of the cheese sauce. Bake it at 375° for about 45 minutes.

BROCCOLI AND BRUSSELS SPROUTS

Cover the vegetables with water and bring them to a good boil. Drain them and add butter and a small amount of water. Then simmer them until tender.

Variations: Place several slices of processed cheese on top of the vegetables. Or sprinkle them with flour and stir, then add a bit of cream.

SOUR CREAM CABBAGE

4 cups very finely grated cabbage
1 tablespoon flour

2 tablespoons sour cream
Salt and pepper

Simmer the cabbage until it is soft in a tightly covered saucepan with very little water. With a flour shaker, sprinkle approximately 1 tablespoon of flour over the cabbage, add the sour cream, and salt and pepper to taste.

BAKED CARROTS

2½ cups cooked, mashed carrots
1 tablespoon onions, minced
2 tablespoons butter
3 eggs, separated
2 cups milk

½ cup minced celery
1 teaspoon salt
Dash of pepper
1 cup bread crumbs

Cook the onions in the butter until they are soft, and add them to the carrots. Add the beaten egg yolks, milk, celery, seasoning and bread crumbs. Then beat the egg whites and fold them in. Place the mixture in a greased baking dish and bake it at 350° for 40 minutes.

Most youngsters who turn up their noses at carrots will love this dish.

SCALLOPED CARROTS

12 carrots
4 tablespoons butter
4 tablespoons flour
2 cups milk
1 diced onion
¼ teaspoon salt

⅛ teaspoon pepper
1 teaspoon mustard
½ cup diced Velveeta cheese
¼ teaspoon celery salt
Crushed potato chips

Slice the carrots and cook them until they are tender but not too soft. Make a basic white sauce (see page 49) with the butter, flour and milk, and add it to the carrots. Also add the onion, salt, pepper, mustard and cheese, then pour this carrot mixture into a casserole. Top it with the potato chips, and bake it at 350° for 45 minutes.

CREAMED CAULIFLOWER

Cook cauliflower in salted water until it is soft. Make a basic white sauce (see page 49) and add cheese (Velveeta is best). Pour the sauce over the cauliflower and serve it hot.

Cheese sauce is good with different vegetables, such as asparagus (with toast).

CREAMED CELERY

1 quart finely cut celery	1 tablespoon flour
½ teaspoon salt	Milk
2 tablespoons sugar	2 tablespoons salad dressing or
2 tablespoons vinegar	mayonnaise

Cook together the celery, salt, sugar and vinegar until the celery is tender, not using more water than necessary. Add a sauce made with the flour and a little milk. Bring everything to a boil, then stir in the salad dressing or mayonnaise.

CORN FRITTERS

6 big ears of corn	Pepper to taste
2 eggs	1 cup flour
½ teaspoon salt	1 cup milk

Cut the corn with a salad cutter and add the rest of the ingredients. Mix it well and drop it by tablespoons into a frying pan with melted butter or lard.

CRUSHED CORN FRITTERS

1 pint crushed corn	2 teaspoons baking powder
2 eggs	Milk to moisten
1 cup flour or cracker crumbs	Salt and pepper to taste
2 tablespoons sugar	

Combine all the ingredients and mix them well. Form the mixture into balls the size of a walnut, and fry them in deep fat.

SCALLOPED CORN

1 quart canned corn
1 cup cracker crumbs
2 eggs, beaten

½ cup milk
Salt and pepper to taste

Place the corn and cracker crumbs in layers in a casserole, keeping a few cracker crumbs for the top. Mix the eggs, milk and seasoning and pour it over the corn. Add more milk until the corn is covered and top it with the reserved crumbs. Bake it at 350° for 20 minutes or until brown. For a taste variation, try adding chopped onions.

This Scalloped Corn recipe may be made on the burner on top of the stove. Simply put all the ingredients into a heavy saucepan and stir them briskly with a fork, heating them on low heat until the corn mixture thickens. Do not stir it while it is heating, as the corn tends to become watery when cooked on the burner.

BAKED CORN

2 tablespoons lard
2 tablespoons flour
1½ cups milk
1 teaspoon salt
¼ teaspoon mustard

Paprika
2 cups corn pulp
1 egg, slightly beaten
1 tablespoon Worcestershire sauce
Buttered crumbs

Make a sauce with the lard, flour, milk and seasonings. Add the corn, egg and Worcestershire sauce. Pour the mixture into a baking dish and cover it with buttered crumbs. Bake it in a moderate oven (350° to 400°) for 15 to 20 minutes.

FRIED CUCUMBERS

1 egg
1 cup milk
2 or 3 cucumbers

2 cups cracker crumbs (approximate),
   finely crushed
Butter or vegetable oil
Salt

Beat the egg and add the milk. Peel and slice the cucumbers, and dip them into the cracker crumbs. Lay the cucumbers out to dry a little, then dip them into the egg/milk mixture and then again into the cracker crumbs. Fry them in butter or vegetable oil, and sprinkle them with salt to taste.

DANDELIONS AND EGGS

Fry dandelion greens in butter until they are crisp. They will turn black but they are not burned, as long as you continue to add butter while frying. Also add salt. If you can still see some green, then they need more frying. When they are done, put eggs on top, cover the pan and turn the burner off. Let them set until the eggs are done.

These greens taste like bacon and eggs, but it takes a little practice to cook them just right. If the dandelion stalk is too mature and bitter, try fixing the flowers in the same manner described above.

FRIED EGGPLANT

½ eggplant
1 egg
¼ cup milk

Cracker crumbs, finely crushed
Crisco
Butter

Pare the eggplant and slice it into ½-inch thicknesses. Dip it into the egg which has been beaten with the milk, then into the cracker crumbs. Fry the eggplant in the Crisco and butter (half and half) until it is nicely browned, but do not fry it too fast.

ONION PATTIES

¾ cup flour
1 tablespoon sugar
1 tablespoon cornmeal
2 teaspoons baking powder

1 teaspoon salt
¾ cup milk
2½ cups finely chopped onions

Mix together the dry ingredients then add the milk. This should make a fairly thick batter. Add the onions and mix it thoroughly. Drop the batter by spoonfuls into deep fat. Flatten them into patties when you turn them.

ONION RINGS

Onions
½ cup flour
¼ teaspoon salt
½ teaspoon baking powder

1 egg, lightly beaten
⅛ cup corn oil
¼ cup milk

Cut onions into rings, dip them into a mixture of the above ingredients, and fry them in deep fat or oil.

FRIED OYSTER PLANT

1 oyster plant
Salt water
Eggs, beaten

Cracker crumbs
Butter

Clean the oyster plant and cook it in salt water until it is soft. Dip it in beaten eggs, roll it in fine cracker crumbs and fry it in butter until it is nicely browned on both sides.

PATCHES

6 medium-sized potatoes, raw
2 tablespoons flour
Milk

Salt and pepper
Parsley (optional)
Onions (optional)

Peel the potatoes, grind or grate them, and drain them in a colander. Stir in the flour and milk to make a thin batter, and add salt and pepper to taste. Parsley and onion may be added. Fry them in a well-oiled, hot skillet.

CRUSTY BAKED POTATOES

6 medium potatoes
4 tablespoons melted butter

½ cup fine cracker crumbs
1 teaspoon salt

Pare the potatoes, wash them and wipe them dry. Cut them in halves and roll them in the melted butter, then in the crumbs to which the salt has been added. Place the potatoes in a greased pan and bake them at 350° for 1 hour.

BASQUE POTATOES

½ cup finely chopped onions
½ cup chopped celery
½ cup shredded carrots
1 clove garlic, minced
Butter

2 cups chicken broth
4 cups potatoes, pared and cubed
Salt and pepper
Parsley, chopped

In a 10-inch skillet, sauté the onions, celery, carrots and garlic in the melted butter until they are tender. Add the chicken broth, potatoes, salt and pepper to the sautéed vegetables, cover them, and simmer for 10 minutes. Then remove the cover, and continue to simmer the vegetables, stirring them occasionally, for 20 minutes more or until the broth thickens. Sprinkle them with parsley. This recipe makes 4 to 6 servings.

FRIED NEW POTATOES

1 quart new potatoes
1 onion
2 tablespoons oil

Grate the unpeeled potatoes, slice in the onion, and fry them together in the oil.

POT LUCK POTATO CASSEROLE

2 pounds jacket-boiled potatoes,
 peeled and chopped
4 tablespoons melted butter
1 teaspoon salt
¼ teaspoon pepper
½ cup chopped onions

1 can cream of chicken soup,
 undiluted
1 pint sour cream
2 cups grated, sharp Cheddar cheese
2 cups crushed cornflakes mixed with
 ¼ cup melted butter

Combine the potatoes and butter in a large mixing bowl. Add the salt, pepper, onions, cream of chicken soup, sour cream and cheese. Blend this mixture thoroughly and pour it into a greased 9 x 13-inch casserole. Cover it with the crushed cornflakes mixed with melted butter. Bake it at 350° for 45 minutes.

SCALLOPED POTATOES

6 cups medium-sized potatoes
3 tablespoons butter
2 tablespoons flour
3 cups top milk or half-and-half
1 teaspoon salt

Pepper to taste
1 teaspoon parsley (optional)
2 tablespoons chopped onions
 (optional)

Slice the potatoes. Make a basic white sauce (see page 49) of the butter, flour and milk. Place half of the potatoes in a greased casserole and cover them with half of the sauce and seasonings. Add the remaining potatoes and seasonings, then the remaining sauce. Cover the casserole and bake it in a moderately hot oven (400°) for about 1 hour. Uncover it and continue baking it until the top forms a brown crust and the potatoes are done.

Variations: To shorten the baking time, potatoes may be boiled for 10 minutes.

Add 5 wieners or 1 cup of diced ham, or 2 to 3 slices of bacon pieces for extra flavor.

Bake the potatoes with 1½ cups of diced Velveeta cheese.

Raw sliced potatoes do not require a sauce when top milk is used.

POTATOES WITH CHEESE SAUCE

Dice a dish of potatoes and cook them in salt water until they are soft. While they are cooking, make a sauce by melting butter in a skillet and adding flour, as for any basic white sauce (see page 49). Next add milk, and when the sauce thickens slightly, add cheese. (Onion may also be added.) Pour the sauce over the hot potatoes and serve.

BAKED SWEET POTATOES

4 cups sweet potatoes, cooked, salted
   and diced
1 cup brown sugar

1 teaspoon flour
½ cup cream
Marshmallow bits

Put the sweet potatoes into a greased casserole, and add the sugar, flour and cream. Bake them at 350° for 20 to 30 minutes or until they are sticky. Cover the top with small marshmallow bits and brown them lightly until they begin to melt.

SPINACH OMELET

Melt butter in a hot skillet. Add spinach, and heat it until it is wilted (about 2 to 3 minutes). Pour 3 or 4 beaten eggs over the spinach. Sprinkle it with salt. Cover it and cook until done.

SQUASH DISHES AND COOKING HINTS

- When cooking corn on the cob, lay slices of peeled squash on top of the corn. Brush the squash with butter and sprinkle it with salt and pepper. By the time the corn is ready, the squash will be soft.

- When baking squash, scoop out the center but don't peel it. Prepare hamburger with your favorite seasoning, and fill the center of the squash with the meat. Cover it with foil and bake it at 350° until the squash is soft.

- If you don't have hamburger, peel and finely grate raw potatoes. Put them into the center of the squash, and add butter, milk, salt and pepper.

- Add leftover squash to caramel pudding.

- Use squash instead of pumpkin for pie.

- To make baked squash, brush squash slices with soft butter. Season them with salt and pepper and with brown sugar if desired. Bake them at 375° until they are brown. Turn the squash slices once to brown both sides.

COCONUT SQUASH

2 cups mashed squash (or pumpkin)
1 cup fine biscuit crumbs, or bread
   crumbs
1½ cups milk
1 cup sugar
½ cup grated coconut

2 egg yolks, well-beaten
3 tablespoons melted butter
1½ grated orange peels (optional)
½ teaspoon nutmeg
¾ teaspoon salt

Mix together all the ingredients thoroughly. In a casserole, bake the mixture at 350° until it thickens and browns slightly. Make a meringue of the egg whites and 2 tablespoons of sugar. Spread it over the squash and brown it.

TOMATO BREAD

1 quart tomato juice, or whole
   tomatoes
Sugar
Pepper
Butter

Heat the tomato juice, and add sugar and pepper to taste, and a lump of butter. Pour it over broken toast or soda crackers just before serving.

TOMATO CASSEROLE

Raw tomatoes, peeled
Green pepper rings
Onion rings
Sugar

Salt
Pepper
Bread crumbs
Butter

Slice the tomatoes and place them in a cake pan. Arrange the pepper rings and onion rings over the tomatoes, and season them with sugar, salt and pepper. Prepare the bread crumbs as you would for filling, seasoning them with salt, pepper and butter. Bake the casserole in a moderate oven (350°) for 1 to 1½ hours.

BAKED TURNIP

1 medium turnip (1½ pounds)
¾ teaspoon salt
1 tablespoon sugar
⅛ teaspoon ginger

2 tablespoons chopped parsley
¼ cup water
3 tablespoons butter

Peel the turnip and cut it into ½-inch thick slices. Put it into a buttered 1-quart baking dish. Combine the seasonings and sprinkle them over the turnip. Pour the water over all and dot it with the butter. Cover the dish tightly and bake it at 425° for 50 minutes or until done. Stir the ingredients with a fork at least once.

AMISH DRESSING

4 eggs
½ teaspoon salt
⅛ teaspoon pepper
½ teaspoon sage
½ teaspoon thyme
3½ or 4 cups milk as needed
1 medium-sized onion, finely chopped

3 stems celery, finely chopped
¾ cup diced, cooked potatoes
2 cups, more or less, diced chicken
½ cup shredded or diced cooked
  carrots (for color)
1 loaf bread, diced and toasted

Put the eggs into a bowl and beat them. Mix in the salt, pepper, sage and thyme. Add 2 cups of the milk, the onion, celery, potatoes, diced chicken and carrots. Add the bread crumbs with enough milk to moisten them well. (Substitute 1 cup of chicken broth for the milk to give it a different flavor.) Bake this mixture in a well-greased casserole at 350° for 1½ hours or until the liquid is of omelet-like texture.

Variations: Try 2 cups of finely cut cooked ham, instead of the chicken. Also try adding 1 large pepper, cut into short narrow strips. Parsley may be added too.

DRESSING FOR GREENS

Bacon
1 tablespoon flour
1 cup water
1 tablespoon sugar
Salt

Vinegar
Sour cream or buttermilk
2 hardcooked eggs, diced
Greens

Cut up a few strips of bacon into a pan and fry them. Use part of the drippings to make a pan gravy with the flour. When it is brown, stir in the water and let it boil before adding the sugar, salt and vinegar to taste. A bit of sour cream or buttermilk may be added. Fold in the hardcooked eggs. Add the greens just before serving. This dressing is good with dandelions, lettuce, endive and other greens.

TOMATO GRAVY

1 cup tomato juice
½ cup water
3 tablespoons flour

½ teaspoon salt
½ cup cream
2 cups milk

Place the juice and water in a saucepan and bring it to a boil. Meanwhile, blend the flour and salt with the cream. (Add 2 tablespoons of sugar if desired.) Add the milk and mix it well. Pour the flour mixture into the hot juice, stirring it constantly until it boils and thickens.

This gravy may be served with bread, toast, crackers or fried potatoes.

LEAH'S TOMATO SAUCE

Butter
1 rounded tablespoon flour

Pure tomato juice
Sugar

Melt butter, the size of a walnut, in a pan. Add the flour, stirring it into the melted butter before adding enough tomato juice to make a slightly thickened sauce. Add sugar to taste. Serve this sauce hot with crackers or over toasted bread.

POTATO GRAVY

Pour the water from boiled potatoes into a saucepan. While it is heating, make a thickening of 1 rounded tablespoon of flour, dampen it with milk, then stir in 1 egg yolk. Mix it well, then add about ½ cup of milk. Add the thickening to the potato water, stirring it constantly. Add enough milk for the right consistency. Add salt and pepper to taste and 1 tablespoon of butter. Serve as any other gravy.

When using the white of an egg instead of the yolk, add about 1 tablespoon of cold water to the yolk to keep it from drying out.

BASIC WHITE SAUCE

2 tablespoons melted butter
2 tablespoons flour
2 cups milk

½ teaspoon salt
⅛ teaspoon pepper (optional)

Melt the butter in a saucepan. Stir in the flour, then add half of the milk. Stir it rapidly to remove all lumps, then add the remainder of the milk, and the salt. Cook it for about 1 minute, stirring constantly.

Variations: Add chopped dried celery leaves to the sauce. Cook it a few minutes, then serve it on boiled potatoes or toast.

Fry small pieces of bacon, then make a white sauce from the bacon grease, or brown a diced onion before making the sauce.

Add parsley or celery leaves and 4 or 5 chopped hardcooked eggs.

CHEESE SAUCE

Make the Basic White Sauce above (but slightly thinner) and add 1 cup of diced cheese. Stir it until the cheese is melted.

Cheese sauce is good with many different vegetables. Pour it over them just before serving.

WHOLE WHEAT SAUCE

3 to 4 tablespoons butter, or oil
2 rounded tablespoons whole wheat
   flour
2 cups milk (approximate)

Herbs
Dash of red pepper
⅛ to ¼ teaspoon basil

Melt the butter (or use oil) and add the flour. Brown it lightly, then add milk (about 2 cups) until the sauce is of the right consistency. Add herb seasonings, the red pepper and basil. This sauce is good over steamed asparagus tips and broken toast, or over string beans, peas, and other vegetables.

ONE DISH MEALS AND CASSEROLES

CHICKEN AND DRESSING

1 chicken, boned and sliced
1 loaf of bread, broken up and toasted
1 large or 2 small onions, chopped
1 cup celery, diced

2 hardcooked eggs, sliced
Salt and pepper to taste
Butter

Make a thin gravy with the chicken broth. Then mix together all the ingredients and put the mixture into a loaf pan or baking dish. Dot the top with butter and bake it at 350° for ¾ to 1 hour.

CHICKEN AND DUMPLINGS

Cook and debone the meat of 2½ pounds of chicken. Put this meat with the broth into a large kettle with a tight-fitting lid.

Dumplings:

1 egg
2 tablespoons milk
½ teaspoon salt

3 teaspoons baking powder
Flour

Beat the above ingredients with enough flour to make a good stiff dough. Drop it by spoonfuls into the boiling broth. Cook the dumplings, covered, for 5 to 8 minutes. It is important that the lid not be removed during this time. Remove the kettle from the stove, take the lid off and serve the chicken and dumplings at once. The dumplings should be light and fluffy.

CHICKEN LOAF

1 cup soft bread crumbs
½ cup sweet milk
3 cups diced cooked chicken
1 teaspoon salt

½ teaspoon pepper
3 eggs, separated
2 tablespoons melted butter
¼ cup chopped pimentos

Let the crumbs stand in the milk for 10 minutes. Then add the chicken, salt, pepper, egg yolks, butter and pimentos. Beat the egg whites until they are stiff and add them to the chicken. Place the mixture in a buttered pan and bake it for 45 minutes at 350°.

CHICKEN AND RICE CASSEROLE

In a flat baking dish, place chicken or hamburger. Add chopped celery or other vegetables, and uncooked rice. Add a can each of cream of celery and cream of chicken soup, or substitute a white sauce. Bake it at 350° until the rice is tender.

VEGETABLE CHICKEN CASSEROLE

According to family size, have on hand enough potatoes, carrots (cut into small pieces) and peas. Cook each vegetable separately until it is almost soft. From a canned chicken, drain off the liquid to make a thin gravy. Cut the chicken off the bone and pour the potatoes, carrots, peas and cut up chicken into a roaster or casserole, pouring the seasoned gravy on top of it. Mix it slightly. Make a biscuit dough, then drop pieces of the dough on top of the mixture. Put it into the oven at 400° for 15 to 20 minutes or until the biscuits are done.

As a short cut, cook all the vegetables together.

BAKED BEEF STEW

2 pounds beef cut into cubes
¼ cup flour
¼ teaspoon celery seed
1¼ teaspoons salt
⅛ teaspoon pepper
4 medium onions, sliced

6 medium potatoes, thinly sliced
2 medium carrots, thinly sliced
1½ cups hot water
4 teaspoons beef bouillon
1 teaspoon Worcestershire sauce
Butter or margarine

Mix together the flour and seasonings and dredge the meat in the mixture. In a large casserole with a tight-fitting cover, arrange in layers the meat and vegetables. Add the bouillon to the hot water, then add the Worcestershire sauce. Pour it evenly over the casserole. Dot the surface with butter, cover the casserole and bake it at 325° for 3 hours.

Leftover beef broth may be used instead of the water and bouillon.

DRIED BEEF CASSEROLE

¼ pound dried beef
Butter
1 can (10 ounces) cream of mushroom
   soup

1 cup milk
8 ounces noodles
Buttered bread crumbs

Fry the beef in butter until it is slightly browned. Add the mushroom soup and milk. Cook the noodles in salted water until they are tender. Drain them, and combine them with the beef in a buttered casserole dish. Cover the top with buttered bread crumbs, and bake it in a moderate oven (350°) until brown.

CHOW MEIN

1 heavy chicken
1 stalk celery, chopped
2 onions, chopped
1 tablespoon butter
1 tablespoon soy sauce

1 tablespoon Worcestershire sauce
Salt and pepper to taste
Sugar (optional)
3 tablespoons cornstarch

Cook the chicken until it is tender, then remove the bones. Fry the celery and onions in butter until they are brown. Add them to the chicken and broth, and cook them until the celery is tender. Add the soy and Worcestershire sauce, salt and pepper, and sugar if desired. Make a thickening with the cornstarch and add it to the chow mein. Serve this dish with chow mein noodles.

LITTLE BEEF PIES

1 beef bouillon cube
2 cups boiling water
3½ cups chopped cooked beef
2 teaspoons Worcestershire sauce
1½ teaspoons salt
1 teaspoon sugar

½ teaspoon paprika
¼ teaspoon pepper
1 package (10 ounces) frozen or
  canned mixed vegetables
¼ cup flour

Dissolve the bouillon cube in the boiling water and add the beef, Worcestershire sauce, salt, sugar, paprika and pepper. Add the vegetables, and cook the mixture for 5 minutes. Combine the flour with enough cold water to make a paste, and slowly stir it into the mixture, cooking it until it thickens. Then spoon it into 6 or 8-ounce oven-proof casseroles.

Pastry;

1 cup flour
½ cup cornmeal
¾ teaspoon salt

⅓ cup shortening
4 tablespoons cold water

Make the pastry by sifting together the flour, cornmeal and salt. Cut in the shortening until the mixture resembles coarse crumbs. Sprinkle the water by tablespoons over the mixture. Stir it lightly with a fork until it is just damp. (If necessary, add another tablespoon of cold water to make the dough hold together.) Form the dough into a ball. Divide it into 6 parts and roll each part to form a circle large enough to fit the top of each casserole. Place the pastry circle over the filling, turn the edges under, and flute them. Make several cuts in the pastry to allow steam to escape. Bake the pies in a preheated oven at 450° for 12 to 15 minutes.

MEAT PIES

Grind 3 or 4 cups of cooked meat. Add hardcooked eggs and chopped onions, and salt and pepper to taste. A desired sauce may be added to moisten the meat, such as salad dressing, ketchup or mayonnaise.

Make a dough with the following ingredients. Mix it lightly.

1 cup milk	2 eggs
2 teaspoons baking powder	2 tablespoons lard
1 teaspoon salt	2 cups all-purpose flour

Roll out the dough and cut it into squares. Put the meat on the squares and fold them over, then press down. Fry them in deep fat.

SUEY STEW

Cut a roast or stewing meat into chunks. Trim off the fat. Cut potatoes into cubes. According to the size of your family, add sufficient carrots and onions, as well as any other vegetable you like. Pour the following ingredients individually over the vegetables and meat;

1 can (10 ounces) cream of celery soup	1 can (10 ounces) cream of chicken soup
½ can water	½ can water

Do not mix the stew. Bake it for 5 hours at 275°.

BEEF AND CHEESE

1½ cups uncooked spaghetti	Seasonings
1 pound ground beef	2 cups milk
1 small onion, chopped	¾ cup grated cheese
2 tablespoons butter	1 cup tomatoes
3 tablespoons flour	

Cook the spaghetti until it is tender, then drain it. In a skillet, brown the beef and onion in the butter. Add the flour, milk and seasonings to taste. Cook it until it is thick. Mix ½ cup of the cheese with the spaghetti, and place ½ of the spaghetti in a baking dish. Add the meat mixture, top it with the tomatoes, and add the rest of the spaghetti. Sprinkle the remaining cheese on top. Bake it at 350° for 25 to 30 minutes.

BUDGET BEEF-NOODLE CASSEROLE

1 pound ground beef
3 tablespoons onions
½ teaspoon salt
½ cup diced cheese
1 egg, beaten

3 cups cooked noodles
1 cup tomato juice
2 teaspoons Worcestershire sauce
¼ cup ketchup

Mix together all the ingredients and pour the mixture into a greased casserole. Top it with ¼ cup of cracker crumbs. Bake the casserole at 350° for 1 hour.

BUSY DAY CASSEROLE

1½ cups cubed ham or hamburger
1 cup diced potatoes
1 cup diced carrots

½ cup peas, canned
½ cup green beans, canned

Brown the ham, then add the potatoes, carrots and water. Cook them until they are tender. Add the peas, beans and enough boiling water to cover them. Stir in 1 tablespoon of flour mixed with a little water. Put this mixture into a large casserole or small cake pan. Top it with your favorite biscuit dough (cheese may be added), dropped by tablespoons into the ham mixture. Bake the casserole at 350° for 20 to 30 minutes, or until done.

CHILI CON CARNE

1 pound ground beef
2 tablespoons shortening
2 onions, minced
½ green pepper

1 small can tomatoes or tomato soup
1 small can kidney beans plus liquid
2 teaspoons salt
1 teaspoon chili powder

Brown the beef in the shortening, and add the onions and diced pepper. Brown these vegetables lightly. Stir in the tomatoes, kidney beans, salt and chili powder. Simmer it for 1 hour, stirring frequently.

DELICIOUS ONE DISH DINNER

Peel potatoes, wash and slice them. Grease a casserole with butter, and put in a layer of potatoes. Add a layer of carrots if you wish, then a layer of sliced onions. Season it with salt and pepper, and put dices of butter on top. Next prepare hamburger patties and put them on top. Add a little water and cover the casserole with aluminum foil. Bake it for 1 hour at 350°.

Variations: Ham may be used instead of hamburger.

Turnips may be added.

Canned tomato soup may be poured over the casserole. Dilute it first with about half water.

FRYING PAN SUPPER

1 pound hamburger
1 small onion, chopped
2 cups potatoes, cut into strips
2 cups shredded cabbage

2 cups finely cut celery
Salt
½ cup water

Fry the hamburger and onion until it changes color, then add the potatoes, cabbage and celery. Sprinkle it with salt and add the water. Cover and simmer it for 20 minutes, or until the vegetables are done.

Canned hamburger or cut up chunk meat may also be used.

GREEN BEAN DISH

4 large potatoes, peeled and sliced
1 pound wieners, cut up, OR
1 pound hamburger, browned
1 quart canned green beans, drained
½ onion, sliced

2 cups milk
½ pound soft cheese
½ cup flour
2 teaspoons salt

Put the first 4 ingredients into a baking dish. Make a sauce by heating the milk enough to melt the cheese, and adding the flour and salt. Pour it over the ingredients in the baking dish, and bake it at 300° for 2 hours.

MEATBALL CHOWDER

2 pounds ground beef
2 teaspoons salt
⅛ teaspoon pepper
2 eggs, beaten
¼ cup chopped parsley
Garlic salt (optional)
½ cup fine cracker or bread crumbs
2 tablespoons milk
3 to 5 tablespoons flour
1 tablespoon salad oil

2 bay leaves (optional)
4 to 6 small onions, cut up
2 or 3 cups diced celery
3 to 4 cups diced potatoes
¼ cup long grain rice
6 cups tomato juice
6 cups water
1 tablespoon sugar
1 teaspoon salt
1½ cups canned corn

Mix thoroughly the meat, salt, pepper, eggs, parsley, garlic salt if desired, crumbs and milk. Form the mixture into balls the size of walnuts. Dip them in flour. In a large kettle, heat the oil, and lightly brown the meatballs on all sides. Add all the remaining ingredients except the corn. Bring the mixture to a boil, cover and cook it slowly until the vegetables are tender. Add the corn last and cook it for 10 minutes more. This recipe serves 12.

Variations: Carrots, peas and celery leaves can be used. Also try V-8 juice with less water.

HAMBURGER CASSEROLE

1 chopped onion
1 pound ground beef, fresh or canned
Salt and pepper
2½ cups canned green beans
1 can (10 ounces) tomato soup

5 potatoes, cooked
½ cup warm milk
1 egg, beaten
Cheese (optional)

Fry the onion and ground beef with salt and pepper to taste until the beef is brown. Mix the beans and soup with the meat. Pour the mixture into a 1½-quart casserole. Mash the potatoes, add the milk and egg, and mix well. Spoon mounds of potatoes onto the meat mixture. Cover it with cheese if desired. Bake the casserole at 350° for 30 minutes.

If leftover mashed potatoes are used, omit the milk.

HANDY CASSEROLE

Put a layer of browned hamburger into a dish. Place over it a layer of sliced potatoes (cooked until almost done), then a layer of canned vegetables. Add 1 can (10 ounces) of mushroom, celery or chicken soup, and top it with a layer of cheese. Cover the casserole with foil and bake it at 350° for 30 minutes.

KINGBURGER KLOPS

1½ pounds hamburger
2 slices bread soaked in water, then
   squeezed dry
3 eggs

1 chopped onion
Salt and pepper to taste
1 bay leaf (optional)

Mix the ingredients together and form the mixture into balls about 2 inches in diameter. Place them in a pan of 1½ quarts of boiling water. Cook them for 10 minutes, then place the balls in a roaster or casserole with 2 quarts of boiled potatoes cut into chunks. Mix together the following ingredients;

1 cup strained water in which the
   meatballs were boiled
1 cup sour cream plus 1 cup cold milk
   OR
2 cups milk

4 tablespoons flour
Salt and pepper to taste

Cook this mixture to make a sauce, then pour it over the meatballs. Bake the casserole at 350° for 45 minutes.

MEATBALL STEW

1½ pounds hamburger
1 cup soft bread crumbs
¼ cup finely chopped onions
1 beaten egg
1 teaspoon salt
½ teaspoon marjoram
¼ teaspoon thyme
2 tablespoons cooking oil

10-ounce can condensed tomato soup
10-ounce can condensed beef broth
4 medium potatoes, pared and quartered
4 carrots, scraped and cut into 1-inch chunks
8 small white onions, peeled
2 tablespoons chopped parsley

Combine the first 7 ingredients, and shape the mixture into 24 meatballs. Brown them in the oil in a 4-quart pan. Add the condensed soups and vegetables. Bring the mixture to a boil, then cover and simmer it for 30 minutes or until the vegetables are tender. Add the parsley. This makes 6 to 8 servings.

PORCUPINE MEATBALLS

½ cup rice
1 pound ground beef
1 teaspoon salt
½ teaspoon pepper

1 onion, minced
1 small can tomato soup
½ cup water

Wash the rice, then combine it with the meat, salt, pepper and onion. Shape the mixture into small balls. Mix together the soup and water and pour it over the meatballs. Using a pressure cooker if possible, cook the meatballs for 12 minutes. Otherwise, cook them, tightly covered, for 30 minutes.

TAMALE PIE

1 can (1 pint) kernel corn
1 pint tomatoes
½ pound ground beef
¼ pound ground pork
1 small onion, chopped

1½ tablespoons butter
1½ teaspoons salt
½ to 1 tablespoon chili powder
½ garlic bud (optional)

Boil together all the ingredients for 15 minutes. Remove the mixture from the heat and add the following;

¾ cup sweet milk
1 cup granulated cornmeal
1 egg, beaten

Mix it well and pour it into a buttered casserole. Bake it for 1 hour in a moderate oven (325°).

MEXICAN MIX-UP

1½ pounds ground beef
1 cup chopped onions
½ cup chopped green pepper
½ tablespoon chili powder
½ clove garlic
2 cups beef gravy

2 cups kidney beans, drained
2 cups cooked macaroni
¼ teaspoon salt
⅛ teaspoon pepper
½ cup shredded Cheddar cheese

In a skillet, brown the beef and cook the onion and green pepper with the chili powder and garlic until the vegetables are tender. Add the gravy, beans, macaroni, salt and pepper. Pour the mixture into a 2-quart baking dish (12 x 8 x 2 inches) and bake it at 450° for 15 minutes. Stir it, top it with the cheese, and bake it until the cheese melts.

SPAGHETTI DINNER

½ quart canned or fresh hamburger
1 pint pizza sauce (see page 264)

½ pound or more spaghetti
Salted water

Cook the hamburger until the liquid is almost taken up. Add the pizza sauce and simmer it a little longer. Meanwhile, cook in boiling, salted water about ½ pound or more of spaghetti until it is tender. Combine the meat sauce and spaghetti before serving.

SPANISH RICE

1 pound hamburger
1 small onion, chopped (optional)
½ cup diced green pepper
1 cup rice
½ cup cheese, diced

Salt and pepper
½ teaspoon chili powder (optional)
Dash of Italian seasoning (optional)
Tomato juice

Brown the hamburger, adding the onion if desired, and the green pepper. Cook the rice until it is soft, then add it to the hamburger and pepper, followed by the cheese, and salt and pepper to taste. Try adding chili powder and a dash of Italian seasoning for a more zesty flavor. Add the tomato juice (diluted with ⅓ water) to cover the ingredients. Bake it for 1 hour at 350°.

Variations: Peppers may be stuffed with the hamburger, rice, cheese, salt and pepper, and set in diluted tomato juice to bake.

MOCK TURKEY

2 pounds hamburger, browned in
    butter
2 cans (10 ounces each) cream of
    chicken soup
1 can (10 ounces) cream of celery soup

4 cups milk
1 loaf bread, broken
Salt and pepper to taste

Mix together the ingredients. Place the mixture in a pan and bake it at 350° for 45 minutes.

YUMMASETTI

1 large package noodles, cooked in
    salted water
3 pounds hamburger, fried in butter
    with 1 chopped onion
1 pint peas
2 cans (10 ounces each) mushroom
    soup

1 can (10 ounces) cream of chicken or
    cream of celery soup
1 cup sour cream
½ loaf toasted buttered bread crumbs

Mix together all the ingredients (reserving some of the bread crumbs) and pour the mixture into a greased baking dish. Top it with the reserved crumbs. Bake it at 350° for 1 hour.

SAUCY WINTER CASSEROLE

¼ pound bacon, diced
½ cup chopped onions
4 teaspoons Worcestershire sauce, OR
4 teaspoons vinegar
1 cup corn syrup
¾ teaspoon salt
¼ teaspoon paprika

¾ cup water
1½ cups tomato sauce
1 pound wieners, cut up
1 tablespoon cornstarch
2 tablespoons water
Cooked spaghetti or macaroni

Combine the bacon and onions in a skillet and fry them until the bacon is crisp and the onion is soft. Drain off extra fat. Stir in the Worcestershire sauce, corn syrup, salt, paprika, water and tomato sauce. Bring the mixture to a boil. Reduce the heat, cover and simmer it for 10 minutes. Add the wieners and simmer until they are hot. Blend the cornstarch with the 2 tablespoons of water, and stir it into the sauce, boiling it for 1 minute. Serve it on hot spaghetti or any macaroni product.

TEXAS HASH

2 large onions, sliced
2 green peppers, finely cut
3 tablespoons shortening
1 pound hamburger

2 cups tomatoes
1 cup spaghetti or macaroni
2 teaspoons salt
¼ teaspoon pepper

Fry the onions and green peppers slowly in the shortening until the onions become yellow. Add the hamburger and cook the mixture until it falls apart. Then add the tomatoes, spaghetti and seasoning, and mix. Put the mixture into a casserole, cover it and bake it at 375° for 45 minutes.

WIGGLERS

5 slices bacon
1½ pounds hamburger
2 onions
1½ cups diced potatoes
1½ cups celery
2 cups peas

1½ cups carrots, diced
1 can (10 ounces) mushroom soup
¾ quart tomato juice
1½ cups spaghetti, cooked
Velveeta cheese

Cut the bacon into small pieces and fry it with the hamburger and sliced onions until brown. Drain off the fat. Cook the potatoes, celery, peas and carrots before putting them into a roaster with the bacon, hamburger and onions. Add the spaghetti, then stir in the soup and juice. Lay slices of Velveeta cheese on top and bake it for 1 hour at 350°.

SCHNITZ UND KNEPP

1 quart dried apples (schnitz)
3 pounds ham
2 tablespoons brown sugar
2 cups flour
1 teaspoon salt

¼ teaspoon pepper
4 teaspoons baking powder
1 egg, well-beaten
Milk
3 tablespoons melted butter

Wash the dried apples then cover them with water to soak overnight. Cover the ham with boiling water and boil it for 3 hours. Add the apples and the water in which they were soaked, and boil it for 1 hour longer. Add the sugar.

Make the dumplings by sifting together the flour, salt, pepper and baking powder. Stir in the beaten egg, milk (enough to make a fairly moist, stiff batter) and butter. Drop the batter by the tablespoon into the hot ham and apples. Cover it and cook it for 15 minutes. Serve it hot.

BAKED PORK CHOPS

Put a layer of thinly sliced potatoes into a baking dish, and cover them with shredded onions, salt and pepper. Lay over this as many pork chops as needed, seasoned well on both sides. Add enough milk to moisten the ingredients, then bake them at 400° until done.

PORKY PIE

4 medium sweet potatoes
1½ teaspoons salt
2 tablespoons butter
1½ teaspoons cinnamon sugar

1 pound ground pork
1½ cups water
2 tablespoons flour
Dash of pepper

Cook the potatoes in water with 1 teaspoon of the salt, then peel them. Mash them slightly and add the butter, cinnamon sugar and the remaining salt. Add a little milk if necessary. Form the pork into patties, brown them, and drain. (Canned sausage works fine, too.) Make a gravy with the pork broth, water, flour and pepper. Pour it over the patties in a shallow baking pan. Spread the sweet potatoes on top, and bake it at 400° for 20 minutes.

CALIFORNIA RICE

1 pound bulk sausage
1 cup chopped celery
1 cup chopped onion
1 cup raw rice

1 cup cooked, diced chicken
1 can (10 ounces) mushroom soup
1 can (10 ounces) water
Salt and pepper

Brown the sausage, celery, onion and rice. (This step may be ignored if you wish.) Add the chicken, mushroom soup, water and seasonings. Put the mixture into a greased casserole. Bake it for 2 hours at 325°.

LIMA BEAN BARBECUE

2 cups dried lima beans, OR
4 cups cooked or canned lima beans
2 teaspoons salt
1 pound pork sausage links
1 tablespoon prepared horseradish

¼ cup liquid from cooked beans
½ cup chopped onions
1 cup ketchup
1 teaspoon Worcestershire sauce

Add salt to the beans and cook them until tender, then drain them. Fry the sausage until it is brown. Mix together all the ingredients except the sausage, then place ½ of this bean mixture in a 1½-quart casserole dish, and cover it with ½ of the sausages. Make another layer of the remaining bean mixture and sausages. Bake it at 400° for 15 minutes.

WASHDAY DINNER

Melt 1 tablespoon of butter in a large casserole. Line the bottom with a thick layer of onions, then add a generous layer of potatoes. Over the potatoes, sift 2 tablespoons of flour and pour a can (1 pint) of tomato juice. Add thinly sliced sausages to cover the top and add boiling water to cover all the ingredients. Add salt to taste. Bake it at 300° for 3 hours. If the sausages get too brown, turn them over.

BAKED MACARONI AND CHEESE

2 cups macaroni
2 teaspoons salt
2½ cups milk
8 ounces cheese (Velveeta)

Pepper
Butter
Bread crumbs

Cook the macaroni until it is tender in salted water. Put it into a casserole dish, add the milk, cheese, pepper to taste, and dot it with butter. Top the macaroni with bread crumbs, and bake it for about 30 minutes at 325° to 350°, or until brown.

Variations: Try adding chopped peppers, onions, celery or parsley.

MACARONI AND CHEESE

3 tablespoons butter
2½ cups uncooked macaroni
½ pound Velveeta cheese

1 teaspoon salt
¼ teaspoon pepper
1 quart milk

Melt the butter in a baking dish and pour the macaroni into the melted butter, stirring it until the macaroni is coated. Slice the cheese, then cut the slices into 4 pieces. Add it with the salt, pepper and milk to the macaroni. Bake it at 325° for 1½ hours. Do not stir the macaroni while it is baking.

TUNA MACARONI

1 pound elbow macaroni
Tuna chunks
10-ounce can mushroom soup

Milk
Bread crumbs
Cheese slices (optional)

Cook the macaroni according to the directions on the package. Pour part of the macaroni into a greased casserole dish. On top of it, place cut up tuna chunks, then pour ⅓ of the can of mushroom soup over it. Repeat this procedure until the dish is full. Pour milk over all until it covers the macaroni. Top it with bread crumbs and bake it for 1 hour in a moderate oven (350°). Cheese slices instead of bread crumbs may be put on top for the last 10 minutes of baking.

SKILLET SUPPER

1 pound bulk sausage (or 1 quart
   canned)
1 onion, chopped
1 green pepper, chopped
1 quart tomatoes

2 cups uncooked macaroni
2 tablespoons sugar
2 teaspoons chili powder
½ cup water or tomato juice
1 teaspoon salt

Brown the sausage, onion and pepper, pouring off the fat as it collects. Stir in the remaining ingredients. Bring the mixture to a boil, cover it and simmer, stirring often until the macaroni is tender. Two cups of sour cream may be added before serving.

Try substituting hamburger for the sausage.

BAKED SPAGHETTI

2 cups spaghetti
Salted water
Butter
2 slices bacon, cut up
1 slice onion

1 pint tomatoes
Salt and pepper
Bread or cracker crumbs
Grated cheese (optional)

Cook the spaghetti in the salted water. Drain it and pour it into a buttered baking dish. Fry the bacon and onion, and add them to the spaghetti. Season the tomatoes with butter, salt and pepper, and pour them over the above ingredients. Sprinkle them thickly with bread or cracker crumbs, and bake at 350° until brown. Grated cheese may be added if desired.

STARK CHEESE SOUFFLE

1 pint milk
¼ cup quick-cooking tapioca
½ pound cheese, grated

1 teaspoon salt
5 eggs, separated

Scald the milk in a double boiler. Add the tapioca and cook it until it is transparent, stirring frequently. Add the grated cheese and stir it until it is melted. Remove this mixture from the boiler and add the salt. Slowly add the tapioca mixture to the thickly beaten egg yolks. Mix it thoroughly, then fold in the stiffly beaten egg whites. Pour it into a well-greased pan, and set the pan in hot water to bake. Bake it at 350° for 45 minutes, or until a knife comes out clean when inserted.

Variations: Instead of grated cheese, add 1 finely cut green or red pepper.

EGG AND POTATO CASSEROLE

White Sauce
Dash of paprika
6 cups cooked grated potatoes
6 hardcooked eggs, sliced

Grated cheese
Buttered bread crumbs or cracker
    crumbs

Make a basic white sauce (see page 49) and mix in a dash of paprika, the potatoes and hard-cooked eggs. Pour the mixture into a greased baking dish, and sprinkle the top with grated cheese, buttered bread crumbs or cracker crumbs. Bake it at 375° for 30 minutes.

EGG DUTCH (OMELET)

5 eggs
1 teaspoon salt
Pepper to taste

1 heaping tablespoon flour
1 cup milk

Put the ingredients into a bowl in the order given and beat them with a rotary beater. Pour the mixture into a heated greased pan, and cover it tightly with a lid. Place it over medium low heat. Cut and turn the omelet when it is about half done, and continue baking it until done.

QUICK LUNCH

½ onion, diced
Margarine
1 pint sweet corn
1 pint tomato juice

Salt
Pepper
Brown sugar
Eggs (1 for each person)

In some margarine, sauté the onion until it is golden. Add the sweet corn and tomato juice, and salt, pepper, and a small amount of brown sugar to taste. Bring the mixture to a boil then break an egg into it for each person. Cover and cook it for about 3 to 4 minutes, until the eggs are softcooked. When using more than 6 eggs, double the amount of corn, tomatoes and onion.

Children enjoy dipping bread or toast into the egg yolk, then you can cut up the remaining egg white and eat it with the soup. This recipe is also good with crackers.

SCRAMBLED EGGS WITH CHEESE

4 eggs
¼ to ½ cup cheese, diced
Salt and pepper

Break the eggs into a bowl and add the cheese, salt and pepper. Pour the mixture into a hot, greased frying pan. Stir it roughly with a fork, breaking the yolks. Fry it, and serve immediately.

STROGANOFF CASSEROLE

2 cans (6 to 7 ounces each) tuna
1 can (10 ounces) cream of chicken
   soup
½ cup sour cream
¾ cup milk
2 tablespoons chopped parsley

2 cups cooked medium noodles
¼ teaspoon salt
Dash of pepper
2 teaspoons melted butter
3 tablespoons dry bread crumbs

Drain the tuna and break it into bite-sized chunks. Blend the soup and sour cream, and stir in the milk. Add the tuna, parsley, noodles and seasonings. Pour the mixture into a greased baking dish, and top it with buttered crumbs. Bake it at 350° for 20 to 25 minutes, or until it is bubbly.

Variations: Cheaper canned fish such as mackerel can be used in fish dishes, but in smaller amounts, as they are a little stronger in taste.

For Sour Cream Substitute, blend cottage cheese by hand or with a blender until it is smooth. Cottage cheese can be used in many recipes instead of sour cream at about half the cost.

VEGETABLE-RICE DISH

Cook together rice, onions to taste, a small amount of carrots and red and green peppers if desired. When the rice is tender and almost dry, add enough milk to make it juicy, then add drained peas, margarine, cubed Velveeta cheese and seasonings to taste. Heat the mixture until the cheese melts, then serve it with fresh bread and butter and a salad or applesauce.

Variations: For variety, substitute diced potatoes, noodles or macaroni for the rice. Add ham, beef chunks, or almost any kind of meat, and green beans or peas. When potatoes are used, instead of adding plain milk, make a white sauce. The combination of the above ingredients and your imagination will make many nourishing meals.

MEATS, SAUCES, PIZZA AND MEAT CURING

HINTS FOR MEATS

- Add vinegar to the water when cold packing meat to keep cans free from grease.

- To stretch hamburger, crumble about 5 or more slices of bread into 1 pound of the meat. Add a little milk or tomato juice, or an egg. Mix and form it into patties, then fry them.

- Roasting time for beef is approximately 30 to 35 minutes per pound. For a boneless, rolled roast, increase the time by 10 minutes per pound.

- Put a handful of soda into scalding water to scald chickens. This will help remove pin feathers.

- To make chickens easier to defeather, the water should be heated to 175°.

- When dressing a quantity of chickens, place 6 fowls (after scalding, picking and singeing), 3 towels and soap in the washing machine and cover them with warm water. Run the machine for 10 minutes. The chickens come out nice and clean.

- When cleaning chickens, use a ball made of nylon netting instead of a knife. Nothing works better.

CANNED CHICKEN

Cut chicken into bite-sized pieces. Add salt, fry the chicken, then can it. When unexpected company arrives, this can be opened, and a thickening added to provide a meat and gravy dish.

OLD-FASHIONED POULTRY STUFFING

1 cup chopped celery
½ cup chopped onions
½ teaspoon poultry seasoning
¼ cup butter or margarine

1 can (10 ounces) condensed cream of
   chicken soup, OR
1¼ cups chicken gravy
8 cups dry bread cubes

Cook the celery, onions and poultry seasoning in the butter until the vegetables are tender. Add the soup. Mix it lightly, adding the bread cubes. This makes about 4 cups of stuffing, or enough for a 5 to 6 pound bird.

CHICKEN COATING MIX

1 cup flour
Pepper (scant)
½ teaspoon salt

2 teaspoons paprika
1 teaspoon baking powder

Mix together the above ingredients. Put the mixture into a plastic bag, then shake it with pieces of chicken to coat them.

BAKED CHICKEN

½ cup flour
2 teaspoons paprika
1 teaspoon pepper
¼ teaspoon dry mustard

3 teaspoons salt
1 cut up broiler or young chicken
¼ pound butter

Mix the dry ingredients well in a plastic bag, then coat the cut up chicken parts with the mixture. In a cake pan, melt the butter. Place the chicken parts in the pan, but do not crowd them. Bake the chicken at 350° for 1½ to 2 hours or until done.

CHICKEN ROLL

Make a biscuit dough. Roll it out, then spread it with cut up cooked chicken. Roll it up as you would to make rolls, then slice it. Place the slices in a greased pan and bake them at 350° until done. Make gravy with the chicken broth, and top the hot slices with it.

Variations: *This recipe can be made with ham, using the same method. For the gravy, use a simple white sauce. Stir in cheese spread while it is hot. Serve it hot over the ham rolls.*

BARBECUED CHICKEN

Cut fryers into serving pieces. Place them in a shallow baking dish, brush them with oil and bake in a moderate oven at 375° for 45 minutes or until browned. Pour barbecue sauce over the chicken and continue to bake it for 45 minutes longer, basting frequently.

CRUNCHY CHICKEN

Using 3 to 4 pounds of broilers, dip pieces of the raw chicken into melted margarine, then roll them in finely crushed equal parts of cracker and cornflake crumbs. Place the chicken in flat, well-oiled baking pans, laying the pieces side by side but not crowding them. Sprinkle them with salt and your favorite chicken seasoning. Bake them at 375° for 1 hour or until the meat is brown and tender.

CHICKEN SALAD FOR SANDWICHES

1 quart cold, boiled chicken
1 pint celery
4 or 5 hardcooked eggs

Mayonnaise or other dressing
Salt and pepper to taste
¾ cup chopped olives (optional)

Put the chicken, celery and eggs through the coarse blade of a food chopper. Mix in the remaining ingredients.

BARBECUE SAUCE

½ cup ketchup
1 tablespoon vinegar
1 tablespoon sugar

1 tablespoon mustard
1 tablespoon Worcestershire sauce

Mix the ingredients together well. If the sauce is too strong, use less ketchup and add some tomato juice.

CHICKEN BARBECUE SAUCE

¼ cup butter, margarine or oil
1 teaspoon salt
Dash of pepper
1 cup water

2 tablespoons vinegar
2 teaspoons brown sugar
2 tablespoons Worcestershire sauce

Mix together the ingredients, then bring the mixture to a boil. Baste the meat with this sauce.

HOT DOG SAUCE

½ green pepper, chopped
1 medium-sized onion, chopped
2 tablespoons prepared mustard
¾ teaspoon salt

2 tablespoons brown sugar
¾ cup ketchup
1 tablespoon Worcestershire sauce

Mix together all the ingredients, then add 1 pint of water. Cook the sauce for 15 minutes, then add wieners and continue cooking it until the wieners are good and hot.

This sauce is very good on top of mashed potatoes.

SPAGHETTI SAUCE

1 small onion, chopped
1 can (7½ ounces) tomato sauce
1 can (10 ounces) tomato soup
1¼ cups water

½ teaspoon garlic salt
¼ teaspoon pepper
1 tablespoon parsley

Mix the onion, tomato sauce and tomato soup with the water. Simmer it for 10 minutes, then mix in the seasoning and parsley. Place meatballs in the sauce and simmer it uncovered for 25 minutes, turning them occasionally. Mix this sauce with hot, cooked spaghetti and top it with grated cheese.

Variations: *This sauce is very good with a cut up stewing hen instead of hamburger. Cook the hen until it is almost done, then finish cooking it in the spaghetti sauce.*

BARBECUED HAMBURGER

Brown 1 pound of hamburger with 1 sliced onion. Add 1 teaspoon of salt and a dash of pepper. When the hamburger is brown, add barbecue sauce and steam it for 10 minutes. Serve this dish with buns.

BEEF BARBECUE (LARGE QUANTITY)

1 large bunch celery
1 pound onions
3 bottles (14 ounces each) ketchup
5 teaspoons Worcestershire sauce
1 cup brown sugar

2 tablespoons chili powder
2 tablespoons salt
1 tablespoon pepper
½ cup flour
5 pounds ground beef, browned

Finely mince the celery and onions and simmer them until they are tender. Add the ketchup, Worcestershire sauce, sugar and seasonings. Make a thickening of the flour, and add it to the celery/onion mixture. Cook it on low heat for 10 minutes. (If placed on high heat, it will burn easily.) Add the browned beef and heat it thoroughly to finish the barbecue.

Beef Barbecue may be refrigerated in a closed container and warmed up as needed.

BEEF ROAST

3-pound roast
2 teaspoons salt
Pepper

2 teaspoons brown sugar
3 tablespoons water (approximate)

Mix together the salt, a small amount of pepper, and the brown sugar, and rub it well into all sides of the meat. Place the meat in a casserole and add a small amount of water (approximately 3 tablespoons). Roast it, covered, at 325° for 1 hour or until done.

YORKSHIRE PUDDING

2 eggs
2 cups sour milk
1 cup sweet milk
2 teaspoons baking powder

1 teaspoon salt
1 tablespoon sugar
2 cups sifted all-purpose flour, or
    enough to make a stiff batter

When the beef you are cooking is almost done, pour out the broth (reserving it), leaving about 1 inch in the pan. Mix together the above ingredients to make a batter, and pour it into the broth around the roast. Bake it for 25 minutes with the meat. Thicken the reserved broth to make gravy. Cut the pudding into blocks, pour the gravy over it, and serve it with the beef.

SAUSAGE LOAF

1½ pounds pork sausage meat
1½ cups bread or cracker crumbs
2 tablespoons grated onions
2 tablespoons ketchup

2 tablespoons horseradish
2 teaspoons prepared mustard
1 egg, slightly beaten
½ cup milk

Mix together the sausage and cracker crumbs, then add the onions, ketchup, horseradish, mustard and egg. Moisten the mixture with the milk, and shape it into a loaf. Bake it at 350° for 1 hour.

SAVORY MEAT LOAF

1¼ pounds ground beef, plus
¼ pound ground pork, OR
2 pounds ground beef (omit the pork)
¼ cup minced onions
1 cup oatmeal or crushed crackers
2½ teaspoons salt

1 beaten egg
¼ teaspoon pepper
1 teaspoon mustard
¼ cup ketchup
1 cup tomato juice
Bacon slices

Mix together the ingredients, then form the mixture into a loaf. Put a few bacon slices on top, and pour additional tomato juice over all. Bake the meat loaf at 350° to 375° for 1 hour.

Variations: *The mixture may be pressed into a cake pan and topped with ketchup. Bake it for about 1 hour.*

Try spreading a glaze over the loaf.

Glaze for Meat Loaf;

½ cup brown sugar
1½ teaspoons prepared mustard
1 tablespoon Worcestershire sauce

Mix together the ingredients and add enough vinegar to make a paste. Spread the glaze over the meat loaf.

HAM LOAF

2 pounds smoked ham (ground)
2 pounds fresh pork (ground)
2 eggs
1½ cups milk

1½ cups bread crumbs
1 teaspoon salt
1 teaspoon pepper

Mix together the ingredients, then form the mixture into a loaf. Pour the following glaze over the top, and bake it at 325° for 2 hours.

Glaze;

Mix together the following ingredients;

1½ cups brown sugar
1 teaspoon dry mustard

½ cup water
½ cup vinegar

POOR MAN'S STEAK

1 pound hamburger
1 cup milk
¼ teaspoon pepper

1 cup cracker crumbs
1 teaspoon salt
1 small onion, finely chopped

Mix the ingredients well and shape the mixture into a narrow loaf. Let it set for at least 8 hours, or overnight. Slice it and fry it until brown. Put the slices in layers in a roaster and spread mushroom soup on each piece, using 1 can (10 ounces) of soup. Bake it for 1 hour at 325°. (Pan gravy may be used with the mushroom soup.)

HAMBURGER PUFFS

1 good-sized onion, chopped
1 tablespoon butter or oil
4 large slices bread
1 cup milk
2 eggs, beaten

½ green pepper, finely chopped
1 teaspoon salt
¼ teaspoon pepper
1 pound ground beef

Sauté the onions in the butter until they are lightly browned. Crumble the bread into the milk and let it stand until the milk is absorbed. Add the onions and the remaining ingredients to the bread and milk. Mix them well and press them into patties in greased muffin tins. Allow the patties to set for 15 minutes, then bake them for 25 to 30 minutes at 400°. Place the muffin tins on cookie sheets if necessary. Serve the puffs with gravy or ketchup. This recipe makes 8 or 9 puffs.

Variations: A can of cream soup heated with ½ can of milk makes a nice sauce to use with the puffs.

VEAL LOAF

1 pound beef, finely ground
1 cup bread or cracker crumbs
½ cup cream
1 teaspoon sugar

2 eggs, beaten
1 teaspoon butter
Salt and pepper to taste

Mix the ingredients well. Make a long loaf, and bake it for 1½ to 2 hours at 350°.

CHUNK BEEF PATTIES

1 quart beef chunks
5 double soda crackers, crushed
2 eggs

Parsley
Hamburger seasoning
Milk

Grind the beef chunks. Mix in the cracker crumbs, eggs, a little parsley, hamburger seasoning, or whatever seasoning your family likes. Add enough milk to make soft patties. Fry them.

HAMBURGER-EGG CASSEROLE

6 eggs, beaten
1 pound ground beef, browned
¼ teaspoon pepper
½ teaspoon dry mustard
12 slices bread, cut up

3 cups milk
1 teaspoon salt
1 teaspoon Worcestershire sauce
6 slices cheese, cut up (optional)

Mix together all the ingredients, then put the mixture into a casserole. Place the casserole in a pan of water, and bake it at 350° for 1¼ hours.

BEANBURGERS

2 pounds ground beef
2 tablespoons oil
1 small onion, chopped
½ cup ketchup
1 teaspoon Worcestershire sauce
Water

1 pint kidney beans, cooked and
    drained
Salt and pepper to taste
½ teaspoon garlic powder
½ teaspoon chili powder, OR
1 teaspoon oregano
Cheese slices

Brown the ground beef in the oil. Add the onion, ketchup and Worcestershire sauce. To prevent burning, add sufficient water and simmer for 20 minutes. Add the kidney beans, salt and pepper, garlic powder and chili powder, or oregano. Continue simmering the ingredients for about 30 minutes more. Serve them on buns, using only ½ of the bun. Top each one with a slice of cheese and melt it in a hot oven. Serve them hot.

MEAT PATTIES

2 pounds ground pork or hamburger
2 eggs
1 onion, chopped
1 cup cracker crumbs

1 cup milk
1 teaspoon salt
½ teaspoon pepper

Mix together the ingredients. Form the mixture into patties and fry them.

SOUPERBURGERS

1 pound ground beef
½ cup chopped onions
1 tablespoon shortening
2 tablespoons ketchup

Dash of pepper
1 can (10 ounces) vegetable soup
1 teaspoon prepared mustard
6 buns split and toasted

In a skillet, brown the beef and onions in the shortening. Stir it to separate the meat. Add the remaining ingredients and cook them for 5 minutes, stirring now and then. Serve this on buns or with mashed potatoes.

SOUR CREAM BEEFBURGERS

1½ pounds ground beef
¼ cup Worcestershire sauce
1½ teaspoons salt

1 cup sour cream
1 tablespoon chopped onions
1½ cups cornflakes or bread crumbs

Mix together the first 5 ingredients, then add the crushed cornflakes or bread crumbs. Form the mixture into patties. Broil them for 5 minutes, then turn them over and broil them for 3 minutes more. This recipe makes 10 to 12 burgers.

WAGON WHEEL HAMBURGER

2 pounds hamburger
½ cup barbecue sauce
½ cup dry bread crumbs
2 beaten eggs

¼ cup chopped onion
¼ cup chopped green pepper
1 teaspoon salt

Combine the ingredients, mix them lightly, and put the mixture into an 8-inch, cast-iron skillet. On top make a spoke design with additional barbecue sauce, and sprinkle a little brown sugar over the entire surface. Bake it at 325° for 50 minutes or until done.

LIVER PATTIES

If the beef liver you are using is tough, try grinding it. Season it with salt, and pepper if desired. Chopped onion and beaten egg may be added. Fry the liver like hamburger patties. Add a little flour if necessary, or sprinkle the patties with flour before turning them.

STEAK SUPREME

2 pounds hamburger
2 eggs
½ cup dry bread crumbs

2 teaspoons salt
6 tablespoons onions, finely chopped
Pepper (optional)

Heat lard in a skillet, then press a mixture of the above ingredients into the skillet to about a 1-inch thickness. Brown it on both sides. Add 1 can (10 ounces) of mushroom soup and the same amount of water. Cover the skillet tightly and simmer for 20 minutes.

HAPPY CHANGE MEATBALLS

1 teaspoon salt
1½ pounds ground beef
¼ teaspoon pepper and nutmeg

   mixture

½ cup cracker crumbs
½ cup milk
2 eggs, slightly beaten

Shape the mixture into small balls, and place them in a large shallow baking pan. Bake the meatballs at 350° for 30 minutes, then drain off excess fat.

In a bowl, combine;

2 cups tomato juice
2 tablespoons flour

Mix them well, then add the following;

¾ cup ketchup
½ teaspoon Worcestershire sauce
¼ cup water

Mix these ingredients until blended, then pour the mixture over the meatballs and bake them for 30 minutes longer.

BEGGAR'S DISH

Use 1 pound or more of hamburger with a bit of onion. Fry it until it is well done. Drain off the liquid from a can (16 ounces) of kidney beans, and add the beans to the meat. Mix it well, and fry it again until well done.

This is an economical dish if meat is too expensive.

Variations: A can of condensed tomato soup may be added with the beans. Delicious!

SLOPPY JOES

1 cup water
2 pounds hamburger
½ cup onions, chopped
½ cup celery, chopped
½ cup vinegar

2 tablespoons dry mustard
1 small bottle ketchup
2 tablespoons brown sugar
1 cup tomato paste
Salt and pepper to taste

Add the water to the hamburger and cook it. Add the rest of the ingredients and continue cooking the hamburger until it is done. Serve it on hamburger buns.

SPARERIBS AND SAUERKRAUT

4 pounds or 2 sides spareribs
Salt and pepper
1 quart sauerkraut
1 apple, chopped

2 tablespoons brown sugar
1 tablespoon caraway seeds
1 onion, sliced
2 cups water

Cut the ribs and brown them in a skillet, adding seasonings. Pour off the fat. Place the sauerkraut mixed with the apple, sugar, caraway and onion in a kettle. Place the ribs on top. Pour the water around the meat and sauerkraut. Cover it tightly and simmer it for 1¼ to 1½ hours or until the ribs are very tender.

BARBECUED SPARERIBS

Add canned ribs to Tennessee Barbecue Sauce and simmer them for 15 to 20 minutes. Sausage may be substituted for the ribs.

Tennessee Barbecue Sauce;

1 bottle (15 ounces) chili sauce
⅔ cup brown sugar
2 tablespoons Worcestershire sauce
3 medium-sized onions, chopped

1 bottle (15 ounces) ketchup
3 tablespoons dry mustard
1½ cups water

Mix together all the ingredients and simmer the mixture for 15 minutes.

HAM SALAD FOR SANDWICHES

2 cups cooked ham
3 stalks celery
1 large dill pickle
¼ teaspoon dry mustard

¼ teaspoon onion powder
½ cup mayonnaise
½ teaspoon salt
1 tablespoon lemon juice

Put the ham, celery and pickle through the coarse blade of a food chopper, add the remaining ingredients and mix.

SCALLOPED HAM

1½ cups ham
½ cup ham broth
2 cups cracker crumbs
3 cups milk

2 eggs, beaten
1 teaspoon salt
Dash of pepper
1 tablespoon butter

Brown the ham and cook it until it is tender, then grind it. Line the bottom of a casserole with a layer of cracker crumbs, then a layer of ½ of the ground ham, then the crackers, making 2 layers of each. Mix the milk, seasonings and eggs, and pour the mixture over the meat. Dot the top with the butter. Bake the casserole at 375° for 30 minutes or until done.

HOT HAM AND CHEESE BUNS

½ pound ham
½ pound sharp cheese
⅓ cup sliced onions
2 hardcooked eggs, sliced

½ cup sliced peppers, OR
½ cup stuffed olives, sliced
3 tablespoons salad dressing
½ cup chili sauce

Cut the ham and cheese into ¼-inch cubes. Combine them with the onions, eggs and peppers or olives. Add the salad dressing blended with the chili sauce, mix it well and spread the mixture in 10 split wiener buns. Wrap each one in foil and twist the ends securely. Bake them for 10 minutes at 400° or until the buns are hot.

SCALLOPED WIENERS

1 pound wieners
Water
5 cups coarsely crushed crackers
2 eggs

2 teaspoons salt
Pepper to taste
4½ cups milk
4 brimming tablespoons butter

Add a small amount of water to the wieners and cook them for 10 minutes. Slice the wieners, and make alternate layers of crackers and wieners in a casserole. Beat the egg and add the seasonings and milk. Pour this mixture over the crackers and wieners, and dot the surface with the butter. Bake the casserole at 350° for 30 minutes or until it is done. This will fill a very large casserole or 2 smaller ones.

PIZZA PIE

1 package yeast
¾ cup warm water

2½ cups biscuit mix

Dissolve the yeast in the water, add the biscuit mix, and mix them well. Knead the dough, roll it out, and put it into a greased pan, letting it rise for ½ hour.

1 pound ground beef, cooked
¾ cup chopped onions
½ cup chopped green peppers

1 teaspoon oregano
Salt and pepper to taste
2 cups tomato sauce

To make the topping, cook the ground beef, onions and pepper together. Add the rest of the ingredients and continue cooking them. Spread this mixture over the crust and bake it at 375° for 30 minutes or until it is done. Cheese and/or mushrooms may be put on top.

YEAST PIZZA

1 package dry yeast
1 cup warm water
1 teaspoon sugar
1½ teaspoons salt

¼ cup salad oil
3 cups flour
1 pound cheese
2 cups tomato sauce

Dissolve the yeast in the warm water, add the sugar, salt and oil, and mix it thoroughly. Add ½ the flour and beat it until there are no lumps. Gradually add the remaining flour. Knead the dough for 5 minutes. Take ½ the dough and roll it out to a circle 12 inches in diameter. Place it on a greased cookie sheet, leaving the edges a little thicker than the middle. Repeat this procedure with the other ½ of the dough and put it on a second cookie sheet. Let the dough rise for 20 to 30 minutes. Brush the top with salad oil. Cut the cheese into fine pieces and sprinkle it over the 2 surfaces. Pour the tomato sauce lightly over the cheese. Bake the pizzas at 450° for 15 minutes or until the edges are brown and the cheese is melted.

CRAZY CRUST PIZZA

1 cup flour	1 quart cooked, drained hamburger
1 teaspoon salt	Onions, chopped
1 teaspoon oregano	Mushrooms, sliced
⅛ teaspoon pepper	1 cup pizza sauce
2 eggs	Velveeta cheese slices
⅔ cup milk	

Mix together the flour, salt, oregano, pepper, eggs and milk. Grease and flour a pizza pan or cookie sheet with sides. Pour in the batter and tilt the pan so that it covers the bottom. Arrange the hamburger over the batter, and add onions and mushrooms. Bake the pizza at 400° for 20 to 25 minutes. Remove it from the oven, drizzle on the pizza sauce, and lay Velveeta cheese slices on top. Bake the pizza again until the cheese melts.

Variations: Instead of pizza sauce, try tomato sauce, 1½ teaspoons of oregano and pepper.

JIFFY PIZZA

Dough;

2 cups flour	⅔ cup milk
1 tablespoon baking powder	⅓ cup salad oil
1 teaspoon salt	

Sauce;

6 ounces tomato paste	2 tablespoons sugar
¼ cup water	1 teaspoon garlic powder (optional)
1 teaspoon oregano	1 pound browned hamburger
¼ teaspoon pepper	Cheese, finely chopped
½ teaspoon salt	

Sift together the flour, baking powder and salt, and add the milk and oil to make a dough. Pat it on the bottom of a pizza pan. Mix the first 7 sauce ingredients and spread the mixture over the dough. Spread the chopped meat over the surface and sprinkle it with the cheese. Bake the pizza for 25 to 30 minutes at 425°. It serves 6 or more.

SWISS STEAK

Salt and pepper a 2 or 3-inch steak, and cover both sides with as much flour as it will hold. Sear both sides of the steak, cover it with sliced onions, and pour over it a small bottle of tomato ketchup. Add enough water to cover the steak and bake it for 2 hours at 400°.

If ketchup is not desired, sear the steak and add 1 tablespoon of vinegar, 1 tablespoon of salt and a small amount of pepper. When the steak is browned, cover it with boiling water or cream and simmer it slowly until very tender.

FRIED OYSTERS

3 dozen oysters
½ cup finely crushed cracker crumbs
½ teaspoon salt

2 eggs, beaten
1 tablespoon water
Butter

Drain the oysters. Dip them in the seasoned crumbs, then in the eggs diluted with the water, then again in the crumbs. Fry the oysters with butter until they are golden brown.

SCALLOPED OYSTERS

4 cups crackers, coarsely crushed
1 can (10 ounces) oysters
2 cups milk
1 teaspoon salt

Pepper to taste
1 egg
⅓ cup butter

In a 1½ quart casserole, place a layer of cracker crumbs on the bottom, then a layer of oysters, then crackers, then oysters, making 2 layers of each. Just before baking, add the milk and seasonings to the egg, then pour it over the casserole ingredients. Arrange the butter in thin strips on top. Bake it in a moderate oven (350°) until it is well heated, approximately ¾ to 1 hour.

CANNED FISH

Cut up and pack fish into a jar. Add ½ teaspoon of salt per pint and about ⅓ cup of vinegar to each quart. Seal and cold pack it for 3½ to 4 hours. (The bones will become soft and edible within 4 weeks.) Serve the fish with a little vinegar and pepper.

SALMON LOAF

Fix Amish Dressing (see page 48), omitting the chicken and chicken broth. Add 1 can of salmon, finely cut. Mix it, and form the mixture into a loaf, or press it into a casserole. Bake it at 350° for 1 to 1½ hours.

FRIED SALMON PATTIES

2 cups cracker crumbs
1 cup salmon
1 teaspoon salt (scant)

2 eggs, beaten
1½ cups milk
Pepper to taste

Roll the crackers until they are finely crushed. Mix them with the other ingredients. Drop the mixture by tablespoons and fry it with butter.

SALMON SOUFFLE

1 can salmon, minced
2 egg yolks
1¼ cups milk

1 cup bread crumbs
½ teaspoon vinegar
2 egg whites

Mix together the first five ingredients, then add the beaten egg whites. Put the mixture into a casserole dish, and bake it for 30 to 40 minutes at 400°.

MEAT CURING

Trim the meat, then chill it thoroughly through and through at 40°, being careful that it does not freeze. Never put salt on the meat before it is thoroughly chilled, as salt tends to block the escape of body heat, causing the inside bones to sour before the salt or cure penetrates.

For 100 pounds of meat, use 7 pounds of salt, 2 pounds of brown sugar and 2 ounces of saltpeter. Apply this only once to the meat. For hams, use ½ the required amount and about a week later, the remaining ½. For bacon use ½ of the cure recipe, and apply it only once. Using a cup measure, fill it to slightly rounding with the cure for every 10 pounds of meat (bacon and hams), putting a second cup on the hams a week later.

MEAT CURE

2 pounds brown sugar
4 gallons water
6 pounds salt

2 ounces pepper
1 ounce saltpeter

Bring the ingredients to a boil, then allow the mixture to cool. Pack meat in a tub or crock as tightly as possible with this brine. Put weight on top to keep the meat in the brine. Leave hams in for 4 weeks, bacon only 5 or 6 days. Then smoke the meat, and wrap it in paper or cloth.

CORNED BEEF

50 pounds beef (roasts, steaks, or any
    choice cut)
3 quarts salt

Place the meat in layers in a large crock or similar suitable container. Salt each layer and let it stand overnight. Roughly rinse off the beef and pack it again in a crock.

Make a brine of;

¼ pound baking soda
¼ pound saltpeter

2 pounds brown sugar
2 tablespoons liquid smoke

Place the meat in the brine with enough water to cover the meat well. It will be cured and ready for use in 2 weeks. It can then be cut into suitable pieces and canned (cold pack for 3 hours) or put into the freezer. If the crock is kept in a cool place, the meat may be kept in brine and used any time within 3 months. The flavor of the meat is improved when kept over 6 weeks.

DRIED BEEF

4½ gallons water
Salt enough to float an egg
1 ounce saltpeter

2 pounds brown sugar
20 pounds beef

Combine the water, salt and sugar to make a brine. Put a weight on top of the meat to keep it in the brine. For large pieces of meat, soak them for 60 hours, and for small pieces, 48 hours. Then smoke the meat.

HAM CURING

When curing hams, poke cure around the bones, especially the shank end, with your fingers and finish by patting the remainder on the meat side. Put the meat into a wooden box which has a few drain holes. Place it in a cool cellar or room, keeping the temperature between 45 and 36°, if at all possible, and not below freezing. Two days for every pound of ham are required for curing. A 25 pound ham requires 50 days. The curing time may be shortened somewhat for a very large ham. Bacon curing time is 1½ days for each pound of meat.

After the meat is cured, soak it in cold water for ½ to 1 hour; then scrub it to remove excess salt and mold which forms if your curing room is too warm. This mold won't hurt the meat.

To smoke the meat, pass a twine through the shank of hams or shoulders. For bacon, push a stiff wire through one end to hold it stiff. Put a twine through the meat under the wire to hang it up. Meat will color better when dipped in hot water a few seconds, and scrubbed briskly.

When the meat is cured and smoked, wrap it in a large paper bag. Double the top over and tie it tightly so no flies can enter. The skipper fly which lays eggs to hatch worms, can't be kept out of a room with regular window screens. Hang the meat in a reasonably dry room as this will prevent it from becoming moldy. If it molds, just brush it off. Never wrap your cured meat in plastic.

After you begin cutting a ham, swab some vegetable oil on the cut. This will to some extent prevent mold. This way hams can be kept a long period of time. Some people say it is better the second year than the first. Preferably, it should be aged several months so it will lose its saltiness. If it is still too salty, soak or cook the ham lightly and pour off the first water.

EASY HAM CURING

Add enough salt to water so that an egg floats. In this brine soak the untreated hams for 6 weeks, then smoke them.

To preserve the ham, slice or cut the ham into pieces. Dip each piece into soft, partly melted lard. Place the ham in a jar. Pour the melted lard on top, completely covering the meat. Put lids on the jars and set them on the cellar floor.

MEAT—TO USE NOW OR LATER

Spine, ribs and bacon can be put into salted water (strong enough to float an egg). To use the meat, soak it in clear water overnight so it will not be too salty.

Hams can also be put into salted water and kept there for 6 weeks before smoking.

BARBECUED BONE MEAT

1½ pounds bone meat
1 cup celery, chopped
2 tablespoons Worcestershire sauce
1 tablespoon brown sugar
Tomato juice (optional)

½ cup onions, chopped
1 cup ketchup
1 tablespoon mustard
¾ teaspoon salt

Mix together the ingredients, then cold pack the mixture for 1 hour. To make a large batch, about 40 pints, use the following quantities;

18 pounds bone meat, ground if
   desired
12 cups celery, chopped
6 cups onions, chopped
¾ cup mustard
3 quarts ketchup

1½ cups Worcestershire sauce
¾ cup brown sugar
3 tablespoons salt

BEEF BARBECUE (FOR CANNING)

10 pounds ground beef
5 cups chopped onions
¼ cup salt
1¼ tablespoons pepper
1 cup vinegar

¾ cup prepared mustard
1½ cups brown sugar
⅔ cup Worcestershire sauce
5 cups ketchup
4 cups beef broth or water

Brown the ground beef and onions. Add the rest of the ingredients with the beef broth or water (using more than 4 cups if necessary). Steam the mixture for 10 minutes. Pack it in jars, seal them, and boil them for 1 to 2 hours. This recipe makes about 9 quarts.

CANNED MEATBALLS

5 pounds hamburger
3 teaspoons salt

⅛ teaspoon pepper

Mix the ingredients together well, and form the mixture into balls the size of walnuts. Fry them until brown in a skillet. Pack the meatballs in jars. Make a brown gravy and divide it among the jars. If it does not fill the jars, add water. Boil them in a pressure cooker at 10 pounds pressure for 1 hour.

To can meatballs for cooking with spaghetti, put them into cans raw but seasoned, and add water. Cook them for 1 hour and 25 minutes at 10 pounds pressure in a pressure cooker.

CANNED MEAT LOAF

15 pounds ground beef
⅓ cup salt
4 slices bread, crumbled
36 soda crackers, crushed

1 cup oatmeal
3 cups water, milk or tomato juice
4 eggs
Chopped onions (optional)

Mix the ingredients well. Pack the mixture into jars, seal them and process them for 3 hours. Or, form the mixture into balls and fry them. Then pack the meatballs into jars, seal them, and process them for 2 hours.

CANNING BEEFBURGER

Brown hamburger as you would for casseroles, and add salt, pepper and whatever other seasonings you prefer (1 cup of salt and 3 tablespoons of pepper to 25 pounds of meat). Add chopped parsley, diced celery, chopped onions or the vegetables of your choice (or none at all). Put the mixture into jars and cold pack them for 1 hour.

This beefburger is very handy to use in many different dishes.

MINCEMEAT (FOR CANNING)

1 quart ground meat
2 quarts sliced apples
2 quarts cider (or grape juice)
1 quart sour cherries (optional)
5 cups sugar
½ teaspoon cinnamon

¼ teaspoon ground cloves
¼ teaspoon allspice
Juice and rind of 2 oranges (optional)
Salt to taste
2 cups raisins

Mix together all the ingredients and cook the mixture for 15 minutes. Stir it frequently to prevent scorching. Add more cider if necessary. Pour it into hot sterilized jars and seal them at once. Process them for 30 minutes in a hot bath.

BRINE FOR CANNING STUFFED SAUSAGE

2 quarts water
¼ cup salt
¼ cup sugar

½ teaspoon pepper
½ teaspoon saltpeter

Combine the ingredients and bring the mixture to a boil before adding the meat. Boil it for 20 minutes, then pack the meat in jars and cover it with the brine in which it was boiled. Cold pack it for 3 hours.

BEEF AND PORK BOLOGNA

60 pounds beef trimmings
40 pounds pork trimmings
3 pounds tenderizer
3 to 4 ounces black pepper

1½ ounces coriander, OR
1 ounce curry powder
1 ounce mace
Onions if desired

Mix 2 pounds of the tenderizer with the chilled beef trimmings, and grind them using the coarse grinding plate. After grinding, spread the meat in a cool place and let it cure for 48 hours. Grind the chilled pork trimmings with 1 pound of the tenderizer and let it cure. After 48 hours, regrind the cured beef, using a ⅛-inch hole plate. Then add the pork and grind the mixture again. Add the seasonings and mix thoroughly—a small amount of water will help. Thirty to 40 minutes is not too long for thorough mixing.

Stuff the meat tightly into beef or muslin casings and allow it to hang in a cool place overnight. Then hang the bologna in a smoke house, heated 110 to 120°, and smoke it to a rich brown color, for about 2 or 3 hours. Immediately put the hot smoked bologna into water heated 160 to 175° and cook it until it floats or until it squeaks when the pressure of your thumb and fingers on the casing is suddenly released. The cooking time ranges from 20 to 90 minutes, depending on the size of the casing. Plunge the cooked sausage into cold water to chill it. Hang it in a cool, dry place for future use.

LEBANON BOLOGNA

50 pounds beef
1 pound salt
3 tablespoons pepper
2 tablespoons nutmeg
1½ tablespoons saltpeter

2½ pounds sugar
1½ pounds salt
½ pound lard or 9 ounces peanut oil,
    per 25 pounds meat

Salt the beef and let it stand for 4 days. The secret to a good bologna is to let the meat season well before grinding and stuffing it. Cut up the meat in order to grind it, then put it into a large container making alternate layers of the meat and the mixed seasonings. Let it stand in a cold place for 5 to 7 days, turning the meat on top every day or so to prevent drying out. Then grind the meat twice to the desired texture, and add the peanut oil or lard. Mix it well in a wooden or enamel container. Stuff the meat and let it hang for 2 or 3 days to settle, then smoke it, being careful not to overheat it with the fire.

CHICKEN BOLOGNA

25 pounds chicken meat
1 pound tenderizer
1 ounce black pepper
½ cup sugar

2 teaspoons saltpeter
2 teaspoons garlic powder
3 tablespoons liquid smoke

Add the tenderizer to the chicken meat and grind it twice. Let it set for 24 hours, then add the black pepper, sugar, saltpeter, garlic powder and liquid smoke. (The liquid smoke may be omitted and the meat smoked after stuffing.) Mix it well, then grind it again and process it as you would any fresh meat (such as sausage or ground beef), or stuff it into cloth bags and boil it in water for 30 minutes. If you have stuffed the meat, then it may be frozen or canned. To can the bologna, slice it and pack it into jars, adding the broth in which it was cooked. Then cold pack it for 2½ hours.

SUMMER BOLOGNA

60 pounds beef
1 teaspoon saltpeter
⅓ cup pepper (scant)
1 quart molasses

1 pound lard
1 quart salt
3 pounds brown sugar

Let the beef stand until it is just a little old. Soak it in strong salted water for about 30 minutes. Smoke it for ½ day. Grind the beef, add the above mixed ingredients, and mix. Grind it again. Stuff the mixture into bologna-sized bags. Smoke the meat for 7 to 10 days.

This recipe is also very good if you substitute venison for the beef.

SUMMER SAUSAGE

25 pounds beef
10 pounds pork
2 tablespoons garlic powder

1 cup white sugar
2 teaspoons saltpeter
1½ cups warm water

Grind the meat and mix in the rest of the above ingredients.

6 cups salt
5 cups brown sugar

6 heaping teaspoons saltpeter
3 gallons water

To make a brine, mix these ingredients together and bring the mixture to a boil. Let it cool. Stuff the meat into long narrow bags (bologna size) then place them in the brine for 3 weeks. Remove them from the brine and place them in cold water overnight. Hang up the meat and smoke it in the bags. When it is smoked, paraffin the bags well, and hang them in a cool place. The bags may be hung in the cellar stairs but not in the cellar. Slice the meat and eat it cold.

SALADS AND SALAD DRESSINGS

CARROT SALAD

1 package (3 ounces) orange gelatin
    powder
½ cup carrots, finely grated
1 cup crushed pineapple

2 tablespoons sugar (optional)
Raisins (optional)

Prepare the gelatin according to the directions on the box, using slightly more water. When the gelatin starts to thicken, add the carrots and pineapple. If more sweetness is desired, add the sugar, and add raisins according to taste. Stir it and let it set.

CARROT CRACKER SALAD

3 cups carrots, grated
1½ cups soda cracker crumbs
3 hardcooked eggs, chopped
1 small onion, chopped

1 tablespoon sugar
Salt and pepper to taste
1 cup mayonnaise (approximate)

Mix the ingredients together, and serve.

COLESLAW

4 cups cabbage, finely shredded
¾ cup sugar
2 tablespoons water

3 tablespoons vinegar (approximate)
½ teaspoon salt

Mix all the ingredients thoroughly until the sugar is dissolved. If desired, add ½ cup of finely chopped celery or peppers.

Coleslaw Dressing;

1 cup salad dressing
½ cup sugar
1 teaspoon garlic powder

1 tablespoon celery seeds
2 tablespoons vinegar
1 teaspoon salt

Blend the ingredients well before serving this dressing on coleslaw.

CABBAGE SLAW

4 quarts shredded cabbage
2 medium onions, chopped

1 pepper, diced (optional)

Mix these ingredients, then pour over them a mixture of the following ingredients after it has been brought to a boil.

1½ cups sugar
¾ cup salad oil
1 teaspoon celery seeds

¾ cup vinegar
1 tablespoon salt

This salad will last indefinitely in the refrigerator.

DUTCH SLAW

1 large head cabbage, chopped
½ cup vinegar
1 cup celery, diced
2 teaspoons salt
½ teaspoon mustard seeds

½ cup chopped onions
2 cups sugar
1 green pepper, diced
1 teaspoon celery seeds

Mix together all the ingredients and put them into a glass jar. Screw on the lid, and refrigerate it until needed. It is ready to serve.

This salad will last a long time if refrigerated.

HAM-RONI SALAD

1 cup diced ham
2 cups cooked macaroni
¾ cup celery, chopped
1 cup grated carrots
¼ cup green peppers, chopped
¼ cup onions, chopped

3 tablespoons mayonnaise
1½ tablespoons barbecue sauce
(optional)
Ketchup (optional)
1 teaspoon prepared mustard
Salt and pepper to taste

Combine the ham, macaroni, celery, carrots, peppers and onions. Combine and mix thoroughly the mayonnaise, barbecue sauce, ketchup and mustard. Then combine the two mixtures.

GOLDEN SALAD

1 envelope unflavored gelatin
¼ cup sugar
¼ teaspoon salt
¾ cup pineapple juice
¾ cup orange juice

¼ cup vinegar
1 cup diced pineapple, drained
½ cup orange sections, cut into small
pieces
½ cup raw carrots, coarsely grated

Mix thoroughly in a saucepan the gelatin, sugar and salt. Add the pineapple juice. Place it over low heat, stirring constantly until the gelatin is dissolved. Stir in the orange juice and vinegar after removing it from the heat. Fold in the pineapple, oranges and carrots. Pour the mixture into a mold and refrigerate it to set.

GREEN BEAN SALAD

1 pound green beans
2 small onions
6 slices bacon

⅓ cup vinegar
2½ tablespoons sugar
½ teaspoon salt

Wash the green beans and cut off and discard the ends. Cut the beans into 1-inch pieces. Cook them for 15 to 20 minutes or until they are tender. Drain them thoroughly and put them into a bowl, keeping them warm. Meanwhile, clean the onions and cut them into ⅛-inch thick slices. Separate the onion rings and put them into the bowl with the beans.

Dice and fry the bacon until it is crisp, without pouring off the drippings. Then add to the bacon the vinegar, sugar and salt. Heat this mixture to boiling, stirring well. Pour the bacon/vinegar mixture over the beans and onions and toss it lightly to coat them thoroughly.

KRAUT SALAD

1 quart sauerkraut, drained
1 cup celery, finely cut
1 small mango, finely cut
1 small onion, finely cut

½ cup cooking oil
1 cup sugar
½ cup vinegar

Mix the ingredients together, and the salad is ready to serve.

MACARONI SALAD

Use well-cooked macaroni instead of potatoes and prepare it the same as you would Potato Salad (see page 93). Macaroni and potatoes may also be combined and used for Macaroni-Potato Salad. Cooked navy beans may also be added.

PEA SALAD

1 cup cooked peas, drained
1 cup celery, finely cut

½ cup sweet pickles, chopped
½ cup diced cheese

Season the ingredients with salt, pepper and sugar, and mix them with a good mayonnaise.

PERFECTION SALAD

1 tablespoon unflavored gelatin
½ cup cold water
1 cup boiling water
½ cup sugar
½ cup mild vinegar
2 tablespoons lemon juice

1 teaspoon salt
1 cup cabbage, finely shredded
2 cups celery, finely cut
2 pimentos, finely cut
¼ cup red or green peppers, finely cut

Soak the gelatin in the cold water for about 5 minutes. Add the boiling water, sugar, vinegar, lemon juice and salt. When the mixture begins to stiffen, add the remaining ingredients. Turn it into a wet mold and chill it. Remove the salad to a bed of lettuce and garnish it with mayonnaise.

QUICK LETTUCE SALAD

Spread lettuce leaves on individual plates. Place a pineapple slice or a spoonful of pineapple chunks on each plate of lettuce, and top it with cottage cheese. On top of the cottage cheese put a spoonful of mayonnaise, and sprinkle it with nutmeats or garnish with a maraschino cherry.

POTATO SALAD

1 quart cooked, salted, diced potatoes
10 (or fewer) hardcooked eggs, sliced
½ cup celery, finely chopped (optional)

2 cups Velvet Salad Dressing
   (see page 101)

1 small onion, minced

Mix the ingredients together, and serve.

SUMMER SALAD

Take several tablespoons of olive oil, cooking oil or sour cream. Add vinegar or lemon juice, then salt to taste. If a sweet salad is desired, honey or sugar may be mixed in with the oil. Add ½ banana, finely diced. Mix these ingredients, then add any of the following vegetables or others of your choice;

Lettuce
Radishes
Cucumber
Celery

Carrots
Tomatoes
Onions
Spinach

Mix them thoroughly then add 1 handful of raisins and a handful of crushed peanuts (optional).

Variations: For a simpler salad, try using only lettuce and onions, or lettuce and diced apples.

THREE-BEAN SALAD

1 cup vinegar
1 cup sugar
2 tablespoons oil
Salt and pepper to taste
1 sweet onion, sliced
1 to 1¼ cups celery, diced

1 quart yellow beans, drained
1 quart green beans, drained
1 small can (1 pint) dark red kidney
   beans, washed and drained
1 green or red sweet pepper, sliced

Mix together the first 4 ingredients, then let the mixture stand while you slice the rest. Mix together all the vegetables, then add the vinegar mixture. Let it stand for 24 hours before serving.

Variations: Salad dressing may be used instead of the vinegar mixture.

TURNIP SALAD

Take 3 cups of finely grated turnips. Add mayonnaise, sugar, salt and pepper to taste. Add enough milk for the right consistency, and mix.

CHRISTMAS SALAD

First Part;

2 packages (3 ounces each) lime gelatin
  powder
3½ cups water

1 medium can crushed pineapple
  (reserve juice)

Prepare the gelatin, using the 3½ cups of water instead of following the package directions. Add the crushed pineapple, and pour it into a 9 x13-inch cake pan. Chill it until firm.

Second Part;

2 packages unflavored gelatin
⅔ cup cold water
1 small package white cream cheese

1 cup whipping cream
Sugar

Bring the reserved pineapple juice to a boil. Soften the gelatin in the cold water and add it to the boiling pineapple juice. Soften the cream cheese and add it to the gelatin mixture. Cool it until it is partially set. Whip the cream and sweeten it to taste. Add it to the pineapple juice/cheese mixture, then pour it over the firm lime gelatin. Refrigerate it until it is firm.

Third Part;

2 packages strawberry gelatin powder
3½ cups water

Mix the gelatin, using the 3½ cups of water instead of following the directions on the package. Chill it until it is partially set. Pour it over the second part and chill the whole salad until it is firm.

Variations: If desired, ½ of the crushed pineapple may be added to the strawberry gelatin instead of putting all of it into the lime gelatin.

COTTAGE CHEESE SALAD

1 small can mandarin oranges
1 small can crushed pineapple
1 package dessert topping mix, OR
1 cup cream, whipped

1 pint creamed cottage cheese
1 package (3 ounces) orange gelatin
  powder

Drain the fruit. Make the dessert topping according to the package directions. Mix the cottage cheese and dry gelatin thoroughly, then add the fruit and whipped topping. Beat the ingredients, then chill. Serve this salad the same day it is prepared.

APRICOT SALAD

Prepare this as you would Three-Layer Salad (see page 94), but use 2 small packages of apricot gelatin powder, 2 diced bananas and 2 cups of mashed apricots for the first layer instead of pineapple.

APPLE SALAD

1 cup white sugar	1 tablespoon butter
2 tablespoons flour	6 apples, diced
1 egg	½ cup celery, diced
Cold water	4 bananas, sliced
1 cup hot water	½ cup nuts, finely chopped (peanuts
Salt	may be used)
Vinegar	

Mix the sugar, flour and egg with enough cold water to make a thickening. Add the hot water and boil it. Add a little salt and vinegar and the butter. Cool the mixture before mixing in the rest of the ingredients.

Variations: Whipped cream, marshmallows and pineapple may also be added.

CROWN JEWEL GELATIN

1 package (3 ounces) raspberry gelatin powder	½ cup cold water per gelatin package
	¼ cup sugar
1 package (3 ounces) lime gelatin powder	1 cup pineapple juice
	1 package strawberry gelatin powder
1 package (3 ounces) black cherry gelatin powder	½ cup cold water
	2 cups whipping cream
1 cup hot water per gelatin package	

Prepare separately the first 3 gelatins. For each package, dissolve the gelatin in 1 cup of hot water, then add ½ cup of cold water. Let the gelatin set until it is firm, then cut it into ½-inch cubes.

Heat the sugar and pineapple juice to boiling. Dissolve the strawberry gelatin in the hot liquid, and add the cold water. Chill it until it is syrupy. Whip the cream and fold it into the syrupy gelatin. When this is well mixed, fold in the gelatin cubes. Pour the mixture into a dish and chill it.

FRUIT SALAD

3 pounds sugar
3 cups water
Yellow food coloring
2 packages gelatin soaked in 1 cup
    water
1 quart crushed pineapple
3 pounds bananas, sliced

1 medium jar maraschino cherries
2 quarts peaches
10 oranges
2 pounds red grapes
2 pounds green grapes

Boil the sugar and water for 2 to 3 minutes. Add a few drops of yellow food coloring and the gelatin soaked in the water. Pour the crushed pineapple over the sliced bananas. Stir it gently so the pineapple juice coats the bananas well—this will keep them from turning brown (lemon juice will do the same). Add the bananas and pineapple to the gelatin mixture. Add the other fruit, then mix and chill the salad.

MARY'S LIME SALAD

16 marshmallows
1 cup milk
1 package (3 ounces) lime gelatin
    powder
2 packages (4-ounce size) cream
    cheese

1 medium can crushed pineapple
1 cup cream, whipped
⅔ cup salad dressing

Melt the marshmallows and milk in a double boiler. Pour this hot mixture over the lime gelatin, stirring it until the gelatin is dissolved. Stir in the cream cheese until it dissolves. Add the pineapple and cool the mixture until it becomes syrupy. Blend in the whipped cream and salad dressing. Chill it until it is firm.

MONOTONY BREAKER

1¼ cups boiling water
1 package (3 ounces) cherry gelatin
    powder
1 cup ground cranberries
1 cup sugar

¼ cup water
1 cup ground apples
1 cup crushed pineapple
Broken nuts

Mix together the 1¼ cups of boiling water and the gelatin. Combine the sugar and ¼ cup of water with the cranberries, and cook this mixture until the cranberries are soft. When it is cool, blend the 2 mixtures and add the apples, pineapple and broken nuts. Spoon it into a prepared 4-cup mold, and chill it until firm.

PINEAPPLE AND CHEESE SALAD

1 package (3 ounces) lime gelatin
   powder
1 small can crushed pineapple, drained

2 cups cottage cheese
½ cup nuts, finely chopped

Prepare the gelatin according to the package instructions. When it begins to set, whip it as you would whipping cream. Fold in the pineapple, cheese and nuts. Chill the salad, and serve.

Variations: Try adding ¼ cup of sugar and 1 can of whipped evaporated milk.

PINEAPPLE FRUIT SALAD

1 tablespoon flour
Cold water
1 egg
½ cup sugar
1 tablespoon butter

1 can (19 ounces) sliced pineapple
   (reserve juice)
6 bananas, sliced
1 dozen marshmallows
1 cup mixed nuts

Mix the flour with the water to make a smooth paste. Stir the egg into the paste. Heat together the reserved pineapple juice, sugar and butter, then mix and boil it until it thickens slightly. Allow it to cool before pouring it over a mixture of the cut up pineapple, bananas, marshmallows and nuts. Serve this salad with whipped cream.

Variations: For Lettuce-Pineapple Salad, follow the above instructions but omit the bananas, nuts and whipped cream. Instead, add cut up lettuce and more marshmallows.

THREE-LAYER SALAD

2 packages (3 ounces each) lime gelatin
   powder
1 cup drained, crushed pineapple
½ cup sugar
2 tablespoons cornstarch
2 egg yolks

½ cup cold water
1½ cups pineapple juice
1 package (8 ounces) white cream
   cheese
1 cup Marvel cheese (see page 289)
1 cup whipping cream, whipped

Fix the gelatin according to the package directions, and add the pineapple. Pour it into an oblong cake pan and let it set until it is firm. Combine the sugar, cornstarch and egg yolks. Blend this mixture with the cold water and pour it into the pineapple juice, which has been heated. Cook it until it is thick. Allow it to cool, then pour it onto the gelatin and chill it. When it is ready to serve, top it with the cream cheese blended with the Marvel cheese and whipped cream. Add sugar to the whipped cream if desired.

RIBBON SALAD

First Layer;

1 package (3 ounces) cherry gelatin
powder

Prepare the gelatin according to package directions, and pour it into an oblong cake pan. Chill it to set.

Second Layer;

⅔ cup milk
16 marshmallows
1 package (8 ounces) cream cheese
1 package (3 ounces) lemon gelatin
powder

1 small can crushed pineapple
⅔ cup nuts
1 cup whipping cream, whipped

Heat the milk, marshmallows and cheese in a double boiler until all is melted, then add the lemon gelatin. Let the mixture cool before adding the pineapple, nuts and whipped cream. Pour it over the first layer of cherry gelatin and chill.

Third Layer;

1 package (3 ounces) orange gelatin
powder

Prepare the orange gelatin according to package directions, then pour it on top of the second layer. Let it set in the refrigerator.

WHITE FRUIT SALAD

2 tablespoons unflavored gelatin
½ cup cold fruit juice (drained from
canned fruit)
1 cup hot fruit juice (drained from
canned fruit)
1 cup mayonnaise
1 cup whipping cream, whipped

¼ cup icing sugar
½ cup pineapple slices, cut into small
pieces
½ can white cherries, cut into small
pieces
½ cup chopped nuts

Soak the gelatin in the cold fruit juice for about 5 minutes, then dissolve it in the hot fruit juice. When the mixture begins to stiffen, add the mayonnaise and fold in the cream and icing sugar. Add the pineapples, cherries and nuts. Pour the mixture into wet molds, and refrigerate. Serve this salad with lettuce, and mayonnaise mixed with a little whipped cream. It serves 12.

TRIPLE TREAT SALAD

First Layer;

1 package (3 ounces) strawberry
gelatin powder
2 bananas

Prepare the gelatin according to the package directions, then pour it into a 9 x 9-inch pan. Slice the bananas into the gelatin and let it set until firm.

Second Layer;

1 package (3 ounces) lemon gelatin
powder
1 cup hot water

4 ounces cream cheese
⅓ cup mayonnaise

Dissolve the lemon gelatin in the hot water. Add the cream cheese and mayonnaise, then beat the mixture well. When it is partially set, pour it over the first layer.

Third Layer;

1 package (3 ounces) lime gelatin
powder
2 cups hot water

½ cup crushed pineapple

Dissolve the lime gelatin in the hot water. When it is cool, add the pineapple. Chill it until it is partially set, then pour it on top of the other two layers.

Slice it into cubes for serving.

FRENCH DRESSING

1 can (10 ounces) condensed tomato
soup
½ cup sugar
1 teaspoon paprika
1 teaspoon salt
1 teaspoon onion salt
1 teaspoon pepper

1 teaspoon garlic salt
1 teaspoon dry mustard
1 teaspoon horseradish (optional)
1 cup cooking oil
¾ cup vinegar

Put all the ingredients into a jar and shake it. Keep the dressing cool.

Variations: Try adding 2 tablespoons of Worcestershire sauce and 1 small chopped onion.

HOMEMADE MUSTARD

½ cup vinegar
½ cup sugar
2 tablespoons flour

½ cup sweet cream
2 tablespoons dry mustard
1 egg

Mix together all the ingredients, then boil the mixture in a double boiler until it is thick. To color the mustard, add a shake of turmeric.

ELLA'S SALAD DRESSING

¼ cup vinegar
½ cup oil
1 teaspoon salt

⅓ cup ketchup
½ cup sugar
1 tablespoon creamy salad dressing

Shake the ingredients together well. This dressing will keep quite awhile in the refrigerator.

HOMEMADE SALAD DRESSING

1 egg plus water to make ¾ cup
⅔ cup flour
1 cup water
½ cup vinegar
¾ cup cooking oil

1 tablespoon lemon juice
⅔ cup sugar
½ teaspoon dry mustard
2 teaspoons salt

Beat the egg and water thoroughly with an egg beater. Bring to a boil in a 1 quart saucepan the flour, water and vinegar, then blend in the egg and the rest of the ingredients. Beat the mixture hard until it is smooth.

PERFECT SALAD DRESSING

½ cup sugar
1 teaspoon salt
2 tablespoons vinegar (scant)

2 tablespoons salad dressing
⅓ cup milk or cream

Mix together the first 4 ingredients, then add the milk or cream. Mix it until the sugar dissolves. Serve this dressing on cut up lettuce.

SALAD DRESSING

1 pint milk
½ cup sugar
½ teaspoon salt
5 tablespoons flour

3 tablespoons vinegar
2 teaspoons mustard
½ teaspoon turmeric
Cream

Heat the milk, sugar and salt. Moisten the flour with milk and stir it into the hot milk mixture. Continue to stir it until it boils. Add the vinegar, mustard and turmeric (dissolved in hot water). Let it stand until it is cold, then beat the mixture and add cream to the consistency desired.

SUSAN'S SIMPLE SALAD DRESSING

1 cup white sugar
½ cup vinegar
¾ cup ketchup
1 tablespoon salt
½ teaspoon paprika

1 cup salad oil
¼ cup lemon juice
3 tablespoons grated onion
1 teaspoon celery seed

Mix together well all the ingredients. Keep this dressing refrigerated.

TOSSED SALAD DRESSING

1⅓ cups white sugar
2 teaspoons paprika
2 tablespoons dry mustard
1 teaspoon celery seed

2 teaspoons salt
1 cup vinegar
1 cup salad oil
1 small onion, grated

Mix together the ingredients and serve on tossed salad.

VELVET SALAD DRESSING

1 egg
1 tablespoon flour
½ cup sugar
1 teaspoon salt

1 teaspoon prepared mustard
4 tablespoons vinegar
1 cup cold water
3 tablespoons butter

Beat the egg well, then add the flour, sugar, salt, mustard, vinegar and water. Cook it in a double boiler until it is thick. Remove it from the heat and beat in the butter.

This dressing is good on lettuce or potato salads. Cream or 2 tablespoons of mayonnaise may be added if preferred.

CRANBERRY SAUCE

1 pound cranberries
8 apples
2 oranges

4 cups sugar
1 can crushed pineapple (optional)

Grind together all the ingredients. Do not heat the mixture. Let it stand in a cool place or refrigerate it for a few days to sweeten.

COOKED CRANBERRY SAUCE

1½ cups water
1 pound cranberries
18 apples

4 or 5 cups sugar
2 oranges

Add the water to the cranberries and apples and boil them together. Put them through a ricer or food mill, and add the sugar, adjusting the quantity according to taste. Stir the mixture while it cools. Grate the orange rind, extract the juice from the oranges, and add both to the mixture when it has cooled.

CAKES

HINTS FOR CAKES

- Much less sugar can be used in several of the cake, cookie or dessert recipes, and the food is no less tasty. In many instances, molasses or honey can be substituted for sugar. Someone said we pay twice for sugar or sweets—once when we buy them, and again when we pay the dentist's bill.

- When making a ready-mix cake, add 1 tablespoon of cooking oil. This brings out more of the flavor and will make the cake more moist.

- When baking, measure shortening before molasses and it will not stick to the cup.

TIPS FOR MAKING ANGEL FOOD CAKES

- Have all the ingredients at room temperature.
- Use cake flour only.
- Egg whites must be clean and should not contain a part of the yolks.
- Have the sugar clean if beaten with the egg whites. Even a bit of flour might damage the cake.
- Fold in the flour and sugar mixture gently, using a cake scraper. DO NOT BEAT it.
- Bake the cake in an ungreased tube pan. When it is done, turn it upside down to cool.
- Be careful not to over-bake.

AMISH CAKE

½ cup butter
2 cups brown sugar, packed
2 cups buttermilk or sour milk

2 teaspoons soda
3 cups all-purpose flour
1 teaspoon vanilla

Cream the butter and brown sugar. Add the buttermilk and soda, then the flour and vanilla. Bake the batter in a greased and floured 9 x 13 x 2-inch baking pan at 375°. Spread the following topping over the cake after it is done. Return it to the oven and bake it until bubbly, or for 1 minute.

Topping;

6 tablespoons soft butter
4 tablespoons milk

1 cup brown sugar
½ cup nuts

Combine these ingredients.

BROWN SUGAR ANGEL FOOD CAKE

2 cups egg whites (14 to 16)
1½ teaspoons cream of tartar
2 teaspoons vanilla

1 teaspoon salt
2 cups brown sugar
1½ cups sifted cake flour

Beat the egg whites with the cream of tartar, vanilla and salt until stiff peaks form. Gradually sift 1 cup of the sugar over the beaten egg whites and beat them again. Sift the remaining sugar with the flour, and fold it into the egg whites. Turn the batter into an ungreased 10-inch tube cake pan. Bake it at 350° for 45 to 50 minutes.

CHOCOLATE ANGEL FOOD CAKE

¾ cup cake flour
¼ cup cocoa
¼ teaspoon salt
1 teaspoon cream of tartar

2 cups egg whites (14 to 16)
1 teaspoon vanilla
1½ cups sugar

Sift together the flour, cocoa and salt. Add the cream of tartar to the egg whites and beat them until they will hold peaks. Add the vanilla, then add the sugar gradually, and fold this mixture into the flour mixture. Put the batter into an ungreased tube pan and bake it for 40 to 45 minutes at 350 to 375°.

WHITE ANGEL FOOD CAKE

1½ cups white sugar
1 cup cake flour
1½ cups egg whites (11 to 12)

½ teaspoon salt
1½ teaspoons cream of tartar
1 teaspoon almond flavoring

Sift together 3 times, ¾ cup of the sugar and the flour. Set it aside. Beat the egg whites until they are frothy, then add the salt and cream of tartar. Beat it until it stands in peaks. Add the rest of the sugar about 3 tablespoons at a time, beating well with an egg beater after each addition. Fold in lightly the sugar/flour mixture about ½ cup at a time, then add the almond flavoring. Bake the batter at 375° for about 35 to 40 minutes or until it is done.

Variations: To make **Nut Angel Food Cake,** *omit the almond extract and add ½ cup of ground walnuts to the flour and sugar mixture.*

For **Maraschino Cherry Angel Food Cake,** *grind the drained contents of 1 small jar of maraschino cherries (about ⅔ cup). Fold it into the batter described above and bake it as directed.*

For **Butterscotch** *or* **Chocolate Chip Angel Food Cake,** *add ¾ cup butterscotch bits or chocolate chips to the batter.*

For **Jelly Angel Food Cake,** *mix in 2 or 3 tablespoons of any fruit flavored gelatin powder.*

CHOCOLATE TWO-EGG CHIFFON CAKE

2 eggs, separated
1½ cups sugar
1¾ cups sifted cake flour
¾ teaspoon soda
¾ teaspoon salt

⅓ cup cooking oil
1 cup buttermilk, or sweet milk
2 squares (2 ounces) unsweetened
    chocolate, melted

Preheat the oven to 350°. Grease well and dust with flour 2 round layer pans (8-inch diameter by at least 1½ inches deep), or 1 oblong pan (13 x 9½ x 2 inches). Beat the egg whites until they are frothy. Gradually beat in ½ cup of the sugar, and continue beating the whites to make a very stiff and glossy meringue.

Sift the remaining sugar, flour, soda and salt into another bowl. Add the oil and ½ of the buttermilk. Beat these ingredients for 1 minute at medium speed on a mixer or for 150 vigorous strokes by hand, scraping the sides and bottom of the bowl constantly. Add the remaining buttermilk, the egg yolks and chocolate. Beat the mixture for 1 minute more, scraping the bowl constantly. Fold in the meringue. Pour the batter into the prepared pans and bake it for 30 to 35 minutes.

APPLE DAPPLE

2 eggs
2 cups white sugar
1 cup cooking oil
3 cups all-purpose flour (scant)
½ teaspoon salt

1 teaspoon soda
3 cups chopped apples
2 teaspoons vanilla
Chopped nuts (optional)

Mix together the eggs, sugar and oil, and add the flour, salt and soda which have been sifted together. Add the chopped apples, vanilla and nuts. Mix the batter well and pour it into a greased cake pan. Bake it at 350° for 45 minutes or until done.

Icing;

1 cup brown sugar
¼ cup milk
¼ cup butter or margarine

Combine the sugar, milk and butter, and cook the mixture for 2½ minutes. Stir it a little after removing it from the stove, but do not beat it. Dribble it over the cake while it and the cake are still hot. A few chopped nuts may be sprinkled over the icing.

APPLESAUCE CAKE

½ cup shortening
1 cup sugar (white or brown)
1 egg
1 cup applesauce
1 cup sifted cake flour
½ teaspoon salt
½ teaspoon baking powder

1 teaspoon soda
½ teaspoon cloves
1 teaspoon cinnamon
1 teaspoon allspice
1 cup raisins
¼ cup chopped nuts

Cream the shortening and add the sugar, beating it until light. Add the egg and beat it until fluffy, then add the applesauce and mix it well. Sift together the flour, salt, baking powder, soda, cloves, cinnamon and allspice, then add the raisins and chopped nuts. Combine the two mixtures. Bake the batter in a greased 8-inch square pan at 350° for 40 to 45 minutes.

Glaze for Applesauce Cake;

½ cup white sugar
2 tablespoons cornstarch
¼ teaspoon cinnamon

½ cup canned applesauce
½ cup water
1 teaspoon lemon juice

In a small saucepan stir together the sugar, cornstarch and cinnamon. Stir in the applesauce, water and lemon juice. Cook this mixture over moderate heat, stirring it constantly until it is thick. Spread it over the cake when it is lukewarm or cold.

ROMAN APPLE CAKE

1 cup brown sugar
½ cup shortening
1 egg
1 teaspoon vanilla
1½ cups all-purpose flour

¼ teaspoon baking powder
¼ teaspoon soda
¼ teaspoon salt
½ cup milk
4 medium apples, chopped

Mix together well all the ingredients but the apples, then fold them in.

Topping;

1 tablespoon melted butter
½ cup brown sugar
½ cup chopped nuts

2 teaspoons cinnamon
2 teaspoons flour

Mix these ingredients together and sprinkle the mixture as crumbs over the batter. Bake it for 45 minutes at 350°. Serve the cake warm.

ROYAL APPLE CAKE

3 cups all-purpose flour	2 eggs
1 teaspoon soda	2 cups sugar
2 teaspoons cinnamon	1 cup water
1 teaspoon baking powder	1 cup nuts
½ teaspoon salt	1 cup raisins
1 teaspoon nutmeg	2 cups diced apples
1 cup oil	

Sift together and set aside the flour, soda, cinnamon, baking powder, salt and nutmeg. Combine and mix well the oil, eggs and sugar, and add the flour mixture alternately with the water. Then add the nuts, raisins and apples. Spread the batter in a greased 9 x 13-inch pan and bake it at 350° until done.

BANANA NUT CAKE

1 cup white sugar	1 teaspoon soda
½ cup butter	2 teaspoons baking powder
2 eggs, well-beaten	Pinch of salt
4 tablespoons sour milk	1 teaspoon cream of tartar
1 teaspoon vanilla	1 cup mashed bananas
2 cups flour	½ cup chopped nuts

Cream the sugar and butter, then add the eggs, milk and vanilla. Add the sifted dry ingredients, then the bananas, and nuts. Bake the batter in a greased and floured 9 x 13 x 2-inch baking pan at 375° for 40 minutes or until done.

BROWN STONE FRONT CAKE

2½ cups all-purpose flour	2 cups brown sugar
1 teaspoon cinnamon	3 egg yolks
½ teaspoon nutmeg	1 cup sour milk or buttermilk
½ teaspoon allspice	1 cup chopped walnuts
1 teaspoon soda	1 cup stewed raisins
½ cup butter	3 egg whites stiffly beaten

Sift together the flour and spices, then add the soda. Cream the butter and sugar, and add the egg yolks. Add the sifted ingredients and milk alternately to this egg mixture. Then add the nuts and raisins and fold in the egg whites. Bake the batter in a greased 9 x 13-inch pan at 350° until it is done, about 30 minutes.

Frost the cake with Creamy Caramel Frosting (see page 132).

BURNT SUGAR CAKE

2¼ cups sifted cake flour
3 teaspoons baking powder
1 teaspoon salt
1 cup sugar
1 cup milk

⅓ cup Burnt Sugar Syrup
  (see page 298)
1 teaspoon almond extract
½ cup shortening
2 eggs, unbeaten

Sift together the flour, baking powder, salt and sugar. Blend together the milk, Burnt Sugar Syrup and almond extract, then add ⅔ of it to the flour mixture. Add the shortening and beat it until the batter is well blended and glossy, then add the remaining liquid. Add the eggs, and beat the batter again until it is very smooth. Bake it in a moderate oven (350°) until done.

Frost the cake with Burnt Sugar Frosting (see page 131).

CARAMEL CAKE

2 cups brown sugar
½ cup lard
2 eggs, unbeaten
1 teaspoon vanilla
2 cups all-purpose flour

1 teaspoon cocoa
2 teaspoons hot water
Sour milk
1 teaspoon soda

Cream together the sugar and lard. Add the eggs, vanilla and flour. Put the cocoa into a cup and add the hot water. Fill the cup with sour milk, then add the soda. Stir this mixture until the cocoa is well dissolved. The cup will run over so be sure to hold it over the mixing bowl while stirring the contents. When the cocoa is dissolved, pour it in with the other mixture and mix it. Bake the batter at 350° until done.

LEMON CHIFFON CAKE

1½ cups sugar
2¼ cups sifted cake flour
3 teaspoons baking powder
1 teaspoon salt
⅓ cup cooking oil

1 cup milk
2 teaspoons lemon juice
Grated rind of 1 lemon
2 eggs, separated

Sift 1 cup of the sugar with the flour, baking powder and salt. Add the oil, ½ of the milk, the lemon juice and rind. Blend this mixture well, then add the egg yolks and the remaining milk, beating it to make a smooth batter.

Beat the egg whites until they are frothy, then gradually beat in the remaining sugar until the mixture is stiff and glossy. Fold this into the batter and pour it into an ungreased 10-inch tube pan. Bake it at 350° for 40 minutes or until done.

CARROT CAKE

2 cups sugar
1½ cups cooking oil
4 eggs
2 cups all-purpose flour
2 teaspoons soda

2 teaspoons baking powder
1 teaspoon salt
2 teaspoons cinnamon
3 cups raw carrots, shredded
½ cup chopped nuts

Cream together the sugar and cooking oil. Add the eggs and beat the mixture well. Sift together the flour, soda, baking powder, salt and cinnamon, and add it to the creamed mixture. Fold in the carrots and nuts. Bake it in a greased 9 x 13-inch pan in a moderate oven (350°) until done.

Cream Cheese Icing;

4 tablespoons butter
8 ounces cream cheese

2 teaspoons vanilla
1 pound icing sugar

Mix together these ingredients until smooth.

ORANGE CARROT CAKE

2 cups whole wheat flour
1 cup brown sugar
1 cup white sugar
2 teaspoons baking powder
2 teaspoons soda
2 teaspoons cinnamon
1 teaspoon nutmeg

1 teaspoon salt
1¼ cups vegetable oil
1 (12-ounce) can frozen, unsweetened
    orange juice (save ¼)
4 eggs
2½ cups grated, raw carrots
½ cup chopped nuts

Sift together the dry ingredients. Add the oil and orange juice (saving ¼ can of the orange juice for the glaze). Mix this well, then add the eggs and beat the mixture well. Stir in the carrots and nuts. Bake the batter at 350° for 1 hour or until it is well done.

Glaze;

6 tablespoons butter
2 cups icing sugar

Brown the butter. Add the juice reserved from the cake recipe, and the icing sugar. Spread this glaze over the cake while it is still warm.

SPICE CHIFFON CAKE

1¾ cups plus 2 tablespoons all-purpose
  flour
1½ cups sugar
3 teaspoons baking powder
1 teaspoon salt
1 teaspoon cinnamon
½ teaspoon nutmeg
½ teaspoon allspice

½ teaspoon cloves
5 egg yolks
¾ cup water
2 teaspoons vanilla
½ cup salad oil
1 cup (7 to 8) egg whites
½ teaspoon cream of tartar

Sift together the flour, sugar, baking powder, salt and spices. Beat well the egg yolks, water and vanilla, then add this mixture with the oil to the sifted dry ingredients. Beat the egg whites with the cream of tartar until they are stiff, and fold them in last. Pour the batter into an ungreased 10-inch tube pan and bake it at 325° for 55 minutes, then at 350° for 10 minutes more.

WHOLE WHEAT COCOA CHIFFON CAKE

½ cup cocoa
¾ cup boiling water
½ teaspoon cream of tartar
7 to 8 eggs, separated
1¾ cups whole wheat flour

1½ cups raw sugar
1 teaspoon salt
3 teaspoons baking powder
½ cup salad oil
1 teaspoon vanilla

Stir together the cocoa and boiling water until smooth, then set it aside to cool. Add the cream of tartar to the egg whites (1 cup) and whip them until they form very stiff peaks.

Blend together the flour, raw sugar, salt and baking powder. Make a well and add in order the oil, egg yolks, cooled cocoa mixture and vanilla, and beat them until the mixture is smooth and creamy. Pour this mixture gradually over the whipped egg whites, folding it in gently with a rubber scraper until it is just blended. Bake the batter in a tube pan at 325° for 55 minutes, then at 350° for 10 to 15 minutes more.

CHOCOLATE MAYONNAISE CAKE

2 cups all-purpose flour
1 cup sugar
½ cup cocoa
2 teaspoons soda

1 cup boiling water
1 teaspoon vanilla
1 cup mayonnaise (or Homemade
  Salad Dressing, see p. 100)

Sift together the flour, sugar, cocoa and soda. Mix this with the rest of the ingredients, and bake the batter in 2 greased and floured 8-inch layer pans at 350° for 30 minutes.

AUNT FRONIE CAKE

2 cups sugar
¼ cup shortening
2 eggs, beaten
2 cups all-purpose flour
1 teaspoon baking powder

½ cup sour milk
4 tablespoons cocoa
½ teaspoon salt
2 teaspoons soda

Cream together the sugar and shortening, then add the rest of the ingredients. Mix them well, then mix in thoroughly 1 cup of boiling water. Bake the batter in a greased 9 x 9-inch pan at 350° for about 30 minutes or until done.

CHOCOLATE MINT DREAM CAKE

2 cups cake flour
¾ teaspoon salt
1½ cups white sugar
3 teaspoons baking powder
½ cup cocoa

⅔ cup shortening
1 cup milk
1 teaspoon vanilla
2 eggs

Sift together the dry ingredients. Add the shortening, milk and vanilla. Mix them, then add the eggs and beat well. Bake the batter in a greased 9-inch spring form pan at 350° for 30 to 35 minutes. Cut off the top of the cake using a thread, and add the following filling, or place the filling on top as icing.

Peppermint Whipped Cream Filling;

1 pint whipping cream
⅓ cup icing sugar

½ teaspoon peppermint flavor
Green food coloring

Beat the whipping cream until it is stiff. Add the icing sugar and peppermint flavoring, and tint it with the food coloring.

COCOA CAKE

6 tablespoons butter or margarine
2 cups sugar
2 cups sour milk or buttermilk
2 teaspoons soda

2 teaspoons vanilla
3 cups cake flour (scant)
½ cup cocoa, or less

Melt the butter and mix it with the sugar. Add the sour milk in which the soda has been dissolved. Add the vanilla, then add the flour and cocoa which have been sifted together. Bake the batter for 40 to 45 minutes at 350°.

EASY CHOCOLATE CAKE

Pan Size;

small (8 x 8 inches)	medium (13 x 9½ inches)	large (14 x 9½ inches)	
1	2	3	Measure and sift together; heaping cups of sifted cake flour
1	2	3	rounded tablespoons of cocoa
1	2	3	teaspoons of soda
⅛	¼	½	teaspoon of baking powder
⅛	¼	½	teaspoon of salt Beat;
1	2	3	eggs Cream together well and add to the eggs;
¼	½	¾	cup of shortening
1	2	3	cups of sugar Add the following mixture alternately with the dry ingredients to the egg mixture, and mix well;
¼	½	¾	cup buttermilk or sour milk
½	1	1½	cups boiling water
1	2	3	teaspoons vanilla

The batter will be thin. Bake it in a hot oven, 375 to 400°.

FIVE STAR FUDGE CAKE

1½ cups butter or margarine
4½ cups sugar
6 eggs
3 teaspoons vanilla
6 (1-ounce) squares unsweetened
  chocolate, melted

6 cups sifted cake flour
3 teaspoons soda
1 heaping teaspoon baking powder
1½ teaspoons salt
3 cups ice water

Cream together the butter, sugar, eggs and vanilla until they are fluffy. Blend in the melted chocolate. Sift together the dry ingredients, and add this mixture alternately with the water to the chocolate mixture. Pour the batter into three 8-inch layer pans which have been greased and lined with waxed paper. Bake it in a moderate oven (350°) for 30 to 35 minutes.

GERMAN SWEET CHOCOLATE CAKE

1 bar (4 ounces) German sweet
  chocolate
½ cup boiling water
1 cup butter or margarine
2 cups sugar
4 egg yolks, unbeaten

1 teaspoon vanilla
2½ cups sifted cake flour
½ teaspoon salt
1 teaspoon soda
1 cup buttermilk
4 egg whites, stiffly beaten

Melt the chocolate in the boiling water, then let it cool. Cream the butter and sugar until they are fluffy. Add the egg yolks one at a time, beating well after each addition. Then add the melted chocolate and the vanilla.

Sift together the flour, salt and soda. Add this alternately with the buttermilk to the chocolate mixture, beating it well until smooth. Fold in the egg whites. Pour the batter into 3 layer pans (8 or 9-inch) which have been lined on the bottom with waxed paper. Bake it in a moderate oven (350°) for 30 to 40 minutes. Allow the cake to cool, then spread it with Coconut-Pecan Frosting (see page 132).

Variations: Instead of German chocolate you can use 6 tablespoons of cocoa, 2 tablespoons of margarine and an extra ½ cup of flour.

DELUXE CHOCOLATE CAKE

½ cup shortening
½ cup brown sugar, firmly packed
2 cups sifted all-purpose flour
1 teaspoon soda
1 cup granulated sugar
⅔ cup sour milk or buttermilk

1 teaspoon vanilla extract
2 eggs
3 (1-ounce) squares unsweetened
  chocolate, melted in ½ cup boiling
  water

Have the shortening a room temperature, and stir it just enough to soften it. Add the brown sugar, forcing it through a sieve to remove lumps if necessary, and mix it well. Add the flour, soda and granulated sugar, then ½ cup of the sour milk, the vanilla and eggs. Mix them until all the flour is dampened, then continue mixing for 1 minute or 100 strokes. Blend in the remaining sour milk and beat the mixture for 1 minute more. Add the chocolate mixture and beat it for another minute. Scrape the bowl and the spoon often to make sure that all the batter is well mixed. Turn the batter into 2 greased and floured 9-inch layer pans, or one loaf pan. Bake it in a moderate oven (350°) for 30 minutes.

MARBLE CAKE

2½ cups cake flour
1½ teaspoons baking powder
1⅔ cups sugar
1½ teaspoons soda
1 teaspoon salt
¾ cup shortening

¾ cup sour milk
2 eggs, unbeaten
1 square (1 ounce) chocolate, melted
2 tablespoons hot water
¼ teaspoon soda
1 tablespoon sugar

First, sift together the flour, baking powder, 1⅔ cups of sugar, 1½ teaspoons of soda and salt. Then sift this mixture into the shortening alternately with the sour milk. Add the eggs and beat the mixture well.

Mix the chocolate, hot water, ¼ teaspoon of soda and 1 tablespoon of sugar, and add this mixture to ¼ of the batter. Pour the batter by large spoonfuls into 2 greased and floured 9-inch layer pans, alternating the plain and chocolate mixtures. With a knife, cut through the batter in a wide zig-zag pattern. Bake the cake at 350° until done.

SUGARLESS CHOCOLATE CAKE

½ cup cocoa
2 teaspoons soda
2¼ cups cake flour
¼ teaspoon salt

1 cup hot water
1 cup melted lard
1 cup table syrup or honey
2 eggs, beaten

Sift together the dry ingredients. Add the hot water, a little at a time, stirring well after each addition. Add the lard, syrup and eggs, mixing well. Bake the batter in a greased and floured 13 x 9 x 12-inch pan at 350° for 30 to 40 minutes.

VELVET CHOCOLATE CAKE

2 cups cake flour
½ teaspoon salt
½ cup cocoa
½ cup shortening
2 cups brown sugar
1 teaspoon vanilla

2 eggs, well-beaten
1 cup cold water
1 teaspoon soda dissolved in 2
    tablespoons boiling water
1 cup chopped nuts (optional)

Sift the flour once, measure it and mix it with the salt and cocoa, and sift it again. Cream the shortening and add the sugar gradually, beating it thoroughly after each addition. Add the vanilla, then add the well-beaten eggs and beat them until the mixture is fluffy. Beat in the flour mixture alternately with the water, then add the dissolved soda and beat it well. If desired, add chopped nuts. Bake the batter in layer cake pans at 350° for 30 to 35 minutes.

LAZY WIFE CAKE

1½ cups pastry flour
¼ teaspoon salt
2 teaspoons soda
3 tablespoons cocoa
1 cup white sugar

1 teaspoon vanilla
7 tablespoons cooking oil
1 tablespoon vinegar
1 cup cold water

Sift the dry ingredients into a 9 x 9-inch ungreased cake pan. Mix them with a fork. Make three holes in this mixture: into one put the vanilla, into the next the oil, and into the third the vinegar. Pour over all of this the cold water. Mix these ingredients with a fork, but do not beat them. Bake the batter at 350° for 25 to 30 minutes or until done.

FRESH BLUEBERRY CAKE

½ cup butter or margarine
1 cup sugar
2 eggs
2 cups all-purpose flour

½ teaspoon salt
3 teaspoons baking powder
1 cup milk
1 cup blueberries

Cream the butter or margarine, then add the sugar a little at a time, and cream it again. Add the eggs and some of the flour, sifted with the salt and baking powder. Blend this slowly, adding the milk and the rest of the flour. Wash the berries, dry them on a towel, then dust them with some flour. Add them to the batter just before baking. Pour the batter into a greased and floured pan, 9 x 13 x 2 inches. Sprinkle it with cinnamon and sugar, nutmeg, cloves or whatever appeals to you. Bake it at 325° for 45 minutes. Serve the cake with whipped cream or ice cream.

If blueberries are scarce, raisins or currants can be substituted.

FRUIT CAKE

8 ounces mixed fruit peel
2¼ cups nuts
3¾ cups golden raisins
½ cup grape juice
2 cups brown sugar
1 teaspoon almond flavoring

½ cup soft butter
5 eggs
2 cups all-purpose flour
½ teaspoon mace
½ teaspoon cinnamon
¼ teaspoon baking powder

In a bowl, mix together the fruit peel, nuts, raisins and grape juice. Let it stand for 1 hour. Then in a large bowl, mix together the sugar, flavoring, butter and eggs. Add to this mixture the flour, mace, cinnamon and baking powder, which have been sifted together. Combine this with the fruit mixture. Pour it into a greased 10-inch tube pan lined with waxed paper. Bake it at 275° until firm and evenly browned, about 3 hours and 20 minutes. Remove it from the oven and let it cool for ½ hour. Turn the cake onto a cooling rack and let it cool thoroughly. Wrap it in vinegar-soaked cloth and store it in an airtight container for one week.

COCOA CRUMB CAKE

2 cups all-purpose flour
1½ cups brown sugar
½ cup butter or margarine
1 egg, beaten

1 cup buttermilk
2 large tablespoons cocoa (optional)
1 teaspoon soda
1 teaspoon vanilla

Mix together the flour, sugar and butter as for a pie crust, reserving ¾ cup for the topping. To the remainder of the crumbs add the egg, buttermilk, cocoa, soda and vanilla. Pour the batter into a cake or pie pan and sprinkle the reserved crumbs on top. Bake it at 350° for 30 to 40 minutes.

FRUIT COCKTAIL CAKE

2 cups all-purpose flour
1⅓ cups sugar
3 teaspoons soda
1 can (19 ounces) fruit cocktail

2 eggs
1 teaspoon vanilla
½ teaspoon salt

Mix together all the ingredients and blend them well. Pour the batter into a 9 x 13-inch pan. Bake it at 350° for 45 minutes or until it breaks away from the pan.

Boil the following ingredients for 5 minutes before spreading the mixture on the cake as topping.

Topping;

8 tablespoons butter
1 cup brown sugar

½ cup milk
Coconut or nuts (optional)

CREME VELVET CAKE

½ cup margarine or shortening
1½ cups sugar
½ teaspoon salt
1 cup water

2½ cups cake flour
2½ teaspoons baking powder
3 egg whites
1 teaspoon vanilla

Cream the margarine and gradually add the sugar, creaming them well. Add the salt and water alternately with the sifted flour and baking powder. Then fold in the stiffly beaten egg whites and vanilla. Bake the batter in 2 greased 8-inch layer pans at 350° for 35 to 40 minutes.

DATE CAKE

1½ cups whole, pitted dates
2 cups boiling water
2 teaspoons soda
1 cup brown sugar
2 tablespoons butter

1 teaspoon salt
2 eggs, beaten
1¼ cups all-purpose flour
Nut meats (optional)

Put the dates and boiling water into a pan over heat. Cook the dates until they are soft. Add the soda, brown sugar, butter and salt. After this mixture has cooled a little, add the eggs, flour and nuts. Bake the batter at 350° until done.

This is a cake that is good without frosting.

FEATHER CAKE

½ cup shortening
2 cups sugar
1 cup milk

3 cups self-rising flour
1 teaspoon vanilla
3 whole eggs or 5 egg whites

Cream the shortening, add the sugar, and cream it again. Add the milk and flour alternately, then the vanilla. Lastly, add the eggs. Mix the batter and bake it at 350° for 30 to 40 minutes in pans of your choice.

If you use all-purpose flour, add 3 teaspoons of baking powder and ½ teaspoon of salt.

GOLDEN FLUFF CAKE

2 cups sifted cake flour
3½ teaspoons baking powder
1 teaspoon salt
1⅓ cups sugar
⅓ cup shortening

½ teaspoon lemon (optional)
½ teaspoon vanilla flavoring
1 cup milk
⅓ cup (4 medium) egg yolks

Sift together the dry ingredients. Add the shortening (which should be at room temperature), lemon, vanilla and ⅔ of the milk. Beat this mixture for 200 strokes before adding the remaining ⅓ cup of milk and the egg yolks. Beat it again for 200 strokes, then pour the batter into 2 greased and floured 8-inch layer pans or 1 loaf pan. Bake it for 30 to 35 minutes in a moderate (350°) oven.

MIRACLE FRUIT CAKE

1½ cups chopped dates
1½ cups raisins
1½ cups brown sugar
⅔ cup butter or substitute
4 tablespoons molasses or corn syrup
1½ cups hot water
2 eggs
Candied fruit

1 cup chopped nuts
3 cups all-purpose flour
1½ cups whole wheat flour
3 teaspoons soda
1½ teaspoons nutmeg
2 teaspoons cinnamon
2 teaspoons baking powder

Combine the first 6 ingredients in a saucepan and boil the mixture gently for 3 minutes. Let it cool in a large mixing bowl. Beat the eggs and add them to the fruit mixture. Add candied fruit (see recipe following) and the chopped nuts.

Sift together 4 times, the flours, soda, nutmeg, cinnamon and baking powder. Add this to the fruit mixture, stirring it well. Pour the batter into loaf pans or bread pans lined with waxed paper. Bake it in a moderate oven (350°) until a toothpick comes out clean when inserted.

Candied Fruit;

½ cup butter or margarine
1 cup brown sugar

2 cups drained cherries (sweet or sour)
1 medium can crushed pineapple

Melt the butter in a saucepan and add the sugar. To this mixture add the cherries and pineapple. Let it stand for about 15 to 20 minutes.

NUT CAKE

2 cups sugar
½ cup butter
3 eggs
1 teaspoon vanilla
2½ cups cake flour

¾ teaspoon salt
2 teaspoons baking powder
1 cup milk
1 cup nuts

Cream the sugar and butter, then add the eggs and vanilla, beating them together well. Sift together the flour, salt and baking powder, and add it alternately with the milk to the egg mixture. Fold in the nuts. Bake the batter in a greased and floured 9 x 13 x 2-inch baking pan at 350° for 30 minutes.

LEMON LAYER CAKE

⅔ cup butter
1¾ cups sugar
2 eggs
1½ teaspoons vanilla

3 cups sifted cake flour
2½ teaspoons baking powder
½ teaspoon salt
1¼ cups milk

Cream the butter and sugar. Add the eggs and vanilla and beat them until they are fluffy. Sift the flour, baking powder and salt, and add this mixture alternately with the milk to the egg mixture, beating after each addition. Beat the batter thoroughly before pouring it into 2 greased and floured 9-inch round pans. Bake it at 350° for 30 to 35 minutes. Allow the cakes to cool, then remove them from the pans. Fill the cakes with Lemon Filling (following), and top the cake with Fluffy White Frosting (see page 133).

Lemon Filling;

¾ cup sugar
2 tablespoons cornstarch
½ teaspoon salt
¾ cup water

2 egg yolks, slightly beaten
3 tablespoons lemon juice
1 teaspoon grated lemon peel
1 tablespoon butter

Combine in a saucepan the sugar, cornstarch and salt. Add the water, egg yolks and lemon juice. Cook and stir this mixture over medium heat until it is thick. Remove it from the heat, then add the lemon peel and butter.

CRUMB CAKE

2 cups brown sugar
2½ cups all-purpose flour
½ cup shortening
2 teaspoons baking powder

1 teaspoon soda
1 cup thick sour milk
2 eggs
1 teaspoon vanilla

Mix together the sugar, flour, shortening, baking powder and soda. Reserve 1 cup of crumbs from this mixture. Mix together and add the remaining ingredients. Pour the batter into a greased 9 x 13 x 2-inch pan, sprinkle the reserved crumbs over top and bake it at 350° for 30 minutes or until done.

HANDY MADE CAKE

½ cup butter or margarine
2 cups sugar
3 eggs, beaten
2½ cups bread flour

3 teaspoons baking powder
1 teaspoon salt
1 cup milk
1 teaspoon vanilla

Cream the butter and sugar. Add the eggs. Sift together the flour, baking powder and salt, then add this alternately with the milk to the egg mixture. Add the vanilla. Bake the batter at 350° for 35 to 40 minutes.

OATMEAL CAKE

1¼ cups boiling water
1 cup instant oatmeal
½ cup shortening
1 cup brown sugar
1 cup white sugar
2 eggs

1½ cups cake flour
1 teaspoon nutmeg, if desired
1 teaspoon cinnamon
1 teaspoon soda
½ teaspoon salt
1 teaspoon vanilla

Pour the boiling water over the oatmeal and let it set for 20 minutes. Cream the shortening and sugars well. Add the unbeaten eggs, one at a time, beating well after each addition. Blend in the oatmeal mixture. Sift together the flour, spices, soda and salt, and fold this mixture in. Add the vanilla. Bake the batter in a greased and floured 9 x 13 x 2-inch pan at 350° for 30 to 35 minutes.

While the cake is still hot from the oven, spread on the following topping and put it under the broiler for about 2 minutes or until it is brown.

⅔ cup brown sugar
1 cup chopped nuts
1 cup coconut

6 tablespoons melted butter
¼ cup cream
1 teaspoon vanilla

Mix these ingredients together well.

OLD TIME MOLASSES CAKE

2 cups all-purpose flour
¾ cup molasses
¼ cup sugar
2 teaspoons soda

1 egg
½ cup buttermilk or sour milk
½ cup hot water

Mix the ingredients thoroughly. Bake the batter at 325 to 350° for 30 to 40 minutes.

SORGHUM MOLASSES CAKE

2 cups sorghum molasses
2 eggs
3 cups self-rising flour
½ teaspoon salt
½ teaspoon allspice
1 teaspoon cinnamon

1 cup cooking oil
1½ cups milk
½ teaspoon cloves
1 teaspoon nutmeg
Raisins or nuts (optional)

Mix together the above ingredients, then bake the batter at 350° for 30 to 35 minutes until done.

CAROB OATMEAL CAKE

1½ cups boiling water
1 cup quick rolled oats
¼ cup carob powder (available in
   health food stores), or cocoa
1 teaspoon soda
¼ teaspoon salt
1 cup flour (½ cup unbleached, ½ cup
   whole wheat, if desired)

⅓ cup cooking oil
1½ cups raw sugar
2 eggs, beaten
1 teaspoon vanilla
Shredded coconut and sunflower
   seeds

Pour the boiling water over the oats and carob powder, stirring it until smooth. Allow it to cool. Sift together the soda, salt and flour. Cream the oil and sugar and add the beaten eggs and vanilla. Then add the carob and flour mixtures to the eggs. Pour the batter into an 8 x 12-inch greased pan, and top it with shredded coconut and sunflower seeds instead of frosting. Bake it at 350° for about 45 minutes.

This cake will stay nice and moist for a week.

PINEAPPLE UPSIDE DOWN CAKE

3 tablespoons brown sugar
3 tablespoons butter
5 slices pineapple

Spread the sugar and butter in a skillet, then heat and melt them. Arrange the pineapple on top, and cover it with the sponge cake batter as follows.

3 egg yolks
½ cup sugar
¼ cup boiling water
½ teaspoon lemon flavoring

¾ cup cake flour
1 teaspoon baking powder
¼ teaspoon salt

Beat the egg yolks thoroughly. Add the sugar, boiling water and lemon flavoring. Mix them for 1 minute. Sift together and add the flour, baking powder and salt. Beat this mixture quickly for about ½ minute before pouring it over the pineapple as instructed above. Bake it for 25 to 30 minutes at 350°. Turn the cake upside down on a plate to serve it.

Variations: Try substituting other fruit for the pineapple.

ORANGE COCONUT CAKE

¾ cup shortening
2 cups sugar
1½ teaspoons grated orange rind
2 egg yolks
½ cup orange juice
¾ cup water

3¼ cups cake flour
½ teaspoon salt
4 teaspoons baking powder
½ cup coconut
4 egg whites

Cream the shortening and add the sugar gradually. Beat it until it is fluffy. Add the orange rind and beaten egg yolks, then beat the mixture again. Mix in the orange juice and water. Sift the flour, salt and baking powder twice, then add these dry ingredients to the mixture. Fold in the coconut and stiffly beaten egg whites. Pour the batter into 9-inch layer pans and bake it at 350° for 30 to 35 minutes.

PENNSYLVANIA DUTCH HUSTLE CAKE

⅓ cup milk
¼ cup sugar
½ teaspoon salt
¼ cup butter or margarine
¼ cup lukewarm water
1 package dry yeast

1 egg, beaten
1⅓ cups sifted all-purpose flour
1½ cups apple slices
2 tablespoons brown sugar
¼ teaspoon cinnamon
¼ teaspoon nutmeg

Scald the milk, then stir in the sugar, salt and half of the butter or margarine. Cool the mixture to lukewarm. In a mixing bowl dissolve the yeast in the lukewarm water, then stir in the lukewarm milk mixture. Add the egg and flour, and beat the dough until it is smooth. Spread it evenly in a greased 9 x 9-inch pan. Arrange the apple slices on top, and sprinkle it with a mixture of the sugar, cinnamon and nutmeg. Dot the top with the remaining butter or margarine. Cover the dough and let it rise in a warm draft-free place for 40 minutes or longer, until it is double in bulk. Bake it at 400° for 25 minutes.

SHOO-FLY CAKE

4 cups all-purpose flour
¾ cup shortening
2 cups brown sugar

2 cups boiling water
1 cup molasses
1 tablespoon soda

Mix thoroughly the flour, shortening and sugar. Reserve 1 cup of the crumbs for the topping. Add to the remaining crumbs the boiling water, molasses and soda. Mix these ingredients well, then pour the batter into a greased cake pan. Sprinkle the reserved crumbs over the batter, then bake it at 350° until done.

PRALINE CAKE

1 cup butter or vegetable shortening	1 teaspoon soda
2 cups sugar	1 cup buttermilk
4 eggs, separated	1 teaspoon cream of tartar
3 cups sifted cake flour	

Cream the shortening and sugar until light. Add the egg yolks, one at a time, and beat them until they are fluffy. Sift together the flour and soda, and add it alternately with the buttermilk and cream of tartar. Fold in the stiffly beaten egg whites. Pour the batter into a 9 x 13 x 2-inch greased and floured cake pan, and bake it at 350° for 50 minutes. Remove the cake from the oven and spread it with Praline Topping (see page 134). Place it under the broiler or in a hot oven for 1 or 2 minutes.

RAISIN NUT LOAF

1 cup cooked raisins	¼ teaspoon salt
1½ cups warm raisin juice	½ teaspoon nutmeg
1½ cups white sugar	½ teaspoon cinnamon
1½ cups brown sugar	1 teaspoon soda
½ cup shortening	3 cups all-purpose flour
2 eggs	1 cup chopped nuts

Cook raisins, using enough water to make 1½ cups of juice when they are done. Cream the sugars and shortening. Add the eggs and beat the mixture well. Add the sifted dry ingredients and warm raisin juice to the egg mixture, then stir in the raisins and nuts. Bake the batter in a greased loaf pan at 350° for 1 hour or until done.

NUT SPICE CAKE

3 cups cake flour	⅔ cup shortening
1½ teaspoons soda	1 cup granulated sugar
¾ teaspoon salt	1 cup brown sugar
¾ teaspoon allspice	3 eggs
¾ teaspoon cloves	1½ cups buttermilk
1½ teaspoons cinnamon	½ cup chopped nuts

Sift the flour, soda, salt and spices together. Cream the shortening and add the sugars gradually. Cream them well. Add the eggs one at a time, and beat the mixture well after each addition. Add the sifted dry ingredients alternately with the buttermilk. Add the nuts with the final addition of the dry ingredients. Pour the batter into 2 greased paper-lined 9-inch layer pans. Bake it at 350° for 35 to 40 minutes.

OLD SPICE CAKE

1 tablespoon or 1 cake yeast
1 cup warm water
1 teaspoon sugar
2 eggs, beaten
½ cup lard, softened
1 cup raisins
2½ cups all-purpose flour

1 cup sugar
1 teaspoon soda
1 teaspoon salt
½ teaspoon cinnamon
½ teaspoon nutmeg
½ teaspoon cloves
½ teaspoon allspice

Dissolve the yeast in the warm water and teaspoon of sugar. Mix together the eggs, lard and raisins, and stir in the yeast. Sift together the rest of the ingredients and add them to the first mixture. Let the batter set in a warm place for about 25 to 30 minutes, then bake it in a greased 9-inch round cake pan at 350° for 30 minutes.

SOUR CREAM SPICE CAKE

½ cup shortening
2 cups brown sugar
3 eggs, separated
1¾ cups cake flour sifted with
½ teaspoon salt
1 teaspoon soda

2 teaspoons cinnamon
1 teaspoon cloves
1 teaspoon allspice
1 cup sour cream
1 teaspoon vanilla

Cream the shortening and sugar, and add the egg yolks. Add the flour, soda and spices, then add the sour cream and beat the mixture well. Add the vanilla and fold in the stiffly beaten egg whites. Bake the batter in greased 8-inch layer pans for 25 minutes at 350°.

SUGARLESS SPICE CAKE

2¼ cups sifted cake flour
2¼ teaspoons baking powder
1¼ teaspoons cinnamon
¼ teaspoon nutmeg
¼ teaspoon cloves
¼ teaspoon salt

½ cup shortening
1 cup corn syrup
2 eggs, unbeaten
½ cup milk
1 teaspoon lemon rind
1 teaspoon vanilla

Sift together the flour, baking powder, spices and salt. Cream the shortening and add a little of the flour mixture at a time until all of it has been stirred in. Add the syrup and eggs and beat the mixture well. Then add the milk, lemon rind and vanilla. Bake the batter for 30 minutes at 350°.

PUMPKIN SPICE CAKE

½ cup shortening
1¼ cups sugar
2 eggs, beaten
2¼ cups sifted cake flour
2½ teaspoons baking powder
½ teaspoon soda
1 teaspoon salt

2 teaspoons cinnamon
½ teaspoon ginger
½ teaspoon nutmeg
1 cup pumpkin
¾ cup milk
½ cup chopped nuts

Cream the shortening, then add the sugar gradually and continue creaming it until it is light and fluffy. Blend in the eggs. Sift together the dry ingredients. Combine the pumpkin and milk. Add the dry ingredients alternately with the pumpkin mixture to the egg mixture, beginning and ending with the dry ingredients. Stir in the chopped nuts. Bake the batter in 2 greased 9-inch layer pans at 350° for about 30 minutes.

Frost the cake with your favorite butter cream icing, using orange juice for the liquid and grated orange rind for added zest.

LEMON SPONGE CAKE

1 cup sifted cake flour
1 teaspoon baking powder
½ teaspoon salt
½ cup cold water
2 teaspoons grated lemon rind

2 egg yolks, beaten
¾ cup plus 2 tablespoons sugar
2 egg whites
1 teaspoon lemon juice

Sift together 4 times, the flour, baking powder and salt. Add the water and lemon rind to the egg yolks and beat them until they are lemon-colored. Add the ¾ cup of sugar (2 tablespoons at a time), beating after each addition. Then add the sifted ingredients, slowly stirring to blend them. Beat the egg whites until they peak, and add the lemon juice and 2 tablespoons of the sugar, beating until they are well blended. Fold this mixture into the rest of the batter, and pour it into a tube pan. Bake it for 1 hour at 350°.

SPONGE CAKE

1½ cups sugar
1½ cups cake flour
1 teaspoon baking powder
¼ teaspoon salt

½ cup cold water
5 eggs, separated, and beaten well
¾ teaspoon cream of tartar

Sift together the first 4 ingredients. Beat the water with the egg yolks until they are thick, then fold them into the dry ingredients. Beat the egg whites with the cream of tartar until they stand in peaks, then fold them into the other mixture. Bake the batter in a tube pan for 1 hour at 350°.

YELLOW SPONGE CAKE

1½ cups sifted cake flour
1½ cups sugar
6 eggs, separated
1 teaspoon vanilla

½ teaspoon baking powder
¼ teaspoon salt
½ cup cold water

Sift together the flour and 1 cup of the sugar. Beat the egg yolks with the rest of the sugar, the vanilla, baking powder and salt until they are fluffy. Then add alternately the flour/sugar mixture and ½ cup of cold water. Fold in the stiffly beaten egg whites. Pour the batter into a tube pan and bake it approximately 1 hour at 350°.

Cooked Icing;

¾ cup milk
⅓ cup flour
½ cup butter or margarine
¾ cup sugar

1 teaspoon vanilla
Coconut, shredded, or ground
nutmeats

Combine the milk and flour and cook the mixture until it is very thick. Let it cool before beating in the butter, sugar and vanilla. Continue to beat the mixture until it is fluffy like whipped cream. Ice the cake with it and cover it with coconut or nutmeats.

TOASTED SPICE CAKE

½ cup shortening
2 cups brown sugar
2 egg yolks
2½ cups cake flour
½ teaspoon salt
1 teaspoon soda

1 teaspoon baking powder
1½ teaspoons cinnamon
1 teaspoon cloves
1¼ cups sour milk
1 teaspoon vanilla

Cream together the shortening and sugar. Add the egg yolks and beat the mixture well. Sift the flour once, then measure and add the salt, soda, baking powder and spices. Sift these again before adding them to the first mixture alternately with the milk and vanilla. Beat the mixture well after each addition. Pour the batter into a greased flat pan (8 x 12 x 1¼ inches).

2 egg whites
1 cup light brown sugar

½ cup nuts, finely chopped, OR
½ cup shredded coconut

Beat the egg whites until they are stiff enough to hold peaks. Slowly add the sugar, beating the mixture until it is smooth. Spread it over the cake batter and sprinkle it with the nuts or coconut before baking it at 350° for 40 minutes.

WHITE AS SNOW CAKE

2½ cups sifted cake flour
4½ teaspoons baking powder
1½ cups sugar
1 teaspoon salt
½ cup shortening

1 cup milk
4 egg whites to make ½ cup, unbeaten
1 teaspoon vanilla extract
Nuts, chopped (optional)

Sift all the dry ingredients into a mixing bowl. Add the shortening (soft but not melted) and ⅔ of the milk. Beat these ingredients 150 strokes by hand to make a well blended and glossy batter. Add the remaining milk, the egg whites and vanilla, and nuts if desired. Beat the batter again until it is smooth, about 150 strokes. Pour it into 2 well-greased and floured 8-inch layer cake pans or 1 loaf pan, and bake it in a moderate oven (350°) for 30 minutes.

ZUCCHINI SQUASH CAKE

1 cup oil
2 cups sugar
3 eggs
3 cups all-purpose flour
1 teaspoon baking powder
1 teaspoon soda

1 teaspoon salt
2 cups peeled, drained zucchini,
    mashed
½ cup raisins
2 teaspoons vanilla
Chopped nuts (optional)

Prepare this recipe the same as you would Pumpkin Spice Cake (see page 125). Pour the batter into 2 small loaf pans or 1 large one, and bake it for 1 hour at 350°.

ANGEL GINGERBREAD

1 cup white sugar
½ cup shortening
½ cup baking molasses
2 eggs
2 cups sifted cake flour
½ teaspoon salt

½ teaspoon ginger
½ teaspoon cinnamon
½ teaspoon nutmeg
¾ cup boiling water
1 teaspoon soda

Mix together the first 9 ingredients, beating them well. Then add the boiling water in which the soda has been dissolved. Bake the batter in a moderate oven (350°) for 25 to 30 minutes or until it is done. Serve the cake with whipped cream.

VELVET CRUMB CAKE

1⅓ cups biscuit mix
¾ cup sugar
3 tablespoons soft shortening

1 egg
¾ cup milk
1 teaspoon vanilla

Preheat the oven to 350°. Grease and flour a square pan (9 x 9 x 1½ inches). Mix the biscuit mix and sugar. Add the shortening, egg and ¼ cup of the milk. Beat these ingredients for 1 minute. Gradually stir in the rest of the milk, then add the vanilla and beat them for ½ minute longer. Pour the batter into the prepared pan and bake it for 35 to 40 minutes. Cover the cake with Broiled Topping while it is warm.

Broiled Topping;

3 tablespoons soft butter
⅓ cup brown sugar, packed
2 tablespoons cream

½ cup shredded coconut or Wheaties
¼ cup chopped nuts

Mix together the butter, brown sugar, cream, coconut and nuts. Spread it over the baked cake, then place it under low heat until the topping is bubbly and brown, for 3 to 5 minutes.

SUNSHINE CAKE

8 eggs
½ teaspoon cream of tartar
1½ cups raw sugar
½ teaspoon salt

1½ teaspoons lemon extract
2 tablespoons water
1 cup whole wheat flour
½ cup chopped nuts

Separate the eggs. Beat the egg whites until they are frothy, then add the cream of tartar. Gradually add 1 cup of the sugar. Continue beating the whites until they form very stiff peaks. Beat the egg yolks until they are very thick, then add the salt, lemon extract and the rest of the sugar. Continue to beat the mixture while adding alternately the water and whole wheat flour. Beat it well. Very gently fold the yolks into the whites, then fold in the nuts. Pour the batter into an ungreased angel food cake pan. Bake it at 325 to 350° for 1½ hours. Invert the cake on a funnel and let it cool for 1 hour. Remove it from the pan. This cake may be eaten unfrosted, or frosted with Seafoam Frosting (see page 135).

COCOA ICING

1 cup sugar
4 teaspoons cocoa
2 tablespoons cornstarch

1 cup boiling water
2 tablespoons butter
Vanilla

Boil the sugar, cocoa, cornstarch and water until thick, then add the butter and vanilla.

TROPICAL GINGERBREAD

½ cup shortening
½ cup sugar
1 egg
2½ cups all-purpose flour
1½ teaspoons soda
1 teaspoon cinnamon

1 teaspoon ginger
½ teaspoon cloves
½ teaspoon salt
1 cup baking molasses
1 cup hot water

Melt the shortening and let it cool. Add the sugar and egg, then beat the mixture well. Sift together the flour, soda, spices and salt. Combine the molasses and hot water. Add this alternately with the flour mixture to the egg mixture. Bake the batter in a 9 x 9 x 2-inch pan at 350° for 50 to 60 minutes.

EASY CHOCOLATE ROLL UP

¼ cup butter
1 cup chopped pecans
1⅓ cups flaked coconut
1 can (15½ ounces) sweetened
  condensed milk
3 eggs
1 cup sugar

⅔ cup all-purpose flour
⅓ cup cocoa
¼ teaspoon salt
¼ teaspoon baking powder
⅓ cup water
1 teaspoon vanilla

Line a 15 x 10-inch jelly roll pan with foil. In the pan, melt the butter and sprinkle the nuts and coconut evenly. Drizzle it with the condensed milk. Beat the eggs at high speed for 2 minutes until they are fluffy. Gradually add the sugar and continue beating them for 2 minutes more. It is not necessary to sift the flour—spoon it into a cup, level it, and add the remaining ingredients. Blend this into the egg mixture for 1 minute, beating it lightly.

Pour the batter evenly into the pan. Bake it at 375° for 20 to 25 minutes until the cake springs back when touched in the center. Sprinkle the cake in the pan with icing sugar. Cover it with a towel and put a cookie sheet lightly over the towel. Invert the cake and remove the pan and foil. Using a towel, roll up the cake jelly roll fashion, starting on the 10-inch side.

ICINGS AND FILLINGS

HINTS FOR ICINGS

- *A teaspoon of vinegar beaten into a boiled frosting when flavoring is added will keep it from being brittle or breaking when cut.*

- *To keep icing soft, add a pinch of baking soda to the whites of eggs before beating them. Then beat them in the usual way and pour hot syrup over them. The frosting will be soft and creamy.*

BEAT'N'EAT FROSTING

1 egg white, unbeaten
¾ cup sugar
¼ teaspoon cream of tartar

1 teaspoon vanilla
¼ cup boiling water

Mix together well the first 4 ingredients. Add the boiling water and beat the mixture rapidly with an egg beater for 4 to 5 minutes until it is thick. This is delicious as a quick topping.

BURNT SUGAR FROSTING

3 tablespoons soft butter or margarine
1 egg yolk, beaten
5 tablespoons Burnt Sugar Syrup (see page 298)

2 tablespoons cream
4 cups sifted icing sugar
1 teaspoon almond extract

Cream together the butter or margarine and egg yolk. Beat in alternately the syrup, cream, sugar, and extract until the frosting is smooth and creamy enough to spread.

BUTTER-CREAM FROSTING

1 pound icing sugar
¼ teaspoon salt
¼ cup butter or margarine

¼ cup cocoa
1 egg
3 tablespoons hot water

Blend together the ingredients and beat the mixture until it is thick enough to spread. This recipe makes enough to frost the top and sides of an 8-inch layer cake.

COCONUT-PECAN FROSTING

1 cup evaporated milk, or cream	1 teaspoon vanilla
½ cup butter or margarine	1⅓ cups shredded coconut
1 cup sugar	1 cup chopped pecans
3 egg yolks	

Combine the milk, butter, sugar, egg yolks and vanilla. Cook and stir the mixture over medium heat until it is thick (about 12 minutes). Add the coconut and pecans, then beat the mixture until it is thick enough to spread. This makes 2½ cups.

CREAM CHEESE FROSTING

8 ounces white cream cheese	1 pound icing sugar
8 tablespoons margarine	2 teaspoons vanilla

Cream together the cheese and margarine, then add the sugar and vanilla and stir it until it is creamy.

CREAMY CARAMEL FROSTING

4 tablespoons margarine	¼ cup whole milk
1 cup brown sugar, firmly packed	2½ cups icing sugar (approximate)
¼ teaspoon salt	½ teaspoon vanilla

Melt the margarine in a saucepan. Blend in the brown sugar and salt. Cook it over low heat, stirring it constantly for 2 minutes. Stir in the milk, and continue stirring until the mixture comes to a boil. Remove it from the heat, and gradually blend in the icing sugar. Add the vanilla. Thin the frosting with a small amount of canned milk if necessary.

CREAMY ICING

¼ cup sugar	1 egg
2 tablespoons water	½ cup Crisco
2⅓ cups icing sugar	1 tablespoon cocoa
1 teaspoon salt	1 teaspoon vanilla

Boil the sugar and water together for 1 minute. Mix together the icing sugar, salt and egg, then blend it with the first mixture. Add the Crisco, cocoa and vanilla, and beat it until it is creamy.

CHOCOLATE FUDGE ICING

2 squares (2 ounces) unsweetened
   chocolate
1¼ cups milk
2 cups sugar

Dash of salt
1 tablespoon light corn syrup
3 tablespoons butter
1½ teaspoons vanilla

Add the chocolate to the milk and place it over low heat. Cook it until it is smooth and blended, stirring constantly. Add the sugar, salt and syrup. Stir it until the sugar is dissolved and the mixture boils. Continue boiling it until the mixture forms a very soft ball when tested in water. Cool it to lukewarm, then add the butter and vanilla and beat it until it can be spread. If it hardens too soon, add a small amount of hot water.

FLUFFY WHITE FROSTING

2 egg whites
½ cup sugar
½ cup white corn syrup

Put the egg whites in the top of a double boiler, and add the sugar and white syrup. Beat the mixture over boiling water until it is thick enough to support the egg beater upright. Then spread it over the cake and swirl it. It will stay soft.

GELATIN FROSTING

3 tablespoons fruit flavored gelatin
   powder
¼ cup water

2 small egg whites
1 cup sugar
⅛ teaspoon cream of tartar

Heat the gelatin and water in the top of a double boiler. Beat the egg whites. Mix together the sugar and cream of tartar, then add it to the gelatin mixture with the egg whites. While it is still over boiling water, beat this mixture until it peaks. Remove it from the heat and beat it for 1 minute before spreading.

LEMON FROSTING

½ cup butter or margarine
Dash of salt
1 teaspoon grated lemon rind

4 cups icing sugar
4 teaspoons lemon juice
⅓ cup milk

Cream the butter, salt and rind. Gradually add part of the sugar. Then add the remaining sugar alternately with the lemon juice and milk until the mixture is of the right consistency to spread.

MAPLE CREAM ICING

1 cup brown sugar
¼ cup butter or margarine
3 tablespoons milk

½ teaspoon maple flavoring (optional)
1 cup icing sugar
1 teaspoon vanilla

Mix together the brown sugar, butter and milk and bring the mixture to a full boil. Remove it from the heat and add the icing sugar and vanilla, stirring until it is of spreading consistency.

MARSHMALLOW FROSTING

1 egg white, unbeaten
⅞ cup sugar
3 tablespoons water

1 teaspoon vanilla
12 marshmallows cut into pieces
1 to 2 cups moist coconut

Put the egg white, sugar and water into a double boiler. Beat the mixture constantly with an egg beater for 6 minutes. Remove it from the heat and add the vanilla and marshmallows. Beat it until it is of a consistency to spread. Add the coconut, reserving enough to sprinkle on top.

PRALINE TOPPING

½ cup brown sugar
1 cup chopped nuts, OR
½ cup shredded coconut

¼ cup melted butter
3 tablespoons cream

Mix together the sugar, nuts, butter and cream. Spread the mixture over the cake, then place it under the broiler or in a hot oven for 1 or 2 minutes.

GRANDMA'S CARAMEL FROSTING

2 cups brown sugar
1 cup top milk
¼ teaspoon cream of tartar

Cook the sugar and top milk over medium heat until it reaches the soft ball stage (230°). Remove it from the heat and add the cream of tartar, stirring it very little to blend. Set the frosting aside to cool to lukewarm but do not let it get too cold. Beat it until it thickens enough to spread on cake. Work fast when it is of the right consistency.

MINUTE FUDGE ICING

¼ cup butter
1 cup sugar

¼ cup cocoa (scant)
¼ cup milk

Melt the butter in a saucepan, then add the rest of the ingredients. Stir the mixture over low heat until all the ingredients are dissolved, then bring it to a rolling boil and boil it for 1 minute. Remove the icing from the heat and beat it until it is creamy enough to spread.

NUT ICING

2 cups brown sugar
1 cup sweet cream
½ cup ground hickory nuts

Lump of butter
1 teaspoon vanilla

Boil together the sugar and cream to the soft ball stage. Set it aside until it is cool, then add the nuts, butter and vanilla. Beat it until it thickens enough to spread on cake. Work fast when the icing is of the right consistency.

SEAFOAM FROSTING

1 egg white
¾ cup raw sugar
Pinch of salt

¼ teaspoon cream of tartar
2 teaspoons honey

Beat these ingredients with an egg beater in the top of a double boiler until peaks form (about 7 minutes).

SIMPLE ORANGE ICING

3 cups icing sugar
4 tablespoons orange juice

Grated rind of 1 orange
2 tablespoons melted butter

Combine the sugar, juice and rind. Beat this mixture well, then add the melted butter. Stir it until it is well blended.

ORANGE ICING

¼ cup margarine or butter
¾ cup granulated sugar
¼ cup orange juice

¼ cup orange gelatin powder
¾ cup sifted icing sugar

Melt the margarine, then add the sugar, orange juice and gelatin. Boil the mixture for 1 minute. When it has cooled slightly, beat in the icing sugar until the icing is of spreading consistency.

CARAMEL FILLING FOR SPONGE CAKE

2 tablespoons white sugar
1 cup water
1 tablespoon butter

1 cup white sugar
3 eggs, beaten
2 tablespoons flour

Melt the 2 tablespoons of sugar in a pan without water. Then add the water and boil it to a syrup. Add the butter and the 1 cup of sugar. Pour over this mixture the eggs which have been combined with the flour. Beat the mixture well, then bring it to a boil, stirring constantly. Spread it on sponge cake.

This or any other filling may be used for gelatin rolls.

SOFT ICING

3 tablespoons flour
⅔ cup milk
¾ cup Crisco

Flavoring
¾ cup granulated sugar

In a saucepan, cook the flour and milk until thick, then allow it to cool. Cream together the Crisco, flavoring of your choice and sugar. Combine the 2 mixtures and beat vigorously until the icing is smooth.

SUGARLESS FROSTING

1¼ cups corn syrup
3 egg whites

1 teaspoon baking powder
2 teaspoons vanilla flavoring

Boil the corn syrup in a saucepan over direct heat until it spins a thread when dripped from a spoon. Beat the egg whites until they are foamy, then add the baking powder and beat them again until stiff. Add the corn syrup slowly while beating vigorously. Add the flavoring and continue beating until the frosting is stiff and stands in peaks. This makes frosting for two 9-inch layers, 1 medium loaf cake, or 16 large cup cakes.

CHOCOLATE FILLING

2 squares (2 ounces) chocolate
1 cup rich milk

1½ cups sugar
Butter the size of an egg

Shave the chocolate finely, then add it to a pan with the milk, sugar and butter. Boil these ingredients to the desired thickness.

CLEAR LEMON FILLING

¾ cup sugar
3 tablespoons cornstarch
⅓ teaspoon salt
1½ tablespoons grated lemon rind

6 tablespoons lemon juice
1½ tablespoons butter
¾ cup water

Mix together in a saucepan the above ingredients. Bring the mixture to a boil and boil it for 1 minute, stirring it constantly. Chill the filling before using it.

CREAM FILLING

1 pint milk
1 egg
½ cup sugar

3 tablespoons cornstarch
1 lump butter

Cook the above ingredients until thick. Cool the mixture and spread it between layers of cake.

ORANGE CAKE FILLING

Juice and rind of 1 orange
1 cup cold water
1 cup sugar

2 egg yolks
1 tablespoon corn starch

Cook the ingredients until the mixture is thick and clear.

COOKIES, BARS, FINGERS AND SQUARES

APPLESAUCE DROP COOKIES

2 cups all-purpose flour
1 teaspoon soda
¼ teaspoon salt
1 teaspoon cinnamon
½ teaspoon nutmeg
½ cup butter
½ cup white sugar

½ cup brown sugar, packed
1 egg
1 cup applesauce
1 cup rolled oats
½ cup raisins
½ cup chopped nuts
½ cup chocolate chips

Sift together the first 5 ingredients, then set the mixture aside. Mix the butter and sugar, add the egg, then blend these ingredients. Add the applesauce with the sifted dry ingredients before adding the rest and mixing well. Drop the batter by teaspoonfuls onto an ungreased cookie sheet, and bake it for 8 minutes at 375°.

BUSHEL OF COOKIES

5 pounds sugar
2½ pounds lard
12 eggs
1 pound salted peanuts, ground coarsely with
1 pound raisins
2 pounds quick cooking oats

1 cup maple syrup
2 ounces or 3 tablespoons soda
2 ounces or 3 tablespoons baking powder
1 quart sweet milk
6 pounds flour

Mix together all the ingredients to make a batter. Drop it by spoonfuls onto a cookie sheet, and bake it at 350°.

Half recipe in cup measures;

7 cups sugar
2½ cups lard
½ pound peanuts, ground coarsely with
½ pound raisins
2 tablespoons soda

2 cups milk
6 eggs
4¾ cups oatmeal
½ cup maple syrup
2 tablespoons baking powder
12 cups flour

APPLESAUCE NUT COOKIES

½ cup shortening
1 cup sugar
1 egg
1 cup thick unsweetened applesauce
2 cups all-purpose flour
½ teaspoon cinnamon

¼ teaspoon cloves
3 teaspoons baking powder
½ teaspoon salt
½ cup raisins
½ cup nuts

Cream the shortening, then add the sugar and egg. Add the applesauce and the dry ingredients before folding in the raisins and nuts. Drop the batter by teaspoonfuls 2 inches apart on a cookie sheet and bake them at 350° for 15 to 20 minutes.

CARROT COOKIES

½ cup shortening
1 cup brown sugar
½ cup granulated sugar
1 teaspoon vanilla
1 egg

1 cup cooked carrots, mashed and
    cooled
2 cups all-purpose flour
½ teaspoon baking powder
Pinch of salt
¾ cup raisins

Cream together the shortening and sugar. Add the vanilla, egg, carrots and the remaining ingredients in the order listed. Drop the batter by spoonfuls onto a cookie sheet and bake it at 375° until done.

CHERRY COOKIES

2¼ cups all-purpose flour
1 teaspoon baking powder
½ teaspoon soda
½ teaspoon salt
¾ cup shortening
1 cup sugar
2 eggs

2 tablespoons milk
1 teaspoon almond extract
1 teaspoon vanilla
1 cup chopped pecans
⅓ cup chopped maraschino cherries
1 cup chopped dates
2½ cups cornflakes

Sift together the flour, baking powder, soda and salt. Combine the shortening and sugar, then blend in the eggs. Add to this mixture the milk, almond extract and vanilla. Blend in the sifted dry ingredients and mix it well. Add the pecans, cherries and dates, and mix it well again. Shape the dough into balls, using 1 level tablespoon per cookie. Crush the cornflakes and roll each ball of dough in them. Place the balls on a greased cookie sheet and top each one with ¼ cherry. Bake them at 375° until done. Do not stack them until they are cold.

BUTTERSCOTCH COOKIES

6 cups brown sugar
1½ cups butter
4 eggs, beaten
1 tablespoon vanilla

1½ teaspoons soda
2 teaspoons baking powder
6 to 7 cups all-purpose flour

Cream together the sugar and butter until smooth, then add the eggs and vanilla. Sift the soda and baking powder with the flour, and add it to the first mixture. Shape the dough into rolls and chill them. Slice them and bake the cookies at 350° for 15 to 20 minutes.

CHOCOLATE MACAROONS

2 egg whites
1 cup sugar
⅛ teaspoon salt
½ teaspoon vanilla

1½ cups shredded coconut
1½ squares (1½ ounces) unsweetened
   chocolate

Beat the egg whites until stiff, then gradually beat in the sugar and salt. Beat the mixture well after the sugar has been added. Add the vanilla, and fold in the coconut and the chocolate which has been melted over hot water. Drop the batter by teaspoons onto a greased cookie sheet. Bake it at 275° for about 30 minutes. This recipe makes 1½ dozen cookies.

CHOCOLATE PEANUT BUTTER COOKIES

2 cups sifted all-purpose flour
½ teaspoon double-acting baking
   powder
¼ teaspoon soda
¼ teaspoon salt
½ cup shortening
½ cup peanut butter

½ cup white sugar
½ cup brown sugar, firmly packed
1 egg, well-beaten
½ cup milk
1 cup (6 ounces) semi-sweet chocolate
   chips

Preheat the oven to 375°. Sift together the flour, baking powder, soda and salt. Cream together the shortening and peanut butter, then blend in the sugars. Add the egg and mix it thoroughly before stirring in the sifted flour mixture alternately with the milk. Mix it well again. Fold in the chips. Drop the batter by spoonfuls onto an ungreased baking sheet and bake it for about 12 minutes. This recipe yields about 3 dozen cookies.

CHOCOLATE PINWHEEL

½ cup sugar
½ cup shortening
1 egg yolk
1½ teaspoons vanilla
1½ cups all purpose flour

¼ teaspoon salt
½ teaspoon baking powder
3 teaspoons milk
1 square (1 ounce) unsweetened
    chocolate, melted

Mix together all the ingredients but the chocolate to make a smooth dough. Divide it into 2 equal portions. To 1 portion add the melted chocolate. Roll the white dough ⅓-inch thick on a floured surface. Roll the chocolate dough the same size and place it on top of the first dough. Roll it like you would a jelly roll. Chill the dough, then cut it into slices and bake it at 350° until done.

CHOCOLATE SANDWICH WAFERS

1¼ cups sugar
2 eggs
1 teaspoon vanilla
½ cup butter
3 squares (3 ounces) chocolate,
    melted

2 cups all-purpose flour
½ teaspoon soda
1½ teaspoons baking powder
½ teaspoon salt

Combine the sugar, eggs, vanilla, butter and chocolate. Beat the mixture until it is creamy, then gradually add the flour, soda, baking powder and salt. Chill the dough well, then roll it out ⅛-inch thick and cut it into rounds. Put them onto an ungreased cookie sheet and bake them at 350° for 8 to 10 minutes. Let them cool, then put them together with your favorite filling.

SOFT CHOCOLATE COOKIES

1 teaspoon salt
1 teaspoon soda
2 teaspoons pure vanilla extract
1 cup shortening
2 cups light brown sugar

3 squares (3 ounces) unsweetened
    chocolate
2 eggs, unbeaten
2½ cups sifted all-purpose flour
¾ cup sour milk
1 cup chopped nuts

Blend the first 3 ingredients with the shortening. Gradually mix in the sugar. Melt the chocolate over hot water and add it to the mixture. Beat in the eggs, then add the flour alternately with the milk. Stir in the nuts. Drop heaping teaspoons of the batter, 2 inches apart on a lightly greased cookie sheet. Bake the cookies in a moderate oven (375°) for 10 to 12 minutes or until done. Let them cool and store them in an airtight container. This recipe yields 5 dozen cookies.

SOFT CHOCOLATE CHIP COOKIES

½ cup shortening
1 cup sugar
2 large eggs, or 3 small
½ cup milk
2½ cups all-purpose flour

1 teaspoon baking powder
¾ teaspoon soda (in milk)
1 small package (6 ounces) chocolate
    chips, or butterscotch morsels

Mix the ingredients to make a batter. Drop it by teaspoons onto a greased cookie sheet and bake it at 400°. When slightly brown around the edges, the cookies are done.

SOUR CREAM CHOCOLATE COOKIES

2 cups brown sugar
¾ cup shortening
2 eggs
1 teaspoon vanilla
2 squares (2 ounces) chocolate

2 teaspoons soda
1 cup sour cream
4 or 5 cups all-purpose flour
Pinch of salt

Cream together the sugar, shortening, eggs and vanilla. Melt the chocolate over hot water and add it to the sugar mixture. Put the soda into ½ cup of the sour cream and add it alternately with the flour and salt and the remaining cream. Make the dough as soft as can be handled. Chill it for a few hours. Roll it out ¼-inch thick, cut it and bake it in a moderate oven (350°) until done.

COCONUT OATMEAL GEMS

1 cup raw sugar
1 cup honey or maple syrup
½ cup vegetable oil
3 eggs
½ cup chopped dates or raisins
3 cups whole wheat flour
1 teaspoon soda

½ teaspoon baking powder
1 cup ground oatmeal or wheat germ
3 cups rolled oats
½ teaspoon salt
1 cup unsweetened coconut
½ cup hickory nuts

Cream together the sugar, honey and oil until light and fluffy. Add the beaten eggs and dates, beating the mixture thoroughly. Add the dry ingredients, coconut and nuts, mixing well after each addition. Drop the batter by spoonfuls onto a cookie sheet, then flatten the cookies with a fork. Bake them at 350° until done.

CHURCH COOKIES

3 tablespoons soda
1 teaspoon salt
1 cup hot water
12 to 15 cups all-purpose flour
5 cups sugar
2½ cups lard

1 cup molasses
4 eggs
2 teaspoons vanilla
2 teaspoons ginger
Dash of cinnamon (optional)
1 teaspoon baking powder

Dissolve the soda and salt in the hot water. Add this to the flour, and mix in the rest of the ingredients in the order they are listed. Roll out the dough, cut it with a cookie cutter, and bake it at 375° until done.

COCONUT COOKIES

2 cups all-purpose flour
1 teaspoon salt
2 teaspoons baking powder
¾ cup sugar

½ cup melted shortening
2 eggs
2 teaspoons vanilla
1 cup shredded coconut

Sift together the flour, salt and baking powder. Blend the sugar and shortening, add the eggs, and stir the mixture well. Stir in the vanilla and coconut, then add the sifted dry ingredients. Form the dough into a roll and chill it. Slice the dough and bake it at 375° until done.

DATE COOKIES

8 cups all-purpose flour
4 cups sugar
2 teaspoons soda
2 teaspoons cream of tartar

1 teaspoon salt
2 cups shortening
6 large eggs

Blend together all the ingredients, and drop the batter by spoonfuls onto a cookie sheet. Bake the cookies at 375° until done. When they have cooled, spread the following date filling between pairs of cookies. The cookies may seem a little hard at first, but several hours after the filling has been spread they will be soft and delicious.

Date Filling;

2 tablespoons cornstarch
2 cups water
1 cup cut-up dates

2 cups brown sugar
Juice of 2 lemons, OR
2 tablespoons Realemon

Bring the ingredients to a boil and cook the mixture until it is thick. Cool it and spread it between pairs of cookies.

COCONUT KRISPIES

1 cup butter, or ¾ cup oil
1 cup raw sugar
½ cup honey
2 eggs
1 teaspoon vanilla
2 cups whole wheat flour
½ cup wheat germ

½ teaspoon soda
¼ teaspoon salt
½ teaspoon baking powder
1 cup shredded coconut, unsweetened
2 cups rolled oats
1 cup bran flakes (optional)

Mix together the ingredients in the order given. Form the dough into balls the size of a walnut. Place them on a greased cookie sheet and bake them at 350° for 10 to 12 minutes.

DATE-FILLED OAT COOKIES

3 cups brown sugar
2 cups shortening, half butter
1 teaspoon vanilla
6 cups all-purpose flour

1 teaspoon salt
2 teaspoons soda
4 cups rolled oats
1 cup buttermilk

Cream together the sugar and shortening. Add the vanilla. Sift and measure the flour, then add the salt, soda and rolled oats. Add these dry ingredients alternately with the buttermilk, and mix thoroughly. Chill the dough for several hours. Turn it onto a lightly floured board and roll it to a ⅛-inch thickness. Cut the dough with a round cookie cutter and place the cookies 1 inch apart on a greased baking sheet. Bake them at 375° until they turn golden brown. This recipe makes 8 dozen cookies.

When they are cold, spread them with the following filling;

2 cups finely chopped dates
1 cup sugar

1 cup water
2 tablespoons cornstarch

Combine the ingredients and cook the mixture until it is thick. Let it cool before spreading on the cookies. Top the filling with another cookie.

CREAM WAFERS

1 cup lard plus 1 cup margarine
8 eggs, beaten
4 teaspoons cream
6 teaspoons soda
4 cups brown sugar

10½ cups all-purpose flour
4 teaspoons cinnamon
Vanilla
Salt

Mix together the ingredients to make a dough. Roll it out and cut it with a cookie cutter or put it through a cookie press. Bake the cookies at 350° until done. Spread them with your favorite frosting and place another cookie on top.

DATE PINWHEELS

Filling;

2½ cups dates
1 cup sugar

1 cup water
1 cup chopped nuts

Cook slowly the dates, sugar and water for 15 minutes. Add the nuts, and allow the mixture to cool.

Dough;

1 cup shortening
2 cups brown sugar
4 eggs

4 to 5½ cups all-purpose flour
½ teaspoon salt
½ teaspoon soda

Cream the shortening and gradually add the brown sugar. Add the well-beaten eggs and beat the mixture until it is smooth. Add the dry ingredients which have been sifted together, and mix it well. Chill the dough thoroughly.

Divide it into 2 parts and roll out each one separately into rectangular shape, less than ¼ inch thick. Spread each piece of the dough with the date filling and roll it up into 2 long rolls as for a jelly roll. Chill the rolls overnight. With a sharp knife slice them into ¼-inch thicknesses. Bake them in a moderately hot oven (400°) for 10 to 20 minutes.

EASY FILLED DROPS

1 cup shortening
1 cup brown sugar
2 eggs
½ cup water, sour milk or buttermilk
1 teaspoon vanilla

3½ cups sifted all-purpose flour
1 teaspoon soda
1 teaspoon salt
⅛ teaspoon cinnamon

Preheat the oven to 400°. Mix together well the shortening, sugar and eggs. Stir in the water and vanilla. Sift together and stir in the flour, soda, salt and cinnamon. Drop the dough by teaspoons onto an ungreased baking sheet. Place ½ teaspoon of date filling (see below) on each cookie and cover it with ½ teaspoon of the dough. Bake the cookies for 10 to 12 minutes. This recipe makes 5 to 6 dozen cookies.

Date Filling;

2 cups dates, cut into small pieces
¾ cup sugar

¾ cup water
½ cup chopped nuts

Cook the dates, sugar and water, stirring constantly until the mixture is thick. Add the nuts, and allow the filling to cool.

GINGER CREAMS

⅔ cup shortening
1¼ cups brown sugar
1 cup molasses
1 teaspoon soda
1 cup hot water
5½ cups flour, OR
4½ cups flour plus 1 cup wheat germ

1 teaspoon cinnamon
½ teaspoon cloves
½ teaspoon salt
1 teaspoon ginger
1 cup raisins
Chopped nuts (optional)

Cream together the shortening and sugar. Add the molasses, then the soda dissolved in the hot water. Add the sifted dry ingredients, then the raisins and nuts. Drop the batter by teaspoonfuls onto a greased baking sheet. Bake the cookies at 350° for 15 to 20 minutes or until done.

OLD-FASHIONED GINGER COOKIES

3 cups baking molasses
1 cup sugar
2 cups shortening
10 cups flour (5 cups pastry, 5 cups
   bread)

1 teaspoon salt
2 tablespoons soda
1 to 2 tablespoons ginger
1 teaspoon cinnamon
2 cups sour milk or buttermilk

Heat together the molasses and sugar, add the shortening and stir the mixture until it is smooth. Remove it from the heat. Sift together the dry ingredients and add this mixture alternately with the sour milk. Stir it to make a smooth dough, then work it with your hands for 5 minutes. Chill the dough and roll it out to ½-inch thickness. Cut it into cookies, and glaze them with a beaten egg. Bake them at 350° for 20 to 25 minutes. This recipe makes 8 dozen cookies.

SOFT GINGER COOKIES

6 to 8 cups all-purpose flour
¾ teaspoon salt
½ teaspoon cinnamon
2 tablespoons ginger
1 cup lard
1 cup sugar

1 egg
2 cups dark baking molasses
2 tablespoons vinegar
4 teaspoons soda
1 cup boiling water

Sift the flour with the salt and spices. Cream the lard and sugar, then add the egg and beat it until light. Add the molasses and vinegar, then the previously sifted dry ingredients, and the soda dissolved in the boiling water. If necessary, add more flour to make a soft dough. Drop it by teaspoons onto a greased cookie sheet. Sprinkle the cookies with sugar, and bake them for 10 minutes in a moderate oven (350°).

GINGER SNAPS

1 cup sugar	1 teaspoon ginger
1 cup dark baking molasses	½ teaspoon cinnamon
1 cup lard	1 teaspoon soda
1 egg	4 to 5 cups all-purpose flour

Heat together the sugar, molasses and lard. Let the mixture cool while stirring frequently. Stir in the egg, then add the combined ginger, cinnamon, soda and flour. Use enough flour to make a stiff dough. Roll it out very thinly, cut it with a cookie cutter and bake the cookies at 400° until done. They will taste like bakery cookies.

GRAHAM GEMS

2 cups dark brown sugar	1 teaspoon soda
½ cup butter or lard	5 tablespoons sour cream
2 eggs	¼ teaspoon salt
4 cups whole wheat flour (or part white)	1 teaspoon vanilla
	½ cup raisins (optional)

Mix together the above ingredients, then drop the batter by teaspoonfuls onto a greased cookie sheet. Bake the cookies at 400° until done.

The raisins add a better flavor if they are cooked in a little water first for a minutes. Then add the raisins and water to the dough. In this case, more flour may be required.

JUBILEE JUMBLES

½ cup soft shortening	3 cups all-purpose flour (scant)
½ cup white sugar	½ teaspoon soda
1 cup brown sugar	1 teaspoon salt
2 eggs	½ cup nuts
1 cup undiluted evaporated milk	½ cup coconut
1 teaspoon vanilla	1 package (12 ounces) chocolate chips

Mix together thoroughly the shortening, sugar and eggs. Stir in the evaporated milk and vanilla. Sift together the flour, soda and salt, and stir this mixture into the first. Blend in the nuts, coconut and chocolate chips. Chill the batter for 1 hour, then drop it by spoonfuls onto a greased baking sheet and bake it for 8 to 12 minutes at 375°. While they are still warm, frost the cookies with a creamy fudge frosting.

LEMON CRISPS

1¾ cups shortening
1 cup granulated sugar
1 cup brown sugar
2 tablespoons lemon juice
2 eggs

2 teaspoons grated lemon rind
5½ cups all-purpose flour
½ teaspoon salt
½ teaspoon soda

Mix the ingredients together well, then form the dough into small balls. Place them on a cookie sheet and flatten them. Bake the cookies at 350° for 10 to 12 minutes.

ORANGE CRISPS; Substitute orange juice and rind for the lemons.

LITTLE HONEY CAKES

1½ cups lard
2 cups sugar
4 eggs, beaten
1 cup molasses
1 cup honey
1 cup hot water

2 teaspoons cinnamon
1 teaspoon ginger
2 teaspoons soda
2 teaspoons baking powder
5 cups all-purpose flour (approximate),
   to stiffen

Cream together the lard and sugar. Add the eggs. Blend in the molasses, honey and hot water. Add the cinnamon, ginger, soda, baking powder and flour. Chill the dough overnight, then roll it out and cut it into cookie shapes, or drop it by the spoonful onto a cookie sheet. Bake the cookies at 350° until brown.

MINCEMEAT COOKIES

1 cup shortening
1 cup brown sugar
1 cup white sugar
3 eggs
3 cups all-purpose flour
1 teaspoon soda

½ teaspoon salt
1 teaspoon cinnamon
½ teaspoon cloves
½ teaspoon nutmeg
1 cup mincemeat
1 cup chopped nuts

Cream together the shortening and sugar. Add the eggs and beat until fluffy. Sift and measure the flour, add the soda, salt and spices, then sift it again. Add these dry ingredients to the creamed mixture and mix it thoroughly. Add the mincemeat and nuts. Drop the batter by teaspoonfuls onto a greased baking sheet, and bake it at 350° until done.

MARY'S SUGAR COOKIES

2 eggs
1½ cups granulated sugar
1 cup lard
1 teaspoon vanilla
1 cup sweet milk

4 cups all-purpose flour
2 teaspoons baking powder
2 teaspoons cream of tartar
2 teaspoons soda (scant)

Beat the eggs for 1 minute. Add the sugar and lard and beat the mixture for 1 minute more. Add the vanilla and milk. Sift together the dry ingredients and combine this mixture with the first. Drop the batter by spoonfuls onto a cookie sheet and bake the cookies at 400° until they are golden brown. When the cookies have cooled, spread the following icing on top.

6 tablespoons butter (room
    temperature)
2 teaspoons vanilla

⅛ teaspoon salt
1 pound icing sugar
4 to 5 tablespoons milk

Put all the ingredients into a bowl and beat the mixture for 1 minute. Divide the icing into several parts and color each part with a different food coloring. This will add variety to one batch of cookies.

MICHIGAN ROCKS

1½ cups brown sugar
¾ cup shortening
4 eggs
3 cups all-purpose flour (scant)
1 teaspoon soda

1 pound dates, finely chopped
1½ cups nut meats
1 teaspoon vanilla
¼ teaspoon salt

Mix together the ingredients, then drop the batter by teaspoonfuls onto a cookie sheet. Bake it at 350° for 6 to 8 minutes or until done.

MOLASSES DROP COOKIES

1 cup lard
1½ cups brown sugar
2 eggs
1 cup molasses
1 cup table syrup

1½ cups sweet milk
3 teaspoons soda
1 teaspoon ginger
2 teaspoons cinnamon
6 cups all-purpose flour

Mix the ingredients together to make a batter. Drop it by spoonfuls onto a greased cookie sheet. Bake the cookies in a moderate oven (350°) until done.

OATMEAL MOLASSES COOKIES

½ cup sugar
½ cup molasses
¾ cup shortening
2 eggs
¼ cup sweet milk
2 teaspoons cinnamon

1 teaspoon cloves
1 teaspoon soda
2 cups all-purpose flour
1 cup raisins
2 cups oatmeal

Mix together the ingredients in the order given. Drop the batter by teaspoons onto a greased cookie sheet. Bake it at 350° until done.

MOLASSES SUGAR COOKIES

1 cup sugar
¾ cup shortening
¼ cup molasses
1 egg
2 cups sifted all-purpose flour

2 teaspoons soda
1 teaspoon cinnamon
½ teaspoon cloves
½ teaspoon ginger
½ teaspoon salt

Cream together the sugar and shortening. Add the molasses and egg, and beat the mixture well. Sift together the flour, soda, cinnamon, cloves, ginger and salt, and add this mixture to the first. Mix it well and chill. Form the dough into 1-inch balls. Roll them in granulated sugar and place them 2 inches apart on greased cookie sheets. Flatten them with a spoon or fork. Bake the cookies at 350° for 8 to 10 minutes. This recipe makes 4 dozen cookies.

SOFT MOLASSES COOKIES

¾ cup shortening
¾ cup brown sugar
2 eggs
¾ cup molasses
¾ cup sour cream

2¼ cups all-purpose flour
2 teaspoons soda
½ teaspoon salt
½ teaspoon cinnamon
1½ teaspoons ginger (optional)

Cream together the shortening and sugar. Add the well-beaten eggs, molasses and sour cream, and stir the mixture until it is smooth. Mix together the dry ingredients, and add this mixture gradually to the first. Chill the dough, then drop it by spoonfuls onto a greased baking pan. Bake the cookies at 350° for about 10 minutes.

NO-BAKE COOKIES

2 cups white sugar
3 tablespoons cocoa
¼ cup butter
½ cup milk

3 cups oatmeal (finely crumbled)
½ cup peanut butter
1 teaspoon vanilla

Boil together the sugar, cocoa, butter and milk. Remove this mixture from the heat and add the oatmeal, peanut butter and vanilla. Drop the batter quickly by teaspoonfuls onto waxed paper.

Variations: Coconut, nuts or chocolate chips may be used instead of the peanut butter.

SOFT OATMEAL DROP COOKIES

¾ cup melted shortening
2 eggs, beaten
¾ cup buttermilk
4 cups oatmeal
1½ cups raisins, OR
½ cup shredded coconut
¼ cup corn oil

⅛ teaspoon salt
2 teaspoons soda
½ cup brown sugar
½ cup raw sugar
½ cup honey
2 cups all-purpose flour
1 teaspoon baking powder

Mix together all the ingredients to make a batter. Drop it by spoonfuls onto a greased cookie sheet. Grease your fingers to press the cookies flat and to make a nice edge. Bake them at 350° until done. This recipe makes 42 cookies.

BANANA OATMEAL COOKIES

1½ cups sifted all-purpose flour
1 cup sugar
½ teaspoon soda
½ teaspoon nutmeg
¾ teaspoon cinnamon

¾ cup shortening
1 egg, well-beaten
1 cup mashed bananas
1¾ cups rolled oats
Nuts

Sift together the dry ingredients. Cut in the shortening, then add the egg, bananas, oats and nuts. Beat the mixture thoroughly until all the ingredients are blended. Drop the batter by teaspoonfuls about 1½ inches apart onto greased cookie sheets. Bake it at 400° for about 15 minutes. This recipe makes 3½ dozen cookies.

NUT COOKIES

½ cup shortening
1½ cups sugar
4 egg yolks, beaten
1 teaspoon vanilla
1¾ cups flour

½ teaspoon baking powder
¼ teaspoon salt
¾ cup chopped nuts
2 teaspoons cinnamon

Cream together the shortening and sugar, then blend in the eggs and vanilla. Sift together the flour, baking powder and salt, then mix this with the creamed mixture. Form the dough into tiny balls, and dip them in a mixture of the nuts and cinnamon. Bake them in a moderate oven (350°) until done.

PEANUT BUTTER COOKIES

½ cup shortening
½ cup peanut butter
½ cup granulated sugar
½ cup brown sugar
1 egg, well-beaten

1 teaspoon vanilla
1¼ cups all-purpose flour
¼ teaspoon salt
½ teaspoon baking powder
¾ teaspoon soda

Thoroughly cream the shortening, peanut butter and sugars. Add the eggs and vanilla, then beat the mixture well. Add the sifted dry ingredients and mix it thoroughly. Chill the dough well, then form it into small balls on a cookie sheet, and flatten them with a fork. Bake the cookies in a moderate oven (375°) for 10 to 15 minutes. This recipe makes 3 to 4 dozen cookies.

PEANUT SURPRISES

1 cup shortening (part butter for flavor)
2 cups brown sugar, packed
2 eggs
2 cups all-purpose flour
1 teaspoon baking powder

1 cup flaked wheat cereal
½ teaspoon salt
1 teaspoon soda
2 cups quick cooking oatmeal
1 cup coarsely chopped salted nuts

Mix together the ingredients, then drop the batter by teaspoonfuls onto a lightly greased baking sheet. Flatten out each cookie with a fork dipped in flour. Bake them for 10 to 12 minutes in a moderate oven (350°).

PEANUT BUTTER OATMEAL COOKIES

1 cup shortening
1 cup peanut butter
2 teaspoons vanilla
2 cups sugar
2 eggs
3 cups all-purpose flour
2 tablespoons baking powder
1 teaspoon salt

2 teaspoons cinnamon
½ teaspoon cloves
½ teaspoon nutmeg
4 cups quick cooking oats, OR
5 cups wheat flake cereal
⅔ cup milk
1 cup chopped nuts (optional)

Cream together the shortening, peanut butter and vanilla, and gradually add the sugar. Continue to cream this mixture until it is light and fluffy, then beat in the eggs. Sift together the flour, baking powder, salt, cinnamon, cloves and nutmeg, then add the oats. Stir this into the creamed mixture alternately with the milk, and blend in the nuts. Spoon the batter onto greased cookie sheets and bake it at 375° for 12 to 15 minutes. This recipe makes 6 dozen cookies.

Variations: *Substitute 1 cup of molasses or honey for the 1 cup of sugar.*

Stir in 2 cups of raisins, or 2 cups of chopped dates, prunes or apricots (uncooked) when adding the nuts.

PUMPKIN COOKIES

1 cup brown sugar
1 cup lard
1 egg
1 cup pumpkin
2 cups all-purpose flour

1 teaspoon soda
½ teaspoon salt
1 teaspoon baking powder
1 teaspoon cinnamon

Mix together the sugar, lard and egg, then add the pumpkin and mix it well. Sift together the dry ingredients and add them to the mixture, beating it well. Drop the batter by spoonfuls onto a cookie sheet and bake it at 350° for 10 to 20 minutes. When the cookies have cooled slightly, frost them with the following icing. This makes a very delicious and moist cookie.

1 tablespoon butter
1 tablespoon milk

¼ cup pumpkin
Icing sugar

Cream the butter, add the milk and pumpkin, then add enough sugar to bring the icing to spreading consistency.

PUMPKIN NUT COOKIES

½ cup shortening
1 cup sugar
2 eggs, beaten
1 cup pumpkin
2 cups sifted all-purpose flour
4 teaspoons baking powder

1 teaspoon salt
2½ teaspoons cinnamon
¼ teaspoon ginger
½ teaspoon nutmeg
1 cup raisins
1 cup chopped nuts

Cream the shortening and gradually add the sugar. Cream this mixture until it is light and fluffy. Add the eggs and pumpkin, and mix it well. Sift together the flour, baking powder, salt and spices. Stir in these dry ingredients and mix until they are blended. Add the raisins and nuts. Drop the batter by teaspoonfuls onto a greased cookie sheet, and bake it at 350° for about 15 minutes. This recipe makes 4 dozen cookies.

RAISIN DROP COOKIES

1 cup raisins
1 cup water
¾ cup margarine
1 cup sugar
1 egg

1 teaspoon vanilla
1 teaspoon soda
3 cups sifted all-purpose flour
1 teaspoon baking powder
Pinch of salt

Combine the raisins and hot water and boil it down to ½ cup of liquid. Cream together the margarine, sugar and egg, then add the vanilla and the combined soda, flour and salt. Mix this alternately with the raisins and liquid. Drop the batter by the tablespoon onto a greased cookie sheet, and bake it at 375° for about 15 minutes.

PINEAPPLE DROP COOKIES

3½ cups all-purpose flour
1 teaspoon baking powder
1 teaspoon soda
⅛ teaspoon salt
1 cup sugar

¾ cup Crisco
¾ cup butter
1 egg
½ cup pineapple juice
½ cup sour cream

In a bowl, measure and sift together the dry ingredients. Then cut in the Crisco and butter as for a pie crust. Add the beaten egg, pineapple juice and sour cream, and stir the mixture only enough to blend it. Drop the batter by spoonfuls onto a greased cookie sheet. Press a small piece of pineapple into each cookie before baking them at 400° for 12 minutes or until light brown.

PINEAPPLE COOKIES

1 cup brown sugar
1 cup granulated sugar
1 cup shortening
2 eggs
1 cup crushed pineapple
1 teaspoon pineapple flavoring

½ teaspoon salt
1½ teaspoons soda
½ teaspoon baking powder
4 cups all-purpose flour (more if
    pineapple undrained)

Combine the ingredients in the order given. Drop the batter into muffin tins and bake it at 350° for 20 minutes.

SNITZ COOKIES

1 cup lard
2 cups brown sugar
2 eggs
1 cup cooked snitz (dried apple pieces)
4 cups all-purpose flour

2 teaspoons baking powder
2 teaspoons soda
1 teaspoon salt
1 teaspoon cinnamon
½ cup raisins

Mix together the lard and sugar, then add the eggs and snitz. Sift together the dry ingredients and stir them in. Add the raisins. Drop the mixture by spoonfuls onto a greased baking sheet and bake the cookies at 350° for 10 to 15 minutes or until done.

SOUR CREAM COOKIES

1 cup lard or shortening
3 cups brown sugar
4 eggs
2 cups thick sour cream
2 teaspoons vanilla

1 teaspoon salt
2 teaspoons soda
2½ teaspoons nutmeg
1 teaspoon baking powder
6 to 7 cups all-purpose flour

Cream well the lard and sugar, then add the eggs, beating well after each addition. Add the sour cream and vanilla. Sift together the dry ingredients and add them to the mixture, mixing it well. Drop the batter by teaspoonfuls onto a greased baking sheet, then bake the cookies at 375° until done. Let them cool, then spread them with the following icing.

Icing;

¾ cup butter, browned
3 cups icing sugar
2 teaspoons vanilla

Mix the ingredients together and add hot water until the mixture is of spreading consistency.

RAISIN FILLED COOKIES

Filling;

2 cups chopped raisins
2 tablespoons flour
1 cup water

1 cup sugar
1 tablespoon lemon juice (optional)

Combine these ingredients and boil the mixture until it is thick.

Dough;

1 cup shortening
2 cups brown sugar
2 eggs
1 cup sweet milk

2 teaspoons vanilla
7 cups all-purpose flour
2 teaspoons soda
2 teaspoons baking powder

Cream the shortening, then add the sugar gradually. Add the well-beaten eggs and beat the mixture until it is smooth. Mix in the milk and vanilla. Add the dry ingredients which have been sifted together, and mix well. Roll out the dough and cut it with a round cutter.

Put 1 teaspoon of the filling on a cookie. Make a hole (with a thimble) in the middle of another cookie, then place it on top of the filling. Do not press the two together. Continue with this procedure until the cookies and filling are used up. Bake the cookies at 350° for 20 minutes or until done.

SNICKERS

½ cup white sugar
1 cup brown sugar
1 cup shortening
2 eggs
2¾ cups all-purpose flour

1 teaspoon soda
2 teaspoons cream of tartar
¼ teaspoon salt
½ cup brown sugar
1 teaspoon cinnamon

Mix together well the first 8 ingredients. Chill the dough overnight, then form it into balls. Roll the balls in a mixture of the ½ cup of brown sugar and the cinnamon. Bake them at 350° for about 10 minutes or until done. This recipe makes 6 dozen cookies.

FAVORITE SOUR CREAMS

5 cups brown sugar
2 cups shortening (scant)
2 cups thick sour cream
4 eggs, beaten
1 cup sweet milk

3 teaspoons baking powder
3 teaspoons soda
1 teaspoon vanilla
All-purpose flour, enough to make a
    soft dough

Mix together the ingredients in the order given. Drop the batter by teaspoonfuls onto a greased baking sheet. Bake the cookies at 350° for 20 minutes or until done. This recipe makes 90 to 100 cookies.

TOLL-HOUSE COOKIES

1 cup shortening
¾ cup brown sugar
¾ cup white sugar
2 eggs, beaten
1 teaspoon hot water
1 teaspoon vanilla
1½ cups sifted all-purpose flour

1 teaspoon soda
1 teaspoon salt
2 cups oatmeal
1 cup chopped nuts
1 package chocolate chips or
    butterscotch chips

Mix together the shortening, sugars, eggs, hot water and vanilla. Sift together and add the flour, soda and salt. Then add the oatmeal, nuts and chocolate chips. Drop the batter by teaspoons onto a greased cookie sheet, and bake the cookies at 350° for 10 to 15 minutes.

WHOLE WHEAT COOKIES

2¼ cups whole wheat flour
1½ cups sifted all-purpose flour
1½ cups brown sugar
1½ teaspoons soda
1½ teaspoons salt
1½ cups sour milk

2 eggs
½ cup melted butter
¼ cup molasses
1½ teaspoons vanilla
1 cup chocolate bits

Measure out the flours, sugar, soda and salt, and mix them together. Make a well and add the milk, eggs, butter, molasses and vanilla. Beat this mixture well and stir in the chocolate bits. Drop the batter by spoonfuls onto a cookie sheet and bake it at 350° for 6 to 8 minutes or until done.

Variations: Omit the vanilla and chocolate bits and add 1½ teaspoons of cinnamon and 1 cup of raisins.

WHOOPIE PIES

2 cups sugar
½ teaspoon salt
1 cup shortening
2 teaspoons vanilla
2 eggs

4 cups all-purpose flour
2 teaspoons soda
1 cup cocoa
1 cup cold water
1 cup thick sour milk

Cream together the sugar, salt, shortening, vanilla and eggs. Sift together the flour, soda and cocoa, and add this to the first mixture alternately with the water and sour milk. Add slightly more flour if the milk is not thick. Drop the batter by teaspoons onto a greased cookie sheet, and bake the cookies at 400° until done. Let them cool, then put them together with the following filling.

Filling;

1 egg white
2 cups icing sugar (as needed)
1 tablespoon vanilla
2 tablespoons flour

2 tablespoons milk
¾ cup Crisco or margarine
Marshmallow Creme (optional—see
    page 228)

Beat the egg white, before adding the remaining ingredients. Beat the mixture well.

A few drops of peppermint flavoring may be used in place of the vanilla.

DATE BARS

1 pound pitted dates
½ cup granulated sugar
¾ cup light corn syrup

¼ cup orange juice
2 teaspoons grated orange rind
¼ teaspoon salt

To make the filling, combine and cook the above ingredients until the dates are softened and the mixture becomes thick. Allow it to cool.

2½ cups all-purpose flour
1 teaspoon soda
1 teaspoon salt
1 cup brown sugar

1 cup soft shortening
½ cup water
2½ cups oatmeal (uncooked)

Sift together into a bowl the flour, soda and salt. Add the brown sugar, shortening and water, and beat the mixture until it is smooth. Fold in the oatmeal. Spread half of the dough over a greased 10 x 15-inch baking sheet. Cover it with the date filling.

Roll out the remaining dough and place it between 2 sheets of waxed paper. Chill it, then remove the top sheet of paper. Place the dough over the filling, and remove the other sheet of waxed paper. Bake it in a moderate oven (350°) for 30 to 35 minutes. Allow it to cool, then cut it into bars.

CHOCOLATE CHIP BARS

2 cups all-purpose flour
2 cups sugar
2 teaspoons baking powder
2 cups chocolate chips

4 eggs
1½ teaspoons salt
½ cup butter, melted
1 teaspoon vanilla

Mix together the ingredients, then spread the batter on a cookie sheet. (If you want a glossy top, beat the eggs first.) Bake it for 25 minutes at 350°, being careful not to overbake. When it has cooled, slice it into bars.

CHOCOLATE REVEL BARS

2½ cups all-purpose flour
2 cups white sugar
1 cup butter or margarine
1 teaspoon salt

2 eggs
2 teaspoons vanilla
1 teaspoon soda
3 cups oatmeal

Mix together the flour, sugar, butter and salt as for pie crumbs. (Reserve some of the crumbs for topping.) Add the eggs, vanilla, soda and oatmeal, and mix the dough until it is smooth. Spread it ⅔-inch thick in a baking pan, and top it with the following filling.

12 ounces chocolate chips
1 can sweetened condensed milk
2 tablespoons butter

½ teaspoon salt
1 cup nuts (optional)

Melt together in a double boiler the chocolate chips, milk, butter, salt and nuts if desired. Spread this over the batter, top it with the reserved crumbs, and bake it at 350° for 25 to 30 minutes.

RAISIN BARS

3½ pounds bread flour
2 pounds white sugar
1 pound shortening
1 teaspoon salt
2 pounds raisins

Water
5 eggs, beaten
1 pint mild molasses
3 tablespoons soda
½ cup boiling water

Mix together the flour, sugar, shortening and salt as for pie crumbs. Cook the raisins in as little water as possible. Allow them to cool before adding them to the crumbs. Then add the eggs, molasses and the soda which has been dissolved in the boiling water.

Mix the dough and let it stand overnight or longer. Form it into long rolls about ½ inch thick. Garnish the top with beaten egg to which a little water has been added. Bake the rolls at 350 to 375°. Let them set a little before slicing them.

MARSHMALLOW BARS

1 cup brown sugar	2 cups flour
½ cup margarine	½ teaspoon soda
1 egg	½ teaspoon salt
1 teaspoon vanilla	½ cup milk
¼ cup cocoa	

Combine the sugar, margarine, egg and vanilla. Add the dry ingredients, then the milk. Spread the batter on a greased cookie sheet. Bake it at 375° for 8 minutes before removing it from the oven. Sprinkle miniature marshmallows over the top, then return it to the oven for 1 minute.

Icing;

⅓ cup butter	¼ cup milk
1 cup brown sugar	Icing sugar
2 tablespoons cocoa	

Combine these ingredients and boil the mixture until it forms large bubbles. Allow it to cool before adding icing sugar to thicken it. Spread the icing thinly over the baked batter, then slice it into bars.

OLD-FASHIONED RAISIN BARS

1 cup seedless raisins	1 teaspoon cinnamon
1 cup water	¼ teaspoon salt
½ cup salad oil, shortening or	1 teaspoon soda
margarine	1 teaspoon nutmeg
1 cup sugar	1 teaspoon allspice
1 slightly beaten egg	½ teaspoon cloves
1¾ cups sifted all-purpose flour	½ cup chopped nuts (optional)

Combine the raisins and water and bring the mixture to the boiling point. Remove it from the heat and stir in the oil. Allow it to cool to lukewarm, then stir in the sugar and egg. Sift together the dry ingredients and beat them into the raisin mixture. Stir in the nuts. Pour the batter into a greased 13 x 9 x 2-inch pan, and bake it at 375° for 20 minutes or until done. When it has cooled, cut it into bars, and dust them with icing sugar.

Variations: For thin, brownie-sized cookies, bake the batter in a greased 15½-inch jelly roll pan for 12 minutes, or until done.

LEMON BARS

1 cup sifted all-purpose flour   ¼ cup icing sugar
½ cup butter or margarine

Mix together these ingredients and pour the mixture into an 8 x 8-inch pan. Bake it for 15 minutes at 350°.

2 eggs, beaten   2 tablespoons flour
2 tablespoons lemon juice   ½ teaspoon baking powder
1 cup sugar   ½ teaspoon lemon flavoring

Combine these ingredients in the order given, then pour the mixture over the baked crust. Bake it for 25 minutes at 350°, then cut it into bars when it has cooled.

ORANGE RAISIN BARS

1 cup raisins   2 cups all-purpose flour
1½ cups water   1 teaspoon baking powder
2 tablespoons shortening   1 teaspoon soda
1 cup sugar   ½ teaspoon nutmeg

Stew the raisins in the water. If there is not enough juice to fill 1 cup, add water. Add the shortening and allow it to cool. Sift and add the sugar, flour, baking powder, soda and nutmeg. Spread the dough on a large greased pan and bake it for 18 to 20 minutes at 375°.

Icing;

1 cup icing sugar   1 tablespoon butter
Orange juice

Mix together these ingredients. Spread the mixture over the baked dough while it is still hot, then cut it into bars.

KEUFELS

1 cup plus 2 tablespoons all-purpose 2 tablespoons melted butter
  flour   1 teaspoon vanilla
½ cup margarine or butter   1 egg, beaten
3 ounces cream cheese   ¼ teaspoon salt
1 cup brown sugar   ¾ cup chopped nuts

To make the dough, mix the first 3 ingredients with a fork. Form the dough into 24 small-sized balls, and with your finger press and shape them into small muffin tins. Then mix the rest of the ingredients and fill the muffin tins with this mixture. Bake it at 350° for 20 minutes.

NUTTY FINGERS

½ cup margarine
¼ cup plus 1 tablespoon icing sugar
1 teaspoon vanilla

1 cup all-purpose flour
1 cup finely chopped nuts

Cream the margarine and add the ¼ cup of icing sugar and vanilla. Then gradually add the flour and nuts. Form cookies the size of a little finger. Bake them at 375° for 8 to 10 minutes or until lightly browned. When they have cooled, roll them in the remaining icing sugar.

This is an easy recipe for little girls and boys to try.

SUNNY GRAHAM CHEWIES

1⅔ cups graham cracker crumbs
2 tablespoons flour
½ cup butter or margarine
1½ cups brown sugar, packed
½ cup nuts

½ teaspoon salt
¼ teaspoon baking powder
2 eggs
1 teaspoon vanilla

Combine 1⅓ cups of the crumbs, the flour and butter in a bowl. Blend this mixture until particles like rice form. Pack it into a greased 9-inch square cake pan, and bake it for 20 minutes at 350°. Then combine the sugar, the remaining crumbs, nuts, salt and baking powder, and blend this mixture. Add the beaten eggs and vanilla, and blend it well again. Pour it over the baked crust before returning it to the oven to bake for 20 minutes or more. When it has cooled, cut it into bars.

TOLL-HOUSE MARBLE SQUARES

1 cup plus 2 tablespoons all-purpose
    flour
½ teaspoon soda
½ teaspoon salt
½ cup soft butter
6 tablespoons white sugar

6 tablespoons brown sugar
½ teaspoon vanilla
¼ teaspoon water
1 egg
12 ounces chocolate morsels
½ cup chopped nuts

Sift together the flour, soda and salt. Blend together the butter, sugar, vanilla and water, then beat in the egg. Mix it with the sifted flour mixture, and add the nuts. Spread the dough in a greased 13 x 9 x 2-inch pan. Sprinkle the chocolate morsels over the dough and place it in the oven for 1 minute. Run a knife through the dough to marbleize it. Bake it at 375° for 12 to 14 minutes, then allow it to cool before cutting it into 24 squares.

GRANOLIES

1½ cups granola cereal
¾ cup unsifted all-purpose flour
1 teaspoon baking powder
¼ teaspoon soda
¼ teaspoon salt
½ cup chopped dates

½ cup chopped nuts
½ cup butter, softened
½ cup sugar
¼ cup molasses
1 egg
½ teaspoon vanilla

Measure out onto waxed paper the cereal, flour, baking powder, soda and salt, then stir to blend the mixture thoroughly. Mix in the dates and nuts. Cream the butter, then beat in the sugar, molasses, egg and vanilla. Stir in the cereal/date/nut mixture and mix it well. Spread the dough in an ungreased 9-inch square pan, and bake it in a preheated 350° oven for 25 to 30 minutes or until done. Allow it to cool before cutting it into squares. This recipe makes 16 to 20 squares.

WALNUT SQUARES

1 egg
1 cup brown sugar
½ teaspoon vanilla
½ cup sifted all-purpose flour

½ teaspoon salt
⅛ teaspoon soda
1 cup chopped walnuts

Beat the egg until it is foamy, then beat in the sugar and vanilla. Sift together and stir in the flour, salt and soda, then mix in the nuts. Spread the batter in a well-greased 8-inch square pan. Bake it at 375° until the top has a dull crust. Cut it into squares while it is still warm. Allow the squares to cool, then remove them from the pan.

PEANUT BUTTER BROWNIES

2 cups sugar
½ cup shortening
1 cup peanut butter
6 eggs
1 tablespoon vanilla

1½ cups brown sugar
4 cups pastry flour
1½ tablespoons baking powder
1½ teaspoons salt
½ cup nuts

Cream together the sugar, shortening and peanut butter. Add the eggs and vanilla, then add the dry ingredients and mix them well. Add the nuts before pressing the dough into 2 cookie sheets and baking it at 350° for 30 minutes. Cut it into bars while it is still warm.

BUTTERSCOTCH BROWNIES

¼ cup butter
1 cup brown sugar
1 egg
1 cup all-purpose flour

1 teaspoon vanilla
½ teaspoon salt
1 teaspoon baking powder
½ cup nuts

Melt the butter in a pan, then stir in the sugar. Heat it until the sugar has melted. Allow it to cool, then add the beaten egg, flour, vanilla, salt and baking powder. Add the nuts last. Bake the dough at 350° for 30 minutes, then cut it into squares while it is still hot. Sprinkle it with icing sugar.

YUM YUM BROWNIES

2 cups granulated sugar
¾ cup butter and lard combined
4 eggs, beaten
1 teaspoon vanilla

½ cup chopped nuts
1 cup all-purpose flour
½ teaspoon salt
½ cup cocoa

Cream together well the sugar and shortening. Add the eggs, vanilla and nuts. Sift together the flour, salt and cocoa, and add this to the sugar mixture. Stir it well. Bake the dough in a greased and floured 9 x 13-inch pan at 350° until the dough shrinks from the edges of the pan. Let it cool before cutting it into squares.

PIES AND PASTRIES

HINTS FOR PIES

- *For best results, pie dough should be worked very lightly after the water has been added.*
- Pie crusts will have a browner crust when milk is used in the dough. Milk can also be brushed over the top before baking.
- When making fruit pies, add the sugar when the pan is half full instead of on top—the pastry will then be lighter.
- Do you have trouble baking custard pies? Try heating the milk to the boiling point before mixing it with the eggs. This also helps keep the undercrust crisp.
- For Streusel Pies, mix together ⅓ cup of peanut butter and ¾ cup of powdered sugar. *Spread this on the bottom of a baked pie shell. Cover it with your favorite cream pie recipe and top it with meringue or whipped cream.*
- To glaze pies or cookies, brush the top with beaten egg, or egg white.
- Add a tablespoon of vinegar to the pie dough and a bit of sugar to keep it from drying out when storing it for later use. Store it in a plastic bag or covered dish in a cool place.

PIE CRUST

3 cups sifted pastry flour
1 cup shortening
½ teaspoon salt

1 egg
5 tablespoons water
1 teaspoon vinegar

Mix together the flour, shortening and salt. Beat the egg, add the water and vinegar, then add enough of this to the flour mixture to make a soft dough. This recipe makes 1 double crust pie or 2 single crust pies.

PIE DOUGH

3 quarts flour (11 cups all-purpose
    flour, or 12 cups pastry flour)
2 tablespoons vinegar

4 cups lard
2 cups water (approximate)
2 teaspoons salt

Mix the ingredients together to crumb consistency, using the vinegar and water to wet the mixture. This will be enough for the top and bottom crusts for 6 pies more or less, depending on the size of the pies and how thinly the dough is rolled out. If all the crumbs are not needed at once, they may be stored in a tight container for future use.

PAN PIE DOUGH

1½ cups all-purpose flour
1½ tablespoons granulated sugar
1 teaspoon salt

½ cup cooking oil (scant)
2 tablespoons milk

Mix together in a pan the first 3 ingredients. Add the cooking oil into which the milk has been stirred. Blend the mixture, then press it on the bottom and sides of the pan.

EGG WHITE PIE CRUST

¾ cup graham cracker crumbs
⅓ cup sugar
½ cup pecan pieces

3 egg whites
⅓ cup sugar
1 teaspoon vanilla

Mix together the crumbs, ⅓ cup of the sugar and the pecans. Beat the egg whites until they are stiff, gradually adding the other ⅓ cup of sugar and the vanilla. Add this to the crumb mixture. Pour it into a greased pie pan and bake it at 350° for 30 minutes. When it has cooled, mash it down to the shape of the pan. Fill the crust with ice cream and freeze it. Thaw it slightly before serving, and top it with your favorite fruit.

Variations: Instead of using ice cream and freezing the pie, just use your favorite filling.

FLAKY PIE CRUST

2 cups sifted whole wheat flour
1 teaspoon salt
2 tablespoons wheat germ

¾ cup margarine
4 to 5 tablespoons ice water

Combine the flour with the salt in a medium-sized bowl, then add the wheat germ. With a pastry blender, cut in the margarine. Sprinkle the ice water over the pastry and mix it with a fork. The pastry should be just moist enough to hold together.

This dough handles like any other using white flour, but it is far more nutritious.

GRAHAM CRACKER CRUST

1 cup graham crackers
3 tablespoons brown sugar

¼ cup melted butter

Crush the graham crackers into fine crumbs. Add the sugar and melted butter, and mix them thoroughly. Press the mixture firmly in an even layer around the bottom and sides of a 9-inch pie plate. Bake it at 375° for 5 to 8 minutes, then let it cool.

NO-BAKE GRAHAM CRACKER CRUST

1 cup (¼ pound) graham crackers
3 tablespoons icing sugar

¼ teaspoon plain gelatin
¼ cup melted butter

Crush the graham crackers finely. Add the sugar, gelatin and butter and mix it thoroughly. Save 2 tablespoons of the mixture for the topping. Press the rest firmly into a 9-inch pie pan, and chill it for 15 minutes.

NEVER FAIL PIE CRUST

6 cups pastry flour, or 5½ cups all-
purpose flour
2 cups lard

1 teaspoon salt
3 teaspoons baking powder
1 egg in cup, filled with water

Mix together the flour, lard, salt and baking powder until the mixture is crumbly. Add the egg and water, and mix it again. Sometimes more water is required. This dough will keep for awhile.

OATMEAL PIE CRUST

1 cup quick-cooking oats
⅓ cup sifted flour
⅓ cup brown sugar

½ teaspoon salt
⅓ cup butter

Combine the oats, flour, sugar and salt. Cut in the butter until the mixture is crumbly. Press it firmly on the bottom and sides of a 9-inch pie plate. Bake it in a moderate oven (375°) for about 15 minutes. Cool the crust completely and fill it with any desired cream filling.

SPOON PIE DOUGH

½ cup boiling water
1 cup lard
3 cups all-purpose flour

1 teaspoon baking powder
1 teaspoon salt

Add the boiling water to the lard, and stir it until the lard is melted. Then add the flour, baking powder and salt. Stir it with a spoon, then chill the dough in the refrigerator for a few hours.

WHOLE WHEAT PIE CRUST

2 cups whole wheat flour
1 cup ground oatmeal
½ teaspoon salt

⅓ cup vegetable oil
½ cup water

Combine the flour, oatmeal and salt in a bowl. Blend in the oil, then add the water.

MERINGUE FOR PIE

2 egg whites
¼ teaspoon cream of tartar
4 tablespoons granulated sugar

½ teaspoon cornstarch
1 teaspoon vanilla

Beat together the egg whites and cream of tartar until soft peaks are formed. Add the sugar to which the cornstarch has been added, then add the vanilla. Beat the mixture until it is stiff.

APPLE CREAM PIE

3 cups finely cut apples
1 cup brown or white sugar
⅔ cup cream or top milk

¼ teaspoon salt
1 rounded tablespoon flour

Mix together the ingredients, then put the mixture into an unbaked pie shell. Sprinkle the top with cinnamon. Bake the pie in a hot oven (450°) for 15 minutes, then reduce the heat to 325° and bake it for 30 to 40 minutes longer. When the pie is about half done, take a knife and push the top apples down to soften them.

Variations: *Elderberries or other fruit may be used instead of apples.*

DUTCH APPLE PIE

3 cups sliced apples
1 cup sugar
3 tablespoons flour
½ teaspoon cinnamon
1 beaten egg

1 cup light cream
1 teaspoon vanilla
½ cup chopped nuts
1 tablespoon butter

Place the apples in a 9-inch unbaked pie shell. Mix together the sugar, flour and cinnamon. Combine the egg, cream and vanilla, then add the sugar mixture and mix it well. Pour it over the apples, then sprinkle it with the nuts and dot it with the butter. Bake the pie in a moderate oven (350°) for 45 to 50 minutes until the apples are tender.

PAPER BAG APPLE PIE

6 cups coarsely sliced or chopped apples
½ cup sugar

2 tablespoons flour
½ teaspoon nutmeg
2 tablespoons lemon juice

Measure the apples into a bowl, and mix them with the sugar, flour, nutmeg and lemon juice. Turn them into an unbaked pie shell and pat them down evenly.

Topping;

½ cup butter
½ cup flour

½ cup brown or white sugar

Measure out the butter, flour and sugar, cutting in the butter with a pastry blender until crumbs are the size of peas. Sprinkle this evenly over the apples and pat it down around the edges. Slide the pie into a brown paper bag and fold the end under the pie. Put it onto a cookie sheet for easy handling. Bake it at 425° for 50 minutes.

The benefit of this method is a pie with no scorched rim, no under-baked apples, no boiling over in your clean oven, and no grief in general!

PLAIN APPLE PIE

2 tablespoons flour
6 medium apples, sliced
1 cup sugar

¼ teaspoon cinnamon
1 tablespoon water
1 teaspoon butter

Mix together the flour, apples, sugar and cinnamon. Pour this mixture into an unbaked pie shell, add the water, and dot the center with the butter. Place ½-inch strips of dough lattice-style over the apples, connecting the strips to the sides of the pie shell. Bake the pie at 400° until the apples are done.

BUTTERSCOTCH PIE

2 tablespoons butter
1 cup brown sugar

⅔ cup hot water

Brown the butter in a heavy saucepan. Add the sugar and stir it until it is melted. Add the hot water and cook the syrup slowly until all the lumps disappear.

2 tablespoons flour
3 tablespoons cornstarch
½ teaspoon salt

2 egg yolks
2 cups milk
1 teaspoon vanilla

Mix together the flour, cornstarch, salt, eggs and milk, then slowly stir this mixture into the hot syrup. Boil it until it thickens, then add the vanilla. Pour it into a baked pie shell and top it with meringue.

Variations: If you wish to use this as a butterscotch pudding or sauce, add ½ cup more milk.

BASIC CREAM PIE

2 cups milk
½ cup sugar
2 tablespoons cornstarch
2 tablespoons flour

½ teaspoon salt
2 eggs, separated
1 tablespoon butter
1 teaspoon vanilla

Scald 1½ cups of the milk in the top of a double boiler. Make a thickening by combining the sugar, cornstarch, flour and salt, then stir in the remaining ½ cup of milk with the egg yolks. Stir this flour mixture into the hot milk and cook it until it thickens. Remove it from the heat and add the butter and vanilla. Let it cool a little before pouring it into a baked pie shell. Cover the pie with meringue.

Variations:

COCONUT PIE; Add ¾ cup of coconut to the Basic Cream Pie filling. Top it with whipped cream and sprinkle it with coconut.

CHOCOLATE PIE; Add 2 to 4 teaspoons of cocoa to the thickening of the Basic Cream Pie recipe.

BANANA PIE: Cover the bottom of a baked pie shell with sliced bananas before adding the Basic Cream Pie filling.

STREUSEL PIE: Mix ⅓ cup of peanut butter with ¾ cup of powdered sugar. Sprinkle it on the bottom of a baked pie shell, saving some crumbs to put on top. Pour in the Basic Cream Pie filling and top it with whipped cream. Sprinkle the reserved crumbs over the whipped cream.

GRAHAM CRACKER PIE; Pour the cream filling into a graham cracker pie crust.

RAISIN CREAM PIE; Add ⅓ cup of raisins and ½ teaspoon of allspice (optional) to the cream filling.

CHOCOLATE MOCHA PIE

1 tablespoon gelatin
¼ cup cold water
1 tablespoon cocoa
⅛ teaspoon salt
1¼ cups milk

¾ cup sugar
1 teaspoon instant coffee
1 cup whipped cream
1 teaspoon vanilla
Chopped nuts

Soak the gelatin in the water. Combine in a saucepan the cocoa, salt, milk, sugar and coffee, and bring the mixture to a boil, stirring it constantly. Remove it from the heat and stir in the gelatin. Cool it until it has slightly thickened, then fold in the whipped cream and vanilla. Pour the mixture into a baked pie crust and top it with chopped nuts.

Variations: Graham cracker pie crust may be used.

Whipped dessert topping may be substituted for the whipped cream.

CHERRY PIE

2 tablespoons tapioca
1/8 teaspoon salt
1 cup sugar
3 cups drained, pitted sour cherries

1/2 cup cherry juice
1/4 teaspoon almond extract
Red food coloring (optional)

Mix together the ingredients and let the mixture stand for 15 minutes. Pour it into a 9-inch pie shell and dot it with 1 tablespoon of butter. Add a top crust, and bake the pie at 425° for 50 minutes.

CHERRY PIE FILLING

4 cups sweet red cherries, pitted
2 cups sugar
1 1/2 cups water

2 heaping tablespoons cornstarch
1 teaspoon almond flavoring
Red food coloring (optional)

Mix together and bring to a boil the cherries, sugar and water. Then mix the cornstarch with enough water to make a thin paste, and slowly add it to the boiling cherry mixture, stirring constantly until it comes to a boil once more. Add the almond flavoring, a few drops of red coloring if desired, and allow it to cool. This recipe makes enough for 2 pies.

BOB ANDY PIE

2 cups brown or white sugar
4 tablespoons flour
1/2 teaspoon cloves
1 teaspoon cinnamon

1 tablespoon butter
3 eggs, separated
2 cups milk

Mix together the dry ingredients, then add the butter, beaten egg yolks and milk. Fold in the beaten egg whites. Pour the mixture into 2 unbaked pie crusts and bake them at 400° for 10 minutes, then reduce the heat to 350° and continue baking them until done.

COCONUT CUSTARD PIE

2 eggs, beaten
1 cup molasses (white or dark)
1 cup milk
1 teaspoon vanilla

1/2 cup sugar
1 tablespoon flour
2 tablespoons melted butter
1 cup coconut

Mix together all the ingredients and pour the mixture into an unbaked pie shell. Bake the pie at 450° for 15 minutes. Reduce the heat to 350° and bake it for 20 to 30 minutes longer.

RAISIN CUSTARD PIE

3 eggs, beaten
1 cup raisins
1 cup molasses

1 tablespoon butter
1 teaspoon vanilla

Mix together the ingredients, then pour the mixture into an unbaked pie shell and bake it at 400° for 10 minutes. Reduce the heat to 350° and bake it 30 minutes longer.

Variations: Walnuts may be substituted for raisins.

VELVETY CUSTARD PIE

4 eggs, slightly beaten
½ cup sugar
¼ teaspoon salt

1 teaspoon vanilla
2½ cups scalded milk

Thoroughly mix together the eggs, sugar, salt and vanilla. Slowly stir into this mixture the scalded milk, then pour it immediately into an unbaked pastry shell. Bake the pie at 475° for 5 minutes, then reduce the heat to 425° and bake it 30 minutes longer, or until a knife inserted halfway between the center and the edge comes out clean.

ELDERBERRY PIE

2½ cups elderberries
1 cup sugar
3 teaspoons lemon juice or vinegar

⅛ teaspoon salt
2 tablespoons flour

Pour the washed elderberries into an unbaked pie crust. Mix together the other ingredients and pour the mixture over the berries. Cover it with a top crust. Bake the pie at 425° for 10 minutes, then reduce the temperature to 350° and bake it 30 minutes longer.

ELDERBERRY CUSTARD PIE

1 cup elderberry juice
4 tablespoons flour
1 cup sugar

¼ teaspoon salt
1 egg, separated
1 cup milk

Bring the juice to a boil. Combine the flour, sugar and salt, then gradually add the egg yolk and milk. Add this mixture to the boiling juice and stir it until it thickens. Fold in the stiffly beaten egg white. Pour the mixture into an unbaked pie shell, then bake it at 350° for 20 to 30 minutes.

CREAM CUSTARD PIE

3 eggs
1 cup brown sugar

1 cup cream
1 teaspoon vanilla

Beat the eggs, then add the brown sugar, cream and vanilla. Pour the mixture into an unbaked pie shell and bake it in a hot oven (450°) for 15 minutes. Reduce the heat to 300° and bake it for 30 to 35 minutes longer. The filling should appear slightly less set in the center than around the edge.

MOTHER'S ELDERBERRY PIE

1 cup sugar
2 eggs, separated
1 cup sour cream

2 cups uncooked elderberries
2 tablespoons cornstarch

Mix the sugar with the egg yolks, then add the sour cream, elderberries and cornstarch. Cook this mixture until it is thick, and pour it into a baked pie shell. Top it with meringue made with the 2 egg whites, then brown it in the oven.

FRUIT CRUMB PIE

Prepare your favorite fruit pie filling—cherry, blueberry, raspberry, elderberry or raisin. Pour it into an unbaked pie shell and top it with the following crumb mixture.

¾ cup flour
¾ cup oatmeal
⅔ cup brown sugar
½ teaspoon soda

¼ teaspoon salt
1 teaspoon cinnamon
½ cup melted butter

In a bowl, mix together the dry ingredients, then add the melted butter and mix it thoroughly until all the ingredients are moistened.

Bake the pie at 425° for 25 to 30 minutes or until the filling boils and the crumbs are nicely browned. This recipe makes enough crumbs for approximately 3 pies.

HAWAII FOOD PIE

1 cup crushed pineapple
1 cup cold water
½ cup sugar

⅛ teaspoon salt
3 tablespoons cornstarch
2 eggs, separated

Cook together until thick the pineapple, water, sugar, salt, cornstarch and egg yolks. Fold in the beaten egg whites while the mixture is hot, then pour it into a baked pie crust.

LEMON PIE

3 tablespoons cornstarch
1½ cups sugar
Juice and grated rind of 1 lemon

1¼ cups boiling water
3 eggs, separated
6 tablespoons sugar

Mix together the cornstarch, 1½ cups of sugar, and lemon juice. Add the beaten egg yolks, followed by the water in which the lemon rind has been boiled. (Discard the rind.) Cook this in a double boiler, then pour it into a baked pie crust. Beat the egg whites until they are stiff with the 6 tablespoons of sugar before spreading this mixture over the pie. Brown it in the oven.

LEMON SPONGE PIE

2 tablespoons flour
1 cup sugar
1 tablespoon butter

1 cup milk
2 eggs, separated
Juice and grated rind of 1 lemon

Sift together the flour and sugar, then cream in the butter. Add the milk with the egg yolks stirred in, then add the lemon, and the well-beaten egg whites last. Pour the mixture into an unbaked pie crust, and bake it in a moderate oven (375 to 400°) until done. This recipe makes 1 good-sized pie.

Variations: Lemon Sponge may be made without the crust. Set it in a pan of hot water to bake.

MAPLE NUT PIE

½ cup milk
1 cup maple syrup (or maple flavored syrup)
2 egg yolks, slightly beaten
1 tablespoon gelatin

Cold water
1 teaspoon maple flavoring
2 egg whites, stiffly beaten
1 cup whipped cream
½ cup chopped nut meats

Heat together the milk and maple syrup. Stir ½ cup of this into the egg yolks and return this mixture gradually to the hot syrup mixture, beating constantly. Cook this mixture a little, then add the gelatin which has been softened in a little cold water. Add the maple flavoring and chill the mixture until it begins to thicken. Fold in the egg whites, then add the whipped cream and chopped nut meats. Pour the mixture into a baked pie shell.

This pie tastes like maple nut ice cream. If you double the recipe, it makes three 8-inch pies.

MONTGOMERY PIE

1 egg	2 cups sugar
1 lemon (juice and rind)	1 cup butter
1 cup sugar	2 eggs
3 tablespoons flour	1 cup milk
1 cup corn syrup	2½ cups flour
1 pint water	2 teaspoons baking powder

Boil the first 6 ingredients until syrupy, then let the syrup cool. Divide it among 3 unbaked pie shells. Cream together the 2 cups of sugar and butter, then beat in the eggs. Sift together the flour and baking powder, and add it alternately with the milk, mixing until well blended. Pour this over the syrup in the pie shells. Bake the pies in a hot oven (450°) for about 10 minutes, then reduce the heat to 350° and bake them until done.

OATMEAL PIE

3 eggs, beaten	⅔ cup oatmeal
⅔ cup white sugar	⅔ cup coconut (optional)
1 cup brown sugar	⅔ cup milk
2 teaspoons margarine, softened	1 teaspoon vanilla

Blend together the ingredients and pour the mixture into an unbaked pie shell. Bake the pie for 30 to 35 minutes at 350°.

Variations: Try adding ½ teaspoon of cinnamon and ½ teaspoon of cloves.

PEACH CRUMB PIE

2½ tablespoons tapioca	⅓ cup packed brown sugar
¾ cup sugar	¼ cup flour
¼ teaspoon salt	½ teaspoon cinnamon
4 cups sliced peaches	2½ tablespoons soft butter

Mix together the first 4 ingredients, then let the mixture set for 5 minutes before pouring it into an unbaked 9-inch pie shell. Mix the rest of the ingredients for the crumb topping, then put it on top of the fruit filling. Bake the pie at 425° for 45 to 50 minutes.

Variations: Other fruit may be used, but this recipe is especially good with apples.

PEACH-PINEAPPLE PIE

1 quart canned sliced peaches
1 small can crushed pineapple
3 tablespoons cornstarch

2 cups sugar
½ teaspoon salt

Cook the ingredients together until the mixture is thick. Bake it between 2 crusts at 400° until the crust is brown. This recipe makes enough for 2 pies.

DOUBLE TREAT PEACH PIE

1 cup sugar
3 tablespoons cornstarch or tapioca
½ cup water

1 tablespoon butter
6 large peaches

Mix together the sugar and cornstarch, then add the water and butter before bringing the mixture to a boil. Dice 3 of the peaches and add them to this syrup, simmering it for 5 minutes or until it thickens. Allow it to cool. Slice the remaining peaches into a baked 9-inch pie shell, and pour the cooled peaches and syrup over it. Top it with whipped cream.

EMMA'S PEACH PIE

½ cup sugar
½ teaspoon salt
2 cups milk
3 tablespoons flour
3 tablespoons cornstarch

1 teaspoon vanilla
½ cup whipping cream, whipped
4 peaches, sliced
¼ cup water
Cornstarch

To make the filling, cook together the first 5 ingredients, then let the mixture cool. Add the vanilla and whipped cream.

To make the glaze, mash half of the peaches and add the water. Boil this for 2 minutes, then strain. Add sugar to taste, and cook it again slightly, thickening it with cornstarch. Put the filling into a baked pie shell. Cover it with the remaining peach slices and top it with the glaze.

FRESH PEACH PIE

Fresh peach halves
1 cup sugar

2 tablespoons butter
3 eggs, partly beaten

Arrange the peaches in an unbaked pie shell. Then mix together the sugar, butter and eggs, and pour this mixture over the peaches. Bake the pie at 350° until the crust is done.

PECAN PIE

2 eggs, beaten
¼ teaspoon salt
½ cup sugar
1 cup molasses (white or dark)
1 tablespoon flour

1 cup milk
1 teaspoon vanilla
2 tablespoons melted butter
1 cup chopped pecans, peanuts or
   coconut

Mix together the above ingredients, then pour the mixture into an unbaked pie shell. Bake the pie for 45 minutes at 350°.

KENTUCKY PECAN PIE

1 cup white corn syrup
½ cup brown sugar
⅓ teaspoon salt
⅓ cup melted butter

1 teaspoon vanilla
3 eggs, slightly beaten
1 cup pecans

Combine the syrup, sugar, salt, butter and vanilla, and mix them well. Add the eggs. Pour the mixture into a 9-inch pie shell, then sprinkle the pecans over all. Bake the pie in a preheated oven at 350° for about 45 minutes.

Variations: This recipe may also be used for tarts.

English walnuts may be used instead of pecans.

OATMEAL PIE; Use ⅔ cup of quick oatmeal instead of nuts.

KRISPIE PIE; Use 1 cup of Rice Krispies instead of nuts.

COCONUT PIE; Use coconut instead of pecans.

The above variations may also be used with Southern Pie (see page 182), omitting the grapenuts.

PINEAPPLE COCONUT PIE

3 eggs
1 cup sugar
1 tablespoon cornstarch
½ cup drained crushed pineapple

½ cup light corn syrup
¼ cup shredded coconut
¼ cup melted butter

Beat the eggs slightly, then add all the remaining ingredients. Blend the mixture well, then pour it into a 9-inch unbaked pie shell. Bake the pie at 350° for 45 to 50 minutes or until it is slightly set.

BETTY'S PUMPKIN PIE

1½ cups brown sugar
1 cup mashed pumpkin
1 tablespoon flour
1 teaspoon cinnamon
3 cups milk

½ teaspoon nutmeg
½ teaspoon allspice
Sprinkle of cloves
5 eggs, separated

Mix the ingredients as you would for a custard pie, beating the egg whites and folding them in last. For an extra rich pie, use part evaporated milk. Bake the pie at 400° for 15 minutes, then reduce the heat to about 350° until done. This recipe makes 2 pies.

MOTHER'S PUMPKIN PIE

⅔ cup sugar
1 tablespoon flour (heaping)
1 tablespoon melted butter
½ cup stewed pumpkin (more for
    stronger flavor)
¼ teaspoon ginger

¼ teaspoon cinnamon
½ teaspoon salt
1 egg, separated
2 or 3 drops vanilla
1½ cups milk

Beat together thoroughly the sugar, flour, butter, spiced pumpkin and egg yolk. Add the vanilla and milk. Beat the egg white and fold it into the mixture. Pour it into an unbaked pie crust and bake it at 400° for 10 minutes, then at 350° until done.

PUMPKIN CHIFFON PIE

1 envelope unflavored gelatin
¼ cup cold water
¾ cup brown sugar
½ teaspoon salt
½ teaspoon nutmeg

1 teaspoon cinnamon
½ cup milk
1 cup cooked pumpkin
3 eggs, separated
¼ cup sugar

Dissolve the gelatin in the water. Mix it in with all the other ingredients except the egg whites and ¼ cup of sugar. Put the mixture into a saucepan over medium heat for 10 minutes, stirring it constantly. Remove it from the heat and let it cool until the mixture is partially set. Then beat the egg whites until stiff, add the ¼ cup of sugar and fold it into the pumpkin mixture. Pour it into a 9-inch baked pie shell. Top the pie with whipped cream before serving.

RHUBARB PIE

2 tablespoons butter
2 cups rhubarb plus ½ cup water, OR
1 pint canned rhubarb (no extra water)
1¼ cups sugar
2 tablespoons cornstarch

⅛ teaspoon salt
2 eggs, separated
¼ cup cream or rich milk

Melt the butter, then add the rhubarb and water (or 1 pint canned rhubarb without water), and 1 cup of the sugar. Cook this mixture slowly until the rhubarb is tender.

Combine ¼ cup of the sugar, the cornstarch, salt, beaten egg yolks and cream. Add this to the rhubarb and cook it until it is thick. Pour this filling into a baked pie crust. Use the egg whites for meringue topping.

Variations: *This recipe may be used for pudding. Fold in the beaten egg whites when the rhubarb has finished cooking, then chill it.*

RHUBARB CREAM PIE

2½ cups cut up rhubarb
2 tablespoons flour
2 eggs, separated
3 tablespoons water

1 cup sugar
1 tablespoon melted butter
2 tablespoons sugar

Beat the egg yolks with the water. Add the 1 cup of sugar mixed with the flour and melted butter. Stir the mixture until it is smooth. Arrange the rhubarb in an unbaked pie shell, and mix in the sugar mixture. Bake the pie in a hot oven (450°) for 15 minutes. Then reduce the heat to 350° and continue baking it until done. Add meringue made of the beaten egg whites and 2 tablespoons of sugar. Brown it in the oven.

RHUBARB CUSTARD PIE

1¼ cups rhubarb
¾ cup sugar
1 tablespoon flour
¼ teaspoon salt

2 eggs
1 cup milk
1 tablespoon butter

Finely cut the rhubarb and put it into an unbaked pie shell. Mix together the sugar, flour, salt, beaten egg yolks, milk and melted butter. Pour this mixture over the rhubarb. Bake the pie at 400° for 10 minutes, then at 350° for 30 minutes longer. Cover it with a meringue made from the beaten egg whites and 1 tablespoon of sugar. Brown it in the oven.

FRENCH RHUBARB PIE

¾ cup flour
½ cup brown sugar
⅓ cup margarine
1 egg

1 cup sugar
1 teaspoon vanilla
2 cups diced rhubarb
2 tablespoons flour

To make the topping, mix together the flour, ½ cup of brown sugar and margarine. In a separate bowl, mix together the rest of the ingredients, then pour this mixture into an unbaked pie shell. Cover it with the topping, and bake it at 400° for 10 minutes. Continue baking the pie at 350° for 30 minutes longer or until done.

OHIO STATE RHUBARB PIE

1 cup sugar
1 tablespoon flour
½ teaspoon salt

1 egg
2 cups rhubarb
1 teaspoon lemon juice

Mix together the sugar, flour, salt and slightly beaten egg. Add the rhubarb and lemon juice. Bake this mixture between rich crusts, at 425° for 15 minutes, then at 350° for 25 to 30 minutes longer.

SOUTHERN PIE

¾ cup grapenuts cereal
½ cup warm water
3 eggs, well-beaten
¾ cup sugar

3 tablespoons dark corn syrup
3 tablespoons butter, melted
1 teaspoon vanilla
⅛ teaspoon salt

Combine the cereal and water, and let it stand until the water is absorbed. Meanwhile, blend the eggs with the sugar. Add the syrup, butter, vanilla and salt, then fold in the softened cereal. Pour the mixture into a 9-inch unbaked pie shell, and bake it at 350° for 50 minutes or until the filling is puffed completely across the top. Let it cool, then garnish it with whipped topping. Sprinkle the pie with additional cereal, if desired.

Variations: *Omit the grapenuts, and substitute the suggested ingredients shown under Variations on Kentucky Pecan Pie (see page 179).*

SHOO-FLY PIE

2 cups molasses
2 cups hot water
1 cup light brown sugar
1 teaspoon soda (scant)
5 cups all-purpose flour

2 cups light brown sugar
1 cup shortening (scant)
½ teaspoon soda
½ teaspoon cream of tartar

To make the syrup, mix together the first 4 ingredients until they are dissolved. (Use 1 cup or more of syrup per 9-inch pie shell.) Then mix the remaining ingredients to crumb consistency. Pour the syrup into unbaked pie crusts and divide the crumbs over top. Bake them for 10 minutes at 450°, for 30 minutes more at 375°, then for 30 minutes longer at 350°. This recipe makes 4 pies.

Variations: Try adding 2 teaspoons of nutmeg and 3 teaspoons of cinnamon to the crumbs.

Lemon Sauce For Shoo-Fly Pie;

2 tablespoons cornstarch
½ cup sugar
¼ teaspoon salt
2 cups boiling water

¼ cup butter or margarine
3 teaspoons lemon juice
1 tablespoon grated lemon rind

Mix together in a saucepan the cornstarch, sugar and salt. Gradually stir in the boiling water. Cook the mixture, stirring it constantly, until it boils and becomes thick and clear. Remove it from the heat, and stir in the remaining ingredients. Serve this sauce warm over Shoo-Fly Pie. This recipe yields 2¼ cups of sauce.

GOOEY SHOO-FLY PIE

Make crumbs by mixing together the following ingredients.

2 cups flour
¾ cup brown sugar
⅓ cup lard or butter

½ teaspoon nutmeg (optional)
1 teaspoon cinnamon (optional)

To make the syrup, combine the following.

1 cup molasses
½ cup brown sugar
2 eggs

1 cup hot water
1 teaspoon soda, dissolved in hot water

Pour ½ of the syrup into a pie crust, then add ½ of the crumbs. Add the remaining syrup and the rest of the crumbs. Bake the pie for 10 minutes at 400°, then reduce the heat to 350° for 50 minutes. This recipe makes enough for 2 pies.

STRAWBERRY PIE

1½ quarts fresh strawberries
2 cups sugar
½ cup cornstarch

Combine the strawberries and sugar and let them stand for 2 hours. Drain off the juice and add water to make 2 cups. Blend in the cornstarch and cook it over low heat until it has thickened. Mix it with the strawberries, then let it cool. Put it into a baked pie crust or graham cracker crust and serve it with whipped cream.

STRAWBERRY CHIFFON PIE

3 eggs, separated
½ cup sugar
1 package gelatin

4 tablespoons cold water
1½ cups crushed fresh strawberries

Beat the egg yolks slightly, then add ¼ cup of the sugar. Put the mixture into the top of a double boiler and cook it, stirring constantly until it thickens. Soak the gelatin in the cold water and add it to the mixture. Remove it from the heat. Stir in the crushed strawberries, mixing well, then chill the mixture until it begins to thicken.

Beat the egg whites until they hold soft peaks. Add the rest of the sugar, beating the mixture until it is stiff. Fold this into the strawberry mixture, then pour it into a baked pie shell. Chill and serve the pie with whipped cream.

Variations: Try substituting ¾ cup of raspberry juice instead of the strawberries.

STRAWBERRY PUDDING PIE

Strawberries
½ small box strawberry gelatin powder

1 cup plus 2 tablespoons boiling water
2 cups Basic Vanilla Pudding (see page 190)

Wash and stem the berries, then slice them into a pie pan. Dissolve the gelatin in the boiling water, and pour it over the strawberries. Let it set until it jells. Make the vanilla pudding, let it cool, then pour it into a baked pie crust. Put the bottom of the pie pan containing the thickened gelatin into a pan of hot water for a moment, until the gelatin loosens. Then slide the gelatin onto the pudding in the crust. Chill the pie. Top it with whipped cream before serving.

Variations: Raspberry or other berry pies may be made with this method, using the same pudding but with gelatin flavors matched accordingly.

FRESH STRAWBERRY CHIFFON PIE

3-ounce package instant vanilla
  pudding or pie filling
1¼ cups crushed strawberries

Prepare the pudding or pie filling according to the package instructions, then blend in the crushed strawberries. Pour the mixture into a graham cracker pie crust and chill it until it is firm. Spread it with whipped cream before serving.

JELLIED STRAWBERRY PIE

2 cups water
1¼ cups sugar
3 tablespoons cornstarch

1 package (3 ounces) strawberry
  gelatin powder
1 pint fresh strawberries, hulled
2 baked pie shells

Cook together the water, sugar and cornstarch until the mixture thickens. Add the dry gelatin powder and let the mixture cool. Pour it over the strawberries in the pie shells, and chill them until firm. Top the pies with whipped cream or your favorite vanilla pudding.

SUSIECUE PIE

1 cup brown sugar
½ cup white sugar
1 tablespoon flour
2 eggs, beaten

1 teaspoon vanilla
2 tablespoons milk
½ cup butter
1 cup pecan or hickory nuts

Mix together the sugars and flour, then add the eggs, vanilla, milk and butter. Beat the mixture until it is thick, then pour it into an unbaked pie crust. Bake it at 375° for 20 minutes, then sprinkle the nuts over the top. Continue baking the pie until the filling has set.

UNION PIE

2 cups sugar (scant)
2 cups sour cream
4 tablespoons flour
1 teaspoon soda

2 cups molasses
2 cups buttermilk
4 eggs, beaten
¾ teaspoon nutmeg

Mix together all the ingredients, then pour the mixture into 4 unbaked pie shells. Bake the pies at 400° for 10 minutes, then at 325° for 20 to 25 minutes or until a knife comes out clean.

FILLED RAISIN PIE

2 cups raisins
4 tablespoons flour
2 cups sugar
2 eggs, separated

2 cups water
1 teaspoon vinegar
1 teaspoon salt

Stew the raisins until they are soft. Add the flour, sugar, egg yolks, water, vinegar and salt. Let the mixture come to a boil while stirring it continuously. Allow it to cool before pouring it into a baked pie crust. Top the pie with meringue.

VANILLA PIE

1 cup molasses or maple syrup
1 cup brown sugar
2 cups hot water
1 egg, beaten
1 cup granulated sugar
½ cup lard

1 egg
1 cup sour milk or cream
2 cups flour
½ teaspoon soda
2 teaspoons baking powder

Cook together the molasses, brown sugar, hot water and beaten egg. Mix together the rest of the ingredients as you would for a cake batter. Divide the batter among 4 unbaked pie shells. Pour the previously prepared syrup over the batter and bake it at 400° for about 10 minutes, then reduce the heat to 350° and bake it until done. The cake will rise to the top during baking.

VANILLA CRUMB PIE

1 cup brown sugar
1 cup maple syrup
2 cups water
2 tablespoons flour

1 egg
1 teaspoon vanilla
½ teaspoon cream of tartar
1 teaspoon soda

Boil together for 1 minute the sugar, syrup, water and flour, then set the mixture aside to cool. In a bowl, beat together the egg, vanilla, cream of tartar and soda, then add this to the syrup mixture. Divide the filling equally into 3 unbaked pie shells. Top the pies with crumbs made from a mixture of the following.

2 cups pastry flour
1 cup brown sugar
½ cup lard

½ teaspoon soda
1 teaspoon cream of tartar

Bake the pies for 45 minutes at 350 to 375°.

GREEN TOMATO PIE

Green tomatoes, peeled, very thinly
   sliced
1½ cups sugar (1 cup white, ½ cup
   brown)

2 tablespoons flour
4 tablespoons vinegar
1 tablespoon butter
1 teaspoon cinnamon

Fill an unbaked pie shell with the tomatoes. (Remove the seeds if you wish.) Mix together the sugar, flour, vinegar, butter and cinnamon, then pour this mixture over the tomatoes. Cover it with a top crust and bake it at 425° for 15 minutes, then at 350° for 30 to 40 minutes.

HALF MOON PIES

1 quart apple snitz (dried pieces)
1½ cups water
1 quart applesauce

1½ cups brown sugar
½ teaspoon cinnamon
½ teaspoon salt

To make the filling, boil the apple snitz in the water until no water remains and the snitz is soft. Drain it in a colander. Add it to the applesauce, sugar, cinnamon and salt.

Make a pie dough (see page 167). For each pie, shape it to the size of a large egg. Roll it out thinly. Fold the dough over to make a crease through the center. Unfold it, and make 2 holes in the top part. On the other half of the dough place ½ cup of the filling. Wet the edges of the dough and fold it over, pressing the edges together. Cut off the remaining dough with a pie crimper. Brush the top with buttermilk or beaten egg, and bake it at 450° until brown.

Snitz Pie;

Put 2 or 2½ cups of this filling into an unbaked pie shell. Place another crust on top and bake it at 400° until the crust is done.

KATIE'S MINCE PIES

6 cups chopped apples
1 pint hamburger
1 cup raisins
3 tablespoons vinegar
1 tablespoon butter, melted

2 cups sugar
1 teaspoon cinnamon
1 teaspoon allspice
Salt to taste

Mix together all the ingredients, then pour the mixture into 2 unbaked pie shells. Bake them at 350° for 25 to 35 minutes.

APPLE FRITTERS

1 cup flour
2 tablespoons sugar
½ cup milk
1½ teaspoons baking powder

½ teaspoon salt
1 egg
5 or 6 apples
Icing sugar, or syrup

Make a batter by combining the flour, sugar, milk, baking powder, salt and egg. Core and peel the apples, then slice them and put them into the batter. Drop them by spoonfuls into 1 inch of fat or oil in a frying pan. Test the apples with a fork—they are done when soft. Drain them on paper towels or in a colander. Sprinkle the fritters with icing sugar or eat them with syrup. This recipe makes about 4 skillets full.

FRIED APPLE TURNOVERS

⅔ cup granulated sugar
½ teaspoon cinnamon
¼ cup butter or margarine
2 cups sliced, pared, tart apples

1 package refrigerator biscuits, or
 biscuit mix (see page 254)
Icing sugar

Combine the granulated sugar, cinnamon, butter and apples in a saucepan. Simmer this mixture, stirring it occasionally until the apples are tender. Separate the biscuits and roll each one to an oval shape, about 5 inches long. Place 1 tablespoon of the apple filling on ½ of the oval, then fold the dough over the filling and seal the edges with a fork. (Be sure they are well sealed or the filling will leak out.) Fry the turnovers in 375° hot deep fat for about 1 minute or until golden brown, turning them once. Drain them and sprinkle them with icing sugar, and serve them warm. This recipe makes 10 turnovers.

DESSERTS AND DESSERT SAUCES

BASIC CUSTARD RECIPE

1 cup scalded milk
1 tablespoon sugar
¼ teaspoon salt

1 beaten egg
1 teaspoon vanilla
Dash of nutmeg (optional)

Mix together the ingredients, then set the mixture in a pan of hot water to bake at 350° until done. To test if the custard is done, insert a knife in the center, and if it comes out clean, the custard is done. Do not let the custard boil.

This recipe may be expanded to suit one's needs.

Variations: *Add chocolate (not cocoa) to the recipe for CHOCOLATE CUSTARD.*

For LOW-CALORIE CUSTARD, use a low-calorie artificial sweetener and skimmed milk.

Try lemon flavoring instead of vanilla.

For CARAMEL CUSTARD, try using brown sugar instead of white.

GRAHAM CRACKER CUSTARD

18 graham crackers
½ cup butter
¼ cup sugar

Crush the crackers, then add the butter and sugar. Line a dish with these crumbs, saving a few to put on top.

¾ cup milk
3 eggs, separated
½ cup sugar

1 package (3 ounces) lemon or orange
  gelatin powder
½ to ¾ cup cream, whipped

Bring the milk to a boil and gradually add it to the egg yolks and sugar. Stir the mixture over low heat until the eggs are cooked, then remove it from the heat and add the gelatin. Stir to dissolve. Allow it to cool and partly set, then fold in the stiffly beaten egg whites and whipped cream. Pour this custard into the crumb-lined dish, sprinkle it with the reserved crumbs and chill it.

BASIC VANILLA PUDDING

¾ cup sugar
⅓ cup cornstarch
½ teaspoon salt
2 eggs, separated

½ cup cold milk
3½ cups milk, scalded
1 teaspoon vanilla
1 tablespoon butter

Combine the dry ingredients, then stir in the beaten egg yolks, and cold milk. Beat it into the hot milk and stir it over medium heat until it thickens. Add the vanilla and butter. Fold in the beaten egg whites, or top the pudding with meringue.

Variations: For COCONUT PUDDING, use the above recipe and add 1 cup of coconut. Top the pudding with meringue and coconut.

BAKED BERRY PUDDING

1 tablespoon butter
½ cup milk
1 teaspoon baking powder
½ cup sugar

1 cup all-purpose flour
1 cup sweetened berries
1 cup boiling water

Mix together the butter, milk, baking powder, sugar and flour to make a dough, then spread it in a greased, deep baking dish. Pour the berries and boiling water over the dough, and bake it at 400° until the cake part is done.

CHOCOLATE PUDDING

1 cup shortening	3 cups all-purpose flour
2 cups sugar	2 teaspoons soda
2 eggs	1 teaspoon salt
1 teaspoon vanilla	⅔ cup cocoa
1 cup buttermilk or sour milk	1 cup hot water

Mix together the ingredients until smooth, then add 1 cup of hot water. Pour this batter into a 13 x 9-inch pan.

1½ cups sugar	¾ to 1 cup hot water
2 tablespoons cocoa	

Mix together the above 3 ingredients, and pour the mixture over the cake batter. Bake it at 350° for 50 to 60 minutes.

This pudding is great with ice cream.

CHOCOLATE FUDGE PUDDING

3 tablespoons shortening	½ cup nuts, chopped
¾ cup sugar	1 cup brown sugar
1 cup all-purpose flour	¼ cup cocoa
½ teaspoon salt	¼ teaspoon salt
1½ teaspoons baking powder	1¼ cups boiling water
½ cup milk	

Cream together the shortening and ¾ cup of sugar. Sift together the flour, ½ teaspoon of salt and baking powder. Add this alternately with the milk to the creamed mixture. Fold in the nuts and pour the batter into an ungreased pan.

Mix together the brown sugar, cocoa and ¼ teaspoon of salt. Sprinkle this mixture over the top of the batter, but do not stir it in. Pour the boiling water over all, and again do not stir it. Bake the pudding at 350° for 40 to 45 minutes. Serve it with whipped cream.

COTTAGE PUDDING

¼ cup butter	2½ cups all-purpose flour
⅔ cup sugar	4 teaspoons baking powder
1 egg	½ teaspoon salt
1 teaspoon vanilla	1 cup milk

Cream together the butter and sugar and add the well-beaten egg and vanilla. Mix it well. Sift together the dry ingredients, then add them alternately with the milk to the first mixture. Pour it into a well-greased cake pan and bake it in a moderate oven (350°) for 35 minutes. Serve it with fruit and milk.

DATE PUDDING

1 cup chopped dates
1 cup boiling water
1 cup sugar
1½ cups all-purpose flour
½ cup chopped nuts

1 teaspoon butter
1 teaspoon vanilla
1 egg
2 teaspoons soda
½ teaspoon salt

Put the dates into a bowl and pour the boiling water over them. Let them set to cool a little, then add the other ingredients. Bake the pudding at 325° for 30 to 40 minutes, then allow it to cool. Chop it up before serving and mix whipped cream through it.

RICH DATE PUDDING

18 graham crackers, crushed
¾ cup chopped dates
¾ cup chopped nuts

12 marshmallows (chopped)
¼ cup cream

Mix the ingredients together well and pack the mixture in a dish or form it into a roll. Let it set for 12 hours in the refrigerator. Slice it and serve it with whipped cream.

DEPRESSION PUDDING

1 cup brown sugar
1 tablespoon butter or margarine
1½ cups raisins
4 cups boiling water
2 teaspoons vanilla
½ cup nuts (optional)

¼ cup butter or margarine
1 cup sugar
2 cups all-purpose flour
1 cup milk
4 teaspoons baking powder

To make the syrup, combine the first 6 ingredients and boil the mixture for 5 minutes. Pour it into a greased loaf pan. Combine the rest of the ingredients to make a batter, and dab it by tablespoons over the syrup. Bake it for 30 to 35 minutes at 350°, then serve it with whipped cream or milk.

Variations: For *CINNAMON PUDDING, prepare the above recipe, but omit the raisins and add 1 teaspoon of cinnamon to the batter. Pour it into a greased pan and pour the syrup on top.*

FLUFFY PUDDING

1 egg, separated
⅓ cup sugar
3 tablespoons tapioca

⅛ teaspoon salt
2 cups milk
¾ teaspoon vanilla

Beat the egg white until it is foamy. Gradually add 2 tablespoons of the sugar and beat it into soft peaks. Mix the rest of the sugar with the egg yolk, tapioca, salt and milk, and bring the mixture to a full boil. Very slowly add it to the beaten egg white, stirring rapidly to blend. Then add the vanilla. Let it cool for 20 minutes, then beat it well.

GRAHAM CRACKER PUDDING

Make alternate layers in a serving dish of graham cracker crumbs, Basic Vanilla Pudding (see page 190), and sliced bananas sprinkled with nuts (optional). Top it with whipped cream or sprinkle it with more crumbs.

Variations: Different desserts may be made by adding pineapple chunks, orange slices, strawberries or other fruit, or grapenuts and whipped cream.

STEAMED GRAHAM PUDDING

1 egg
1 cup sugar
1 cup sour milk
1 cup white flour
½ cup raisins

1 cup whole wheat flour
1 teaspoon soda
1 teaspoon cinnamon
2 tablespoons molasses
½ teaspoon salt

Mix together the above ingredients, and steam the mixture on top of the stove, preferably using a greased angel food cake pan covered and set in a large covered kettle. Simmer it for 1 to 1½ hours, then serve it warm with milk.

This is a delicious and economically made pudding.

STEAMED BANANA PUDDING

1¼ cups sugar
1 egg
¼ cup shortening
2 tablespoons molasses
2 cups pastry flour
2 cups mashed bananas

1 teaspoon baking powder
½ teaspoon soda
¼ cup milk
Cloves, cinnamon, ginger and nutmeg
to taste

Mix together all the ingredients. Put the mixture into a pan and set it in hot water in a covered dish to steam for 2 hours.

CHERRY PUDDING

3 cups all-purpose flour
9 tablespoons butter
9 tablespoons sugar
1 teaspoon salt
3 teaspoons baking powder
1½ cups milk

1 teaspoon vanilla
3 cups pitted cherries
1½ cups water
¼ cup sugar
2 tablespoons flour

Work the first 5 ingredients together as you would for pie crumbs, then add the milk and vanilla. Stir this mixture with a fork until a soft dough is formed. Boil together the remaining ingredients before pouring the mixture into a pan and putting the dough on top. Bake it at 350° for about 1 hour or until done, then serve it hot with milk.

Variations: Other fruit may be used instead of the cherries. And instead of the dough, try using Biscuit Mix (see page 254).

RHUBARB PUDDING

1 egg
1 cup sugar
2 cups all-purpose flour
1 cup milk
2 teaspoons baking powder

1 teaspoon vanilla
4 cups rhubarb
2 cups sugar
2 cups boiling water

Mix together the egg, 1 cup of the sugar, the flour, milk, baking powder and vanilla. Place this dough in the bottom of a cake pan. Then mix together the rhubarb, 2 cups of the sugar and the boiling water. Pour this over the dough and bake it at 350 to 375° for 40 minutes or until done.

SODA CRACKER PUDDING

¼ cup butter
2 tablespoons peanut butter

½ cup brown sugar
18 square soda biscuits, crushed

Melt together the butter and peanut butter, then add it to a mixture of the sugar and cracker crumbs. Mix it well. Wet a bowl and press this mixture around the side and bottom. Reserve ¼ cup of the crumbs for the top.

Filling;

3 cups milk
2 eggs
2 tablespoons cornstarch

1 cup white sugar
1 teaspoon vanilla
½ cup coconut

Boil together until thick the first 4 ingredients, then add the vanilla and coconut. Pour this slowly onto the crumbs. When it has cooled, sprinkle it with the reserved crumbs.

STEAMED CHOCOLATE PUDDING

3 tablespoons melted butter
⅔ cup sugar
1 egg
1⅛ cups cake flour
2 teaspoons baking powder

⅛ teaspoon salt
¾ cup milk
4 tablespoons cocoa
1 teaspoon vanilla

Mix together the ingredients in the order given, then pour the mixture into a buttered double boiler. Cover and steam it for 2 hours.

RAISIN-NUT PUDDING

1 cup brown sugar
2 cups hot water
2 teaspoons butter
1 tablespoon cornstarch
½ cup sugar
2 tablespoons butter

1 cup milk
1 cup all-purpose flour
2 teaspoons baking powder
½ teaspoon salt
½ cup raisins
¼ cup nuts

Boil together for 5 minutes the first 4 ingredients, then pour this syrup into a cake pan. Mix the rest of the ingredients as you would a cake. Pour the batter onto the syrup. Bake it at 350° until a knife inserted comes out clean. Serve this pudding warm with milk or whipped cream.

CROW'S-NEST PUDDING

Make a cake batter with Basic Cake Mix (see page 251) or Handy Made Cake (see page 119). Pour 1 quart of sliced peaches into a buttered baking dish. Sprinkle 1 tablespoon of flour over them. Top this with the cake batter and bake it at 350° for 30 to 40 minutes. Serve it warm with top milk.

Variations: *Try substituting other fruit for the peaches.*

APPLE-CRANBERRY DUMPLINGS

Syrup;

2 cups water
2 cups sugar
½ teaspoon cinnamon

½ teaspoon cloves
½ cup butter

Combine the first 4 ingredients and boil the mixture for 5 minutes. Remove this syrup from the heat and add the butter.

Biscuit Dough;

2 cups all-purpose flour, sifted
1 teaspoon salt
1 tablespoon baking powder

2 tablespoons sugar
½ cup shortening
¾ cup milk

Sift together the dry ingredients and cut in the shortening. Gradually add the milk, tossing the mixture to make a soft dough. Roll it out on a floured board to form an 18 x 12-inch rectangle.

Filling;

4 cups grated, peeled apples
1 cup cooked, drained whole
    cranberries, OR
1 cup whole cranberry sauce

½ cup black walnuts, chopped

Spread the dough with the apples, cranberries and nuts. Roll it up like a jelly roll and cut it into 1-inch slices. Place them in a 13 x 9 x 2-inch pan. Pour the hot syrup over all and bake them in a hot oven (425°) for 40 minutes. Serve the dumplings warm.

APPLE GOODIE

½ cup sugar
2 tablespoons flour
¼ teaspoon salt
1 teaspoon cinnamon
1½ quarts apples, sliced
1 cup oatmeal

1 cup brown sugar
1 cup flour
¼ teaspoon soda
⅓ teaspoon baking powder
⅔ cup butter

Mix together the sugar, flour, salt and cinnamon, then add this mixture to the apples and mix it again. Put it on the bottom of a greased pan. Combine the rest of the ingredients until crumbly, then put this mixture on top of the apple mixture, and pat it firmly. Bake it at 350° until brown and a crust forms. Serve it with milk or cream.

Variations: For Rhubarb Goodie, use the above recipe but substitute 3 cups of diced rhubarb for the apples, and add 1 teaspoon of nutmeg and an extra cup of sugar.

APPLE DUMPLINGS

2 cups all-purpose flour
2½ teaspoons baking powder
½ teaspoon salt
⅔ cup shortening
½ cup milk

6 apples, peeled and halved
2 cups brown sugar
2 cups water
¼ cup butter
½ teaspoon cinnamon

Combine the first 5 ingredients to make a dough. Roll it out and cut it into squares, then place ½ apple on each square. Wet the edges of the dough and press it around the apple to form a ball. Set these dumplings in a pan.

Combine the rest of the ingredients to make the sauce. Pour it over the dumplings and bake them at 350° until the apples are soft and the dough is golden brown.

APPLE RICE BETTY

½ cup honey
¼ teaspoon cloves
1 teaspoon salt
¼ teaspoon cinnamon

1 cup cooked brown rice
4 large apples
½ cup chopped walnuts
2 tablespoons oil

Mix the honey with the spices. Grease a baking dish and place a thin layer of the rice in it. Add a layer of thinly sliced apples, and sprinkle it with the spiced honey and nuts. Repeat the layers until all the ingredients are used, saving some of the honey and nuts for the top. Pour the oil over the surface. Bake it at 350° until the apples are soft. This can be served hot or cold.

APPLE SURPRISE

1 package (3 ounces) gelatin powder
  (any flavor)
½ cup chopped celery
½ cup chopped dates

½ cup diced apples
1 cup drained pineapple
¼ cup chopped nuts
½ cup whipping cream, whipped

Prepare the gelatin according to the package instructions, then let it cool. When it has thickened slightly, fold in the fruit and the rest of the ingredients, adding the whipped cream last. Pour the mixture into a mold and refrigerate it. To serve, garnish it with mayonnaise.

MY OWN APPLE DESSERT

4 quarts washed, sliced cooking apples
1 cup raisins
1 teaspoon cinnamon

1½ cups sugar
2 tablespoons cornstarch
5 or 6 bananas

Put the apples into a large kettle and add the raisins, cinnamon, sugar and enough water to almost cover the fruit. Bring the mixture to a boil.

Mix the cornstarch with a little water, add it to the fruit mixture, then boil it until it thickens. Allow it to cool before slicing in the bananas.

APPLE-RHUBARB CRISP

2 cups finely cut apples
2 cups finely cut rhubarb
1 egg, beaten
¾ cup white sugar

¼ teaspoon nutmeg
½ cup butter or margarine
1 cup flour
1 cup brown sugar

Mix together the apples, rhubarb, egg, white sugar and nutmeg, then place the mixture in a glass baking dish. Combine the butter, flour and brown sugar to crumb consistency. Pack this over the apple/rhubarb mixture and bake it at 375° for 30 minutes. Serve it with sweetened milk or whipped cream.

Variations: *Use 4 cups of apples and omit the rhubarb. Add ½ cup of nuts if desired.*

SPICED APPLE DESSERT

1 cup brown sugar
1 cup all-purpose flour
½ teaspoon soda
1 teaspoon cinnamon
½ teaspoon baking powder
1 teaspoon nutmeg

1 teaspoon cloves
½ teaspoon salt
4 large apples, cubed or sliced
2 eggs, beaten
4 tablespoons butter

Combine the dry ingredients, then add the apples, egg and butter. Bake this mixture for 45 minutes at 350°. Serve it with milk and sugar when it has cooled.

AUNT CLARA'S DESSERT

1 package (3 ounces) raspberry gelatin
   powder
1 cup boiling water
1 cup pineapple juice
¼ cup butter
1½ cups icing sugar

2 eggs, separated
½ cup melted butter
¼ cup brown sugar
16 graham crackers, crushed
1 cup drained crushed pineapple

Dissolve the gelatin in the boiling water, then add the pineapple juice. Chill the mixture until it is slightly thickened. Cream together the ¼ cup of butter and icing sugar, and blend in the well-beaten egg yolks. Beat the egg whites until they are stiff but not dry, then fold them into the creamed mixture.

Combine the melted butter and brown sugar with the cracker crumbs. Put ½ of the crumb mixture into the bottom of a buttered 9-inch square pan. Spread it evenly with the egg mixture, then spread the pineapple over this filling. Sprinkle on the remaining crumbs, and pour the gelatin over top. Chill it until it is set, then cut it into squares. Top each serving with whipped cream. This recipe serves 9.

RAW APPLE PUDDING

Mix several cups of diced apples, about ¼ cup of chocolate shavings (or chips), nuts and broken homemade graham crackers with whipped cream.

BUTTERSCOTCH NUT TORTE

6 eggs, separated
1½ cups sugar
1 teaspoon baking powder
2 teaspoons vanilla
1 teaspoon almond extract

2 cups graham cracker crumbs
1 cup broken nuts
1 pint whipping cream
3 tablespoons icing sugar

Beat the egg yolks well before adding the 1½ cups of sugar, baking powder, vanilla and almond extract. Then beat the egg whites enough to hold a peak. Fold them into the egg yolk mixture, then add the crumbs and nuts. Line two 9-inch layer pans with waxed paper. Pour in the cake batter and bake it at 325° for 30 to 35 minutes. Allow the cake to cool. Whip the cream and sweeten it with the icing sugar before putting it between layers and on the top and sides. Cover the top with the following sauce.

1 cup brown sugar
¼ cup butter
¼ cup water
1 tablespoon flour

¼ cup orange juice
1 well-beaten egg
½ teaspoon vanilla

Mix the ingredients together well and boil the mixture until it is syrupy. When it has cooled, pour it over the whipped cream on the cake.

CHEESE CAKE

¾ cup graham crackers
½ cup sugar
¼ cup margarine
2 eggs

16 ounces cream cheese
1 teaspoon vanilla
1 cup sugar

Line the bottom of a 9 x 9-inch pan with crumbs made with the graham crackers, ½ cup of sugar and the margarine. Then beat the eggs, add the cream cheese and whip this mixture until it is smooth. Add the vanilla and 1 cup of sugar, then pour it on top of the crumbs. Bake it for 45 to 50 minutes at 300° or until the center is almost set. Top the cake with your favorite fruit pie filling—cherry, blueberry, raspberry, strawberry or any other fruit. Refrigerate it for several hours.

LEMON CHEESE CAKE

1 package (3 ounces) lemon gelatin
   powder
1 cup hot water
30 graham crackers
½ cup margarine

8 ounces cream cheese
1 cup sugar
1 teaspoon vanilla
1 large can evaporated milk, chilled, or
   1 cup whipping cream

Dissolve the gelatin powder in the hot water, then let it stand to thicken. Meanwhile, crush the graham crackers and blend in the butter. Line the bottom of two 8-inch cake pans with the crumbs, saving a few for the top. Soften the cream cheese and add the sugar and vanilla. Whip the cream or evaporated milk until it is thick. Add the cheese mixture and whipped cream to the gelatin which has by this time almost thickened. Beat this mixture until it is fluffy. Pour it into the pans lined with the graham cracker crumbs, and top it with the remaining crumbs. Refrigerate the cakes.

CORN PONE

1 cup corn meal
¼ cup all-purpose flour
1½ teaspoons baking powder
½ teaspoon salt

2 eggs
4 tablespoons sugar
½ cup milk
4 tablespoons shortening, melted

Mix together and sift the dry ingredients, except the sugar. Beat the eggs, then stir in the sugar and milk. Add the sifted dry ingredients and the shortening to the egg mixture. Bake it in a well-greased 9-inch-square pan at 425° for 25 minutes.

WHOLE WHEAT CORN BREAD

Dissolve 1 package or 1 tablespoon of yeast in 1 cup of lukewarm water. Let it set.

3 cups cornmeal
2 cups whole wheat flour
2 cups all-purpose flour
½ teaspoon soda
1 teaspoon salt
1 cup sweet milk

¾ cup soft homemade butter
6 unbeaten eggs
¼ cup baking molasses
¾ cup honey
¾ cup grapefruit juice, OR
¼ cup sweet pickle juice

Mix together the above ingredients and add the yeast. Then pour it into 2 greased 13 x 9 x 2-inch cake pans, let it set until double in size, and bake it at 350° for about 30 minutes or until done. Serve this bread with strawberries or honey. It can be frozen after it has been baked.

Variations: *If you use pickle juice in this recipe, add approximately 1½ cups of water instead of milk to make a medium thick cake batter.*

CHERRY CRISP

2 tablespoons flour
1 cup sugar
1 teaspoon grated lemon rind
　(optional)

½ cup cherry juice
2 cups drained, unsweetened cherries

Mix together the flour, sugar, lemon rind and juice. Add this to the cherries and put the mixture into a buttered baking dish. Mix lightly into crumbs the following ingredients, and spread it over the cherry mixture.

1 cup sugar
¾ cup flour

7 tablespoons butter
¼ teaspoon nutmeg

Bake this for about 30 minutes in a medium hot oven (375°), and serve it with whipped cream or sweet milk.

Variations: Other fruit besides cherries may be used.

CHERRY ROLLS

1 egg
¾ cup sour cream
2 cups all-purpose flour
¾ teaspoon salt
¼ teaspoon soda

2½ teaspoons baking powder
2 tablespoons butter
2 cups drained cherries
2 tablespoons sugar
1 teaspoon cinnamon

Beat the egg, then add the sour cream. Sift the flour, and add the salt, soda and baking powder before sifting this mixture again. Add it to the egg mixture and stir well. Toss the dough onto a slightly floured board and roll it into an oblong piece ¼ inch thick. Spread it lightly with the soft butter, cover it with the cherries, and sprinkle it with the sugar and cinnamon. Roll it up like a jelly roll and cut it into 1½-inch thick slices. Place them cut side up, close together in a greased 9-inch-square baking pan.

⅓ cup brown sugar
⅓ cup white sugar
1½ tablespoons cornstarch
1½ cups cherry juice

Red coloring, a few drops
½ teaspoon almond flavoring
1½ tablespoons butter

Combine the dry ingredients before adding the liquid, coloring and flavoring. Bring this mixture to a boil, and when it has thickened slightly, add the butter and pour it over the slices in the baking pan. Bake them at 375° for 25 minutes. This recipe makes 12 cherry rolls.

EASY MILK DESSERT

Boil a can of sweetened condensed milk in a kettle of water for 3½ hours. Set it in a cool place to chill, then open both ends and push out the contents. Slice it and put each slice on top of pineapple slices. Add a spoonful of whipped cream, and garnish it with a red maraschino cherry.

This is a handy dessert. You can boil as many as you wish and set them on your pantry shelf for unexpected company.

GRAHAM CRACKER FLUFF

Filling;

1 package gelatin
⅓ cup cold water
½ cup sugar
¾ cup rich milk

2 eggs, separated
1 teaspoon vanilla
1 cup cream, whipped

Soak the gelatin in the cold water. Mix together the sugar, milk and egg yolks. Cook this mixture in a double boiler until the egg yolks are cooked (10 minutes), stirring it constantly. Remove it from the heat, then add the gelatin and vanilla. Chill it until the mixture begins to thicken. Then fold in the egg whites which have been beaten until stiff and the whipped cream.

Crumbs;

1½ tablespoons butter
3 tablespoons brown sugar

12 graham crackers, crushed

Melt together the butter and brown sugar, and mix it with the graham cracker crumbs. Line the bottom of a dish with ½ of the crumbs, then pour in the filling. Put the remaining crumbs on top, and set it in a cool place to chill.

MAPLE SPONGE

2 cups brown sugar
1½ cups hot water
½ teaspoon maple flavoring
1 package gelatin

½ cup cold water
Vanilla pudding
1 cup whipped cream

Boil together for 10 minutes the sugar, hot water and maple flavoring. Soak the gelatin in the cold water for a few minutes, then mix it with the hot syrup. Let it set until it is almost firm, then whip it until it is light and fluffy. Using this sponge, your favorite vanilla pudding, and the whipped cream, put spoonfuls of the three alternately into a serving dish. Nuts or bananas may also be added.

MISSISSIPPI MUD

1 tablespoon butter (heaping)	4 tablespoons flour
1½ cups brown sugar	2½ cups milk
½ cup water	1 teaspoon vanilla
3 eggs, separated	12 graham crackers

Melt the butter and brown it. Add the sugar and water and boil it to make a syrup. Mix the egg yolks, flour and milk. Gradually add ½ cup of hot syrup to the egg mixture and return the whole mixture to the syrup, beating constantly. Bring it to a boil and cook it until thickened. Add the vanilla, then put it into a dish. Roll the graham crackers and spread the crumbs on top. Spread it with the beaten egg whites and a few graham cracker crumbs. Brown it slightly.

OATMEAL BROWN BETTY

1 cup whole wheat flour	½ cup shortening, scant
½ teaspoon salt	2½ cups sliced apples
½ cup brown sugar	¼ cup raisins
½ teaspoon soda	Butter
1 cup rolled oats	½ cup corn syrup or honey

Mix together the dry ingredients, then cut in the shortening until the mixture is crumbly. Spread ½ of it in a baking dish, and cover it with the apples and raisins. Put the remainder of the crumbs on the top to cover the apples and raisins. Dot the top with butter, and drip the corn syrup or honey over it. Bake it in a moderate oven (350°) for 35 minutes or until the apples are soft. Serve it with milk.

Variations: *Other fruit may be substituted for the apples.*

PEACH PETZ

1 cup all-purpose flour	2 tablespoons butter
½ teaspoon baking powder	¾ cup sugar
¼ teaspoon salt	⅓ cup flour
⅓ cup shortening	14 peach halves (canned)
3 to 5 tablespoons cold water	

Combine the 1 cup of flour, baking powder and salt. Cut the shortening into this mixture, then add the water slowly and mix it, using only enough water to hold the dough together. Chill it, then roll it out a little thicker than pie dough and put it into a large pie plate or cake pan.

Mix together the butter, sugar and ⅓ cup of flour for the filling. Sprinkle ½ of this mixture over the dough. Place the peaches (cut side down) on the dough and cover them with the remaining crumbs. Pour the peach juice over top. Bake it at 375° for 35 minutes or until the crust is brown. Serve it with milk.

TWO-EGG BOSTON CREAM PIE

1 cup sugar
1 egg
½ cup sour cream
½ cup milk

1¾ cups cake flour
1 teaspoon soda
2 teaspoons baking powder

Mix the ingredients to make a batter, then bake it at 350° in 2 layer cake pans. When the cakes have cooled, split the layers and fill them with the following filling.

¾ cup sugar
1 egg yolk
1 tablespoon cornstarch

1 pint milk
1 tablespoon flour
Vanilla

Mix these ingredients in a saucepan and cook the mixture until it is thick and smooth. Cover the pie with brown sugar frosting.

Variations: *Try adding 1½ teaspoons of grated lemon peel, lemon extract or 4½ teaspoons of lemon juice to the filling.*

QUICK SYRUP KNEPP

1 cup brown sugar or maple syrup
2½ cups water

1 tablespoon butter
1 teaspoon vanilla

To make the syrup, bring the above ingredients to a boil in a 10-inch-wide cooker.

2 cups all-purpose flour
½ cup brown sugar
3 tablespoons lard
¾ cup milk

4 teaspoons baking powder
½ teaspoon salt
1 egg

To make the dough, mix the above ingredients as you would for biscuits or pie dough, stirring the mixture lightly. Add it by the spoonful to the boiling syrup. Cover it and let it simmer for 20 minutes. Do not remove the cover at any time during the cooking process. Serve it with milk.

Variations: *Cocoa may be added to the syrup or the dough, or both. When you add cocoa to the dough, peaches are especially good in the syrup.*

Try adding sliced apples to the syrup.

Make the above dough without the sugar, and drop it onto hot stewed fruit. Follow the cooking directions above.

RASPBERRIES WITH KNEPP

2 cups whole raspberries or juice
¾ cup sugar
2 cups water
3 level tablespoons cornstarch
1 cup all-purpose flour

5 teaspoons baking powder
3 teaspoons sugar
¼ teaspoon salt
1 cup milk

Bring the first 3 ingredients to a boil. Mix the cornstarch with enough water to make a smooth sauce, then stir it into the hot raspberry mixture and bring it to a boil.

Mix together the rest of the ingredients to make a dough, and drop it by spoonfuls into the boiling raspberry mixture. Cover it with a tight lid and let it boil slowly for 20 minutes. Do not uncover it during the boiling period. Serve it with milk.

Variations: Elderberries or other fruit may be used instead of raspberries.

RHUBARB CRUNCH

1 cup whole wheat flour
1 cup brown sugar
1 teaspoon cinnamon

¾ cup oatmeal
½ cup melted butter

Mix together the above ingredients until crumbly, and put ½ of the mixture into a greased 9-inch pan. Cover it with 4 cups of diced rhubarb.

1 cup sugar
2 tablespoons cornstarch

1 cup water
1 teaspoon vanilla

Combine these ingredients and cook the mixture until it is clear. Pour it over the rhubarb. Top it with the remaining crumbs and bake it at 350° for 45 minutes or until the rhubarb is tender.

RHUBARB TAPIOCA

1 cup tapioca (pearl)
2 cups cold water
Cinnamon (optional)
3 cups hot water

2 cups rhubarb
2 cups sugar
1 can (14 ounces) crushed pineapple

Soak the tapioca in the cold water overnight or for a couple of hours. Then add cinnamon if desired, and the remaining ingredients. Cook this mixture, stirring it constantly until the tapioca is clear or nearly clear.

SARAH SCHWARTZ'S RHUBARB ROLLS

2 cups flour
1 teaspoon salt
2 teaspoons baking powder
3 tablespoons lard
⅞ cup sweet milk
Soft butter
Granulated sugar

Rhubarb, finely cut
Dash of nutmeg
1 cup sugar
1 heaping tablespoon flour
¼ teaspoon salt
1 cup hot water
Small lump of butter

Sift together the flour, salt and baking powder. Cut the lard into this mixture, add the milk and mix it well. Roll this dough out ¼ inch thick, spread it thickly with soft butter, granulated sugar and rhubarb, and sprinkle it with nutmeg. Roll up the dough as you would cinnamon rolls and cut it into 1½ to 2-inch slices.

Mix together the rest of the ingredients and boil the mixture for 3 minutes to make a sweet sauce. Place the dough slices in a pan and pour this sauce over and around them. Bake them at 350° until brown.

Variations: Diced apples may be used instead of rhubarb.

FRUIT TAPIOCA

1 small package gelatin powder
   (any flavor)
¼ cup minute tapioca
2½ cups water, fruit juice, or syrup
   from canned fruit

¼ teaspoon salt
½ to ¾ cup sugar

Mix together the ingredients and let the mixture stand for 5 minutes. Bring it to a boil over medium heat, stirring it often. Allow it to cool for 20 minutes, then add any fruit desired. This recipe makes 6 servings.

WEDDING TAPIOCA

9 cups water
½ teaspoon salt
1½ cups tapioca (baby pearl)
1 cup sugar

2 small packages pineapple gelatin
   powder
1 small package orange gelatin powder
1 small package lemon gelatin powder

Bring the water and salt to the boiling point. Add the tapioca and boil it until it is clear, stirring it constantly. Remove it from the heat and stir in the sugar and gelatin. Chill this mixture.

Variations: Whipped cream, nuts or fruit such as pineapple, bananas or orange slices may be added if desired.

VANILLA SOUFFLE

¼ cup butter, melted
¼ cup flour
1 cup milk, scalded

¼ cup sugar
3 eggs, separated
1 teaspoon vanilla

Make a white sauce of the butter, flour, milk and sugar. Add the beaten egg yolks and vanilla, and mix these ingredients thoroughly. Then fold in the stiffly beaten egg whites. Pour the mixture into a greased soufflé dish, set it in a pan of hot water and bake it in a moderate oven (350°) for 40 to 45 minutes or until the soufflé is firm to the touch.

SHORTCAKE

2 cups all-purpose flour
4 teaspoons baking powder
¾ teaspoon salt
1 tablespoon sugar

⅓ cup shortening
⅔ cup milk
1 egg, beaten

Make crumbs with the flour, baking powder, salt, sugar and shortening. Add the milk and egg to the crumbs, then spread the mixture into a small cake pan. Make the following topping and spread it on top of the batter before baking it at 350° until done. Serve this cake with fresh fruit and milk.

½ cup sugar
½ cup flour
3 tablespoons butter

Mix together these ingredients.

WHOLE WHEAT SHORTCAKE

1 pound granulated sugar
1 pound whole wheat flour
1 pound pastry flour
1 teaspoon salt

1 quart buttermilk or sour milk
1 tablespoon soda
1 teaspoon vanilla
2 tablespoons melted butter

Put the dry ingredients, except for the soda, into a bowl. Combine the buttermilk and soda, then add it to the dry ingredients. Add the vanilla and butter last. Mix it well to create a dough that is not too thick. Bake it at 350° until done, then serve it with milk.

SUDDEN COMPANY DESSERT

Pour 3 cups of canned, thickened cherries into a graham cracker crust. Top it with whipped dessert topping, or whipped cream mixed with white cream cheese. Sprinkle graham cracker crumbs on top.

CREAMY VANILLA SAUCE

¼ cup sugar
⅛ teaspoon salt
1 teaspoon flour

1 egg, beaten
1 cup light cream or top milk
1 teaspoon vanilla

Combine the sugar, salt and flour, then stir in the egg. Gradually stir in the cream or top milk. Cook this mixture over medium heat, stirring it constantly until it thickens and coats a spoon. Remove it from the heat and stir in the vanilla. This recipe makes 1⅓ cups.

VANILLA TOPPING

2 egg whites
1 teaspoon vanilla
¾ cup light corn syrup

Beat together the egg whites and vanilla, and gradually add the syrup while still beating. Continue to beat the mixture until it is stiff and holds peaks.

This topping may be used on pies and desserts as a substitute for whipped cream.

DANISH FRUIT DESSERT SAUCE

1½ cups juice or water
¼ cup gelatin powder (any flavor)
⅓ cup white sugar

¼ teaspoon salt
1½ tablespoons cornstarch

Heat to boiling 1 cup of the juice or water. Combine the gelatin, sugar, salt and cornstarch. Make a paste of it with the remaining ½ cup of liquid, then stir it into the boiling juice until it is thick and clear. Cook it for about 1 minute, then pour it over a mixture of drained, canned fruit. Chill it well.

ICE CREAM AND TOPPINGS

HINTS FOR ICE CREAM AND TOPPINGS

- Chill the prepared ice cream mix in the refrigerator at least an hour before freezing.
- Scald the freezer can before using and rinse it with cold water.
- Crush the ice in a canvas bag with a mallet.
- Use coarse rock salt to layer with the crushed ice. Measure the ice and plan to use 1 part of salt to 8 parts of ice. After the ice cream is made and you are repacking ice around the can to hold it, use 1 part of salt to 4 parts of ice. (Using the higher proportion of salt during mixing causes ice crystals to form too quickly.)
- With the can and dasher in place, fill the can only ⅔ full. Cover and test the crank, then fill the tub to the same level with layers of the measured ice and salt. Crank the ice cream until it becomes difficult to turn. Drain off the salt water, wipe off the lid and remove it and the dasher from the can. Repack it with ice mix to hold for 1 to 2 hours.

ICE CREAM

4 quarts rich milk
4 cups sugar (brown or white)
¾ teaspoon salt
2 tablespoons flour

2 tablespoons cornstarch
4 eggs, beaten
Cream or canned milk (optional)

Heat together the 4 quarts of milk, the sugar and salt. Mix the flour, cornstarch and eggs with enough cream or milk to make a smooth sauce, then stir it into the heated milk mixture and bring it to a boil. Add the vanilla and allow it to cool thoroughly before freezing. This recipe makes 6 quarts.

CHOCOLATE CHIP ICE CREAM

2 teaspoons melted butter
2 squares (2 ounces) sweet chocolate
2 teaspoons sugar

Mix the ingredients together in a saucepan. Put it on medium heat and stir it until the chocolate is melted. After the ice cream you have made is frozen (see Vanilla Ice Cream, page 211), open the freezer can, and with a long spoon make several holes on each side of the dasher as far down as you can. Dribble in the chocolate mixture and quickly close the freezer, giving it a few turns to turn the chocolate back into chips. This recipe makes enough chocolate for 1½ gallons of ice cream.

DAIRY QUEEN

2 envelopes unflavored gelatin
½ cup cold water
4 cups whole milk
2 cups sugar

2 teaspoons vanilla
1 teaspoon salt
3 cups cream

Soak the gelatin in the cold water. Heat the milk until it is hot but not boiling, then remove it from the heat. Add the gelatin, with the sugar, vanilla and salt. Let it cool before adding the cream. Chill it in the refrigerator for 5 or 6 hours before freezing.

This recipe makes 1 gallon. The ingredients may be varied to suit your taste.

Gelatin can be bought by the pound at some health food stores. It is much cheaper that way.

JUNKET ICE CREAM

1 quart cream, OR
1 pint cream plus 1 pint top milk
18 large marshmallows
5 eggs, well-beaten
2 cups sugar

2 tablespoons vanilla
½ gallon milk
½ teaspoon salt
6 junket tablets
¼ cup lukewarm water

Heat together but do not boil the cream and marshmallows until the marshmallows are melted. Add the combined eggs, sugar and vanilla, then the milk and salt. Pour this mixture into an ice cream freezer can. Add the junket tablets to the lukewarm water, then add this to the ice cream in the freezer can. Let it set for about 20 minutes before freezing it.

Variations: *Two boxes of junket mix or instant pudding may be used instead of the junket tablets.*

ORANGE PINEAPPLE ICE CREAM

9 eggs (or fewer), beaten
3¾ cups white sugar
½ package orange drink mix
14 ounces crushed pineapple or juice

1 quart rich milk
Cream or milk
3 junket tablets, dissolved

Beat together thoroughly the eggs and sugar, then add the drink mix and pineapple. Pour this mixture into an ice cream freezer can followed by the heated rich milk. Add cream or milk to fill the can to several inches from the top. Add the dissolved junket tablets and stir. Let it set for 15 minutes, then freeze it. This recipe makes 6 quarts.

Variations: *Omit the pineapple and orange drink mix and use vanilla or lemon flavoring.*

Try brown sugar instead of white.

GELATIN ICE CREAM

4 cups milk
5 eggs
2 tablespoons flour
2½ cups sugar
2 envelopes unflavored gelatin

1 cup cold water
2 cups whipping cream
2 tablespoons vanilla
Milk

Heat the 4 cups of milk to boiling. Beat the eggs together and add the flour and ½ cup of the sugar. Stir this into the boiling milk and cook it for 1 minute, stirring constantly. Pour it over the remaining sugar which has been measured into a large bowl. Dissolve the gelatin in the cold water, and pour it into the egg mixture. Add the cream and vanilla and enough milk to fill a 1 gallon ice cream freezer can to within 2 inches of the top. Freeze it. This makes 4 quarts.

Variations: The eggs may be omitted and 2 more cups of cream added. Or this can be made without any cream at all for a less rich ice cream.

Any flavor of gelatin may be used, using 1 box (3 ounces) of fruit gelatin powder for 1 envelope of unflavored gelatin.

VANILLA ICE CREAM

1 quart milk
2 cups sugar
½ cup cornstarch
¼ teaspoon salt
1 cup cold milk
4 egg yolks

2 tablespoons milk
1 package unflavored gelatin
3 teaspoons cold milk
1 quart thick cream
1 teaspoon vanilla
4 egg whites, well-beaten

Scald the 1 quart of milk, then add the sugar, cornstarch and salt which have been blended into the 1 cup of cold milk. Cook this mixture until it is thick. Add the egg yolks which have been mixed with the 2 tablespoons of milk, then cook it for 1 minute. Add the gelatin which has been soaked in the 3 teaspoons of cold milk. Remove the cooked custard from the stove and let it cool. Add the cream, vanilla and well-beaten egg whites, then freeze it. This recipe makes 1 gallon.

Variations: For CHOCOLATE ICE CREAM, mix ½ cup of cocoa with a little boiling water, and add it to the above recipe before freezing it.

Instead of cocoa, try adding crushed fruit.

FROZEN CUSTARD

1 quart milk
6 to 8 egg yolks, well-beaten
1 cup white sugar
1 cup brown sugar
½ teaspoon salt
1 pint milk

1 cup white sugar
1 package unflavored gelatin
½ cup cold water
1 large can evaporated milk
1 pint cream

Put the 1 quart of milk into a double boiler and add the egg yolks, 1 cup of white sugar, 1 cup of brown sugar and salt. Cook this mixture until it coats a spoon. In another pan heat the 1 pint of milk and add the 1 cup of white sugar, and the gelatin which has been soaked in the cold water. Combine the mixtures and add the milk and cream. Freeze it.

CHOCOLATE TOPPING

1 cup hot chocolate mix
⅓ cup milk

1 teaspoon vanilla
1 tablespoon butter

Mix the chocolate powder and milk. Cook it over medium heat until it boils, then boil it for 3 minutes, stirring it constantly. Remove it from the heat, add the vanilla and butter, and allow it to cool.

HOT CHOCOLATE SAUCE

1 cup white sugar
3 tablespoons cocoa
½ teaspoon salt

1 cup water
3 tablespoons flour
1 teaspoon vanilla

Combine the sugar, cocoa, salt, water and flour. Cook the mixture for 3 minutes before adding the vanilla.

BUTTERSCOTCH TOPPING

1 cup brown sugar
2 tablespoons corn syrup

¼ cup rich milk
3 tablespoons butter

Combine the ingredients and heat the mixture until it boils, stirring constantly. Then simmer it for 3 minutes.

HOT FUDGE SAUCE

1½ cups evaporated milk
2 cups sugar
4 squares (4 ounces) unsweetened
    chocolate or cocoa, or less

½ teaspoon salt
¼ cup butter
1 teaspoon vanilla

Heat the milk and sugar to a rolling boil, stirring constantly. Boil it for 1 minute. Add the chocolate and salt, stirring the mixture until the chocolate is melted. Then beat it with a rotary beater until it is smooth. Remove it from the heat and stir in the butter and vanilla. Serve this sauce hot on ice cream, or chill it if desired. This recipe makes about 3 cups.

STRAWBERRY TOPPING

1 quart mashed strawberries
1 quart sugar

1 package pectin crystals
1 cup boiling water

Stir together the strawberries and sugar until the sugar is melted. Dissolve the pectin crystals in the boiling water, bring it to a boil and immediately stir it into the berry mixture. Stir it for 5 minutes, then put it into jars and freeze it.

BREAKFAST TREATS

BUCKWHEAT CAKES

2 cups buckwheat flour
2 eggs, beaten
2 teaspoons sugar
2 teaspoons baking powder

⅛ teaspoon salt
1½ cups milk
½ cup water

Mix together the ingredients and bake the batter on a hot griddle.

YEAST BUCKWHEAT CAKES

1 cake yeast
1 quart lukewarm water (approximate)
2 tablespoons sugar or molasses
2 teaspoons salt
2 tablespoons melted shortening

1 pint sifted buckwheat flour
1 pint sifted whole wheat flour
½ teaspoon soda
2 tablespoons warm water

Dissolve the yeast in 1 cup of the lukewarm water, add 1 teaspoon of the sugar and let it set for about 5 minutes. Dissolve the salt and the rest of the sugar in the remaining water, then add the shortening, dry ingredients and yeast mixture. Beat it until it is smooth. Let it rise in a warm place until it is light and full of bubbles. This will take about 1 hour or more depending on the temperature. Then dissolve the soda in the warm water and stir it into the batter. Bake the cakes thoroughly on a heated griddle and serve them with butter and syrup.

If the cakes are wanted for breakfast, prepare the batter the evening before, using only ½ cake of yeast. Do not keep it too warm. Add the soda and 2 tablespoons of warm water in the morning before baking.

EASY PANCAKES

2 cups self-rising flour
½ cup buttermilk
2 eggs

2 tablespoons sugar
1 tablespoon melted shortening
Milk

Mix together the ingredients and add enough milk to make a batter of the right consistency. Fry the pancakes on a lightly greased griddle.

CORNMEAL PANCAKES

2 cups all-purpose flour
½ cup cornmeal
½ cup whole wheat flour
1 teaspoon soda

½ teaspoon salt
2 eggs, beaten
Buttermilk or sour milk

Combine the ingredients and add buttermilk or sour milk for the desired batter consistency: use more milk for thinner cakes, less for thick cakes.

Syrup;

Bring to a boil 2 parts brown sugar to 1 part water. Add maple flavoring. Use the syrup while it is warm.

GRAHAM CAKES

1 cake yeast
2 cups warm milk
2 teaspoons brown sugar or molasses

3 eggs, separated
3 tablespoons shortening, melted
1¼ cups whole wheat flour

Dissolve the yeast in the warm milk with the brown sugar or molasses. Stir together the egg yolks, shortening and flour, then add the yeast mixture. Set it in a warm place to rise for 2 hours. Fold in the beaten egg whites just before frying.

GRIDDLE CAKES

1⅓ cups all-purpose flour
2 tablespoons sugar
3 teaspoons baking powder
3 tablespoons melted shortening or oil

1 egg
¾ teaspoon salt
1¼ cups milk

Combine all the ingredients and mix them well. Lightly grease a skillet for the first griddle cakes only. Fry them until they are puffy and bubbly, turning to brown the other side. Then serve them hot with butter and maple syrup. This recipe yields ten 6-inch griddle cakes.

PANCAKE SYRUP

1¼ cups brown sugar
¾ cup white sugar
⅓ cup molasses or corn syrup

1 cup water
1 teaspoon vanilla
Maple flavoring (optional)

Bring the sugars, molasses and water to a boil, stirring the mixture constantly. Simmer it on low heat for 5 minutes. Remove it from the heat and add the vanilla.

OATMEAL PANCAKES

2 cups all-purpose flour
2 cups whole wheat flour
2 cups quick oats
1 tablespoon each of baking powder,
    soda, salt

3 eggs, separated
½ cup cooking oil
1½ quarts sweet milk (approximate),
    warmed to lukewarm

Mix together thoroughly the dry ingredients. Add the egg yolks, oil and lukewarm milk, and mix. Fold in the beaten egg whites. Pour the batter onto a preheated, ungreased griddle, using about ¼ cup for each pancake. Turn the pancakes once.

WHOLE WHEAT PANCAKES

1½ cups whole wheat flour
½ tablespoon baking powder
¾ teaspoon salt
1 teaspoon soda

3 tablespoons brown sugar
2 eggs, beaten
1½ cups buttermilk
3 tablespoons melted shortening

Thoroughly mix together the dry ingredients. Combine the eggs, buttermilk and shortening, then add this mixture to the dry ingredients, and mix it until it is smooth. Fry the pancakes on a hot, lightly-greased griddle.

WAFFLES (CORNMEAL, RYE OR WHOLEWHEAT)

	Cornmeal	Rye	Whole Wheat
all-purpose flour	1½ cups	1 cup	
other flour	1½ cups cornmeal	2 cups rye	2 cups whole wheat
baking powder	1 tablespoon	1 tablespoon	2 teaspoons
salt	1½ teaspoons	1½ teaspoons	1 teaspoon
oil	⅓ cup	⅓ cup	¼ cup
milk	3 cups	3 cups	2 cups
eggs	5	5	4

Make a batter with the flours, baking powder, salt, oil and milk. Separate the eggs and add the yolks to the batter, then beat the whites until stiff and fold them. Bake the batter using a waffle iron. For pancakes, use a little less liquid.

GRANOLA

10 cups oatmeal
2 cups wheat germ
2 cups coconut
1 to 2 cups brown sugar
1 small package almonds

½ cup vegetable oil
½ cup honey
2 teaspoons vanilla
1 teaspoon salt

Mix together the ingredients and pour the mixture into shallow pans. Toast it at 275° for 30 to 40 minutes or until golden brown, stirring it occasionally.

Variations: There is no end of ideas on how the Granola recipe can be altered. Each person changes it according to his or her family's tastes. Following are a few suggestions.

—*For PEANUT BUTTER GRANOLA, heat the oil and honey until it is lukewarm, then stir in ⅓ to ½ cup of peanut butter.*

—*Add nuts (walnuts, pecans or whatever you prefer), wheat germ or coconut after the Granola has been toasted.*

—*Add about 1½ cups of water to the Granola and mix it, then toast.*

—*Omit the wet ingredients.*

—*Add any of the following: whole wheat flour, sesame seeds, sunflower seeds or 1 to 2 teaspoons of cinnamon.*

—*Coarse rolled oats can be used to make Granola more crunchy.*

—*Raisins and dates are also a delicious addition.*

COOKED GRAHAM CEREAL

1 cup cracked whole wheat kernels
4 cups boiling water
1 teaspoon salt

Into a pan measure the cracked whole wheat kernels, boiling water and salt. Boil this mixture for ¼ to ½ hour, stirring it occasionally. Remove it from the heat and cover it. Let it stand until it is ready to serve. Continue cooking it if the desired texture has not been reached. Serve this cereal hot with sugar and milk.

Variations: Graham Meal is also delicious. The flavor is greatly improved by using freshly ground whole wheat flour. Follow the above directions, but note that this need not be cooked so thoroughly.

Some people prefer Whole Kernel Wheat Cereal. It takes longer to cook but is an old-fashioned, chewy breakfast cereal.

Cooking the brown sugar with the cereal gives it a caramel flavor.

KALONA GRAPENUTS

5 cups flour
2 cups sugar
3 teaspoons salt
3 cups sour milk

6 cups graham flour
2½ cups cane molasses
3 teaspoons soda

Combine the ingredients to make a dough that is thick and hard to stir. Spread it in a shallow pan, and bake it at 250° for 1½ to 2 hours.

Put this into a plastic bag to avoid hard crusts. When needed, crumble it into grapenuts according to the Sieve directions (see page 219).

TOBE'S GRAPENUTS

5 pounds brown sugar
8 pounds whole wheat flour
1¼ tablespoons salt
2 tablespoons soda

2½ quarts buttermilk or sour milk
¾ pound margarine (melted)
1½ teaspoons maple flavoring
2 tablespoons vanilla

Put all the dry ingredients but the soda into a bowl, then add the milk in which the soda has been dissolved. Add the margarine and flavorings last. Mix this well. The thickness varies a little with your own whole wheat flour and store bought flour.

The dough should be fairly thick. If it is too thick, add a little more milk, and if it is not thick enough, add more whole wheat flour until it is of the right consistency.

Put the dough into pans and spread it evenly with a spoon or spatula. Bake it at 350° until done, then crumble it into grapenuts according to the Sieve instructions (see page 219). This recipe makes approximately 15 pounds.

SIEVE

This implement is required to crumble the grapenuts you have made. Make a strong rigid frame, approximately 14 x 14 inches. Over the top of this, stretch a ¼-inch wire mesh. Tack it in place, then put the frame over a large pan.

Cut the grapenuts into small pieces and rub them through the wire screen as soon as they have cooled. Spread the crumbs in pans and put them into a slow oven (250°) to toast to a golden brown. Stir them occasionally.

An inverted deep fat frying basket can also be used as a sieve.

Variations: *A crumbling sieve is handy for cleaning shelled peas. Roll the peas over the screen and the dirt will fall through.*

BREAKFAST CRUNCH

1 cup rolled oats
1 cup cornmeal
3 cups whole wheat flour
½ cup sugar
2 teaspoons baking powder

1 teaspoon soda
2 teaspoons salt
1½ cups milk
¾ cup molasses

Mix together the dry ingredients. Heat the milk and add the molasses, then mix it with the dry ingredients. Bake this mixture in a shallow pan in a moderate oven (350°). Let it cool and slice it into strips, then when it is dry, grind it finely.

CREAMY OATMEAL

2 cups coarse oatmeal
½ teaspoon salt
1 quart cold milk

Heat water in the bottom of a double boiler to boiling. Into the top part put the oatmeal, salt and milk, then put it over the boiling water for 30 minutes. It may be stirred once or twice, if desired.

COFFEE CAKE

½ cup very warm (not hot) water
1 teaspoon white sugar
1 tablespoon yeast
2 eggs
1 teaspoon salt

1 cup milk
1 cup lukewarm water
¾ cup oil or other shortening
1 cup white sugar
3 cups all-purpose flour

Stir the teaspoon of white sugar into the very warm water, then add the yeast. Let it set in a warm place while beating the eggs. Add the salt, milk, lukewarm water, oil and 1 cup of white sugar. Stir in the yeast mixture, then add the egg mixture. Mix in the flour, slowly adding more until the dough is smooth and elastic. Let it rise until it is double in size, then punch it down. Let it rise again before cutting and putting it into 4 round pans. Bake it at 350° for 20 to 30 minutes. Sprinkle brown sugar, cinnamon or nutmeg on top if desired.

EGG ON TOAST

Spread 1 tablespoon of butter over the bottom of a small hot frying pan. Lay a piece of bread in the butter and break an egg on top of it. With a fork break the yolk and spread the egg over the bread. Sprinkle it with salt and pepper. When the bread is toasted, turn it over to fry the egg side for 1 or 2 minutes.

This is good served at lunch with mayonnaise and lettuce on top of the egg.

GOLDEN EGG

Make a Basic White Sauce (see page 49) while 4 pieces of bread are toasting. When the sauce is done, slice in 4 hardcooked eggs, reserving 1 yolk. Pour the sauce over the toast on individual plates. Press the remaining yolk through a strainer and sprinkle it over the sauce as a garnish.

Variations: Chipped beef or ham may be added to the sauce.

FRENCH TOAST

2 eggs   Butter
¾ cup milk   Salt
Bread slices

Beat the eggs before adding the milk, then dip pieces of bread into the mixture. Melt and lightly brown butter in a pan, and add the coated bread pieces, sprinkling them with salt. Fry them until brown on both sides. Serve French Toast with syrup or jam.

CANDIES

BUCKEYES

1 pound peanut butter
1½ pounds icing sugar
1 cup margarine

1 package (12 ounces) chocolate chips
½ stick paraffin

Mix the peanut butter and sugar like pie dough, then add the margarine. Roll the mixture into balls and chill them thoroughly. Then melt the chocolate chips and paraffin, and dip the balls into this mixture.

CANDY KISSES

3 cups brown sugar
½ cup water
Pinch of salt

1½ teaspoons rootbeer extract
1 egg white

Cook the sugar, water and salt until it spins a thread when dropped from a spoon. Add the extract and pour it over the stiffly beaten egg white, beating while pouring. Continue to beat it until the mixture is quite stiff, then drop it by teaspoonfuls onto waxed paper.

Variations: Instead of 3 cups of brown sugar, 2 cups of maple sugar and 1 cup of brown sugar may be used.

CARAMEL CORN

2 cups white sugar
¾ cup white corn syrup or sorghum
2 tablespoons vinegar
2 tablespoons water

¼ teaspoon salt
1 teaspoon soda
1 cup peanuts (whole or chopped)
5 quarts popped corn

Melt and lightly brown the sugar. Place it over low heat when it is almost finished to prevent scorching. Then add the syrup, vinegar, water and salt. Boil the mixture to a very hard ball when tested in cold water, so that it can be snapped into pieces. Remove it from the heat, add the soda and peanuts and stir it well. Pour it immediately over the warm popped corn. Stir it a few minutes until all the popcorn is coated, then stir it occasionally until it is cold.

CARAMELS

1 cup white sugar
½ cup brown sugar (firmly packed)
½ cup light corn syrup

½ cup cream
1 cup milk
¼ cup butter

Combine the ingredients and cook the mixture over low heat to 246°, stirring it constantly. Add 2 teaspoons of vanilla and pour it into an 8-inch square greased cake pan. Let it cool, then turn it out and cut it into squares. Wrap each piece in waxed paper.

GOLDEN POPCORN

1 cup sugar
½ cup baking molasses (dark)
½ cup corn syrup
1 tablespoon butter
2 tablespoons water

1 teaspoon vinegar
¼ teaspoon soda
5 quarts popped corn
1 cup peanuts

Mix together the sugar, molasses, syrup, butter, water and vinegar. Cook the mixture until it forms a hard ball (265°) when dropped into cold water. Stir it frequently during the last part of cooking to prevent scorching. Remove it from the heat and add the soda, then stir it lightly. While it is still foaming, pour it over the popcorn and peanuts and mix them together. Pour the mixture into a buttered, flat pan, and when it has cooled, crumble it into small pieces.

POPCORN TREAT

1 quart corn syrup
3 cups white sugar
2 cups brown sugar

½ pound butter
1 teaspoon cream of tartar
Salt to taste

Boil the ingredients together to the hard crack stage (290°) on a candy thermometer. Into a large, buttered bowl pour the mixture over a lard can (4 gallons) of popped corn and stir it.

The popcorn may also be made into balls. Grease your hands well with butter or margarine and shape it into balls immediately, before the coated popcorn cools.

Use the following measurements with 2 gallons of popcorn.

2 cups corn syrup
1½ cups sugar
1 cup brown sugar

¼ pound butter
½ teaspoon cream of tartar
1 teaspoon salt

POPCORN BALLS

1 cup sugar
½ cup white or dark corn syrup
⅓ cup water
¼ cup butter

¾ teaspoon salt
¾ teaspoon vanilla
3 quarts popped corn

Keep the popcorn hot in a slow oven. Stir and cook together the sugar, corn syrup, water, butter and salt until the sugar is dissolved. Continue cooking the mixture without stirring it until the syrup forms a soft ball (236°). Add the vanilla, then pour this syrup slowly over the popped corn. Mix it well to coat every kernel. Grease your hands well with butter before shaping the mixture into balls. This recipe makes 12 medium-sized balls.

CHEERIOS BARS

½ cup light corn syrup
1 package (6 ounces) semi-sweet
  chocolate pieces

1 teaspoon vanilla
4 cups Cheerios

Heat the syrup to boiling, then remove it from the heat. Stir in the chocolate pieces and vanilla until the chocolate is melted. Add the Cheerios and stir them until they are well coated. Put the mixture into a 9 x 9 x 2-inch buttered pan. Let it cool for 1 hour before slicing it into bars. This recipe makes 3 dozen.

CHOCOLATE BALLS

1 square (1 ounce) unsweetened
  chocolate
1 can sweetened condensed milk

12 to 18 graham crackers, crushed
Coconut, shredded

In a double boiler, melt the chocolate, adding the milk. Remove it from the heat and add the crushed crackers. Form the mixture into balls and roll them in the coconut.

CHOCOLATE CANDY

3 cups sugar
3 cups milk
5 tablespoons cocoa

1 tablespoon butter
1 teaspoon vanilla

Boil together the sugar, milk and cocoa, stirring it while it is on the stove. Boil the mixture to the soft ball stage. Remove it from the heat and add the butter and vanilla. Stir it until it is creamy, then pour it onto a buttered plate and cut it into squares when it has cooled.

CHOCOLATE-COVERED CHERRIES

1 cup sifted all-purpose flour
⅓ cup brown sugar
½ cup butter or margarine
¼ teaspoon salt

18 maraschino cherries, well drained
  and halved
6 squares (6 ounces) semi-sweet
  chocolate, melted

Combine the flour and sugar. Cut the butter and salt into the flour mixture until it resembles a pie dough. Press it into an 8 x 8 x 2-inch pan, and bake it at 350° for 20 minutes. While it is warm, cut it into 36 squares. Cool and place them in a pan lined with waxed paper. Place a cherry half on each square and cover each cherry with a spoonful of melted chocolate. Chill them for a few minutes until the chocolate hardens.

YUMMY CHOCOLATE SQUARES

1 package marshmallows
1 package (12 ounces) semi-sweet
  chocolate bits
3 tablespoons butter

1 teaspoon vanilla
1 cup broken walnut meats
½ teaspoon salt
1 cup crisp rice cereal

Melt the marshmallows, chocolate and butter over low heat, stirring the mixture constantly until all is melted. Mix in the remaining ingredients and spread it in a well-buttered 8-inch pan. Cut it into squares after it sets.

FUDGE MELTAWAYS

½ cup butter
1 square (1 ounce) unsweetened
  chocolate
¼ cup sugar
1 teaspoon vanilla

1 egg, beaten
2 cups graham cracker crumbs
1 cup shredded coconut
½ cup chopped nuts

Melt the butter and chocolate in a saucepan. Blend the sugar, vanilla, egg, graham cracker crumbs, coconut and nuts into the butter/chocolate mixture. Mix it thoroughly and press it into an 11½ x 7½ x 1½ baking dish or a 9 x 9-inch square pan. Refrigerate it while making the filling as follows.

¼ cup butter
1 tablespoon milk or cream
2 cups sifted icing sugar

1 teaspoon vanilla
1½ squares (1½ ounces) unsweetened
  chocolate, melted

Cream together the butter, milk, sugar and vanilla. Mix and spread it over the crumb mixture, then chill it in the refrigerator. Pour the melted chocolate over the chilled mixture and spread it evenly.

CREAMY-SURE FUDGE

⅔ cup (1 small can) evaporated milk
16 marshmallows, OR
1 cup Marshmallow Creme
  (see page 228)
1⅓ cups sugar

¼ cup butter or margarine
¼ teaspoon salt
2 cups semi-sweet chocolate pieces
1 teaspoon vanilla
1 cup coarsely chopped walnuts

Mix the first 5 ingredients in a saucepan, stirring the mixture constantly. Heat it to boiling and boil it for 5 minutes only. Remove it from the heat, then add the chocolate, stirring until it is melted. Stir in the vanilla and walnuts. Spread the mixture in an 8-inch pan and cool it until firm. This recipe makes about 2 pounds of fudge.

SNOWY FUDGE

2 cups sugar
⅔ cup milk
1½ cups peanut butter

1 cup Marshmallow Creme
  (see page 228)
1 teaspoon vanilla

Cook the sugar and milk to 234° or until the syrup forms a soft ball which flattens when removed from water. Add the other ingredients and mix them well. Pour the mixture into a buttered 8 x 6 x 2-inch pan.

This candy can be stored for months and still be soft and edible.

STORE-AWAY FUDGE

4½ cups sugar
½ cup butter or margarine
1 can condensed milk
2 large chocolate bars
2 cups chocolate chips

1 pint marshmallows
1 teaspoon vanilla
½ teaspoon black walnut flavoring
  (optional)
½ cup chopped nuts (optional)

Bring the first 3 ingredients to a boil, then boil the mixture for 7 minutes or until the soft ball stage. Remove it from the heat and add the chocolate bars (cut into small pieces), chocolate chips, marshmallows (cut into pieces), vanilla, and flavoring and nuts if desired. Beat the mixture until it is smooth and pour it into a pan as you would regular fudge.

MARSHMALLOWS

2 cups sugar
¾ cup boiling water
2 envelopes unflavored gelatin
½ cup cold water
½ teaspoon salt

1 teaspoon vanilla
Icing sugar
Chopped nuts (optional)
Coconut (optional)

Boil together the sugar and water until a thread forms when the syrup is dropped from a spoon. Remove it from the heat. Soften the gelatin in the cold water, then add it to the hot syrup and stir it until the gelatin is dissolved. Let it stand until it is partly cool, then add the salt and flavoring. Beat it until the mixture becomes thick, fluffy and soft.

Pour it into an 8 x 4-inch pan thickly covered with icing sugar. Have the mixture 1 inch in depth. Let it stand in the refrigerator until it is thoroughly chilled. With a sharp, wet knife, loosen it around the edges of the pan. Turn it out onto a board lightly floured with icing sugar. Cut it into squares and roll them in icing sugar, chopped nuts or coconut.

MARSHMALLOW CRÈME

2 cups sugar
2½ cups corn syrup
1 cup water

½ cup warm corn syrup
3 or 4 egg whites
1 teaspoon vanilla

Cook the sugar, corn syrup and water to 242° (a medium-hard ball when tested in cold water). While this is cooking, place in a mixing bowl the warm syrup and the egg whites. Beat them slowly until they are mixed, then beat the mixture hard until it is light and fluffy. Pour the first mixture into this in a fine stream. When all is mixed, beat it hard for 3 minutes before adding the vanilla. Store it in cans or jars, but do not cover it until it is cold.

MINT CANDY

2 cups sugar
¼ cup butter
⅔ cup cold water

Mint flavoring
Food coloring

Boil the ingredients to 267 to 270°, then add flavoring and coloring. Pour the mixture onto a buttered marble slab or greased cookie sheet. Pull it like taffy, then roll it in icing sugar on brown paper. Cut the candy into squares and put it into jars. It will mellow in a day or two.

The candy can be made in different flavors—anise, wintergreen, peppermint and so on, and the coloring can be added according to the flavor.

HARD TACK CANDY

1¾ pounds white sugar
1 cup water
1 cup corn syrup

Cook the ingredients together to 280°, then add coloring. Leave the mixture on the heat until it reaches 290°, then remove it and add ⅛ ounce of the chosen flavoring (peppermint, spearmint, wintergreen, thyme, anise, cinnamon etc.—make each flavor a different color). Pour it at once onto a greased cookie sheet or marble slab. As soon as it is cool enough to work with (you can begin cutting at the edges almost immediately) cut it with scissors into strips and various-sized pieces.

IDA'S FONDANT CANDY

3 cups sugar
1 cup corn syrup
½ cup hot water

1 cup sugar
½ cup hot water
2 egg whites

Combine the first 3 ingredients in a saucepan and boil the mixture until it spins a thread. Do the same for the next 2 ingredients. Whip the egg whites until they are stiff, then slowly beat in the second mixture until it stiffens again. Add the first mixture to this, and beat it until it cools.

It may then be divided into parts so that different flavors can be added as desired. Then form the candy into shapes and dip it into melted chocolate.

MACAROONS

⅔ cup sweetened condensed milk
3 cups shredded coconut
1 teaspoon vanilla

Mix together the milk and coconut. Add the vanilla and drop the mixture by spoonfuls about 1 inch apart onto a greased baking sheet. Bake them in a moderate oven (350°) for 10 minutes or until delicately browned. Remove the macaroons from the pan at once. This recipe makes 30 macaroons.

OPERA CREAMS

1½ cups sugar
½ cup cream

2 tablespoons butter
1 square (1 ounce) chocolate

Boil the ingredients together to a soft ball (236°), testing it in cold water. Remove it from the heat and add 1 teaspoon of vanilla. Let it cool without stirring, then beat it until it becomes light in color. Drop it onto waxed paper.

PEANUT BRITTLE

1½ cups sugar
½ cup white corn syrup
⅔ cup water
1½ cups raw peanuts

½ teaspoon salt
2 tablespoons butter
1 teaspoon soda
1 teaspoon vanilla

In a 4-quart saucepan, combine the sugar, corn syrup and water. Cook this mixture to the soft ball stage (238°) on a candy thermometer, stirring it only until the sugar is dissolved. Add the peanuts and salt. Cook the mixture to the hard crack stage (290°), then remove it from the heat. Add the butter, soda and vanilla. Stir it thoroughly and pour it at once onto a well-buttered sheet or slab. Spread it thinly and let it cool before breaking the candy into pieces.

CHOCOLATE PEANUT CLUSTERS

½ pound sweet chocolate
⅔ cup sweetened condensed milk
1 cup peanuts

Melt the chocolate in the top of a double boiler over boiling water. Remove it from the heat, add the condensed milk and peanuts, and mix them well. Drop the mixture by teaspoons onto waxed paper, and allow it to cool.

NUTTY BARS

2 cups white sugar
1 cup corn syrup

1 cup water
¾ cup peanut butter

Cook the above ingredients until the mixture forms a hard ball when tested in cold water. Let it stand until cool, then add the peanut butter. Stir it until it is cold. Shape the mixture into rolls as thick as your thumb and 2 inches long.

1 cup corn syrup
½ cup brown sugar

2 pounds ground peanuts
Melted semi-sweet chocolate

Cook the syrup and sugar together until the mixture forms a hard ball when tested in cold water. Dip the previously prepared rolls into this mixture, then roll them in the ground peanuts while the coating is still hot. Coat them with melted semi-sweet chocolate.

SWEETENED CONDENSED MILK

Boil together 1 part sugar to 2 parts milk until the mixture thickens. This should occur at 225°, or 'jelly' on a candy thermometer.

ROCKY ROAD SQUARES

3 pounds milk chocolate
½ pound soft butter

10 ounces miniature marshmallows
3 pounds walnuts, broken

Melt the chocolate and stir it until it is smooth. Add the butter and mix it well (it will be thick but warm). Set the mixture in a cold place until it thickens around the edges, stirring it occasionally while it cools. Then put it in a warm place and stir it for 5 to 10 minutes until it becomes creamy and thinner. Add the marshmallows and walnuts. Pour the mixture onto a waxed paper-lined cookie sheet, and press it to a ¾-inch thickness. Let it cool to room temperature, then cut it into squares.

TAFFY

1 quart white sugar
1 pint cream
1 tablespoon gelatin dissolved in
¼ cup cold water

1 tablespoon paraffin
1 pint light corn syrup

Combine all the ingredients and boil the mixture until it forms a hard ball in cold water when dropped from a tablespoon (250° on a candy thermometer). Pour it onto a well-greased cookie sheet. When it is cool enough to handle, start pulling it. When an ivory color is obtained, pull the taffy into a long thin rope and cut it with kitchen scissors.

DRINKS

CANNING APPLE OR PEAR JUICE

Heat the juice, but do not boil it. Remove any scum with a spoon. Fill bottles or jars and seal them. Set them in hot water and bring them to the boiling point, then remove them from the water immediately.

By not boiling apple juice, it retains its fresh flavor.

CHOCOLATE SYRUP

4 cups brown sugar
2 cups cocoa
½ cup corn syrup
4 cups white sugar

2 cups water
2 cups water
4 tablespoons or ¼ cup vanilla

Mix the first 5 ingredients in a 6-quart kettle until all are blended. Add the remaining 2 cups of water and stir the mixture again. Bring it to a boil and boil it for 5 minutes. (Be careful as it is likely to boil over.) Add the vanilla. If you do not can the syrup, cover it until it is cool or a crust will form over the top. This makes approximately 3 quarts.

It will keep for 8 months (or through the school year) if it is put boiling hot into jars and sealed.

GRAPE JUICE

5 pounds grapes
1 pound sugar
1 quart water

Wash and stem the grapes, then add the water and boil them for 10 minutes. Strain, but do not press them. Add the sugar, stirring until it is dissolved, then bring the mixture to a boil. Bottle the juice. Add water before serving, about 50%.

Concord or Fredonia grapes are best for juice.

Variations: For GRAPE SAUCE, put the pulp through the sieve, add sugar to taste, and can the sauce.

CONCORD GRAPE JUICE

Wash fully ripened Concord grapes and spoon them into a quart jar until it is ⅓ full. Add 1 cup of sugar and water to fill the jar. Seal it and boil for 10 minutes.

FRUIT PUNCH

3 cups sugar
3 quarts water
4 large cans frozen orange juice

4 large cans frozen lemonade
1½ cups strong tea
4 quarts ginger ale

Boil together the sugar and water. Let it stand until it is cool, then add the frozen orange juice, frozen lemonade, tea and ginger ale. Add water to taste. This recipe makes enough for 75 people.

RHUBARB JUICE

Cut rhubarb coarsely. Cover it with water and boil it for 2 minutes. Drain off the juice. Cover the cooked rhubarb a second time with water, then bring it to a boil and drain it again. The rhubarb may be sweetened for canning.

Rhubarb juice may be added to other fruit juices, or with a little lemon juice to meadow tea for a deliciously refreshing cold drink.

QUICK ROOT BEER

2 cups white sugar
1 gallon lukewarm water

4 teaspoons root beer extract
1 teaspoon dry yeast

Dissolve the sugar in some hot water, then combine it with the rest of the ingredients. Put the mixture into jars, cover them and set them in the sun for 4 hours. The root beer will be ready to serve the next day. Chill it before serving. (There is no need to bottle it.)

ICED TEA SYRUP

4 cups boiling water
1 cup loose tea
2½ cups sugar

Let the tea steep in the boiling water for 15 minutes. Strain it, then add the sugar and boil it for about 10 minutes. This will make a quart of syrup, or 1 gallon of iced tea, depending on the strength desired.

To use it, put 1 tablespoon of the syrup in a glass, then fill it with water and ice.

GOLDEN PUNCH

7 packages orange drink mix
4 large cans frozen orange juice
5 large bottles (28 ounces each) lemon-
  lime soft drink

Mix the drink mix according to package instructions, then combine it with the rest of the ingredients. This makes 5 gallons.

GOOD LUCK PUNCH

1 quart rhubarb (2 dozen stalks)   Juice of 6 lemons
Water to cover   1 cup pineapple juice
3 cups sugar   Rhubarb juice
2 cups water   1 quart ginger ale

Cut the rhubarb into 1-inch pieces. Add enough water to cover it. Cook it until soft, for about 10 minutes, then drain it through a cheesecloth bag. This should produce approximately 3 quarts of juice. Dissolve the sugar in the 2 cups of water and cook it for 10 minutes to make a syrup. Add the lemon, pineapple and rhubarb juices. Pour this over a chunk of ice in a punch bowl, and just before serving, add the ginger ale. This recipe makes 1 gallon of punch.

SUMMER SPARKLE PUNCH

2 packages (3 ounces each) strawberry   2 cans (12 ounces each) frozen
  gelatin powder   lemonade, slightly thawed
2 cups boiling water   3 bottles (28 ounces each) ginger ale

Dissolve the gelatin powder in the water, stir in the lemonade and add the ginger ale. This recipe makes 1 gallon.

PEPPERMINT WATER

Sweeten a pitcher of cold water. Dip a toothpick into a bottle of peppermint oil, then swish it off in the water. Do this a few times until the right strength is obtained. Stir the water before tasting it. (Synthetic peppermint oil is not recommended.)

This is a healthy drink and good on hot days for people working under the sun.

INSTANT SPICED TEA

2½ cups sugar
2 cups instant powdered orange drink
½ cup instant tea

2 teaspoons cinnamon
2 teaspoons cloves
2 large packages instant lemonade mix

Mix the ingredients together, and store the mixture in tightly sealed containers. To use it, place approximately 2 teaspoons of the mix into each cup of boiling water.

This is sometimes called Russian Tea. You may add to or reduce the amount of spices and lemonade mix according to family taste.

TOMATO COCKTAIL

1 peck tomatoes
2 bunches celery
2 green peppers
1 bunch parsley

6 small onions
1 cup sugar
¼ cup salt
½ teaspoon pepper (scant)

Cook the vegetables together until they are soft, then put them through a sieve. To the vegetable juice add the sugar, salt and pepper, then pour the liquid into sterilized jars. Cold pack them for a few minutes.

VEGETABLE DRINK

2 quarts celery
2 to 4 red beets
6 carrots
4 onions

Juice of 3 lemons, plus grated rind
2 gallons tomato juice
Salt to taste

Cook the celery, beets, carrots and onions separately until they are very soft. Mash them very finely, strain and add the lemon juice and rind and tomato juice. Add salt to taste, then cold pack the juice in jars for 10 minutes.

LEFTOVERS

LEFTOVER BREAD

Cut leftover bread into cubes and toast it in pans in the oven, stirring it a few times. When it is toasted and well dried out, store it in tightly sealed containers. It can be used in soups, dressings, tossed salads (adding them just before serving) and many other dishes.

Leftover bread can also be dried out completely over the stove, and stored in lard cans or jars. When you are ready to use it, place the bread slices in the steamer and steam them until they are heated through. Serve the bread warm. If you have no steamer, use a colander over a pan of hot water, and keep it covered.

You can pour bacon grease over pieces of leftover bread or toast, then let it harden. Put a string through the center of the bread and tie it to a tree branch for birds.

CHOCOLATE BREAD CUSTARD

2 squares (2 ounces) unsweetened
   chocolate
3 cups scalded milk
4 cups bread crumbs

$\frac{3}{4}$ cup sugar
$\frac{1}{4}$ teaspoon salt
3 eggs, well-beaten

Combine the chocolate and milk, then heat and stir the mixture until the chocolate melts. Add the bread, sugar and salt. Slowly stir this into the beaten eggs. Pour it into a greased 10 x 6 x 2-inch pan and set this pan in a pan of hot water. Bake it in a moderate oven (350°) for about 50 minutes or until a knife inserted comes out clean. Serve this custard warm with Creamy Vanilla Sauce (see page 208).

Old-Fashioned Bread Custard;

Omit the chocolate and add 1 teaspoon of nutmeg. Less sugar may be used if desired ($\frac{1}{3}$ cup).

LEFTOVER BUTTERMILK

Pour 1 cup of fresh water into your leftover buttermilk before storing it. Pour off the water which comes to the top when you are ready to use the buttermilk again.

LEFTOVER CAKE

Make large crumbs of leftover cake and put them into a serving dish. Cover them with the following sauce.

Nutmeg Sauce;

2 cups water   2 tablespoons butter
¼ cup sugar   ⅛ teaspoon nutmeg
3 tablespoons flour

Mix the first 3 ingredients and bring them to a boil. Boil the mixture for a few minutes, stirring it constantly. Add the butter and nutmeg. Let it cool before pouring it over the cake crumbs. Sliced bananas or nuts may be added.

LEFTOVER HOMEMADE CANDY

Leftover candy and candy that did not turn out right can be used for cake frosting. Add water or milk to the candy and place it over low heat to melt it. Mix it to the right consistency.

LEFTOVER COOKED CEREAL

Stir milk into leftover cooked cereal before storing it. Serve it as a dessert by adding whipped cream, apples, raisins or other raw fruit. Leftover cake crumbs or apple roll may also be added.

LEFTOVER CREAM OF WHEAT OR ROLLED OATS

These may be added to hamburger or sausage. Mix it thoroughly and make it into patties or a loaf.

LEFTOVER CHEESE

Old cheese turns into a delicious spread when it is processed through a meat grinder with several chunks of onion.

LEFTOVER MACARONI

If there is not enough macaroni to go around, toast bread cubes in butter in a frying pan. Add the macaroni and enough milk to soak into the bread and to keep the macaroni from burning. Heat the mixture.

Leftover macaroni may also be added to vegetable soup, chili soup, potato salad or stews.

LEFTOVER COLESLAW

This is good when it is cooked before serving. Add a white sauce made with 1 tablespoon of flour and ½ cup of cream.

LEFTOVER FRUIT

FRUIT CAKE

1½ cups brown sugar	2 cups fruit (canned or fresh), mashed
2 teaspoons soda	2 eggs
2 cups all-purpose flour	½ cup salad oil
½ teaspoon salt	

Sift together the brown sugar, soda, flour and salt. Make a well and add the fruit, eggs and oil. Mix these ingredients, then bake the batter at 350°. When it is done, top it with the following icing and return it to the oven for a few minutes.

¼ pound butter	¾ cup brown sugar
¼ cup evaporated milk	¾ cup chopped nuts

Combine the butter, milk and brown sugar, and cook the mixture for 1 minute before adding the nuts.

To use up leftover fruit syrup from canned fruit, add an equal amount of water to the syrup and thicken it with tapioca (3 tablespoons tapioca to 1 pint of liquid). A pinch of salt and a package of flavored gelatin powder adds to the taste. Whipped cream may also be blended into the cooled tapioca.

LEFTOVER PANCAKE BATTER

Do not throw out leftover batter. Add a little milk to make it thinner, then dip your hamburgers or other meat into the batter and fry them in hot oil.

LEFTOVER PICKLE JUICE

Save your leftover pickle juice for recanning. Use it for making relish, sandwich spread, or to can red beets (adding more vinegar, sugar, etc.) or make salad dressing. When you use the juice in salad dressing, omit the vinegar and sugar in the recipe.

LEFTOVER PICKLED BEET JUICE

Hardcooked eggs are good when left overnight in pickled beet juice.

LEFTOVER CHURCH CHEESE

Cut up the cheese and put it in the top of a double boiler. Add 2 tablespoons of margarine or butter and 1 tablespoon of water. Boil it until the cheese is melted. Pour it into wide-mouthed jars and seal them. Cold pack the jars for ½ hour, or until the cheese looks smooth. When you are ready to use it, put the jar into warm water until the cheese loosens from the sides of the jar—it will slide out easily. Slice and serve it.

LEFTOVER MACARONI AND CHEESE

Beat 2 eggs and add a little salt and 1½ cups of milk. Pour this over 4 to 5 cups of macaroni and bake it at 350° until brown. Extra cheese may be sprinkled on top if desired.

LEFTOVER NOODLES

Put about 1 or 2 tablespoons of grease into a frying pan. When it has melted, sprinkle in about 1 tablespoon of flour with a flour shaker. Cut the leftover noodles into slices and lay them in the floury grease. Fry them.

Leftover noodles are also good when added to vegetable soup.

LEFTOVER PIE DOUGH
HANS WASCHTLIN

Roll out the dough thinly. Spread it with apple butter and roll it up like a jelly roll. Cut it into ½-inch slices. Lay them on a pie pan with the cut side down, and bake them at 350° for 20 to 25 minutes.

These are a real treat for children.

SUGAR PIES

Roll out the dough thinly, then fit it into a small tin foil pan or any 4 to 6-inch pan. Onto the crust put 2 tablespoons of brown sugar, 1 tablespoon of flour, ½ cup of water and nutmeg to taste. A bit of cream may be added. Mix it with your finger or the back of a spoon, and bake it at 350° until the crust is done.

This makes a great treat for children.

BROKEN, BAKED PIE CRUSTS

These can be refreshed by putting them into the oven for a few minutes. Add them to applesauce just before serving. Then stir in cream (whipped or unwhipped) and blend. Cinnamon may also be added.

LEFTOVER POTATOES

To make Potato Filling with leftover mashed potatoes, cook the greenest part of 1 stalk of celery and 1 chopped onion. With juice and all, pour it over the mashed potatoes and mix. Add 2 eggs and milk according to the amount of potatoes used. Then add 4 or 5 slices of cubed bread which have been toasted in 2 tablespoons of butter. Pour the mixture into a buttered baking dish and bake it for about 1 hour at 350°. Leftover corn, peas, lima beans or diced meat may be added.

To approximately 2 cups of leftover mashed potatoes, add 3 eggs, ⅓ cup milk, 1 small chopped onion, 2 or 3 slices of bread made into crumbs and salt and pepper to taste. Mix everything together and put it into a hot, buttered skillet. Cover the mixture and heat it slowly.

Cold sweet potatoes are good when sliced very thinly, dipped into a beaten egg with a little salt added, then into flour. Quickly brown the slices in a skillet. Other potatoes may be treated in the same way.

Potato Salad may be made with leftover mashed potatoes, adding other ingredients the same as you do for salad made with diced potatoes.

FRIED POTATOES

Use fried, cooked or mashed potatoes. Put them into a hot greased frying pan and chop them. Beat an egg or two with a fork, pour it over the potatoes and fry them. (One tablespoon of flour blended with 1 beaten egg and ¾ cup of milk may be added instead of the 2 beaten eggs.) If there are not enough potatoes, toast bread cubes in the pan first, then add the potatoes. Add salt and pepper.

POTATO CAKES

2 cups medium grated, peeled, cooked
   potatoes, or mashed potatoes
2 eggs
½ teaspoon salt

1 medium onion, chopped
Dash of pepper
⅛ to ¼ cup chopped, leftover bologna
   or dried beef (optional)

Mix together the above ingredients, then fry the mixture as you would pancakes.

POTATO CHEESE PIE

Crust;

2 to 2½ cups leftover mashed potatoes
2 tablespoons flour
1 teaspoon baking powder

1 egg
2 tablespoons melted butter
Salt and pepper

Mix the ingredients thoroughly, then pat the mixture into a large, greased pie plate as you would dough.

Filling;

2 eggs
1 cup cream

Salt and pepper
¾ cup grated Velveeta cheese

Beat the eggs, then stir in the cream and seasonings. Pour this into the potato crust and sprinkle the top with the cheese. Bake it at 350° for 20 minutes or until a knife inserted in the center comes out clean.

POTATO PUFFS

1 cup leftover mashed potatoes
1 or 2 beaten eggs
¼ teaspoon salt

¼ to ½ cup flour
1 teaspoon baking powder

Mix the ingredients together well and drop the mixture by the ½ teaspoon into deep fat. Fry the puffs until brown on both sides.

POTATO SOUP

Cook a small chopped onion until it is soft. Add milk as desired. When it is hot, mix some in with leftover mashed potatoes until blended. Pour all back into the remainder of the milk, and heat it to the boiling point. Add a chunk of butter and a bit of chopped parsley, salt and pepper.

LEFTOVER SQUASH

Squash may be added to caramel pudding by mashing it and adding it to the milk.

It can also be used in pumpkin pie recipes, or made into custard by eliminating the crust. Just set the casserole into a pan of hot water to bake.

LEFTOVER RICE

This, like leftover cereal, can be prepared as a dessert. Prepare the Basic Custard Recipe (see page 189) then add leftover rice, and bake.

GLORIFIED RICE

2 cups boiled rice
1 cup pineapple, cubed or crushed
½ cup sugar

24 marshmallows
1 cup chopped apples
1 cup whipped cream

Cook the rice until it is soft, but not mushy. Let it cool. (Leftover rice can be used.) Mix together all the ingredients but the whipped cream and let it stand for 1 hour. Fold the whipped cream into the mixture just before serving. Garnish it with candied cherries.

LEFTOVER VEGETABLE AND MEAT DISHES

Use your leftover meat, potatoes, gravy and vegetables by placing them in layers in a pan or casserole. Add meat broth or tomato juice, herbs or spices. Make a plain biscuit dough and drop it by spoonfuls into the mixture and bake. Serve it with applesauce.

Mix together all your leftovers. Add beaten eggs, some milk and diced onions, and season the mixture well. Put it into a greased baking dish and bake it at 350° until bubbly.

Leftover meat, potatoes and vegetables can be made into dressing by adding diced toast, eggs, milk and seasoning.

Add canned hamburger to leftover meat gravy or tomato gravy. Add leftover string beans, put leftover potatoes on top and sprinkle paprika over the potatoes. Bake it at 350° until it is heated through.

Bits of leftover ham can be ground and mixed with bread crumbs which have been soaked in a milk and egg mixture. Shape the mixture into patties and fry them. This makes real hamburgers.

LEFTOVER CHICKEN

Cook macaroni until it is soft. Mix it with diced leftover chicken and gravy. Put the mixture into a baking dish and add milk to cover it. Season it with salt and pepper and top it with bread crumbs. Bake it at 350° for about 20 to 30 minutes.

LEFTOVER BEEF

Grind any leftover beef. Brown butter in a saucepan and add a little milk. To this, add the ground beef and enough milk to make the meat stick together. Stir in 1 tablespoon of flour and 1 egg. Drop the mixture by tablespoons into cracker or bread crumbs, coating it well. Then fry it in hot fat.

LEFTOVER ROAST BEEF

Prepare 1 package of onion soup mix according to the package directions, and add peeled chopped carrots. Cook it until the carrots are tender. Thicken it with a flour and water paste. Add sliced, cooked roast beef, then pour it into a greased casserole. Top it with mashed potatoes. Brush it with butter and brown it in the oven. Serve this with a crisp green salad and French bread.

SHEPHERD'S PIE

In a greased baking dish, spread out leftover meat. Top it with leftover vegetables and dot these with leftover mashed potatoes. Pour gravy over all. Bake this until it is heated through.

Tomato juice or ½ cup of milk blended with 1 beaten egg may be poured over the top before baking, instead of the gravy.

LEFTOVER WIENERS

Cook sliced potatoes in water, adding salt to taste. Add sliced wieners for the last 5 or 10 minutes of cooking. When they are about done, add a small amount of cream.

Instead of wieners, sliced smoked pork sausage is good. Cook the sausage with the potatoes.

CORNED BEEF PUDDING

3 eggs, slightly beaten
2 or 3 cups corn (fresh, frozen or
   canned)
4 tablespoons flour (scant)
¼ teaspoon pepper

1 teaspoon salt
2 cups rich milk
1 cup diced, cooked beef (or other
   meat)
2 tablespoons butter

Add the eggs to the corn. Stir in the flour and season it as desired. Add the milk and meat and pour it into a buttered baking dish, dotting the top with butter. Set the baking dish in a pan of warm water and bake it at 350° for about 35 minutes or until a knife inserted comes out clean.

TRAMP'S HASH

Cut up leftover sausage or beef. Cook 6 medium-sized potatoes (or according to family size) and 2 sliced onions with the meat and meat stock until they are soft. Before serving, add enough bread crumbs to soak up the meat stock.

OLD-FASHIONED POT PIE

Add 2 diced potatoes, 1 cup of finely cut celery and 2 tablespoons of minced onions (optional) to 1 quart of leftover meat broth (ham, beef or chicken). While this is boiling, make a dough of 2 beaten eggs, ¼ teaspoon of salt, ½ cup of milk, ¼ teaspoon of baking powder and enough flour to make a stiff biscuit-like dough. Roll it out thinly and cut it into squares. Drop it into the meat broth and cook it for 10 to 15 minutes. Add parsley before serving.

The dough may also be made as follows. Combine 2 beaten eggs, ¼ cup of water, 1 tablespoon of shortening and enough flour to make a thick dough. Roll it out, cut it into squares, then add it to the broth.

CORN FRITTERS

Separate 2 eggs for each cup of drained corn. Beat the egg whites until they are stiff, then add the corn and yolks. Form the mixture into patties and fry them in butter.

STRING BEAN CASSEROLE

Cook together until partly soft 1 quart of string beans cut into small pieces, 1 quart of diced potatoes and 1 or 2 diced carrots. Then mix in leftover beef and gravy, seasoned salt and salt to taste. Pour this into a casserole and bake it at 350° for 45 minutes. Serve this with a salad and dessert.

LEFTOVER GRAVY

Leftover tomato or meat gravy may be mixed with vegetable soup or stews.

TOMATO GRAVY

Chunk 1 quart of canned hamburger into a heavy skillet. Add leftover tomato gravy. If it is too thick, thin it with milk or tomato juice, or a little cream. This is good with corn bread or hot biscuits, or with cooked navy beans and applesauce. (If you have a small amount of fresh strawberries, mix them with the applesauce.)

LEFTOVER SOUP

Leftover soup which was made with hot milk and bread may be mixed with eggs and more bread crumbs if it is too thin, and fried in patties like pancakes.

SCHOOL LUNCHES

HINTS FOR SCHOOL LUNCHES

- *Do not cut lettuce wedges unless you want to use the remainder of the lettuce within a few hours. The edges of the cut lettuce will turn brown. With head lettuce, use it leaf by leaf and it will keep better*

- *Be sure that eggs are freshly cooked when you put them in a lunch bucket. When hardcooked eggs become too old, they may cause serious stomach disorders.*

SANDWICH OR SALAD SUGGESTIONS

Following are various ideas on the different combinations of foods that may be mixed with mayonnaise for a sandwich or salad.

—2 chopped, hardcooked eggs, 2 chopped pickles and a handful of peanuts, lightly crushed

—mashed cooked eggs (egg salad)

—flaked tuna and hardcooked eggs (tuna salad)

—ham, chicken, ground canned beef, liverwurst, or any meat which may be diced

—a variety of flavors may be added to ground meat: diced onions, dash of garlic, sprouts, pickles (with some pickle juice), grated carrots, finely diced celery, lettuce and chopped cabbage, as well as spices, seasonings or herbs, parsley, dill, chives, Worcestershire sauce and sage

—grind 1 tongue, chop 2 medium-sized sweet pickles and 1 large sweet apple, adding salt to taste (tongue salad)

—½ cup grated Cheddar cheese, 1 tablespoon of honey, ½ cup of pitted, chopped dates, mixed with milk, cream or mayonnaise

Spread peanut butter on bread. Top it with mayonnaise and lightly chopped or thinly sliced bananas.

Put salad dressing in the sandwich, and the lettuce in a plastic bag so that the child can add the lettuce at school. It will be crisper this way.

Try softening a package of cream cheese and adding some chopped nuts. Spread it on slices of Date and Nut Bread (see page 23).

For unusual flavor treats, try creaming one of your favorite seasonings into the butter. Mustard, horseradish, parsley, chives, curry powder, minced onion, celery salt and even a light hint of garlic will bring a welcome touch of flavor to the sandwiches.

247

ADDITIONAL SUGGESTIONS

—ice cream in a wide-mouthed thermos, served with a piece of pie

—freezer cabbage slaw

—cabbage wedges, with or without peanut butter

—carrot sticks

—grated carrots on buttered bread

—celery sticks filled with peanut butter or soft cheese

—apple halves filled with peanut butter

—prunes stuffed with cream cheese or nut paste

—dates, raisins, figs or dried apples

—sliced radishes on buttered bread

—popcorn

—hotdogs, sliced lengthwise, in a thermos, with ketchup or mustard on bread

—applesauce with strawberry gelatin

—cottage cheese, topped with applesauce

—cottage cheese with raisins and nuts

—soda crackers with peanut butter

—custard or pumpkin custard made in custard cups (set in hot water to bake)

—different kinds of bread for variety

—ground raisins, dates and nuts mixed with coconut

DESSERT SUGGESTIONS

DANISH DESSERT

Add 3 or 4 cups of water plus sugar to taste to 2 pints frozen or 1 quart canned strawberries. Let this come to the boiling point, then add enough cornstarch so that it is a little runny. Remove it from the heat and add 5 rounded tablespoons of fruit flavored gelatin. (This is cheaper when you buy it by the pound.)

Fill a week's supply of baby food jars with this dessert or with hot cooked caramel pudding. Keep it refrigerated. The jars often seal, which keeps the pudding from spoiling.

SCHOOL ICE CREAM

By the time winter rolls around, the young scholars are tired of the same things in their lunch buckets. A simple, yet delicious dessert can be made by cooking cornstarch (see Basic Vanilla Pudding, page 190). Cool it, then add whipped cream. Spoon it into a tumbler with a lid. When the children get to school, they set the tumbler outside and let it freeze (for those of you in northern climes!).

THERMOS POTATO SOUP

Dice and cook potatoes with parsley and onions. While they are cooking, melt a few tablespoons of margarine or butter in a pan. Add a heaping tablespoon of flour. Brown it slowly, then add milk, stirring it all the time. Let it boil then pour it over the soft potatoes. Grated hardcooked eggs may be added.

Variations: Fry bacon, then use the grease to make a pan sauce. Proceed as above, and add the bacon to the soup.

ADDITIONAL SUGGESTIONS

Crunchy or smooth peanut butter mixed in with leftover frosting, milk and icing sugar makes a very delicious snack. Put it between graham crackers.

Make a paste of icing sugar and milk. Add peanut butter to taste. Spread it between graham crackers.

Make Iced Tea Syrup (see page 234), then follow the simple directions for a quick tea to take to school in a thermos.

Homemade cereal is good to take to school. Send along a thermos with cold milk.

MIXES

BASIC CAKE MIX

10 cups all-purpose flour
5 tablespoons double-acting baking
    powder
5 teaspoons salt

7 cups sugar
1 cup dry milk
2½ cups shortening

Sift together the dry ingredients 3 times. Rub the shortening into this mixture until it takes on a cornmeal texture. Lift it lightly into containers and store it at room temperature. It may be kept for up to 3 months. (Dry milk may be omitted if whole milk is used instead of water for the batter.)

With this mixture you can make the following cakes.

Plain Cake;

4½ cups mix
2 teaspoons vanilla

1 cup milk or water
2 eggs

Bake the batter for 25 to 30 minutes at 375°.

White Cake;

Use the Plain Cake recipe, substituting 3 egg whites for the 2 whole eggs.

Buttermilk Cake;

In place of the milk in the Plain Cake recipe, use buttermilk, and add 1 teaspoon of soda.

Orange Cake;

Add to the Plain Cake recipe 1 tablespoon of orange rind, and omit the 1 cup of milk. Use ¾ cup of water and ¼ cup of orange juice.

Chocolate Cake;

Use the recipe for Plain Cake, and add ¼ cup of cocoa before any of the liquid.

Spice Cake;

Add to the Plain Cake recipe 2 teaspoons of cinnamon, ½ teaspoon of cloves and ½ teaspoon of allspice.

Applesauce Cake;

Omit the liquid from the Plain Cake recipe, and add the following.

¾ cup brown sugar
½ teaspoon cloves
½ teaspoon nutmeg
Raisins or nuts (optional)

1 teaspoon soda
2 teaspoons cinnamon
2 cups applesauce

Applesauce Raisin Bars;

Add to the Applesauce Cake ingredients ½ cup of margarine. After adding all the other ingredients, add 4 eggs, one at a time, and beat the mixture well. Add as many raisins as desired, cut up, whole or ground. Pour the batter into two 9 x 13-inch pans, and bake it at 400° for 30 minutes. Frost the bars with a powdered sugar icing.

Pineapple Upside-Down Cake;

Mix and pour the following ingredients into a greased 9 x 13-inch pan.

⅔ cup melted butter	1 cup brown sugar
¼ cup nuts	6 tablespoons pineapple juice
1 tablespoon flour	6 to 8 pineapple slices

Arrange pineapple slices in the bottom of the pan. Pour the Basic Cake Mix batter over the pineapple and bake it at 375° until done. Invert it on a large plate, then serve it with whipped cream or another topping.

Dessert;

Put fruit pie filling in the bottom of a cake pan. Top it with the Plain Cake batter and bake it at 375°. Use almond in the cake when cherry pie filling is used. Serve it with whipped cream, top milk or ice cream.

Chocolate Cinnamon Bars;

4½ cups Basic Cake Mix	3 teaspoons cinnamon
1 egg	1 egg yolk
½ cup margarine	

Mix together the above ingredients and press the dough into a greased 9 x 12 or 15 x 10-inch pan. Beat 1 egg white slightly and brush it over the dough, then sprinkle over it the following topping. Bake it at 350° for 25 minutes. Allow it to cool, then cut it into bars.

1 teaspoon cinnamon	1 cup chocolate chips
⅓ cup sugar	½ cup nuts

CHOCOLATE CHIP COOKIES

4½ cups Basic Cake Mix	2 eggs
2 tablespoons flour	1 small package chocolate chips
¾ cup brown sugar	Chopped nuts
⅓ cup cooking oil	

Mix together all the ingredients. Shape the dough into balls. Bake them at 375° for 10 to 12 minutes on an ungreased cookie sheet.

BASIC COOKIE MIX

10 cups all-purpose flour
7½ cups sugar
4 tablespoons baking powder

4½ teaspoons salt
3⅓ cups shortening

Measure the flour into a large bowl. Add the sugar, baking powder and salt. Blend these thoroughly, then add the shortening and work it into the mixture until it is uniformly blended. Put it into a tightly sealed container but do not pack it down. Store it at room temperature.

Mincemeat Bars;

3 cups Basic Cookie Mix
1 large egg
1 cup mincemeat

Mix together thoroughly all the ingredients. Spread the mixture in a greased 9 x 13 x 2-inch pan. Bake it at 400° for 30 minutes. If desired, sprinkle white sugar over the top while it is still hot. Let it cool in the pan, then slice it into bars. This recipe yields 36 (2-inch) bars.

Banana Coconut Bars;

3 cups Basic Cookie Mix
1 large egg
½ cup coconut
1 teaspoon vanilla

1 cup mashed bananas
¼ cup finely chopped candied cherries
⅔ cup chopped nuts

Follow the Mincemeat Bars recipe, but sprinkle part of the nuts on top.

Orange Date Nut Sticks;

3 cups Basic Cookie Mix
1 tablespoon grated orange rind
¼ cup orange juice

2 eggs
1 cup chopped dates
1 cup finely chopped nuts

Follow the same directions as for Mincemeat Bars, but cut the sticks about 1 x 2½ inches.

LYDIA'S PIE DOUGH MIX

9 pounds all-purpose flour
4 pounds lard
1 cup cornstarch

1 tablespoon baking powder
2 cups sugar, icing or brown, sifted
1 tablespoon salt

Use about 1½ cups of this mix for 1 pie crust. Wet it with water or milk.

BISCUIT MIX

8 cups all-purpose flour
8 teaspoons sugar
2 teaspoons salt
⅓ cup baking powder

2 teaspoons cream of tartar
1 cup powdered milk
1¾ cups shortening

Sift the dry ingredients together 3 times, then cut in the shortening. Pack the mixture loosely in an airtight container.

To make biscuits, add 1 cup of this mix to ⅓ cup of water. Bake the dough at 450° for 10 to 12 minutes.

You may omit powdered milk from the mix if using milk instead of water.

This biscuit mix may be used with the Cherry Pudding recipe (see page 194) and the Pizza Pie recipe (see page 78).

Custard Pie;

4 eggs, separated
½ cup Biscuit Mix
⅓ cup sugar
2 cups milk

3 tablespoons butter
1 teaspoon vanilla
½ cup coconut (optional)

Beat the egg whites until they are stiff, then add the remaining ingredients and beat the mixture well. Pour it into a buttered pie pan and bake it for 25 to 30 minutes at 400°, or until the pie is golden brown. The mix forms its own crust.

CRUNCH MIX

5 cups oatmeal
5 cups brown sugar
1½ teaspoons baking powder
5 cups flour

1½ teaspoons soda
½ teaspoon salt
2 teaspoons cinnamon.

Mix these ingredients together, and store the mixture in a tightly sealed container.

Method;

1 quart sweetened, slightly thickened
  fruit
3 cups Crunch Mix
⅔ cup butter

Place the fruit in the bottom of a buttered baking dish. Mix together the Crunch Mix and butter, then pour this mixture over the fruit, patting it down. Bake it at 350° for about 30 to 45 minutes. Serve it with milk or cream.

GINGERBREAD MIX

8 cups all-purpose flour
2¼ cups sugar
2½ teaspoons soda
2 tablespoons baking powder
3 tablespoons ginger

3 tablespoons cinnamon
1 teaspoon cloves
1 tablespoon salt
2¼ cups shortening

Sift together all the dry ingredients, then cut in the shortening. Store the mixture in a gallon jar, tightly covered, in a cold place. It will keep for about 3 months.

Method;

2 cups Gingerbread Mix
1 egg, beaten

½ cup molasses
½ cup boiling water

Put the mix into a bowl. Combine the rest of the ingredients and stir them into the mix. Blend this mixture until it is smooth, then pour it into a greased 8 x 8-inch pan. Bake it at 350° for 35 minutes. Serve it warm with whipped cream.

Maple Gingerbread;

⅔ cup maple syrup
⅓ cup sour cream

2 cups Gingerbread Mix
1 egg, well-beaten

Heat the maple syrup, then combine it with the sour cream, and stir it into the mix. Add the egg before pouring the mixture into a greased 8 x 8-inch pan and baking it at 350° for 40 minutes.

THREE-FLOUR MUFFIN MIX

12 cups fine whole wheat flour
6 cups sifted, all-purpose flour
6 cups oatmeal
3 tablespoons salt

8 tablespoons baking powder
3 cups sugar
3 cups lard

Mix together the dry ingredients, then cut in the lard to make a very fine, meal-like mixture. Store it in a cold place.

Method;

2¾ cups Three-Flour Muffin Mix
1 cup milk
1 egg, beaten

Mix the ingredients until moistened. Bake the batter at 425° for 20 to 25 minutes. This makes 12 medium-sized muffins.

Variations: *Add raisins and carob flour, and bake the batter in an oblong pan like corn bread.*

PANCAKE MIX

12 cups all-purpose flour
¾ cup sugar
4 cups milk powder

2 tablespoons salt
¾ cup baking powder

Mix together well the above ingredients and store the mixture in a tightly sealed container.

To make pancakes, combine the following ingredients.

1½ cups of the above mix
1 egg, beaten

1 cup water
2 tablespoons salad oil

Variations: Buckwheat or whole wheat flour may be used as part of the flour.

Milk powder can be omitted if whole milk is used in place of the water.

PANCAKE AND WAFFLE MIX

4 cups all-purpose flour
2 cups cornmeal
3 teaspoons salt
4 teaspoons baking powder
⅔ cup liquid shortening (½ the amount
   for pancakes)

2 cups buckwheat flour
1 cup raw wheat germ
4 teaspoons soda

Mix together thoroughly the above ingredients. This mixture may be used immediately or stored in a cool place for future use. When using it, take equal amounts of the mix and milk (sour milk is best). For pancakes, use 1 egg to 1 or 2 cups of the mix. For waffles, use 1 egg to 1 cup of the mix.

FEATHER-LIGHT PANCAKES

8 cups all-purpose flour
1 cup sugar

2 tablespoons soda
2 teaspoons salt

Mix these ingredients, and store the mixture in a tightly sealed container.

2 eggs
¼ cup vinegar

2 cups milk
¼ cup soft shortening

To make pancakes, beat the eggs well and add the vinegar, milk and shortening. Then add 2¼ cups of the prepared dry mix (making the ¼ cup quite full).

When dry milk is added to the mix, water instead of milk is required in preparing the pancakes.

WHOLE WHEAT MUFFIN MIX

24 cups finely ground whole wheat
flour
3 tablespoons salt

3 cups sugar
8 tablespoons baking powder
3 cups lard

Mix together the dry ingredients, then cut in the lard to make a very fine, meal-like texture. Store it in a cold place.

Method;

2¾ cups Whole Wheat Muffin Mix
1 cup milk
1 egg, beaten

Mix the ingredients until moistened. Bake the batter at 425° for 20 to 25 minutes. This recipe makes 12 medium-sized muffins.

PUDDING MIX

½ cup cornstarch
1 cup flour

1½ cups sugar
1 teaspoon salt

Mix the ingredients together well and store the mixture in a tightly sealed container.

Vanilla Pudding;

3 cups milk
¾ cup Pudding Mix
2 eggs, beaten

2 tablespoons butter
2 teaspoons vanilla

Heat 2½ cups of the milk. While it is heating, make a paste of the Pudding Mix, ½ cup of the milk and the eggs. Add it to the hot milk with the butter and vanilla and cook it for 1 minute.

Chocolate Pudding;

3 cups milk
¾ cup Pudding Mix
5 tablespoons cocoa
¼ cup sugar

2 eggs
2 tablespoons butter
2 teaspoons vanilla

Cook these ingredients as directed in the Vanilla Pudding recipe, adding the cocoa and sugar to the Pudding Mix.

Butterscotch Pudding;

3 cups milk
¾ cup Pudding Mix
½ cup brown sugar

2 eggs
4 tablespoons butter
1 tablespoon vanilla

Cook these ingredients as directed in the Vanilla Pudding recipe, and top the pudding with nuts.

SHOO-FLY CRUMB MIX

4 pounds all-purpose flour
1 pound lard
2 pounds brown sugar

Mix these ingredients as you would for a pie crust, and store the mixture in a tightly sealed container.

Shoo-fly Cake;

2 cups Shoo-fly Crumb Mix   ¾ cup molasses
¾ cup hot water   1 teaspoon soda (scant)

Mix together the above ingredients, then pour the mixture into a greased 9 x 9-inch cake pan. Top it with dry Shoo-fly Crumbs. Bake it at 450° for 10 minutes, then at 375° for about 40 minutes or until done.

Shoo-fly Pie;

For pie, pour the batter into an unbaked pie shell and bake it at 450° for 10 minutes, then at 375° for about 40 minutes or until done.

CANNING

MARASCHINO CHERRIES

4½ pounds pitted, white cherries
2 tablespoons salt

1 teaspoon alum
Water to cover

Soak the cherries overnight in a brine made from the 3 remaining ingredients.

3 cups water
Juice of 1 lemon
4½ pounds sugar

1 ounce red coloring
1 ounce almond extract

The next day, drain and rinse the cherries in water. Add the 3 cups of water, juice, sugar and coloring. Heat the mixture to the boiling point, then let it set for 24 hours. Bring it to a boil again the third day, and add the almond extract. Jar and seal the cherries.

COLD PACKING HUCKLEBERRIES

2 cups sugar
1 cup boiling water

Make a syrup of the sugar and water. Pack berries in a jar and add the syrup. Place the jars in water until the water starts to boil, then remove them from the heat and seal.

SPICED MELONS

2 cups sugar
½ cup vinegar
1 cup water

¾ teaspoon salt
1 tablespoon whole cloves

Boil the ingredients for 20 minutes to get the taste of the cloves. Put muskmelons in jars and pour the syrup over them. Cook them for 20 minutes. Do not can the cloves as they will color the melons.

CANNING PRUNES WITH SODA

Use 2 tablespoons of soda to 1 gallon of water. Bring the water to a boil, then drop in the prunes a handful at a time. When they rise to the top, ladle them out into a clean jar. When the jar is full of prunes, fill it with the hot syrup, then seal.

RHUBARB

There are many variations in canning rhubarb—some with pineapple and some without, and some with different flavors of gelatin powder. Use 2 small packages of gelatin powder to 6 quarts of cooked rhubarb. On each can write what flavor it contains so you can decide which flavor your family enjoys the most. While the rhubarb is boiling hot, pour it into jars and seal.

Rhubarb may also be canned for pies by putting the raw, diced fruit into jars and filling them with cold water. It need not be heated, as the acid in the fruit keeps it from spoiling.

CANNED STRAWBERRIES

3 quarts strawberries
2 cups sugar
½ cup water

The strawberries may be lightly mashed if desired. Boil the ingredients together for 8 minutes, then put the strawberries into sterilized jars while still hot, and seal them.

BAKED BEANS

8 pounds navy beans
4½ quarts tomato juice
1 pound brown sugar
½ teaspoon black pepper
1 tablespoon ground mustard

1½ pounds bacon or ham, finely cut
8 tablespoons salt
1 cup molasses
1 tablespoon cinnamon

Soak the beans overnight. Cook them until they are soft, then drain. Mix together the other ingredients, cook them a few minutes, then add them to the beans. Put the mixture into jars and cold pack them for 1½ to 2 hours. This makes 14 quarts.

Variations: Three pounds of wieners may be used instead of bacon. Slice and fry them before adding

The tomato juice may be doubled, or part of the juice from cooking may be added.

WATERLESS STRING BEANS

Wash the beans and pack them in jars. Drain off all the water and seal them, then cold pack them for 3 hours. There will be enough juice in the jars from the beans that no water need be added when preparing the beans for a meal.

To prepare the beans, melt a little butter in a saucepan. Then add the beans with some salt and sauté them.

CANNED CORN

Cut the corn off the ears, cover it with water and cook it for 5 minutes. Put the corn and liquid into pint jars. Add to each pint 1 teaspoon of salt, 1 teaspoon of sugar and 1 teaspoon of lemon juice. Boil the jars in a hot water bath for 3 hours.

CANNED PEPPERS

Clean peppers (cut them into strips if desired) and pack them in jars. Add 1 teaspoon of vegetable oil and 1 teaspoon of salt to each quart jar.

Syrup;

1 pint vinegar
3 cups water
3 cups sugar

Mix these ingredients then pour the syrup over the peppers while they are boiling hot. Seal the jars and cold pack them until the boiling point.

GREEN PEPPERS

Dice and fry green peppers in butter. Put them into small jelly jars and cold pack them until the boiling point, then remove them from the stove.

This is good for one-dish meals and casseroles.

Peppers for Casseroles;

These can also be diced and packed in small jars, adding about ¼ teaspoon of salt to 1 cup of peppers. Fill the jars with water and cold pack them. Bring them to the boiling point before removing them from the stove.

HOMINY

In a large kettle bring 1½ gallons of water and 3 tablespoons of lye to a boil. Then add 1 gallon of clean corn and simmer it for 10 minutes (no need to stir). Remove it from the heat and let it set for 25 minutes.

Drain off the lye water and add clean water. Wash the corn repeatedly until all the black ends are loose, changing the water often. Soak it overnight and follow the Hominy Canning recipe.

After the black ends are off, the corn can also be dried and kept in a cool place.

Hominy Canning;

Boil Hominy until it is almost tender. Fill jars ¾ full. Add 1 teaspoon of salt to each quart and fill the jars with boiling water. Process them for 3 hours in a boiler, or for 90 minutes in a pressure cooker.

Hominy with Soda;

Use 2 tablespoons of soda and 2 quarts of water for each quart of corn. Follow the same procedure as the Hominy recipe.

Household lime can also be used to remove hulls. Cook corn in lime water for 2 hours or until the hulls loosen.

Hominy Making Hints;

- *Always use stainless steel, iron or enamelware for making hominy.*
- *Stir it with a wooden spoon.*
- *The black ends may be removed by rubbing over a cloth on a washboard or by using a churn.*
- *Hominy is delicious even if the hulls and centers are not all removed.*
- *Hominy may be used in meat loaf.*
- *Do not inhale the steam from the lye water.*

STUFFED LITTLE PEPPERS

Make your favorite cole slaw and stuff it into small green, red and yellow peppers. Pack them into jars and cold pack them for 3 hours.

This makes a delightful and colorful addition to your salad plate.

CANNING POTATOES

Do not let newly-dug small potatoes go to waste. Scrape them, pack them into a jar, and add 1 teaspoon of salt. Cold pack them for 3 hours. To use, drain off the water and fry the potatoes in butter.

QUICK STEPS FOR CANNING PUMPKIN

Wash the pumpkins, remove the seeds and put the pumpkins into a pressure cooker with a very small amount of water. Cook them for 10 minutes, timing them after the cooking starts. The shell then comes off easily and the pumpkins are soft and ready to use. This eliminates peeling and cubing, and the pumpkins are nice in texture and not water soaked. If desired, the pumpkins may be put through a Foley food mill. Put them into jars and cold pack them for 1 hour.

CROCK KRAUT

Measure 3 tablespoons of pure granulated salt and sprinkle it over 5 pounds of shredded cabbage. Allow the salted cabbage to stand a few minutes to wilt slightly. Mix it well with clean hands or a spoon to distribute the salt uniformly. Pack the salted cabbage into a large crock. Press it down firmly with a potato masher until the juices drawn out will just cover the shredded cabbage. Place a water-filled plastic bag on top of the cabbage. This fits snugly against the cabbage and against the sides of the container and prevents exposure to air. Place the crock in a room with a temperature of 68 to 72°F.

Instead of covering the cabbage with a plastic bag you may cover it with a clean, thin, white cloth (such as muslin) and tuck the edges down against the inside of the container. Cover it with a plate or round paraffined board that just fits inside the container so that the cabbage is not exposed to air. Put a weight on top of the cover so the brine comes to the cover but not over it. A glass jar filled with water makes a good weight.

When fermentation is complete, remove the sauerkraut from the crock and heat it in a kettle to simmering. Pack the hot sauerkraut into clean, hot jars and cover it with the hot juice to ½ inch from the top of the jars. Adjust the lids. Place the jars in a boiling water bath and process them 15 minutes for pints and 20 minutes for quarts. Start to count the processing time as soon as the hot jars are placed into the actively boiling water.

Remove the jars from the canner and complete the seals if necessary. Set the jars upright, several inches apart on a wire rack to cool. An off odor indicates that the sauerkraut may be spoiled. It rots when it is not covered sufficiently to keep out the air.

EASY SAUERKRAUT

For this recipe it is best to use large bursted heads of cabbage. Shred and chop the cabbage, then pack it in jars. Add 1 teaspoon of salt to each jar, then fill them with boiling water. Do not seal them tightly. Let the cabbage stand about 10 days to ferment. Then turn the lids tightly and store the jars.

SIMPLE SAUERKRAUT

Shred cabbage and pack it loosely into a jar. Make a hole down through the middle with a wooden spoon or similar utensil and add 1 tablespoon of salt for each quart. Then fill it with boiling water and immediately seal the jar tightly. This will be ready to use in 4 to 6 weeks. More salt may be added if desired.

MARY'S TOMATO SOUP

1 peck ripe tomatoes	½ cup sugar
10 small onions	¼ cup salt
5 sprigs parsley	1 teaspoon pepper
3 bunches celery	½ cup flour
2 red peppers	½ cup butter

Cook the tomatoes and put them through a sieve. Boil down the pulp to nearly half. Grind the onions, parsley, celery and peppers through a food chopper and pour the mixture into the tomatoes. Add the sugar, salt and pepper. Make a thickening with the flour and enough water to make it smooth, then stir it into the pulp and tomato juice and boil it for ½ hour. Add the butter before removing it from the heat. Can the soup while it is hot. This makes 6 to 7 pints. To prepare it, add milk and heat.

PIZZA SAUCE

Cook ½ bushel of tomatoes and 3 pounds of onions for 2½ to 3 hours. Put them through a sieve, then add the following.

4 hot peppers, OR	1 tablespoon oregano
1½ teaspoons red pepper	1½ cups white sugar
2 cups vegetable oil	½ cup salt
1 tablespoon basil leaves	

Boil this mixture for 1 hour, then add 48 ounces (four 12-ounce cans) of tomato paste. Bring it to a boil, then pack it in hot jars and seal them. This makes 20 pints.

TOMATO SAUCE FOR PIZZA PIE

1 peck tomatoes
3 red peppers, seeded
3 onions

Cook the above ingredients together until they are soft. Drain them well then put them through a colander. Add the following ingredients.

2 tablespoons salt
½ teaspoon pepper
½ cup vinegar

2 teaspoons dried celery leaves
¼ teaspoon red pepper (optional)
2 teaspoons oregano (optional)

Put this into pint jars, seal and boil them for 30 minutes.

CHICKEN SOUP

4 chickens
Salt to taste
1 gallon noodles, cooked

Cook separately until nearly done ½ gallon of each of; celery, carrots and potatoes, all chopped. One cup of chopped onions may be added. Combine all the ingredients and cold pack the soup for 2 hours.

CHILI SOUP

1 pound hamburger
2 tablespoons butter
1 cup chopped onions
2 pints kidney beans
½ teaspoon chili powder

1 tablespoon salt
2 tablespoons prepared mustard
Pinch of black pepper
2 quarts tomato juice

Mix these ingredients as you would other Chili Soup (see page 000), then cold pack the soup for 3 hours. This makes 3 quarts.

BYLERS' CHILI SOUP

8 pounds hamburger
2 quarts red kidney beans
2 to 4 red peppers

6 quarts strained tomatoes
24 small onions
1½ teaspoons chili powder

Cook each ingredient except the spice separately, then mix all together. Put the soup into jars and seal them, then cold pack them for 2 hours.

MIXED VEGETABLES

Cook separately, carrots (diced small), lima beans, string beans, corn, soup beans, peas, potatoes (diced small) and green peppers (small amount). Salt each vegetable when cooking, then mix them together. (Be careful not to overcook them.) Cold pack the vegetables for 1 hour.

This recipe is good if you like variety in canning. The vegetables resemble frozen mixed vegetables available in stores. This is also delicious with meat broth for soup.

VALLEY TOMATO SOUP

1 peck tomatoes
8 onions fried in 2 tablespoons butter
6 sweet peppers, seeded
5 teaspoons salt
5 tablespoons sugar

4 cloves
1 stick cinnamon
4 bay leaves
2 quarts water

Boil together all the ingredients before running them through a sieve. Put the mixture over heat again and bring it to a boil. Add 5 teaspoons of cornstarch mixed with ½ cup of cold water, and boil it for 15 minutes longer. Can the soup.

To serve, heat the soup and an equal amount of milk in separate pans, adding ¼ teaspoon of soda to 1 quart of soup. Mix the milk into the soup and let it come to a boil. Serve it with crackers.

VEGETABLE SOUP

10 carrots
2 heads cabbage
10 peppers
½ gallon potatoes or macaroni
½ gallon navy beans

½ bushel tomatoes, strained
6 bunches celery
10 onions
3 pounds hamburger or cut up chicken
1 pound butter

Cook each vegetable separately. Fry the onions and hamburger in the butter, then mix all together. Season it with salt, pepper and sugar to taste. Cold pack the soup for 1 hour. This makes 20 quarts.

PRESERVED BUTTER

Form butter into patties, then place them in a crock with salty brine strong enough to float an egg. Keep it in a cool place. In this way the butter can be kept for several months.

CANNED CREAM

When there is an overabundance of cream during the summer months, can it and keep it for the winter. First cook the cream, then seal it in pint or quart jars. Cold pack them for 1 hour. This cream can be whipped and used the same as fresh cream, and it has a good flavor.

CANNED NUTMEATS

Put nutmeats into cans with 2-piece lids. Heat them to 250° on a grate or rack in the oven for ¾ hour, then turn off the heat and let them cool on the grate.

INSTANT PUDDING

Thicken any kind of fruit or fruit combination such as pears and pineapple, sour cherries and raspberries or apples and raisins, using tapioca or cornstarch (tapioca should not be cooked until clear). As soon as the cooked fruit has reached the boiling point, fill the jars, seal them, and put them into the pressure cooker. Heat them to 5 pounds pressure. Let the steam out and the jars will seal. A hot water bath may also be used, or the jars may be placed in a hot oven for a few minutes.

This thickened fruit may be used for puddings or pie filling when unexpected company arrives.

CANNING SWEET CIDER

Never boil cider in a kettle to can it. Pour the fresh apple juice into bottles or cans, filling them to the top. Place them in a canner with cold water that reaches to the neck of the cans. Leave the cans uncovered. Bring the water to a boil. With a spoon or small ladle remove the scum that rises to the top. Continue to boil the cans until no scum appears. Then remove them from the water and seal.

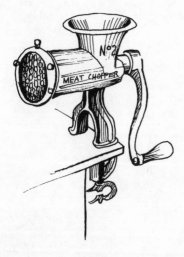

PICKLED FOODS, RELISHES, KETCHUP AND SPREADS

CHERRY PICKLES

1½ gallons cold water
1 cup salt
1 quart sweet cherry leaves

Place cucumbers in a mixture of the above ingredients and let them stand for 8 days. Remove, wash and cut them into desired pieces. Heat them in weak vinegar, then pack them in jars and drain. Cook together the following.

4 cups sugar
2 cups vinegar

2 cups water
1 tablespoon mixed spices

Pour this over the pickles and seal the jars.

CHUNK PICKLES

1 gallon cucumber chunks
½ cup salt
Boiling water to cover
3 cups sugar
3 cups vinegar
1 cup water

1 teaspoon allspice
1 teaspoon dry mustard
1 teaspoon mustard seed
1 teaspoon celery seed
½ teaspoon turmeric

Cut the medium-sized cucumbers into 1-inch chunks. Add the salt and cover them with the boiling water. Let them stand overnight then drain them. Combine the sugar, vinegar, 1 cup of water and spices, bring them to a boil and add the pickles. Green food coloring may be added if desired. Heat the pickles again to a boil, then can and seal.

CLARA'S PICKLES

Chunk 1 gallon of cucumbers. Add 1 cup of salt and enough boiling water to cover them. Let them stand overnight. The next morning drain them. Mix 3 cups of white sugar, 1 teaspoon turmeric, 1 teaspoon of mustard seed and 1 quart of vinegar, diluted. Pour this over the pickles and heat but do not boil them. Pack them in jars and cover them with the syrup. Seal the jars.

COLD PACKED PICKLES

Pack cucumbers in jars. To each quart add ⅓ cup of vinegar, 1 heaping tablespoon of salt and ½ teaspoon of sugar. Fill the jars with water, seal them and set them in cold water in a boiler. Heat the jars until the color of the pickles is completely changed or until the water boils.

CRISP PICKLES

1 gallon cucumbers, sliced ⅛-inch thick	⅓ cup salt
6 medium-sized onions, thinly sliced	Cold water

Combine the above ingredients and let them stand for 3 hours before draining. Pack them in jars for cold packing.

1 cup water
⅔ cup strong vinegar
1¾ cups raw sugar (scant)

Make a syrup of the above ingredients.

½ teaspoon turmeric
½ teaspoon celery seeds
2 teaspoons mustard seeds

Tie the above seeds in a muslin bag and place it in the syrup. Cook the syrup a few minutes then lift out the seed bag. Add ½ cup of water extra and ⅛ cup more vinegar. When the syrup has cooled, pour it over the cucumbers and onions. Cold pack them 5 minutes, no longer. Use the leftover syrup for the next batch of cucumbers, but refrigerate it until then.

DOLLAR BREAD AND BUTTER PICKLES

4 quarts sliced cucumbers (40 to 50)	1 tablespoon turmeric (optional)
½ cup salt	1 quart vinegar
2 quarts sliced onions	1 tablespoon celery seed
4 cups sugar	1 tablespoon ginger
2 tablespoons mustard	

Gently stir the salt into the thinly sliced cucumbers. Cover them with ice cubes and let them stand for 2 or 3 hours until the cucumbers are crisp and cold. Add more ice if it melts. Drain the cucumbers and add the onions. Combine the remaining ingredients and bring the mixture quickly to a boil, boiling it for 10 minutes. Add the cucumber and onion slices and bring them to the boiling point. Pack them at once in hot jars. Process them in a boiling water bath for 30 minutes. Remove the jars from the canner and complete sealing. This makes 8 pints.

EXCELLENT UNCOOKED PICKLES

Select good small cucumbers, and wash and dry them. Pack them into jars, then fill the jars with vinegar sweetened with saccharin to suit your taste. Do not make the vinegar too sweet or the pickles will wrinkle. Seal the jars as you would for cold packing. Put them into a boiler in cold water and bring the water to a boil. When it starts to boil, remove the jars and tighten the lids. This makes a very crisp pickle.

FROZEN CUCUMBERS

7 cups cucumbers, sliced thinly
1 cup peppers, diced
1 cup onions, diced

Mix these ingredients, then add the following vinegar solution.

1 tablespoon salt   2 cups sugar
1 teaspoon celery seeds   1 cup white vinegar

Let the cucumbers stand in the refrigerator for 4 or 5 days, stirring them every day. Then freeze them.

ICICLE PICKLES

2 gallons large cucumbers
1 pint salt
Water enough to cover

Mix the cucumbers, salt and water, and let them stand for 4 days. Drain and add boiling water to the cucumbers, then let them stand for 24 hours. Drain and cut them into strips. Pour water over them again, adding a lump of alum the size of an egg. Let them stand for 24 hours, then drain them again and pack them in jars.

Syrup;

2½ quarts vinegar   1 tablespoon salt
8 pints sugar (or less)   1 handful mixed whole spices (scant)

Boil these ingredients together to make a syrup. While it is hot, pour it over the pickles in jars before sealing them.

LIME PICKLES

7 pounds cucumbers, unpeeled, sliced
   into 1-inch or thinner chunks
2 cups lime
2 gallons cold water
9 cups sugar (or less)

2 quarts vinegar
1 teaspoon mixed spices
1 tablespoon salt
1 tablespoon celery seeds
1 tablespoon whole cloves

Mix together the lime and water and pour the mixture over the cucumbers. Let them stand for 24 hours before thoroughly washing out the lime. Cover them with the sugar, vinegar and spice mixture. Do not heat the cucumbers at this time. The next morning simmer them for 40 minutes. Put them into hot jars and seal them. These pickles stay good and crisp.

MIXED PICKLES

8 cups sliced cucumbers
2 cups sliced onions
4 green peppers, sliced

1½ quarts cooked lima beans
¾ cup cooked carrots (or more)

Soak for 1 hour the cucumbers, onions and peppers separately in hot salted water, using 1 cup of salt for each gallon of hot water. Drain them, add the beans and carrots, then add a mixture of the following.

1 teaspoon turmeric
2 cups vinegar
2 to 3 cups sugar

1 teaspoon celery seed
1 stick cinnamon
Salt if needed

Boil the vegetables in this liquid for 20 minutes. Pack them in jars, fill with the liquid, and seal the jars while they are hot.

DELAWARE MIXED PICKLES

2 quarts carrots
2 quarts corn
2 quarts cabbage
2 quarts celery

2 quarts beans
2 quarts cucumbers
4 or 5 peppers
1 quart onions

Cook the above vegetables separately until they are tender, except for the cucumbers, peppers and onions. Mix the following ingredients and bring the mixture to a boil.

3 tablespoons mustard
3 pints sugar
1 cup flour
3 pints water

2 tablespoons turmeric
1 tablespoon salt
3 pints vinegar

Combine all the ingredients, then pack the vegetables in jars, filling them with the syrup. Cold pack them for 1 hour.

MUSTARD PICKLES

1 gallon vinegar
1 cup sugar (or use part saccharin)
1 cup dry mustard

1 cup salt
1 tablespoon mixed pickling spices

Boil together the above ingredients, then allow the mixture to cool. Put about 2 gallons of small cucumbers into a crock and cover them with the brine. (Make sure the cucumbers dry thoroughly after washing or they will become moldy.) Weight them down to keep them in the brine. Cover the crock with a cloth.

OVERNIGHT DILL PICKLES

Wash 20 to 25 dill-sized (4-inch) cucumbers. Put them into a pan of cold water and let them stand overnight. The next morning, pack them in hot sterile jars. Into each quart measure ⅛ teaspoon of powdered alum. Add 2 heads of dill (fresh with seed) and 1 small hot red pepper.

Combine 4 cups of vinegar, 1 cup of pure salt and 3 quarts of water. Heat the mixture to boiling, then fill the jars with this liquid. Seal them and allow them to stand for 6 weeks. A washed grape leaf or two can be put on the top for green coloring.

POLISH PICKLES

Cut 2 dozen cucumbers into quarters. Place them in salted water (1 tablespoon of salt to each quart of water) and let them stand overnight. Drain and pack them in jars. Fill the jars with the following syrup, which has been boiled for 3 minutes.

1½ pints vinegar
1½ pints sugar

¼ teaspoon red pepper
½ teaspoon turmeric

Put ¼ teaspoon of alum and a slice of onion on top of each jar before sealing.

REFRIGERATOR PICKLES

4 cups vinegar
1½ teaspoons celery seeds
1½ teaspoons turmeric

4 cups sugar
1½ teaspoons mustard seeds
¼ cup salt

This needs no boiling. Just pour a mixture of these ingredients over cucumbers and put them in the refrigerator. They will keep for months.

SEVEN DAY SWEET PICKLES

Day 1—Wash 7 pounds of medium-sized green cucumbers and cover them with boiling water.

Day 2—Drain them and cover them with fresh boiling water.

Day 3—Repeat procedure.

Day 4—Repeat procedure.

Day 5—Cut the pickles into ¼-inch rings.

Combine the following.

1 quart white vinegar	2 tablespoons salt
8 cups granulated sugar	2 tablespoons mixed pickle spices

Bring this mixture to a full boil and pour it over the sliced pickles.

Day 6—Drain the brine from the pickles, bring it to a full boil and pour it over the pickles again.

Day 7—Repeat Day 6 procedure, then jar and seal.

SOUR PICKLES

3 quarts water	3 tablespoons salt
1 quart white vinegar	7 tablespoons sugar

Soak cucumbers overnight in a mixture of the above ingredients. Then heat but do not boil them in this mixture. Pack the pickles in jars. Boil the liquid and pour it over the pickles before sealing the jars.

SWEET DILLS

Fill jars with sliced cucumbers, adding 2 bunches of dill and 3 or 4 garlic cloves to each quart. Pour the following liquid over the pickles.

1 quart weakened vinegar (may be ½ water)	¼ cup salt
1 pint water	4 cups sugar

Bring the mixture to a boil. Fill jars, then put on the lids. Set the jars in hot water and bring it to a boil, just long enough to seal.

CHOW CHOW

1 pint green beans
1 pint yellow beans
1 pint cucumbers
1 pint lima beans

1 pint carrots
1 head cauliflower
1 pint corn
3 or 4 stalks celery

Cook the above ingredients until they are just tender. Chop them to a uniform size, then salt and drain them. Chop and salt ½ dozen green tomatoes, and 3 red and 3 large yellow mangoes. Mix them well with the first ingredients and add the mixture to a boiling syrup made from the following.

3 quarts vinegar
5 cups sugar
1 tablespoon celery seed

1 tablespoon mustard seed
Other spices as desired
Onions (optional)

Heat, jar and seal.

PICKLED BEETS

3 quarts small beets
3 cups vinegar
2 tablespoons salt

4 cups sugar
1½ cups water
2 cinnamon sticks (optional)

Cook the beets. Combine the rest of the ingredients and boil them to a syrup. Pour the boiling syrup over the beets in hot jars, then seal them. Cold pack them for 10 to 15 minutes.

SPICED RED BEETS

2 cups sugar (raw if desired)
1 cup vinegar
½ teaspoon cinnamon
½ teaspoon cloves

3 cups water or beet juice
Juice of 1 lemon
½ teaspoon allspice
Salt to taste

Mix the above ingredients and pour the mixture over 1 gallon of cooked beets. Simmer them for 15 minutes. Then pack the beets in jars (without the syrup), and reheat the syrup to boiling. Pour it over the beets and seal the jars.

PICKLED PEPPERS

Into a clean cold jar, put pieces of green peppers (red peppers get mushy), or hot peppers. Add 1 tablespoon of pickling salt, and spices, garlic, pieces of celery or dried red peppers if desired. Fill the jar ⅔ full with cold water, then fill it to the top with cold white vinegar. Seal the jar with a screw cap and lid. These peppers will be ready to eat after 2 weeks, and they keep indefinitely.

CUCUMBER RELISH

4 quarts cucumbers, thinly sliced,
  unpeeled
6 large onions, sliced
½ cup salt

Mix these ingredients together and let them stand overnight. The next morning, wash them in clear water and drain. Make a syrup with the following ingredients.

4 cups sugar
1 teaspoon turmeric
1 teaspoon mustard seeds

1 quart vinegar (diluted if desired)
1 teaspoon celery seeds

When the syrup is hot, add the cucumbers and onions. Boil them together for about 15 minutes. Then make a paste with 3 tablespoons of flour and some vinegar, and add it to the pickles. Can the relish while it is hot.

RIPE TOMATO RELISH

18 firm, ripe tomatoes
1 stalk celery
4 medium onions
2 green peppers
2 red peppers
⅓ cup salt

2½ cups sugar (scant)
½ teaspoon cloves
2 tablespoons mustard seeds
½ teaspoon pepper
2 teaspoons cinnamon
1½ cups vinegar

Peel the tomatoes and chop them into small pieces. Chop the celery, onions and peppers in a food chopper with a coarse blade. Combine the celery, onions, peppers, tomatoes and salt. Let them stand in the refrigerator overnight, then drain them well the next morning. Mix together the sugar, spices and vinegar, then add this to the tomato mixture. Mix them well before putting the mixture into sterile jars. Cap the jars.

This will keep for up to 5 months in the refrigerator. It is very good on hamburgers, on different kinds of meat and on fried potatoes.

TOMATO CORN RELISH

12 ears corn
2 quarts ripe tomatoes
2 bunches celery, finely cut
2 cups vinegar

1 tablespoon salt
3 cups white sugar
6 onions, finely cut
¼ teaspoon red pepper (or less)

Cut corn off the cobs. Peel the tomatoes and cut them into small pieces. Add the rest of the ingredients and boil them for 50 minutes. Put the relish into small jars and seal them.

TOMATO PEPPER RELISH

½ peck green tomatoes
8 red peppers
2 or more large onions

Put the above ingredients through a food chopper. Boil them for 15 minutes, then remove them from the heat and add salt. Boil them again for 15 minutes. Drain them through a colander, then add the following ingredients.

1 pint vinegar
1 pint sugar
2 sticks cinnamon

2 tablespoons allspice
2 tablespoons whole cloves

Boil the mixture rapidly, then add 1 tablespoon of celery seeds and 1 teaspoon of mustard seeds. Jar and seal.

SWEET PEPPER RELISH

2 ounces celery seeds
1 dozen sweet red peppers

1 dozen green peppers
1 dozen onions

Grind these ingredients in a food chopper, soak them for 10 minutes in boiling water, then drain them. Put the following into a kettle over heat.

1½ pints vinegar
2 pounds brown sugar (or less)
3 tablespoons salt

½ teaspoon pepper
1 teaspoon cinnamon
2 tablespoons mustard seeds

Add the chopped ingredients and boil them for about 10 to 15 minutes, then jar and seal.

CORN RELISH

12 ears corn
1 head cabbage
6 peppers
2 stalks celery
1 teaspoon celery seeds

1 teaspoon mustard seed
1 cup sugar
¼ cup salt
1 pint vinegar

Cut the corn from the cobs. Chop the cabbage, seeded peppers and celery in a food chopper using the coarse blade. Mix these with the rest of the ingredients and boil the mixture for 30 minutes. Jar and seal.

PICKLED GREEN TOMATOES

1 quart vinegar
2 tablespoons salt
2 tablespoons sugar

5 quarts green tomatoes (large if
possible)

Mix together the vinegar, salt and sugar. Heat the mixture and add it to the green tomatoes and garlic. Bring it to a boil, then put it into jars. Before sealing them add 2 dill sprigs or 2 teaspoons of dill to each quart.

Can the tomatoes whole, then slice them to use in sandwiches.

STORE-LIKE KETCHUP

½ bushel tomatoes
½ cup salt
4 cups sugar
2 cups vinegar

Dash of pepper
2 grated onions
1 ounce ketchup spices
Cornstarch (optional)

Mix the tomatoes and salt in a large crock. Weigh down the tomatoes and let them stand for 5 days. Each day dip off the water. On the fifth day, remove the white top and put the tomatoes through a colander. Add the sugar, vinegar, small amount of pepper, onions and the ketchup spices tied in a bag. Cook this for ¾ hour before removing the bag. The tomatoes may be thickened with cornstarch if desired. Put the ketchup into bottles or jars and seal them.

WINTER KETCHUP

5 quarts tomato juice
1 pint applesauce
2 cups sugar
2 tablespoons pickling spices

6 onions
1 pint vinegar
Salt to taste

Cook the onions and put them through a sieve. Tie the pickling spices in a cloth and cook them with all the ingredients for 1½ hours. Remove the pickling spices, then thicken the mixture with 1¼ cups of cornstarch. Cook it for 15 to 20 minutes. Put the ketchup into jars or bottles, and dip the tops of them into melted paraffin to be sure they seal.

This ketchup can be made in the winter months.

PICKLE KETCHUP

1 pint onions, finely chopped
4 quarts peeled cucumbers, finely
  chopped
1 teaspoon pepper
½ teaspoon celery seeds
½ teaspoon turmeric
1 cup vinegar

1 small head cauliflower, finely
  chopped
1 bunch celery, finely chopped
2 cups white sugar
1 tablespoon salt
1 tablespoon dry mustard
1 tablespoon flour

Mix together all the ingredients and bring them to a boil. Put the ketchup into jars and seal them.

TOMATO KETCHUP

4 quarts tomatoes, finely cut
2 cups vinegar
2 tablespoons salt
1 tablespoon ketchup spices

3 cups sugar
½ teaspoon red pepper
1 teaspoon dry mustard
1 stick cinnamon

Boil the ingredients together for 2 hours. Put the mixture through a sieve and thicken it with approximately 3 tablespoons of cornstarch moistened with a little vinegar. Boil it for 10 minutes before sealing it in sterilized jars.

KETCHUP

1 peck tomatoes
1 tablespoon mixed pickling spices
4 onions
3 red peppers
6 peach leaves

1 cup vinegar
3 cups sugar
1 tablespoon salt
1 tablespoon turmeric
¼ teaspoon pepper

Peel the tomatoes and cook them until they are soft. Put them through a sieve. Tie the pickling spices in a bag, and add it with the remaining ingredients to the tomatoes, boiling the mixture until it is thick. Remove the bag. Put the hot ketchup into jars or bottles and seal them.

MUSTARD SANDWICH SPREAD

6 green peppers
6 red tomatoes
6 cucumbers

6 red peppers
6 onions

Grind together all the ingredients. Add 2 tablespoons of salt and let it stand for 2 hours. Drain it well, then mix the following and add it to the vegetables.

½ cup flour
4 cups sugar

2 tablespoons turmeric
2 cups vinegar

Cook everything together for 15 minutes, then add 1 quart of prepared mustard and cook it for 5 minutes more, stirring all the time to prevent burning. Put it into hot jars and seal.

SANDWICH SPREAD

3 to 4 quarts green tomatoes
1 quart onions

12 large peppers
2 large stalks celery

Grind the ingredients together and add 1 cup of salt. Drain the mixture overnight in a cloth bag, and press the remaining juice out in the morning. Add 1 quart of vinegar and 1½ quarts of sugar, then boil it for 25 to 30 minutes. When it has cooled, add 1 quart of mayonnaise (more if desired) and ½ small jar of mustard (optional).

PRESERVES

SIMPLE APPLE BUTTER

4 gallons apples, unpeeled, quartered
1 gallon corn syrup
6 pounds sugar

Put the apples into a heavy kettle or canner with a tight-fitting lid. Pour the syrup and sugar over the apples and let them set overnight to form juice. Bring the mixture to a slow boil and cook it, covered, for 3 hours. Do not open the lid or stir the mixture during the entire cooking period. Put it through a strainer.

Cider Apple Butter;

3 gallons snitz (dried apple pieces)   ½ gallon corn syrup
1 gallon sweet cider   4 pounds sugar

Follow the directions above.

STOCKMAN'S APPLE BUTTER

10 gallons fresh cider
8 gallons apples, peeled and cored
20 pounds sugar

Bring the cider to a boil in a copper kettle. Add the apples and bring it to a boil again. Add a lump of butter to keep it from boiling over. After the apples are well cooked, add the sugar and keep stirring it until it thickens. This makes 6 gallons of apple butter. When it is done, quickly remove it from the kettle.

GRAPE BUTTER

1 quart whole grapes
1 quart sugar
2 tablespoons water

Cook the ingredients for 20 minutes, then put them through a fruit press or colander. Pour this into jars and seal the tops with paraffin.

LEMON BUTTER

¼ cup lemon juice
Grated rind of 1 lemon
1 cup sugar

2 eggs, well-beaten
½ tablespoon butter

Cook the ingredients in a double boiler until the mixture thickens. Then pour it into jars and seal.

APRICOT JAM

2 pounds dried apricots
2 quarts water
8½ cups sugar

Wash the apricots and put them through the coarse blade of a food grinder. Then put the ground apricots with the water, into a large bowl. Let the mixture stand in a cool place for 48 hours, stirring it occasionally. Cook it for 15 minutes, then add the sugar and cook it slowly for 1 hour, stirring frequently until it thickens.

WILD GRAPE JELLY

Wash grape clusters and put them into a large kettle with enough water to cover them. Boil them for about 15 minutes. Pour the grapes into a cloth bag and squeeze out all the juice. Then add an equal amount of water to the juice. This is now ready for jelly making. Use 5 cups of juice, 7 cups of sugar and 1 package of pectin crystals.

Put the remaining juice into quart cans with ½ cup sugar per quart, and process it for 10 minutes at 10 pounds pressure, or for 30 minutes in a boiling water bath for later use.

PEACH AND PINEAPPLE PRESERVES

6 cups sliced peaches
2 cups crushed pineapple
6 cups sugar

2 small packages orange gelatin
   powder

Cook the first 3 ingredients together for 20 minutes, then add the gelatin powder. Pour the preserves into jars and seal.

In early spring, jams and jellies may be scarce. This recipe may be the answer to this problem.

PEACH PRESERVES

3 cups peaches, peeled and diced
3 oranges, diced or chopped
4½ cups sugar

Boil the ingredients until the mixture sheets from a spoon, about 20 to 30 minutes. Remove it from the heat and add a few chopped maraschino cherries. Pour it into jars and seal.

1-2-3-4 RASPBERRY SPREAD

1 cup water
2 cups red raspberries

3 cups chopped apples
4 cups white sugar

Cook the ingredients together for 10 minutes. Put the spread into jars and seal them with paraffin.

When choosing apples to use, Northern Spy work well with this recipe.

RHUBARB JAM

5 cups rhubarb, finely cut
4 cups sugar

Mix together the above ingredients and let them stand overnight. In the morning, boil the mixture for 5 minutes, then add 1 small package of strawberry gelatin powder. Boil it for 3 minutes, then pour it into jars and seal.

Variations: Try adding 1 small can of pineapple. Then only 4 cups of rhubarb are required instead of 5.

PEACH MARMALADE

5 cups sliced peaches
1 small can crushed pineapple
7 cups sugar

Cook the ingredients together for 15 minutes. Add 1 large or 2 small packages of orange or strawberry gelatin powder, and cook this mixture until the gelatin is dissolved. Pour it into jars and seal them. Use paraffin if desired.

PEAR BUTTER

Boil ½ gallon of pears. Then mash them as you would apples for apple sauce. Add 1 quart of white sugar and 1 quart of light corn syrup. Nutmeg or cinnamon may be added at this time. Bake the mixture in a moderate oven (350°) or simmer it on top of the stove until it is of the right consistency.

When cooking it on the stove, extreme care must be taken to avoid scorching.

FRESH STRAWBERRY JAM

3 cups strawberries, well crushed
6 cups sugar

1 package Certo crystals
1 cup water

Mix the strawberries and sugar together and let the mixture stand for 20 minutes. Stir it several times. Combine the Certo crystals and water. Boil this for 1 minute, stirring constantly. Mix it with the berries and stir it for 2 minutes. Put it into jars and cold pack them a few minutes to seal them. Store them in the freezer.

Variations: Other fruit may be used instead of strawberries.

STRAWBERRY JAM

1 cup strawberries, crushed or whole
2 cups sugar

Boil the ingredients for 3 minutes. Remove the mixture from the heat and stir in 1 teaspoon of Epsom salts. Pour it into jars and seal them.

STRAWBERRY PRESERVES

1 quart strawberries
2 cups sugar

Boil the ingredients for 5 minutes, then add 2 more cups of sugar and 2 teaspoons of lemon juice. Boil the mixture for 10 minutes more. Let it stand for 24 hours, then put it into glasses and seal them while cold with paraffin, or cover them with lids.

CARAMEL SPREAD

2 cups brown sugar
2 cups granulated sugar

1 cup corn syrup
1 cup water

Cook the ingredients together, bringing the mixture to a full boil. Then let it cool. Add 2 egg whites beaten stiff. Stir them together well and add maple flavoring.

PINEAPPLE HONEY

6 pounds sugar
5 pounds corn syrup
2 (19-ounce) cans (1 quart) crushed
    pineapple

Mix the ingredients well and bring the mixture to a boil. There is no need to boil it longer. Pour it into jars and seal. This recipe makes 1 gallon.

QUINCE HONEY

¼ cup corn syrup
1 cup water
3 cups sugar

2 cups quince, ground, OR
1 cup quince plus 1 cup apples, ground

Cook the ingredients together for approximately 5 minutes. Pour the mixture into jars and seal.

MAPLE SYRUP

4 cups brown sugar
2 cups boiling water

¼ cup corn syrup
2 teaspoons maple flavoring

Mix together the first 3 ingredients and bring the mixture to a good boil. Remove it from the heat and add the maple flavoring

Variations: *Double this recipe plus ½, and mix it with 5 or 6 pounds of peanut butter. If it becomes too stringy at this point, add a bit of cold water. Then add 2 quarts of Marshmallow Creme (see page 228) to almost fill an 8-quart bowl.*

GRAPE MOLASSES

1 pint corn syrup
1 pint grape juice
3 pounds granulated sugar

Boil the ingredients for a few minutes until the mixture is of the right consistency. Pour it into jars and seal them.

Variations: *Raspberries, blackberries or elderberries may be used instead of grapes.*

CHEESE

HINTS FOR CHEESE

- One gallon of curds produces approximately 1 pound of cheese.
- To make hard, dry cheese, press it with 25 to 30 pound weights.
- If mold forms on cheese that is being used, just trim it off.
- Cheese may be kept longer while it is being used if it is kept in a large container with a cup of vinegar beside it. Cover the container tightly and set it in a cool place. Do not set vinegar with cheese while the cheese is aging.
- Rennet tablets and coloring may be purchased at drug or grocery stores. If they are not available in your area, they may be ordered from—

  Hansen's Laboratory, Inc., 9015 West Maple Street, Milwaukee, Wisconsin, U.S.A. 53200

  OR

  Horan Lilly Company Limited, 26 Kelfield Street, Rexdale, Ontario, Canada.
- Try scalding your milk for cottage cheese in a waterless cooker. The cooker has an insulated base. The milk will then require less watching and with a low fire is not apt to be overheated.

EQUIPMENT NEEDED TO MAKE SOLID CHEESE

rennet tablet
yellow food coloring (for yellow cheese)
wooden spoon

sharp knife with long blade
thermometer (a clean weather
  thermometer is sufficient)

To press the cheese, use an old lard press, or 2 canners which fit together like a double boiler (put water into the upper one for weight), or a lard or jam bucket which can be obtained from restaurants. Holes (about 18) should then be punched from the inside out into the one side of the bucket bottom to drain off whey. Set it on the table with the holes extending over the edge. Place a bucket beneath to catch the whey. Put a lid over the cheese with bricks on top.

GENERAL DIRECTIONS FOR CHEESE MAKING

1. Let milk set in a cool place overnight to ripen. A commercial starter may be added to hasten ripening, using 1 cup per gallon of milk.

2. The next morning warm the milk slowly to 86°.

3. Dissolve the cheese color tablet in ¼ cup of water and add it to the milk. Use ¾ tablet for 10 gallons of milk. Never mix the cheese coloring with the rennet tablet solution.

4. Dissolve the cheese rennet tablet in ¼ cup of cold water. Mix it with the milk at 86°. Ice cream junket tablets may be used instead of the rennet.

5. Remove the milk from the stove. Stir it gently but thoroughly with a wooden spoon for 2 minutes.

6. Cover the container and let it stand by a warm stove for 1 hour or until it is thick enough. To test it, put your finger into the milk and bring it up like a hook. If the curd breaks clean across your finger like jelly, it is thick enough.

7. Cut the curds into cubes using a long-bladed knife that extends to the bottom of the kettle. Cut ½-inch squares, then cut them diagonally. A wire bent in a U-shape may be used to cut the curds horizontally, using the 2 ends as handles. Cutting should give a clear whey.

8. Let the curds stand for 5 minutes. Return them to the stove, then stir them slowly and gently to keep the pieces from sticking together while the temperature is slowly raised to 100 to 102°, and kept there. Then stir them only occasionally so the pieces will not stick together.

   Instead of returning the curds to the stove, some of the whey may be taken from the top, strained into a dipper, then brought to a boil. Slowly pour the hot whey back into the curds, stirring the curds all the time. Continue this process until the temperature has risen to 100 to 102°. The curds are ready when a handful, squeezed firmly, does not squirt out between your fingers, but almost falls apart when your hand is opened. This takes about 1 hour.

9. Pour the heated curds into a colander which has been lined with cheese cloth, organdy or gauze diaper cloth. Catch the whey; it is a healthy drink, it may be used in recipes calling for water, and it is also a good tonic for flowers.

10. Gently work salt into the curds, about 1 tablespoon to 2 gallons of milk, or according to taste.

11. Leave the curds in the cloth, with only 1 thickness over the top, and place them in the prepared press—a lard press, bucket or cans. Do not use an aluminum container. Place the lid on top of the cheese. Weigh it down with 2 bricks, or the equivalent in weight. In the evening turn the cheese and double the weight. The next morning, remove the cheese from the press. Keep it in a warm room for 36 to 48 hours. Laying it in the sun by a window for ½ day will hasten the aging process.

12. Seal the cheese by brushing it with smoking hot paraffin, but be careful, for hot paraffin catches fire like oil. If the cheese is not solid, do not seal it. Instead of paraffin, vegetable or mineral oil may be rubbed into the cheese to keep it from becoming moldy. Another method to prevent mold is to mix only ½ of the salt into the cheese, then rub salt over it every few days. If mold appears, wash the cheese in warm salt water and salt it again. Turn it every few days.

13. Place the cheese in a room (cellar) with a temperature of about 60° and turn it every other day for 3 to 6 weeks. If it is kept longer, turn it twice a week. Cheese may be kept for several months. The longer it is cured, the sharper it becomes.

BUTTERMILK CHEESE

Let a quart of buttermilk set until it is thick. Pour 1 quart of boiling water over it, stirring it at the same time. Let it set for a few minutes. The cheese will go to the bottom. Pour off the water. Put the cheese into a cloth to drain for ½ day. Add salt according to taste.

CREAM CHEESE

1 quart light cream of good flavor
¼ cup fresh sour milk

Mix the ingredients well in the top of a double boiler or stainless steel bowl. Cover the mixture and let it stand at room temperature until it is thick. Skim the thin layer off the top if necessary. Cut it into squares and heat it over warm water to 110°. Make a few strokes across the bottom while warming. Handle it carefully so the cream does not get thin and drain off with the whey. Pour it into a cloth bag. After 15 minutes place the bag on a rack in the refrigerator with a bowl underneath to catch the whey. Drain it for 10 hours or so. Press the curds with a weight on top of the bag, until the curds are pasty. Turn them into a bowl, and with a fork or mixer, work in salt to taste (about ¾ teaspoon). Mix it thoroughly.

This cheese is good with crushed pineapple, or served on drained pear chunks.

MARVEL CREAM CHEESE

Make yogurt (see page 293). One quart makes about 6 to 8 ounces of Marvel Cream Cheese. Instead of refrigerating the yogurt once it has formed, pour it into a colander lined with a triple thickness of cheese cloth, or an old clean gauze diaper. Catch the whey by placing a bowl under the colander. Allow the whey to drip for 1 minute, then lift up the 4 corners of the cheese cloth and tie them together. Hang the bag at the sink faucet or elsewhere and let the whey drip for 6 to 8 hours. It is then ready to be removed from the bag and stored in the refrigerator. This cheese is almost identical to commercial brands of cream cheese.

CROCK CHEESE

Place a gallon of thickened sour milk on the stove. Stir it constantly and heat it to about 102° until you can press curds of milk together with your hand. Pour the curds into cheese cloth and thoroughly press out the whey. Melt 2 tablespoons of butter in a hot skillet, then add the curds, 1 teaspoon of soda and salt (approximately 1 teaspoon or according to taste). Stir it with a potato masher. Cook it until it is smooth, then add cream or milk to the thickness desired. Pour it into a bowl and it is ready to serve.

MUENSTER CHEESE

Let 2½ gallons of sour milk set until it is thick like junket. Scald it until it is too hot to hold your hand in, then pour it into cheese cloth. Let it hang until the curds are dry, overnight or for about 12 hours. Crumble the curds and mix 2 heaping teaspoons of soda and ½ cup of butter into them. Let them set for 2 hours then put them into a double boiler. Add 1 cup of sour cream and melt the cheese. When melted, add another cup of sour cream and 1 tablespoon of salt. Mix it well. Pour it into a buttered mold and let it set until it is completely cold before slicing it.

PROCESSED CHEESE

Let 5 gallons of skimmed milk sour until it is thick. Then scald it on top of the stove until it is hot enough to be uncomfortable for your hand, or until you can squeeze the whey out of the cheese with your hand. Then strain it through a cloth and squeeze it until it is very dry.

Grind the cheese finely in a food grinder. Then cook 5 cups of this dry cheese with the following in a double boiler until it is smooth (for approximately 1 hour or a little more.)

1 teaspoon soda	½ cup butter
2 teaspoons salt	1 to 1½ cups cream or milk

Stir it occasionally while it is cooling. To make a softer cheese add more milk. This recipe makes approximately 3 quarts.

SMEAR KASE

Take drained dry cheese and add salt, pepper and milk or cream. Mix it until it is smooth, then spread it on bread. It may be topped with molasses or apple butter.

STINK KASE

Put about 5 cups of dry curds into a dish. Mix in 1 teaspoon of soda and let it stand in a warm room until mold has begun to form over the top. The older it is, the stronger the flavor. Add 1 teaspoon of salt and then proceed with the same directions as for Crock Cheese (see page 289), by heating and adding milk or cream.

SOFT CHEESE

Select a quantity of very rich milk. Mix with this 3 to 5% of its bulk in clean well-soured skim milk or this amount of a commercial starter. Add dissolved rennet (2 ounces for each 10 pounds of milk) and set the mixture at 80°. When it is well thickened, cool it down to 60° by placing it in the refrigerator or by letting cold water run around the container. Care should be taken not to break the curd. After it has cooled for 24 hours, turn it into a cheese cloth sack and allow it to drain for another 24 hours. Add salt to taste. (The presence of fat makes a smooth, soft cheese.) This cheese can be molded into balls or printed in a butter printer and wrapped in oil paper or aluminum foil.

SPREADING CHEESE

Let 2½ gallons of skimmed milk sour until it is very thick, then heat it until it is too hot to hold your hand in, but not boiling. Drain it through a coarse cloth bag, putting only ½ of the milk through at a time, so as to be able to squeeze out as much water as possible. (If it is too hot, hold the bag under running water a minute to cool it.) Put it into a bowl and crumble it. This makes 4 cups or a little more of crumbs. Let it set at room temperature for 2 to 3 days, or longer if a stronger taste is desired.

To 4 cups of the crumbs add 2 teaspoons of soda, and mix. Let it stand for about 30 minutes, then stir in 1½ cups of warm water (scant). Set the bowl in a dishpan of boiling water or use a double boiler. Heat the mixture to the boiling point, then stir it vigorously. Add ⅓ cup of butter and 2 level teaspoons of salt. Add 1 cup of hot water, a little at a time, stirring after each addition. Cook it for 10 to 12 minutes longer or until the crumbs are mostly dissolved. If necessary, put it through a strainer. Stir it occasionally until it is cold. This makes approximately 1½ quarts of cheese.

Variations: Use milk instead of water with only 1 teaspoon of soda. One cup of hot cream may also be added.

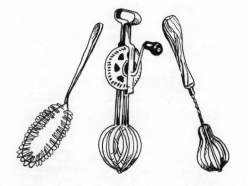

MISCELLANEOUS

MAKING YOGURT

Add 3 tablespoons of yogurt culture to 1 quart of warm milk. Set it in a warm place (about 100°) until it thickens. Do not serve all of the yogurt but let at least 3 tablespoons remain. To this add 1 pint of milk. Set it in a warm place until it thickens, then it is ready to serve. Repeat this process to make more yogurt from yogurt. Eventually it is necessary to buy fresh yogurt again as a starter.

YOGURT

To make yogurt, simply buy a small quantity of plain yogurt and stir 3 tablespoons into 1 quart of milk that has been slowly warmed to 98°. Keep the milk in a warm room for 5 to 6 hours. When it has thickened, the yogurt is ready to use. Keep it refrigerated.

More yogurt can be made from this yogurt by following the simple directions above.

JAR YEAST (SOURDOUGH)

4 medium-sized potatoes
3 pints boiling water
½ cup bread flour
½ cup sugar

2 teaspoons salt
1 cake yeast, dissolved in
¼ cup water

Pare the potatoes and boil them in the boiling water until they are soft. Mash them, or put them through a strainer, then return them to the water. Use the hot water mixture to scald the flour, sugar and salt. Let it cool, then add the yeast and set it aside to rise. There should be 1 quart of this mixture. (Use 1 cup of sourdough (jar yeast) instead of 1 cake of yeast.)

Always save 2 cups of starter from each baking. To this, add the same amount of water that was used from the jar and store it in a cool place for the next baking. This may be done for a long time, but occasionally a fresh starter needs to be made.

JAR YEAST (YOGURT CULTURE)

Heat 1 cup of milk to lukewarm, then add ⅛ cake of yeast. Cover it and set it in a warm place until the next day (24 hours). Take ½ the liquid and pour in 1 cup of warm milk. For 7 days add ½ cup of warm milk to ½ the liquid. Always keep the yeast milk in a warm place. On the 7th day use all the yeast milk and add 2 cups of warm milk. Let it set for another 24 hours. This makes 3 cups of yogurt starter.

HOW TO FREEZE EGGS

Stir up 2 or 3 eggs at a time as for scrambled eggs, and freeze them in small containers. They can be used later for baking, but not for any other purpose.

PRESERVING ELDERBERRIES

2 gallons elderberries
1 pint vinegar
4 pounds sugar

Boil the ingredients until thick. This can be used for pie. Store it in crocks.

Plums can also be cooked this way but they need no vinegar as they are sour. Water should be added before putting plums into a pie crust.

BATTER FOR DEEP FRYING

1 cup flour
¼ teaspoon salt
2 teaspoons baking powder

2 eggs, separated
⅔ cup sweet milk
1 tablespoon melted butter

Sift and measure the flour. Add the salt and baking powder and sift it again. Add the beaten egg yolks and milk, then the beaten egg whites and melted butter. This is good for fish or cooked chicken. Two batches make enough for 3 fryers.

TEETHING COOKIES

Break 2 eggs into a bowl. Stir them in one direction until they are creamy. Add 1 cup of sugar. Continue stirring in the same direction. Gradually stir 2 to 2½ cups of sifted flour into the mixture and continue stirring it until the mixture is stiff. Roll out the dough with a rolling pin, between 2 lightly floured sheets of waxed paper, to a thickness of ¾ inch. Use a drinking glass and a salt shaker to cut out doughnut shaped cookies. Place the cookies on a lightly buttered cookie sheet. Let the formed cookies stand overnight (10 to 12 hours). Bake them in a preheated oven at 325° until they are lightly browned and hard. This recipe makes approximately 12 durable and relatively crumb-proof teething biscuits.

GRAHAM CRACKERS

2 cups sugar
4 cups graham flour
1 teaspoon soda
1 teaspoon salt
1 teaspoon vanilla

2 cups all-purpose flour
1 cup shortening
1 teaspoon baking powder
1 cup milk

Make a dough with the ingredients, then roll it out thinly. Cut it and prick it with a fork. Bake it at 350° until nice and brown.

SOFT PRETZELS

1 envelope yeast
1¼ cups warm water
1 teaspoon sugar
2 teaspoons salt

4 to 5 cups all-purpose flour
Butter as needed
4 teaspoons soda
Coarse salt for sprinkling

Dissolve the yeast in ¼ cup of the water. Then stir in an additional cup of warm water, and the sugar. Pour the yeast mixture into a bowl and add the salt. Beat in the flour to make a stiff dough. Knead it for 10 minutes or until the dough is elastic. Place it in a bowl and spread it with butter. Cover it and let it rise for 45 minutes or until double in size. Shape the dough into sticks or twists. Make it ½ the thickness of the desired finished pretzel.

Bring 4 cups of water to boiling with the soda. Drop in 3 pretzels at a time. Boil them for 1 minute or until they float. Remove and drain them, and place them on buttered cookie sheets. Sprinkle them with coarse salt. Bake the pretzels at 475° for 12 minutes or until golden brown. To make them crisp, lay them on a cookie sheet and place them in a warm oven (200°) for 2 hours.

NOODLES

6 egg yolks
6 tablespoons water

3 cups all-purpose flour (approximate)
1 teaspoon salt

Beat the egg yolks and water for a few minutes. Add the flour to make a dough as stiff as possible but still workable. Divide it into 4 balls, then roll them very thinly. Lay them separately on a cloth to dry. They are ready to cut when they are almost dry and do not stick together.

How to Quick Cut Noodles;

Put as many as 12 sheets of noodles on top of each other when they are dry enough to cut. Roll them tightly and cut them with a sharp butcher knife. After they are cut, lay them out on a table in a warm place, cover them with a cloth and let them dry thoroughly. Store them in a tightly closed container.

HOW TO DRY CORN

Cook corn for 10 minutes as for roasting ears. Cut it from the cob. To each gallon of cut corn add ¾ cup of sweet cream (optional), ½ cup of white sugar (optional) and salt to taste. Pour it into flat pans and place them in the oven at 200° to dry. Stir the corn often so it will dry more evenly.

When using the oven for drying, do not forget to leave the oven door open.

CORNMEAL

Dry selected ears of field corn or sweet corn in a slow (275°) open-door oven for several days, or until the corn shells easily by hand. The cornmeal is tasty when the corn has been slightly browned. Shell the corn, then take it to a mill to have it ground. Put it into an oblong pan and bake it in a slow oven for a more toasted flavor. Stir it occasionally. Place the cornmeal in a tightly covered container when it is cool.

CORN MUSH

Bring 3 cups of water to a boil. Make a thickening with 1 cup of cornmeal, 1 teaspoon of salt and 1 cup of milk. Add it to the boiling water. Stir it until it has reached the boiling point, then stir it occasionally. Cook it for 15 to 20 minutes then pour it into a deep baking dish. Let it cool, then slice and fry it.

To clean the mush kettle after the mush has been poured out, put 1 or 2 cups of water into the kettle. Add 1 teaspoon of soda. Cover it, then bring it to the boiling point. Set the kettle aside, but keep it covered until dishwashing time.

DRIED FRUIT

These are lunch box treats for children as they are naturally sweet.

Pears—Take firm pears, peel them, then make small snitz (dried pieces). Dry them as you would other fruit.

Peaches—Cut them into quarters, unpeeled, then dry them. They can also be mashed, spread in a thin layer on pie plates and dried in the oven. This is called PEACH LEATHER and is a great snack.

Prune plums—Cut them in half. Remove the pits. Place them in a dryer.

Apricots—Cut them in half, remove the pits and dry them.

Plums—These can be dried but if they get too hot, they become mushy.

Apples—Quarter peeled slices, then lay them on a dryer. When put through a food cutter and dried they make a delicious snack or addition to breakfast cereals.

Elderberries—They can be dried in the sun on a warm, sunny day. Spread them thinly on a sugar bag or a brown paper bag in a warm, dry, sunny place.

DRIED TOMATOES

Pour boiling water over ripe tomatoes. Let them stand for a few minutes. Slip the skins off then cut them into pieces. Put them through a Foley food mill. Fill greased pie pans with them about ½ full, then put them into a slow oven (275°). After they are dried only a thin layer is left. Fold them and put them into a dry container. When ready to use, add water and cook them up again.

DRIED GREEN BEANS

Cook beans for 15 to 30 minutes or until the green color disappears. Spread the beans in thin layers on pans. Dry them in a slow oven at 250° until dry. Store them in a tightly sealed container for winter use.

How to Use Dried Beans;

Fry ¼ pound of bacon. Pour off the grease then add 3 cups of dried beans, 1 teaspoon of salt and water to cover them. Cook them until the beans are soft and most of the water is absorbed; OR

Pour boiling water over 2 or 3 cups of dried beans. Let them set for several hours, then drain them. Add water to cover them and cook for 1 to 1½ hours. The cooked beans may be added to meat and gravy and vegetables as a one dish meal.

HOW TO ROAST SOYBEANS

People have different methods of roasting soybeans. Even if they do not quite agree on method, they all agree that roasted soybeans are delicious as well as nutritious. Here the different ways of preparing them are all merged into one recipe. The reader can decide his or her own method of roasting them.

Wash the beans in cold water and remove the debris. Some soak the beans overnight, some 6 hours, others 3 hours and some only 10 minutes in warm water. Drain them well by placing them on a towel. (Some prefer to cover the soybeans with water and freeze them, thawing them before roasting.) Place the soybeans in oil that has been preheated to 375 to 400°. (They may be put into a colander to set in the oil.) Cook them until they begin to crack in ½ and float to the top and the oil stops bubbling—some keep them in for 3 minutes, others for 10 minutes, and still others for 20 minutes. Watch closely, for soybeans burn easily. Drain them and add salt. (Add more oil if the beans cook dry.)

Oven-Roasted Soybeans;

Soak washed soybeans overnight. Boil them for 1 hour in salted water. Spread them in a shallow pan and roast them at 350° until brown. Sprinkle them with salt while warm.

GREEN TOMATOES FOR PIE

Wash and trim out the stalks from 1 gallon of green tomatoes. Slice them quite thinly. Add ½ crock of white sugar and boil this mixture until it is thick. Add 2 lemons, thinly sliced, about 15 minutes before removing it from the stove. This can be kept in crocks and used as needed.

Before putting the tomato mixture into a pie shell, add water to make them thinner. Place a crust on top.

CORN COB SYRUP

Boil 6 red corn cobs, washed, for 1 hour in 3 quarts of water. Strain them, then add 3 pounds of brown sugar and water enough to make 3 quarts. Boil this mixture until it is the consistency of maple syrup.

Be sure to select clean corn cobs, free from mold. Light colored cobs will make a lighter syrup and give a better flavor.

BURNT SUGAR SYRUP

Into a heavy skillet that heats uniformly, pour 2 cups of granulated sugar. Melt the sugar over low heat, stirring it constantly with a wooden spoon to prevent scorching. When the sugar becomes a clear brown syrup, remove it from the heat. Slowly stir in 1 cup of boiling water and return it to a low heat, stirring the syrup until it is smooth again. Let it cool, then pour it into a clean pint jar. Cover it tightly and store it at room temperature. It keeps for 6 to 8 weeks. This recipe makes 1⅓ cups of syrup.

INDEX

301

BREAD AND ROSES TOO

Also by Jack Newfield

A PROPHETIC MINORITY

ROBERT KENNEDY: A MEMOIR

JACK NEWFIELD

Bread and Roses Too

E. P. Dutton & Co., Inc. | *New York* | *1971*

Published simultaneously in Canada by Clarke, Irwin & Company Limited,
Toronto and Vancouver

Library of Congress Catalog Card Number: 73-148476

SBN: 0-525-07085-0

for Dan, Hal, Janie, and my Mother

Contents

NINE SOME PEOPLE I LIKED

Author's Preface

This is a collection of journalism. Most of the pieces were written for *The Village Voice* against a deadline of a few days or a few hours. Rereading them now I occasionally wish I had taken more time to polish the language, to develop fragments of thought, to interview more people for background information.

But as an advocacy journalist, these pieces were flares defined by their immediacy and engagement. So I have resisted the temptation to tidy them up because to do so would make them something else. The only changes I have made were the correction of factual errors. I have not tried to reconcile contradictions or update opinions I no longer hold.

Several of the longer pieces were written for publications other than *The Voice*. In most cases, I was lucky enough to work with exceptional editors: Steve Gelman at *Life*, Carey McWilliams at *The Nation*, Clay Felker and Sheldon Zalaznick at *New York* magazine. And, of course, Ross Wetzsteon, the unsung hero of *The Voice*.

I would also like to acknowledge the debt I feel to some friends from whom I have learned so much over the last five years: Paul and Rachel Cowan, Paul Gorman, Fred Gardner, Pete Hamill, Harold Ickes, Jerry Kretchmer, Jeff Greenfield, Tom Hayden, and James Breslin.

Introduction

Over the five years that these pieces were experienced and written, I slowly learned a few useful lessons, and they gradually congealed into a few deeply felt ideas. And like most writers, I find I have been repeating these essential themes in different forms.

The mass media—television and the newsmagazines—do not tell us the truth. The most powerful influence in this country distorts, usually subtly, in the direction of authority, fashion, and advertisers.

Socialism and democracy must be united. Unless radicalism is yoked to freedom and reason, unless it wears a human face, it will fail and will deserve to fail.

If we are at all serious, we have to find out who we are, and not ride every little manufactured tide, from the occult, to Camp and Pop, to hot pants and acid rock. If fascism ever comes to America, it will come as a fad dressed in lovebeads and hyped by *Esquire* magazine.

Character is more important than politics. It is more important how people treat each other, that they tell the truth and be open-minded and compassionate, than that they hold the precisely correct ideological position on every issue.

And the most basic idea of all, the idea that underlies so many of these pieces and gives this collection whatever unity and cohesion it has: the Center cannot hold.

By the Center I mean the unions, the Congress and the courts; the Ford Foundation and the RAND Corporation; and politicians like Nelson Rockefeller and Hubert Humphrey. I mean intellectuals like Daniel Moynihan, Irving Kristol, and Henry Kissinger, organizations like the Bar Association, and General Motors. I mean the notion that America is getting better, that our problems are being exaggerated, that the Peace Corps, or the OEO, or revenue sharing by creative federalists can actually heal the structural ills of poverty, racism, and war.

And I mean that the guiding philosophy of the Center—
liberal anticommunism—is the name of the problem.

The liberal anticommunism of unions like the Building
Trades and the United Federation of Teachers would make Joe
Hill weep. The liberal anticommunism of those "tough-minded"
professors like Bundy, Rostow, Roche, and Kissinger has become
no different from the kill-ratio projections of computers. Liberal
anticommunism has become a barrier to social change, a dead
hand preventing the liberation of new ideas, new programs, new
movements, new dreams.

After zigzagging ambiguously through the 1930s and '40s, the
American electoral Left fell off the track entirely in about 1950,
and we are still paying the backbreaking price.

We are paying that price most painfully and obviously with
the war in Indochina. It is, as so many commentators have said,
"the liberals' war," begun by John Kennedy and his circle of liberal intellectual advisers, and then escalated by Lyndon Johnson,
Hubert Humphrey, Adlai Stevenson, Arthur Goldberg, and Robert McNamara.

One reason we stumbled into such a monstrous mistake as
Vietnam without any national debate prior to 1965, is that those
liberals who should have been organizing the opposition, were
busy making the policy. The official rationale for Vietnam—
global anticommunism wed to the rhetoric of social reform and
renamed counterinsurgency—was the heart of the mistake made
by the Kennedy Administration. And this was considered on the
New Frontier to be a humanistic advance over some of Dulles's
theories.

We are also paying a terrible price in the consequences that
flow from an AFL-CIO leadership that stands to the right of the
Catholic Church and the *Wall Street Journal* on many questions
of public policy: from all-out support for the war in Vietnam, to
snickering at Women's Liberation, to the toleration of racism
within major member unions. The most liberal thing the AFL-
CIO has done in ten years was prevent their members from voting for George Wallace in 1968. And one cannot help but notice
that the morality of the unions did not improve after the Reds
and fellow travelers were all kicked out in the late 1940s.*

* Irving Howe and Lewis Coser wrote in their landmark study of American
Communism, "Granting the desirability of eliminating communist influence
from the trade union movement, one might still have argued that mass ex-

And last, we are paying that price in the unnatural isolation of the student, black, and antiwar movements of the 1960s, which were forced to start from scratch, ignored and often opposed by the generation that should have been their historical big brothers.

The point being that during the 1950s liberalism lost its will to fight and accepted the basic economic and foreign policy assumptions of the Right. And this pulled the center of gravity of American politics decisively away from the Left.

During the 1950s, when liberalism was out of power, and should have been insurgent, the leading liberals betrayed their own tradition of Jefferson, Jackson, Lincoln, Brandeis, and Roosevelt by embracing a wide range of antidemocratic and militaristic policies of the Right while claiming to represent the Left. And although liberals, from Wilson to FDR, had lost many of their struggles with business and the corporations, during the 1950s they gave up even proposing economic reforms to improve the conditions of Roosevelt's "one third of a nation ill-fed, ill-housed, and ill-clothed."

The reason for liberalism's failure was not just the Cold War, or McCarthyism, or that the unions purged all their radicals. It was that the central intellectual formulations of liberal anticommunism were mistaken. Or at least much more transient and exaggerated than their messianic architects realized.

I do not say the liberals of the 1950s were badly motivated, or uncommonly corrupt, or that any significant numbers were caught in the web of conspiracy weaved by the CIA spider. All I say is that they were in error, and their poor judgment has had grievous historical consequences.

They were wrong, first, in their total, fanatical anticommunism, which permitted no possibility for change in the Soviet bloc, and blinded them to obvious injustices within their own society, and within the so-called "free world."

Sidney Hook was able to write in *Partisan Review* in 1952:

"I cannot understand why American intellectuals should be apologetic about the fact that they are limited in their effective historical choice between endorsing a system of total terror, and *critically* supporting our own imperfect democratic culture . . ." (Italics in original.)

pulsions were not only a poor way of achieving this end, but constituted a threat to democratic values and procedures."

That was never the either/or choice intellectuals faced. There were always the independent alternatives of democratic radicalism, or neutralism in the cold war, or the movements against colonialism then being born in the womb of the Third World, movements from Vietnam to Cuba that almost all the cold war liberals ignored in their preoccupation with white Western Europe.

The second theoretical mistake the '50s liberals made was the "end of ideology" mischief, popularized by Daniel Bell's book bearing that axiom. That theory held the remarkable idea that all the large problems of America had been solved, and all that was required now was small adjustments, some minor technological tinkering with the soft machine at the top.

The foolishness of this theory has been proven many times over by the mass movements of the 1960s. But the same problems were all there during the '50s, too. Poverty, the growth of the arms budget, imperialism, McCarthyism, the oppression of women, migrant farm workers, slums, the destruction of the environment, and most clearly, the racism of the South. But the intellectuals did not care to look.

Bell's book was published in 1960, five years after Martin Luther King's bus boycott in Montgomery baptized the southern movement. Yet in Bell's large index there are only four passing references to Negroes, the longest one dealing with crime statistics. None referred to the civil rights movement.

The "end of ideology" now seems to have been merely an autobiographical epitaph for one generation of weary sociologists who lost the capacity to imagine new radical movements growing within affluent America. It was an elitist generalization totally inapplicable to blacks, the Third World, or even the generation of Americans in high school in 1960.

It would, however, be unfair to place the whole burden for this theory on Bell's shoulders. Professor S. M. Lipsit was equally persuasive and probably more energetic in his promotion of it. It was Professor Lipsit who wrote in the last chapter of his book, *Political Man* (1959): ". . . the fundamental political problems of the industrial revolution have been solved . . . This very triumph of the democratic social revolution in the West ends domestic politics for those intellectuals who must have ideologies or utopias to motivate them to political action."

The third false premise of the 1950s was the popular notion

that the "quality of life" was the next great question facing liberalism, since only "pockets of poverty" remained to be mopped up. The advocates of this middle-class notion argued that identity and fulfillment in a mass society was the urgent issue of the day.

I believe the "new issue" that faced liberalism in 1956, and faces it today, is the unequal distribution of wealth and land and power in America. Liberals have become absolute geniuses at inventing causes and novelties to evade the fundamental question of distribution of wealth.* They have made the abolition of HUAC, legalization of marijuana, ecology, school busing, admission of mainland China to the UN, almost anything else their central concern, to avoid facing up to the economic question the Populists had placed first on the agenda of justice.

Unemployment, rotten housing, inadequate health care, no land, inferior education, lousy sanitation, disease—all the same old boring crap—but still the heart of the matter. The pop sociologists might call it a "spiritual crisis," or a "crisis in confidence," but what it all comes down to is too many poor people excluded from an economy of astounding abundance.

The last erroneous pillar of anticommunist liberalism was the idea—put forward by Sidney Hook, Irving Kristol, and many others—that the united front against Stalinism had made all the traditional distinctions between Left, Right, and Center irrelevant. Again, I think this was an overreaction to the undeniable evil of Stalinism. But the fact is the Left has always had a sense of outrage against poverty and injustice, and the Right has always defended order and property out of a sense of tradition. And that distinction has never been erased.

* * *

Basically what happened during the 1950s was that some liberals who called themselves socialists became conservatives, partly out of guilt for once having been Marxists.

They went from one failed God to a bright new religion called anticommunism without the smallest flirtation with agnosticism

---

* According to Gus Tyler, the ILGWU's resident intellectual, 1 percent of the American population owns 36 percent of the national wealth, including land. And according to G. William Domhoff's *Who Rules America?*, 90,000 American families own between two thirds and three quarters of all corporate stock.

or doubt. Major intellectual figures like Hook and Reinhold Nie-
buhr became as dogmatic as liberals as they had been as Marxists. The first warning signal that liberalism's mood was about to
shift toward accommodation and diminished goals came as early
as 1948. That spring the leaders of the just-born ADA tried to
draft General Dwight Eisenhower (yes, Ike!) to challenge Harry
Truman for the Democratic nomination for president. This is
not an episode liberal journalists tend to remember, but it is recited straightforwardly by Cabell Phillips in his book, *The Truman Presidency* (Macmillan, 1966). Phillips lists among those
plotting the overthrow of Truman for Eisenhower: Hubert Humphrey, ADA chairman Leon Henderson, "the Liberal Party in
New York," James Roosevelt, Senator Paul Douglas, Walter
Reuther, Chester Bowles, and the ADA's Wilson Wyatt. The
boom for Ike folded a week before the convention opened in
Philadelphia when he issued a Sherman-type declaration of non-
candidacy from Morningside Heights. Yet these liberals must have
sensed something in Eisenhower, perhaps his lack of politics, that
struck a barely conscious chord in them.

The new "realistic" mood among intellectuals crystallized with
the founding of The Congress for Cultural Freedom in West Berlin in June of 1950. The original sponsors of this new organization included Sidney Hook, Arthur Schlesinger, Elliot Cohen,
Walter Reuther, Arthur Koestler, Melvin Lasky, James Burnham, James T. Farrell, and Franz Borkenau of Austria. Koestler, Hook, Burnham, and Borkenau had all been Communists
during the 1930s, and their repentant anticommunism (an ideology itself) dominated the CCF's opening assembly. Commitment
and Socialism came under heavy attack in speeches given and papers delivered. Socialism was turned into a synonym for Stalinism, and political passion was ridiculed as a sign of immaturity.
"Pragmatism" was much praised.

The CCF quickly became the fashionable center—pure anti-
Stalinism, divorced from any radical critique of capitalism, and
put forward by men who continued to describe themselves as socialists.

Although the fierceness of the CCF's anti-Stalinism was
unique, its more general stance of pro-American political and
cultural analysis came to dominate the entire intellectual community.

In 1952 *Partisan Review* began its famous three-part symposium on "Our Country and Our Culture," in which most of the
twenty-five participants managed to appreciate the Kitsch culture
that was beginning to make them affluent and semifamous with
professorships, book contracts, foundation grants, assignments
from mass circulation magazines, and free airplane tickets to international conferences. Only four of the contributors—C.
Wright Mills, Norman Mailer, Philip Rahv, and Irving Howe—
directly challenged the new fashion of acceptance.*

Lionel Trilling spoke for the satisfied majority when he
wrote:

> Even the most disaffected intellectual must respond
> . . . to the growing isolation of his country amid the
> hostility which is directed against it. He has become
> aware of the virtual uniqueness of American security
> and well-being, and at the same time, of the danger
> in which they stand. . . . There is an unmistakable
> improvement in the present American cultural situa-
> tion over that of, say thirty years ago. . . . Intellect
> has associated itself with power as perhaps never before
> in our history, and is now conceded to be itself a kind
> of power.

C. Wright Mills represented the unreconciled rebels with
prophetic power:

> American intellectuals seem quite decisively to have
> shifted their attitude toward America . . . from a politi-
> cal and critical orientation toward life and letters to a
> more literary and less politically critical view. Or: gener-
> ally to a shrinking deference to the status quo; often to
> a soft and anxious compliance, and always a synthetic
> and feeble search to justify this intellectual conduct,
> without searching for alternatives, and sometimes with-
> out even political good sense . . . And I would, of
> course, impute the leveling and the frenzy effects of
> mass culture in this country not to "democracy" but to

---

* The contributions by Delmore Schwartz and William Phillips were less
political and combative, but also dissented from the majority, and stand the
test of time very well.

capitalist commercialism which manipulates people into
standardized tastes and then exploits these tastes . . . as
marketable brands. . . .

 I also believe, as an amateur historian, that one
should never allow one's values to be overwhelmed in
the short runs of time: that is the way of the literary
faddist and the technician of the cultural chic. One just
has to wait, as others before one have, while remembering that what in one decade is utopian may in the next
be implementable . . . In the meantime, we must bear
with the fact that in many circles impatience with
things as they are in America is judged to be either mu-
tinous or utopian.

By 1956 *Time* magazine could put a certified intellectual on its
cover—Jacques Barzun—to celebrate the arrival of the "Man of
Affirmation" to replace the outdated "Man of Protest."

"In 1956," the Timeniks wrote, "it would seem the intellectual
has ceased weeping . . . Many have come at last to realize that
they are true and proud participants in the American Dream."

An excessive conformity among intellectuals, or compliance
with a trend, is something that is legitimately open to critical debate. Even the giving of names of communists to congressional
committees, the way writers of the stature of James Wechsler *
and Granville Hicks did, is perhaps understandable given the
context of history. (Wechsler, at least, continued to attack
McCarthy in print, before and after he bent in private before the
committee's subpoena.) But what is much harder to forgive, or
understand, is the actual justification some intellectuals and journals lent to McCarthyism, on the basis that it was a necessary
evil.

Irving Kristol could write in the March 1952 issue of *Commentary:* "There is one thing that the American people know about
Senator McCarthy: he, like them, is unequivocally anti-Commu-
nist. About the spokesmen for American liberalism, they feel they
know no such thing."

As late as July of 1954, Alan Westin could publish an essay in

---

* See *The Haunted Fifties,* by I. F. Stone, pages 44 and 50. Also, for a full
discussion of Wechsler's submission of 60 names to McCarthy and his failure
to defend fellow editor Cedric Belfrage when McCarthy had him deported,
see James Aronson's book, "The Press and The Cold War," pages 87–102.

Commentary warning that the communists are exploiting the issue of McCarthyism. And Leslie Fiedler published a piece in the August 1954 issue of *Encounter* mocking "the loud fears of intellectuals" and again attacking the "outlived illusions of the Left."

In 1951 an American Committee for Cultural Freedom (ACCF) was launched by Hook, Schlesinger, Bell, and Diana Trilling. And acting on their freshly minted theory that anti-Stalinism had rendered all the old distinctions between Left and Right outdated, the American group recruited actual right-wingers like Ralph de Toledano (now a Nixon biographer and friend), John Chamberlain, John Dos Passos, and Whittaker Chambers. They helped cement the new consensus based on the atrophy of change and the death of class conflict.

But because the American group (just like the communists) viewed culture primarily as a political weapon in the cold war, it was not successful in recruiting the real cultural innovators of the '50s like Norman Mailer, Robert Lowell, Allen Ginsberg, Paul Goodman, Miles Davis, Lenny Bruce, Ralph Ellison, and Nelson Algren. Film-makers, satirists, sculptors, architects, musicians, jazzmen, and composers were outside the organization's political concept of culture. Its mainstays were intellectual pols like Hook, Kristol, and Daniel Bell.

One of the most cogent criticisms of the American group was published by Michael Harrington in a 1955 issue of *Dissent*. I quote it here, partly because Harrington's own anticommunism is beyond question. Harrington wrote:

> Under the guidance of [Sidney] Hook and the leadership of [Irving] Kristol, who supported Hook's general outlook, the American Committee [for Cultural Freedom] cast its weight not so much in defense of those civil liberties which were steadily being nibbled away, but rather against those few remaining fellow travelers who tried to exploit the civil liberties issue.
>
> At times this had an almost comic aspect. When Irving Kristol was executive secretary of the ACCF, one learned to expect from him silence on those issues that were agitating the whole intellectual and academic world, and enraged communiqués on the outrages performed by people like Arthur Miller and Bertrand Rus-

sell in exaggerating the dangers to civil liberties in the
U.S. . . .

One of the crippling assumptions of the Committee
has been that it would not intervene in cases where Stalinists or accused Stalinists were involved. It has rested
this position on the academic argument . . . that Stalinists, being enemies of democracy, have no "right" to
democratic privileges. . . . But the actual problem is
not the metaphysical one of whether enemies of democracy [as the Stalinists clearly are] have a "right" to democratic privileges. What matters is that the drive against
cultural freedom and civil liberties takes on the guise of
anti-Stalinism.

It now all seems incredible. An organization conceived to defend cultural freedom doing McCarthy's work for him! An
organization of the outstanding intellectuals in the land failing
to take the lead in defending the freedoms of speech, association,
and thought when under direct attack from an anti-intellectual
Republican demagogue!

In 1967 a fragment of the reason came out. The Congress for
Cultural Freedom, and its American affiliate, and its sponsored
magazine *Encounter* were all the recipients of secret funds from
the CIA. A CIA agent (Michael Josselson) helped start, and later
as executive director, helped run the Congress. And, according to
Thomas Braden, the man who directed the CIA's cultural activities, "Another agent became an editor of *Encounter*." *

It is easy to slip into a reverse McCarthyism about the CIA's
role in all this. But it seems clear that most of the contributors to
Encounter, and most of those who joined the CCF were not
aware of all the facts, that most of them were, in McCarthy's preferred phrase, duped.

The point, however, is that they did not have to be "witting."
Most of them independently agreed with the cold war analysis of
culture as politics.

It is also easy to make rhetoric about an organization started
to defend truth ending up being based on a great lie. But I think
the deeper issue here, and the one usually overlooked in the

---

* See Braden's article, "I'm Glad the CIA Is Immoral," *Saturday Evening
Post,* May 20, 1967.

flights of rhetoric, is the one of values Jason Epstein explored in his *New York Review of Books* essay in April of 1967:

> It was not a matter of [The CIA] buying off and subverting individual writers and scholars, but of setting up an arbitrary and factitious system of values by which academic personnel were advanced, magazine editors appointed, and scholars subsidized and published, not necessarily on their merits . . . but because of their allegiances. The fault of the CIA was not that it corrupted the innocent, but that it tried, in collusion with a group of insiders, to corner a free market. . . .
>
> The CIA and the Ford Foundation, among other agencies, had set up and were financing an apparatus of intellectuals selected for their correct cold war positions, as an alternative to what might be called a free intellectual market, where ideology was presumed to count far less than individual talent and achievement, and where doubts about established orthodoxies were taken to be the beginning of all inquiry.

If the intellectuals * defaulted so shamelessly, how much resistance to McCarthyism could reasonably be expected from the professional politicians?

Not much. It seems almost unnecessary at this late date to document the default once again, but reading the faded yellow clippings of the early '50s, one aches for the chance to replay history with a few pinch-hitters.

When the United States Senate passed the bill making it a crime to belong to the Communist Party, only one member— Estes Kefauver of Tennessee—voted against it. Humphrey, Morse, Douglas, the rest of the liberals, voted Yes.

In February of 1954 the Senate voted $214,000 for McCarthy's committee. This was two years after McCarthy had accused the Democrats of "twenty years of treason," and called Adlai Stevenson a "Communist dupe." But only a single vote was cast against the subsidy—by J. William Fulbright of Arkansas.

In July of 1953 the Senate passed a new McCarran Act, which in effect, repealed the Fifth Amendment. The bill compelled wit-

---

* There were, of course, noble exceptions like Lillian Hellman, Paul Goodman, Arthur Miller, and I. F. Stone.

nesses before investigative committees to surrender constitutional right against self-incrimination, to testify on the basis of immunity from prosecution; in other words, coercion to inform.

Only ten Senators voted against the legislation, and some of them were right-wing Democrats: Stennis, McClellan, and Kerr of Oklahoma. The only two liberals among them were Herbert Lehman of New York and John Sherman Cooper of Kentucky.* The rest—Humphrey, John Kennedy, Douglas—went along, trying to prove still their own anticommunism.

In foreign policy most of the political liberals were mute; mute as the CIA overthrew the leftist government of Guatemala, mute at the CIA's intervention in Iran, mute about the support for Chiang, Battista, Diem, Trujillo, and other "free world" dictators, mute as the arms budget grew like Topsy.

And without the intellectuals providing a better example, without sustained criticism and analysis from the Left, the liberal Democrats enlisted as privates in the cold war to prove themselves "tough-minded" and "realistic." But they were too clever by half.

When they woke up, the permanent war economy and the military-industrial complex were an impregnable reality. Their own anticommunist rhetoric became the official justification for Vietnam. And a new generation wanted to hold them accountable for their actions: the politicians for their votes, and the intellectuals for their judgment.

What I've tried to say here is not that the liberals should have acted like radicals during the 1950s, but that *they didn't even act like liberals*. They were not true to their own tradition. They did not defend freedom and reason when McCarthy began his witch hunt. They informed and compromised and voted freedoms away just like the moderates and the reactionaries. And that's what all the jabber about "consensus" and "end of ideology" really meant.

Something else, something less obvious, happened to liberalism during the 1950s. The Democratic Party, the essential instrument of liberalism, began to move away from the working masses and became snobbish and elitist.

---

* In the end it was conservative Republican senators like Ralph Flanders of Vermont and Margaret Chase Smith of Maine who brought McCarthy down, with the help of a conservative Secretary of the Army.

On the issues of the cold war and civil liberties, Adlai Stevenson conducted himself better than most public men of his time. He was an attractive man of taste and decency. His campaign speeches, often drafted by Schlesinger or Galbraith, danced with wit and elegant phrases. He was a magnificent Tory.

But with Stevenson's two campaigns, the Democrats began to drift away from their traditional role of representing the needs of the lower middle class—the workers. Part of it was Stevenson's patrician style, the impression he gave of not really liking people or politics. And part of it was programmatic. Stevenson did not talk much about economic problems, what the pols like to call "bread and butter issues," despite the flagging economic growth rate and the two mini-recessions of the '50s.

He was very good talking about the United Nations and the atom bomb. But one reads his old speeches in vain looking for a passion for raising the minimum wage, or public ownership, or building more low-income housing, or protecting consumers, or attacking corporate price fixing and corruption, or getting tax reform to help families with incomes of under $10,000 a year, or regulating big business.

In 1954 Irving Howe published an excellent essay in *Dissent* trying to deflate the Stevenson cult then so powerful among liberal intellectuals.

> Stevenson, [Howe wrote] was the first of the liberal candidates in the post-Wilson era who made no effort to align himself with the plebeian tradition or plebeian sentiments. . . .
>
> Just as Stevenson bewitched the intellectuals by miming, from on high, their political impulses, so did he fail to attract very much enthusiasm among the workers. By and large they voted for him, but with little of the fervor they felt for Roosevelt and Truman. . . . Truman was one of the plebes, and after his triumph over Dewey there was a remarkable elation in the Detroit auto plants. . . . A striking characteristic of Stevenson's campaign, as distinct from Roosevelt's or Truman's, was that he did not speak in the name of the poor or the workers. . . . The conservative press was always delighted to praise him for not indulging in Truman's "demagogy," that is, for not employing Truman's "anti-plutocrat" vocabulary.

Howe correctly pointed out that "Truman was, if anything, slightly to the left of Stevenson." But the intellectuals fell in love with Stevenson for reasons even now difficult to understand. Part of it might have been Stevenson's weariness, his civilized stance of being *above politics, beyond ideology*. Part of it was surely his personal qualities of reason and wit.

But what I can't understand is why a similar affection was not forthcoming for Stevenson's great rival, Estes Kefauver, a better liberal and a better politician. Kefauver, who stood in the tradition of Southern Populism, did talk about the things the workers cared about, and if he had been nominated in 1952 or 1956, I think the Democratic Party might not have begun the process of alienating the white workers who now vote for Wallace and cheer for Agnew.

Kefauver, bereft of polish or style, or the tragic quality many saw in Stevenson, fought hard for the people Dos Passos called "the working stiffs."

Kefauver led the fight to prevent the "private power crowd" from taking over the Tennessee Valley Authority. He attacked the steel industry and the auto industry for overpricing. He beat the giant drug lobby and made the drug companies lower the price of medicines for the sick and the aged. In 1950 Congress passed the Kefauver-Celler antitrust law, and in 1962 Kefauver got Congress to tighten the pure food and drug laws. In the Senate, he opposed the seniority system, and, perhaps, in his most famous crusade, he went after the Mafia in 1950, even though it embarrassed a lot of big-city Democrats and helped retire Mayor O'Dwyer of New York.

But Kefauver was poor, and his crusades antagonized all the vested interests that control the Democratic Party, so he was never nominated for President.*

From 1960 to 1968 the liberal Democrats had a chance to govern again. But that whole time they were unable to think up a single large programmatic idea that ventured beyond the familiar formulas of the New Deal.† Liberalism had become just a set of bureaucratic routines to defend, rather than a new vision to

---

* In 1952 Kefauver won thirteen and fourteen primaries, including New Hampshire, when he upset President Truman. Stevenson entered no primaries, but was drafted at the Convention by Truman, the unions, and the city organizations.

† It required Richard Nixon to propose the family assistance program.

fight for. In fact, the army of liberal bureaucrats and technocrats found more ways to make things even worse for the working stiff; first, by building up ghetto hopes with a symphony of speeches promising an end to poverty. But when the poverty program, in every city I know anything about, turned out just to be just another patronage hustle, the disappointed hopes fell back into rage, and aroused taste for a better tomorrow spilled into the streets.

In August of 1970 Congresswoman Edith Green of Oregon finally blew the whistle on the poverty hucksters. She said that billions of dollars intended for the poor had been diverted into private research companies "more interested in 'profits than poverty." Much of the money, she said, went to $100-a-day consultants, "many of whom used to be high level government officials in Washington." She added that "since 1965, the government has spent almost $500 million on studies by experts. . . . Most of the antipoverty money never gets in the hands of the poor."

The liberal Democrats also ignored the very real problems of millions of white workers who earn between $5,000 and $10,000 a year. These families are not part of the media's "affluent society," although they see all the products of that abundance each day on television: cars, appliances, vacations to Hawaii and Europe. These people saw no new antipoverty programs launched in their rundown areas. In New York City, John Lindsay set up neighborhood task forces for all the black and Puerto Rican communities in 1966, but he didn't begin them in low-income white sections until after he began to run for reelection in 1969. What the liberals failed to do, while they had the chance to govern, was devise programs like national health insurance, or a guaranteed annual income, or free child care centers, or effective taxes on major polluters, programs *that helped blacks and poor whites alike.*

By promising and not delivering to the blacks, and by forgetting the low-income whites, the liberal Democrats managed to anger and polarize both halves of the other America. And although in power for eight years, they failed to make any significant improvement in the day-to-day life of America's thirty to forty million poor. The reason for this, I suspect, is that the Ivy League experts who fed the computers never knew how ordinary working people lived out their days.

And while ethnic whites and slum blacks competed bitterly

for the same scarce jobs, and the same scarce admissions to colleges, the large corporations, the insurance companies, the utilities, the defense contractors, the conglomerates, and the large banks continued to make immense profits. And the federal regulatory agencies—the ICC, FCC, CAB, FTC, the FDA—continued to be dominated by the very industries and corporations they were supposed to be supervising in the name of the consumers.

And all the while the frustration and resentment among the people we would come to call the Silent Majority began to rise and swell because they were being asked to bear the burden of change. They saw the liberal bureaucrats construct all those antipoverty programs for Watts and Harlem, but none for the white sections. They heard the Kerner Commission tell them the number one problem in America was "white racism," while their children couldn't get into college, and they owed money on the house, and there were layoffs at the plant. They saw the faddish media romanticize the Woodstock Nation, while making fun of their own culture of bars, the *Daily News,* and the roller derby.

The elitism of the liberals reached its apotheosis in Eugene McCarthy's campaign in the spring of 1968. He had the almost unanimous support of the rich, white elite I have previously named the "boutique guerrillas."

McCarthy was not comfortable in the company of the poor, black or white. He twice told campaign audiences in Oregon please to notice that "the educated people vote for me, and the less educated people vote for my opponent, and I think you ought to bear that in mind as you go to the polls here on Tuesday."

I campaigned hard for Robert Kennedy that spring for several reasons, the most important being that Kennedy understood that poverty was the heart of the matter and, by communicating his passion to the white working masses, made it possible to forge a new interracial majority of the victimized. Kennedy, like Kefauver, offered liberalism a second chance to stand again with Roosevelt's "one third of a nation," gas station attendants as well as Indians, cops as well as Chicanos.

The conventional wisdom, from the *New Republic* to the *National Review,* now has it that the ethnic workers have moved to

the right in backlash against student demonstrators, hippies, and blacks.

Although that of course has been a factor, I do not believe it has been the major one. The workers have gone to the right because the old liberalism has made their life worse, worse with inflation, worse by ignoring them and making promises to the blacks, worse with bureaucracy, worse with Vietnam. And quietly laughing at their life style ("greasers, hicks, philistines") all the while.

But the record shows that when new-style Populists have attempted to talk directly to the blue-collar class they have been remarkably successful. The white workers are open to a fresh alternative to Wallace, but old-fashioned liberals can't provide that alternative because their past record of mistakes robs them of credibility. And there are other examples besides Robert Kennedy's 1968 campaign.

In 1969, forty-four-year-old Pete Flaherty was elected the new Mayor of Pittsburgh, a tough steel town that is not known as a bastion of reform. He won in a campaign that forged a coalition of blacks, students, and low-income whites behind Flaherty's attacks on the "Mellons and Carnegies," on the "union bosses," and on the "corrupt political machine."

The day after Flaherty was elected, with 59 percent of the vote, the Pittsburgh *Press* carried this account of his headquarters:

"At one stage in the night the oldest person to be found in a Flaherty vote counting room was eighteen years old.

"Typical of the youthful Flaherty followers was Barbara Lembersky, nineteen, a Pitt student from Squirrel Hill.

"She's been typing, stuffing envelopes and talking up her man for months. 'I like the way he responds to people,' was the reason she gave for her loyalty.

"And then there was the fifty-five-year-old man who voted for Wallace for President, and then threw his support to Pete for Mayor.

" 'I just wanted to rock the boat,' he explained."

In other model Populist campaigns last year, Mrs. Bella Abzug unseated fourteen-year Congressman Leonard Farbstein in Manhattan. Father Robert Drinan defeated the seventy-two-year-old Philip Philbin, formerly the number two man on the House Armed Services Committee, in the Massachusetts primary. And

Ron Dellums upset five-term Congressman Jeffrey Cohelan in California.

And in November of 1970 those liberal Democrats who ran hard on economic issues defied the pundits who were predicting a sharp swing to the Right, and scored important victories. John Gilligan in Ohio, Philip Hart in Michigan and William Proxmire in Wisconsin, all refused to act as if they were running for sheriff of Tombstone, and were vindicated by the electorate.

Let me try and be more concrete about what I mean by a new Populist program.

The enormous wealth of America is unequally distributed among its citizens; 20 percent of American families earn between $1,000 and $4,000, and 75 percent of these families are white.* Our laws and institutions favor the rich, from expense accounts, to the cost of lawyers and doctors, to the influence of lobbyists, to the tax structure, to bail, to access to unions and colleges, to the composition of draft boards and grand juries. We have an economic system that Charles Abrams has described as "socialism for the rich, and free enterprise for the poor."

This is how Supreme Court Justice William O. Douglas put it in his book *Points of Rebellion*:

> The great welfare scandal of the age concerns the dole we give rich people. Percentage depletion for oil interests is, of course, the most notorious. . . . When we get deeply into the subject we learn that the cost of public housing for the poorest twenty percent of the people is picayune compared to the federal subsidy of the housing costs of the wealthiest twenty percent. . . .
> The 1968 Report of the National Commission on Civil Disorders tells us that during a thirty year period when the federal government was subsidizing *650,000* units of low income housing, it provided invisible supports, such as cheap credit and tax deductions, for the construction

---

* According to the U.S. Department of Labor statistics released in August of 1970, ten million blue-collar workers earn between $5,000 and $10,000 a year.

of more than *10 million* units of middle and upper class housing. . . .

Like examples are numerous in our tax laws, each marking a victory for some powerful lobby. The upside-down system of welfare helps the rich get richer and the poor, poorer.

"Other subsidies receive a greater reverence. Railroads, airlines, shipping—these are all subsidized; and those companies' doors are not kicked down at night.

Publishers get a handsome subsidy in the form of low second class mail rates, and publishers' rights are meticulously honored.

The subsidies given farmers are not treated as gratuities, but as matters of entitlement. . . .

In one year Texas producers [large farmers] who constitute .02 percent of the Texas population, received 250 million dollars in subsidies, while the Texas poor, who constitute 28.8 percent of the Texas population, received 7 *million dollars* in food assistance.

The litany of tax injustices is endless. There are millionaires, as Philip Stern showed in his book *The Great Treasury Raid,* who pay no taxes at all, while poor people sometimes go into debt to pay their taxes.

Yet this tax system has grown more unequal while liberal Democrats like Kennedy and Johnson were in power. It would seem to me that the first plank in a new Populist platform would be a radical restructuring in our tax laws; the end of government subsidies to giant corporations and industries; the increase in corporate, inheritance, stock transfer, and bank assets taxes, and the reduction of taxes for all families earning less than $10,000 a year. The beneficiaries of such a reform would be mostly blue-collar families, whose lives now can be wrecked by sudden illness, death, unemployment, or divorce. Recently such families have voted their fears because so few politicians have offered the countervailing incentive of a larger share of America's affluence. The only possible way to compete with a Nixon or a Wallace, who appeals to their racism and paranoia, is to appeal directly to their pocketbooks, to their self-interest.

But lacking the imagination and commitment for this approach, many liberal politicians instead have played on, and fed,

the fear and hate of the workers, thus again moving the center of gravity of American politics one more notch to the Right, as conservative theoretician Kevin Phillips shrewdly noted in a recent Washington *Post* column (September 25, 1970).

Let me suggest two more forgotten areas where a new Populist movement might do some good. One is the alphabet soup of federal regulatory agencies. Many of them were started during the New Deal to protect the ordinary consumer from price fixing, inferior products, misleading advertising, and other corporate abuses.

Ralph Nader and his Raiders have now published four books on these agencies and they contain all the evidence—hard cold facts—anyone needs to prove that these bureaucracies have all been failures.

A book on the Interstate Commerce Commission (ICC) edited by Robert Fellmeth, *The Interstate Commerce Omission* (Grossman), documents how the ICC has become "an elephants' graveyard for political hacks," how the public is excluded from the decision-making process; how important studies of transportation problems have been suppressed, how railroad mergers are rubber-stamped; how conglomerates cheat the consumer; how truck-driving safety regulations go unenforced; how rate bureaus encourage "monopolistic" price fixing.

A report by Raiders Edward Cox, Robert Fellmeth, and John Schulz, asserted, "There is little doubt that toothpastes, mouthwashes, deodorants, cleansers, soaps and so on are priced between five and twenty times their cost of production. The American people mus eventually grow tired of paying $1 for a tube of toothpaste that costs no more than fifteen cents to make."

Nader himself, in speeches and articles, has revealed that "Consolidated Edison of New York pays its board chairman more in salary in a single year, than it spent on pollution control research in the last five years."

And that "Caltec Citrus paid a fine of $6,000 when it was charged with adulterating and watering its orange juice. Estimated company profits as a result of this practice were one million dollars." Which is a little like putting a dime in a parking meter, and then sticking up a bank.

The point seems clear. The huge corporations are cheating consumers, mostly low-income people, and the federal regulatory

agencies are not doing much about it, although such protection is supposed to be their only function.

Another problem the unions and the traditional politicians have ignored is industrial safety. According to the Department of Labor, two million injuries and fourteen thousand deaths occur every year in the workplace. And according to Ralph Nader, who is preparing a book on the subject, many companies suppress or underestimate their safety statistics.

Many of the deaths and diseases that strike industrial workers are caused by the environment they work in. Steelworkers get silicosis, a condition that causes paroxysms of coughing. More than a hundred thousand of the country's one million textile workers have contracted byssinosis, or brown lung disease, caused by inhaling cotton dust. And thousands of coal miners suffer from black lung, or pneumoconiosis.

Unions like the United Mine Workers (UMW) have been as indifferent to this slow murder as the mine owners and the politicians.

According to the August 17, 1970, issue of *Newsweek*:

> The generally unimpressive industrial record in the U.S. has a good many causes, none of them reflecting much credit on those responsible. Union leaders too often willing to barter safety for a wage hike. Employers tend to coax a little more life from worn-out and unsafe machinery. State safety standards are too often antiquated and ineffective, and there aren't enough inspectors to enforce the ones on the books. . . .

A tax system that favors the rich and punishes the poor, federal regulatory agencies dominated by rich corporations, factories and mines that killed more Americans in 1969 than the war in Vietnam. A sorry bunch of monuments left by liberal Democrats who have governed us for so much of the last forty years.

And the remedies are as obvious as they are radical. In the concise and precise words of John Kenneth Galbraith, they are, "taxing the rich, nationalizing industries, regulating private enterprise, and redeeming power and policy from military and civilian bureaucracy."

Amen.

And what needs to be done now is to transcend the cold war

liberalism of military intervention (Bay of Pigs, Dominican Republic, Vietnam) by becoming internationalists once again. And as Christopher Lasch * has pointed out, we need to go back and rediscover the deeper roots of the indigenous American Left in fragments of the Populist, black, abolitionist, progressive, feminist, and socialist movements in the early part of this century, and late nineteenth century.

No radical movement has ever succeeded that was rooted in hatred of its own country, and parts of the New Left (Weathermen, Yippies) are guilty of this fatal mistake. By picking up the standard of the Left before it was corrupted by the cold war, we give the postlinear kids something inside their own nation to identify with, so they won't have to import fantasy notions of revolution from Bolivia or North Korea.

And by reconnecting with the old Populist attack on "the interests"—private corporate power—we will again place a liberalism which has grown dangerously elitist on the side of the white workingman, who has been ignored since Truman's time, and the black underclass, which has been brutalized beyond words.

Populism would also turn liberalism back in the direction of its Jeffersonian beginnings, back toward local participation and decentralization, and away from the impersonal, centralized bureaucracy of the last thirty years. It would also help reclaim liberalism from the technocrats and computers, and help restore its shriveled humanism.

I am not an ideologue. There is no single system of thought that seems nearly adequate to me. I know there are no total answers, no total solutions; only endless, ambiguous struggle. I can define myself only as a radical and as a democrat, as a writer and a Jew, as an activist and a skeptic. I would identify with Antonio Gramsci, the Italian revolutionary who described himself as a "pessimist of the intelligence and an optimist of the will."

I have tried to argue here that the old orthodoxy of cold war liberalism is used up, that it is a dying hand on the present. I

---

* I would differ from Lasch, however, to the extent that I view these earlier mass movements only as the most general examples, rather than as specific models for the future.

have also suggested that we need to rediscover a usable past within America to help chart the radical future.

If I have learned anything in these years since I joined SDS in 1961, it is that movements make history; movements of ordinary citizens, and not organizations, or personalities, people in motion generating energy move time forward and change consciousness; movements like civil rights, antiwar, the grape strike, and women's liberation.

And there are a variety of mass movements in the American experience we might identify with and learn from. The American Revolution itself with its models of Tom Paine and Sam Adams. The abolitionists, the Populists, and the socialism of Debs. Susan B. Anthony and the feminist movement that won the vote. The black radicalism of Du Bois, Malcolm X, and Martin Luther King. The literary radicalism of Thoreau, Whitman, Mark Twain, Lincoln Steffens, and Heywood Broun. And an older liberalism, symbolized by La Guardia and Brandeis, committed to liberty and equality, before it became spoiled by the cold war and the small compromises of power.

And a school not recently in fashion—the Anarchists, and the Wobblies of Joe Hill. Perhaps we should now confront Nixon and his band of babbitts behind the banner the IWW marched with during the great textile strike at Lawrence, Massachusetts, in 1912: "Bread and roses too."

November, 1970

ONE

WHITE POWER/BLACK RAGE

The first couple of pieces in this section are about SNCC and the old civil rights movement, which was where I met many of the best human beings I know. A couple of them like Bob Parris Moses, Carol Rogoff, Marshall Ganz, and E. W. Steptoe are described in the first piece on Amite County. But there were others like Casey Hayden, Mendy Samstein, John Lewis, and Charley Cobb I never wrote about as much as I should have. Moses, the most remarkable of them all, has simply fallen out of history since late 1965 when he changed his name to Parris and visited Africa.

When the veterans of McComb and Greenwood and Selma reassemble they still talk about Moses as a legendary figure and exchange rumors about where he is now. Someone told me he was in Tanzania. Someone else told me the grotesque rumor that he was now a welfare caseworker in Harlem. The younger kids who became political with Vietnam, or McCarthy, or Kent State, never seem to have heard of Moses. I hope this piece at least tells this generation of the New Left where they come from.

The three pieces on lead poisoning were part of an experiment in activist journalism. I learned about the problem when an old college friend turned community organizer, Paul Du Brul, took me to lunch and gave me some literature about the poisoning of ghetto children. At about the same time Ralph Nader had mentioned to me that the one failure of the muckraking journalists like Steffens was that they never followed up their written exposés with direct action.

So I began to agitate in the Voice week after week about lead poisoning. At the same time I went on television and radio programs, talked to acquaintances who worked at City Hall, prodded other journalists to join the crusade, and spoke to Mayor Lindsay about it between campaign stops one night in Brooklyn. Finally, early in 1970, Lindsay announced a 2.4 million appro-

priation for a special program to combat lead poisoning. A mass screening program was begun in the slums, and in nine months almost 3000 poisoned children were found and treated.

The theme of most of these pieces turn out to be the systemic nature of white racism, how it saturates American life, from politics, to journalism, to sports. I didn't start out with that generalization in mind, but the work on each seperate story over five years led me, step by step, to that ineluctable conclusion.

[1.]
Amite County

I'm going back out before the rain starts a-falling;
I'll walk to the depths of the deepest dark forest
where the people are many and their hands are all empty
where the pellets of poison are flooding their waters
where the home in the valley meets the damp dirty prison
where the executioner's face is always well hidden
where hunger is ugly, where souls are forgotten
where black is the color, where none is the number

—Bob Dylan

When you're in Mississippi, the rest of America doesn't seem real.
And when you're in the rest of America, Mississippi doesn't seem
real.

—Bob Parris Moses

In the mythology of the movement, Amite County is a synonym for the Ninth Circle of Hell.

It was to impoverished, remote Amite County, in southwest Mississippi, that SNCC's Bob Parris came in August of 1961, to attempt SNCC's pilot project in voter registration. Beaten twice and jailed three times, Parris left for the state capital in Jackson after four melancholy months.

It was in Amite that Herbert Lee, a fifty-two-year-old father of nine children, was murdered by E. H. Hurst, a member of the Mississippi state legislature.

It was in Amite that farmer Louis Allen, a witness to Lee's slaying, was shotgunned to death in his home, after he had spoken to the Justice Department about the Lee murder.

It was Amite that saw not a single white volunteer during the 1964 Summer Project because of its legacy of lawlessness.

It was Amite that until July of 1965 had only one registered

Negro voter in the whole county, despite a Negro population majority of 55 percent.

It is Amite that twelve years after *Brown* v. *Board of Education* does not have a single classroom desegregated, two years after the 1964 civil rights act does not have a single public facility desegregated, and a year after the 1965 act does not have a federal voting registrar.

It is Amite that has never experienced a civil-rights march, a sit-in, or even a picket line.

It is in rural, red-clayed Amite that the movement has bled itself dry trying to break the century-old trap of terror, poverty, and fear.

Amite is about eighty miles south of Jackson on the Louisiana border. Its county seat is the hamlet of Liberty, population 652.

More than half of the total population of the county is Negro, but only 40 percent of the 13,000 eligible voters are Negro. Because of the hopeless cycle of poverty, many Negroes escape to Baton Rouge, New Orleans, and Chicago while still in their teens. Sociologists have estimated that Negro emigration from Mississippi is 40 percent. Amite is becoming a place for the very old and the very young.

Although many Negroes in Amite own their own farms, most of them are marginal. Attendance at all-Negro Central High each autumn falls below 50 percent because so many children are required to chop cane and pick cotton on the farms. While this makes the farmer less vulnerable to economic reprisals, it does lead to frequent acts of physical violence.

More than 90 percent of the Negro homes have no heating system or indoor toilet. Only a few have telephones. Almost all rely on hand-dug wells for water. Food must be purchased in Liberty, where Negroes are still beaten up on the street on whim, and where no white has ever stood trial for violence against a Negro.

The sheriff of Amite is six feet, five inch Daniel Jones. His father, Brian Jones, is the Klan leader in the county.

Amite does not have a white, business-oriented middle class that has made Greenville, in the delta, an oasis of decency, or a merchant class that finally, in 1965, helped halt the reign of terror in nearby McComb. It was Hodding Carter's *Greenville Delta-Democrat Times,* and later, Oliver Emmerich's *McComb*

Enterprise-Journal, that spread the message of compliance and moderation. The only newspaper in Amite is a racist sheet called the *Liberty Herald.*

Amite seems outside the flow of history, a backward enclave insulated from the passage of time. It has not only missed the civil-rights movement, but the Industrial Revolution as well. There are no factories, no shopping centers, no unions in the county. The longed-for educated, civilized white moderate isn't in hiding; *he doesn't exist in Amite.*

This chapter is an attempt to chronicle the descent of three young Dantes into this one particular hell. This trio of pioneers did not abandon hope, but brought hope to this Ninth Circle.

Liberty is one of the oldest towns in Mississippi, its founding dating back to 1805. Among the earliest settlers in Amite were the poor whites—the "peckerwoods"—who were pushed out of the area around Natchez by the cotton-plantation-owning class of aristocrats. As the South moved toward the Civil War, great tensions developed between the rural peckerwoods of Amite and the affluent, genteel planters of Natchez. When the war began, the residents of Natchez voted to remain in the Union, while the poor whites of Amite chose secession.

After the Civil War, Amite was over 60 percent Negro. There were Negro sheriffs and a powerful Republican Party organization. But after the historic Compromise of 1876 ended Reconstruction, the pattern of Negro disenfranchisement came to Amite, as it did to all of the South. Negroes were lynched, driven off land they owned, beaten, and their right to vote taken away. Most Negroes who own their own land in Amite today do so only because one of their ancestors fought for it with guns or fists. Most of the Amite Negroes, however, fled to the rich soil of the delta, where cheap labor was needed to clear the swamps for the future plantations.

The diminution of Negro power in the county has continued all through the twentieth century. The only Negro resistance to this trend came during the 1930s when several of Huey Long's Share the Wealth Leagues sprang up in the area, but they were violently suppressed. The remote rurality and the backward poverty of Amite have been the jaws of the vise that has bled the Amite Negro since Reconstruction.

Robert Parris Moses grew up in a housing project on the edge
of Harlem. But somehow he was not swallowed up by the
squalor and violence of the ghetto like so many of his contempo-
raries. Instead, gifted with a philosophical and poetic mind, he
went downtown at age thirteen, as a result of high grades on a
competitive examination, to virtually all-white, academically superior Stuyvesant High School. There Parris not only compiled
outstanding grades, but was captain of Stuyvesant's championship basketball quintet, and vice president of his graduating
class.

Parris then went, on a scholarship, to predominantly white
Hamilton College in Clinton, New York, where again he excelled
in both scholarship and sports. It was at Hamilton that a French
instructor introduced him to the writings of Albert Camus,
whose melancholy morality was to make a lasting impact on his
thinking. Almost a decade later, addressing volunteers at Oxford,
Ohio, for the Mississippi Summer Project, Parris compared racism to Camus's plague, and the volunteers to the sanitary squads.

From Hamilton, Parris went on to graduate school at Harvard, and received a master's degree in philosophy in 1957. After-
ward Parris began to teach math at one of New York City's elite
private schools—Horace Mann, in the Riverdale section of the
Bronx. Nothing in his first twenty-four years—spent increasingly
in the white world—seemed to indicate that Parris was destined
to become a myth-shrouded legend to thousands of young radicals, and to have his picture hang in a sharecropper shack in the
delta next to Abraham Lincoln's and John F. Kennedy's.

Folk singer Bob Cohen, who lived with Parris in Manhattan
from September of 1960 until he left for Amite in July of 1961,
remembers him as "extraordinarily quiet, gentle, abstract . . .
really involved with his students and reading a lot—Bertrand
Russell, and Camus in French. . . . Yet, I always had the sense
he was very busy in his head all the time."

Cohen met Parris at the Maine Folk Dance Camp in June of
1960, and recalls, "One of the few times I can remember Bob's
face really lit up was when he was folk dancing. He loved it. I remember sometimes we would be coming home late from a party
or something, and if Bob had had a good time, he would start
dancing down Amsterdam Avenue. He could be very free and
gay then."

Cohen, who named his first child after his roommate, says,

"Bob hardly ever talked about going back South after his trip in June of 1960. . . . The only hint I got of the deep feeling he had about going back South was that he would sit for hours and listen to a record of Odetta singing, 'I'm Going Back to the Red Clay Country.' "

Nineteen hundred and sixty-one, when Parris went back to the red clay of Amite and Pike counties, marked the first time a SNCC worker tried to live in and become part of a community. It was the first time SNCC engaged in voter registration. It was probably the most creative and heroic single act anyone in the New Left has attempted. Certainly much of the subsequent history of the New Left has flowed from that existential act of Parris disappearing alone into the most violent and desolate section of Mississippi.

As a consequence of that deed and his own selfless personality, Parris occupies a legendary niche in the New Left. He has been compared to Danilo Dolci, Hesse's Siddhartha, and Prince Kropotkin. Perhaps the reverential feeling about this shy, often sad prophet was best expressed by Dick Gregory when he introduced Parris to the mammoth Berkeley teach-in in May of 1965 with these words:

> I refused to do my act a few minutes ago because it was too light. Now it's dark enough, but I looked over my shoulder and found some light that I must get rid of first. This is a young man who has done more for my life without even knowing it to make me commit my life for right over wrong. Thank goodness I happened to be in the right place at the right time when he was speaking in his own little way. Many times I listened to him when he thought I was asleep in jail; many times I overheard him in the sharecropping fields of Mississippi. I'd like to postpone my act for another few minutes and bring to the stand a man who to me and to many people, will stand up among the greatest human beings who have ever walked the face of the earth. I don't have to say any more. I would like to present to you a *man*—Bob Parris.

The series of events that propelled Parris into the Ninth Circle of Amite began during the summer of 1960. It was then that Parris, while traveling through Mississippi trying to recruit Negro

students to attend SNCC's October founding conference, met Amzie Moore, the indomitable leader of the NAACP chapter in Cleveland, Mississippi. In the course of several conversations Moore convinced the twenty-five-year-old SNCC field secretary he should quit his teaching job and return to the delta the following summer to begin a voter-registration campaign. Parris agreed, and in November the popular Negro magazine *Jet* printed a short item describing the projected venture. Amite County's NAACP founder and leader, E. W. Steptoe, saw the *Jet* item, and along with Pike County leader C. C. Bryant, wrote a letter to Parris in New York, suggesting he change his plans and try to organize a project in southwest Mississippi. At that point only thirty-eight of 9,000 Pike County Negroes were registered to vote, and one of 5,500 in Amite was eligible to vote, according to Civil Rights Commission figures.

Parris, who was encountering unexpected difficulty in finding a church willing to house a voter-registration school in the delta, agreed to come to the Amite-Pike region.

Civil-rights workers had not even tried to enter Mississippi until 1952. According to Elizabeth Sutherland, in her *Letters from Mississippi,* the "first 'agitator' was shot and killed, the second was shot and run out of the state." Next came Bob Parris in July, of 1961, without a grand scheme, lacking any concrete experience in voter registration.

On August 7 the SNCC Pike County voter-registration school opened up in a hamlet called Burglundtown in a two-story structure, which included a grocery below and a Masonic meeting hall above. The only teacher was Parris, and the student body consisted of about twenty Negroes, half of them too young to vote.

After the first class four persons went to the registrar's office in nearby Magnolia, the county seat, and three of them registered without incident. Three Negroes went down on August 9, and two registered successfully. Nine journeyed to Magnolia on August 20, and one was registered. The next night one of the Pike County Negroes who had attempted to register was shot at by a white farmer. The next day only two people showed up at the voter-registration school.

Parris then went into Amite, living on Steptoe's farm. On August 15, he accompanied an old farmer named Ernest Isaac and two middle-aged women, Bertha Lee Hughes and Matilda

Schoby, to the courthouse in Liberty. The trio managed to fill out a form, but not to take the test. As they were driving out of Liberty, toward McComb, their car was flagged down by a highway patrolman, who told Isaac, the driver, to get out and come into the police car. Isaac quickly complied, but Parris also got out of the car and asked the officer why. He was pushed and ordered back into the car. At that point the patrolman arrested Parris for "impeding an officer in the discharge of his duties." Taken to McComb, Parris was fined fifty dollars, and for the first of many times saw the inside of a Mississippi jail, as he spent two days in prison, fasting, rather than pay the fine.

On Monday, August 28, Parris started a voter-registration class at Mount Pilgrim Church, the first in the history of Amite County. The next day he went with Reverend Alfred Knox and Curtis Dawson to the courthouse in Liberty to try to register. A block from the courthouse they were met by Billy Jack Caston, a cousin of the sheriff and the son-in-law of state representative E. H. Hurst. Without saying a word, Caston walked up to Parris and knocked him down with a punch to the temple. He then proceeded to pummel Parris for several minutes with punches to the head and ribs. Parris just sat in the street trying to protect himself as best he could in the traditional nonviolent position, his head between his knees and his arms shielding his face. Reverend Knox tried to pull Caston off his victim, but white bystanders ordered him not to intervene.

Knox and Dawson never made it to the courthouse. Instead they picked up the semiconscious Parris and drove him to Steptoe's farm. Steptoe later recalled, "I didn't recognize Bob at first he was so bloody. I just took off his tee shirt and wrung out the blood like it had just been washed." Then Steptoe drove Parris to a Negro doctor in McComb, who took eight stitches in his scalp.

The next day Amite experienced another first: Parris filed assault and battery charges against Caston, the first time in that area a Negro had challenged the right of a white man to beat him up at will. The warrant was made out by the county district attorney after the county judge refused.

The trial was held in the Liberty courthouse on August 31. More than 100 whites, many of them openly armed, jammed the courtroom for the spectacle. While on the stand, Parris was asked by Caston's attorney whether he had participated in riots the

year before in Japan or San Francisco. After his testimony Parris —the plaintiff—was told by the sheriff he had better leave the courtroom because he could not guarantee his safety. So before the trial ended in Caston's acquittal, Parris was given a police escort to the Pike County line.

Meanwhile, two other crucial events were happening during the month of August. One was a SNCC staff meeting at the Highlander Folk School in Tennessee. At that meeting the fledgling organization was divided into two camps, one favoring direct action on the order of the sit-ins and the freedom rides, and the other suggesting the innovation of voter registration. Hints from the Kennedy Administration that it would look favorably on voter-registration activities, plus financial support from the New World and other foundations, strengthened the voter-registration group in SNCC. After prolonged debate, SNCC decided to adopt "an all-out revolutionary program encompassing both mass direct action and voter registration drives."

The second thing to happen during August was the gradual emergence from jail in Jackson of the first group of freedom riders. Four of these freedom riders, Reggie Robinson of Baltimore, John Hardy of Nashville, Travis Britt of New York, and MacArthur Cotton of Jackson, were to join Parris before the month was over. Also, direct-action partisans like Marion Barry came to McComb during August and sparked a series of sit-ins and protest marches. A fifteen-year-old McComb high school student, Brenda Travis, and five friends sat in and were arrested. Her companions were sentenced to eight months for "breach of peace," and Brenda was turned over to juvenile authorities and sentenced to one year in the state school for delinquents. Later, more than 100 of Brenda's classmates at Burgland High School marched through McComb to protest her severe sentence and expulsion from school. They were all arrested as they knelt praying at the steps of the city hall.

More violence in Liberty.

On September 5, Parris and Travis Britt accompanied four Negroes to the courthouse. In his pamphlet, *Revolution in Mississippi,* Tom Hayden recorded Britt's terse description of the events that followed:

> There was a clerk directly across the hall who came rushing out while we were waiting, and ordered us to

leave the hallway. He said he didn't want a bunch of people congregating in the hallway. So we left and walked around the building to the courthouse, near the registrar's window. By the time we reached the back of the building a group of white men had filed into the hall. . . . They were talking belligerently. Finally one of the white men came to the end of the hall as if looking for someone. He asked us if we knew Mr. Brown. We said no. He said you boys must not be from around here. We said he was correct. This conversation was interrupted by another white man who approached Bob Moses (Parris) and started preaching to him: how he should be ashamed of coming down here from New York stirring up trouble, causing poor innocent people to lose their homes and jobs, and how he (Bob) was lower than dirt on the ground for doing such things, and how he should get down on his knees and ask God forgiveness for every sin in his lifetime. Bob asked him why the people should lose their homes just because they wanted to register and vote. The white gentleman did not answer the question, but continued to preach. He said that the Negro men were raping the white women up North, and that he wouldn't allow such a thing to start down here in Mississippi. . . . At this point Bob turned away and sat on the stoop of the courthouse porch, and the man talking to him took a squatting position. Nobody was saying anything. I reached into my pocket and took out a cigarette. A tall white man, about middle-aged, wearing a khaki shirt and pants stepped up to me and asked, "Boy, what's your business?" at which point I knew I was in trouble. The clerk from the hallway came to the back door leading to the courthouse with a smile on his face and called to the white man, "Wait a minute, wait a minute!" At this point the white man, who they called Bryant, hit me on my right eye. Then I saw this clerk motion his head as if to call the rest of the whites. They came and all circled around me, and this fellow that was called Bryant hit me on my jaw and then on my chin. Then he slammed me down; instead of falling I stumbled onto the courthouse lawn. The crowd (about

15, I think) followed, making comments. He was holding me so tight around the collar, I put my hands on my collar to ease the choking. This set off a reaction of punches from this fellow they called Bryant; I counted fifteen; he just kept hitting and shouting, "Why don't you hit me, nigger?" I was beaten into a semiconscious state. My vision was blurred by the punch to the eye. I heard Bob yell to cover my head to avoid any further blows to my face. . . . Bob took me by the arm and took me to the street, walking cautiously to avoid any further kicks or blows. The Negro fellow that had been taking the registration test gave up in the excitement, and we saw him in his truck. . . .

This incident, in the heart of the hell Bob Parris says isn't real unless you're there, went unreported in the national press. This was still three years before the Summer Project, and such beatings administered to blacks were so commonplace as not to fit the definition of news. Such beatings, however, turned out to have considerable news content in 1964, when the bloodied recipients were white students from "good families" in the North. In 1961 the blood of Parris and Britt was invisible.

The beating had its desired effect. Attendance at meetings and voter-registration classes dwindled to almost nothing. The small group of SNCC workers walked the back roads from dawn to dusk in a vain search for Negroes willing to try to register in Liberty. "But the farmers were no longer willing to go down," Parris later recalled, "and for the rest of the month of September we just had a rough time."

Amite's unchecked, legally sanctioned violence became murder on September 25, when Herbert Lee was shot to death in front of the Liberty cotton gin by E. H. Hurst.

The day before, Parris had met with Steptoe and John Doar of the Justice Department at Steptoe's farm. Steptoe had told Doar that Hurst, whose land is adjacent to his, had publicly threatened to kill him and Herbert Lee. Lee had attended voter-registration classes and had volunteered a few days before to attempt to register in Liberty, the first individual to do so since the beating of Britt.

Lee was shot once in the brain by Hurst's .38 caliber revolver. It happened about noon in front of a dozen witnesses, including

several Negroes. Lee, wearing his farmer's overalls and field boots, was sitting in the cab of his pickup truck, and fell out into the gutter when he was shot. For two hours his body lay in a pool of blood, uncovered and swarmed over by insects. Finally, a coroner from McComb came and picked it up. That same afternoon a coroner's jury in Liberty met, and ruled that Lee was killed in self-defense.

Parris felt responsible for Lee's death, just as three years later he was to feel himself responsible for the deaths of Goodman, Chaney, and Schwerner. For the next three nights, from sundown till almost sunup, he walked and rode through the mist-shrouded rolling hills of Amite, knocking on strange doors, seeking the three Negro witnesses. Fighting off exhaustion, waking up families that had to get up at 5 A.M., Parris finally found the Negro farmers who had witnessed the slaying. But none was willing to tell a grand jury the truth. Instead they told Parris that the sheriff and deputy sheriff had warned them to tell everyone that Lee, who was about five feet four, had tried to hit Hurst, who is six feet three, with a tire iron.

One of the three witnesses was a farmer named Louis Allen. Late in October a federal grand jury convened to consider an indictment of Hurst. It was then that Allen drove to McComb to inform Parris he had changed his mind, and would tell the truth about Lee's death if he was guaranteed federal protection.

Parris called the Justice Department in Washington but was told it was "impossible" to provide Allen with protection. So Allen testified to the federal jury that Hurst had killed Lee in self-protection. Six months later a deputy sheriff told Allen he knew he had contacted the Justice Department, and he broke Allen's jaw with a flashlight. On January 31, 1964, Allen was found dead on his front porch as a result of three shotgun blasts.

Tormented by the shadows of guilt, Parris has tried to make Herbert Lee a symbol for all the hundreds of Mississippi Negroes who have been lawlessly murdered by whites. Whenever he spoke in the North in 1961 or 1962 he would talk about Herbert Lee, and soon thousands of young people knew of this one murder out of many. Lee was also memorialized in a song, "Never Turn Back," written in 1963 by Bertha Gober, a wide-eyed teen-ager from Albany, Georgia. For a while the song, a dirge sung at a slow, elegiac tempo, was the "We Shall Overcome" of the SNCC workers in Mississippi. Its final verse goes:

We have hung our heads and cried
Cried for those like Lee who died
Died for you and died for me
Died for the cause of equality
No, we'll never turn back
No, we'll never turn back
Until we've all been freed
And we have equality
And we have equality

The murder of Lee broke the back of whatever had been stirring in Amite. Few Negroes were willing to be seen talking to Parris or to the other "freedom riders," as they were called by both Negroes and whites. The tiny flicker of hope from Parris's candle went out, and Amite's Negroes were left to curse the darkness.

A month later Parris went to jail for two months in Pike County for leading a march of 118 high school students to the McComb city hall. From the Magnolia jail he smuggled out a note to the SNCC office in Atlanta. The last few paragraphs illuminate Parris's speculative and poetic turn of mind.

Later on, Hollis [Hollis Watkins, now a member of SNCC's executive committee] will lead out with a clear tenor into a freedom song, Talbert and Lewis will supply jokes, and McDew [Chuck McDew, then SNCC's chairman] will discourse on the history of the black man and the Jew. McDew—a black by birth and a Jew by choice, and a revolutionary by necessity—has taken on the deep loves and the deep hates which America, and the world, reserve for those who dare to stand in a strong sun and cast a sharp shadow.

In the words of Judge Brumfield, who sentenced us, we are "cold calculators" who design to disrupt the racial harmony (harmonious since 1619) of McComb into racial strife and rioting; we, he said, are the leaders who are causing young children to be led like sheep to the pen and be slaughtered (in a legal manner). "Robert," he was addressing me, "haven't some of the people from your school been able to go down and register without violence here in Pike County?" I thought to myself that Southerners are most exposed when they boast. . . .

This is Mississippi, in the middle of the iceberg. Hollis is leading off with his tenor, "Michael row the boat ashore, Alleluia; Christian brothers don't be slow, Alleluia; Mississippi's next to go, Alleluia." This is a tremor in the middle of the iceberg—from a stone that the builders rejected.

In January Parris left southwest Mississippi, melancholy and depressed, to begin a pilgrimage that was to lead to the Mississippi Summer Project, the Freedom Democratic Party, and a 100 percent rise in Negro registration in the state by the end of 1965 (25,000 to 50,000).

But for three years Amite was to remain that base of the iceberg most submerged beneath the ocean of terror. Nobody tried to register in Liberty after the murder of Herbert Lee. No SNCC project was attempted in the county. No summer volunteer was sent into the hills and woods of Amite. For three years a pattern of life incomprehensible to an outsider endured without assault. Negroes were beaten and killed. Whites, a minority of the county, continued to make every political and economic decision. No word was written about the iceberg, and the tiny crack Parris had made froze over.

E. W. Steptoe, a small, reedlike man with a time-trampled face has lived in Amite all his fifty-six years. He was there trying to register before Parris came; he was there after Parris moved on to Jackson and Greenwood; and he is there today, shaming, cajoling, bullying Negroes into registering.

Steptoe is not a saint. He is a violent man and an egotistical one. He can be demagogic at meetings, and he can con reporters and naïve visitors. But there are few men like him in the whole state of Mississippi. His courage, his commonsense wisdom, his bittersweet wit and love, are the special qualities of the rural Mississippi Negro, who lives by his wits to survive, and whose life depends on human bonds with others.

Steptoe first tried to register in 1953 and was told he flunked the test. In 1954, after reading about the Supreme Court's desegregation decision, he organized an Amite County chapter of the NAACP. Its third meeting, however, was broken up by armed Klansmen with the help of the deputy sheriff.

"My uncle was so scared after that meeting," Steptoe recalls,

"he ran into the woods and stayed there for a week, living on raw food. Then he finally came out and left the county."

In June of 1964 Amite sheriff Daniel Jones visited a score of Negro homes, making it clear there would be reprisals if they put up white summer volunteers. Steptoe was the only Negro in the county who said he would house "as many white civil rights workers that will fit in my house." The final decision not to send any volunteers to Amite County was made in Jackson after Goodman, Chaney, and Schwerner were reported missing in Neshoba County.

One of the 650 summer volunteers was a rabbi's son from Bakersfield, California, named Marshall Ganz. During the summer Ganz worked in McComb on one of the more effective SNCC projects, along with Curtis Hayes, Mendy Samstein, J. D. Smith, and Dennis Sweeney. Their freedom house was bombed in August, and Hayes narrowly escaped death. At the end of the summer Ganz was one of the 150 who chose to remain.

Elizabeth Sutherland remembers the first time she met Ganz in July of 1964:

> As soon as I saw him I knew he would be one of those volunteers who would stay in the state. Marshall seemed more mature and more sophisticated than most of the other volunteers. He was an economic radical, but more important, he had a sensitive, literary kind of mind. He was the type of person who was driven to become part of people's lives in a deep way. He seemed more concerned with human relationships than with staging big demonstrations. I think Marshall could be a fine novelist if he ever had the time to reflect on his experiences.

So in January of 1965 Ganz moved to Steptoe's farm to become the first full-time SNCC worker since Parris in Amite County. Miss Sutherland now suspects it was Ganz's "passion for human contact" that led him to abandon the "impersonalization of a city like McComb, to live directly with the poor farmers in Amite."

In McComb, Ganz had lived in a freedom house with about ten other staff members, and had been somewhat removed from the rhythm of life in the Negro community. But at Steptoe's farm he was at the vortex of it, and intimately involved in people's everyday life.

For six months Ganz canvassed alone in Amite; tedious, repetitive, frustrating drudgery. Hour after hour, day after day, he would walk the deserted gravel roads of the county, talking, visiting, joking with people who had never seen a friendly white face before in their lives. For six months all he did was try to find local Negroes who were willing to act against the system that emasculated them.

Early in July two more SNCC staff members—both girls—joined Ganz and Steptoe in Amite. One was twenty-year-old Hazel Lee, a Negro from Panola County and a veteran of six arrests and a hundred picket lines. Hazel came, she says, "because I heard that Amite was a really rough place where there had been a lot of killings. I felt I had to go there."

The other was a Jewish girl from Brooklyn named Carol Rogoff, a 1963 graduate of Beaver College near Philadelphia. Carol did not come to fashionable Beaver a rebel. But during the summer of 1963 she became active in the SNCC-ignited movement in Cambridge, Maryland. She was almost expelled from college, and there were tensions with her conservative family, but she continued to work in the movement after the summer in Cambridge.

In 1965 Carol was in charge of organizing high school students in New York City. During the Easter vacation she escorted a group of those students on a visit to McComb, repaying a trip made by a group of McComb students to New York the previous Christmas. While in McComb, Carol made a few trips to Steptoe's farm, and was so touched by the pure, slow movement being built in Amite she decided to return there as a SNCC field secretary in July.

Ganz, Rogoff, and Lee were all part of the SNCC faction most committed to decentralization and grass-roots decision-making, and most antagonistic to flashy demonstrations and leader-oriented mass rallies. All agreed the movement in Amite must be built slowly and with care, from the bottom up.

"A big influx of volunteers would smother the movement here," said Carol, "as it did in McComb. If anything is to be built in Amite it must be inward, rather than outside-oriented. What has to be done is to build a community of local people who trust each other and are willing to act on their grievances; local Negroes who are willing to take responsibility and make decisions democratically."

After weeks of canvassing and church meetings of thirty and

forty people, it was finally decided a group of Negroes would try to register on July 22 at the Liberty courthouse. By then the voting rights act was about to be signed by the President, and the Mississippi legislature had passed a new law liberalizing the procedures for voter registration, to prevent application of the federal law to Mississippi. Marshall Ganz called the Justice Department in Washington and the FBI in McComb to inform them of the registration bid, but in order to thwart dependence on whites, none of the SNCC workers accompanied the twenty-two Amite Negroes to Liberty on July 22.

At 9 A.M. they were lined up outside the courthouse, only a few yards from the spot where Herbert Lee's body had lain for two hours. The group included Steptoe, making his eighth attempt to register; Reverend Knox, who had made that first bloody trip to Liberty with Bob Parris in 1961; Ben Faust, a seventy-seven-year-old farmer who once spent five years in the infamous Parchman Prison for allegedly stealing a cow; and William Weathersby, a militant farmer who had attended registration classes in 1961.

"Okay, who's first?" asked Sheriff Jones, his hand ominously fingering his gun.

Silence.

Then William Sibley, a farmer, stepped forward and announced, "Me."

By dusk all twenty-two had been registered to vote.

A month later about 200 Negroes were registered, including the widow of Herbert Lee and one of his nine children.

All summer Ganz, Rogoff, and Lee worked hard winning slowly the confidence of the community, then its respect, and finally, its love. When they ate, it was a meal forced on them by the community, by those who had less than enough to feed their own families. Local whites began to spread dozens of nails each night in Steptoe's gravel driveway, and the project's one beat-up car suffered from a series of flat tires. The car was a necessity in the completely rural county, and calls would go out in the middle of the night to friends in New York and California, asking for money needed to fix the flats so that as few days as possible would be wasted.

In September, Marshall left Amite, planning to return after a few months' rest, perhaps with a tape recorder to document the saga of the Ninth Circle. But instead, Marshall went to California

to help in the dramatic grape-pickers' strike near Delano. He quickly involved other SNCC workers in the strike and became a close aide to strike leader Cesar Chavez, whom *The New Republic*'s Andrew Kopkind has compared to Bob Parris.

In November I visited Amite.

As one drives from Jackson to Amite along fog-clouded Highway 51, the abstract sociological term "rural" becomes concretized. The sense of desolation and backwardness grows with each mile on the speedometer. There are no cities except for McComb, whose thirteen thousand inhabitants make it a metropolis by Mississippi standards. Next to Jackson, the capital, the biggest city in the state is Meridian, population fifty thousand. Perhaps one of the reasons for Mississippi's primitive racism is the absence of a cultured urban center that might civilize the population from within. Georgia has Atlanta, Louisiana has New Orleans, even Alabama has Montgomery. But Mississippi has Meridian, where the killers of Goodman, Chaney, and Schwerner are still free.

Even a short stay in Amite is a bruising experience. Old Negroes with bent spines and work-swollen fingers lie to the SNCC workers, inventing ailments and appointments, rather than face the local registrar in Liberty. A meeting in a broken-down shack called a church approaches Gandhian *agape* with the singing of religious hymns and the preachments of love thy enemy. A home with no toilet, no telephone, and no heat, and with six children crowded into three small rooms, is spotlessly clean, and a magnificent meal is prepared for a dozen people in two hours. An old farmer named Willie Bates recalls how his cousin was castrated in 1962 and asks whether "there is any place on earth where colored peoples is treated meaner than in Amite County?"

Fear and Love.

These are the two polarities upon which the fragile, embryonic movement in Amite rests.

The movement in Amite is in an earlier stage than anywhere else in Mississippi. Even the most rebellious local Negroes think a public demonstration in Liberty must wait for another age. The protest in Amite is pure and religious, uncontaminated by organizational in-fighting or Mau Mau militancy. It is just two outside organizers and perhaps 200 or 300 local Negroes. The

right to protest has not yet been won, much less the tokens of desegregation or the utopian goal of equality. For a Negro to talk
to another Negro active in the movement requires courage; to
come to a meeting is authentic heroism. There is not much talk
about Herbert Lee, but there is a lot of remembering.

The daily routine of Steptoe, Carol, and Hazel is "boring,
shitty" work, as Carol puts it. It is canvassing from sunup until
twilight, and then often a meeting in a church. There is nothing
dramatic about the work. There are no emotional releases. The
tension is constant: every passing car is a threat, every white face
a mask for violence, every back road a potential trap. There is no
freedom house in Amite, where drink, talk, or sex can be shared
with other organizers. There is nothing more intellectual than
the *McComb Enterprise Journal* to read. By November both Carol
and Hazel had been there for five months and both were preparing to leave, burned out by the tension, the exhaustion, the frustration, of day-to-day work.

Religion is the source of love in Amite. Baptist churches are
the only possible places to hold meetings. Several of the indigenous leaders developing in Amite, like Reverend Knox, are ministers, or, at least, deacons in their church, like Curtis Dawson.
The people themselves are deeply religious.

There is no tradition of freedom singing in Amite. Few Negroes even know the words to "We Shall Overcome." The four
meetings I attended while in the county were all begun with the
singing of Baptist hymns and a prayer. There were none of the
fiery call-and-response chants of "Freedom now" or of the improvised freedom songs that characterize the movement in urban
centers.

One of the meetings I attended was in Mount Pilgrim Baptist
Church on Steptoe's land, where Parris had conducted his first
voter-registration class in 1961. Herbert Lee is buried in the
churchyard, and his handsome fifteen-year-old son, Herbert, Jr.,
was among the fifty people present at the meeting.

Mount Pilgrim has no pulpit. There are just ten rows of spare
wooden benches in the center, and four rows on either side. It is
lighted by only three bulbs. Outside it was forty-five degrees, and
until the warmth from the small heater spread throughout the
room, few people took off their jackets. A hand-drawn tablet
with the Ten Commandments was on the wall.

One by one, individuals began drifting in, some in blue denim

field overalls and mud-caked boots, others in sports jackets and
shirts open at the neck. The men and women segregated themselves by sex.

The meeting began with the singing of two hymns: "Lord,
Come By Here," and "Jesus, Hold My Hand While I Run This
Race." Then there was a prayer by Reverend A. D. Hackett, an
itinerant preacher without a permanent church. "God is going to
cure our troubles through somebody," he said in a prophecy that
synthesized the Bible with the movement.

I had come to Amite with young folk singer Eric Andersen.
We, along with Carol, were the only whites at the meeting, and
Steptoe used our faces as his text for the evening. (Steptoe is one
of the few local Negroes who is not religious.)

"White people come down here and do everything for us," he
began. "But you have to do just one thing for them—and that's
to redish."

Chants of "Amen," and "That's right," welled up from the
benches.

"We're going through something here now that should have
happened years ago. I've been in the struggle since 1953 and now
I can see the first change happening."

More amens greeted that affirmative observation.

"You all have to go down and redish now. You should want to
make this a better county to live in. You have to take that first
step. You get the key to freedom when you redish. To be a re-
dished *voter* means you are an American, a first-class citizen. It
will keep bullets out of your body and clubs away from your
head."

Curtis Dawson, with a morose, bespectacled face, not unlike
Bob Parris's, spoke in the same vein of civic virtue and racial reconciliation. It was a sermon of love no Harlem hustler could
comprehend.

"We must love everybody," he started.

From that opening statement he began to build, the way a
blues singer states, restates, and then embroiders on a basic
theme.

"White people care more about us than we care about ourselves," Deacon Dawson added, the counterpoint of amens and
"Say it, brother," rising from the benches.

"They do everything for us. They go farther with us than we
go with ourselves. But we have to redish for our own selves."

With that, the amens swelled up again.

And then, as is often done in Amite, a political point was cloaked in a biblical analogy.

"God told Moses," Dawson said, "to pick up a stick. But Moses said it was a snake. But the Lord insisted he pick it up, and when Moses did, it turned out to be a sword. And that's how going to the courthouse in Liberty seems. Right now it looks like picking up a snake. But once you pick it up, it will become the sword of freedom."

Then Carol Rogoff, sitting in the last row, began to sing, "This Little Light of Mine." And the younger people in the church, some of whom had gone to jail in Jackson in June, joined in, and Eric Andersen began to contribute a guitar accompaniment.

"This little light of mine we're gonna let it shine. . . ."

The words filled the church and spilled out into the frosty night. With modulating fervor, each new chorus was sung.

"All over Mississippi, we're gonna let it shine. . . .

"All over the courthouse, we're gonna let it shine. . . .

"All over Sheriff Jones, we're gonna let it shine. . . .

"All over the highway, we're gonna let it shine. . . .

"All over Liberty, we're gonna let it shine /oh, we've got the light of freedom/we're gonna let it shine."

Most of the older people had left, since Amite farmers must get up at 5 A.M. But a cluster of teen-agers remained around Eric, singing the songs they had learned in jail.

After a while Herbert Lee, Jr., began to sing:

"Oh, my father was a freedom fighter/I'm a freedom fighter too. . . ."

Fear.

That's the other emotion always just beneath the surface of life in Amite. It is there whenever you stop for gas in Liberty; whenever the dogs start barking in the night and someone is approaching the house; whenever you notice the gun Steptoe always keeps within reach.

One incident that happened to me helped demonstrate the total vulnerability of Amite Negroes to random violence. Four of us—Carol, Hazel, a local woman named Juanitta Griffin, and I —were nailing up posters on trees for the Agricultural Stabilization and Conservation election. The ASC county committees de-

cide local cotton allotments, who gets extra acreage, and who gets community credit corporation loans. Until Carol and Hazel came to work in Amite, Negro farmers didn't know they were eligible to run in this election even if they weren't registered to vote in political elections. The Federal Government hadn't bothered to inform them of their right to participate.

I had just nailed a poster to a tree and we were driving away when we noticed a pick-up truck stop and the driver tear down the poster. For about a quarter of a mile the truck followed us on the deserted, narrow gravel road. We noticed it had no license plate. The driver had a woman, a child, and a Negro in the cab with him. Suddenly he came up on us very fast, trying to drive us off the road. He barely missed. He drove on a few hundred yards to discharge his three passengers. Then he began to come up on us again from behind, making a second pass, again coming very close to forcing us off the road. By this time we were growing frightened, realizing that we didn't know where we were and that the driver of the tagless pick-up truck had us at his mercy.

Carol, who was driving, suggested we try to make it to a paved road less than a mile away. Just then the pick-up truck bore down on us, head-on, at about sixty miles an hour. Carol swerved, and our car landed in a ditch.

We were destroying all the lists of local Negroes we had in the car when the driver of the pick-up truck pulled up alongside. He had a face from central casting, like all the faces I had watched in newsreels spitting on little girls in Little Rock and unleashing snarling police dogs in Birmingham.

"You-all need any help?" he asked mockingly.

"No, thank you," Carol replied.

"Well, if you-all did, I'd tell you-all to call Martin Luther," the face said, and drove off to a dairy barn up the road.

The four of us quickly got out and began to walk as fast as we could in the direction of the main road. As we walked past the dairy barn, the driver, now with a friend and a pack of dogs, began shouting at us.

"White trash . . . nigger lovers . . . degenerates. . . ."

We kept walking, heads down, and he began following us, cursing and threatening.

Before he caught up to us we reached the main road and flagged down a log truck with three Negroes. But the Negroes

were afraid to pick up our integrated group. Only several minutes of pleading convinced them to take us to a nearby home, where Carol called FBI agent R. L. Timmons, stationed in McComb.

Agent Timmons said he was busy just then, but would come to Steptoe's farm the next morning to hear our stories.

Within a few hours the grapevine in the Negro community reported back that the man who had chased us was named Dan "Buster" Wells, and that he had a long history of brutality against Negroes. The Negro originally in the truck with Wells was also spoken to, but he wouldn't talk to us, much less to the FBI. The Negroes in Amite remember Louis Allen, too.

The next morning Agent Timmons arrived exactly on time, wearing a businessman's blue suit. He carefully took down all our statements, but added he didn't think "anything would come of them."

"We don't have any jurisdiction," he said, incanting the phrase that has made FBI agents despised by civil-rights workers. "Why didn't you call Sheriff Jones when this happened?" he asked.

Carol reminded Agent Timmons that many local Negroes believed that Sheriff Jones had personally murdered Louis Allen, and that he had never arrested a white man for violence against a Negro.

The next day, on the street in McComb, we accidentally ran into Timmons's assistant, Sy Hoglund. While Timmons grew up in Louisiana and is clearly hostile to the movement, Hoglund is a Northerner who went to law school at the University of Wisconsin. He reluctantly admitted that since we were working on the federal ASC election when the incident occurred, "there might be jurisdiction . . . but we will not do anything more than file a report unless the Justice Department specifically instructs us to proceed further in the case."

Bob Parris, Marshall Ganz, and Carol Rogoff are all complex, city-bred, middle-class intellectuals. That Amite should attract and sustain such people is, I suspect, an insight into one of the New Left's most tangled threads. That thread is the revolt against the IBM card, against urban impersonalization and the alienation of mass society; a revolt rooted in the void, which cries out for the kind of human generosity and vitality that exists among rural Mississippi Negroes.

Many civil-rights workers in the state rage passionately against the life-style they left behind in the comfortable North: suburbia, status commodities, nine-to-five jobs. But in Amite people are judged not by their manners, or their fathers' income, or what fraternity they belong to, but by their integrity, their work, and their courage.

Although it is too often sentimentalized, there is a special quality to the Negroes of Amite County that is missing elsewhere. The routinized middle class doesn't have it, the cynical Northern-ghetto Negro doesn't have it, and the violent, poor Southern white doesn't have it. In part this distinctive quality comes from living in a totally rural environment, removed from the criminality, corruption, and violence in the cities. In part it derives from the strength of the Baptist Church with its embracing of the values of both the Sermon on the Mount and the Ten Commandments. And in part it comes from a people that has achieved an authentic nobility in one hundred years of stoic suffering.

In *Letters from Mississippi,* a few of the volunteers reached for an explanation for their love of a culture they had been taught, in America's best schools, was slow and primitive.

"One sees freedom here," one volunteer wrote, "that is so much more than the ironical fact that enslaved people are, at least relatively, the liberated ones. Some 'white' people sit at their feet wondering at this sorrow freed and made beautiful. . . ."

Another summer worker wrote home: "When I see these simple people living lives of relative inner peace, love, honor, courage, and humor, I lose patience with people who sit and ponder their belly buttons. . . ."

Still another volunteer observed: "There is some strong ambivalence which goes with this work. I sometimes fear that I am only helping to integrate some beautiful people into modern white society with all of its depersonalization (I suppose that has something to do with its industrial nature). It isn't nineteenth century pastoral romanticism which I feel, but a genuine respect and admiration for a culture which, for all the trouble, still isn't as commercialized and depersonalized as our Northern mass culture."

What I am trying to suggest is the ultimate irony of the New Left's assault on the Closed Society. It is that the liberators have so far benefited more from the struggle than those in bondage, that for all the enormity of their heroism, Parris, Ganz, and Ro-

goff have gotten more than they have given. And it may be an enduring paradox that all through Mississippi the lives of the white volunteers have been more enriched, and more fundamentally changed, than the lives of the maids and tenant farmers whom they came to help.

Such a tentative suggestion, finally, flows from a suffocating pessimism about the future of Amite County.

Pessimistic because Amite is such a desperately poor place to begin with. Pessimistic because so many of the young Negroes leave, and the bright and rebellious handful that stays is likely to be recruited into the Government's million-dollar antipoverty Headstart program or else die in Vietnam. Throughout the state the potential second generation of the movement is being absorbed by such programs and the draft. Pessimistic because SNCC probably left Mississippi a year too soon, and the MFDP has expended too much of its energy in Washington, and not enough in remote outposts like Amite.

Nevertheless, three young Dantes, all under thirty years of age, have helped bring substantial change since July of 1961. The right to hold meetings and the right of civil-rights workers to move freely around the county have been won. The pattern of fear and submissiveness in the Negro community has been broken. Local leadership is developing. About 500 Negroes are registered, and at least 1,000 will be on the voting rolls by the time of the next countywide election in 1967. Such voting strength is, at least, enough to dilute the arbitrary terror.

Still, no Negro's life has been materially improved. Nor is there any visible possibility of such improvement. Amite remains the bottom of the iceberg, which only massive outside intervention, backed by the Federal Government, can shatter.

On my last night in Amite an old Negro preacher asked me what could possibly change the "conditions of my people?"

The only answer I could give him was the absurd fantasy that one day Lyndon Johnson, traveling in disguise as did Peter the Great, might come to Amite, and live for a few days on Steptoe's farm.

NOVEMBER, 1965

[2.]
Marching to Montgomery:
The Cradle Did Rock

MONTGOMERY, Ala.—It was the Ecumenical Council, a hootenanny, a happening, and a revolution all rolled into one. And it happened in Montgomery, the "Cradle of the Confederacy."

A broken-down hipster, the *Realist* sticking out of his dungarees, marched alongside an Episcopal bishop clutching the Holy Bible. There were the kamikazes of the Student Nonviolent Coordinating Committee—SNCC—in their blue denim overalls, mud-caked boots and crash helmets, next to middle-class housewives who won't ride the subways after dark. There were nuns in flowing black habits arm in arm with jowly labor leaders who discriminate in their unions.

There were rabbis, junkies, schoolboys, actors, sharecroppers, intellectuals, maids, novelists, folk-singers and politicians—10,000 motives and 40,000 people marching to Montgomery behind James Forman who hates the oppressor and Martin Luther King who loves the oppressed.

There were hundreds of high school and college youngsters—that new breed of revolutionary that has somehow grown up inside the bowels of prosperous America. There were kids who rioted against HUAC, vigiled against the Bomb, invaded Mississippi last summer, and turned Berkeley upside down. They are a new generation of insurgents, nourished not by Marx or Trotsky, but by Camus, Lenny Bruce, Bob Dylan, and SNCC. Their revolution is not against capitalism, but against what they deem to be the values of an enlightened America—Brotherhood Weeks, factories called colleges, desperation called success, and sex twice a week.

And there were thousands of clergymen symbolizing the revolution within a revolution—the nun with suntan cream on her face who marched all the way from Selma, priests, ministers, rabbis

with yarmulkas. There was a huge sign: "Lutherans are Here Because Christ Cared." Another read: "Kansas Mennonites Support Civil Rights." And another: "SMU Marches for Freedom."

On the streets of the Confederacy's cradle, that "coalition of conscience" Bayard Rustin and Michael Harrington have tried to will into existence, materialized spontaneously. A line of marchers, strung out as far as the eye could see, sang "America, the Beautiful" and made it sound like a revolutionary anthem.

The day that was to end in triumph and tragedy began in sleepy whimsy at 4 A.M. last Thursday for the 104 participants in the Village Independent Democrats' "Fly-In" as they pulled out of the West Side Airlines Terminal singing ironic songs about their pilgrimage.

They sang in spirited atonality that quickly disintegrated into anarchy songs like "Stars Fell on Alabama" and "I'm Alabamy Bound" and "Swanee" and "Dixie."

"Alabama, here I come," roared Bill Tatum, "VIDers, don't be late, open up that capitol gate. Alabama, here I come, right back where I started from . . ."

The "Welcome to Montgomery" sign at Dannelly Airport reinforced the ironic mood of the pilgrims, especially for those who noticed that billboard just outside the airport that read: "Get the U.S. out of the U.N. or get the U.N. out of the U.S."

Within twenty minutes the small airport lounge became congested as flights from Boston and St. Louis also landed, disgorging eager, smiling, scrubbed and middle-class faces, some on top of clerical collars.

A white minister from Martin Luther King's Southern Christian Leadership Conference (SCLC) greeted new arrivals, urged them to leave the city "as soon as the rally is over because it will be dangerous," and directed them to shuttle buses to the City of St. Jude, a Roman Catholic complex where the marchers had camped the night before. On the SCLC minister's lapel was a button that said "GROW." He explained it stood for "Get Rid of Wallace."

At St. Jude the predominant mood was gaiety, as thousands upon thousands of visitors swelled the great serpentine line of march that coiled around the vast, muddy athletic field.

Small clusters sang freedom songs during the two hours it took for the whole line to unwind onto the streets toward the capitol, four miles away. The visitors sang off-key versions of better-

known freedom songs, while local Negroes, led by either SNCC or SCLC staff members, sang raucous, sassy, taunting songs that came out of the Movement in Alabama's Black Belt. A group of about 5,000 from St. Louis stood in a large circle, one small Negro woman calling out chorus after chorus of "We Shall Overcome."

Other demonstrators milled around the staging area like conventioneers, wearing name tags and introducing themselves to strangers, pronouncing their home towns with accents of pride— Montreal, Berkeley, Boston, Detroit—and their association with equal pride—ADA, the United Auto Workers, NAACP, the University of Virginia, the American Legion (Gramercy Park chapter).

At noon, under one of the day's brief showers, the procession began to move out, with the bloody-shoed 300 who had marched all the way in the vanguard. With them were barefoot Joan Baez; James Baldwin, nervously smiling, just back from Scandinavia; the angelic-looking Montgomery seamstress Rosa Parks, who ignited the mythic bus boycott a decade ago; and SNCC's John Lewis, who walked the whole way from Selma and who had suffered head injuries on "Bloody Sunday" at the Alabama River Bridge. And there was Martin Luther King, to whom Negroes of the Black Belt now sing "Glory, Glory Hallelujah" and then kiss his hand.

The streets in the Negro slums of Montgomery were of mud and clay. There were row upon row of rundown shacks, with the very old, the very young, the unemployed sitting on porches.

At first the nonmarchers were timid and shy. It was as if shame made them look down rather than at the masses that surged past them. But slowly they looked up, to wave, and when the marchers began to shout, "Join us, come on," many accepted the invitation and probably protested their plight for the first time in their lives. Marching through the slums was like taking LSD for the soul.

One bent old woman ran off her porch and kissed a white marcher. Children, dirty and scrawny, ran alongside, singing the songs and chanting the slogans of freedom. A very old man, his cane resting between his legs, sat on his porch steps and wept.

About a mile from the capitol we reached the downtown section of Montgomery, with its banks, hotels, movies, stores, office buildings, and clean asphalt streets. The sidewalks were almost

deserted except for a sprinkling of hecklers and the federal troops at each intersection, standing at attention, their rifles at their sides.

But against the windows of the office buildings were pressed the white faces of the South. Some shook their heads "no" or gave the thumbs-down sign when the marchers waved to them. A beautiful woman of about twenty-five stood on the balcony of the Jefferson Davis Hotel, and when the demonstrators waved at her, this flower of Southern womanhood made the traditional obscene gesture of one finger up.

On the lawn of an elegant home a hunched, elderly maid stood in the midst of her sullen employers. She was smiling and waving a white handkerchief at the procession. One wonders what was happening in the minds of her employers at that moment.

Remarked Edward Koch, the Village Democratic leader: "Walking through the Negro section made me feel like I was marching through Paris again with the liberation army. The white section was what it must have been like marching through Germany."

From the window of the Alabama Bible Society Building hung a blow-up of the picture Senator Eastland introduced into the *Congressional Record* prior to the March on Washington to prove Martin Luther King was "part of the Communist conspiracy." The photograph shows King at a rally in 1957 at the Highlander Folk School.

Dexter Avenue is the eight-lane street that leads to the white stone capitol building. As the procession turned the corner of that final leg of the journey, the marchers suddenly broke into "America the Beautiful" and sang it was a passion normally associated in the Movement with "We Shall Overcome."

"America, America, God shed his grace on thee; and crown thy good with brotherhood, from sea to shining sea," they sang. Hundreds of schoolchildren waved little American flags. Ahead loomed the dome of the capitol with its Alabama and Confederate flags blowing in the breeze.

By 2 P.M. all 40,000 marchers, including about 10,000 whites, arrived at the foot of the capitol and stretched several blocks down Dexter Avenue. The symbolism of the scene was inescapable. At the spot where Jefferson Davis was inaugurated, where George Wallace shouted in his inaugural in 1961, "Segregation

now, segregation tomorrow, segregation forever," the largest civil-rights demonstration in the history of the South sang "We Shall Overcome"—black and white together—"We are not afraid today."

In the shadow of the red-brick Dexter Avenue Baptist Church, from whose pulpit Martin Luther King led the bus boycott ten years earlier, the huge rally was turned into a kind of coronation of Dr. King.

"Who is your leader?" the Reverend Ralph Abernathy asked the throng. The answer swelled up, "Martin Luther King!" The only exceptions were veterans of SNCC, who yelled, "De Lawd of Slick." But even that invidious distortion of SCLC was probably shouted as much in respect as in cynicism.

(The bitterness lurking in the background was based on the fact that SNCC, which had been alone in Dallas County since late 1962, had great difficulty working in harness with King after SCLC took over the Selma campaign in January. There had been serious disputes over strategy and tactics, since King's basic goal is integration and SNCC's is a revolution.)

After two hours of speeches by every major leader of the civil-rights movement, King was finally introduced to the crowd. Like the multitude in Washington in 1963, they had become fatigued and restless; many had been awake as long as twenty hours. Overhead, a helicopter and a Piper Cub circled noisily. Behind the platform two dozen green-helmeted Alabama conservation police guarded the steps of the capitol building. Behind them stood a number of members of the Alabama legislature.

Then King began, his resonant voice and preacher's alliterative rhythm slowly rousing the crowd from boredom. From behind him on the platform came counterpoints of "Amen" and "Tell it, Brother" from the other ministers.

In Washington he invoked the phrase, "I have a dream," the way a blues singer repeats a key phrase. In Montgomery, facing the capitol, it was, "We are on the move now," that became the launching pad for a series of crescendolike thrusts.

"We are on the move now," he said. "The burning of our churches will not deter us. We are on the move now. The bombing of our homes will not dissuade us. We are on the move now." Now the throng responded with shouts of "Yes, Lord" and "Amen".

"The beating of our clergymen will not divert us. We are on

the move now. Yes, we are on the move now, and no wave of racism can stop us."

King climaxed his speech by repeating four times with rising fervor, "Glory Glory Hallelujah." And then the cooks, maids, and janitors were crying and cheering at the same time.

There were supposed to be twenty-six shuttle buses waiting after the rally to ferry demonstrators from the capitol to the airport five miles away. But twenty-one of the drivers called in sick, and for two hours thousands milled around in a muddy lot a block behind the capitol while five buses tried to do all the work. There was pushing, shoving, and maneuvering each time a bus pulled in. Finally a SNCC worker with a walkie-talkie told the crowd, "Come on, you're acting like kids. This ain't the New York subway."

By dusk the troops had disappeared and the last handful waited unprotected in the lot, feeling fear for the first time during the day.

Chaos reigned at the airport. Hundreds sprawled on the lawn, picnicking, sleeping, and singing. Huge lines pointed to the lavatories and phones; there were no snack counters. All outgoing flights were late.

After an hour's delay the VID flight was ready to be boarded, except that there was no ladder available. So for another hour the 104 weary passengers stood in a cramped line, twenty yards away from the plane, while a ladder was searched for—or, as some suspected, hidden.

Meanwhile, a few yards away, the dean of all civil-rights leaders, seventy-seven-year-old Asa Philip Randolph, had collapsed from exhaustion, and Bayard Rustin and Michael Harrington tended him while dispatching friends to find a doctor. The Montgomery police seemed uninterested.

"It's my fault," Rustin mumbled. "I never should have gotten him up at 2 A.M., and he never should have walked those four miles."

At 10:45 New York time, the VID flight left the Cradle of the Confederacy amid complaints to the Civil Aeronautics Board about the delay and caustic reflections on "Southern hospitality." There was no singing on the flight back. Most of the passengers slept. A few talked about the future of the civil-rights movement, agreeing at the outset that Montgomery was just a skirmish in a long war whose end still lies beyond the rim of history.

Steve Berger, an aide to reform Congressman Jonathan Bingham, said the new voting rights bill was "pretty bad and very poorly drawn." Others, activists of the Movement, thought no legislation could possibly deal with the specter of firing, beating, and murder that faces any Negro who tries to register to vote in the Black Belt. Other militants spoke eagerly of the next battle—the continuing attempt to unseat the five Congressmen from Mississippi by the Freedom Democratic Party.

Elizabeth Sutherland, who works for SNCC in New York, sat reading a private legal memorandum on the proposed voting bill, pointing out all its flaws and loopholes. "I just hope the registrars don't get their hands on this memo," she said.

And there was speculation about what would happen in the Black Belt now that the "civil-rights tourists," Dr. King, the federal troops, and the outside journalists were leaving, and the Negroes were left alone to confront the Jim Clarks, the racist registrars, and those terrible faces that looked down from those windows.

When the plane landed at Kennedy Airport, its passengers were told it had already happened—murder. Nobody said anything memorable or poetic. They just cursed.

MARCH, 1965

[3.]
Two Months Later—A Dream Deferred

MONTGOMERY, Ala.—While the whole world watched, this Cradle of the Confederacy rocked to the beat of "Oh, Freedom" two months ago.

Most of the crack organizers of the Student Nonviolent Coordinating Committee (SNCC) converged on this city of 160,000 from all over the South, after Martin Luther King had secured control of the movement in Selma, fifty-four miles away. With the movement's marines-in-overalls came scores of hip radicals, who had rushed to Selma to march and not to pray. Waiting for them were thousands of young Negroes—at George Washington Carver and Booker T. Washington High Schools, and at Tuskegee Institute and Alabama State College.

These volatile elements quickly fused and generated a series of dramatic street demonstrations in the downtown section of the city. Once docile Negro schoolchildren sang "No More Wallace Over Me," as mounted policemen beat them with whips and clubs. Negro "block boys" who joined one SNCC march on the state capital pelted the police with bricks and bottles. For two rainy nights hundreds of students slept in the streets in a vigil for the dying Unitarian minister James Reeb. Several hundred undergraduates from segregated Alabama State marched on the home of their conservative Negro president and presented him with a list of demands, the first being that he resign immediately. Between March 10 and 27, more than 250 people went to jail here, and thousands of others were swept into motion for the first time in their lives.

SNCC's storefront headquarters at 908 High Street was the nerve center for this almost totally spontaneous movement. Dozens of people slept in the cluttered office. The mimeograph machine pitched out an endless flow of leaflets and manifestoes. The telephones never stopped ringing. The street outside was jammed

with floodlights, sound trucks, reporters, demonstrators, camera-men, and FBI agents. Clerical workers labored around the clock trying to keep track of the new arrivals as they were taken off to jail. Others canvassed the Negro section trying to raise bail in pennies and dimes.

But last week the SNCC office was a cage for hot, bored people to pace. The used mimeograph stencils of March hung like wrinkled flypapers on the walls, symbol of a deferred dream.

"Nothin' shakin' here, baby," said a volunteer worker. The militancy, the passion, and the hope of the march were gone. Montgomery's Negro community of 35,000 had slipped back into apathy, demoralization, and fratricide.

Four full-time SNCC field secretaries, plus eight volunteers, sleep, work, and—when they have money—eat in the storefront headquarters. Worn clothes, unmade cots, and crumpled cigarette packs are everywhere. There is a cheap phonograph. The records are mostly Tony Bennett and Brook Benton. The reading material in the office reflects SNCC's diversity. There is the nationalistic *Liberator,* the British Labour-oriented *New Statesman, Jet,* and a lot of comic books. Staff member Fred Meely, twenty-three and a veteran of Natchez, Greenwood, and Holly Springs, is reading Camus's *The Rebel.* After a few minutes he dozes off, the worn book still in his callused hands.

The project workers are tired, frustrated, and dirty. They are desperate for information about the movement—the Freedom Democratic Party Congressional challenge, the voting suit in Sunflower County.

They explain that *The New York Times* has been virtually unavailable in the state since the libel suit against the paper was lost last year.

"It's a wonder we don't get brainwashed ourselves," Willie Ricks said. "All you can read is the Montgomery and Birmingham papers and all you can see is the three local television channels. . . . This is really a closed society."

The project workers admit they have no active program under way, nor do they have any concrete plans. They say the Negroes of Montgomery are "exhausted by ten years of demonstrating without any change in their lives" and that the city is "overorganized by an entrenched and conservative leadership."

Twenty-two-year-old white volunteer Bruce Bramson spent eight days fasting in prison. Now he says reluctantly: "I think we

might have to close this project down and go back into the back counties, like Wilcox and Lowndes." (In rural Lowndes County Negroes outnumber whites five to one, but, as of May 20, only eleven of 15,200 Negroes were registered to vote.)

"But this is one project," Bramson emphasized, "I still believe SNCC's basic philosophy of developing indigenous leadership, rather than creating synthetic crises, is the right one. . . . Maybe we just aren't experienced enough yet to take on the cities, that's all."

Handsome, shrewd, twenty-year-old Doug McCass spends almost all his spare time hanging around the SNCC office. Although he has only a B average, he has the highest IQ of any student of all-Negro Alabama State College. And like many others like him across the South, his only ambition after he graduates in January is to work for SNCC at $10.00 a week.

"What else can I do that will satisfy me?" he asks. "I know I can get a good job in public relations downtown, but I would be ashamed."

Doug, however, disagrees with SNCC's urban strategy of trying to organize those most damaged by the society—criminals, alcoholics, junkies, dropouts, teen-age toughs, the unemployed—the lumpen proletariat.

"There is no movement in this town," he asserted. "And part of the reason is that SNCC is making some big mistakes. First of all, they got to get organized themselves. Then they got to stop messing with them cats in the bars and on the street corners—all of them winos got guns, man. They got to organize the bourgeoisie and the intellectuals first in a city like this."

But Fred Meely, an intellectual and a revolutionary, retains hope that the movement in Montgomery can be rekindled.

"All summer," he explained, "we might just sit here and build a base in the community, letting people know we are here, becoming involved in their lives, finding out what they want us to do—you know it's no shit when we say programs come from the people—that's the way we work. After all, it took a year for Bob [Moses] to get something moving in Mississippi. The summer project came only after he was there for three years. We've been here just since the march—and that was the worst possible time to begin a grass-roots movement.

"SNCC is just now beginning to deal with the problems of the cities," Meely continued. "Up until this year all our experience

has been in rural places like the delta, Arkansas, and southwest
Georgia. Montgomery represents a whole new set of problems for
us. Its size, for one. It's a fact that there is already an existing
middle-class Negro leadership that is very corrupt. Also, in a city
like this Negroes seem much less open to the idea of nonviolence.
There is a hard core of hate and violence in every black man in
this city. Sometimes I'm even afraid to walk through the Negro
section on a Saturday night. And you watch, the people who
come in here asking for help will be angry and hostile, looking
for a fight."

A walk through black Montgomery confirmed all that Meely
said. An extraordinary number of people were either on crutches
or bandaged in some way. It seemed as if half the community
had been wounded by the other half the week before. A thir-
teen-year-old schoolboy had bloody patches of gauze on his
forearm and neck; a handsome woman of about forty was scarred
all over her face and neck. Few people look you in the eye, and,
contrary to folk mythology, nobody hums freedom songs. The atmosphere is depressed and sullen—like Harlem a few days after
last summer's riots.

One man, a laborer, said he wished "SNCC would get its ass
out of the community. They're just a bunch of kids." Another
complained: "The fools think you get something with nonviolence. That's plain craziness!"

And a third commented on the interracial character of the project: "It don't bother me none, but people here don't like to see
them white girls jazzing around with colored boys."

In addition to the Montgomery experiment, a quartet of
SNCC organizers are quietly investigating the situation in Birmingham, the industrial center 100 miles to the north. And in
Atlanta SNCC's only published poet, Julian Bond, recently won
the Democratic Party primary for the state legislature, despite
the opposition of the "black power structure." Bond's campaign
manager, SNCC veteran Ivanhoe Donaldson, believes a grass-
roots movement will now finally spring up in Atlanta, "because
Julian will go to the people, make them think, and involve them
in basic decision-making. . . . He will get them talking to each
other, instead of talking to him, the way a conventional politician
would do."

But in Montgomery it was different. A symptom of the decline
of the movement was the fact that last week there was not one

lawyer in the whole city willing to argue a hearing in federal district court on a motion to remove the trials of the 250 demonstrators jailed in March to a federal court.

The only Negro attorney in the city who regularly accepted civil-rights cases had become estranged from the movement because "it had begun to wreck my practice, which runs about $30,000 a year." So Village Independent Democrats president Martin Berger volunteered to fly to Montgomery to plead the case before Judge Frank Johnson, the Eisenhower appointee who approved the Selma-to-Montgomery march.

After several phone calls, this city's disgruntled civil-rights lawyer finally agreed to confer with Berger and brief him on the case. Most of their three-hour conference, however, was spent with the local attorney trying to dissuade Berger from raising any erudite points of constitutional law during the hearing. "Judge Johnson don't put up with any of that nonsense," he warned the VID president.

"You know, I have to live in this town after you go back to New York. I'm now in a position here where I can call the Governor [George Wallace] any time I want and get him on the phone. He knows we disagree on some matters, but that we are friends."

Then Montgomery's most militant Negro lawyer drove off in his Thunderbird, and Berger walked back to the Negro motel next to the SNCC office.

On the day before the hearing Berger worked from dawn until after midnight finding his student defendants, interviewing them, calming their fears, subpoenaing local records and city officials, reading law books and the sketchy files on the case.

At about 1 A.M. Berger finished, yawned, ground his fingers into his eyes, and said: "It's tragic the way these kids are afraid to talk to me because I'm white. The scars they've been given down here will never heal."

Then he fell asleep while the SNCC staff and five Alabama State students stayed up until 5 A.M. debating the existence of God.

Thus the SNCC visionaries confront the repressive, complex urban South. Dr. King, the press, the clergy, the lawyers, the civil-rights tourists, the hung-up student radicals float in and out of Montgomery. But the faceless pioneers like Fred Meely, Doug McCass, and Bruce Bramson remain to endure, flounder, experi-

ment, learn, grow, and perhaps, someday, carry the movement to a new plateau.

For as SNCC's happy warrior Stokely Carmichael says, "Man, as soon as we crack Montgomery and Birmingham—man, I'm splittin' for Harlem."

MAY, 1965

[4.]
The End of the Road Is Just the Beginning

When President Johnson signed the voting-rights bill into law on August 6 and handed the pen to Martin Luther King, many liberals believed he had fulfilled the basic goals of the civil-rights movement. The barriers to equality, built up over 100 years, they thought, had been knocked down with the flourish of a pen.

Now, two months later, according to the Justice Department, more than 65,000 Southern Negroes have been added to the voting rolls in the hard-core racist bastions of Mississippi, Alabama, Louisiana, and Georgia. Thirty thousand have been registered in Mississippi, doubling the total number of registered Negroes in that closed society. Almost 10,000 have been added to the books in Alabama. The results seem impressive, but the negative side of the picture is overwhelming.

Registration of Negroes has doubled in Mississippi, but 360,-000 remain voteless, afraid to risk life, home, and job for the privilege of marking a ballot that may never be counted by white election officials. Federal examiners have been assigned to only nine of eighty-two Mississippi counties. The same is true in Alabama, where 330,000 Negroes eligible to vote are unregistered. In the eleven states of the Old Confederacy, about 1.9 million Negroes are registered and 3.1 million not registered, according to the Justice Department.

In mid-August, in counties where there were Federal examiners, like Madison and Leflore in Mississippi, registration went as high as 2000 a day. Now, registration is down to about 150 a day in these places, and declining. It is only in the old centers of civil-rights activity, like southwest Georgia, Selma, Alabama, and Greenwood, Mississippi, that Negro registration has continued at a steady pace. This seems to indicate that only in those few communities where the field workers of Southern Christian Leadership Conference (SCLC) and the Student Nonviolent Coordinating Committee (SNCC) have dug in and worked for years, where

a movement exists, will Negroes take that heroic march to the courthouse.

The recent elections in Atlanta appear to make clear the fact that the first generation of Negroes who win the ballot—at the end use that ballot to elect highly progressive lawmakers. Atlanta Negroes elected twenty-six-year-old poet and SNCC worker Julian Bond to the state's Lower House. They also elected twenty-six-year-old NAACP militant Ben Brown and blunt-talking John Hood, twenty-seven, to the legislature. Men of such militant character were probably elected because Atlanta was one of the earliest centers of sit-in activity, and is now the home of SNCC and Martin Luther King's SCLC.

Nevertheless, despite the passage of the voting-rights bill and the Atlanta elections, the civil-rights movement now seems at its lowest ebb since 1963 when the Birmingham violence, the Medgar Evers assassination, and the March on Washington helped to forge a national consensus for civil rights.

The Watts riots have contributed to the decline of sympathy for the movement. So has the idea that the last two civil-rights bills "solved the problem." But part of the blame seems to rest in the movement itself.

The movement has now reached its first plateau. Five years of moral leadership and brilliant tactics by Martin Luther King and incredible boldness and sacrifice by SNCC workers have won, on paper, equal voting rights and equal access to public accommodations.

The movement is now beginning to realize that deeper regard is needed for unemployed youths in cities and for farmers being automated off their land. Protection against murderous sheriffs is needed. And, above all, a method of giving the vote to the 3.1 million unregistered Southern Negroes living in communities untouched by the civil-rights movement.

The voting law puts the initiative for registering on the Negro, but it offers him no protection. It does not take into account the century-old legacy of apathy and fear that exists in the Negro community. After all, Federal examiners are present in only 1 percent of the counties of the Deep South.

Violence, though little headlined, is still used as a deterrent to Negro voting. In three of the nine counties into which Federal examiners were sent, Negroes were killed during August under mysterious circumstances. None of them was involved in civil-

rights activity and their deaths may have been accidental, but it had the effect of frightening local Negroes.

In southwest Mississippi the practice of having young Negro toughs beat up Negroes who register has developed. The toughs are often paid by local whites to do this.

Then, too, the courthouse, where they must register, has always been the symbol of barbarism to the Southern Negro. The courthouse is where Negroes are beaten and killed. Early in life the Negro learns what goes on in the basement of the courthouse.

But besides outright violence, there is the less-visible weapon of economic reprisal. Under Mississippi law the names of all applicants for registration must be published in the local newspaper, ensuring that the employer knows which of his Negro employees has the temerity to register. Most Mississippi Negroes work for whites. A few farmers work their own land, and they are the backbone of the local movements because of their relative economic independence. In Tallahatchie County, white bank president Ned Rice was quoted recently in the *Wall Street Journal* as estimating that "about 98 per cent of local Negroes are employed by whites."

According to A. D. Beittel, who works in Mississippi for the American Friends Service Committee, "economic intimidation is a far more powerful deterrent to voting by Negroes than outright violence. You read more about violence, but economic intimidation is the thing these people live with every day."

And in Alabama, Governor George Wallace is now drafting a bill to gerrymander the state legislature so that there are no Negro majorities in any state legislative district. This will require ingenious map-drawing since in places like Lowndes County, Negroes outnumber whites four to one.

Adding to the inadequacy of the voting-rights law are the internal problems that now beset the Southern freedom movement.

Stalled at its current plateau, the movement has failed to develop a program or strategy to deal with the problem of poverty or the problem of organizing politically the major cities of the South. Up to now SNCC has worked almost exclusively in rural counties. Tentative efforts to organize in Montgomery and Birmingham have ended in failure.

Secondly, SNCC and some SCLC field projects seem to be falling apart. Day to day life on a project imposes hardships few outside the movement can comprehend. For a SNCC worker, one

meal a day sometimes consists of grits. They often sleep on floors in shabby offices. There is always tension, intellectual starvation, self-doubt, and petty harassment, like slashed tires or midnight phone calls for Andy Goodman.

Such a life, not of danger or drama, but of tedium and frustration, is turning many project workers to marijuana, surrealist poetry writing, dreams of guerrilla warfare, or the creation of a separate "countercommunity" of all Negro institutions in the Black Belt.

This year's summer projects, sponsored by both SNCC and SCLC, were much less successful than last summer's. SNCC staff member Elizabeth Sutherland, writing recently in the *Nation,* admitted, "the volunteers seemed to me often a poorer quality than last year's: less inspired and more frustrated. In fairness . . . it should be said that SCOPE's workers in Alabama recruited by the Southern Christian Leadership Conference—seemed no better off."

Paul Good, writing in last week's *Reporter* magazine, summed the dilemma up well, saying, "it would seem that many of the SCOPE people arrived a summer too late, as many of the SNCC workers stayed a summer too long."

Part of the tragedy of the civil-rights movement is that it has developed at an unfortunate moment in history. In the decade of rising automation, it's every man for himself and the Negro take the hindmost. There is no Populist movement in which the Negro can find a political home although there are plenty of panacea pushers, left and right. The labor movement of the 1930s has become an analogue of Milovan Djilas's "new class" of fat commissars. The Negroes, students, a few professors, a few clergymen are, at this moment, no countervailing force to the corporations, the military, and the radical right.

Perhaps the best advice has been given by Bayard Rustin at a civil-rights convention.

"In the past you could both call attention to an evil and correct it with a handful of people who were prepared to go to jail," he said. "When you come to housing, to schools, to jobs, no demonstration can do more than call attention to an evil. It is a political problem requiring a political strategy, numbers, planning, reading, requiring knowing something about the nature of revolution. . . . From now on we are going to have to sit down and become thinkers as well as actors."

OCTOBER, 1965

Lead Poisoning: Silent Epidemic in the Slums

Except for its ironic name, Tiffany Street looks like a hundred other decaying streets in the Southeast Bronx. Mounds of uncollected garbage strewn all over. Idle young black and Puerto Rican men sitting on crumbling stoops. Mangy dogs looking through the garbage for scraps. Boarded-up, burnt-out houses freckled with graffiti.

At number 1051, on the fourth floor of a tenement whose dark halls stink from urine, Brenda Scurry was sitting in her clean, neat apartment telling me how her twenty-three-month-old daughter Janet had died of lead poisoning in April.

Brenda, twenty-three, is pretty, street smart, and black. She writes informed and angry letters to President Nixon—and gets back impersonal form letters thanking her for interest in the "New Federalism." She has two other children, four- and five-year-old boys. Her husband works in the garment center, and sometimes lives at home. That morning Brenda had gone to the local public school, discovered her five-year-old sitting in a third-grade class, and had to explain to the indifferent teacher that her child belonged in kindergarten.

"I used to live at 1113 Teller Avenue," she began quietly, but with a bittersweet edge to her voice. "Plaster from the walls started falling all over the place last November. I asked the landlord a couple times to do something about it, but he never did. Then in April one morning my daughter wouldn't eat anything. She started trembling and couldn't breathe. I got scared and she started to change color. A neighbor called a policeman, and we took her to Morrisania Hospital. A doctor looked at her and told me to go home, that she would be okay. They didn't know what it was, but they sent me home. They asked me if Janet ever ate paint or plaster, and I told them yes. I went home but her temperature kept going up and down. After five days they gave her a

blood test for lead poisoning. And then she died the next day. The day after she died, the blood test came back positive. . . . Later they sent me a death certificate that said Janet died of natural causes. The doctors did an autopsy, but I still haven't got the results. I called the administrative director of the hospital twice, and they still haven't sent it to me. The hospital doesn't want to say it was lead, I guess.

"I asked welfare if they would pay for Janet's funeral, but they made me fill out a bunch of forms. So I paid for the funeral with the rent money. Then I asked welfare to pay for the rent. They said I had to fill out some other papers and that it would take a while. Then I got an eviction notice. I went to the central welfare office with it, but they still wouldn't give me any money. So I borrowed some money and moved out because I didn't want that landlord to put me on the street."

Lead poisoning is a disease endemic to the slums. The victims are hungry, unsupervised children between the ages of one and six, who get it by eating pieces of paint and plaster from flaking walls. Lead in paint was outlawed twenty years ago, but the bottom layers of walls in 800,000 run-down dwelling units in New York City still contain poisonous lead.

The city estimates that about 30,000 children each year suffer lead poisoning, but only 600 cases were reported during each of the last three years. (There are probably 300,000 victims nationally.) The early symptoms are vague—nausea, lethargy, vomiting, crankiness—and doctors and nurses are not trained to look for it since they are told that lead has been outlawed as a paint ingredient. Ghetto parents are also ignorant of the disease. In three years, Harlem Hospital has not reported a single case of lead poisoning.

But surveys by researchers and activists keep discovering thousands of undiagnosed cases living in the ghettoes; lead poisoning has been called "the silent epidemic" by microbiologist Dr. René Dubos of Rockefeller University, a Pulitzer Prize winner last year.

According to doctors, 5 percent of the children who eat lead die. Of those who survive, about 40 percent suffer permanent brain damage, mental retardation, and deterioration of intelligence. A recent Chicago study of 425 children who had been treated for lead poisoning showed that 39 percent had neurologi-

cal disorders years later, and 22 percent suffered from mental retardation as adults.

Two young, white, middle-class radicals have taken up the
cause of lead poisoning, and for a year now have been waging a
lonely crusade, bereft of money, manpower, or organizational
support, to pressure the city and the health establishment, and to
alert parents. One is red-haired, thirty-year-old Paul Du Brul, the
housing director of the University Settlement House on the
Lower East Side. The other is bearded, twenty-four-year-old
Glenn Paulson, cochairman of the Scientists' Committee for Public Information.

Du Brul met me for lunch two weeks ago. He was particularly
frustrated that day over the media's failure to take an interest in
lead poisoning. He had called the *Post*'s Joe Kahn earlier that
morning, and Kahn had apologized, but the city desk wasn't interested in a story without a hard news peg. *The Times* had
printed a story a few months before, but it had been buried in
the real estate section on a Sunday, "where only landlords would
see it."

Mrs. Scurry had written a personal letter to the *Times* man
who wrote the Sunday story, telling him of her experience with
her landlord, the hospital, and the Welfare Department. And he
wrote back a moving letter how he felt lead poisoning was a
tragic problem, but there just wasn't a news story in her case because the hospital denied lead was the cause of her daughter's
death.

And lead was a story hard to make visible or dramatic for the
television networks. It didn't involve famous leaders, or exotic
militants, or public violence. How do you show a *process,* how
do you show indifference, how do you show invisible, institutionalized injustice, in two minutes on Huntley-Brinkley? How do
you induce the news department of a television network to get
outraged about nameless black babies eating tenement paint,
when the public health profession, schoolteachers, housing experts, scientists, the NAACP, and the politicians haven't given a
damn?

Du Brul then began to explore some of the ramifications of
this silent epidemic.

"Look," he said, "doctors say the effect of lead poisoning is to
damage the nervous system. Kids can't concentrate. They become
disruptive and lose points on I.Q. tests. So I think some of Jen-

sen's findings [geneticist Arthur Jensen] about race and chromosomes might just be the effects of environmental conditions like lead poisoning. In the last ten years, 300,000 slum kids have been sent into the New York City public school system with lead poisoning. They're not culturally inferior; they're sick. What are now considered problems of remedial education might be doctor's problems, not teacher's problems."

Two nights later Du Brul and Paulson went to Judson Church on Washington Square to speak to a meeting of about seventy-five doctors, nurses, interns, and radical students sponsored by Health-PAC (Policy Advisory Center). Here the discussion focused on tactics, on how to fight the problems, how to make it visible.

Du Brul proposed a "fill the hospitals" strategy, coupled with the demand that every slum child between one and six receive a free laboratory test to determine if there is lead in his system. He said Chicago and Baltimore had been using a test that has proved 90 percent effective, and the Lindsay Administration was holding back because of "bureaucratic bungling."

Some of the radical young doctors at the meeting disagreed. They said the hospitals would not, and could not, absorb the 30,000 walking cases in the city. They argued that such a tactic would collapse the already fragile hospital system. A few proposed rent strikes to force landlords to remove the paint or cover it up. Others suggested direct action at hospitals, particularly at Lincoln Hospital, which has lead on its own peeling walls. And still others urged a direct attack on the "slum system" as the root cause of lead poisoning. The meeting broke up at about 11 P.M., with even those few motivated on the issue divided over what to do first.

I spent the next few days working up an interior rage, trying to find out if anyone, with any responsibility, was doing anything about lead poisoning.

The NAACP had no program, nor any plans for any. The Department of Health, Education, and Welfare (the "good guys" in Nixonland) had no existing program and no funds allocated for any future program, but they did have a twenty-one-page pamphlet. I could not find a copy of the pamphlet in any ghetto health office and had to acquire a copy from Glenn Paulson. The pamphlet turned out to be written in an opaque jargon that would hardly enlighten a second-year medical student, much less

a welfare mother. The following is the second sentence on the first page:

"Its etiology, pathogenesis, patho-physiology, and epidemiology are known."

Nineteen Congressmen, including William F. Ryan, have introduced a package of three bills to provide federal funds for a mass testing program in the slums. But the bills are given no chance of emerging from the limbo of committee, or even generating public hearings.

I also called the United Federation of Teachers to see if they were doing anything to detect cases in the schools, but no one called back.

Werner Kramarsky, Mayor Lindsay's staff man in the health field, advised me to call Health Commissioner Mary McLaughlin, to find out officially what the city was doing. When I called her, I was told the commissioner was not in, so I left a message. The next day the commissioner's press secretary called me and said I couldn't under any circumstances have a direct interview with the commissioner, but that he would answer any questions. I gave him a list of four.

After three days Dr. Felicia Oliver-Smith, the department's lead specialist, called back and reported that 1) the city had tested 7000 children last year, compared to 35,000 in Chicago; 2) the city "hoped to" have a mobile testing unit "within one year"; 3) there were 725 cases last year, and more than 7000 already so far this year; 4) "We have no legal authority to make a landlord remove lead-based paint from tenement walls."

The only politician in the city who seems genuinely involved in the issue is Carter Burden, the Democratic-Liberal candidate for City Council in the polyglot East Harlem-Silk Stocking district. Burden has written angry letters to Lindsay, called press conferences, talked up the problem, and tried to energize grassroots groups.

"It's terribly frustrating," Burden said last week. "The press just isn't interested at all. When I held a press conference in March on lead poisoning, not one daily paper and not one television station showed up. Just yesterday I had lunch with one of the religious leaders in East Harlem, and I tried to turn him on about lead. But he told me it was a phony issue, that *asthma* was a bigger community problem. . . . Kramarsky promised us three months ago there would be a crash program of 40,000 tests in the

slums, but it didn't happen. Now I hear the city is about to start, but the summer is over, and 80 percent of the cases develop during the summer. There was no reason for the delay."

Burden also revealed that a private blood test for lead poisoning had just been conducted in his district—in the new, middle-income cooperative Franklin Plaza, which was completed *after* lead was banned from paint.

"That's a scandal," he said. "Of course there are no cases of lead poisoning in Franklin Plaza. But now they can release the results of the survey to prove lead is not a real problem in the slums." The survey was sponsored by Metropolitan Hospital and the American Cancer Society.

Some minimal testing program seems ready to be announced by the municipal bureaucracy. But it is not clear how the test will be distributed, or if it will reach the children who need it. And no one seems about to challenge the landlords to remove the deadly paint. And no one is doing anything about the hundreds of children now living in slum apartments with lead in the walls.

Today there is still lead in the walls of the apartment where Janet Scurry lived on Teller Avenue. There is lead in the two other tenements on the same block, owned by the same landlord who sent Mrs. Scurry the eviction notice. There is still lead in the crumbling walls of Lincoln Hospital, where lead victims are sent. There are still thousands of undiagnosed, lead-poisoned children walking the streets, sitting in classrooms.

As Dr. René Dubos said at a conference on lead poisoning earlier this year: "The problem is so well defined, so neatly packaged with both causes and cures known, that if we don't eliminate this social crime, our society deserves all the disasters that have been forecast for it."

SEPTEMBER, 1969

Young Lords Do City's Work in the Barrio

Free urine tests to detect lead poisoning were given door-to-door last Tuesday to the children who live along East 112th Street in El Barrio.

But this was accomplished only after an unpublicized three-hour sit-in at the Health Department last week by thirty members of the Young Lords Organization, health workers, nurses, and medical students forced the city to release the testing kits to the community.

In October, during the mayoralty campaign, the Health Department put out a press release announcing a crash testing program of 40,000 free tests. But the city never actually bothered to pick up any of the testing kits that were donated by the Bio-Rad Laboratories. The Health Department also never devised a method of getting the tests distributed in the slum neighborhoods where lead poisoning has reached epidemic proportions.

The Young Lords are the Latin equivalent of the Black Panthers. Like the Panthers, their motto is "Serve the People," and like the Panthers, many of their leaders discovered their politics in jail cells. They are now part of the Rainbow Coalition, which includes the Panthers, and the Young Patriots, a group of revolutionary poor white youth.

The Lords began as a Puerto Rican street gang in Chicago. Gradually, they became radicalized, and chapters began to develop in other cities, with a national leadership based in Chicago.

The Lords began to organize last summer in New York City, first around the issue of more frequent garbage collection in the ghettos; they organized several clean-ups of their own in East Harlem. Next they launched a free breakfast program for school children on the Lower East Side and in East Harlem. More re-

cently, the Lords have gotten involved in health problems, demanding "community worker control of hospitals," and trying to educate teen-agers against heroin addiction.

As part of their involvement in neighborhood health problems, they extracted a promise from Metropolitan Hospital last month for 200 free kits to test for lead poisoning. Medical authorities estimate there are 30,000 undiagnosed cases of lead poisoning each year in the city. The victims are usually children between the ages of one and six, who eat flaking or peeling paint from tenement walls. Lead poisoning can cause mental retardation, and in severe cases is fatal.

For several weeks the Lords prepared for their testing program, distributing leaflets along East 112th Street that read: "We are operating our own lead poisoning detection program with students from New York Medical College, beginning Tuesday, November 25, on 112th Street. The Young Lords and medical personnel will knock on your door Tuesday and ask to test your children for lead poison. Do not turn them away. Help save your children."

On Friday, November 21, Metropolitan Hospital suddenly reneged on its promise of free tests. Members of the Young Lords immediately called Health Commissioner Mary McLaughlin several times, but she would not take their calls.

So at 10 A.M. on Monday, November 24, a delegation of Young Lords, interns, nurses, and health workers appeared at the Health Department offices downtown to force a confrontation.

According to Gene Straus, the chief medical resident at Metropolitan Hospital, who participated in the sit-in:

"We got there at 10 A.M., but none of the commissioners or assistant commissioners came to work until after 11 A.M. Finally, Dr. David Harris [an assistant commissioner] showed up at about 11.15 A.M. At first he said he would only see two representatives of our delegation. But we insisted he see us all. So we went into his office, which was quite spacious, and had comfortable chairs for everybody.

"After we settled in, he asked us why we weren't satisfied with the city's lead poisoning program. We gave him a lot of reasons, and he seemed to be pretty uptight. At one point his secretary passed him a note she said was urgent. The note said there was a man on the phone who wanted to know what color the commissioner wanted his car. He seemed more worried about his

new car than about the children dying of lead poisoning in this city. .˙. .

"After a while he admitted the city's press release about 40,000 free tests was just a press release. When we told him we wouldn't leave unless we got the 200 tests Metropolitan Hospital promised us, he immediately sent someone right over to the laboratory [at 22 Jones Street] to pick up the tests. The tests were just sitting there for a month, while kids were getting sick all over the city. . . . When we were about to leave with the tests, Dr. Harris and Dr. Donald Conwell [another assistant commissioner] gave us a little lecture about observing proper procedures, and the proper amenities next time."

At 11.30 A.M. on Friday, November 28, I phoned Commissioner McLaughlin, who lives in Manhasset, and earns $35,000 a year. Her secretary told me she wouldn't be at work until the following Thursday because she was "attending a conference." When I said I wanted to ask her some questions about the city's lead poisoning program, she said. "Dr. Harris is in charge of that. But he's out today too. But I can switch you to his office."

Click, click, click.

"Dr. Harris's office, can I help you?"

"Yes. I'm Jack Newfield of *The Village Voice* and I'd like to talk to Dr. Harris about lead poisoning."

"Dr. Harris has nothing to do with lead poisoning. You should talk to Dr. Conwell."

"But the commissioner's office said that Dr. Harris has responsibility in this area."

"I know they always say that, I'm getting a little annoyed by it, but I'm afraid it's really Dr. Conwell who you should talk to. Shall I switch you?"

"Yes, please."

Click, click, click.

"Dr. Conwell's office."

"Is Dr. Conwell in?"

"No, he's taken today off. I think he'll be around on Monday. I'll have him call you." (He never called back.)

Later on Friday I spoke to a sales representative for Bio-Rad Laboratories, who requested anonymity because of his relationship with the city.

"It's hard to understand," he said, "but the Health Department just isn't doing anything it should be doing about this problem. Neighborhood groups keep calling us up to get the tests, but we can't give them to them. Our arrangement was to give the tests to the city. It was up to the city to tell us how and when they wanted the kits. But Dr. Harris never called us to arrange for the details. I don't think the Health Department has really thought about how you get these tests out to the people who really need them the most. . . .

"Kings County Hospital in Brooklyn is giving 200 blood tests for lead poisoning every week. If one hospital can give 200 tests each week, the city should at least be able to do that much. But they just never bothered to do any follow-up."

By Monday of this week the results of the lab tests on the first day's batch of urine samples were in. At least two positives were found among the forty-four tests, including one two-year-old child with a history of convulsions.

The Young Lords now plan to go out one night every week, collecting urine samples door to door in El Barrio, and then testing them over the weekend in a laboratory.

For the next few weeks, the Lords will be doing for free what some people get paid $35,000 a year by the city to do, but don't.

DECEMBER, 1969

Fighting an Epidemic of the Environment

After spending three months digging into the problem of lead poisoning, I have concluded that the heart of the matter is accountability, naming the anonymous individuals responsible for this tragic situation: city officials, landlords, newspaper editors.

The basic facts of the problem are now obvious: an environmental epidemic (as distinct from a virus epidemic) that strikes at least 30,000 black and Puerto Rican children each year, causing mental retardation, brain damage, and death.

In August of 1968, the Citizens Committee to End Lead Poisoning was founded at a church in Bedford-Stuyvesant. Subsequently, Congressman William F. Ryan introduced three bills that would provide federal funds to find and treat victims of lead poisoning, and get rid of leaded paint from tenement walls.

Last June, after twenty-three-month-old Janet Scurry died of lead poisoning in the Bronx, Representative Edward Koch and City Councilman Carter Burden wrote personal letters to Mayor Lindsay, alerting him to the growing crisis. Koch's letter informed the Mayor how Chicago—yes, Daleyland!—has had a lead testing and educational program in operation for two years, and that the number of severely poisoned children had been cut in half.

In September, Representative Koch wrote me a letter saying that the city had never even applied to HEW for money available *under existing legislation* to subsidize a lead poisoning program.

But the Lindsay administration did not act, despite Janet Scurry's death, despite the warnings, public and private, from Ryan, Koch, Burden, and many others.

In one sense this is obviously Lindsay's fault. He's elected Mayor, and he's responsible. But it is more directly the fault of the little-known individuals he appointed, who have direct re-

sponsibility for health care: Commissioner Mary McLaughlin and mayoral assistant Werner Kramarsky.

Neither has cared enough, has taken the trouble, to come up with a program since June. Both are liberal bureaucrats, but cut off from the dailiness of injustice by their positions and life styles. Neither has ever even bothered to go to Chicago to see how successfully the lead program is working.

Last May, Bio-Rad Laboratories offered the city 40,000 free urine tests for lead poisoning. But nothing happened (see the letter to the editor in last week's *Voice* from Bio-Rad salesman Henry Intili). In October, during the election campaign, the Health Department announced a testing program. But they never even bothered to pick up the tests, much less distribute them to community groups like the Young Lords who were eager to use them. Several children died of lead poisoning during this period of bureaucratic buck-passing and delay. Dozens more went into convulsions, comas, and suffered permanent brain damage. Responsibility for those small, unreported daily tragedies is as easy to fix as it is for war crimes committed in Vietnam.

Also implicated in the city's failure is the daily press, which has ignored the issue because, in the words of one city editor, "it doesn't have a hard news peg."

But I believe racism is also a factor here. If lead poisoning affected white, middle-class children, it would be covered on the front page of *The New York Times*. When there are ten cases of polio in the suburbs, it is a crisis that receives urgent coverage. But 30,000 undiagnosed cases of lead poisoning, living in Bed-Stuy, El Barrio, and the South Bronx, is not news. Just like worms and larvae in the water supply of Harlem is fit to print on page 64. But if those worms were coming out of taps on Park Avenue, I think I know where *that* story would be placed.

Similarly, if lead poisoning primarily affected old Jewish ladies, the *Post* would already have begun a seventeen-part series on the problem, naming landlords, profiling the victims, attacking the hospital system. But Janet Scurry was invisible and nobody knew her name because she lived on Teller Avenue in the Bronx.

The Lindsay administration still has not announced a program against lead poisoning. Werner Kramarsky is conniving to

be promoted to deputy mayor. Dr. McLaughlin is leaking stories to *The Times* exaggerating her good works in an effort to save her job.

So here, Mr. Mayor, is a simple, minimal, five-point program you could adopt:

1. Launch an immediate, free, mass testing program in all ghetto neighborhoods, to find the poisoned children, and get them treated in hospitals.

2. Endorse, and lobby for, the passage of Representative Ryan's three bills—H. R. 9191, 13254, and 14735. (Ryan told me on Tuesday, "I've never seen any evidence that the Mayor's office, either in New York or Washington, has tried to do anything to help my legislation get out of committee or pass the House."

3. Declare a health emergency in East Harlem, Harlem, Bedford-Stuyvesant, Brownsville, the South Bronx because of lead poisoning.

4. Give families with a history of lead poisoning immediate shelter elsewhere, and first priority for public housing.

5. Force landlords, through city ordinance or new legislation, to make repairs and board over with plywood peeling walls in any apartment where there is a danger of a child ingesting leaded paint.

You could begin this program tomorrow, Mr. Mayor, without waiting for the next batch of vague memos. In fact begin it today.

DECEMBER, 1969

[8.]
Muhammad Ali's Return:
The Great Black Hope *

What white America demands in her black champions is a brilliant, powerful body and a dull bestial mind—a tiger in the ring and a pussycat outside the ring. . . . A slave in private life, a king in public—this is the life that every black champion has had to lead—until the coming of Muhammad Ali.

Muhammad Ali was the first "free" black champion ever to confront white America. In the context of boxing, he is a genuine revolutionary, the black Fidel Castro of boxing. . . .

Essentially, every black champion until Muhammad Ali has been a puppet, manipulated by whites in his private life to control his public image. . . . For every white man, feeling himself superior to every black man, it was a serious blow to his self-image; because Muhammad Ali, by the very fact he leads an autonomous private life, cannot fulfill the psychological needs of whites.

—Eldridge Cleaver
Soul on Ice

On April 28, 1967, Lyndon Johnson was still the President of the United States, the Vietnam War was still popular, the Black Muslims seemed as menacing as the Black Panthers seem today, and Muhammad Ali was the undefeated heavyweight boxing champion of the planet. That morning in Houston, Texas, Ali refused to take the traditional "one step forward" symbolic of induction into the United States Army.

Within an hour the New York State Athletic Commission withdrew its recognition of Ali as world champion and suspended his license to box in New York. Ali was not yet arraigned, indicted, tried, or convicted. There was no hearing by the Com-

* Several days after this piece was completed, Federal Judge Walter Mansfield ruled the N.Y. Athletic Commission had been arbitrary and discriminatory in denying Ali a license.

mission. After defeating all comers easily and gracefully in the ring, Ali lost his championship in a press release.

What has happened during the three and a half years since then is well known. Ali was convicted of draft refusal in Houston and sentenced to five years in jail. His first appeal to the Supreme Court was rejected, and his new one is still under review. All recognized boxing authorities in "the free world" followed New York's example and stripped Ali of his title. Ali and his lawyers went like vagabonds all over the land looking for a place for the champ to fight, and seventy-two different cities refused to license him. Some like Miami, Seattle, and Detroit were ready to say yes, but then the patriots and vigilantes went to work, and another rejection was fashioned. No political leader defended Ali. Finally Joe Frazier knocked out Jimmy Ellis and was declared the new heavyweight king.

Ali, meanwhile, tried to keep busy. He spoke on hundreds of campuses, starred in a Broadway musical production of "Big Time Buck White," got remarried and fathered three daughters, and quietly drifted apart from the Muslims. Then last week it was announced that Ali, now broke and fifteen or twenty pounds over his fighting weight, would box Jerry Quarry, the best white heavyweight around, in a fifteen-rounder in Atlanta on October 26.

Through it all, through the tangled legal maneuvers, through the comings and goings of lawyers and trainers, through the failures and frustrations to get a license, the first and clearest injustice done to Ali was by the New York State boxing commission. And Ali is now suing in federal court to be licensed again in this state.

In his time Ali was a magical fighter. No one ever defeated him. He brought laughter and passion to a seamy and declining sport. He not only "floated like a butterfly and stung like a bee," he danced like Nureyev and stabbed like Manolete. He destroyed Sonny Liston, Floyd Patterson, Zora Folley, and Cleveland Williams without taking a single solid punch. He outclassed his generation of fighters as totally as Ray Robinson or Joe Louis did. He even managed to predict in poetry the round many of his opponents would fall. And in his idle moments, he invented the Ali Shuffle.

Ali was finally dethroned and exiled not by any fighter, but by the three old, white, political boxing commissioners of the state

of New York: Chairman Edwin Dooley, a former Republican congressman from Westchester; Raymond Lee, the former president of the Lockport Felt Company and a business partner of Barry Goldwater's running mate, William Miller; and Albert Berkowitz, a former Republican state senator from Granville, New York, where he is now a lawyer. All three men are political appointees of Governor Nelson Rockefeller.

Ali applied to be relicensed in New York on September 22 of last year. On October 14 the three boxing commissioners voted unanimously to refuse Ali a new license, and chairman Dooley wrote him a letter saying: ". . . Your refusal to enter the service, and your conviction in violation of federal law is regarded by the Commission to be detrimental to the best interest of boxing, or to the public interest, convenience, or necessity."

Ali's New York attorney, Michael Meltsner of Columbia University and the NAACP's Legal Defense Fund, then filed suit in federal court, claiming the Commission was in violation of Ali's constitutional rights in refusing him a license, citing the equal protection clause of the Fourteenth Amendment, as well as the First Amendment.

In court the boxing commission claimed it was denying Ali a license because he was a convicted felon, "who had not yet paid his debt to society."

But Meltsner has now come up with a list of almost 100 convicted felons the boxing commission has licensed over the last decade. The list includes murderers, rapists, child molesters, sodomists, and arsonists. It also licensed men on parole and probation. And of most direct legal significance, Meltsner has documented that the commission "has granted licenses with knowledge that the applicant had a criminal charge pending against him, or has taken no action upon learning of the arrest of a licensed boxer, and has subsequently renewed his license without attempting to learn the disposition of the arrest."

Meltsner's brief, now being considered by Federal Judge Walter Mansfield, also points out that many of the licensed felons were, like Ali, of championship caliber (LaMotta, Graziano, Giardello) and that many were also convicted of "military related offenses . . . such as desertion while members of the armed forces, and who received dishonorable or undesirable discharges."

Racism has always been built into the structure of boxing. The people who make a nice living off the game—the managers,

the promoters, the gamblers, the mobsters, the commissioners, the writers—have always been white. And the kids who bleed, and end up half blind and pissing blood, are almost always black, or Puerto Rican, or Mexican. Johnny Bratton and Johnny Saxton, two black champions controlled by the Mafia, are both now in mental institutions. Hurricane Jackson, his brains scrambled, now gives shoe shines on Third Avenue for quarters. But a lot of white people got rich off Hurricane for a while.

And because of its rich mythic implications, as Cleaver suggests, the heavyweight championship has always been the pivot of racism in sports. The legendary John L. Sullivan said he would never "fight a colored man," and refused to give his logical challenger, Peter Jackson, a chance to win the title. Jack Dempsey's most feared contemporary was Harry Wills, but Dempsey would never fight him, just as he would never meet the other great black heavyweight of that era, Sam Langford. Jack Johnson's exile and persecution were fully recalled in Howard Sackler's play *The Great White Hope.*

Since Jack Johnson's tragic fall, most black heavyweight champions have been incongruously timid, humble "credit to their race" types like Ezzard Charles, Joe Walcott, and Floyd Patterson. In recent years it has seemed like the only black men in America who did not show rage or pride in public have been heavyweight boxing champions. But as Cleaver says, "Ali was the first 'free' black champion ever to confront white America."

The individual probably most responsible for Ali's exile has been the chairman of the New York Commission, Edwin Dooley. As commission chairman, Dooley receives an annual salary from the taxpayers of $28,000 a year; the two other commission members are paid on a per diem basis. Now sixty-five, Dooley was appointed chairman after he lost the Republican primary for Congress in 1962 to Ogden Reid.

Jose Torres, the former lightheavyweight champ, told me, "Dooley doesn't even know what he's doing most of the time." Howard Cosell, the ABC-TV sportscaster, was even blunter. "Dooley is a dope," he said. "I like him personally. He's an affable fellow. But he is a weakling. He'll do anything for popularity. He took Ali's title and license away because he knew it was a popular thing to do in 1967. He has no idea of the terrible injustice he's done."

Cosell continued: "The boxing commission here is pitiful. It's been moribund for years. It's a rubber stamp for the promoters.

But they're so spineless that I'm sure they'll reverse themselves on Ali if there is enough pressure the other way. Up to now it's been a popular move among fans and writers. My mail still runs ten to one against Ali, and the establishment sports writers like Dick Young and Gene Ward have been incredibly vindictive."

(During the last few weeks Ward, the Procaccino of sportswriting, has written several emotional attacks on Ali in the *Daily News*. He recently devoted most of one column to reprinting a letter from a mother who lost a son in Vietnam and who said that if Ali is permitted to fight it would affront the memory of her dead son. In another column, Ward predicted the "American public" would not permit the Quarry bout to take place, and added that Ali was a second-rate fighter "who can't punch.")

Dooley displayed his immense capacities as commissioner two weeks ago at a luncheon to promote the Floyd Patterson-Devil Green fight at Madison Square Garden. Green's wife showed up to ask for a license to appear as a second in her husband's corner, a nice publicity gimmick to ride the women's lib tide.

Commissioner Dooley told Mrs. Green, "I can't make a decision about that myself. I have to consult the other commissioners. We will have a meeting on September 17."

At that point several smiling boxing writers had to point out to the commissioner the fight was scheduled for September 15. Dooley, after harrumphing for a minute, finally told the assembled writers that he would poll the other commissioners by phone.

Another measure of Dooley's judgment is that he sees nothing wrong with Jake LaMotta being introduced from the ring before all the big fights at the Garden to the cheers of the fans. All Jake LaMotta did was admit to the Kefauver Committee that he threw his fight with Blackjack Billy Fox in the old Garden. LaMotta is only a dumper, so he can be held up as a model. Poor Ali just beat everyone cleanly and fairly, so he becomes an unperson, a bad example to youth, "detrimental to the best interests of boxing," as the commissioner put it.

Muhammad Ali, the manchild evicted from the promised land, was at the ABC television studio on West Fifty-eighth Street last Friday afternoon to tape a show with his old friend Howard Cosell. He arrived exactly on time, and for a while stood around, quietly and softly answering questions and waiting for the taping to begin. He seemed possessed of a remarkable serenity while the

electricians, camera crews, and engineers scurried frenetically about the studio.

Cosell, as playful and talkative as the old Cassius Clay, began to needle Ali about his poor-mouthing his chances with Quarry.

"It may be suicide for you," Cosell said with a wink, "to fight Quarry on six weeks' notice after a three-year lay-off. You're just a shell of your former self."

"I *am* just a shell," Ali admitted in a barely audible whisper. "But I'm fast enough for Frazier," his pride made him add.

"How long can you last with Quarry?" Cosell asked, winking again.

"I can't make no predictions no more. That's what got me into trouble."

"What would you do if you lost, were knocked out?"

"I never think about losing," the professional in Ali said.

Suddenly, Cosell began to laugh and squared off against Ali. "You want to box me five rounds, you big black phony?"

In mock anger Ali replied, "Listen, whitey, I'm gonna call the Black Panthers, have them burn your house down." His eyes flashed the old comic exuberance.

After making Ali change his shirt from blue to yellow to suit the color cameras, it seemed the taping would begin, and Cosell and Ali sat down on the spare set. Ali was again somber and withdrawn, apparently under instructions not to appear threatening or boastful, lest the vigilantes get stirred up again. But Ali is still a natural wit, and as the waiting grew longer, he started to relax.

It took ten minutes to adjust the lights, and ten more to set up the tape of Ali's last fight with Zora Folley. Ali and Cosell watched it on a monitor, so they would be prepared when it was played on the show.

As Ali knocked Folley flat on his face with one right hand to the jaw, the champ exclaimed, "Oh wow, I'm the baddest nigger in the world."

Another long wait, and Ali began to build up the Quarry fight for the crew in the studio. "They got me a white hope to fight, just like they got one for Jack Johnson. They sent Jack Johnson into exile and brought him back out of shape. They're tryin' to do that to me now. And they're makin' me fight this white hope in *Georgia* yet! I hear the Klan has bought up the first row already!"

Ali laughed, Cosell laughed, and most of the cameramen and technicians laughed. Ali was loosening up now and starting to put on a show.

He saw a long-haired stagehand in purple vest and blue bell-bottom pants and called out, "Hey, Abbie Hoffman, could you get me a soda please." Then to Cosell: "They all look alike, they all look just like that Abbie Hoffman."

A false start, and more confusion about starting the tape.

Cosell in mock interview style: "Tell me champ, why do you hate the Jews?"

Ali countered in his best Walter Cronkite serious voice, looking into the dead camera: "Muhammad Ali has just taken Howard Cosell hostage, folks, and is holding him for ransom here just outside of Lebanon."

The crew broke up in roaring laughter.

Ali was now his old preexile self. He made up a rhyme: "Ali will do the shuffle and that will be the end of the scuffle." Cosell recalled Ali's poem before he beat Sonny Liston: "Don't bet on Sonny, and save your money."

More delay. A stagehand brought Ali a different tie. The lighting was changed a little. The soda arrived in a paper bag and Ali announced "I'd show the label if they would pay me."

Ali began to imitate an old Southerner's voice: "I can just see all those cats down in Alabama and Georgia sayin' get me some tickets, honey, I wanna see that uppity nigger get his now."

"Ten seconds till we roll it, all quiet on the set," a voice from the control booth boomed out.

Ali threw a playful right that stopped just short of Cosell's nose. He made a grimace and a V-sign to the camera, and took a deep breath. The camera went on, and Ali went as dull and as plastic as Joe Walcott or Richard Nixon. During the taping he answered Cosell's questions quietly and meekly. The once and future king acted as tranquilized as MacMurphy after his second or third electric shock treatment from Big Nurse in *One Flew Over the Cuckoo's Nest*. And that's what this country has been doing to Muhammad Ali, punishing him until his dignity and zest are amputated. But luckily, he is smart enough to Tom it up for the media, while keeping his interior self whole.

Ali remains one of the few authentic heroes left in this country. He was the absolute best at his chosen craft, and then he

threw it all away for a principle. After being denied a livelihood for three years by the patriots and politicans, he now seems about to dance the glory road back.

But it's hard to envisage a happy ending to Ali's new journey. He has been robbed of the three best years of his career, the years between twenty-five and twenty-eight. He can never get them back. Ten years ago when he won a gold medal for America in the Olympics, he was a joyous kid with the fastest hands in the world and a determination not to conform to the old rules. Now, nearing twenty-nine, he goes on television carefully acting meek, so he might be "allowed" to fight again and climb out of debt. Just like Connie Hawkins being "allowed" to play in the NBA at twenty-nine, after leaving his greatest games in blacktop schoolyards in Bed-Stuy. Or Satchell Paige being "allowed" into the major leagues after his magnificent arm was half gone.

Although he should take Quarry, I doubt if Ali can beat Joe Frazier, who is a superb fighting machine. Ali would go into that superfight symbolizing everything valuable and heroic, but I'm afraid he's getting the chance too late, after too many years of idleness.

I hope I'm wrong. I hope Ali comes back. I hope he beats Frazier because he is the great black hope for all of us who want to see boxing redeemed, for just one night, from all the politicians, and gangsters, and hustlers, and Babbitts like Commissioner Dooley.

SEPTEMBER, 1970

[TWO]
THE KIDS: TWO CHEERS FOR THE FREAKING FAG REVOLUTION

The best of the kids are the best thing about this wounded dino-saur of a country. And it is for that reason that the trend toward terrorism among a fringe during the last few years troubles me so much. I agree that the total violence of the New Left doesn't equal one B-52 bombing raid over Vietnam. But precisely be-cause I agree with the radical goals of the New Left, I feel a special responsibility to raise moral questions about the new tac-tics of blowing up buildings, or shooting firemen from ambush.

Such acts are inhuman, cowardly, elitist, and counterpro-ductive. The life of Robert Fassnacht, who died when the math building at Madison was blown up, is equally as precious as the life of Allison Krouse, who died at Kent State. Their real affect is to sicken everyone, and create the possibility of a new apathy, a new privatism, on the campuses.

I know it is hard to build a movement that does not incorpo-rate the characteristics of the nation it is trying to redeem. But if the name of our desire is socialism, then we must begin with a democratic faith, and a reverence for human life, or else we will fail as miserably as communism. I don't want the bread without the roses.

[1.]
One Cheer for the Hippies

Politics is dead. Culture is dead. The world stinks.

—Emmett Grogan, founder of the Diggers

I am a Roman Senator, not a Digger.

—Paul Goodman

The hippies are happening. Ed Sanders of the Fugs is on a cover of *Life*. Tulsa, Oklahoma, which went for Barry Goldwater by 30,000 votes, recently had its first love-in. Gray Line sight-seeing buses detour through Haight-Ashbury to display the local "freaks" to the Babbitts. Squares (not hippies) pay $4.00 to see the psychedelic Billy Graham—Dr. Timothy Leary—preach his "turn on, tune in, drop out" sermons. Hollywood has adopted the vibrating, "acid art" poster style of the Fillmore Auditorium, using it in ads to promote the big-budget James Bond film, *Casino Royale*. And the folk-rock group, Jefferson Airplane, has recorded a commercial for white Levi denims—even as 460 of that company's employees strike in Blue Ridge, Georgia, against the chronically exploitive conditions of Southern textile mills.

Individually, the hippies are beautiful. They know a lot of things the squares don't. They know that marijuana is mildly pleasant and doesn't give you lung cancer; that Bob Dylan, John Lennon, and Leonard Cohen are authentic poetic voices for all those who have grown up absurd; that it is better to make love than war; that most things taught in college must be unlearned later in life; that it is healthier to be spontaneous, communal, and tolerant than repressed, materialistic, and bigoted; and that it is groovy to read Herman Hesse, Snoopy, and Allen Ginsberg.

All this being eagerly granted, the point must now be made that the hippies have been overrated. Their ultimate vision is in

no way superior to that of the New Left, of Mailer, Camus, or Pynchon. The hippies will not change America because change means pain, and the hippie subculture is rooted in the pleasure principle. They have an intellectual flabbiness that permits them to equate an original talent like Kenneth Anger with a put-on like Andy Warhol. For this reason they are vulnerable to the kind of exploitation symbolized by the Jefferson Airplane commercial. They lack the energy, stability, and private pain to serve as the "new proletariat" that some in the New Left perceive them to be. Bananas, incense, and pointing love rays toward the Pentagon have nothing to do with redeeming and renovating America; Leary's call to "drop out" is really a call to cop out.

The whole hippie contagion seems to be a recoil from the idea of politics itself; it is not merely apolitical but antipolitical. "Civil rights is a game for squares," one hippie told me. "Why should I demonstrate to get the spades all the things I'm rejecting?" And the *Berkeley Barb,* one of the best of the dozen underground weeklies, scorned the April 15 antiwar Mobilization for being "deadly serious, militant, and political."

The hippies, in fact, have more in common with the nihilism of the 1950 beats, than with the activism of their generational comrades in the New Left. The beats opted out of a repressive, materialistic society because they felt impotent to change it. Ike, McCarthyism, Korea, Madison Avenue, the cold war, the defeats of Stevenson made politics appear impossible to the alienated young of the 1950s. Without hope, they sought escape by withdrawing into Eastern religions, sex, jazz, drugs and madness. It required foreign examples of effective student radicalism—in Korea, Japan, Cuba, and Turkey, all in 1959—to inspire the young here.

The New Left took root in 1960 and 1961 because social change through political activism suddenly seemed possible with the election of John Kennedy. There were sit-ins, and lunch counters were desegregated. There were freedom rides, and bus terminals were desegregated. There were heroism and death in the Deep South, and a Civil Rights Act was drafted. There was a free-speech movement at Berkeley, and educational reform of the dehumanizing multiversity became a fashionable symposium topic. SDS organized around the ideal of participatory democracy, and the "maximum feasible participation of the poor" clause was written into the antipoverty program. For a time

there appeared to be in Washington a higher moral authority which would respond humanely to protest.

But just as the beats did not develop in a vacuum, neither have the government's; their growth has been in direct correlation to the country's drift to the right since the Gulf of Tonkin "incident" and the Watts "rebellion." The young who once idolized JFK perceive his successor—correctly, I think—as an antidemocratic manipulator who has stultified the possibility of change through dissenting politics. Johnson has become a depressing Ike figure, and Vietnam the monstrously swollen equivalent of the Korean police action. In 1963 Bob Dylan sang of changes "blowin' in the wind"; today he chants: "Although the masters make the rules/for the wise men and the fools/I've got nothin', Ma, to live up to." In 1962 more Harvard seniors wanted to volunteer for the Peace Corps than wanted to work for a large corporation; this is no longer the case. The Haight-Ashbury scene jumped into national prominence in the same month that the voters were sanctioning Reagan, Wallace, and Maddox, and the Vietnamese War turned a corner into its present open-ended escalation. Suddenly, it seemed more possible to change private reality with LSD than America's reality with SDS.

My own quarrel with the hippie ethic can be summarized in five arguments.

The first is that I don't think it will be permanently impossible to alter America through radical political action. The hippies seem to side with de Sade when he says. "And why should you care about the world outside? For me the only reality is imagination, the world inside myself. The revolution no longer interests me." But the New Left is closer to Marat, who answers (in Peter Weiss's *Marat/Sade*): "Against nature's silence I use action. . . . I don't watch unmoved; I intervene and say this and this are wrong, and I work to alter and improve them. The important thing is to pull yourself up by your own hair, to turn yourself inside out, and see the whole world with fresh eyes."

What the hippies forget is how unlikely social change seemed in 1957 and 1958. It took a new generation of kids, who had not read *On the Road,* to prove that America had not congealed into a static cage. Reform will become possible again, especially once the Vietnamese War ends. What the pleasure-oriented hippies can't accept is that political action is a painful, Sisyphean task that includes sacrifice, boredom, and defeat.

My second point against the hippies is that precisely because they are *not a real threat to anything* they are used to goose a lifeless middle class, and are even widely imitated. Thus they create the illusion of influence when the jet set adopts their fashions, slang, and music. But it is huckster America that profits by merchandising everything from "psychedelic salami" to "psychedelic earrings."

Third, the hippies think their vision of a drug-induced, homogenized love is an original panacea. One hippie even told me: "Man, I love everything. That fire hydrant, LBJ, Wallace, all them cats."

America is surely short on love, but the love the hippies invoke is so generalized and impersonal as to be meaningless. And as an observer I don't detect any greater love content in relations within the hippie subculture; they are just as exploitive and ego-centered and neurotic as the rest of us.

Fourth, the philosophical rationale the hippies cite for dropping out is that life is essentially absurd anyway, and since it has no meaning, it is pointless to try to change events. It is better, they say, again echoing de Sade, to savor all possible personal experience instead.

Evidence certainly mounts to support an absurdist interpretation of recent history, beginning with the assassination in Dallas, through the CIA's secret life, up to Byron de la Beckwith now running for lieutenant governor of Mississippi. Yet both Sartre and Camus accepted—and then transcended—absurdity and were able to embrace an even deeper engagement and commitment. Sartre and Camus did not "turn on and drop out" when the Nazis marched across France; they both joined the underground.

Finally, there is the dilemma of LSD. I have read several research papers and find much of the evidence is contradictory. Clearly, LSD has been useful, in a therapeutic sense, in treating problems like homosexuality, impotence, and alcoholism. But LSD has also caused plenty of mental damage, recurring hallucinations, freak-outs and visits to hospital emergency wards by teeny-boppers who think they are giraffes. And, in general, the effect of acid on activists is to make them fugitives from the system, instead of insurgents against the system. Acid-heads tend to withdraw from politics (as Dr. Leary recommends), pursue private or politically unrealistic goals, and become disruptive if they

remain inside activist organizations. They lack the patience and stability for the drudgery of organizing and scholarship.

The alternative to the hippies remains the New Left, which contrary to some reports, seems still to be growing. The spring semester indicated how deep the roots of student discontent have penetrated, with major campus rebellions at Long Island University, Texas, Drew University, Catholic University, Howard, Jackson State and Oklahoma. In May, card-carrying SDS members were freely elected student body presidents at Indiana and Northwestern. More than 350 students have signed an ad in the *Harvard Crimson* asserting that they will defy the draft. Vietnam Summer claims to have 2,000 organizers in the field.

Undeniably, the hippies represent an important break with the past and have considerable merit. Their musical innovations will, I suspect, ultimately prove as rich as the bop revolution forged by Bird, Dizzy, and Monk in the 1940's. The diggers, who run the indigenous mission halls for their hippie brethren, are closer to St. Francis than to Cardinal Spellman.

But, finally, Dylan, pot and bright colors are the *hippies'* liberation. The poor, the voteless, the manipulated, the spiritually undernourished—they are oppressed by injustice that is crystallized in institutions. Only a radical political movement can liberate *them*. I want to save the squares too.

Junε, 1967

[2.]
Outside the Arena: Prelims Are Bloody *

CHICAGO—The lid blew off Monday night.

In the Amphitheatre:

Hubert Humphrey made his pact with the South and John Connally became his Strom Thurmond.

Eugene McCarthy's badly organized campaign continued to unravel.

The boomlet for Teddy Kennedy turned out to be a fantasy of Bobby's orphans.

In the street:

The cops chased, Maced, tear-gassed, and shot blanks at the kids who were in Lincoln Park an hour after the curfew.

All over the city people were randomly stopped and questioned.

Tom Hayden was arrested on charges that three witnesses including two lawyers insisted were false.

By 3 A.M. Tuesday the liberals had been routed at the convention, the kids had been repulsed on the street. Everywhere you walked, from midnight on, there were plainclothesmen. They frisked you with their eyes like whores strip potential clients, and if you looked the least bit suspicious they tailed you as you continued down the street. Almost every noise was martial: fire sirens, the squawking of two-way radios, cop cars racing from place to place, the idle chatter of police on duty.

We were with Tom Hayden when he got arrested, at 11:55 P.M. in front of the Hilton Hotel. He had come by for a few minutes, intending to go straight on to Lincoln Park, when he ran into some friends who were staying in the hotel. They invited him up to their room, but as Hayden sought to enter the hotel through

---

* I wrote this piece with Paul Cowan between 4 A.M. and 6 A.M. on Tuesday, August 27. It is included here more as a historical document than as an example of good reporting.

its revolving doors a middle-aged man in street clothes stopped him.

"We don't want this man here," he told Hayden's friends.

"But he's our guest," one of them answered.

"No, he's not welcome at this hotel," the security officer insisted.

One of Hayden's friends followed the security officer into the hotel to complain about the decision to his superiors. For a few minutes Tom stood around talking with a small group of people. Then suddenly, Ralph Bell, a plainclothesman dressed in khakis and a red and yellow checked shirt, came running down Michigan Avenue yelling, "He's our man, arrest that man." A uniformed policeman who had been directing traffic grabbed Hayden and threw him on the ground. He was arrested, according to the arrest form at the 11th Precinct Station in Chicago, because he "called the police names and spit at them." We were present during the entire scene and we are certain that Hayden never called the police a name. Since he was grabbed from behind it would have been difficult for him to spit at the arresting officer.

It is clear that the moment that Hotel Hilton's security officer saw Hayden he decided to call the police. Since this was Hayden's second arrest of the day on extremely tenuous charges, it is apparent that the Chicago police have decided to harass the Mobilization leader throughout the convention week.

For three weeks both Hayden and Rennie Davis have been followed twenty-four hours a day by detectives. Hayden says that his tail has repeatedly threatened to kill him. But the police's harassment of the Mobilization is far more extensive than that. Photographs of Hayden, Davis, and other key figures in the radical movement have been distributed to all hotel doormen in the city, and at bus terminals, train stations, airports. (The "Red Squad" of the Chicago police force is one of the most efficient in the country, according to people who live here. During a demonstration against the House Un-American Activities Committee three years ago, for example, policemen took pictures of every participant and put them in a film of people who were likely to assassinate the President or Vice-President of the United States, the *Chicago American* reported at the time.

Now the harassment seems to extend to people who are just casually involved with the radical movement. A taxi driver who took a young couple to the office of the National Mobilization

Against the War in Vietnam was questioned by police about the conversations he had overheard. It is widely assumed here that the telephones of everyone connected with the Mobilization are tapped.

We got to the precinct station where Hayden was booked and were let inside because we had come to bail him out. We overheard the police mocking the kids they had arrested. "We had to fumigate this place after we led all those animals through," said one. An officer apparently nicknamed "Killer," who carried a revolver on each hip and smoked a long cigar, was complaining that he had been scheduled to screw two airline stewardesses that night. "I'm going to kill those Yippies who lost me that good lay," he said. Ten minutes later he came back into the room. "Well, one of them said she would meet me later on. I guess I can wait till tomorrow night to get me some action."

We stood around the precinct station for two hours waiting for Hayden's bail to be set. Finally, one of the police told us that the procedure would take at least two hours more while Hayden was fingerprinted. "But he was already arrested once today," Newfield said. "Oh, we didn't know that," the officer answered. "Since that's the case we'll bring him down here right away."

We spent the next hour walking with Hayden through downtown Chicago, trying to dodge his tail. Every few minutes we would hear fire trucks setting out to chase down some false alarm that had been set off by the hippies. After one particularly complicated trek through back alleys and down side streets we were stopped by two detectives who got out of their car to ask us where we were going. It wasn't clear whether they recognized Hayden or suspected any stranger who walked along an unusual route. James Ridgeway of the *New Republic* showed the detective his White House Press pass and Newfield took out his official press pass to the convention. "We're just trying to show this friend of ours the back streets of Chicago," he explained.

Walking down Clark Street we met a black pimp and two black whores, all of them wearing McCarthy buttons. The women were wearing gaudy pink sunglasses. "Say, man, you want to meet some girls?" the pimp asked, "No, not tonight, man," said Hayden, "I just got out of jail."

"Oh, yeah, what jail?" the pimp asked. "The 11th Precinct Station," Tom replied. "Man, I know those parts real well. I've been in every jail in this city," the pimp said.

At about 3:30 Tom got into a taxi, hoping to evade the tail who threatened to murder him. We went back to the lobby of the Hilton Hotel where we ran into a weary and depressed Fred Dutton, former aide to RFK and JFK. Dutton told us that he saw no hope for stopping Humphrey. He had just spoken to Edward Kennedy, he said, he was convinced that the movement to draft the Massachusetts senator was a pipe dream.

Dutton, who surely must have felt that if Robert Kennedy had lived this convention would be nominating him, showed his despair with the events of the evening. He had been listening to Nick Von Hoffmann, a reporter for the *Washington Post* who had been watching the police beat the Yippies on the Near North Side. Von Hoffmann was visibly angry. "I was over at the pig palace watching the pig master at work," he said. "But I got too disgusted so I decided to watch his hired sadists on the beat. You know that they don't make arrests any more. They can't be bothered with lawyers, courts, any of that stuff."

"Yeah, they just maim people and leave them hidden," added a delegate from New York.

Dutton turned to Von Hoffmann and told him passionately that "it's up to you guys to keep reporting that stuff. There's not much we can do any more—not the politicians, not even the kids. You have to keep telling the public what's going on."

Meanwhile, a cherubic-faced teen-ager walked between the drunks and the celebrants, trying to distribute Ted Kennedy for President leaflets. There were few takers.

AUGUST, 1968

[3.]
The Streets of Daleyland: A Riot by the Cops

CHICAGO—Pigs. Until Wednesday night this was just a Movement nickname for the police. A satisfying exaggeration. An example of in-group argot. A verbal gesture of solidarity with the Black Panthers. But Wednesday night on the streets of Daleyland, pigs became a precise description. The Chicago police, with their thick heads, small eyes, and beery jowls, actually resemble pigs. And they surely behaved like animals in this city famous for its stockyards.

Wednesday at twilight the pigs rioted against the people. The police charged into about 5000 antiwar demonstrators; they did not try to arrest people, but tried to maim people. They gleefully used fists, nightsticks, and tear gas against unarmed students, girls, and photographers who did not offer any resistance.

The light gray smoke from the exploding tear gas canisters was the first omen of violence. The suffocating, burning tear gas curled lazily up toward the upper floors of the Hilton and Blackstone hotels. The young demonstrators began choking, covering their faces with handkerchiefs and jackets, and grudgingly retreated. Then the blue-helmeted police charged into the coughing, tearing people, swinging indiscriminately at Yippies, pedestrians, priests, photographers, girls, doctors, and middle-aged women.

At the southwest entrance to the Hilton a skinny, long-haired kid of about seventeen skidded down on the sidewalk, and four overweight cops leaped on him, bringing their long black nightsticks down in short, chopping strokes on his head. His hair flew from the force of the blows. A dozen small rivulets of blood began to cascade down the kid's temple and onto the sidewalk. He was not crying or screaming, but crawling in a stupor toward the gutter. When he saw a photographer taking a picture, he made a V sign with his fingers.

A doctor in a white uniform and Red Cross arm band began to run toward the kid, but two other cops caught him from behind and knocked him down. One of them jammed his knee into the doctor's throat and began clubbing his rib cage. The doctor squirmed away, but the cops followed him, swinging hard, sometimes missing.

A few feet away a phalanx of police charged into a group of women, reporters, and young McCarthy activists standing idly against the window of the Hilton Hotel's Haymarket bar. The terrified people began to go down under the unexpected police charge, when the plate glass window of the bar shattered, and the people tumbled backward through the glass. The police then climbed through the broken window and began to beat people, some of whom had been drinking quietly in the hotel bar.

At the side entrance of the Hilton Hotel four cops were chasing one frightened kid of about seventeen. Suddenly, Fred Dutton, a former aide to Robert Kennedy, moved out from under the marquee and interposed his body between the kid and the police.

"He's my guest in this hotel," Dutton told the cops.

The police started to club the kid.

Dutton screamed for the first cop's name and badge number. The cop grabbed Dutton and began to arrest him, until a *Washington Post* reporter identified Dutton as a former RFK aide.

Demonstrators, reporters, McCarthy workers, doctors, all began to stagger into the Hilton lobby, blood streaming from face and head wounds. The lobby smelled from tear gas, and stink bombs dropped by the Yippies. A few people began to direct the wounded to a makeshift hospital on the fifteenth floor, the McCarthy staff headquarters.

Fred Dutton was screaming at the police, and at the journalists to report all the "sadism and brutality." Richard Goodwin, the ashen nub of a cigar sticking out of his fatigued face, mumbled, "This is just the beginning. There'll be four years of this."

The defiant kids began a slow, orderly retreat back up Michigan Avenue. They did not run. They did not panic. They did not fight back. As they fell back they helped pick up fallen comrades who were beaten or gassed. Suddenly, a plainclothesman dressed as a soldier moved out of the shadows and knocked one kid down with an overhand punch. The kid squatted on the pavement of Michigan Avenue, trying to cover his face, while the

Chicago plainclothesman punched him with savage accuracy. Thud, thud, thud. Blotches of blood spread over the kid's face. Two photographers moved in. Several police formed a closed circle around the beating to prevent pictures. One of the policemen then squirted Chemical Mace at the photographers, who dispersed. The plainclothsman melted into the line of police. And the kid sat in a dazed crouch on the sidewalk, bleeding, cursing the "pigs."

Back at the Hilton, a pretty girl, a campaign worker for Senator McGovern, began to cross the narrow street between the Blackstone and Hilton hotels. She was on errand for the Senator. Without warning, two plainclothesmen ran into her, knocking her down, and then kneed her in the neck.

Upstairs on the fifteenth floor, the girls who worked for Senator McCarthy were treating the bloody and the sick. They were ripping up Conrad Hilton's bedsheets and using them as gauze and bandages. Jerome Grossman, a bureaucrat in the McCarthy campaign, asked them not to destroy hotel property, but nobody paid attention to him. A lot of the girls had bloodstains on their dresses, legs, and arms.

On the sixteenth floor an incensed reporter was throwing hotel ashtrays at the police below. When he tried to wave a sheet out of the window at the kids, the uptight *Newsweek* editors threw him out of their workroom.

An hour after the police riot, the kids began to straggle back to the Hilton Hotel in twos and threes. They had balls, but no bravado. They hadn't slept for days, and most of them were still in their teens. Slowly, they began to form a circle on the grass across the street in Grant Park, a few feet away from a grim line of 400 National Guardsmen. As the darkness deepened, the group of battered demonstrators began to grow from 50, to 200, to more than 1000. They chanted "oink, oink" at the pigs. They chanted "join us, join us" to the McCarthy staffers inside the Hilton. And they sang songs like "This Land Is Your Land" and "Blowin' in the Wind," as Hubert Humphrey was being nominated six miles away on the votes supplied by Mayor Daley, Governor Connally, and George Meany.

The Left should regard Humphrey's nomination as undemocratic and illegitimate.* He was unwilling to face the voters in a

---

* Like many others, I now regret not voting for Humphrey in 1968.

single primary election. In Indiana, South Dakota, California, and New York, where his stand-ins were on the ballot, they received, on the average, less than 20 percent of the vote. In South Dakota, Humphrey's native state, Robert Kennedy won more than 50 percent of the vote. At the convention itself, Governor Connally, Mayor Daley, and George Meany controlled the votes of more delegates than did the seven million Democrats who voted for Senators McCarthy and Kennedy in the Presidential primaries.

In other examples of the totalitarian atmosphere and mood of the convention, the public—except for Daley supporters—were barred from sitting in the galleries. Humphrey refused to debate his opponents. Mayor Daley denied citizens the right of peaceful assembly and free speech. Television cameras were barred from the streets. Newsmen and photographers were beaten by police. Pro-McCarthy delegates were harassed on the floor of the convention. Allard Lowenstein was prevented from seconding Julian Bond's nomination for Vice-President. Microphones of dissenting delegates were turned off by the convention managers on the podium. And in the final burst of police state arrogance, McCarthy's staff members were beaten in their rooms.

The commentators of the plastic center—men like Bill Moyers and Eric Sevareid—now talk as if blame for the violence is to be distributed equally, like food on a platter, and that Humphrey's nomination is to be accepted. They admit "some police overreacted," and try to balance that with mathematical fairness by accepting Mayor Daley's description of the demonstration leaders as "terrorists and assassins."

But we believe that the police were responsible for the violence, and Humphrey's nomination should not be accepted as legitimate. The people in the streets were unarmed and did not come to assassinate anyone. They came to march, and Mayor Daley would not give them a permit or even a place to hold a public rally. It was Mayor Daley and the convention's managers who violated law and order. The spirit of democracy was more alive in Grant Park than inside the convention.

All that's left now is to act on the illegitimacy of Humphrey's nomination, and treat him like a pretender rather than a nominee.

SEPTEMBER, 1968

[4.]
Letter to an Ex-Radical

Dear Ex-Radical,

For the last month I have been trying to compose an essay for *Evergreen,* calling attention to some disturbing currents within the student radical movement. I had been upset by several recent events, and by the tendency of students to act like revolutionaries when clearly there is no revolutionary situation. I was upset, as well, by the anti-Biafra propaganda by black militants, who called it a puppet of "imperialist Israel"; by the psychedelic Maoists and the Motherfuckers disrupting the rallies of peace candidate Paul O'Dwyer; by the arson during the student strike at N.Y.U.; by the McCarthyism of the Left in some of the underground papers, accusing professors, without evidence, of CIA connections, and trying to discredit their politics by listing their institutional affiliations.

But every time I would get into the essay, *your friends* would do something so outrageous that I stopped writing, paralyzed by guilt and fury. Could I, in good conscience, criticize a movement at the moment it was under such unfair, ignorant assault in the mass media, and in the intellectual journals of your generation? I finally decided that the prevailing atmosphere prevented my making an open, detached analysis of the strengths and weaknesses of the New Left; that because of the new, ugly mood of the country, and the polemics of your friends, the young radicals were now exiled in a separate country, defined by generation and belief. And despite my serious disagreements with some of their more flamboyant leaders, I was part of their country—not yours. And to attack them—even fraternally—would be treason.

The mood in your country seems increasingly repressive. According to public opinion polls, 70 percent of the people supported the gleeful riot by Mayor Daley's police in Chicago. When HUAC subpoenaed Tom Hayden, Jerry Rubin, Rennie

Davis, etc., there was no roar of rage. The paranoia in the white press about the Black Panthers is another symptom of sickness. Huey Newton is in jail, and Dr. Spock, Eldridge Cleaver, Muhammad Ali, and Jerry Rubin are free only on bond. The first foul odors of a new McCarthyism are already alerting the nostrils.

And yet, at the very moment these portentous omens are becoming apparent, your generation of intellectuals seems to have declared war on the New Left. The lead articles in four of the last six issues of *Commentary* have been attacks on the New Left. The fall issue of *The Public Interest* (edited by Daniel Bell and Irving Kristol) is devoted almost exclusively to unsympathetic dissections of international campus radicalism. Bayard Rustin, after advising Hubert Humphrey so brilliantly in Chicago, is now coaching Albert Shanker on how to destroy school decentralization in New York City. Venerable George Kennan, an otherwise sensible diplomat and historian, has published an entire book attacking the inhabitants of my country for their beards, language, "lack of humor," and even their love life, which he describes as "tense, anxious, defiant, and joyless." And Irving Howe has hastened to warn the readers of the *Sunday Times Magazine* against "confrontation politics." If that's not breaking down a door that is already open, I don't know what is.

I ask you not to believe what these old liberals and ex-radicals are telling you. It is uninformed and emotional. They have little life experience with the complex and mysterious interior life of the Movement. Their information comes largely from television and is therefore naturally distorted in the direction of the violent and bizarre.

I recently had a long and unpleasant argument with Norman Podhoretz, the editor of *Commentary*. He said the "gravest threat to the fabric of the culture" came, not from George Wallace or the military-industrial complex, but from the New Left. He maintained the New Left had "contributed nothing" in the last few years to ending the Vietnam war, to exposing poverty and racism, to democratizing the university. "All you people have done is to help the Right," he exclaimed.

But when I asked Podhoretz whether he had read Carl Oglesby's book on imperialism or Tom Hayden's book on Newark, he said No. Had he attended SDS meetings or Resistance workshops? No. He *had* read the 1962 *Port Huron Statement* of SDS

and told me in great detail how Stokely Carmichael had called him a "racist" in a 1966 speech. "That was all I have to know about you people," the author of *Making It* told me.

To understand us, you must first understand how much the world has changed since the days when you leafleted and picketed. Thirty years ago the labor unions were a powerful force for progressive change in America. Now they are cheerleaders for the Vietnam war, exclude Negroes from their locals, work intimately with the CIA in Latin America, and instruct their people to vote for Hubert Humphrey in national conventions. Twenty years ago Stalin was alive and Communism was a conspiratorial monolith bent on expansion. Now there is Tito, and Soviet troops in Prague, and democratic theorists like Leszek Kolakowski, and an Italian Communist Party that can criticize Soviet foreign policy. My generation remembers the Bay of Pigs and Vietnam more clearly than it recalls Hungary. And we believe that the engine for change in the Third World is anticolonialism and nationalism, and not Communism. Twenty years ago public housing and welfare gave promise of healing some of our social ills. But today public housing projects are merely barricades to the liberated children of Malcolm X, and welfare has become demeaning and dehumanizing to its recipients.

The second thing you must do to understand us, is read the unhappy history of the last eight years carefully, and recognize that *we have been proved right on most of the great public issues.* We were organizing Negroes in the Delta when John Kennedy was still saying there was no need for new civil-rights legislation. We sat in at Berkeley while Clark Kerr and Sidney Hook were claiming we had no moral or legal case against the remote power of the multiversity. We marched and organized teach-ins against the Vietnam war in the spring of 1965, while Richard Goodwin, Bill Moyers, and McGeorge Bundy were still working in LBJ's White House. Now we say the draft is unnecessary and undemocratic, and the military and security establishments have too much power, and decentralization is an imperative. We say now that it was more honorable to have been with Che Guevara than with the CIA in Bolivia, and it was more honorable to be with Tom Hayden than with Mayor Daley in Chicago.

The New Left is a large, diffuse, contradictory movement. *Movement* is a key word, because that's what it is, rather than a

party or an organization. There are perhaps two or three million young people who actively identify with the New Left. Most of them have humanistic and democratic values. Many of them are still in high school, with their politics still not entirely developed. They are not duped by communists, and their hearts go out to the people of Prague.

There are some *leaders* of the New Left I do not agree with. Particularly within SDS, there are trends, like antirationalism, manipulative tactics, and a mindless fascination with violence, that trouble me. But SDS is only 20,000 people. Most of the activists, given their anarchist bias, do not join *any* organization. They are free-lance radicals, and their style is *ad hoc*. Measure the New Left by the 1000 diverse people who "liberated" the five buildings at Columbia, not by Mark Rudd. Measure the New Left by the 10,000 who demonstrated in Chicago, not by the put-on rhetoric of Jerry Rubin. Don't be misled, like Podhoretz, by the mass-media guerrillas. Listen to, and talk to, the average kid, who might even have worked for McCarthy or Kennedy, after having burned his draft card. Kenneth Keniston's studies * show that the radical activists are the most intelligent, best adjusted, most sensitive students on the campuses. The Cox Commission Report on Columbia said the same thing. Even McGeorge Bundy said it in a speech at DePauw University. If you want to understand what the average campus rebel is like, do not draw your conclusions from those exhibitionists who perform thirty-second "bits" on Huntley-Brinkley. Forget personalities. Judge my generation by our analyses, our values, and our actions. Judge us by the consequences of our march on the Pentagon, by the uprising at Columbia, and by the fact that both Lyndon Johnson and Grayson Kirk are today in retirement.

I am afraid this missive has been too narrowly political. Perhaps at the bottom of what we call the generation gap are cultural † and sociological differences. Perhaps that is what divides me from you.

You listened to Leadbelly and Woody Guthrie, and I listen to the Band and the Fugs. You read Dos Passos and Steinbeck, and I read Heller and Pynchon. You did not smoke marijuana, or dress freaky, or wear your hair long, or live with a girl while you

---

* See *The Young Radicals,* Harcourt, Brace and World.

† Read Richard Poirier's piece in the October 1968 issue of the *Atlantic,* which makes this point brilliantly.

were still in high school. Affluence, television, the proliferation of birth control devices and drugs have liberated this generation. You may not like it—I certainly don't like being panhandled by sixteen-year-old urchins with parents in Scarsdale—but it is here.

This liberation has led to perhaps the most critical difference between our generations—the choice of career and life styles. We don't want to live out lives of quiet desperation in split-level suburbia. We don't want to make it on Wall Street, or contribute *anything* to the corporate-military-security nexus. We don't even want to join the Peace Corps anymore, because Vietnam taught us that is only a mask for the ugly warts of interventionism and imperialism. In short, we reject the root values of the culture— religion, materialism, patriotism, and status. And this is probably much more revolutionary than rejecting the cold war or the New Deal.

I don't know where this leaves us. I hope you understand us a little better. I hope you are more skeptical of what you read about us in *Commentary*. I'm not that sure we're right about everything, and on many questions we are badly split among ourselves.

But in Norman Mailer's prophetic phrase, "there is a shitstorm coming." And I think we are going to have to help each other in shoveling some of that shit off the flowers that have just begun to grow.

Yours truly,
Jack Newfield

JANUARY, 1969

[5.]
SDS: *From Port Huron to La Chinoise*

For more than a year now I have intentionally avoided writing about SDS (Students for a Democratic Society). In my travels around the nation's campuses I kept running into SDS members (usually "leaders") who seemed to me increasingly attracted to street fighting, coupled with a Marxist-Leninist-Maoist dogmatism. I read the SDS newspaper, *New Left Notes,* each week and found myself regularly repelled by a hermetic sectarianism, increasingly remote from the everyday needs and problems of most students, and most people. Turgid propagandistic writing, quotations from Lin Piao, General Giap, Nguyen Van Troi, and Chairman Mao, articles advocating "armed struggle" in the U.S., proliferated. One front-page story glorified a five-year-old boy who had derailed a passenger train with a rock. And during this period most of the organization's policies and tactics seemed to me wildly wrongheaded: support for the Arab guerrillas against Israel, bitter hostility to the McCarthy and Kennedy campaigns, rejection of building a broad-based popular movement against the Vietnam war in favor of playing the role of a pure "anti-imperialist vanguard."

But I kept quiet. I had once been a member of SDS, from 1961 till 1964. I had written a book on the New Left and was credited with some authority on the subject by the establishment media. And I was determined not to let anyone use my specific disagreements with the current national officers of SDS out of context in order to bludgeon the whole student rebellion. Mark Rudd and the dominant Weatherman faction may be crazy, I thought, but they weren't killing anyone, and SDS was, in Paul Glusman's pungent phrase, "on the nation's shit list." So I spent my anger at SDS in private conversations with friends, rather than let it spill over into print.

There was also the problem of cultural lag. I knew about the

unhappy trends inside SDS (violence, dogmatism, vanguardism) mostly because I still had friends in the Movement, and read internal Movement publications. Because I had friends in SSOC (the Southern Student Organizing Committee), I knew how, through pressure politics, SDS had forced that promising grouping of Southern intellectuals and radicals to absorb itself into SDS because it was "not revolutionary enough." Because I still had contact with the earlier founders and members of SDS, I was aware that they spoke privately of their disillusionment and frustrations with the new SDS that emerged from the blood and ruin of the 1968 Democratic Convention.

But, at the same time, for many people in the middle of the country, SDS was a shining symbol of insurgence and resistance. It was this to sensitive high school kids in Florida and to nice, retired old leftists in Colorado, just as it was a symbol of "violence and lawlessness" to the editorial writers on *The New York Times,* to the bureaucrats in the Justice Department, and to the investigators from the McClellan Committee. Was it possible to write something that meant the same thing to all three groups, that tried to grope for some truth about SDS, without giving aid and comfort to all the enemies of social change and student activism?

I decided it probably wasn't, so I found other things to write about through the flat middle of 1969—Ralph Nader, Theodore White's disappointing book, the new journalism, the problem of lead poisoning of children in the slums. Late in June, SDS met in convention, threw Little Red Books at each other, chanted slogans, and then the *minority* expelled the *majority* because, among other reasons, it didn't support the *Albanian* revolution! From what I could gather from the daily press, it seemed an absurd parody on the worst of the Old Left. Oh, how Max Schachtman must have roared! But the stories in the antiestablishment press seemed tentatively positive and optimistic: Andrew Kopkind in *Hard Times,* Dotson Rader in *The Village Voice,* and Jeff Shero in *Rat.* Here is an example of Rader in *The Voice:*

> I thought of these brave young people in the Coliseum, and how much they had, and will have to pay before they make their revolution. And I thought them beautiful, and I loved them. . . . I read the *Chicago Sun-Times* with a bullshit article about how SDS was

done, friend, over with for good. And I thought, bullshit!

But a few months later I read something else that made more sense, that touched me much more deeply. It was the final paragraph of a piece by Harvey Swados on Eldridge Cleaver. It said:

> For if anything is clear in a confusing time, it is that the best of our people are sick to death of the killing, everywhere, and of the lies that go with the killing, everywhere; of the conformity, everywhere. Any writer who ignores this, who opts for selective killing, selective lies, selective conformity, selective compulsion, dooms himself to what is perhaps an even worse fate than exile: irrelevance.

So, as I write these words it is now three months since Mark Rudd and the Weatherman faction moved into the SDS national office, and every sign and portent I see indicates that SDS has become even more estranged from reality, even more sectarian, and even more caught up in proving its revolutionary purity, rather than organizing students around the real, felt discontents of the war, the draft, universities, racism, and the rest of the familiar litany of issues.

A few grotesque examples: at New York University, SDS and Progressive Labor members got into a chain-throwing brawl at a meeting that ended with ten students injured and the *police* being summoned to restore *order*. The two SDS factions also engaged in a free-for-all in Cambridge, where both have large chapters. On other campuses this fall, two and even three rival groups are calling themselves the "real SDS," and are spending their time and energy debating and fighting with each other. *The Wall Street Journal* reported that university presidents think this factionalism will reduce "campus unrest." In Pittsburgh, the women's liberation caucus of SDS took over a Friends Service Committee office, threatened its occupants with karate and held them hostage while leaflets for a high school "jailbreak" were mimeographed and run off. In Detroit, another SDS karate-trained cadre roughed up teachers and students in a high school, and were later chastised by a group of Black Panther women, who reminded them of the slogan "Serve the People." The new SDS national leaders—Rudd, Bill Ayers, and Jeff Jones—have been put-

ting down the Chicago Eight (Hayden, Rubin, Seale, etc.), Newsreel, the Yippies, and some underground papers as revisionist and even as counterrevolutionary!

As a result, many radicals and activists have become openly critical of the incumbent SDS national leaders. Julius Lester wrote a trenchant column on SDS in the April 19, 1969, issue of *The Guardian;* Staughton Lynd wrote a painfully honest and gentle rebuke to SDS in the June issue of *Liberation. Rolling Stone* recently quoted Ken Kelley, the nineteen-year-old editor of the *Ann Arbor Argus,* as saying, "Fuck SDS. They're getting more and more absurd. They missed their chance because they never listen to what people want, what people are into, and now SDS is just into rhetoric. Everything else is going on, and all they see is rhetoric."

Paul Glusman, a leader of the People's Park Movement, and Todd Gitlin, former SDS president (1963), both wrote generally critical analyses of SDS in the September issue of *Ramparts.* And a brilliant critique of the current SDS by another former president, Carl Oglesby (1965), was published in the September issue of *Liberation.* A less rational assault on SDS by Abbie Hoffman was printed in the *Los Angeles Free Press* (September 12, 1969). Abbie criticized SDS for being "racist" and "elitist," and added that *"New Left Notes* makes good toilet paper."

These criticisms are very different from those of tenured liberal academics like Nathan Glazer, Daniel Boorstin, George Kennan, or even socialist Irving Howe. They come from full-time radical activists and organizers, all of whom would describe themselves as part of the New Left. Yet Oglesby can conclude his lucid, original essay by saying, ". . . if SDS continues the past year's vanguarditis, then it . . . will have precious little future at all. For what this movement needs is a swelling base, not a vanguard."

In the beginning SDS was multi-issue, activist, and wide open. It had been started in direct response to the failures of the old student Left, the Stalinism and sterility of the Marxist tribes, the caution and careerism of the liberal groups, and the single-issue orientation of CORE and the Student Peace Union (SPU). Its fluid politics were rooted in actual experience, and no one was excluded, not even Soviet-style communists, not even liberals.

Recently I spent an evening rereading my creased, mimeographed copy of the Port Huron Statement, SDS's founding manifesto, drafted by Tom Hayden in the spring of 1962. It remains, more than seven convulsive years later, a remarkably prophetic and instructive document. It warns against the growing power of the CIA and "the intermingling of Big Military and Big Industry." It criticizes John Kennedy for his support of "dictators" like Ngo Diem in Vietnam. It singles out university students as the most likely catalytic agent of social change during the 1960s. It proposes a "program to abolish poverty." It urges "experiments in decentralization based on the vision of man as master of his machines and his society."

How did SDS go sour? Was it inevitable that it end up repeating the mistakes of the 1930s, breaking up other people's meetings, impatiently giving in to fantasies of guerrilla warfare, memorizing the Chairman's maxims, purging its own membership on abstract ideological issues?

One of the reasons SDS took the road *east* rather than *left* was foreshadowed at its birth: *the collective failure of nerve of American labor and liberalism starting with the cold war and McCarthyism.* The unionists and Social Democrats of the League for Industrial Democracy (LID), the parent group of SDS, objected to the political content of the Port Huron Statement and tried to abort SDS in its cradle. The LID changed the lock on the SDS office after the founding convention in Michigan, refused to permit its student affiliate to distribute the Port Huron manifesto, and censured Hayden and the other founders for politics "outside the basic tradition and principles of the LID."

But this generational conflict was merely a symptom of a much deeper historical problem—the discontinuity of radical generations in America; the absence of credible fathers for these children of Watts, Vietnam, and Chicago; the absence of a creative, combative liberalism that might have provided allies and examples. If labor and liberalism had not been implicated in counter-insurgency, red-baiting, the Bay of Pigs, the CIA, the Vietnam war, it might have provided an alternative for the best of the young. If the unions had not supported the war, excluded blacks, and forced the presidential nomination of Hubert Humphrey, things might have turned out differently.

This liberal abdication began during the 1950s, while Daniel Bell was announcing "the end of ideology" and most of the cur-

rent generation of activists were not yet in high school. As Paul Goodman has written, "the young are honorable and see the problems, but we have not taught them anything." Goodman attributes this to "the failure of the intellectuals during the late forties and fifties [who] allowed themselves to be co-opted by the CIA, the Rand Corporation, and the universities [in which they] were kept busy, were able to esteem themselves as in the swim and thereby did not devote themselves to their normal business —to create new programs for the future."

Progressive Labor was founded by a group expelled from the Communist Party in 1962 as a tightly disciplined Marxist-Leninist organization that regarded China as the model for all revolutions. It viewed the proletariat (rather than youth or middle-class intellectuals) as the agency of change, and tried for several years to organize industrial workers, without much success.

In 1964, PL set up a front group called the May 2nd Movement, to rally students against the Vietnam war and eventually funnel them into PL. But in 1966, PL dissolved the still minuscule M-2-M, and in a disciplined, semisecret fashion, began to infiltrate the much larger SDS across the country at the local chapter level. It was this move that injected ideology, factionalism, Old Left slogans, and the idea of the working class into SDS, at a time when it was still communitarian, decentralized, and without much theory, though undoubtedly well beyond liberalism.

PL members tended not to be very bright or likable, but skilled at maneuver, filled with Marxist-Leninist clichés, and very dedicated. SDS members tended to be moralistic, long haired, and eager for direct action and community organizing, but not very intellectual or ideological. In such a situation PL's disciplined cadre was bound to have an impact beyond its members.

So it was in tactical reaction to PL's flooding of SDS that the SDS leaders hastily began their quest for a counterideology. Up to that point the early SDS leaders—Hayden, Oglesby, Gitlin, Paul Potter—had improvised their radicalism in action, borrowing ideas, as they seemed relevant, from C. Wright Mills, from Marcuse, from William Appelman Williams, Paul Goodman, SNCC, and Fanon. But under the pressure of PL's factional challenge, SDS's leaders went directly to the only existing body of prepackaged revolutionary doctrine—Marxism-Leninism. And in an effort to seem even more militant than PL, SDS went looking

for positions and prophets even more revolutionary than Mao. Failed guerrillas like Che and Debray were quoted in support of various domestic analyses.

Thus by the start of 1969 the rhetoric of all SDS factions was Maoist. Instant ideology invented a vanguard and let a thousand factions bloom. Suddenly SDS was swept up in internal debate over revisionism, Trotskyism, and guerrilla warfare. There was even a hot debate over whether the black colony could secede *after the Revolution!* (Although to their lasting discredit, SDSers never displayed much interest in, or solidarity with, the student rebels in Prague who were resisting, in the name of liberty, a resurgent Stalinism—not in theory but in the streets.) The group that had begun in 1962 with the notion of discovering its politics existentially through action and experience was now importing its slogans from China, North Korea, and Bolivia. Participatory democracy, the ability to communicate with ordinary students, the distinctively American quality of SDS were all lost in the shuffle. Liberals, anarchists, and radicals who were not Marxist-Leninist were called names like racist and revisionist and pushed out of local chapters. Hippies and cultural radicals, sensing the bad vibes and heavy rhetoric, split for Taos, rock festivals, or any place exempt from the great grass famine. SDS forgot that politics starts with how people treat each other.

By the time of the June convention, SDS had grown to fifty thousand members, but it had become indistinguishable from an Old Left sect. The Weatherman faction takes its name from Dylan's line, *"You don't need a weatherman to know which way the wind blows."* But perhaps more appropriate is another Dylan line: *"What price do you have to pay to get out of going through all these things twice?"*

The venality and passivity of established liberalism, and the intervention of PL, are the two most important factors in the rigidification of SDS. But there have been other reasons too. One has obviously been the Vietnam war, which over four murderous years has increased student bitterness and frustration, and provided some with the model of using violence to achieve one's ends. Another impetus to violence has been the ghetto riots, the Panthers, and the influence of Third World theorists like Fanon, Mao, and Debray. My own view on violence is admittedly ambiguous. I am not a pacifist. I think people have a right to self-de-

fense. It is clear to me that ghetto violence has been effective in winning minimal reforms, and I am certainly in favor of civil disobedience, boycotts, strikes, draft resistance, and the physical occupation of property. But at the same time I do not believe America is anywhere near a "revolutionary situation." I think violence tends to alienate potential sympathizers and brutalizes those who employ it. I am skeptical about it because it doesn't work. And the state and the police are much better at it than we are. Morever, while violence may be useful in dramatizing an existing evil, it is not a substitute for a program or analysis.

There is also the problem inherent in any student movement —the lack of continuity. Students always graduate, freshmen always have to be recruited, the campus is inevitably isolated from the larger society. Early on, SDS lost its self-confidence in the role of radical intellectuals. They tried to forget books and become blacks, instead of trying to find ways of organizing young adult professionals. I think the Port Huron Statement was right in the first place—youth and intellectuals are the catalysts of change in America. Psychic and spiritual oppression affects more people than economic oppression in this vinyl culture. The recent expressions of radicalism among lawyers, doctors, sociologists, political scientists, and English professors at their annual conventions show that young radicals are finding ways to maintain their politics after they graduate and enter the middle class. Thus SDS's own anti-intellectualism and romanticizing of the under class— two disturbing trends I mentioned in *A Prophetic Minority,* published in 1966, have also contributed to the current shape of SDS.

SDS has been caught inside a contradiction. They are probably right in perceiving class distinctions—distribution of basic income, power, and wealth—as the root of the problem, rather than racism, or just a variety of mistaken policies, as liberals do. But the American white working class is just not liberal, much less revolutionary. There are certain obvious reasons for the unique backwardness of the American proletariat: the capitalist character of the American labor movement; the purge of radicals from the CIO unions during the 1940s and '50s; the absence of a mass Socialist Party; the threat posed by angry blacks competing for jobs; the fact that on account of the cold war, America is the most anticommunist country on the planet. So, for all these reasons, I suspect that SDS has made an error in neglecting the mass

of restless students and middle-class professionals (Bazelon's New Class) in favor of trying to rally the white proletariat, and in some cases the bikers and street gangs of the lumpenproletariat. All this is doing is making SDS even more violent and anti-intellectual as it takes on the least attractive qualities of a class it can't organize.

The Movement is much bigger than any single organization. The Movement is a *movement*—a spontaneous contagion of energy rooted in attitudes, values, and life styles, and fueled by objective conditions. It is based on a hundred different evils in a hundred different places.

In my visits to college campuses I have noticed many students, probably a numerical majority on the large, urban campuses, who are alienated and dissatisfied, and willing to act on certain vague liberal/radical notions: immediate, unconditional withdrawal from Vietnam; less repressive laws concerning drugs, sex, and abortion; less bureaucracy; abolition of the draft; more relevant college curricula and more student influence in the running of the university; a passion to eliminate hunger and racism; fury at the programmed, hollow man in the White House. This seems to me to be the general mood of the current campus generation. Meanwhile, very few of this moralistic mass of students join SDS, and most seem to disagree with SDS's tactics and rhetoric.

The media, because of its own need for personalities and simplification, has tried to identify SDS with all campus dissent, to use it almost as a synonym for the New Left, just as the cold war intellectuals of the 1950s tried to make Stalinism a synonym for revolution and socialism. But in fact most of the New Left's most memorable confrontations have been conducted independently of SDS. Berkeley's FSM (Free Speech Movement), VDC (Vietnam Day Committee), and People's Park Movement were all *ad hoc* coalitions in which SDSers played a negligible role. Most of the outstanding Berkeley radicals have never been active in SDS: Frank Bardacke, Charley Palmer, Bob Scheer, Mario Savio.

The October 1967 March on the Pentagon and the demonstrations at the 1968 Democratic Convention were conceived and organized by older radicals like Dave Dellinger and Mitchell Goodman, and by first generation SDS alumni like Tom Hayden and Rennie Davis. Neither action was even endorsed by SDS. The frontal challenge to the draft has been mounted by the Resis-

tance. SDSers had only contempt for those thousands of students who volunteered for the McCarthy and Kennedy campaigns. Blacks and Third World students generated most of last spring's major campus protests at Cornell, at San Francisco State, at Brandeis, at Duke.

The grape strike, the GI organizing movement, the Black Lung Movement in West Virginia, Chicano demands in the Southwest for land and dignity, the New Universities Conference, the underground papers, the women's liberation groups, the Dodge Revolutionary Union Movement (DRUM) have all sprung, without guidance from any vanguard, from local conditions that ruin and stunt people's lives. All these groups may not have exactly the "correct line," but they are moving and acting, and that is what is important.

The Movement is now a decade old. In the context of the total culture it still appears powerless and isolated. It has not generated a new political party or elected one congressman.

But among the young it is influential and growing; it is certainly larger now than was the student movement during the national ferment of the 1930s. And it has won some notable battles —the retirement of Lyndon Johnson, the reversal of national opinion on the war, reforms in admissions policies and decision-making, and black studies programs at scores of universities: the creations of millions of living, walking radicals in this affluent country.

The Movement's future remains problematic. Repression and backlash menace it from the Right, factionalism and fantasy from within. Since the murder of Robert Kennedy, I have been deeply pessimistic about the chances for immediate change in America. I still see no leader worth following, no political coalition that can command a new majority for social reconstruction, no conventional politician with any creative connection to an insurgent movement. But if there is any hope at all for building a more democratic, humane future it lies with the nonwhite poor and the dissatisfied young—the Movement in its largest sense.

Part of my very tentative, long-range hopefulness comes from my enduring agreement with the basic assumptions and myths of the Movement. The country *is* in crisis. Youth *is* a new kind of class. The United States *does* have an imperialist stake in those nonwhite continents now striving for independence. Power and

income *are* unequally distributed. The environment—air, water, mines, factories—is being poisoned and polluted for profit. Racism *is* entrenched in institutions. And the traditional corporate liberal institutions—the AFL-CIO, Harvard, the Peace Corps, ADA, IBM, the Ford Foundation, Urban League, OEO, Reform Democrats—cannot solve these basic structural inequities.

The young will be a permanent and increasing constituency for change. Biology and time are on the side of the Movement. As Tom Hayden often tells adult audiences: "We will not bury you: we will just outlive you."

Perhaps we will get even with McNamara, and Hayakawa, and Sidney Hook through their children. Perhaps the Movement is now like a time bomb, ticking away inside young heads. Perhaps its full, final impact can't be known until the millions now in college and high school go into the professions, build their own institutions, publish their books, and start voting. Perhaps we will overcome, despite the absurdity of SDS. Perhaps.

SEPTEMBER, 1969

[6.]
The Prophetic Minority Is Ten Years Old
A NEW INTRODUCTION

When did it all begin? Was it the Youth March for Integrated Schools in April of 1959, when 20,000 members of the Silent Generation unexpectedly assembled in the shadow of the Lincoln Memorial? Was it the first student lunch-counter sit-in at Greensboro, North Carolina, on February 1, 1960? Was it the student demonstrations against the House Un-American Activities Committee in Berkeley three months later? Or was it the publication C. Wright Mills's prophetic "Letter to the New Left" in the *New Left Review* of September-October 1960? Or was it the election of John Kennedy as President that really generated the fertile climate for conception? Or was it the visionary monologues of Lenny Bruce, or the examples of Castro's triumph in Cuba, or the founding of Students for a Democratic Society by Tom Hayden and Al Haber?

No matter. Something called the New Left exists, is now one decade old, and is growing. The January 1960 issue of *Fortune* magazine published the results of an in-depth survey of young people between the ages of eighteen and twenty-four. The study indicated that about 750,000 of the nation's 6.7 million college students now "identify with the New Left," and that two fifths of that group—about *three million*—"are defined . . . mainly by their lack of concern about making money." This study neglected movement alumni over twenty-five now in the professions, and ignored the volatile high school consistency, which in urban centers is probably even more alienated and rebellious than the university students. As a writer for the *Berkeley Barb* recently put it, "The high schools are uncontainable. Che Guevara is thirteen years old, and he is not doing his homework."

The New Left is real. It can't be comfortably dismissed as merely the ritual Freudian revolt against fathers, or as the infantile equivalent of panty raids, or as the manipulated conspiracy

of Maoist cadres. The activists generally come from liberal middle- and upper-class families and tend to be the brightest and most sensitive members of their generation. This fact has been documented in studies by Yale psychologist Kenneth Keniston and published in his book *Young Radicals*. The Cox Commission Report on the student movement at Columbia University concluded, "The present generation of young people in our universities is the best informed, the most intelligent, and the most idealistic this country has ever known. . . . It is also the most sensitive to public issues." And Robert Kennedy wrote in his book *To Seek a Newer World:* "Not since the founding of the Republic . . . has there been a younger generation of Americans brighter, better educated, or more highly motivated than this one. In the Peace Corps, in the Northern Student Movement, in Appalachia, on dusty roads in Mississippi and narrow trails in the Andes, this generation of young people has shown an idealism and a devotion to country matched in few nations and excelled in none."

The Cox Commission, Dr. Keniston, and Senator Kennedy had in mind the typical restive, morally concerned activist. They were not talking about the small lunatic fringe that quotes mindlessly from Mao's little Red Book, breaks up meetings, or dogmatically "supports" Albania while "opposing" Israel—and neither am I. Part of the problem in understanding the young radicals is that the mass media have perceived no legitimate political or historical space between Eugene McCarthy and Abbie Hoffman, between voting and violence, between the Democratic Party and SDS. The media—the networks and the weekly news magazines in particular—have painted a tyrannizing caricature of the student rioter. He has long, dirty hair, an insatiable libido, and a vocabulary plagiarized from *Portnoy's Complaint*. He is violent, irrational, and antidemocratic. He is humorless and hates America.

But this caricature actually fits only the few activists who are revolutionaries. There are only about 30,000 SDS members—out of an alienated youth constituency of three million—and not everyone in SDS endorses violence or has memorized the quotations of Chairman Mao. The caricature, created by the needs and biases of the mass media, fails to take into account all the creative, extraparliamentary *but nonviolent* movements and programs young activists participate in.

Some specifics. There is grudging, undramatic community organizing going on every day of the poor and the powerless. Attempts at mobilizing peaceful resistance to the Vietnam war within the army itself. New institutions like high school student unions, free universities, and underground newspapers are being started. Activists in their late twenties and thirties are trying to radicalize the professions—lawyers, doctors, dentists, psychologists. Other activists support the grape boycotts or work with social reformers like Saul Alinsky or Ralph Nader or Rev. Jesse Jackson. Books and articles about community control, women's liberation, rock music, and ecology are being written. Demonstrations are being organized against university complicity with the military establishment, against repression of dissent, for more black students and faculty, and for an end to the endless war in Vietnam. These demonstrations are certainly less violent than the union strikes and sit-downs of the 1930s, and seem to me a legitimate part of democratic process. They are the only countervailing pressure available to students and poor people against an establishment that can hire professional press agents and lobbyists, bribe Senators and Supreme Court Justices, plant sympathetic magazine stories, take newspaper ads, make large financial contributions to political candidates, and, in general, use their position and wealth to get their point of view across between elections.

Perhaps the most distinctive quality of the student movement is that its politics are existential—open-ended, invented spontaneously in direct action, mistrustful of dogma and responsive to intuitive passions. Most young radicals at this transitional juncture in time, seem to feel no abiding allegiance to any existing national leader, party, or organization. Their style is free-lance and ad hoc. Many of the same students who burned their draft cards in 1967 shaved their beards to work inside the system for Eugene McCarthy in 1968. After they were beaten by the Chicago police and saw Humphrey nominated even though he won not a single Presidential primary, they voted for Eldridge Cleaver for President.

They are neither reformers nor revolutionaries. They are just as likely to follow Tom Hayden as Teddy Kennedy in 1972. Their values are still changing, and their minds are still open. No caricature can enclose them.

There are significant evils in American society that should be actively protested—war, poverty, racism, and violence. It is now

more than four years since the Vietnam war was expanded and Americanized by Lyndon Johnson. There are now 39,000 dead Americans, approximately a million dead Vietnamese, and more than two million homeless Vietnamese refugees. The government we support in Saigon is as corrupt and antidemocratic as ever. And the endless, criminal war goes on and on. They say, with justice, if the Vietnam war is not wrong, then *nothing* is wrong. If we have burned down a whole country, why can't they seize one administration building?

Students and blacks and their national spokesmen are overwhelmingly the *victims* rather than the *perpetrators* of violence. More than 100 young people, mostly partisans of Eugene McCarthy, were hospitalized as a result of the "police riot" during the Democratic convention in Chicago last August. Dozens of students were injured when police broke up the Columbia sit-in last spring. (Both the Walker Report and the Cox Commission Report criticized excessive police violence in those two situations.) Three black college students were killed—shot in the back—by state troopers at Orangeburg, South Carolina, last year. Black Panther leader Bobby Hutton was killed by Oakland police last April after he walked out of a building with his hands held above his head. James Rector was killed by Berkeley police in the battle of People's Park. The very best who have sought to reform the system from within—John Kennedy, Medgar Evers, Martin Luther King, and Robert Kennedy—have all been assassinated. In addition, this generation has grown up watching its own government kill a million people to gain its goals in Vietnam.

But the violence of the American system is systemic. It goes on casually, invisibly, everyday. Only it can't be filmed and put on Walter Cronkite. It is *systematic violence*. It is a rat biting a baby in Bedford-Stuyvesant. It is an Indian committing suicide on a reservation because he can't find work or dignity. It is a draft board sending an eighteen-year-old to Vietnam. It is a child suffering from lead poisoning because he ate the peeling walls of a Watts tenement. It is General Motors building unsafe cars. It is the Pentagon killing 6,000 sheep in Utah by testing germ-warfare weapons. It is a judiciary system that punishes the black and the poor because they can't afford fixes by high-priced lawyers.

One of the clearest examples of the Establishment's double standard about the use of violence came in the pamphlet *Concerning Dissent and Civil Disobedience* by Justice Abe Fortas. At

one point Justice Fortas lectures students protesting the war that "violent activities, in my judgment, should be regarded and treated as intolerable." But a few pages later he says of the American police action in Korea, "It cost us over 150,000 casualties. . . . But I think it is a fairly universal opinion in the Western world that the war was a necessary action."

Is it any wonder, then, that Rap Brown can say, "Violence is as American as cherry pie"?

The university is implicated in all these evils, particularly with the military-scientific-industrial complex. The American university is not a disinterested community of scholars. It offers courses for credit in ROTC training. It conducts secret chemical, biological, and germ warfare research. It has covert relations with the CIA. It cooperates with draft boards and the FBI. It permits student recruiting by the Marines and Dow Chemical. According to James Ridgeway's superb book *The Closed Corporation,* two thirds of all university research funds come from the Defense Department, the Atomic Energy Commission, and NASA. MIT and Johns Hopkins run centers that design missiles. The dean of students at Princeton and the former treasurer of Yale were CIA recruiters. The University of Michigan was subsidized by the government to conduct secret studies in counterinsurgency. Columbia University conducted research projects secretly funded by the CIA.

Until students exposed these covert institutional arrangements, university administrators flatly denied their existence. This was specifically true at Columbia University, where both former president Grayson Kirk and current president Andrew Cordier in 1967 issued false disclaimers to both faculty members and to the *Columbia Spectator,* the student newspaper. The Cox Commission, which probed the student disorders at Columbia, concluded, "Although both President Kirk and Dean (now President) Cordier may have sincerely believed that their statements were accurate, their remarks impaired confidence in the Administration, both at that time (1967) and through constant repetition."

The history of the last eight years vindicates the actions and analysis of the New Left much more than it does the Democratic Party liberals. It was not the stylish Kennedy administration, but college students, black and white, who first drew attention to the

racism and violence in the South. It was SNCC, and the Freedom Riders, and the martyred Goodman, Chaney, and Schwerner, not a benevolent federal bureaucracy, that first stirred the national conscience enough to pass two civil-rights bills.

It was SDS and a few professors who began the opposition movement to the Vietnam war in April of 1965, while Richard Goodwin, Bill Moyers, and Eric Goldman were still working in LBJ's White House. It was the Northern Student Movement and SDS that first drew attention to the sickness of the cities, five years before the Kerner Commission Report was released. It was the students of the Free Speech Movement, in Berkeley in 1964, who first challenged the computerized authority of the soulless multiversity, while Clark Kerr and Governor Brown insisted there was no problem. It was students who began to work in the "Dump Johnson" movement, and later the McCarthy and Kennedy campaigns, while the unions and the old-line Negro leaders like Bayard Rustin supported Lyndon Johnson and then Hubert Humphrey. While young people were struggling to start dozens of underground newspapers across the country, it was revealed that *Encounter* had received a secret stipened from the CIA. To a whole new generation, official liberalism has come to be symbolized by Hubert Humphrey embracing Mayor Daley, Lyndon Johnson embracing General Ky, and university presidents embracing the National Guard.

What is happening now is not that the country is becoming more conservative, *but that liberalism is becoming more conservative.* The problem is that more and more liberals are placing a higher priority on order than on justice.

The roots of the student disaffection are probably more cultural than political. What is most radical and self-liberating about the activists is their rejection of the most basic middle-class values of American society. Money and material wealth, as the *Fortune* survey indicated, are unimportant to them. Also unimportant are conventional definitions of patriotism, religion, puritanism, and status. They desire a totally new life style and new career options. They don't want a meaningless nine-to-five corporate job, or to live out lives of quiet desperation in split-level suburbia. They don't want to join the Peace Corps. They don't want to be bright young men writing memos in federal agencies. It is this break with traditional majority culture that makes political pro-

test like draft resistance and community organizing so accessible.

What the activists are doing is trying to create a new, adversary culture based on community and psychic liberation. Drugs, rock music, underground papers, long hair, colorful dress, and liberated sex are all part of it. Some of the vessels of these new values are Dylan's songs, Marcuse's books, Goddard's films, and Ginsberg's life style.

At the center of this cultural insurgency, I think, is the perception that adult society is *literally absurd,* that America is threatening to become a giant lunatic asylum. Some recent Orwellian examples: thousands of Americans died in Vietnam while their government debated the shape of a table in Paris; the American government can send 20,000 marines to the Dominican Republic because there are fifty-seven communists there, but it can't send food stamps to Mississippi, where thousands of Americans are suffering from hunger and malnutrition; the President can welcome the Senate's passage of the nuclear nonproliferation treaty one day and the very next day announce America will build a nuclear antiballistic missile system.

The young have literally grown up absurd, listening to Eichmann, CIA recruiters, Billy Graham, General LeMay, Richard Speck, Jack Ruby, and Dean Rusk. So it is quite natural that the young should draw their ethic and sensibility primarily from the artists of the absurd. From the songs of Dylan, the Stones, the Beatles, the Mothers of Invention, and Phil Ochs. From novelists like Joseph Heller, Thomas Pynchon, Ken Kesey, and Terry Southern. From films like *Alice's Restaurant, Putney Swope, Dr. Strangelove,* and *A Hard Day's Night.* From plays like *MacBird!* and *Little Murders.*

It is a symptom of just how badly the student generation is misunderstood that George Kennan, in his book *Democracy and the Student Left,* can lecture the young on their "inability to see and enjoy the element of absurdity in human behavior." Such a comment by an otherwise sensible historian and diplomat is just another reason why the activists so often feel like characters in Kesey's novel *One Flew Over the Cuckoo's Nest,* where the inmates of the mental hospital are saner than the guards. They simply don't want to participate in a culture that kills a million Vietnamese, attempts to put Benjamin Spock and Muhammad Ali in jail for opposing that slaughter, and then places Ronald

Reagan, John Mitchell, and Lester Maddox in positions of authority over their lives.

There are some ideas, tactics, and fashions on the margins of the activist movement that I find morally insupportable and politically counterproductive. Among a small minority of the student activists there is a romantic view of violence and revolution derived from a misreading of Fanon, Che, Debray, and Mao. I am among those who happen to believe that Che Guevera might have been a second Jesus Christ for Latin America. But I don't think anything he or the others wrote is applicable to a nuclear, technological octopus like the United States. Given the government's monopoly of violence, and the prosperity of a majority of Americans, I think the idea of violent revolution here is an infantile fantasy. I agree with Noam Chomsky when he writes in his new book *American Power and the New Mandarins:* "Resistance to the war should remain strictly nonviolent. . . . If there will be a 'revolution' in America today, it will no doubt be a movement toward some variety of fascism. We must guard against the kind of rhetoric that would have had Karl Marx burn down the British Museum because it was merely a part of a repressive society. It would be criminal to overlook the serious flaws and inadequacies in our institutions, or to fail to utilize the substantial degree of freedom that most of us enjoy, within the framework of these institutions, to modify them or even replace them by a better social order. One who pays some attention to history will not be surprised if those who cry most loudly that we must smash and destroy are later found among the administrators of some new system of repression."

Or, as Marcus Raskin asks, "What do you do with the gunmen after the revolution?"

So I am opposed to the tactic of violence against people because it is counterproductive, and it dehumanizes the executioner as much as the victim. But it is also necessary to understand that sit-ins, picket lines, boycotts, or the physical occupation of property are *not* violence. Those tactics are in the classic and noble tradition of Paine, Thoreau, Gandhi, Martin Luther King, Cesar Chavez, Danilo Dolci—and even Walter Reuther thirty years ago. Violence is dropping napalm on civilians or clubbing an unarmed sixteen-year-old demonstrator into unconsciousness.

Also, some of the younger, freakier activists don't seem to realize who the real enemy is. In the last few months in New York, public speeches by maverick journalist I. F. Stone, former Senator Wayne Morse, and Paul O'Dwyer have been disrupted by the Yippies. But Stone, Morse, and O'Dwyer are not the enemy— they were critics of the Vietnam war from the start. The enemy is the banks and absentee landlords who own Harlem; the warrior caste in the Pentagon and State Department; the Telephone Company and Con Edison; the AFL-CIO bureaucracy; Columbia University and the Democratic Party organization; and the FBI. The enemy is *institutions.*

Some of the activists think that liberalism is the primary enemy because liberals have been in power since 1960 and have been directly responsible for the Bay of Pigs, Vietnam, the fraud the war on poverty turned out to be, and the police riot in Chicago. But it has been other liberals who were the first to realize the students were right on so many issues. Liberalism is not monolithic. Both George Orwell and George Meany are liberals. It is necessary to distinguish, in Eldridge Cleaver's phrase, who is part of the problem and who is part of the solution. It seems obvious to me that Melvin Laird is part of the problem and I. F. Stone part of the solution. We should keep in mind that while some liberals like John Kennedy, Hubert Humphrey, and McGeorge Bundy bear much of the guilt for Vietnam, other liberals, like Robert Kennedy, Eugene McCarthy, and George McGovern, tried to stop the war. And it has been conservatives like Senator Strom Thurmond, Ronald Reagan, and Governor Connally who have always wanted to escalate it.

All this said, I would still maintain that on balance the young left—from McCarthy volunteers to draft resisters—is more worthy of support than any competing movement, including the hippie dropouts, the older NATO liberals, or the careerists of the New Politics, who have no vision beyond the 1972 elections.

The student protest movement is now in serious danger of repression by the Nixon administration. America is not likely to give birth to another generation so humanistic and generous in its impulses as this one for many years. This is a generation that values people above things and that has jeopardized its own safe careers to save a small nation 10,000 miles away from the fate of genocide. They have been called cowards for refusing the draft,

but thousands risked their lives to register Negro voters in the South. This is a generation that has witnessed its most respected adult sympathizers assassinated in a systematic horror show but still refuses to withdraw into a painless privatism.

Now there is the possibility that the best of this generation will be jailed, or driven underground, in a paranoid paroxysm of repression. Eight New Left leaders are now on trial in Chicago on charges of conspiracy because of the demonstrations that took place during the Democratic Convention, although if the grand jury had bothered to read the Walker Report they would have indicted Mayor Daley instead. The Justice Department is supporting prevention detention and increased wiretapping. President Nixon has put out an antistudent statement, and every state legislature in the country has been flooded with antistudent bills. Richard Kleindienst, the Assistant Attorney General, talks of "concentration camps" for "ideological criminals." Tom Hayden is followed twenty-four hours a day, his phone tapped, and his mail is opened. Eldridge Cleaver is in exile. The Black Panthers are the victims of continual harassment and intimidation; more than 100 of their members have been jailed in twenty different cities in the last three months. Twenty-seven soldiers who held a nonviolent sit-down at the Presidio to protest inhuman conditions in the stockade were charged with "mutiny" and given four- and five-year jail terms. The first foul odors of a new McCarthyism are in the air. And many liberals seem willing to quietly pay the ransom of a little repression to buy some tranquillity and time, just like the 1950s, when intellectuals like Sidney Hook saw no problem with Senator McCarthy, as long as he left his friends alone.

My reflex is to end this piece with an inspirational quote from Paine or Jefferson or with an optimistic summons to some barricade, but that would be too easy and unfaithful to my mood most of the time these days. Things are getting worse, not better. Nixon's recent decisions on the war, Justice Haynsworth, the ABM, the poverty program, and the Chicago indictments prove that our darkest suspicions about him have been too generous.

What I want to say in conclusion is simple and blunt. The student activists are the best young this nation will produce for generations. They are right on most specific issues. There is no moral adult authority in the country that deserves their trust. Their new political and cultural institutions are the seeds of a

better future. The government, the courts, the police, the FBI, and the college administrations may finally have the institutional power to forcefully repress this beginning movement. But if that happens, America will become a poorer and meaner country.

JANUARY, 1970

[THREE]
VIETNAM: THIS ENDLESS WAR

I can no longer recall a time when I was not preoccupied by the war in Indochina. The first time I can remember thinking seriously about the war was when Bob Moses talked about it at a memorial service for Goodman, Chaney, and Schwerner at the site of a burned out church in Meridian, Mississippi, in 1964.

Since then I've signed all those antiwar ads where my name is inevitably sandwiched between Jay Neugeboren and Grace Paley. The marches all run together in my mind, but I remember vividly the cardboard name of the dead soldier I carried in the cold at 3 A.M. from Arlington Cemetery to the Capitol in November of 1969. The name was Everett Foster, and I imagine that he was black, and that he probably came from Bed-Stuy, where I grew up.

I won't apologize for the rage that is in most of these pieces. It is how I feel. We have killed babies and old women, and bombed half of Indochina into a moonscape for no reason. And I am no longer embarrassed about expressing my sympathy for the NLF. They have been fighting for their own country for a generation against different imperialist armies, and I wish them well.

[1.]

No Taxation Without De-escalation

I am no revolutionary, and on some days I don't think I am even a radical. Melodramatic gestures are not natural to me, and emotional rhetoric by others turns me off. Stokely Carmichael makes me laugh, not cry, and Lord Russell embarrasses me. But this year I will refuse to pay 20 percent of my federal income tax —the percentage that goes to subsidize the Vietnam war.

Three things led me to this decision: watching Lyndon Johnson on live television deliver his address to the Tennessee legislature three weeks ago; having to write a closely reasoned speech for a college symposium on my view of America; and a friend asking me what I was doing personally to stop the war.

For a half hour I looked into the President's face on the television screen and could only think of Camus's comment that "every man over forty is responsible for his own face." The face I saw offended and appalled me.

The earnest words that afternoon—and on too many afternoons—were lies. They enlarged what is euphemistically called the "credibility gap" by the mass circulation press.

He spoke of the growing freedom and democracy in South Vietnam at the moment neutralists—much less NLF sympathizers—were being barred from participating in the election for the Constituent Assembly. He said he was going to Guam to discuss the nonmilitary aspects of the war, but he raced madly across four time zones for no apparent reason except to act as if he was doing something. Earlier, he said we were not bombing civilians, and we were. And once he even said he "wanted no wider war." When he said it he was running for reelection as a man of peace.

I voted for him in 1964, and now I don't believe a word he says. But the polls show 70 percent of the country supports him on the bombings, and, depending on the wording of the ques-

tion, endorses his general conduct of the war. I am a Democrat, so the thing to do is to defeat him next year. The conventional wisdom among politicians these days is that LBJ's political strength has been underestimated. They feel that he is now gaining in popularity, much the way Nelson Rockefeller did before he was reelected Governor in 1966, and that he will defeat any Republican candidate next year.

I disagree. My perception of LBJ is that, like Sonny Liston, he is a bully with a quitter's heart, that he will not run if he thinks he cannot win. The public, I believe, senses his character as it did Nixon's. If these latent feelings are given the chance to concretize by not eliminating all hope of an alternative candidate, there is a real possibility that the President will withdraw from the race.

Last week I began preparing a speech on my view of America, and in the course of writing it I recognized that the events of the last eighteen months have substantiated much of what the radicals think of America and little of what liberals think.

If, two years ago, someone told me that the Warren Report was incorrect, the CIA was subsidizing the National Student Association and a dozen unions, that LBJ would adopt Goldwater's Vietnam policy, that actor Ronald Reagan would soon be Governor of the largest state in the country, and that Congress would vote to throw out Adam Clayton Powell, I would have said such a person was insane. But all the impossibles became possible. There is a madness in America—and it is much worse than liberals are ready to believe. Absurdity is becoming more and more institutionalized. The trend is toward greater injustice, not less. The problem is not just a matter of replacing Dean Rusk.

The corollary, then, is that liberal solutions are inadequate. The editorials in *The New York Times,* the letters of the Peace Corps returnees, the speeches of Fulbright and Kennedy, the vigils of the clergymen are all good, but they are insufficient. It required civil disobedience—the illiberal defiance of law—to bring France's war against the Algerians to an end, and it took civil disobedience to ignite the civil-rights movement and the New Left. The sit-in people, the freedom riders, the Berkeley kids, the travelers to Hanoi, the draft card burners, all of them were right. And so was Sartre in 1957 when he urged French youth to defy the draft, and so were Thoreau and Paine.

Liberalism is falling apart, and as Yeats once wrote, "The cen-

ter cannot hold." The New Deal coalition is fragmenting. The South is gone as the solid base of the Democratic Party. The union leaders cannot deliver their backlashing rank and file, the precinct captains of the urban machines cannot deliver the new middle-class voters, the Negro preachers cannot deliver their angry alienated. And the new coalition—the one in prospect—is yet to coalesce. The young, the urban reformers, the minorities, the ecumenical clergy, the new generation of academics and labor leaders, liberal politicians, and technocrats have not yet come together.

Vietnam is the liberals' war. Stevenson, Roche, Goldberg, Humphrey, Harriman—they are all liberals and they all made their commitment to the cold war myth.

So, finally, a friend asked, "What are you doing?" I told him I had joined the committee to defend the Fort Hood Three, and then I laughed at myself.

I am too old to defy the draft, too content to volunteer as a hostage in North Vietnam, too everything to fight for the Cong. So, I will withhold 20 percent of my taxes this year.

At Auschwitz a child who knew he was about to die, screamed at a German guard, "You won't be forgiven!"

This is my way of saying the same thing to Lyndon Johnson. He is not my President. This is not my war.

APRIL, 1967

[2.]

Catch 23: No Meditation in a Martial Society

COLUMBIA, South Carolina—This characterless state capital, where General Westmoreland was born, and where Dr. Howard Levy was court-martialed, experienced an obscure but perhaps prophetic demonstration against the Vietnam war last Tuesday night. About thirty uniformed soldiers tried to hold a "meditation" to express their "doubts" about the war at the interfaith chapel on the 30,000-man Fort Jackson army base. Military police barred the entrance to the chapel, and forcibly took five of the soldiers into custody. Two of them now face court-martial.

The event did not make much impact on the media, partially because the Fort Jackson Public Information Office pretended ignorance to inquiring reporters. Also, the protesters do not fit any of the existing stereotypes, are anonymous, and have no access to mimeograph machines. But what they did is as portentous—and as invisible—as the first civil rights sit-in, staged in Greensboro, North Carolina, eight years ago this month.

Ordinary, unpolitical soldiers, trapped inside the hermetic military machine, with nothing in their environment to reinforce their doubts, are beginning to rebel against their regimented fate. Two privates—Denis Adelsberger and Robert Mears—are being held under maximum security guard at Fort Gordon, Georgia, for refusing, in protest against the war, to wear their uniforms. Private George Davis voluntarily returned from AWOL to refuse a direct order to go to Vietnam, and is now in the stockade at the Presidio. An underground antiwar newspaper, written by soldiers, is being distributed clandestinely at Fort Ord. The paper, called *The Soldier's Manual of Free Thinking*, notifies its readers that "this paper is written on Army machines, with Army ink, on Army paper." The Pentagon officially admitted last week that desertion convictions in the Navy, Marines, and Air Force in 1967 were higher than in any of the five preced-

ing years. Thirteen antiwar deserters have sought asylum in Sweden. And the case of the Fort Hood three has already received wide publicity.

Steve Kline seemed to be the leader of the group of soldiers involved in the protest here. He is twenty years old, an enlisted man, and an optical specialist in the base hospital where Dr. Levy worked. He graduated from Seton Hall High School, and spent a semester at Villanova University. His classical Catholic education has given him a logical and detached approach to problems, uncluttered by either academic or political abstractions.

"I decided I just had to do something, even if it meant jail or a ruined career," he says, "when Bobby Kennedy said he wouldn't run. Somebody had to try."

About ten days ago Kline and five buddies agreed some show of opposition to the war had to be made "by the people most affected by it." None had been political activists in civilian life, and none wanted to make an apocalyptic gesture. Says Kline, "I didn't want to go to jail, go AWOL, or go into exile. I wanted to do something legal, something all the soldiers could participate in. And I felt the idea of refusing to serve in Vietnam might be interpreted as an act of cowardice."

The group decided the most reasonable thing to do was to hold a "meditation service" in the base chapel. The oldest member of the group, Martin Blumsack, who used to visit Dr. Levy daily, was chosen to request permission for the use of the chapel. The request was granted, and last weekend 1300 leaflets announcing the meeting were distributed by soldiers and South Carolina University students in Columbia. The leaflet read:

"Is God on our side?

"We are soldiers like millions of other Americans who have grave doubts about the war in Vietnam.

"It is time we made those doubts known.

"We'd like to invite those of you who share our concern to join us in Chapel 1 at 7:30 P.M., Tuesday, for an hour of meditation."

The Columbia newspaper and television station got hold of the leaflet and called Colonel Chester Davis, administrative officer of the Fort Jackson hospital. On Tuesday morning, Colonel Davis called in Blumsack and told him that unless he canceled the meeting, "you will end up in prison like Dr. Levy."

Davis then ordered Blumsack, who had only 102 days to serve, to stand outside the chapel and inform anyone who showed up that the meditation was canceled. The post press office then told all the media the meditation was off, and not to bother to come.

At 6:30 P.M., an hour before the chapel meeting, all entrances to the huge post were sealed. The lights inside the chapel were shut off—a violation of army regulations. About twenty-five MPs were positioned on the perimeter of the Chapel, some equipped with tear gas. An MP van was parked in front.

At 7.30, about thirty soldiers—many in freshly pressed olive green dress uniforms, appeared out of the darkness. Blumsack, flanked by two MPs, dutifully said in a monotone that the meeting was canceled. Kline and several of the originators of the protest then approached the chapel and were ordered to "move on" by the uptight MPs.

"Why?" asked Kline. "Don't I have the right to free assembly?"

"Move on, that's an order," snapped a robot MP.

Suddenly, two crew-cut basic trainees, who no one knew, appeared and began screaming at the MPs.

"I don't want to fight for fascism! Why should we kill babies for General Ky? We want to have a free meeting!" They were shaking with rage.

The two—named Rosenbaum and Rivera—were swiftly taken into custody and driven to the other end of the base.

Then Kline and his buddy Bob Tatar simply walked away from the surprised MPs and knelt in prayer on the lawn in front of the darkened chapel. A flashbulb went off, and they were roughly hustled into an MP car and driven off. An MP told the few local reporters who managed to get on the base that no one was under arrest, no charges would be lodged, and "there was no story." Quickly, the MPs dispersed the confused soldiers who had come to attend the meeting. Many said they came only because they had read or heard about the leaflet. They didn't know the organizers of the meditation, but felt they had a constitutional right to discuss the war. Others said they wanted to talk about the epidemic of spinal meningitis at the base.

At 9 P.M. I called the base press office. They said they didn't know any details about "the incident," but suggested I call a Captain Asmus. The captain, who was outside the chapel, said, "nothing much happened. The boys were all turned over to their commanding officers. I don't know their names, but no charges

were made." He apparently told the same thing to the wire service reporters, who were busy in Orangeburg, forty miles away, and had to call in for the story.

After midnight I managed to see Kline and Tatar. Like the early sit-in kids, they both seemed high from the exhilaration of what they had done, even though both had been charged with refusing to obey a direct order, disorderly conduct, and wearing an improper uniform. This charge was tacked on, in a *Catch* 22-like example of the military mind, when the MPs noticed their socks did not match their dress uniforms.

Kline, in rapid, clipped speech, described how he was interrogated by five different police and security agencies, including the FBI, and then told he would face a court-martial.

"It was funny," he recalled, the way the MPs tried to argue with us. One of them asked me how come if I was so much against the war I didn't vote against it. So I told him I was only twenty years old. I could just get killed, but I couldn't even attend a meditation expressing my doubts.

"If we're not locked up," he added, "we're going to try again next week to have a legal meeting in the chapel. I think a lot of guys on this base would come if they weren't afraid to express themselves."

FEBRUARY, 1968

[3.]
The Silent Resignations
of "Decent Americans"

Clark Clifford, the personification of the military-industrial complex, has been named Secretary of Defense. Four H-bombs have been lost off the coast of Greenland. A State of the Union address has been delivered by a President who sounded like a Texas sheriff up for reelection. We are involved in a confrontation with North Korea in which our government is probably lying. And, yet, Lyndon Johnson has never seemed more likely to be reelected.

There is something wrong, the system is not working. The accents of apocalypse and paranoia are suddenly symptoms of sanity. We are trapped not just in a Vietnam crisis or in a crisis of the cities, but also in an electoral crisis. People are now questioning representative democracy itself. The power of the Senate to advise and consent has been emasculated. The draft is being used to coerce campus dissenters. The Democratic National Committee is without influence. And as for electoral politics, McCarthy can't and Kennedy won't. And the Republicans are exposing the true nature of their politics by trooping to the banner of Richard Nixon. Meanwhile, LBJ continues to tell lies as if by instinct. On December 3, when the McNamara switch was leaked, he told reporters, "Nobody else is planning to leave my cabinet. Those are rumors spread by some kids" (widely interpreted as a reference to the Kennedy brothers). "Most of them are not as close to the situation as they might be, or might desire to be." Last week John W. Gardner quit as Secretary of Health, Education, and Welfare, and others are waiting in the wings.

At the moment when the institutions of democracy have become so atrophied, it has become sadly clear that one of the remaining methods of legitimate dissent—the political resignation —has been abdicated. Robert McNamara and John Gardner have quit the government, and Arthur Goldberg will leave soon.

All three men are, in some measure, against escalation of the Vietnam war, but not one will publicly admit that this contributed to his leaving. They are America's equivalent of the "good Germans." They know, but they won't say. Their crime is silence.

If these men, particularly McNamara, won't speak, won't use "legitimate" methods of dissent, then they have lost the moral right to tell people not to use the streets. If Robert Kennedy will not run, then he has forfeited the right to criticize the demonstration that will take place outside the Democratic convention next August. If powerful, decent men will not use legitimate means, then the definitions of legitimacy must change. If America must choose among Johnson, Nixon, and Wallace, then the streets are legitimate, and the jails are shrines.

McNamara, Gardner, and Goldberg are not monsters. They are liberal, sophisticated, and, in McNamara's case, sensitive men. They tell their friends how they dislike the bombings and how dangerous some of the President's "other advisers" are. But they leave in silence. McNamara was fired, but he played out the demeaning charade of a switch in jobs, even though he learned of the switch from a *New York Times* columnist. These three men, if they said in public what they say in private, could probably prevent Lyndon Johnson's reelection. But they remain loyal to the mentality of the club. And, also, they don't want to burn all their bridges.

They act as if political resignations never happened before. They apparently choose to forget that James A. Farley quit FDR's cabinet and Henry Wallace and James F. Byrnes quit Truman's on policy issues and then took those issues to the country. They forget that Winston Churchill and Aneurin Bevan quit the British government on issues of principle. The cold-war liberals have always—and with justice—invoked the specter of Milovan Djilas voluntarily giving up the vice-presidency of Yugoslavia to go to jail, rather than keep silent about Tito's abuses of democracy.

McNamara was, in conventional terms, a remarkable Secretary of Defense. He asserted civilian primacy over the military. He opposed military boondoggles, like the Skybolt air-to-ground missile and the ABM system. The official *Defense Department Digest,* dated February 1, 1965, quoted McNamara as saying, "I think it would be a tremendous opportunity for us economically

and socially to eliminate defense entirely. It would be a social good." To judge him a "good German" now is a confession of disappointment in a man who did not fit the bloody stereotype the Left had of him. It is to say he knows better, but is willing to butcher his conscience, just as Adlai Stevenson did before him.

Gardner, who resigned last week, is a man almost as impressive as McNamara. The power elite is not monolithic, and for each apostle of escalation and repression, there are decent men like Gardner, a Republican, who argued inside the administration that cities were more important than Hill 875. He is the man who said only last month in a widely quoted speech, "We are in deep trouble as a people. And history is not going to deal kindly with a rich nation that will not tax itself to cure its miseries."

History's judgment of "good Germans" like McNamara, Gardner, and Goldberg might well incorporate words Dwight Macdonald wrote twenty years ago about the original good Germans:

"Only those who are willing to resist authority themselves when it conflicts too intolerably with their personal moral code, only they will have the right to condemn the death-camp paymaster."

FEBRUARY, 1968

[4.]
The Shelling of the President, '69

RALEIGH, North Carolina—On Moratorium Day I spoke with
Dr. Howard Levy at the basketball factory called the University
of North Carolina, and at Duke University, Richard Nixon's old
law school.

On the plane flying down I fussed with my speech, fearing my
flat out endorsement of the NLF might be provocative or offensive in Dixie. But when I got off the plane, Richie Leonard, of
Welcome, North Carolina, gave me a copy of the Duke student
paper, whose lead editorial began:

"We believe a careful study of history shows that the war in
Vietnam is an imperialistic conflict."

And concluded:

"And we support the struggle of the Vietnamese people for
their own liberation."

And when I read my speech at Chapel Hill, and said, "The
United States has already lost this war. The United States lost it
because we fought on the wrong side. We fought on the side of a
decadent landlord elite, instead of with the legitimate movement
of national liberation," these sons and daughters of the Southern
business elite, these polite, short-haired children of parents who
voted for Richard Nixon in 1960, stood up and roared and made
a forest of V signs with their fingers.

And when I got to Duke University, a Methodist school of
8000, more than 1500 students cheered when I suggested a national tax strike next April 15 if the war is not over.

So while the "national significance" of M-Day will be debated
endlessly inside the insight industry, and none of us can know if
it had any impact on the policy makers in Washington, I can report that a new generation is rising in the South that is leaping
over thirty years of safe, sterile New Deal politics. In four years,
thousands of white Southern students are jumping from the rac-

ism and militarism of their heredity and environment, into iden-
tification with the Vietnamese, and acceptance of civil disobedience.

North Carolina University was a famous enclave of Southern
liberalism in the 1940s when Dr. Frank Graham was its president. During the 1950s, when Frank McGuire was the basketball
coach, the pipeline from Brooklyn's blacktop schoolyards sent up
such all-stars as Lennie Rosenbluth, Doug Moe, and Harvey Salz.

(I began my speech by remarking that "Dr. Levy and myself
are probably the first two Jews from Brooklyn ever to come here
without a basketball scholarship.")

In the last few years, NCU has become more reflective of its region. The state legislature imposed a speaker ban on communists. Dr. Graham's absence was felt in terms of mood and leadership. Few Northern students were accepted by the admissions
office under mandate from the state legislature. The chancellor
of the university said he might speak at the Moratorium rally
three weeks ago, but pressure from alumni, trustees, and the state
legislature forced him to retract, and he did not appear.

"Up until five years ago," one Duke student told me, "this
place was just a sleepy old Southern college that mass-produced
business executives. Then last year we had a student strike that
won higher wages for the black cafeteria employes, and a black
studies program. But the college has sabotaged the black studies
program, and let five white professors design it. So now all of
Duke's seventy-five blacks are boycotting it, and setting up their
own Malcolm X Liberation School with church money."

But the level of antiwar activity at both colleges had been low.
The students estimated that only ten students from NCU and
twenty from Duke went to the Pentagon in 1967. Neither campus
has an SDS chapter. When college opened a month ago, the few
activists here anticipated only token participation in the Moratorium.

Then came the great national tidal shift in public opinion
about the war, the internal Tet offensive of the doves, the con-
version of Roswell Gilpatric, Averell Harriman, half of Wall
Street, Fred Harris, Tom Seaver, and Melvin Laird's son. The
Gallup Poll showed 57 percent of the country in favor of the
Goodell bill.

And here students like Wib and Dub Gulley from Little Rock,

Arkansas, and George Bulter from Clinton, North Carolina, and Buck Goldstein from Miami, kids who had nothing to do with SDS or the Mobe, or any national organization, these kids began to organize on their own, and discover far more support than they dreamed of.

The daily paper in Greensboro, North Carolina, came out for withdrawal, and the editor agreed to speak at an M-Day rally. Two rival petitions began to be circulated in the Duke Law School, Nixon's old law school. One called for immediate withdrawal, and the other urged support for the President. Withdrawal won, 102 to 75. The local Congressman, Nick Galifinakas, a hardline hawk last year, voted on Tuesday night with the liberal minority to keep the House open all night for the marathon antiwar talk-in. And on M-Day, more than half of Chapel Hill's high school students joined the Moratorium.

Moratorium activities began here at midnight in the eerie light of a thousand flickering candles in the chapel of the Duke Divinity School. There a student read the names of the fourteen Duke graduates who have died in Vietnam, and after each name the bell in the chapel steeple tolled in the night.

At 12:30 A.M. an ecumenical memorial service began, and 3000 solemn students filled the chapel, 2000 more than anyone expected. The Duke chaplain again read the fourteen names, and said, "Let us remember those who once walked the warm stones and green pastures of this campus." And then Cantor Elias Rochbarg chanted the Kaddish.

M-Day started at NCU at 9 A.M. with a liberation class on "Does War Come Naturally" in the Carolina Union. About two hundred students attended, and Richie Leonard said, "Gosh, no professor here *ever* got 200 people for a 9 A.M. class."

By 10 A.M. it was clear M-Day would be a wild success in Chapel Hill. Attendance at classes was less than 50 percent, and 1000 students crowded into a teach-in called "Latin America: Parallel to Vietnam?"

Between 11 A.M. and 3 P.M. there were films, folk singing, poetry readings, liberation classes, and a peace vigil dispersed all over the green, rolling campus. A row of mock graves was put up in front of the ROTC building. Also, in front of the ROTC building, students kept calling out the names of the NCU dead in Vietnam. A few ROTC types and jocks came down and started read-

ing the names of NCU "war heroes in Vietnam." A lot of the names were the same.

Then at 4 P.M. Dr. Levy and I led a march down Franklin Street, to Memorial Hall. And behind us, on this cool, cloudy day, 5000 people marched against the war, and smiled at the supporting signs in the store and shop windows along Franklin Street. The line was many blocks long, and it took fifteen minutes for the back of the line to reach the hall, after the front part had filled the 2500 seats. When I asked Todd Cohen, the editor of the student paper, why they had not arranged for a bigger hall, he answered, "Two weeks ago we were afraid we couldn't fill this. But then it just grew, like Woodstock."

Some problems of public policy are complex and difficult to solve. Democratizing the mass media is a complicated matter. Finding an alternative to the draft is not easy. I don't know how to make sure the garbage gets collected every day in the ghettos. But Vietnam is simple. As Pete Hamill put it, "You get out of Vietnam by getting out of Vietnam." You get out unconditionally, totally, immediately—"by ships and planes."

The President is scheduled to go on national television on November 3, and the inside dopesters tell us he will announce his "Vietnamization" plan, whereby the U.S. will withdraw perhaps 200,000 troops over the next twelve months, and leave 300,000 behind around Saigon, while the South Vietnamese do most of the fighting.

But I don't think the kids I met at Duke, and at NCU, will buy this gimmick, just like they weren't fooled by the last token withdrawal of 30,000, and the firing of General Hershey.

These serious, decent kids with Republican manners want us out of Southeast Asia—Thailand, Taiwan, Laos—out of it, now.

They have brooded about this on a lot of long nights. All the boys face the draft. All of them, boys and girls, know a family that has received that terrible telegram and had a son sent home in a wooden box.

These kids are years ahead of cynical politicians like Ed Muskie and Fred Harris. They are out in front of Sam Brown and the initiators of the Moratorium. In one hour at Duke, 100 of them signed a statement pledging draft resistance.

And so many of them are coming to Washington on November 15, they might have to hide out Richard Nixon at Amherst, just like he gave sanctuary to David and Julie at the White

House last week. And no single organization, no faction, and no leader can control or contain these kids from Little Rock and Welcome, North Carolina. The movement for withdrawal is now a contagion of consciousness.

The shelling of the President has begun. And all his advertising agency hucksters, and all his McLuhanist manipulators immortalized by Joe McGinniss, can't put his cracked image back together again.

OCTOBER, 1969

[5.]
The Accidental President:
"McLuhanizing" the War

"... And Agnew himself, my God. He says all the wrong things."

"What we need is a shade less truth and a little more pragmatism," Trevlean said.

"I think Dexedrine is the answer," Garment said.

"One bright spot," Trevlean said, "you see Agnew and it makes you realize how good Nixon is."

—The President's media experts, Harry Trevlean and Leonard Garment, as quoted by Joe McGinniss in *The Selling of the President 1968*.

Thoughts while watching the President of the United States address the nation on the issue of Vietnam on Monday night.

Nixon, you are giving plastic a bad name. You are a Zeitgeist from an obsolete decade. You remind me of Eddie Fisher and John Cameron Swayze. You are the Howdy Doody of the new politics.

Nixon, you act like you secretly suspect you are only playing the President in some great Genet fantasy factory. Perhaps you sense you are an accident, that you're the President only because Nelson Rockefeller got divorced, and two Kennedys were murdered.

So now you are coming on TV, election eve in New Jersey, New York, and Virginia, to try and deter people from coming to Washington on November 15. It's just like you to try this—a slick media gimmick without vision or substance. It's like when you announced your bland, WASP cabinet on live television. Or when you suddenly intruded on the split screen to talk to the astronauts the night they landed on the moon. You think like the assistant producer of the David Susskind Show. That's

why you hired Ron Ziegler, whose last account at J. Walter Thompson was Disneyland, as your press secretary.

I'm starting to figure you out. For eight years you plotted and connived to get elected President, to heal your hurt of 1960. That's all you thought about all those loner years when you traveled around the country, speaking at Republican county dinners in places like Topeka and Tulsa. But you never thought about what you would do *after* you got elected. You are the archetypal plodder; getting there is everything. But now you're there, and you have no place to lead us, because your mind is bereft of vision or imagination.

You thought you could rule by the same grubby techniques you used to get the nomination—manipulation, deceit, image-making, sophisticated publicity. Only you can't. You think the image is the message, and saying the words makes it so, but you're wrong.

You and your McLuhan mafia, think any problem can be solved by the "right presentation" or "proper management." I bet you thought it was a brainstorm to rename the ABM system "Safeguard," like it was some cake of soap to be cleverly packaged and marketed.

I've been thinking about the slogans you've been pushing. "Lower your voices." "Bring us together." "The American dream doesn't come to he who is asleep."

They are all passive, defensive. You have absolutely no notion of what you want the country to be like except for your halycon memories of the 1950s with Ike. JFK had a particular vision of the future. Even Goldwater and Johnson had a program they were seeking power for. But you have no reason to want to be President, except assuaging your own feelings of inferiority and rejection.

Nixon, you are a total political animal. You sit there in your Oval Office, brooding about the "Emerging Republican Majority" and the "Southern Strategy"; you sit there building up files on Ted Kennedy and George Wallace; you sit there scheming for 1972, and meanwhile, you have no social programs to heal the millions of Americans who are poor, powerless, and enraged.

I really had hopes you would declare a cease fire and announce a systematic timetable for withdrawal. When dovish senators like

Fulbright, Mansfield, and Aiken suddenly stopped criticizing you, I thought that was a portent of a bold new policy you had promised them in private. When influential centrists like Clark Clifford, Hugh Scott, and Ed Muskie started urging a cease fire, that nourished my optimism.

I really thought you were a Weatherman, that you could tell which way the wind was blowing. But it turns out you're the same old stubborn, out-of-touch Nixon, who thinks repetition is reason.

The speech was you. It said nothing, carefully. It tried to be everything, so it ended up being nothing. It ducked the hard, tough specifics, like a coalition government in Saigon that includes the NLF, and it dwelled on airy generalities. Why did you give it, if you had nothing new to say? I thought I was watching a summer rerun of Dean Rusk. And at the end, I expected a voice to say, "The preceding was a paid political advertisement by the antiwar movement." You probably persuaded another 100,000 people to go to Washington on November 15.

Nixon, you are trying to have it both ways as usual. You send Agnew to Republican fund-raising dinners to call us "impudent snobs" and "ideological eunuchs." Your Attorney General went on "Meet the Press" on Sunday to say he would use even stronger language than Agnew to describe the organizers of the November 15 march. Now you come on the tube, hands cleaner than Pilate, playing the troubled statesman, huckstering unity.

Nixon, you are jiving the country. You don't have a secret plan to end the war, as you told us last election autumn. You are just stalling for time. Your press releases say you are pulling out 60,000 troops by December 15. Well, that still leaves 475,000 American soldiers on Vietnamese soil. At that rate, we'll be out of Vietnam by 1977. And that is halfway to 1984.

How can you expect us to believe your optimism? Don't you think we remember Robert McNamara saying in 1963 that we would be out of Vietnam by Christmas of 1965? Don't you think we remember Walt Rostow saying in 1965 that the bombing of the North would "make the NLF come crawling to us for peace talks in six weeks?" Don't you think we remember General Westmoreland—the Custer of Asia—saying in 1968 the V. C. was collapsing, a week before the V. C. came into the Saigon Embassy and liberated the general's mimeograph machine?

And what does "Vietnamization" mean? The word sounds like it came out of a Madison Avenue computer. I think it really means Occupation. Defense Secretary Laird says we plan to keep a "residual force" in Vietnam, even *after* the war is over, a violation of the Geneva accord of 1954. We still have 60,000 troops in South Korea, and with your 1953 mind, you probably think we can draw a line across Vietnam too. But the NLF's one nonnegotiable demand is that no American troops remain in South Vietnam after the war is ended. So could it be that you still secretly think the U.S. can insure a regime in Saigon that excludes the NLF? In that case, Vietnamization is a word totally bereft of meaning.

We have given you a gentleman's nine months to redeem your campaign pledges to find an end to this war. More than 8000 Americans have come home in wooden boxes during that time —100 last week.

So now the Armies of the Night are marching back to Washington, and this time we are the majority. You can't smear, or con, or coopt this army because it is based on an idea, and so it doesn't need any generals.

Speeches drafted by committees of former advertising copy writers, hound-dog stares into the television camera, cornball appeals to national destiny, patronizing "the young people," quoting JFK—none of it will satisfy this army of privates, until, as Martin Nolan has phrased it, the last round eye walks up the gangplank at Cam Ranh Bay, and comes home.

NOVEMBER, 1969

[FOUR]
NEW YORK POLITICS: A CLOWN SHOW

I think politics is a con game and I do not like politicians. The successful ones all lie too gracefully, are too narcissistic, and are too uncommitted to be trusted.

Perhaps for these reasons, one of my favorite pieces in this collection is the essay on Nelson Rockefeller, who struck me as personalizing everything false and cheap about politics.

On the other hand, John Lindsay has always been a chore for me to write about. Partly because I can't make up my mind about him, and partly because his true nature is so concealed. In the end, my ambivalence about Lindsay was best summed up by my friend Tom Johnston, who said, "Face it, Jack. Lindsay is our Eisenhower."

[1.]
"Stop the Election, I Want to Get Off"

BUFFALO, New York—Imagine Cicero, Illinois—conservative, provincial, corrupt, drab. Then magnify it by seven, put on the gloss of urban complexity, and you have an idea of what Buffalo is like.

Here in the state's second largest city antiwar pickets are regularly harassed and jailed by a little HUAC within the police department. The city is declining in vitality as the young leave and the old remain. Local journalists joke about the Mafia's subterranean power over city affairs.

Apart from the fact that he dances with a fine passion at the festivities of all the city's minority groups, Mayor Frank Sedita's only other claim on the public's interest is the persistence of the rumor that he is about to be indicted by a grand jury. His county leader has already been summoned twice before that body.

New York's Democrats climaxed their convention last week by bestowing on Mayor Sedita the privilege of running for the office of Attorney General.

The convention opened last Wednesday. The only excitement of the afternoon was generated by a group of Reformers who sought to insert an antiwar plank into the rather enlightened state platform. They hoped for at least a declaration favoring cessation of the bombings and direct negotiations with the National Liberation Front in Vietnam, a position accepted by about one-fifth of the United States Senate.

For a few hours it seemed that the Reformers and their allies from the suburban counties of Nassau and Westchester would gallantly lose their crusade for a principle, getting perhaps 200 of the convention's 1145 delegates to associate themselves with the lost cause.

But the peace plank menaced the surface tranquillity of the

convention. Brooklyn Congressman Abraham Multer and Congresswoman Edna Kelly drafted a "hawk" resolution going even beyond the Administration's strong position. National Committeeman Edwin Weisl then contacted the White House, and the President—reportedly in a tantrum—ordered Averell Harriman to crush the revolt. So Harriman, architect of the nuclear test-ban treaty, came before the Reform Democrats to say, "You can't rat on our boys in the trenches."

The Reformers then caucused, ignoring their potential allies in other delegations, and voted, after a fierce debate, 52 to 14 to accept a compromise approved by the White House, that "commended the President as a man of peace," but that also said that it "respects the rights of all Americans to hold opinions of their own and the free right of dissent." Former Councilman Paul O'Dwyer, West Side District Leader Victor Kovner, and all the delegates from the Village Independent Democrats and the Riverside Democrats voted against the compromise. All the Reform leaders who were delegates, including the legislators, voted for it.

The Reform establishment, rooted in the Lexington Club and stretching into the Bronx, claimed the compromise resolution was an historic victory. "They took us seriously, they negotiated with us, they had to deal with us," one delegate boasted. But late that night Senator Robert F. Kennedy told a Reform Assemblyman, "You gave up too easily. That resolution praised the President." The senator, however, had not given the Reforms any encouragement in their hour of confrontation with the White House.

Wednesday evening the delegates assembled at six to do their instructed duty of nominating Frank O'Connor for governor. The whole evening was carefully choreographed to the minute, so that O'Connor could deliver his acceptance address in the prime television hour between 10 and 11 P.M.

The hours passed in intolerable boredom. Delegates with jowly Broderick Crawford faces and $200 silk suits gossiped and joked, while terrible speeches were rasped into a microphone that had gone dead; but no one seemed to notice. In three hours of speechmaking there was not one interesting idea to violate the banality, not an original phrase; even bossism had become automated. A guaranteed annual income? Organize the welfare recipients? Pay dropouts to go to school? The Democrats never heard of such heresies.

The only creativity New York's Democrats have left is in the realm of shrewdness. In order to have Stanley Steingut's 154 delegates not vote for O'Connor, the roll was called backward, so that when Staten Island gave O'Connor a majority at 9:50 P.M., Samuels rushed to the podium to concede, and candidate O'Connor could say in truth he was nominated without the votes of Stanley Steingut. If the roll had been called in the traditional manner O'Connor would have been nominated without a single upstate vote.

It was Robert Kennedy's burden to introduce O'Connor. The senator is deeply bored by the kaleidoscopic tribalisms of New York politics. His is the mind of the curious novelist, rather than the mechanic absorbed by details; his span of concentration is brief when it becomes focused on tactical intrigues divorced from substantive issues. According to those who know him best, the senator finds almost all of the party's aspirants for glory uninteresting; Howard Samuels no more nor less than Robert Wagner or Abraham Beame. Kennedy specifically is skeptical about some of the affluent backroom types like Abraham Lindenbaum, the defrocked City Planning Commission member, who mingle in O'Connor's pluralistic entourage with producer Dore Schary. The senator's introduction of O'Connor to the convention was correct and proper, but nothing more. Later one of the nominee's less cerebral hangers-on would call it "chicken shit."

The O'Connor camp, for its part, has little love for Kennedy. There is about the O'Connor inner circle the cold fanaticism of men driven to redeem all the hurts they have suffered since 1962, by Wagner, by Screvane, by the Reformers, by Kennedy.

During O'Connor's acceptance speech Kennedy, standing a few feet behind, looked like a child attending his first funeral, testing a solemn look, not sure it was working. But the senator is a pro, and in the last week of October will be in the streets, charming and goading the multitudes to vote for O'Connor, just as he did for Beame last autumn. But, still, the senator knows of O'Connor's dream of becoming Hubert Humphrey's running mate in 1972.

The candidate's speech was overlong by twenty-five minutes, bereft of either music or the backbone of ideas. It limped along on phrases about getting New York moving again. It was apparent the O'Connor campaign would be fueled by Irish charm and the hope of exploiting the vague discontent with Rockefeller's

taxes and broken promises, just as the governor will exploit the vague mistrust of the bosses. And against both of them, Franklin D. Roosevelt, Jr., will cast the first stone.

On Thursday morning there was a revealing incident in front of the War Memorial Auditorium that most of the press ignored. There was a small, orderly antiwar picket line organized by Youth Against War and Fascism to dim the glory of Vice President Hubert Humphrey's appearance before the convention. Suddenly and without provocation, members of Buffalo's Office of Security Investigation (the equivalent of New York's red squad) arrested two of the pickets, one of them a young telephone operator on her lunch hour. A few Reformers, including Stanley Geller and Martin Berger of the VID, heard of the arrests and rushed to the police station to remind the city of Buffalo the Democratic Party had just endorsed the right of peaceful dissent. They threatened to carry the issue to the floor of the convention, and thereby embarrass Mayor Sedita, whose supporters, led by Comptroller Mario Procaccino in the "Italian caucus," were vowing a walkout if Sedita was not nominated for lieutenant governor. The mayor rushed from the convention to the courtroom, discovered the telephone operator used to date his son, and persuaded the judge, who happened to be his brother, to dismiss the case, while the cops looked on in impotent fury. So shaken was Sedita that he even agreed to dismiss charges against another group of students who were jailed for picketing the Vice-President the last time he visited Buffalo, to address the Polish Millennium of Christianity.

At noon, the Vice-President of the United States stood before the convention. The liberal Democrats gazed into that once reassuring face—the rosy cheeks, the furtive eyes, the rubbery smile—seeking some hint of the man they once knew.

In *The Making of the President—1964,* Theodore White quotes John Kennedy as remarking in deep melancholy of his decision to invade Cuba, ". . . It went around the table and everyone said 'yes,' but I was the last to speak, and I said 'yes.' I learned a lot from it. It would almost be worth what I learned from it—except that I can't get those 1200 men in prison out of my mind."

Does Hubert Humphrey's obsession with himself permit the kind of self-doubt that gave John Kennedy his extra dimension? Does the Vice-President, in the solitude of night, see images of na-

palm searing flesh? Is there, in the darkest corner of his mind, the half-formed idea that he might forsake his succession to the Presidency in order to denounce the most unexplainable war in his nation's history?

The answers came in the words Humphrey spoke. William Butler Yeats wrote that out of our arguments with others we make rhetoric, but out of our arguments with ourselves we make poetry. Humphrey spoke rhetoric.

The answer also came in the labyrinthian alliances secreted in the bowels of the Democratic Party. Hubert Humphrey, hero of the 1948 civil-rights revolt of the Democratic Convention, father of the ADA, was in Buffalo the ally of the worst in the Democratic Party: the fat cats and county leaders, the establishment men, the Steinguts and the O'Connors. He was the enemy of the best: the Reformers, the good government types, the peaceniks, the Kennedy faction. In the scorebook of presidential politics, Humphrey won in Buffalo and Robert Kennedy lost.

The convention adjourned after Humphrey's speech, scheduled to resume again at 3 P.M., as the leaders of the party met in the Statler Hotel to pick the rest of the ticket. In a single air-conditioned suite assembled Edward Weisl, the President's man; Marvin Rosenberg, an old ADAer, now representing Humphrey's interests; the powerful county leaders, Crangle of Erie, English of Nassau, Steingut of Brooklyn, Mayor Erastus Corning, the ambassador of seventy-seven-year-old Dan O'Connell's sheikdom called Albany County; O'Connor and his advisers; and state chairman John Burns. Senator Kennedy remained aloof in his suite, asking to be consulted and for the right of veto, but pushing no one except the imaginative choice of Columbia law school professor Jack Weinstein for Attorney General. "I'd like to see new faces, young people on the ticket," Kennedy told those who asked. He was to leave the city before the revolt on the convention floor against the ticket.

For two hours the county leaders bickered, more in panic than hate, among themselves. Manhattan Reformer Manfred Ohrenstein had already turned down an offer to run for Attorney General because O'Connor would not permit him to accept the endorsement of the Liberal Party. The leaders knew they needed a Reform type to legitimize the ticket, and they finally settled on Orin Lehman to run for Lieutenant Governor.

"Smart," shouted Steingut to Reformer Justin Feldman.

"No, mechanical," Feldman answered.

What had happened was that Reform leaders Richard Brown, an aide to Congressman James Scheuer, and Russell Hemenway, the chairman of the Reform Council for Democratic voters, had pushed Lehman in backroom negotiations, while never informing the Reform rank and file, who saw Lehman as weak, inexperienced, and cursed with the smell of a loser. They also resented the top-level, bureaucratic method of Lehman's would-be empire builders.

To appease the Italian caucus and balance the ticket geographically the leaders chose Mayor Sedita for Attorney General. They could not quite give him what he wanted, the lieutenant governor spot.

The first leader to break against the ticket was Manhattan's J. Raymond Jones—and for the worst of motives. The party leaders had awarded a $10,000 plum of delegate to the constitutional convention to Robert Carter of the NAACP, a Kennedy man. Jones exploded, and demanded the nomination go to NAACP leader Roy Wilkins, who had endorsed Tammany's Arthur Klein against RFK's Samuel Silverman last June.

The second recruit to the floor revolt against the ticket was Jack English, the tough, liberal leader of Nassau County. English, hurt when Eugene Nickerson's candidacy failed, was raging when the leaders turned down Jack Weinstein, a Nassau political activist, for the Attorney General's spot.

The third element in the revolt was two dozen small upstate counties, energized by parochial fury against Babylon on the Hudson. They wanted Samuels because he had visited their hamlets for the last four years, and they knew him as one of their own.

Even the Reformers rebelled against Lehman, whom they remembered as a two-time loser. Samuels seemed more deserving to them, and his defeat by O'Connor gave him the appealing scent of the victim.

By the time the county leaders arrived at the convention hall it was 5 P.M.; for two hours the delegates had waited, sensing indecision at the top. They rebelled, for good and bad motives, for Samuels. At 5:15 Lehman arrived at the convention, his acceptance speech already written. The O'Connor forces told him of the floor revolt and vowed they would still put him over with the votes of the county leaders, not the liberals or the Reformers.

Lehman gracefully withdrew and a Reform leader, mostly in sadness, said, "Poor Orin, he can't even win a fixed fight."

Back at the Statler Hotel, an inebriated delegate, a court clerk from Albany County, chewing on a cigar stump and wearing a straw hat, was bragging. "I don't know what the hell happened. I had to call my wife. She saw it all on the TV, and she explained what happened."

And Hulan Jack jubilantly was informing a friend, "This year we've got a great ticket."

SEPTEMBER, 1966

[2.]
Lindsay: A Year Later

November 2, 1965—The Hotel Roosevelt, just after 2 A.M. About 6000 people are rush-hour jammed into the plush grand ballroom. They are young, healthy, fashionably dressed; Princeton and Radcliffe etched in their Scott Fitzgerald faces. A Benny Goodman-style band is bathing the room in white swing. John Lindsay, after a seesaw duel, has just sprinted 90,000 votes up on Abe Beame on the ballots cast by middle-class, college-educated Jews from Brooklyn. Someone lobbed in copies of the last edition of the late *Herald Tribune,* whose banner headline proclaimed Lindsay the new mayor of New York. The glowing Scott Fitzgerald characters ripped up the papers and joyfully tossed the confetti into the electrified, smoky air.

Suddenly, a deep-throated animal yowl went up, starting at the entrance on the right and sweeping through the mob, recalling the special thunder of a fight crowd at an outdoor match when the champion pops out of the dugout and starts jiggling toward the ring pitched at second base. Forty-three-year-old John Lindsay, movie-idol handsome, radiating energy, was pushing in behind a wedge of cops towards the jungle of microphones on the podium. People, mostly young people, embraced, screamed, and a few wept for joy. John Lindsay, that ballsy Boy Scout, had somehow vanquished the whole malignant establishment of New York: Tammany, the union oligarchy, the civil service bureaucracy, the church, the underworld. In the gray transition weeks that followed there was born the flickering hope that New York City's cycle of riot-strike-blackout-shortage-apathy-resignation might somehow be broken; that sloth and cynicism had not yet congealed into the essence of our politics; that the city would regain its morale, its spirit, its zest for adventure.

At the moment Lindsay was sworn in last New Year's Eve, 550,000 of his constituents were on welfare. One million were liv-

ing in houses built in 1900. Water was scarce and the air polluted. About 850,000 whites had fled the city during the preceding decade. Two citizens were murdered each day and four women raped. The city had to borrow $250 million to balance the 1965 budget. And worst of all, under Robert Wagner, the city's eight million inhabitants had come to accept the nostrum that their city was permanently ungovernable. Five hours after Lindsay took his oath of office, the transit strike began.

Cut to election night, 1966. Lindsay was being blamed for departmental scandals that were not his fault. He was pale and exhausted from a recent virus infection. The magical rise of Robert Kennedy was casting an existential shadow across his own vague national ambitions. Some of his most trusted aides were preparing to quit, and he had not had time to begin seeking substitutes. In California, the old ladies in tennis sneakers were electing a new face to paste over the Goldwater movement. And his civilian review board was being washed away by the ugly backlash, nourished by the votes of the same middle-class Jewish districts that helped elect him the year before.

John Lindsay is as decent a human being as endures in the swamp of our national politics, one of the best since Stevenson: courageous, considerate, truthful, ethical, idealistic. One felt a little like a vulture dogging his trail on the night of his despair. The Irish-faced cops outside Gracie Mansion started joking early about "the mayor crying in his beer."

A little after 9 P.M. he took a ride to the FAIR headquarters at the Governor Clinton Hotel. There, the corridors and cubicles were clogged not with glowing Fitzgerald heroes, but with kids, sixteen and seventeen years old, hardly the troops of triumph. The mayor quickly disappeared into the office of campaign manager David Garth, while his wife Mary chatted warmly with the volunteers, loving them the way a general loves a vanquished platoon.

The first return of the night told the tale: a mere six to five edge for the review board in a heavily Negro and Puerto Rican assembly district in the South Bronx. Lindsay's face masked the sorrow. He fled quickly, Mary in tow, down the elevator, into the street. He did not see his limousine immediately, and for a few painfully symbolic seconds, the mayor of New York stood in the drizzle, in the middle of Seventh Avenue, trying to hail a taxi,

but they all sped past him, as if he were some Negro in Harlem.

Finally, an aide found the limousine around the corner, and Lindsay got in for the ride back to the Mansion. Speeding uptown he flicked on the portable television set in the car, watching the returns pour in.

Paul Adams, the Conservative Party candidate, the only one to oppose the review board, came on to goad the lagging Liberals, and spirited Mary Lindsay observed, "He looks like Hitler, doesn't he?"

Lindsay nervously switched the channel, and there was a popular interviewer's hard face.

". . . We have spoken to aides of the mayor," he was saying, "and none of them can explain why the review board is doing so badly in minority group areas . . ."

"You can explain, because you stabbed us in the back," Lindsay said to the television screen, his tone knifelike.

Then more national returns. The leads piled up by Agnew in Maryland and Percy in Illinois pleased Lindsay; Rockefeller's plurality seemed a more complex blessing.

The car phone rang and it was one of the Lindsay children calling from the FAIR headquarters; she wanted to stay out a little later. Lindsay the parent passed the phone to his wife, leaving it to Mary to negotiate one further hour with the child. The suggestion for a parental review drew a hearty laugh from Mary, and a stare from the mayor.

At 10 P.M. the limousine pulled into the Mansion driveway and Lindsay greeted the policeman on duty. Then, with the rain dribbling down, he disappeared into the Mansion, bigger than life but terribly vulnerable, not unlike the old Dodger first baseman Gil Hodges, trudging back to the bench after popping out with the bases loaded.

It was a graphic counterpoint to the scene of last year. Loneliness instead of adulation, silence instead of the crushing mobs, private pain instead of public pleasure.

More than anything else, Lindsay's first eleven months in office call to mind Ernest Hemingway's fable of the old man, Santiago, and the implacable sea. It was election night, 1966, that Lindsay caught his great fish. But the moment he turned toward port with his reward, all the uncountable piranha fish in the sea of politics began to follow him and strip the fish down to its fleshless skeleton, robbing him of its sweet taste.

It began with trade union oligarchs like Quill and Van Arsdale. Then city-hating, upstate, stone-age pols like Earl Brydges joined the pack. Then came Governor Rockefeller, Sargent Shriver, LBJ, Frank O'Connor and the two thirds of the city government pledged to emasculate Lindsay. Then came Robert Wagner, the righteous reformers, Kennedy and the backroom boys who still run his own party in the provinces outside Manhattan. And then the men he called the power brokers started biting into his prize: Robert Moses, Keith Funston, David Rockefeller. Lindsay possesses a noble Periclean vision of New York as a modern Athens, but after all the piranhas got finished stripping that vision, he was reduced to bending his knee before the P. B. A.'s John Cassese and, earlier, during the last newspaper strike, 308 members of the pressmen's union. Lindsay wants to revolutionize New York, but the columnists joke about Fun City. As Ruskin once remarked, "I show men their plain duty and they reply that my style is charming."

In terms of his day-to-day decisions and long-term innovations, Lindsay's first eleven months in office have been courageous. He killed the Lower Manhattan Expressway and blocked Huntington Hartford's park cafe. He began to breathe life into the city's sleepy bureaucracy. He has begun to humanize the police department and he broke up the ethnic mafia that ran it. He ended the department's cynical policy of entrapment of homosexuals and prostitutes. He initiated eleven low-income housing projects to be built in white, middle-class ghettos in the Bronx and Queens. He has begun to liquidate the obsolete civil defense bureaucracy. He has given the Department of Investigations greater independent powers. He has made repeated visits to the slums to lend visibility to the invisible men and dignity to those whose names nobody knows. He opened up a lobbying office in Washington for the city. He established the precedent of taxing commuters who earn their incomes in the city. He challenged the power of Con Edison and the Stock Exchange. He attracted the movie industry and boxing back to the city. His authentic concern helped prevent a major race riot last summer. He has even criticized the Vietnam war, saying several times, "It is about time we started asking what are the priorities in this country, Vietnam or Brownsville?"

Even Lindsay's appointments have been, on the whole, first rate. Thomas Hoving has sent an electric current of creativity through the Parks Department. Mitchell Ginsberg has begun to

modernize the antiquated procedures of the Welfare Department, cutting caseloads, trying to deal realistically with the problem of contraception. In Housing, abrasive Charles Moerdler has stepped up inspections, rooted out graft and led a top-down inspection of the city's schools. William Booth, the Human Rights commissioner, has gone after cabs who refuse to pick up Negroes and the entrenched bigotry of the construction unions. Mitchell Sviridoff, with his theory of centralized planning and decentralized administration, may yet reunify the floundering poverty program.

But for all this well directed energy Lindsay still looks like Gil Hodges—bigger than life, but vulnerable—for two reasons. One, the basic one, is that ultimately the root problems of the city—unemployment, housing, schools, finances—can no longer be solved within the city; they can only be solved in Washington with buckets full of federal money and a coherent policy of national reform. And two, Lindsay has made his share of mistakes, stemming mostly from inexperience and a stiff, unyielding personality.

His first blooper, one that disoriented his administration at birth, was his handling of the transit strike. His Billy Budd innocence made him underestimate the malevolent intent of Mike Quill. He kept aloof from the negotiations too long and during the collective bargaining kept confusing the words "arbitration" and "mediation."

His pathological dislike of "ideals" and "arrangements" victimized him during the intricate negotiations over his tax package in Albany.

If he had been more subtle and less combative he might have convinced Vincent Broderick, a man of uncommon decency, to accept the review board, stay on as police commissioner, and avoid the debacle of election day, 1966.

If there is another quibble with Lindsay's first eleven months, it is in the murky terrain of personality and psyche. It is his exasperating squareness, his puritan innocence, his Boy Scout pep talks. Occasionally Lindsay gives the impression (false, I suspect) that he believes old-fashioned good will and appeals to high-minded civic virtue can alleviate social problems built into the fabric of the system and defended by powerful forces. (The boys in the press room at City Hall alternate between calling the mayor Batman and Mr. Clean.)

Nowhere during Lindsay's painless pilgrimage from Buckley School to St. Paul's to Yale to Congress did he learn to hate with a radical's passion. Lindsay, because he is a humane and civilized man, is offended by bias and poverty and abridgements of the sacred First Amendment. But he lacks the bowel-churning hatred of slum dehumanization that punishes the brain until it makes a leap of intuition to assault a problem. Lindsay—and this can only be a guess—does not seem to be in touch with his own deepest feelings or his unconscious, the crucibles of imagination and passion. He seems too repressed, too stiff, too hard to talk to, too little introspective. Also, he seems too untouched by personal pain or grief to harness those secret inner resources that propelled FDR and John F. Kennedy to glory, and now seem to fuel Robert Kennedy's presidential happening. One of the mayor's aides calls him "a square saint," and another conjectures:

"I'll tell you what kind of guy Lindsay is. He's the type who, when he was at St. Paul's, would go down to New York drinking with the boys, but he would be the first one to get sick. And then he would go out for the lacrosse team, instead of football."

But, as with Hemingway's hero, Lindsay's basic problem is really not himself, or the lesser fish endlessly chewing away at his epic prize: it is the overwhelming size of the sea itself. It is the small-mindedness of politics and the frailties of human nature. Even if Lindsay's judgment is wise and his policies just, the catastrophe of the American city in 1966 is every bit as great as old man Santiago's sea was wide.

The phrase "crisis of the cities" is now a permanent fixture in our vocabulary, along with overkill and credibility gap and all the rest of the jargon of politics. Last August 21, however, when Lindsay testified before the Ribicoff Senate subcommittee probing that crisis, and asked for "50 billion dollars to transform New York in the next decade into a thoroughly livable and exciting place," the senators reacted as if he were Allen Ginsberg requesting the legalization of LSD.

Some of America's best politicians are now mayors: Lee in New Haven, Cavanaugh in Detroit and Lindsay here. But these men are victims caught in the fateful confluence of a conservative Congress, bigoted suburbs, backlash, inflation and the financial drain of the Vietnam war; like Santiago, prisoners of forces literally beyond their control.

What is Lindsay to do?

The voters have abolished his civilian review board, and if New York has its first winter riot now, they will still blame Lindsay. Lindsay wants more low- and middle-income housing, but in November 1965 the state's voters rejected a bond issue to subsidize the program. Lindsay wants money to raise the war on poverty above the level of the PR gimmick, but the President has let Congress cut the heart out of the teacher corps, water pollution, and demonstration city bills. These are the insatiable fish tearing the flesh from Lindsay's vision of a great, civilized city.

Compared to former Mayors Wagner and Impelliteri, compared to Yorty in Los Angeles, Locher in Cleveland, Daley in Chicago, John Lindsay *is* Pericles. But, measured against the horizon of urban decay, Lindsay seems more like Hemingway's solitary, tragic hero, displaying grace under pressure, against a hostile universe.

NOVEMBER, 1966

[3.]
John Vliet Lindsay: Uptight White Knight

Even now, two years after he took office, it is difficult to write about John Lindsay. He is so uninteresting. He is an example of the banality of decency. He is like an Andy Warhol sculpture—everything is on the gleaming surface. No subterranean dimension is suggested. The man and the image are one. There is no sense of mystery.

So even now, in the pit of the Marcus explosion and on the eve of the 1968 presidential campaign, the nation's only attractive Republican remains a chore to write about. Even his first press conference after the scandal broke across five columns in *The New York Times* was bereft of the unexpected, bereft of anything truly dramatic or spontaneous. There is something about this uptight White Knight which seems unrelievedly programmed. Even his considerable wit seems rehearsed first before some private mirror. He seems incapable, like those totally WASP characters in the fiction of John Updike and John Cheever, of making contact with his own deepest and truest feelings. He is forever Rock Hudson playing mayor.

The ritualistic judging of his mayoral performance, now at mid-passage, is also difficult, because one feels compelled to preface each clause of criticism with another clause acknowledging that no Democrat in town could do as well. One doesn't really like Lindsay, but one feels an urge to protect him.

Lindsay's actual achievements are not insignificant. Decentralization of the bureaucracy—local city halls and the Bundy Report are good examples—is not a dramatic cause, but he is far ahead of the Democrats on the issue. Richard Goodwin, the late President Kennedy's aide, has written that the issue of decentralization will dominate the politics of the 1970s. Despite the Marcus situation, the endless petty grafters of the Wagner administration have been thrown on the defensive if not completely rooted out.

The city now has trouble letting contracts because the competing firms figure that if no bribes are involved, it is too hard to figure out who's making the decisions, and still harder to work mutually advantageous arrangements.

Further, Lindsay has humanized the Police Department. Sadism is in retreat because City Hall is not hiding behind the camouflage of "no political interference with the Police Department." Largely because of Samuel Kearing, the Sanitation Department is more efficient and honest than it was under Wagner. And the city's spirit—its myth of itself—is no longer congealed by cynicism and despair, as it was under Fighting Bob.

That no progress has been made in the nitty-gritty areas of poverty and housing, Lindsay himself would find it hard to deny. These have been his twin failures. But they are primarily America's failures. It is Lyndon Johnson, Sargent Shriver, and John McCormack who have murdered the dream of a war on poverty. If there is no national will, no national funds, no national programs to attack poverty, what can a mayor do? Where can the resources come from?

If Lindsay does have one root flaw, it is his judgment of people. He is an innocent who assumes that everyone is as uncomplicated as he is.

For Lindsay to have chosen James Marcus over Samuel Kearing—just two months ago—to head the new environmental control superagency still makes the mind boggle. How could he have so misread the two men's characters? How many other Sammy Glicks does Lindsay have in his entourage?

The debilitating suspicion, common among Lindsay aides, testifies to the unhealthy atmosphere such doubtful operators can create. They still speak of "Price people" and "Lindsay people," in tribute to the former deputy mayor's puckish genius for intrigue. One of the mayor's most talented aides was in the doghouse for six months because his enemies in the administration convinced Lindsay he was leaking stories to *The Voice*.

It has long been a political cliché to compare Lindsay to John Kennedy because of surface similarities of style, politics, and attractiveness. But for Lindsay there is another potential equally possible. He can end up like former Massachusetts Governor Endicott Peabody, a decent, handsome WASP, who had an unfortunate weakness for questionable aides. What Lindsay seems to lack is Kennedy's large dose of irony and skepticism.

But there comes the inevitable need to compare Lindsay to his possible rivals in 1969. There is Representative John Murphy, slandering the antiwar movement (Lindsay is a dove). And there's Mario Procaccino, slasher of the municipal budget. And Frank O'Connor, who lined up with the Patrolmen's Benevolent Association against Lindsay.

The unfortunate thing about John Lindsay is that he is prissy and uptight, and I gather he is too little acquainted with the kinds of sins committed by other than gentlemen. These qualities and lacks reduce the magnitude of the man, rob him of dimension. But that's a matter of aesthetics or metaphysics.

What it all comes down to in the here and now is that Lindsay gets cheered in Harlem and Berkeley and cursed by taxi drivers and cops.

MAY, 1967

[4.]
Man of La Gotham: A Walker in the City

CAMBRIDGE, Mass.—At the start of every long, hot summer, people begin thinking about John Lindsay running for President. In the collective American fantasy of *High Noon* updated, tall, grim Lindsay strides down Lenox Avenue, into a subsiding storm of bricks. It is a comforting fantasy Lindsay has earned because he is the only white mayor in America, and a Republican mayor at that, to have the grudging trust of the black underclass.

As a congressman from an affluent, white district, Lindsay fought against the Kennedy and Johnson administrations to strengthen the 1964 Civil Rights Act. As a fusion candidate for mayor, he spent the last exhausting hours of his campaign on a Negro radio station, talking to the ghetto. As a leader of the Republican Party, Lindsay deserves most of the credit for the humane final version of the riot commission report. On the night of Martin Luther King's assassination, Lindsay and Kennedy were the only two white politicians in the land who could—or would—go into the ghetto.

But now, time is finally running out, even for John Lindsay. The racism of the suburbs, the indifference of the Congress, and the anticity bias of the state legislature, are converging to threaten the city's poverty program, and even its economy. Soon white America will have to surrender its Lindsay fantasy. Soon not even Lindsay will be able to walk the ghetto, because community service and antipoverty projects will begin to close for lack of funds.

America is now congratulating itself for enacting a misnamed open housing law that mostly is an antiriot law. But what is much more significant is that the current 90th Congress has cut $27 million out of the Headstart program, cut back ghetto health centers by another $27 million, butchered legal services by $9

million, community action programs by $30 million, the Job Corps by $10 million, and the Neighborhood Youth Program by $30 million. The rent supplement program has been reduced by 75 percent. Only last week, the Republican-Dixiecrat coalition led by Representative Ford sliced New York City's summer programs budget from $9 million to $5 million.

And in Albany, which has greater control over the city's economy, the cuts have been even more destructive—$60 million has been cut from state assistance to the city, 89 percent of the money to finance the narcotics program has been cut, and the Medicaid program has been slashed by $300 million, which means 700,000 city residents are no longer eligible for benefits (the same week, however, the legislature voted to increase its own pension benefits).

Two weeks ago Lindsay told an unresponsive luncheon of 1000 businessmen exactly what these budget cuts will mean for the poor of the city:

"Four city hospitals will have to be phased out. . . . 700 narcotics addicts will be returned to the streets uncured. . . . All state-assisted community education programs, after-school study halls and adult education programs will have to eliminated. . . . The staffs of 100 parks and playgrounds will be eliminated, and 100 child health clinics will close."

The effect of all this has been to make Lindsay the most alienated of our conventional politicians this season. It may be just a transient mood, but the mayor seems liberated these days. He acts the way Robert Kennedy acted in his angry autumn of 1966. Future events will probably trap Lindsay into compromises, like endorsing Richard Nixon, but right now he is swinging free.

He attacks GOP leader Gerald Ford, Speaker Travia, anyone he thinks is screwing the ghettos. He breaks protocol and goes after America's senior mayor, Richard Daley, for urging his policemen to shoot looters. Two weeks ago he tried to push cautious Otto Kerner into reconvening the riot commission. Last week he criticized Governor Rockefeller's timid urban program. This Saturday Lindsay will speak to the big antiwar march in the park, something McCarthy and Kennedy refused to do.

Last Friday Lindsay flew to Boston to speak at a $50-a-plate Republican fund-raising dinner, and at Harvard the next day. As

the press waited for the 4 P.M. shuttle to start boarding, they raided the airport newsstand, which happened to be loaded with Lindsay propaganda. A *New York Post* columnist praised him for his sensitive handling of the ghettos. *The Nation* nominated him for President. And *New York* published a cover story re-creation of Lindsay's actions in the hours following Dr. King's assassination. The Boston papers were naturally full of Lindsay.

There were no visible symbols of a national campaign. Lindsay was traveling with only two aides and his wife, Mary. There was no manufactured crowd to greet him at Boston's Logan Airport. The Lindsay staff did not even advance the trip; Sid Davidoff arrived in Boston only two hours before the mayor. But the idea of the Presidency, nevertheless, hung over Lindsay every minute he was in Boston.

At two abbreviated press conferences he was asked if he planned to run this year. At the Republican dinner, Representative Margaret Heckler called Lindsay "my favorite dark horse candidate for President." And Senator Edward Brooke, in his remarks, sounded like he was nominating Lindsay for President on the spot.

In his speech to 3500 white, upper-class, mostly surburban Republicans, Lindsay chose to speak about the value of the black youth in the ghetto.

"In the center cities," he said, "there are young men—mostly black—living their own special kind of street life. They miss something and they wish for something that has not yet been discovered on the streets.

"These young men are not a resource to be feared. There is no warmer, sounder, or firmer ally to have. These young men have lost contact with most of the institutions of our society, including the Republican and Democratic parties. They are not a politically captive group. The regular politicians, behind the drawn curtains of the old clubhouses, are just beginning to discover the power of this force."

At Harvard, at Saturday noon, Lindsay gave one of his best speeches in months. A half hour before he was scheduled to arrive, Sanders Theatre was filled with 1200 students, while another several hundred milled outside trying to get in. An editor of the *Crimson* and an activist from Students for a Democratic Society both estimated that next to Eugene McCarthy, Lindsay was the most popular politician among the Cambridge under-

graduates. When he arrived, twenty minutes late because he spoke briefly to those students who couldn't get in, Lindsay was applauded for almost two minutes.

The mayor began by speaking about "honesty in politics." "How many of the government officials," he asked, "who issued proclamations in city halls and state capitals across the nation on the death of Dr. King ever bothered to meet with him during his life, to talk with him, speak out for him, or walk with him? How many of the corporations that sponsored public memorials after his death had been willing to contribute those funds during his life to his organization, or to the cause he championed?"

But Lindsay, whose public speaking style remains tight and preachy, did not evoke spontaneous applause from his audience, that so plainly came to applaud him, until twenty-five minutes into his speech, until he began to speak of Vietnam.

"America has been guilty of deception and blindness in our involvement in Vietnam," he said, "in our refusal to acknowledge civilian casualties from the bombing of the North, in our unwillingness to admit the existence of the National Liberation Front. . . . We cannot spend more than $24 billion a year in Vietnam and still rebuild our cities. We cannot speak of nonviolence at home, when we are displacing, maiming, and killing thousands of Asians. . . ."

Then he closed with two paragraphs that came close to the nuance and music of poetry:

"The President talks of peace, but the war and the draft go on. Commitments have been renewed, but a man, and perhaps a movement, lie dead in Atlanta. And in our cities it is almost summer again.

"So I think you had better keep moving. I think you had better demand more than what you have gotten so far, until America comes home again."

The students stood and clapped for ninety seconds, just clapped, without stomping or screaming, or doing anything contrived. Then they followed the mayor out to his car. Boys with green and blue McCarthy buttons and Radcliffe girls in miniskirts shouted out embarrassed pleas that he run for President as his car began to pull away.

During some distant summer, John Lindsay will probably be running for President. But right now he is trapped between the

fantasy that he can personally cool the ghetto indefinitely, and the reality of projects and services being cut in Albany and Washington.

Lindsay's staff and family say that he sometimes wakes up in the middle of the night, and half awake, calls police headquarters to be reassured that all is tranquil. Some hot night he may be told that the fire has come to New York this time. But if that night ever comes, Lindsay will understand that it is Earl Brydges and Anthony Travia who should be indicted for inciting that riot, and not Stokely or Rap.

MAY, 1968

[5.]
There Was No Mystery

Columnists and politicians seem intent on extracting cosmic meanings from John Lindsay's reelection victory. They see the end of the two-party system, a mandate for more state aid and peace in Vietnam, proof the Jews are still liberals, proof the Jews are bigots, the glorification of the Liberal Party, and much more.

But I think it is foolish to draw any broad conclusions from any Election Day that saw a Republican elected governor of Virginia, the eighteen-year-old vote rejected in New Jersey, a working-class reformer elected mayor of Pittsburgh, and Carl Stokes reelected in Cleveland.

Locally, I would draw only one hard lesson from John Lindsay's victory. The mayor is a great campaigner, and Mario Procaccino was a lousy one. Period.

The Lindsay experience cannot be generalized to other cities, where there are not large black and Jewish voting blocs, and where no equivalent of the Liberal Party exists.

And I would not confuse Lindsay's *campaign* with Lindsay's *administration*.

Lindsay's reelection drive was well financed, well paced, well planned, and perfectly executed by the candidate. Lindsay is a terrific racehorse. He looks good. He likes crowds. He knows how to shade and twist the facts to put the best face on any situation. He has enormous physical stamina. And he has pride and toughness beneath his Billy Budd exterior.

But the reason the campaign was so effective is that none of the regular city commissioners had anything to do with it. Of the five key campaign strategists, only one, Sid Davidoff, was part of the first Lindsay administration. The others—Dick Aurelio, David Garth, Mrs. Ronnie Eldridge, and Alex Rose—were all outside City Hall. And Lindsay himself is just much better as a campaigner than as an executive. In Professor James Q. Wilson's

useful categories, Lindsay has always been more interested in his "audience" than in his "constituency."

No one can ignore the dramatic dimensions of Lindsay's comeback from the far side of oblivion. Last winter his aides took a private poll that showed 74 percent of the city "disapproved" of Lindsay's performance as mayor. His wife and his press secretary were urging him not to run again, citing the examples of his friends Ivan Allen in Atlanta, Richard Lee in New Haven, and Jerome Cavanaugh in Detroit. Last February 6, I went to the Forest Hills Jewish Center with Lindsay, and watched middle-class Jews who had voted for Lehman, Wagner, and Robert Kennedy call Lindsay redneck names under the shadow of the Torah. And after he lost the Republican primary to John Marchi, syndicated columnist Russell Kirk wrote that Lindsay had "no chance" of being reelected, and that his career "was finished!"

But it turned out that Lindsay's defeat in the primary was, in Alex Rose's words, "a blessing *not* in disguise." Defeat liberated Lindsay from his past, from the Republican Party nationally, and from his own arrogance.

The afternoon after the primary he started calling up liberal Democrats, and meeting with them, and listening to them, and learning what really went on in remote neighborhoods, and learning that not everything his own commissioners told him was the truth. And he went out to Bayside and Flatbush, and talked to community groups, and began to get some idea of what the daily lives of clerks, and factory workers, and secretaries were actually like.

At the start of the campaign on Labor Day, Lindsay was probably 200,000 votes behind Procaccino. But soon he started to get every possible break, beginning with an unsolicited testimonial from Manhattan District Attorney Frank Hogan, which helped defuse the law and order issue. Then Procaccino made the mistake of agreeing to the *The New York Times* minidebate, which generated professional envy among the electronic reporters, who quickly made Procaccino's ducking of a live television debate an issue. And soon after college opened, hundreds of students were recruited to work on "issue canvassing." And they impressed many voters with their dedication, if not their arguments.

Next came the steady flow of endorsements from liberal Jewish Democrats—Arthur Goldberg, Ben Rosenthal, Arthur Katzman, and others. The Vietnam Moratorium on October 15 made the war rather than race the most deeply felt issue in the city, and underscored Lindsay's long-held antiwar convictions.

The *Daily News* poll showing Lindsay far in the lead appeared on October 23, and this loosened up a lot of money for Lindsay in the home stretch. On election eve the Knicks won their eleventh game in twelve starts. And then Robert Wagner decided to vote early on Election Day.

And in the end, what also won it was Lindsay's own toughness as a long distance runner, the thousands of people who volunteered to canvass and poll-watch for him, the incredible political consciousness in the ghettos that gave Lindsay 85 percent of the black vote without the benefit of the Democratic Party line. And the fact that Lindsay actually became a better mayor after the primary, and this is what gave credibility to his campaign themes of humility and reconciliation.

The postelection fashion, however, to mythicize the Liberal Party seems to me too simplistic. Alex Rose is clearly some sort of tactical wizard, but the Liberal Party as an institution is just a franchise and an employment agency. As Pete Hamill says, "Do you know anybody who has been in a Liberal Party clubhouse?"

Ideally, the Liberal Party should just be one partner in the Lindsay fusion coalition, along with the NDC; the neighborhood groups like the task forces, planning boards, and "little city halls"; and humanist unions like the hospital workers, District 65, and Victor Gotbaums's Local 37. This is the alliance that will have to keep the pressure on Lindsay to redeem his campaign pledges on decentralization, rent control, the maintenance of the 20-cent fare, and his political independence.

Now the problem facing the Mayor is to translate the energy and expertise of the campaign to his second administration.

He clearly made his share of blunders the first time around. As many observers have pointed out, he should have experimented with school decentralization first in white middle-class neighborhoods, so the UFT couldn't have twisted it into a racial issue instead of an educational issue. There were concrete administrative reasons the snow wasn't collected in Queens last winter. There was sabotage, and there was sloth, and there was corruption.

Also, Lindsay's judgment on appointments in the past was too often swayed by inflated but false reputations. Of his fifteen top commissioners, only four have impressed me: Fred Hayes in budget, Howard Leary in police, Ken Patton in Commerce, and Bess Myerson Grant in Consumer Affairs. New blood seems particularly required in the Parks Department, in HRA, and on the City Planning Commission if Lindsay is to have a new beginning as an executive.

But the fact remains that John Lindsay is now the only national political figure independent of both parties, and with a following among the urban, peace, black, and youth constituencies.

I have followed Lindsay's person and career closely since his days as a maverick Congressman. The first piece I ever published in *The Voice,* in November of 1963, was one promoting Lindsay for mayor.

I have since then sporadically regretted that flight of fancy: the night he seconded Agnew's nomination, his days of ambivalence during the second and third school strikes, his lingering failure to identify with the frustrations of low-income whites.

But I now think that Lindsay has fundamentally been changed for the better by the events of the last nine months. He has become more humble, more skeptical, more open—and less Republican. He has been educated by his painful journey through the boroughs, and humbled by his need to reach out for fusion with his recent critics.

With the diminished stature of both Ted Kennedy and Eugene McCarthy, Lindsay's future seems limited only by fate and his own frailties.

But first, and now, he must prove his worth in the bankrupt battle pit of City Hall. And this time he had better do it right, because no one has ever heard of a Third Coming, either in religion or politics.

NOVEMBER, 1969

[6.]
The Case Against Nelson Rockefeller

[1]

Let me tell you about the very rich, they are different
from you and me. They possess and enjoy early, and it
does something to them. It makes them soft where we
are hard, and cynical where we are trustful. . . . They
think, deep in their hearts, that they are better than we
are.

—F. SCOTT FITZGERALD

[2]

It was in the middle of January, and the subway fare had just
been raised to 30 cents, and the sun was slanting through the
windows in silver shafts, and John Lindsay was sitting behind his
desk, his glasses on top of his head.

"They tell me you're doing a piece on Nelson," the mayor said.
"I'll give you a title for it. You should call it 'The Last Colonialist,' because that's what Nelson is all about.

"He just doesn't believe in local participation, in the common
sense of ordinary people. He thinks he knows what's best for
everyone. So he walks right in and builds things, big things. He's
a colonialist."

Lindsay was right. He cut to the core of Nelson Rockefeller, to
the central distinctive quality of the governor's sensibility. Perhaps *paternalist,* or *technocrat,* or *elitist* is a better word, but the
idea is the same. It is a set of mind and character beyond the
postures of politics. It is the sensibility behind Lincoln Center;
the new billion-dollar Mall in Albany; the report to President
Nixon on Latin America, justifying close relations with military
dictatorships; his criticism of Eisenhower in 1960 for not building more modern missiles and submarines. It is his indifference

to the idea of community control or participation. It is his stacking of the Metropolitan Transportation Authority with white, rich, suburban bankers and corporation executives. It is, in sum, his elitist social engineering, bereft of soul and blind to the consequences his manipulations lead to.

[3]

Most people think that Nelson Rockefeller is a liberal. Even the restless college campuses thought that in the hopeful spring of 1968. That's Rockefeller's image.

To many voters he is still "Rocky," campaigning lustily among the masses in 1958, gulping bagels, blintzes, and pizza, personifying *machismo* and modernity in contrast to poor wooden Averell Harriman. To many voters he is still the spokesman and symbol of the progressive wing of the Republican Party—the gallant, hurt man standing up to the torrent of abuse from the Goldwater yahoos at the 1964 Republican National Convention, playing noble Christian to the lions while the world watched on the tube. In 1966, running for reelection, he was the "liberal" candidate, endorsed by the *New York Post,* no less. In 1968, he was the last-chance avatar of the "new politics," who picked up the banner after Robert Kennedy was assassinated and Eugene McCarthy faltered. (In *The Making of the President 1968,* Theodore H. White simplistically equated Rockefeller's campaign with Kennedy's: "The crowds were the same. The message was the same.")

Such was, and perhaps still is, Rockefeller's reputation. I can still remember the summer of 1968 and all those rolling *New York Times* editorials lionizing the Governor, and all the chic cocktail chatter around the West Side, cheering him on, even speculating for a few weeks about a Rockefeller-McCarthy "dream ticket."

But the fact is that Nelson Rockefeller has grown increasingly conservative and out-of-touch over the years. Though his rhetoric still goes through seasonal cycles of enlightenment—an election year quickens whatever liberal impulses remain—his actions and decisions are at odds with his image:

On the transcendent issue of our time, Vietnam, Rockefeller has been a plainclothes hawk.

He passionately supported the deployment of the antiballistic

missile system, even lobbying with Republican Senators to vote for it.

One of the richest men on the planet, he coldly slashed welfare for mothers with children to 66 cents a day.

In 1965 he vetoed a bill guaranteeing a $1.50-an-hour minimum wage.

While millions of people in the state live in substandard housing, he was an evangelist for a cockeyed cold war scheme to build fallout shelters.

Under his strong leadership, the State Legislature passed legislation giving police the right to shoot to kill a fleeing suspect, as long as the cop "reasonably believes" the suspect is armed. He also sponsored the notorious "no knock" and "stop and frisk" bills and consistently backed legislation mandating civil commitment of narcotics addicts.

In 1966 he refused to join Lindsay, Javits, and Robert Kennedy in supporting a civilian complaint review board for cases of alleged police brutality.

He supported John Marchi over John Lindsay after the Republican primary last year, even though Republicans like Senator Charles Goodell and Congressman Ogden Reid found it possible to break party ranks and endorse Liberal Lindsay.

He posed for pictures on a balcony with Haitian dictator François Duvalier, in a tropical parody of the Humphrey-Maddox embrace.

He forced New York City to raise bus and subway fares by 50 percent while spending billions for upstate highways.

And in January of this year, Rockefeller backed up Richard Nixon's veto of the $19.7-billion education appropriation bill.

The record shows that Rockefeller has officially taken liberal positions on the eighteen-year-old vote, on pollution, and on abortion reform. But a closer look reveals these positions as mere posturing—some style, but no substance. On these issues he doesn't *really* push and lobby when it can make a difference. For part of Rockefeller's considerable skill as a politician is his ability to function at multiple levels of seriousness and deception.

Says Assemblyman Albert Blumenthal, who had devoted three futile years to trying to pass an abortion-reform bill:

"The Governor *said* he supported my bills, but he didn't *mean* it. It was an *act*. Behind the scenes, where it counted, he didn't help. And he controls those Republicans in the legislature. Ev-

erytime he really wants something, he gets it. He's so damn *cynical.*"

Says Westchester Congressman Richard Ottinger, a long-time critic of Con Edison's Storm King hydroelectric power project and Rockefeller's proposed $250-million six-lane Hudson River Expressway:

"Rockefeller is the most cynical politician I know of. He announced that he would clear up all the waters of New York State by 1970. But he *knew* that was impossible. Now he *says* the program is going beautifully, and that gets into all the papers. But he's committed only $46 million out of a billion-dollar bond issue to solving the pollution problem. He just *says* something, and because the numbers are so complicated, the press doesn't follow up. He just wants to give the appearance of doing something about a very difficult problem, without bothering to really *change* conditions."

[4]

Nevertheless, the image of Rocky the liberal endures, for several reasons.

First, he once really *was* a liberal.

Second, he is smart. He rewards his friends. He has a good sense of timing (except in deciding when to announce for President). He has mastered an essential element in political life—the art of behaving as if no one has any memory. He can contradict himself and praise men he loathes. He is, in short, a very good politician.

Third, the press genuinely likes him. His resources permit him to treat the working press royally. He has a private jet. On trips he feeds reporters wine and steak. Mayor Lindsay doesn't even provide coffee at his twice-weekly City Hall press conferences. Rockefeller's staff, the best money can buy, is generally helpful and accessible. It is *pleasant* to cover him.

Fourth, as governor, Rockefeller can insulate himself from the more irreverent press and alienated public whenever he cares to. Often the press doesn't even know where he is—Albany? Manhattan? Tarrytown? Washington?

Finally, there is the specter of the Rockefeller billions. As one important Democrat summarizes it:

"Nelson's personal fortune, plus the bank [Chase Manhattan, whose chairman is brother David], plus IBEC*, plus the Rockefeller Foundation, plus the Rockefeller Brothers Fund and other charities, and all that corporate clout, can buy *anything*—black militants, unions, congressmen, publishers, *anything*. Nelson once donated $300,000 to a college to win over a powerful publisher who was an alumnus of the college. Chase Manhattan gives mortgages to a lot of black churches, whose ministers always endorse the governor. The family has paid off heavy statewide debts of the Republican Party for years. He uses the Foundation to supplement salaries and help out guys after he's used them up, to make sure they don't turn against him. In 1966 he spent at least $20 million. You just can't beat that kind of money."

[5]

Alignment with the inanimate is the mark of a Bad Guy.

—THOMAS PYNCHON, *V*

They couldn't keep Nelson off the construction site of Rockefeller Center when he was a youngster. He walked around with a workman's hard hat, and he loved every minute of it.

—A REPUBLICAN CONGRESSMAN

Some call it an Edifice Complex. What they mean is that Nelson Rockefeller loves to build things, big, well-designed, highly visible *things*—office buildings, roads (more than 15,000 miles of highway since 1958), cultural complexes, like those in Saratoga and Niagara Falls, that serve the consumers of kitsch. Even functional things. Rockefeller has probably changed the physical face of New York more than any governor since DeWitt Clinton built the Erie Canal.

* IBEC—International Basic Economy Corp., founded by the Rockefeller brothers in 1947. In 1967 IBEC produced a profit of $3.6 million from projects like supermarket chains in Venezuela and Peru, and housing construction in Puerto Rico and Mexico. The Rockefeller Brothers Fund has about $150 million in assets and is one of the fifteen largest foundations in the country. This is different from the Rockefeller Foundation, which is the second biggest, next to Ford. All these institutions have offices in Rockefeller Center.

But, there is a *but.* Local communities, the powerless and usually black families who live in the path of the bulldozer juggernaut, have never had any say about this construction, and thousands have been uprooted and dumped even deeper inside the other America. The governor has appropriated a lot of money to construct hospitals, but the new $5.2-million Children's Hospital in the Bronx is now standing two-thirds empty, manned by a skeleton staff because there was no money left in the budget for the less visible component of nurses, doctors and equipment. He produced a budget surplus last year, but the cities paid for it, not the corporations, not the landlords.

The new South Mall in downtown Albany will be modern and convenient, but it is being built by construction unions that have imported hundreds of white workers from Canada to avoid employing local black labor. The billion dollars being spent on this complex of state office buildings could be used to build a new high school in every school district in the state—thirty-one new high schools in New York City alone. (When the Mall project was first announced in 1964, Rockefeller said it would cost only $250 million.)

Rockefeller's passion for buildings results in jobs for the building trades unions, which in turn support Nelson Rockefeller politically. In 1966, when Rockefeller almost carried New York City against Frank O'Connor, there were signs on many construction sites that read: "Protect Your Job—Vote Rockefeller."

Peter Brennan of the building trades and Harry Van Arsdale, president of the New York City Central Labor Council, endorsed Republican Rockefeller in 1966 and will probably do so again this year. Murray Kempton once summed up the building trades leadership by saying, "They would build gas ovens if it was steady work."

All that state money, all those taxpayers' millions ($895 million in 1968), is spent on things for the middle class. There is not enough money for Medicaid, or welfare, or rent subsidies, or a subsidy for the subways, or enough financial aid to stop the inner cities from their slide toward rot and racial polarization.

[6]

The time Nelson Rockefeller didn't keep a deal with John Lindsay.

First, some background. In September of 1966 Rockefeller decreed—confidently, like a good colonial administrator—that the state would build a $20-million state office building and cultural and civic center in Harlem, at 125th Street and Seventh Avenue. The next year the State Legislature refused to appropriate the funds for the civic-cultural center, but the governor decided to push ahead anyway with his office building. Slowly, resentment against the planned twenty-three-story structure grew in Harlem, fed by the state's cavalier cuts in *human programs* for welfare, Medicaid and education. Last June some squatters and street militants began camping out on the site, demanding that public housing or a school be built instead. At the time, *The New York Times* quoted Harlem State Senator Basil Paterson as saying, "Rockefeller never discussed this thing with the Harlem community. The only discussion was when they set up a committee of about thirty-two people to discuss the site of this thing. But it was a *fait accompli*. They decided beforehand what they were going to put there. It was done without ever determining what are the needs of the community." Finally, last summer, Rockefeller ordered construction temporarily suspended.

Cut to September 22, 1969. Rockefeller has now decided to get on with the job and to use the police to clear the site of the squatters. Mayor Lindsay, making his underdog's run for reelection, is objecting, saying the community has not been involved in the decision-making. And besides, a bust now could trigger violence, which could hurt his campaign. Rockefeller counters by saying the Harlem community now supports his position, and stage-manages endorsement from "community leaders"—Hulan Jack, Charles Rangel, and some businessmen and ministers.

So on the afternoon of September 22, there is a private meeting between the mayor and the governor to settle the dispute. Present are Deputy Mayor Robert Sweet, Police Commissioner Howard Leary, Lindsay aides Ted Gross and Barry Gottehrer, Al Marshall, one of Rockefeller's top staff members, and Benjamin Frank, a consultant to the governor.

The Lindsay people argued first that Rockefeller postpone the bust until after the November election. Marshall said no. Then they urged the governor to use the injunctive court process to evict the demonstrators, but Marshall again said no, the state would file criminal trespass charges, and the police raid would be made the next morning. After the meeting broke up, Sweet wrote

the following memorandum to Marshall summarizing the agreement he thought he had reached:

". . . The city has requested the state to provide an authorized state official on the scene [of the bust] to deal initially with any interference with construction, to file any charges which may be appropriate, to proceed continuously with construction in order to minimize any interference with the undertaking, and to provide sufficient security to insure that the site and the equipment on the site remain secure. I understand that the state will comply with these requests, and that it is the present intention of the State Office of General Services to commence work on the site at 7 A.M., September 23."

Four simple conditions to try to prevent violence, and to show clearly that Rockefeller, not Lindsay, had chosen to call in the police. Four simple promises, and every one of them was broken. Says Lindsay, "They didn't keep their word on one of the four points. It was almost a disaster. They just wanted to screw me."

Adds one the Lindsay men present at the meeting: "The governor lied to us and lied to the police. His guy never showed up. The construction didn't begin until noon. They only sent six security men instead of the twenty-five they promised. His press guy split. They arrested people who never spent an hour on the site. They did everything wrong. And that night there was a lot of bottle-throwing in Harlem. It could have been very bad, and we were just lucky. All because Rockefeller wanted to get his way and make Lindsay look bad. Then came the last straw. Rockefeller's people leaked a story to the *Times* that *we* were afraid to act decisively. We were so mad that we just opened up our files to the *Times*. The *Times* never printed *that* story."

[7]

Their hero was one of the wealthiest men in the world; he was one of the most stubborn men in the world; he was also one of the most high principled. His enemies called him, quite simply, the most ruthless man in politics. But what in other men could be simply arrogance, was in Rockefeller the direct and abrupt expression of motives, which, since he knew them to be good, he expected all other men to accept as good also.

—THEODORE H. WHITE, *The Making of the President 1964*

[8]

All successful liberal politicians, to some degree, twist the truth, display arrogance or pettiness, and act in a ruthless way against political adversaries. This was true of FDR, Harry Truman, and the Kennedy brothers. It is the ransom good guys pay for winning elections, and it is the reason real saints either become poets, lead nonviolent movements, or go nuts. But what is distinctive about Nelson Rockefeller is that he has been ruthless to achieve dubious ends, all the while keeping his liberal credentials. Rockefeller has not been a bully against an obstructionist Supreme Court, or against a disobedient five-star general, or against U.S. Steel, or against the Mafia, or against the California grape-growers. His arrogance has asserted itself for regressive sales taxes and against decent political foes.

In 1962, the central theme in Rockefeller's reelection campaign against Robert Morgenthau was that the state's fiscal structure was sound, and that there would be no need for new taxes during his second administration. Soon after he was reelected Rockefeller did raise taxes, only he called them "fees." A few years later, he admitted his no-tax pledge was "my greatest blooper." So through chutzpah and counterfeit humility, he won a third term.

Last year, Nelson Rockefeller was in trouble and badly needed two Democratic votes in the Assembly to pass his budget. So two Democrats—Charles Stockmeister of Rochester and Albert Hausbeck of Buffalo—changed their minds overnight and decided to vote for the governor's new sales tax, which hits the welfare mother and the corporation executive equally hard. On July 3, when few people buy papers, much less read them, a press release went out from Albany announcing the appointment of Assemblyman Stockmeister to a $26,000-a-year job on the Civil Service Commission. After the appointment, an important Democratic politician said: "It's a good example of Rockefeller's high-handedness. It isn't that he's corrupt. He's just so used to authority, so convinced of his own superior view of the public good, that he thinks his methods are fair play."

Then there is the case of Nelson Rockefeller's smear campaign in the media against Frank O'Connor in 1966. To begin with,

Rockefeller was able to outspend O'Connor twenty to one in that election. According to James M. Perry's excellent book *The New Politics: The Expanding Technology of Political Manipulation,* Rockefeller put 3,027 paid commercials on television during the campaign. His organization distributed 27 million brochures, buttons, and broadsides—four-and-a-half pieces per voter. His paid campaign staff totaled over three hundred. O'Connor had fewer than twenty.

One of Rockefeller's slick, brilliant television spots, which dominated the airwaves in the last weeks of the campaign, said: "Frank O'Connor, the man who led the fight against the New York State Thruway, is running for governor. Get in your car. Drive down to the polls, and vote." The fact is that O'Connor did not "lead" any fight against building the Thruway. He was only a Queens state senator at the time. His actual position was that the Thruway should be *free.* Rockefeller had insisted on tolls.

On the complex, volatile issue of narcotics, Rockefeller out-Goldwatered Goldwater. Early in the 1966 campaign he kept playing a television commercial that began with a police car cruising down a dark, deserted street. Then the announcer said: "If you walk home at night, or if there's a teen-ager in your family, you should be worried. Governor Rockefeller is worried. As much as half the crime in New York is caused by addicts. That's why the governor has sponsored a tough new law that can get addicts off the street for up to three years. . . ."

Then in the final days of the campaign, Rockefeller talked directly into the camera in an early-evening saturation campaign. "If you want to keep the crime rates high," he said, "O'Connor is your man."

O'Connor's opposition to Rockefeller's punitive rather than curative narcotics program made sense, and was shared by doctors, civil liberties groups, and Reform Democrats. But O'Connor never had enough money to get his side of a very problematic issue across to the voters. When the campaign was all over, most people forgot about the governor's cleverly packaged appeals to fear.

[9]

Nelson came up to me at a dinner the other night and
asked me why I was giving him such a hard time on the
fare increase. He said I knew he was right.
—THEODORE KHEEL, FEBRUARY 1970

They should make that rich bum give up his airplane,
give up his helicopter, give up his limousine, and make
him just once ride a subway to Ozone Park at rush hour.
—JIMMY BRESLIN, FEBRUARY 1970

The story of exactly why New York City's mass transit fare was
raised 50 percent by the MTA in January of 1970 must begin with
a simple list of those MTA board members (all appointed by Nelson Rockefeller) who voted for the fare increase without even
holding a public hearing:

Leonard Braun, President of the Newport Petroleum Company
of Mineola, Long Island;

William Butcher, chairman of the board, the County Trust
Company of White Plains;

Eben W. Pyne, senior vice-president, First National City Bank,
who lives in Old Westbury, Long Island;

William J. Ronan, chairman of the MTA, who for seven years
was secretary and adviser to Rockefeller.

The MTA includes no commuter, no poor person, no woman,
no student, no black or Puerto Rican, no union representative.*
It consists exclusively of affluent people who rarely use the dirty,
unreliable, overcrowded, cold, dangerous New York City subways.

In the chaotic days immediately after the fare hike went into
operation, Lindsay and Rockefeller each tried to place the onus
on the other. This left the public confused, and generally thinking all "politicians" were at fault. And some politically sophisticated people I spoke to, like David Gelber of *Liberation* magazine, and my *Voice* colleague Mary Nichols, tended to be angrier
at Lindsay than at Rockefeller for not being more skillful
and/or forceful.

* In 1969, Rockefeller vetoed a bill that would have added four commuters
to the board of directors of the Long Island Rail Road.

But Ted Kheel told me: "The mayor did everything possible to save the 20-cent fare. He endorsed my suggestion for an increase in the gasoline tax, an increase in auto registration fees, and an increase in the bridge and tunnel tolls into Manhattan. On some of those things we needed the State Legislature's approval. But the MTA could have raised the bridge and tunnel tolls on its own. . . . Dr. Ronan just refused, and never gave us a reason for it. . . . On the other parts of my proposal, the governor said the legislative leadership wouldn't go along, but he was obviously not really for them himself. . . . If the MTA had just doubled the bridge and tunnel tolls we might have kept the fare at 25 cents, but at least we could have improved the quality of the ride."

I asked Kheel whether there was any political tension within the MTA during the negotiations. He replied, "No, not really. Ronan controls a clear majority there, and he was apparently in close touch with the governor all the time."

[10]

Winning the fight for freedom in Vietnam is essential to the survival of freedom in all of Asia. The communist Vietcong guerrillas must be defeated. . . . The Administration should declare without reservation that it will withdraw no more American forces from Vietnam until the military situation justifies such action. The Administration should make clear that it supports the existing government in Saigon, and should cease from criticizing it. . . .

—NELSON ROCKEFELLER, CAMPAIGNING
IN OREGON, APRIL 27, 1964

Nelson Rockefeller is one of the few governors who have a distinct foreign policy. Mostly Rockefeller implements his foreign policy away from public scrutiny, through the Chase Manhattan Bank and IBEC, through reports and private meetings with the President, through getting his friends appointed to jobs in the State Department and the White House staff. The records show that he is one of the most unreconstructed cold warriors remaining in American politics. He is probably more military-oriented and more rigidly anticommunist than even Richard Nixon.

Rockefeller has been a hard-liner since the 1950s. In the spring of 1960, after the U-2 crisis, when he was trying to jar the Presidential nomination loose from Nixon, he began attacking Nixon for not doing enough about defense spending. Rockefeller asked for more submarines, more missile bases. He demanded that the government spend at least $3 billion more for modern weaponry. He called for a greater sense of urgency about waging the cold war. Rockefeller wanted more experts, more efficiency, put into the Defense Department. He was a premature McNamara.

In 1961 Rockefeller tried to promote his fallout-shelter scheme as part of his notion of total preparedness, of maximum mobilization in case the Russians were coming. Queens state senator Jack Bronston, who has watched the governor operate for a decade in Albany, recalls the shelter craze: "Fallout shelters was the single policy most consistent with Nelson's real personality. Despite strong opposition, he fought for his plan with everything he had. His program was literally a $200 bomb shelter in everybody's backyard. I remember one afternoon when he invited a bunch of us into the red room at the mansion in Albany, and he had all these maps on the wall. And these maps had nuclear bombs exploding all over them in color. And he gave us a long, emotional lecture on how many lives the shelters could save in case of nuclear attack. I think he was more sincerely committed to that shelter program than anything since then."

Through the volcanic 1960s the cold war thawed. The Sino-Soviet split grew into a bitter ideological struggle. Relations between the U.S. and the Soviet Union grew warmer, despite the Vietnam War. The Nuclear Test Ban Treaty was signed and not violated. But Nelson Rockefeller remained frozen in his 1950s stance. Last year he supported the Safeguard system of nuclear-missile defense. Ogden Reid told me that Rockefeller even lobbied behind the scenes in Washington to delay American participation in the arms limitations talks (SALT) with the Soviet Union in Geneva.

In his lengthy report to the President on Latin America last year, Rockefeller offered this rationalization for doing business with right-wing dictatorships:

"The authoritarian and hierarchal tradition, which has conditioned and formed the cultures of most of these societies, does not lend itself to the particular kind of popular government we are used to. Few of these countries, moreover, have achieved the

sufficiently advanced social and economic systems required to support a consistently democratic system. For many of these societies, therefore, the question is less one of democracy, or lack of it, than it is simply of orderly ways of getting along."

And there has been Vietnam.

The Vietnam war has been an agony for this country for almost ten years now. More than 40,000 Americans have died in that war. It has divided the nation as much as any issue since the Civil War itself.

The politicians who have reached for national or moral leadership during the 1960s have all been tested on this great moral issue of our time. The best of them—Fulbright, Lindsay, Kennedy, McGovern, McCarthy—all risked something by speaking plainly against the government's policies.

Of all our national political figures, Nelson Rockefeller has perhaps the shabbiest record on this issue, because he has not even been true to himself.

Rockefeller has been a hawk all along. He believed in the original commitment, in the domino theory, in the pacification program, in the sending of American combat troops, in the search-and-destroy missions, in the various regimes in Saigon, in the bombings of the North, and now in Vietnamization. He has said this privately, and on rare occasions, as during the Oregon primary, he said it in public. From 1964 until 1968, however, he told the press that he had "no position" on the issue that was tearing the country apart.

But for two months in 1968, between Robert Kennedy's assassination and the Republican National Convention, Nelson Rockefeller sounded like a dove. He bought full-page newspaper ads and sixty-second television spots urging peace. He recited the slogans of the peace movement as he campaigned at universities and in the suburbs. But the moment Richard Nixon and Spiro Agnew were nominated at Miami Beach, Rockefeller became a hawk again.

Last fall, when the antiwar movement swelled again for the Moratorium and the November 15 Washington demonstration, Rockefeller was on television praising the President's "handling of the war." Again Rockefeller counted on no memory to recall his new politics masquerade of 1968.

[11]

Not without regret, McManus told me that the governor refused to cooperate with me. The story in *Esquire,* he said, had been "unfriendly," so there would be no interview for *Good Housekeeping.* . . .

I went to an outdoor telephone booth and called Ray Robinson, the editor with whom I had been working at *Good Housekeeping.* I told him what happened, calling his attention to the fact that Rockefeller and McManus had waited until the day before the election to announce their decision. They could be sure any objection I might raise would not affect the governor's charisma.

Robinson told me that he had been calling me all morning to cancel the assignment. He had been so instructed by the editor-in-chief, Wade Nichols, who said he was acting on orders from Richard Berlin, chairman of the board of the Hearst Corporation. Berlin, Robinson said, had told Nichols that Rockefeller did not want me around him. . . .

I won't speculate on who told Berlin that Rockefeller did not want me around him. . . . One of my hobbies is collecting newspaper clippings of speeches that Nelson Rockefeller has made since November, 1962, to various publishers and journalists about freedom of the press.
         —TOM MORGAN, *Self-Creations:*
                  13 Impersonalties

I was skeptical from the start about whether the governor would actually see me. I had heard that he granted private audiences only to journalists who were certified as sympathetic and that he ducked writers who might give him a hard time. Also, Tom Morgan had talked to me about his frustrating experience. And back in 1966, I had written an unflattering piece on the governor for *The Village Voice.*

After I had interviewed about twenty-five people, read through six volumes of Rockefeller's public papers, and read a dozen long magazine pieces about him, I finally phoned his press assistant, Warren Gardner, on February 2, primed to quote the First Amendment, John Peter Zenger, A. J. Liebling, and Tom Morgan.

I told Gardner I was researching a piece on the governor for
New York, and that I was formally requesting about a forty-five-
minute sit-down interview with the governor sometime in the
next two weeks, either in Manhattan or Albany. He said he
would get back to me in a few days.

During the next five days I managed to interview Richard Salant, the president of CBS News, labor mediator Theodore Kheel,
Mayor Lindsay, and Congressman Ogden Reid without difficulty. But the governor's office never called back. So on Friday
afternoon, February 7, I called Gardner's assistant, informed her
of my casual access to equally busy if less powerful men, and told
her that I thought I was being discriminated against because of
my politics, and that I still expected Mr. Gardner to call me
back, as he'd promised. Nothing happened.

So on February 10, I called Ronald Maiorana, who runs the
governor's press office in Albany. Gloria Steinem had assured me
he was a "decent guy." He was busy on another phone, so I recited my problems to his assistant, saying that if I was not going
to be permitted to see the governor, at least I should flatly be
told, so that I did not waste so much of my time dialing ten dig-
its to Albany and waiting on hold buttons. She said I should call
Mr. Maiorana back "tomorrow morning."

I did, but he was still busy on another phone, and I was connected with another assistant.

I told Maiorana's assistant my situation, and he asked me,
"What sort of questions do you think you might ask the governor?"

"Oh, basic ones like local control, the 30-cent fare, the Albany
Mall, Vietnam, and colonialism in Latin America," I answered.

"You understand the governor is a very busy man these days.
It might be rough to see him for a while. But I'll call you back
when it's possible."

I hung up and immediately began writing this article. I had
joined Tom Morgan in the Pariah Club.

[12]

Rockefeller was not a man who would normally inspire warmth. He had a strong, decent face, and something tough as the rubber in a handball to his makeup,
but his eyes had been punched out a long time ago—
they had the distant lunar glow of the small sad eyes

you see in a caged chimpanzee or gorilla. Even when
hearty he gave an impression the private man was remote as an astronaut on a lost orbit.

—NORMAN MAILER, "CANNIBALS AND CHRISTIANS," 1965

[13]

Fifteen years ago, maybe even ten years ago, Nelson Rockefeller appeared to be a vanguard politician, a potential President
ahead of his party and ahead of his time. He was deeply committed to integration and civil rights. As a freshman governor he
spent millions of dollars to modernize New York's bankrupt
higher education system. He cared about the arts and good archi-
tecture. He was an internationalist. He drew up the blueprint
that led to a separate cabinet post for HEW.

But now, after three bitter disappointments over the Presidency, after an ugly divorce and remarriage, it has all turned
sour. The best part of him has shriveled up from the hurt. He is
sixty-two years old now, and he has been governor for twelve
years, and he has long ago stopped believing in any idea larger
than himself. He has lost the young man's impulse to risk and in-
novate. He has become closed to the moral claims of issues. Bal-
ancing budgets, building things and getting reelected have become both ends and means.

Today Rockefeller stands in polar antagonism to the fragile,
hopeful new politics of McCarthy and Kennedy. His 1968 campaign rhetoric about "participatory democracy" is mocked by his
bulldozer approach to new construction and his power-elite appointments to the MTA. His faddish 1968 talk about "new priorities" is mocked by his support for the war in Vietnam, ABM, and
MIRV, while he is cutting welfare payments and ignoring the
housing, transit, and education needs of the cities. While the citizen activists of the new politics try to challenge the regular party
apparatus from below, Rockefeller stands at the barricades with
Nixon, Agnew, and Marchi.

What I am saying, finally, is not that it is sad that Rockefeller
was once a nice guy, once part of the solution, and that now he
has become part of that vague plague called the problem. I am
saying that Nelson Rockefeller—elitist, hawk, organization man,
and "last colonialist"—has become a precise personification of
the problem.

MARCH, 1969

[7.]
Theodore Sorensen: A Burnt-Out Case

The thing wrong with Theodore Sorensen is the thing wrong with American politics.

The thing is not easy to distill into a few words. It is an elusive mix of personal ambition divorced from values or passion or ideas, old-fashioned venality, and a huckster's cynical obsession with technique and media image-making. All of which is covered over by the most reasonable public rhetoric no sane person could disagree with. It is the invisibility of evil, the concealment of character.

So first, a few raw facts about Theodore Chaikin Sorensen.

In 1967, Sorensen advised Robert Kennedy not to speak out against the bombing of North Vietnam because it might harm his career. In 1966, Sorensen accepted a large legal fee to represent General Motors against the consumer's tribune, Ralph Nader. Also as a lawyer, Sorensen went to work for the statewide association of doctors who tried to discredit and sabotage the state's Medicaid program of free medical care for the indigent. At the 1968 Democratic Convention, Sorensen, while publicly aligned with the antiwar delegates, worked secretly in hotel rooms and on telephones for Hubert Humphrey, and tried to undercut the doves during the peace plank fight.

But those are just the big political things. There are also the little things, the little flashes into a man's character.

There is Sorensen, tortuously rationalizing and justifying John F. Kennedy's Vietnam policies in his book *Kennedy,* published in 1965, now telling audiences, "I didn't have anything to do with foreign policy when I served President Kennedy." There is Sorensen taking out full-page newspaper ads during the recent epidemic of ghetto heroin deaths, implying his opponents have ignored the problem while he has been working hard on it for years. There is Sorensen flying to Moscow on the eve of Passover

to score cheap political points with New York's Jewish voters by having the remarkable courage to attack Soviet anti-Semitism. There is Sorensen giving inspirational sermons about moral clarity in times of crisis, and then trying to explain away his failure to endorse John Lindsay against Mario Procaccino, or explain why he pleaded with Robert Kennedy not to run in 1968. There is Sorensen writing Ted Kennedy's wretched television speech after Chappaquiddick, and then, when it doesn't wash, going on the David Frost television show to deny he ever wrote it and claiming his only role at Hyannis Port was "preventing misstatements of fact." There is Sorensen, quoting the Kennedys, writing books about the Kennedys, trying to link his name to their magic, but ask anyone who works full-time in any cause, in any movement in the country what Sorensen has done to help them even privately, and the answer is always nothing. Talk to the antiwar organizers or the welfare rights organization, talk to the Young Lords, talk to the grape strikers, ask Dr. Spock, Bill Kunstler, Jesse Jackson, Saul Alinsky, or Ralph Nader, ask anyone who really spends his life working for change, and they will all tell you they have no use for Sorensen.

I don't know of any other figure in American politics whose public reputation and real worth are at such variance. To suburban housewives in Huntington who have time only to read *Newsweek* once a week, to upstate county leaders who have only heard about him by reputation, to journeymen reporters based in Moscow who have never actually met him, Sorensen symbolizes the paradise lost of the New Frontier: social reform, style, idealism, wit, intelligence.

But those professionals who know Sorensen, who have worked day-to-day with him, who have sat in meetings with him and drafted statements with him, or those seasoned political journalists who have observed him closely over a decade—to them Sorensen is an impostor. Just as you had to *know* Robert Kennedy to appreciate him, you have to *know* Sorensen to be appalled by him.

Dun Gifford until recently was on Ted Kennedy's Washington staff. In 1968, he worked in Robert Kennedy's campaign. He knows Sorensen very well. Usually a bright staff man like Gifford will not talk on the record about a colleague like Sorensen. But Gifford feels the responsibility to share his insider's knowledge, the urge to correct the mistaken image.

"Sorensen," Gifford says, "has an infatuation with technique. He only cares about the appearances of things. He is a great technician. He knows how to write a speech in an hour that will make 6000 steelworkers applaud. He knows how to draft a letter to De Gaulle that will please all sides. And I have a great respect for this skill. But I have never seen him show any emotion about any cause or any issue. He has a love of management. What he knows best is how to put a cosmetic on any situation, how to make up the best excuse."

Jeff Greenfield also got to know Sorensen as a comrade when they worked side by side in Robert Kennedy's truncated 1968 campaign. Greenfield says: "Ted Sorensen reminds me of Richard Nixon. His speeches never look you in the eye and tell you what's *really* going on. They always twist the truth. . . . He has a fascination with power in a tight-assed way, just like Nixon. Sorensen believes in manipulation rather than participation. . . . Sorensen will never admit he was wrong. Bobby admitted he was wrong on Vietnam and shouldered all the blame. But Sorensen's basic skill is that of a rhetorician, at papering over real differences with phony language. He uses words as a gimmick. His hang-up on all iteration indicates how he only cares about gimmicks and not the guts of anything."

Fred Dutton worked in the White House with Sorensen during the early 1960s, and worked closely with him in the 1968 campaign. He says, "When I first came into the White House in 1961, I had heard that Ted Sorensen was the great liberal intellectual. But in practice, it was Ken O'Donnell, who was supposed to be the cold Irish pol, who would push on civil rights, who would ask 'is it good for people?' while Sorensen would always ask 'Is it smart politics?' "

Peter Maas, author of *The Valachi Papers,* has been close to the Kennedys for almost ten years. He knew Bobby when he was attorney general. He covered Kennedy's 1964 Senate campaign in New York. He has watched Sorensen operate in public and private for a long time. "Ted Sorensen is pathetic," Maas says. "He is totally used up. In the speech he wrote for Teddy after Chappaquiddick, he lifted three paragraphs right out of *Profiles in Courage.* And then at Grossinger's he paraphrased JFK's inaugural address. He's living in the past."

Two little-publicized episodes will, I think, shed some useful light on the real Sorensen who has lived for years behind the

protective mythology of Camelot. One concerns Sorensen's conduct at the tumultuous 1968 Democratic Convention, and the other centers on the book he published last year called *The Kennedy Legacy*.

During the Chicago Convention, I had a few drinks with Paul Gorman, a speechwriter for Eugene McCarthy. Gorman angrily told me Sorensen was "trying to double-cross the peace people" through some complicated and devious maneuvers over the drafting of the minority antiwar, anti-LBJ plank for the platform. But my mind was on the violent streets, and I didn't really follow Gorman's intricate tale of betrayal. A few months later it completely left my mind.

But I recently came into possession of a private memorandum drafted by author and Presidential adviser Richard Goodwin that chronicles in Byzantine detail Sorensen's double game at the 1968 convention. Because of its importance, and in the vagrant hope the daily press will pick it up, I quote from Goodwin's memo, dated September 10, 1968, at some length.

"I arrived in Chicago the evening of Thursday, August 22, and was greeted with the following appalling news: the doves on the platform committee—about thirty-five people including some who were obviously not doves—had set up a separate group. There were five or six McCarthy delegates on this committee, one McGovern man, and the rest were 'uncommitted,' including Ted Sorensen. The drafting committee met and [John] Gilligan said, 'I don't know who should be chairman of this meeting, I suppose you've had the most experience, Ted. You do It.' Ted modestly accepted, and pointed out that a group can't write a platform, so he will parcel out assignments, and they can all meet tomorrow to consider the drafts. He asks a professor—one of our delegates—to write something about Czechoslovakia, [William] Clark to write a preamble about how bad the war is, someone else to do 'no more Vietnams,' and then he says, 'And I'll do the Vietnam plank.' Everyone nods and it is decided. The McCarthy delegates at this meeting are fine, intelligent people but with almost no political sophistication at all. They really believe everyone there is solely motivated by the desire to end the war in Vietnam.

"When I heard this I practically fell out of my chair. The whole charade had clearly been prearranged in order to take the peace issue away from the two candidates for President who represented that issue, and even prevent the issue from ever reaching

the floor. I called Frank Mankiewicz in Washington, who was working for McGovern. I told him the facts and asked him what he thought was happening. 'I know goddam well what's happening,' he said. 'They're trying to steal the peace issue.' We agreed the only way to counter was to draft a peace plank that was agreed to by both McCarthy and McGovern, and present that agreed draft to the informal 'dove' committee when they reconvened to consider the Sorensen draft. Frank suggested I call [Pierre] Salinger who was in Chicago to work for McGovern. I told Pierre what had gone on. His only comment was 'Sorensen is screwing.' . . .

"Friday morning the draft was read over the phone to McCarthy and McGovern. We gave it to Shields [Gilligan's campaign manager in Ohio] thinking Gilligan would present it as the agreed-upon position of the major candidates. That should take care of the Sorensen effort, which ostensibly only represented his personal views. But I was still uneasy, called Salinger, and said, 'Those guys might pull anything, we better go to that meeting.' We drove to the Stockyards Inn and entered the meeting room. We came as representatives of McGovern and McCarthy and were both delegates to the convention. As soon as Sorensen saw us, he had us thrown out on the grounds that we were not on his committee, which, of course, was itself a purely informal and ad hoc group.

"We spent the day sitting around the Stockyards Inn, talking to reporters and having our delegates come out and report to us periodically. No sooner had we left [the meeting] than the McCarthy-McGovern draft was pocketed—not even shown to the committee—and the Sorensen draft was placed on the table. We asked for a copy of the draft and were refused. But our delegates came out and told us the substance of the proposals. They consisted of the administration position, stated more gently and with slightly more ambiguity than Dean Rusk, although there was no substantive proposal that Rusk could not agree with. Pierre then started to brief the press intensively—telling them that the whole committee ploy was an effort to destroy the peace forces on behalf of Humphrey. He was brutal—and it was true. . . .

"Finally, at about 3 P.M., we got them [the McCarthy delegates] to protest our exclusion. There was a vote and we were allowed in just as the Sorensen draft was being retyped to reflect the day's debate. Ted handed it over silently as we came in. The

preamble was strong, and good—written by Clark—and my first reaction was maybe we won't have a clash at all. But as I continued reading, it was clear that it was the administration position all over again. The bombing halt required a quid pro quo, and even worse, any American withdrawal of forces was conditioned on a cease fire. In other words, we wouldn't take out any troops until the war was over. . . . Not only did the draft cut the heart out of the peace position, but it destroyed the proposal for withdrawal which Ted Kennedy had just made. . . . And Sorensen had worked on that speech. . . .

"Of course, in retrospect, we know LBJ wasn't going to let Humphrey even sound different on Vietnam. He wanted a complete vindication of his policies, which he got. But Humphrey did want a plank of his own, and one that would isolate the McCarthy and McGovern forces, making them appear like extremists or rigid ideologues. In this effort, Sorensen was Humphrey's agent, while asserting his independence, and even his fidelity to the completely different policies of Robert Kennedy. . . ."

Then there is the matter of Sorensen's book *The Kennedy Legacy*. *The New York Times* originally invited me to review this book. I read it in galleys and was so disgusted I called the *Times* and told them I didn't want to write the review because the book was boring and worthless, and I was reluctant to say so because I had just published my own Kennedy book and feared people would attribute my hostility to competitive instincts.

But now that Sorensen has been nominated for the United States Senate, I feel free to make a few comments about the book.

First, Sorensen, after advising Ted Kennedy about Chappaquiddick, after ghosting his television speech, then, at great expense to his publisher, changed the galleys of his book to edit out favorable references to Kennedy when the Senator's popularity began to plummet.

In the galleys I read for the *Times,* Sorensen quoted a telephone conversation he had with Ted Kennedy during the 1968 convention: "As certain as anything could be certain in politics, I told Ted, he was young enough to have more and even better opportunities for the Presidency in the future."

That quote does not appear in the book.

In the galleys, Sorensen concluded a long section on youth and

students with a quotation from Ted Kennedy: "As Senator Edward Kennedy has stated . . ."

That innocuous quote, too, mysteriously vanished after Chappaquiddick.

In the galleys, Sorensen criticized Eugene McCarthy because of "his vote against Ted Kennedy for Senate whip." Sorensen changed the sentence to read because of "his vote for Russell Long for Senate whip." That was the only change in the paragraph.

The mythology of Ted Sorensen as a Kennedy liberal still endures in many places—largely because journalists are so conformist and lazy it usually takes years for a politician's reputation to catch up with his reality.

I don't know when Sorensen began to turn sour. Some people who know him say he never was very committed or courageous. Others say it was the trauma of Dallas that made him cynical and self-centered.

But the lesson is that no man can spend a lifetime working in the orbit of a family like the Kennedys and retain sure sense of who he really is.

Sorensen might have spent the years since Dallas differently. He might have spent time in Bed-Stuy, or in the Mississippi Delta, or in Appalachia, learning from the same raw experiences that transformed Robert Kennedy. He might have worked for Ralph Nader instead of General Motors. He might have gone to the campuses to listen, instead of just picking up lecture fees for his campaign chest. He might have renewed his humanist reflexes by joining a cause, helping the Vietnam Moratorium like Galbraith and Dutton, working with the McCarthy kids in New Hampshire like Goodwin, improving a newspaper like Bill Moyers, becoming a witness for the Chicago Conspiracy like Ramsey Clark.

But Sorensen just served corporation clients, played politics, took no unpopular positions, gave bad advice to the Kennedys—and became a burnt-out case.

APRIL, 1970

[8.]
The Liberal Party Today:
Alex in Wonderland

Newspeak has hardly waited until 1984 to make its debut. The vocabulary of our politics has been Orwellianized for some time now. It was, in fact, a great help to me as a young journalist to figure out that the actual name given to most things in politics means the exact opposite.

Of course the free world is made up of dictatorships. Of course the House of Representatives is unrepresentative. Of course the Justice Department is a factory of injustice.

As soon as Nelson Rockefeller said he was a "peace candidate," I knew he was still the war candidate. As soon as Nixon said there were no CIA agents in Laos, I knew there were at least 1000.

And of course the Liberal Party has little to do with liberalism, and nothing to do with democracy. The definition of a Liberal Party primary is Alex Rose having an argument with his maid.

If it was called the Patronage Party, I wouldn't mind. If it was called the Alex Rose Party, that at least would be honest. But the *Liberal* Party, that's what gets Orwell aficionados like me and Hamill and Hentoff so angry. It's like taking stale rainwater and selling it under the generic name of perfume. I have nothing against rainwater, it's the devious label that troubles me.

The Liberal Party was fathered twenty-six years ago by that most conservative of passions—anticommunism. Hatters union leader Alex Rose, garment worker's union president David Dubinsky, and Ben Davidson thought the American Labor Party, then led by Sidney Hillman of the Amalgamated Clothing Workers, had gone too far to the left. So they split away from the ALP to create their own trade union line on the ballot for FDR in the 1944 Presidential election. They got 330,000 votes for FDR and

spent their first years purging commies and red-baiting Vito Marcantonio, Paul O'Dwyer, and the ALP. In 1949, when Marcantonio ran for mayor and polled 350,000 votes, the Liberals gave their line on the ballot to Republican Newbold Morris.

(The anticommie phobia runs so deep in the party that when a group of young Puerto Ricans began a sit-in in Ben Davidson's office last month, his secretary shouted at them, "Go back to Russia where you belong.")

During the early 1950s the Liberal Party flashed a promise of living up to its name. The party briefly became the most independent and rebellious force in the city's political life. In 1951 the Liberals ran Rudolph Halley for City Council president on an anticorruption platform against Democrat and Republican ciphers. Halley, who had been counsel to the crime-busting Populist Senator Estes Kefauver, won in a big upset. And quickly thousands of young, middle-class citizen activists flocked into the Liberal Party. Neighborhood clubs were organized. Ideas were debated. Energies were liberated. People like NAACP's labor secretary Herbert Hill, who would become the ILGWU's most effective critic, went to work for Halley as a speechwriter.

In 1953 the membership of the party nominated Halley for mayor over the objections of Dubinsky. Halley lost badly to Robert Wagner. End of the Liberal Party's liberal epoch.

Through the 1950s and into the '60s, the Party lived off its Halley image. In 1960, as a gesture against Tammany, and in favor of good government, I innocently registered to vote for the first time, and enrolled in the Liberal Party. Meanwhile, the party did become the true balance of power in the state between the Democrats and Republicans. The Liberal line on the ballot was the margin of victory in Herbert Lehman's election to the Senate in 1950, in Averell Harriman's election as governor in 1954, and in John Kennedy's winning New York's electoral votes in 1960.

Such a balance of power role naturally generated prestige, patronage, entry to the White House, and all the little goodies of high politics. Then in 1961 the Liberal Party attained a newer zenith of power when Alex Rose ingeniously wrote the scenario for what Murray Kempton called Mayor Wagner's reelection campaign against his own record.

It was all a castle built on thin air because people believed they were actually getting liberalism when they voted Liberal,

that the nice bottle labeled perfume could not possibly be filled
with dirty old rainwater. People, conditioned by the media, believed the Liberal Party endorsement was a neutral expression of
virtue, that it had a mystical authority the Citizens Union or the
hatters union by itself did not have. What it was, though, was a
franchising hustle to stamp friends "kosher" and foes "traife."

By the time Wagner was reelected, the Liberal Party had
begun to deteriorate deep inside. The mass media and the voters
could not see it yet, but the few liberal columnists and politicians saw it. From the beginning the party was fearful and en-
vious of the Reform Democrats, who were growing quickly in
Manhattan in the early 1960s. Younger voters began to register
Democratic because of the excitement of young, attractive candidates and white hat/black hat primaries. So the Liberals did everything they could to undercut the Reformers, without being too
blatant about it. In 1960, the Liberals endorsed Tammany's Lud-
wig Teller against William F. Ryan, when Ryan first won his
Congressional seat on the West Side. In 1962 the Liberals endorsed William Passannante when Edward Koch challenged him
for the Village Assembly seat. When Jerome Kretchmer first ran
for the Assembly that same year on the West Side, the Liberals
red-baited him and endorsed someone else. In the outer boroughs, they continued to endorse almost anyone who voted right
on tariff legislation that concerned the ILGWU. Even John
Rooney. And in 1963, when David Livingston and Paul O'Dwyer
helped make the $1.50 minimum wage an issue, the Liberals qui-
etly opposed it, because they feared its passage might drive the
sweatshop garment center operators out of town and destroy the
party's base, the 400,000-member ILGWU.

One can now read the 1964 Liberal Party platform as a piece
of camp literature. It urges the "economic and diplomatic isolation of the Castro tyranny." It says, "We recognize the necessity
of giving the President authority to grant military aid wherever
the interests of freedom demand it." This is apparently intended
to mean Vietnam, since there is no other reference to Vietnam in
the platform. In 1964 the Liberals were also in favor of "strength-
ening NATO," and "condemned" Soviet anti-Semitism. The
platform, however, did not include a plank on American civil
liberties.

The second piece I wrote after joining the staff of *The Voice*
was a critical analysis of the Liberal Party ("Empty Ideals, Full

Pockets," December 10, 1964), and even then the central problem with the party was clear. *It was a benevolent dictatorship.* The same three men—Rose, Dubinsky, and Davidson—had controlled the party for twenty years. There was no participation in decision-making by the membership. It was just like Tito's Communist Party.

The whole thing stuck together so well because Alex Rose is a wizard. People talk about Steve Smith or Robert Price being brilliant political managers, but Rose has had nothing to work with, no candidate, no family fortune, no major party, and still he has built an empire. His base has been the tiny 20,000-member hatters union, that's all. But his judgment on the big ones has been superb. He can smell the mood of the electorate because he has none of his own. And so by supporting John Lindsay for mayor in 1965 and 1969, and Sam Silverman for surrogate in 1966, Rose both did the good deed and preserved his party's external liberal image and its internal sources of jobs on the public payroll; although as Paul O'Dwyer told *The New York Times* last week, when Rose decided to throw in with Wagner in 1961 and Lindsay in 1969, it was actual ratios of jobs that he carefully negotiated in exchange for the kosher label, not any commitment to ideas or programs.

Rose gets away with things that Meade Esposito or Joe Crangle would get crucified for. *The Post* and *Times* (though not the *Daily News*) still identify Rose as the Liberal Party "tactician" or "chief strategist," while people might have gotten the impression that "boss" was poor Charley Buckley's first name.

In the last couple of months, however, Rose's franchising hustle has begun to arouse more suspicion than usual.

First came some of the Liberal Party's endorsements for 1970. They endorsed the Republican candidate and radio personality Barry Farber for Congress in Manhattan's 19th C. D. before Bella Abzug, the moral equivalent of General Patton, won the Democratic primary. I have been a guest on Farber's midnight radio program, and he is pleasant enough, but rather a cold warrior in foreign policy, and antistudent domestically. The Liberals have no plan to reconsider their endorsement.

And for attorney general, the Liberals gave the kosher label to the undistinguished Republican incumbent Louis Lefkowitz, rather than his younger, more liberal challenger Adam Walinsky.

And as bad as the substance of that decision was, the procedure that produced it was even worse.

Unlike the "boss-controlled Democrats," the Liberal Party did not have any public forums across the state where party members might hear all the candidates. Instead the agents of good government held a tightly controlled convention. The four leaders of the party had enough proxies in their hands to nominate anyone they wanted. Walinsky was not even permitted to address the delegates, a request he made since he was not invited to meet with the party's policy committee before it endorsed Lefkowitz. Lefkowitz's principal backers were Mike Dontzin and Simeon Golar, both of whom owe their major posts in the Lindsay administration to Alex Rose. And finally Walinsky was told he could not run in a Liberal Party primary against Lefkowitz because he is not a registered Liberal.

But two weeks ago, Alex might have gone too far. He engineered a purge of the Liberal Party's Manhattan organization. It was not necessary because the Manhattan organization, like all the other county organizations, has no power. It was pure vindictiveness, like the new Czech Stalinists purging Alexander Dubcek from his ceremonial post as ambassador to Turkey.

The purge took place two weeks ago at a secret county committee meeting. The new county leader is Edward Morrison, the $25,000-a-year special counsel to Mayor Lindsay. (In 1965, when he was running as a reformer for mayor, Lindsay invented the Lindsay Pledge, which said that it was not ethical for anyone in a high city job to also maintain a high position within a political party.)

At the same meeting, the Liberals elected eighteen new county officers. Fifteen of them are on the city payroll; they owe their livelihoods to Alex Rose. The secretary of the county is now Elaine Morrison, Edward's wife. She has a $10,000-a-year job with the Economic Development Administration, although one of the top administrators in that agency told me she only "comes to work once or twice a week."

Among the new officers of the county are Herb Rose, Alex's son; Eve Davidson, Ben's wife, who has a city job with HDA; Abraham Fuss, a city tax commissioner and a former law partner of Morrison; Charles Kee, who has a patronage job in the Department of Relocation; Alan Moss, who has a patronage job

with the Parks Department; and Walter Kirschenbaum, who had a patronage job in the Finance Administrator's office, and who is the party's biggest anticommunist nut.

The ousted county leader is Arthur Brook, a young lawyer who does not owe his job to the party. Until two weeks ago he was so regular that he had not even aligned himself with the growing reform faction within the Liberal Party led by Dr. Paul Siminoff, Manhattan Councilman-at-large Eldon Clingan, and Bruce Roberts. Brook, however, did support Eugene McCarthy in 1968, while Rose was backing first Lyndon Johnson and then Hubert Humphrey. And in April, Brook supported Adam Walinsky for attorney general.

I spoke to Brook this week, and he told me his story.

"My sin was that I was neutral between the rebels and management [Rose]. I'm not a member of Liberals for New Politics. I'm not a rebel. I tried to work constructively from within. All I said was I thought dissent within the party was a healthy thing, and dissenters should not be punished. . . .

"I really don't know why Alex and Ed Morrison are doing this. Maybe they're afraid of the few new young people in the party who are motivated by issues, and not just jobs and judgeships. But there are so few of them.

"The heart of the problem is that the Liberal Party is not democratic. Alex's motives are not bad, but he's just not a democrat. Look, I was a county chairman. I was one of the twenty members of the statewide Policy Committee. And *I* didn't know what was going on. Nobody has any power in the party except Alex. The state committee has no power, and the county chairmen have no power. I had no power. I still can't figure out why they went to all the trouble of purging me. They even told people who worked for the city they would lose their jobs if they didn't vote the right way."

Over the last two weeks I have interviewed about twenty people about Alex Rose and have meditated a good deal about him.

At one level, it is difficult to think of him as an evil man. He did save the city from the worst of the old-line Democrats in 1961, and he did save John Lindsay's career last year. And it is perhaps unfair to expect him to be any different from all the other union leaders of his generation who bought the whole cold war demonology.

But at another level, Rose deserves to be called accountable for his actions. No matter how many times Rose calls the Democrats "boss-controlled," no matter how many of those silly columns James Wechsler writes rationalizing Rose's every decision, the fact is that Rose is the boss of all bosses, and his party is the least democratic of the four in the state.

Rose has never been issue-oriented. No one can recall him ever making a speech against the war in Vietnam. He has built a third party not on ideas but on patronage, not on idealism, but on organization. And so the party has become filled up with soulless careerists, living off Alex's credit card, and doing anything he wants them to do. Nominate Lefkowitz, throw out Arthur Brook, oppose Bella Abzug, anything if Alex wants it, because Alex owns them.

Flattery has corrupted Rose as much as power. His politics, at bottom, is to support the King, whoever the King happens to be.

Sidney Zion, who used to cover the Liberal Party for the *Times*, told me, "Alex is an old-time hero-worshipper. He loves people he thinks have *stature*. He lives his whole life for his influence on important politicians. That's why he loves to be with a winner so much."

When John Kennedy wanted Rose to endorse James Donovan for the Senate in 1962, he did it. When Lyndon Johnson wanted his support for the war in Vietnam, he gave it. When it looked like Humphrey was going to be nominated in 1968, Alex went along. Royalty gets anything it asks for at Alex's Restaurant. As one of his former assistants told me, "Alex goes for winners first. If they happen to coincide with good government and liberalism, then it's a mitzvah. But he is always smart enough to invent a plausible cover story for whatever atrocity he commits. That's part of his secret."

But the puzzle remains: Why is Rose doing what he's doing now? He is seventy-two years old and he must know the Liberal Party cannot survive without new leadership. The party's base—the hatters union—is shrinking with a dying industry. From his own point of view, Rose should understand the only way his party can survive is to attract new, young members, and keep the handful it has.

But then he makes kosher an old hack like Lefkowitz, whom the party had never endorsed before, instead of an exciting liberal candidate like Walinsky. And then he throws out a young,

moderate lawyer like Brook, who had joined the party because of what he thought it stood for. Brook was one of the few visible members of the party who wasn't there only to hustle a city job. The Liberal Party might have done so much. It might have given wise leadership to the antiwar movement. It might have identified itself with great social reforms like peace, or free health care, or a guaranteed income, as third parties have done before it. But instead, it leaves to the younger generation a legacy of one-man rule and a bunch of city jobs. Alex Rose could have been so much better than that.

JULY, 1970

[9.]
An Open Letter To John Lindsay*

Dear John

Something very deep and very ugly is going on in America. Spiro Agnew is spreading a poison we are going to spend a generation seeking an antidote for. He is doing it with a White House plane, and with Nixon's speechwriters, and he is getting away with it.

And you have been quiet. You seconded his nomination in 1968. You are not up for election this year, and this gives you a certain freedom. But the only time you ever refer to Agnew is by inference, at Goodell rallies, or at the Liberal Party dinner in Manhattan.

But you have to go into the heartland of this wounded dinosaur of a country, you have to go to Colorado, or Oklahoma, or Maryland (Yes, Spiro's backyard), and stand up and attack and expose Agnew. You have to do it with a hundred facts. You have to do to him what Ed Murrow did to Joe McCarthy.

Because he has the President's secret, tacit support, Agnew is a much greater menace than Joe McCarthy, who was only a committee chairman disliked by the President of his own party.

What Agnew is doing to the country I'm sure you understand as well as I do. He has called Joe Montoya, the Senator from New Mexico, a "radical liberal." You and I know that is absurd. But now Nelson Gross has called Harrison Williams a "radical liberal" in New Jersey, and it will sound credible, and gain him votes.

Agnew has said Teddy Kennedy doesn't understand what violence is doing to America. If Don Rickles said that, it would be

* Twelve days after this piece appeared, one week before the election, Lindsay delivered a major address at the Family of Man Dinner attacking Agnew and Nixon for "spreading a cloud of mistrust and suspicion over the nation."

considered a sick joke. But Agnew says it, with his institutional credibility.

Agnew last week said Reverend Joe Duffey, the antiwar Senate candidate in Connecticut, described himself as a "revisionist Marxist." It was a lie. Duffey never said it. But, as you know, the denial never catches up to the smear.

Agnew is a political thug. He is spreading poisons that may doom your own career. If Reagan and Murphy and Jim Buckley and Ralph Smith all win in November, this country will be in mortgage to madness. The Agnews and Mitchells and Chotiners will have a license for repression.

You can't stand aside from this. You carry that special responsibility because of what you did in Miami in 1968.

Vague rhetoric about polarization and divisiveness is not enough. No one has called Agnew on all his lies and smears by name, date, and place. There is no fight left in all of liberalism. If you did it, then Muskie and Kennedy and Bayh and all the other liberal sheep would follow.

It is the moral thing to do, and it is the political thing to do. You will not become President by taking the safe middle road. Muskie has that already. You can only become President by standing for something larger than yourself. You can only become President by liberating the passion and commitment that Kennedy and McCarthy briefly touched in 1968. You will not be the candidate of the insiders, of the unions and bosses and big contributors. You can only be nominated if you symbolize a cause and run in the primaries, and stand for a different America, not a slightly better managed America.

You have disappointed me a lot lately. I haven't heard you talk about the war since the hardhat riot. You made the wrong decision on Con Edison's Astoria plant. You shouldn't have endorsed Louis Lefkowitz, but if you did that on the human grounds that he helped you last year, then how can you even hesitate about endorsing Goldberg? And I'm still waiting for you to indict the correction officers who beat the inmates with baseball bats while you were inside the Long Island City prison. I'm sure you saw the pictures in the *Daily News.*

But these are all small, transient things. The gunmen have had their days, and you may be the last hope we have.

In the past you have made liberty and freedom your special concern. You opposed HUAC as a congressman when it wasn't

safe or fashionable. You were the only national politician to attack Judge Hoffman while the Chicago conspiracy defendants were still in jail for contempt. I was there when you gave that superb speech in Berkeley last April, when you warned of a new wave of repression gathering at the horizon. So that is why I address you now, out of respect for your biography.

And if you give this speech, it should be more than a rebuttal to Agnew: it should be a restatement of the humanist agenda for a generation. Agnew is distorting the political spectrum by defining Duffey and Kennedy outside of legitimacy; he is moving the center of political gravity still another notch toward the right. So what you must also do is remind the country again of racism, of the dispossessed, of the need of a new minimum wage law, of tax reform, of money for public housing, of all the things we have forgotten in the silly discussion over whether Joe Montoya is a "radical liberal."

So don't wait for election results to see if the country is going to the right or not. That's nothing but opportunism. You have a moral obligation to affect this process before it is final. No one is really answering Agnew. Liberalism has capitulated. Time is running out. The disease he is spreading will infect our politics for years to come. If you pretend to have any claim on the allegiance of people like myself, then go out now to Middle America, yes, risk a little bit of your future, go out of Manhattan, and stand up and say it straight. Before it's too late.

Peace,
Jack Newfield

OCTOBER, 1970

[FIVE]
THE MEDIA: MEDIUM FOOL

The only point I would underline here is Agnew. The networks, the media in general, invented him, have overcovered him, and in the end have been profoundly intimidated by him. This intimidation—self-censorship, really—is important because television is so important; the tube has become a surrogate reality for half this country. And the conformity of the networks is probably the best example of what I mean by the Center not holding.

[1.]
Good-bye, Dolly!

I have popular taste myself. I generally feel the way a
majority of people feel. Crime sells better than housing,
say. I'm interested in gossip. I enjoy reading Doris Lilly,
Earl Wilson, and Leonard Lyons.

—Mrs. Dorothy Schiff*

The most exhilarating week I spent in college came in my
sophomore year, in 1958, when we made the April Fool's Day
edition of the Hunter College *Arrow* into a parody of the New
York *Post.* The *Post* had been, in Jerry Tallmer's perfect image,
my warm, humanitarian, Jewish mother all through high school
and college. The indignant editorials tasted like chicken broth.
Max Lerner moralized like a reform rabbi. And all the sentimental girl reporters reminded me of Marjorie Morningstar.

Whatever Herbert Lehman or David Ben-Gurion said was big
news. Each new president of the United Jewish Appeal was the
subject of a long profile. There were gossipy "inside stories"
about Jewish celebrities, from Bess Myerson to Einstein. Columnists like Milton Gross, Leonard Lyons, Sidney Skolsky, Max
Lerner, and Dr. Rose Franzblau gave the paper an unmistakable
urban Jewish flavor. Even the regular letter writers—Allen Klein
and Martin Wolfson—were Jewish. Even the biggest ads were
Jewish—Klein's and Abraham & Straus.

I devoured the paper every day. I learned to hate Joe McCarthy and revere Eleanor Roosevelt. I learned that rapists and reform Democrats played a larger role in the affairs of the world
than the *Times* let on. And I learned from Jimmy Cannon that
sportswriting could be both cynical and lyrical, and from Murray
Kempton that political analysis could call on Freud, Sartre, and
even Yeats. Would the editor and the publisher disagree again

* As quoted by Geoffrey Hellman in a *New Yorker* profile.

over whom to endorse for governor? Would Sugar Ray forgive
Jimmy Cannon for telling him to retire? Would a week pass
without the word "dreary" appearing in an editorial? Would the
paper ever hire a proofreader who didn't derive perverse pleasure
from typos and dropped lines? My first published words were a
letter to the *Post* that said, "I read your paper every single day.
Why can't your proofreaders do the same?"

So when the staff of the Hunter *Arrow* put together its *Post*
parody, I submitted three appropriately sophomoric satires. Pop
therapist Dr. Rose Franzblau: "Dear Madam: Certainly your 16-
year-old can sleep with a rooster—if he loves it." And my two
superheroes—Hemingwayesque Jimmy Cannon: "You're God.
Most people don't believe in you anymore. Sometimes, late at
night, you even doubt your own existence. But you're a game
guy. You keep going against the tide, and you don't say much.
You're God, and tonight you try a comeback at St. Nicholas
Arena. . . ."

And mandarin, victim-oriented Murray Kempton: "Henry
James would have understood poor Jimmy Hoffa. The liberals,
because they hate their class, and want to flee it, don't believe in
wiretapping. But I prefer pariahs who accept their class, because
they all have the surly dignity of Sal Maglie. . . ."

The publication of the parody paper marked the zenith of my
infatuation with the Jewish Momma. A few weeks later Jimmy
Cannon departed mysteriously and went to Hearst's *Journal-
American*. That should have been my equivalent of the Hitler-
Stalin pact. But it wasn't. I remained loyal to the *Post* even
though they fired me after a tryout in 1964, and even though
Kempton and James Wechsler both wrote columns in the *Post* last
spring attacking me for supporting Robert Kennedy rather than
Eugene McCarthy. But what is a Jewish mother for, except to
kvetch a little?

I did not leave my Jewish Momma's house, in fact, until February of 1969, when one morning *The New York Times* reported
that Kempton, Jimmy Breslin, and Jules Feiffer were all leaving
the *Post*. It was a *pogrom!* Even Breslin, the genius *Shabbes goy,*
was going! It was as if my Jewish mother had suddenly dyed her
gray hair blonde, dropped her Liberal Party registration, and
run off to Las Vegas with the vice-president of Lord & Taylor.
But at last, I was liberated enough to try and write about *her,*

now that, in plump middle age, she had decided to assimilate into Richard Nixon's weatherless 1950s America.

The New York *Post* is the oldest newspaper in the United States still published today. It was founded in 1801 by Alexander Hamilton, and began with a circulation of 600 in a city of 80,-000. Through the first century of its existence, the *Post* was a voice of vanguard populism. The poet, William Cullen Bryant, was editor from 1829 to 1878, and he aligned the publication with Andrew Jackson in 1832 and Abraham Lincoln in 1860. Carl Schurz became its editor in 1881 and ignited the municipal campaign that led to the creation of Central Park.

In 1923 the *Post* became the property of Cyrus Curtis, who converted it into a staid organ for conservatism and upper-class fashion. Maverick publisher J. David Stern took it over in 1932 and returned it to its earthy liberal roots. And in 1939, with the paper badly in debt and losing money, Mr. and Mrs. George Backer bought it. Mr. Backer, active in liberal Democratic politics, became president and editor, and his wife, the former Dorothy Schiff, became vice-president and treasurer.

The Backers lost $800,000 the first year, and a million dollars the next. So in 1942 Mrs. Backer wisely concluded the paper should be converted into a tabloid and made less ideological. Her husband disagreed, and they were divorced. Mrs. Schiff took over control of the paper, and the next year married her executive editor, Ted Thackrey, and the *Post* went into the black. But in 1948 Mrs. Thackrey supported Tom Dewey for President, while Mr. Thackrey backed Henry Wallace. The *Post,* in the final week of the campaign, dramatically endorsed Dewey. In 1949 Mrs. Schiff divorced her third husband, and became the publisher of the New York *Post.*

From about 1954 to 1961 the *Post* was probably the most exciting daily tabloid in the country. It was staffed by good young writers. It won prizes for its investigative reporting. Its editorial politics were at the cutting edge of cold war liberalism during a bland, conservative time. And James Wechsler, as editor, gave the paper both sex and spirit, while keeping it strongly anticommunist.

Al Aronowitz was the first daily journalist to explore the saintly lunacy of the Beat underground. Bill Haddad and Joe Kahn raked muck about master pol Carmine DeSapio and mas-

ter builder Robert Moses, and won the George Polk and Heywood Broun awards. Joe Barry covered the anticolonial war in Algeria with sensitivity and insight. Pete Hamill, then a brash kid off the docks, had the raunchy rhythm of the streets in his typewriter. Murray Kempton and Ted Poston went South and sent back prose poems about Dr. King's first generation of marching children. William V. Shannon and Robert Spivack wrote needling, original copy out of the Washington of Eisenhower, Dulles, and Senator Joseph McCarthy. Gene Grove and Normand Poirier, working on night rewrite, would make enterprising phone calls to update yesterday's news. Dave Gelman and Gael Greene were feature writers of considerable imagination. And there were frequent six- and twelve-part series, written by teams of reporters, challenging sacred cows like the FBI, Walter Winchell, and Joe McCarthy.

"There was a great sense of family on the *Post* in the late fifties," Al Aronowitz says. "We were all Jewish, liberal police reporters. We were all friends. We visited each other's homes. We drank together. We were into each other's heads. . . . The *Post* in those days had the craziness of a family. It was a lot of fun. We used to play football in the city room with a rolled up newspaper. Paul Sann [now executive editor] played pranks like answering the switchboard. . . . The *Post* was the only paper I wanted to work for. It was the avant-garde paper for young people in those days."

Bill Haddad shares the same nostalgic feelings. "There was a great pride in working for the *Post* in the late fifties," he says. "We were the best paper in town. The other six papers were afraid of us. We were there because we respected Wechsler. He was down in the city room all the time, working with writers, coming up with new ideas. And he backed you up in any showdown. He was never frightened by any threat of a libel suit. And when they dumped Wechsler, they killed it."

The bureaucratic intrigues and conspiracies of the *Post* are at least as Byzantine as the Vatican's or the State Department's. So there is no definitive chronicle of James Wechsler's sudden fall from grace in 1961. But there is a consensus oral history of the event that almost everyone on the paper at the time subscribes to. And that is that the *Post*'s publisher, Dolly Schiff, was disturbed both at a drop in circulation below 300,000 (the lowest of the city's seven dailies) and by the image of the *Post* as too pro-

Negro, which, she felt, deterred the classier department stores from advertising.

So in an overnight coup, probably encouraged by Wechsler's old-fashioned nonpolitical rivals in the city room, Mrs. Schiff demoted Wechsler to columnist and editor of the editorial page, ending his influence on news coverage, detailed series, and hiring policies. Mrs. Schiff gave herself the title of editor-in-chief, while day-to-day control of the paper passed to Paul Sann, a contradictory character straight out of *Front Page*—sentimental about the 1930s tough-guy school of journalism. Sann came to power on a platform of "neutral journalism," in an effort to get the *Post* out of the red. Almost immediately the crusading exposés vanished from the paper. Out-of-town stringers were cut from the staff. Coverage of civil-rights activity gradually declined. And reporters like Ted Poston and Joe Kahn, who were closely identified with the Wechsler regime, began to receive makework assignments of little significance that often never got into the paper.

Then came the 114-day printers' strike of 1962–63, which killed off the *Daily Mirror*. Under normal circumstances that strike should have closed down the *Post,* the most vulnerable of the city's papers. But Mrs. Schiff resigned from the Publishers' Association in the middle of the strike, made a separate peace with the union, and the *Post* became the only daily to publish as the strike dragged on. This brilliant stroke of class treason gained Mrs. Schiff about 50,000 new readers. Next came the 140-day newspaper strike of 1965 which forced the *Herald Tribune, World-Telegram and Sun,* and *Journal-American* to merge into a hybrid with a permanent identity crisis called the *World Journal Tribune*. When the sickly "widget" folded in May of 1967, the *Post,* incredibly, became the only afternoon newspaper publishing in New York, with more than double its anemic 1960 circulation, and no competition. But during the same period, commercial and entertainment values became enshrined in the city room, at the expense of literary and political values. And the editorials had gone from chicken broth to oatmeal mush.

One reason the *Post* defeated the *World Journal Tribune* in its hand-to-hand competition was simple logistics. The "widget" was never able to get the full run of its last Wall Street edition to the downtown newsstands before the commuters left work. The veteran *Post* truck drivers knew the maze of narrow, one-way streets downtown, and managed to get the last edition to the

stands in time. The "widget," meanwhile, inevitably had to dump thousands of copies of its last edition. Nevertheless, during 1967, three separate publishing institutions—Time-Life, Inc., the New York *Daily News* and *The New York Times*—all explored the possibility of going into competition with the *Post,* and all independently decided in the negative. It was this crucial series of decisions that protected the *Post* from the pressures of competition.

A Time, Inc., executive, who insists on anonymity, says, "Look, the *Post* is a terrible paper, we all know that. It is not connected with the population. It is removed from all the new and inventive things in the culture. It has no character or personality, and what charm it does have is left over from another era. . . .

"We got interested in entering the afternoon field before the *World Journal* folded. Time, Inc., has had a long-standing appetite to get into daily journalism. We set up a research group of five or six executives, and they worked full-time for three months exploring the possibility of starting an afternoon paper in New York. Our idea was a long-term project and was independent of what the *Times* and *News* were doing. But we finally decided against it for a variety of reasons. The unions were not very cooperative. Technology and distribution would be a problem. The *Times* was here in the morning, and finding a good staff would be difficult."

Executives at the *Times,* meanwhile, say they decided not to start an afternoon paper for slightly different reasons. The first was that of defining a stylistic and staff relationship with the competing morning *Times,* while sharing the same corporate ownership. A second reason was financial; the *Times* was not willing to risk so much capital in a situation where a new strike could prove fatal. And third, two experimental dummies of the proposed new paper failed to create a distinctive character and approach to journalism. It was still too much like the good, gray lady of the morning.

In July of 1964, in mid-passage of the *Post*'s conversion from Jewish Mother to Establishment Matron, I had a three months' tryout there as a reporter and nightside rewrite man. Largely on the basis of that experience, supplemented by interviews with past and present members of the *Post* staff, I offer three theories

to explain the paper's current condition, a condition shared by many other American dailies though none is in such a potentially strong position as the only afternoon paper in the nation's principal city:

The Candy Store Syndrome: Most people who have worked for the *Post* call it—with some affection—a "candy store" because of its general grubbiness, because of its grab-bag quality, because of its lingering Jewishness, and because it is *schlock*—unprofessional and cheap.

The first thing that strikes any visitor to the *Post* is the cramped, grubby quality of the second-floor city room. In the summer, when I worked there, it is unbearably hot; the paper is not air conditioned. The city room is filled with dust, dirt, and big fruit flies, since the *Post* is located right on the busy docks of West Street. There are only two small fans around the city desk, and there are frequent debates over which way they should face. The chairs are steel backed and uncomfortable, somewhat like bar stools. Many of the typewriters are old and decrepit. The men's room reeks of urine; many of the toilets are backed up; and the roll of sanitary towels is often used up by the day shift, so the entire nightside staff dries its inky hands on the same soiled stretch of cloth. This physical grubbiness long ago was absorbed into the pores of the paper, and into the psyche of its staff. "That city room is an outhouse," Jimmy Breslin says. "You can get black lung just by working on the rewrite desk for a week. They should pass a law against the joint."

The absence of pride or professionalism is a central element in the paper's decline. Usually three—just three—rewrite men sit in the *Post's* city room night after night, rewriting, virtually *retyping,* stories lifted not only from the *Times,* but also from the often well written *Daily News.* When I was at the *Post,* a copyboy was sent to Times Square every night at about one o'clock to pick up copies of the final edition of the *News.* Almost all the hard news copy in the *Post's* first edition, which comes off the presses at 9:00 A.M., is generated either in this parasitic fashion, or else by deskmen simply editing copy that comes in over wireservice machines. There is no original reporting after midnight, since the *Post* has no one prowling the city for news. But the passivity extends even into the city room. One night, when I wanted to telephone Bill Veeck for his reaction to the purchase of the

Yankees by CBS, night city editor Bob Friedman told me, "We don't do that anymore. Just rewrite the *Times*. And ask the morgue to send down the clips."

On the night of the bloody ghetto riot in Philadelphia, I was handed the *Times, News, Tribune,* and wire-service copy, and told to "do two and a half books," meaning about nine, one- or two-sentence paragraphs. Since I was not in Philadelphia, there was no revealing detail in the story, no feeling, no sense of specific place, only the number arrested, the estimated property damage, and a few predictable quotes from the "leaders" of the city and the civil-rights organizations. It was a little like making an egg cream. But the story became the lead on page five the next morning.

It is the same defeated attitude that accounts for the legendary number of typos and dropped lines in the *Post*. No one cares as long as they are not blamed. A *Post* copyboy, Ray Schultz, captured this burnt-out mood in a marvelous little memoir he wrote for the now dead New York *Free Press* (January 9, 1969):

> Many people consider the *Post* to be the sloppiest of New York's daily papers, and they say sadly, it is not the sloppiness of adventure or overconfidence, it is the sloppiness of exhaustion, of a racehorse faltering, of a fighter unable to exploit the openings. . . . On October 15th, when the wrong dateline, October 11th, was printed on page three, the men on the copy desk shrugged their shoulders and said, "I'm covered" to each other. It was the same reaction they gave when they put the wrong name of one of the Supremes on page one. "I'm covered."

Jules Feiffer was paid $20.00 per cartoon strip. Pete Hamill received $75.00 per column. Larry Merchant is paid $250 a week for four sports columns.* The *Post* did not even assign a reporter to travel regularly with the McCarthy and Kennedy campaigns last spring, although almost all their readers were turned on by the two antiwar candidacies. And according to Jimmy Breslin, the reason his popular column was secreted away on page sixteen every day was that the *Post* could charge special rates to advertisers for appearing on that inside page with him.

---

* The top *reporters* on *The New York Times* earn between $400 and $500 a week.

The Front Page Syndrome: The editors who put out the *Post* each day are all products of the Ben Hecht-1930s-*Front Page* era of journalism. Executive editor Paul Sann is a high school dropout who went to work for the *Post* thirty-eight years ago as a copyboy. The managing editor is Stan Opotowsky, whose values were shaped by his seasons with United Press and the Marines. "Opotowsky has a drill sergeant's approach to journalism," a former staff writer has complained. "All he's interested in is speed and good form. He just isn't interested in good writing." City editor Johnny Bott and sports editor Ike Gellis are both well into their fifties, and long ago stopped fighting the system at the *Post*. And the rigid seniority system protects them all.

As products of the Depression, all these editors share an anti-intellectual, protabloid bias. Most of them never went to college, and began working in "the business" for $12.00 or $15.00 a week. They resent the younger, college-educated reporters. They believe the *Post* should be geared to the lowest-common-denominator readership of the Bronx. And, above all, they believe in the sacred inverted-pyramid formula of journalism. Who, what, when, why in the lead. Then short, factual paragraphs that can be cut from the bottom with a meat cleaver. Longer pieces with a personal point of view, which have become something of a trend in our better papers, are *verboten*. Imaginative use of language is more often punished rather than rewarded. Bang It Out Quick is the motto of the desk, and almost no news story runs more than five hundred words. Reporters are not assigned to beats they have special feelings about. Attempts at unconventional approaches to stories inevitably get aborted by the mechanistic editors.

Pete Hamill recalls: "In 1963, when I was a reporter, I was sent to cover the last execution at Sing Sing. It really got to me. It was an Irish kid who grew up in Chelsea. So I came back to the city room and wrote a piece telling exactly how it was, with the urine running down the guy's pants leg as the electricity shot through his body. But Bob Friedman made me rewrite the whole thing. He just wanted a nice, straight news lead. Who died, what time, how many minutes. That's when I decided to quit the first time."

This is an era in which the journalistic form is exploding. What William Burroughs did to the novel, and what Bob Dylan did to the popular song, Norman Mailer has done to journalism.

The best young writers want to escape the prison of "two and a half books" and follow their instincts. But the *Front Page* generation at the *Post* is oblivious to this energy.

The *Front Page* types also impose an outdated puritanism on the prose of their writers. When Larry Merchant heard Norman Mailer say of the late Robert Kennedy, "He was a rich kid who gave a shit," it came out in the *Post* as a "rich kid who gave a damn," making Mailer sound like a shill for the Urban Coalition. And when I was on the *Post,* the copy desk changed "half-*naked* kids" to "half-*dressed* kids" in a feature I did on Bedford-Stuyvesant.

During the 1950s, the *Post* was a writers' newspaper. Irony, realism, original form, and creative use of language were encouraged. There was space to compose longer, personal stories. Individual styles were appreciated by the editors. Younger reporters were coached and encouraged by the veterans. But today the *Post* is an editors' paper. No reporter has an individual style. The news stories are all the same, each conforming to the ritual formula. And this trend seems to be what Mrs. Schiff desires; she recently told a friend, "We don't want any stars on the *Post.* After a while they get bigger than the paper." Perhaps the most damning thing about the *Post,* in hard, professional terms, has been its failure to develop, or keep, any young writer of distinction. Pete Hamill was probably the last one, and he was hired in 1960, and has quit the *Post* twice since then. But under the Sann-Schiff regime, the *Post* has not developed a single younger journalist of the quality of Mike Royko of the Chicago *Daily News,* or Anthony Lukas of *The New York Times,* or Nicholas von Hoffman of the Washington *Post.* In the last five years, every reporter who has been one notch above a formula robot, has quit. Leonard Koppett left to go to the *Times.* Bernard Lefkowitz quit to go to Columbia University and write a book. Gerald Nachman went to the Oakland *Tribune.* Nora Ephron quit to free-lance.

A textbook case of the *Post's* pettiness was the way it responded to the Norman Mailer-Jimmy Breslin mayoral campaign in New York City last spring. The Boston *Globe* broke the story on April 10. *The New York Times* and Washington *Post* ran long feature stories on it. Papers in London, Tokyo, and Toronto published stories. *Time* and *Newsweek* reported on it. But until the end of April the *Post* blacked it out of its news col-

umns, while giving Norman Frank and Vito Battista generous space.

One night at 2:00 A.M., *Post* reporter Jay Levin telephoned me to interview me about the campaign, since I was Breslin's press secretary. A few minutes later he called Gloria Steinem and Peter Maas, two other organizers of this effort at citizen politics. But the next morning no story appeared in the *Post*. When I called a friendly reporter there to ask for an explanation, he said, after getting a pledge of anonymity, "Sann killed the story when he came in at seven. He resents Breslin for quitting, and didn't want to give him any free publicity. Levin's story was dummied and in type, and Sann just killed it because of a grudge." A few days later Pamela Howard, a young *Post* reporter, asked the city desk if she could do a feature on Mailer and Breslin campaigning in the city's Reform Democratic clubs. But she was informed by an editor that Sann had ordered a blackout on Breslin.

On May 5, Mailer and Breslin held the first press conference of their campaign. Both wire services, the *Times,* NBC television, and several radio stations assigned reporters to cover it. But the *Post* boycott was still going strong. The next day, May 6, Mailer conducted a press conference on the occasion of his winning the Pulitzer Prize, and attacked the press for "not giving me a fair shake." He itemized complaints against the *Times, News, Village Voice,* and *Post*. The conference was attended by a hip, young *Post* reporter, John Garabedien. When he got back to the city room he was told by city editor Johnny Bott not to write a story, but rather a memo for the publisher on everything Mailer had said. After reading the memo, Mrs. Schiff ordered no story printed on Mailer's charges of press unfairness, although the next day, the *Times, News,* and *Voice* all published Mailer's critical remarks.

The Catch-22 Syndrome: Dorothy Schiff, at sixty-six, still a womanly woman, runs the *Post* with capricious, impersonal authority. She has fired two assistants to the publisher, one editor, one managing editor, and countless columnists in the last eight years. She keeps her aging incumbent editors in fear of their jobs, and trying hard to anticipate her whims, with a legendary flood of daily memos, typed on yellow onionskin paper.

Why was Jackie Onassis' picture in the paper three times in the last nine days? Why was this year's history of Passover not as

interesting as last year's? I want Golda Meir to be this week's Woman in the News Saturday feature. Let's do an interview with Philip Roth's mother. Mrs. Schiff, it seems, is preoccupied, often quite imaginatively, with trivia and gossip. Thus, she pays almost no attention to the essentials of the paper, and often does not interfere in its political direction. As a result, the staff is never sure who has made a particular decision—Dolly? Sann? A copyboy? Or what the logic is behind that decision, or whether another decision can be appealed.

Leonard Schecter, who spent twenty years at the *Post,* from copyboy to columnist, puts the blame on the publisher. "The root of the problem," he says, "is that Dolly really doesn't know that Murray Kempton writes better than Earl Wilson. Her own taste is the gossip column. That is the level of her sensibility, and that gets communicated to the rest of the paper. After all, she does own it."

Al Aronowitz, however, who quit the *Post* during the 1962–63 strike, still defends his old family and blames the business of daily journalism. "Everything Dolly has done," he says, "has been instinctively right. She was right to dump Wechsler. She has kept it alive, and she deserves credit for that. If there wasn't a *Post* at all, then you would appreciate what it is. If all you had was the *Journal-American,* then you would miss the *Post.* She's outlasted them all. She's infallible. The problem is the daily newspaper business itself. It can't compete with television and magazines. Newspapers can't pay the salaries that guys like Breslin and Kempton are worth. There's not enough room for a writer to really stretch out. There's not enough time to think. Daily journalism just has its own set of built-in space, time, and economic limitations."

Her friends, victims, and rivals all admit Dorothy Hall Backer Thackrey Sonneborn Schiff is a formidable woman. She has outlasted four husbands, plus Hearst, Whitney, and Scripps-Howard to become the sole owner of the biggest afternoon newspaper in the land. Kings, bankers, and presidents court her whims. She is almost certainly one of the five most powerful woman in New York City.

Mrs. Schiff's parents both died in the early 1930s, bequeathing her an estate worth millions while she was still in her twenties. She was raised as a Republican; Roosevelt made her a Democrat;

and in 1938, she ran as a delegate to the state constitutional convention, but lost to Robert Moses.

When people who know her socially are asked to describe her, the same narrow litany of adjectives is invoked: intuitive, eccentric, feminine, shrewd. Blair Clark, Eugene McCarthy's 1968 campaign manager, who was associate publisher at the *Post* for nine months in 1965–66, says, "Dolly is an inspired amateur. Her time is taken up with the business side of the paper, and she tries to edit it with one hand. So it's very haphazard and unprofessional. . . . The basic problem there is that her formative experience was the brutal competitive situation the *Post* used to be in. She's so used to the economic squeeze that she doesn't know how to use the elbowroom she has now. She doesn't know how to make it a class newspaper, or how to compete with television. She has no idea of expanding now that the *Post* is a monopoly, because she made the paper a success by cutting corners."

Part of the *Catch-22* feeling at the *Post* comes from Dolly's Olympian aloofness, coupled with her absolute power, which is focused on trivia. Mrs. Schiff rarely appears in the city room, choosing to communicate with her editors almost exclusively by memo. Most staff members have never met her, even those with ten and fifteen years' service at the *Post*. It took Schecter twenty years to meet her, and Vic Ziegel is now in his tenth year on the paper without ever being introduced. Dave Gelman was on the *Post* for nineteen years before he first met her. The occasion was Gelman's request for a leave of absence, which was denied. So he quit. Pete Hamill, in the company of Robert Kennedy, one night in June of 1966, arrived at Mrs. Schiff's apartment, only to be asked by the publisher, "And who are you, young man?"

"I'm one of your columnists," explained Hamill.

Also contributing to this mood is the way departing executives and columnists are treated. As in Stalin's Russia, they just vanish from the paper without explanation, and become nonpersons. When Schecter's column was dropped, not one word of farewell or explanation appeared in the *Post*. The same is true when Hamill gave up his popular column in 1966. When Blair Clark ceased to be the associate publisher, his name just vanished from the masthead one day without a trace. Although the *Times* printed a lengthy news story about Breslin, Kempton, and Feiffer leaving, not one word appeared in the *Post*.

I met Mrs. Schiff just once, four years ago. At that time, only nine months after I was rejected as a night rewrite man, she invited me up to her penthouse office, and suggested I write a daily column in the *Post*. It was at this point I started to feel like Yossarian.

My meeting with Mrs. Schiff, I have subsequently discovered, was quite typical. She began by asking me bluntly if I was a communist. When I assured her I wasn't, she mixed me a strong drink, kittenishly curled up on a sofa, and free-associated for thirty charming minutes about her summers at Palm Beach with the Kennedys. Then she offered me the column, "four times a week, financial details to be arranged later."

After thinking it over for three weeks, I wrote Mrs. Schiff a respectful note, explaining that I felt no one could be programmed to write at a predetermined rhythm, for a predetermined space, suggesting that the traditional concept of the daily column was obsolete. I added that I felt the *Voice* was more congenial to the longer advocacy reportage I was interested in doing.

Mrs. Schiff never answered my letter. When I called a friendly columnist at the *Post,* he told me that he had heard that the publisher had changed her mind and decided to withdraw the offer to me. Had I been rejected again? Or had I the honor of refusing a column at the New York *Post?* I didn't know. But I felt very empathetic with Yossarian's attempts to relate to the remote colonels in the Pentagon.

The archetypal *Post* feature has become an interview with the distraught mother of a mass murderer, or with the sobbing wife of a miner trapped in a mine disaster. Over the years, *Post* reporters have been forced to transform personal sorrow into macabre inquisitions for a readership conditioned to titillation. No victim's privacy is respected. However, when I tried to see the three top executives at the *Post* for this piece, all three flatly refused to grant me interviews.

James Wechsler said, "I'd rather not . . . I might get into trouble." Paul Sann explained, "I have a policy of never giving interviews about the *Post*." And two days after I requested an audience with Mrs. Schiff, I received a registered letter turning me down. Mrs. Schiff's letter referred to an article I had written for the August 4, 1966, issue of the *Voice*, whose facts, she complained, I had neglected to check before publication. Her missive concluded: ". . . I cannot have any confidence in your objectiv-

ity or fairness as a reporter on matters relating to the *Post*. . . ."
I found the thought that Mrs. Schiff had a three-year-old clip-
ping of mine from the *Voice* in her private files chilling and
suggestive.

The *Post* makes enormous profits today, but with Kempton's
departure, it publishes no more columnists of distinction, and
very few younger journalists of promise. (Exceptions are sports-
writers Larry Merchant and Vic Ziegel, and reporters Ken Gross
and Tim Lee. Of the older reporters Helen Dudar is the best, as
her coverage of the Sirhan Sirhan trial proved again.)

The *Post* today has a circulation of over 700,000, but it doesn't
go home. Many readers require only the brief subway ride home
from work to finish it, and then leave it behind on their seats for
the subway scavengers. The paper has become like Muzak in an
elevator, present but not heard by its captive audience. It is currently investing more than $13 million in a new plant, and new
color printing presses, in renovating the old *Journal-American*
building on South Street. But it has even dropped its subscrip-
tion to the AP local wire.

Cannon, Hamill, Breslin, Shannon, Feiffer, and Kempton are
all gone now. In their places appear syndicated columnists like
Drew Pearson, Evans and Novak, William F. Buckley, and Clayton Fritchey. Gone are street-smart stylists like Aronowitz, Grove,
Poirier, Gelman, and Greene, replaced by homogenized wire-service copy, and those "two-book" stories lifted out of the *Times* and
News. There are no more prize-winning exposés. There are no
investigative reporters or specialists on the staff. The *Post* has no
pop culture critic in the city that is the capital of pop culture.
New York City has 700,000 Puerto Ricans, but the *Post* has only
one Spanish-speaking reporter—Tim Lee—and he never is assigned to cover stories in the *barrio*. The *Post* has no reporter
based in Queens or the Bronx, much less a man in Saigon.

Despite its monopoly, despite its profits, despite its soon-to-be-
completed new plant, the *Post* is an institution going through a
slow internal death of its moral authority. It could be a newspaper that was a singular force for reform and renewal in a decaying city. The city's activist high school and college students don't
identify with the *Post* anymore, preferring the underground papers and postlinear extensions of man like records and films.
Young committed writers no longer ache to work for the *Post*.
Instead they send their long, nonobjective, first-person pieces on

the city off to *The Village Voice* or *New York* magazine. The new, rapidly growing class of college-educated professionals in New York now get their hard information from television, or the *Times,* and get their cultural values from *Commentary,* or the *New York Review of Books.* The hard core of *Post* readers now buy the paper for Leonard Lyons' gossip column, the stock market tables, and the late sports results from the West Coast. The Jewish Mother of us all is gone, and there are few mourners around to say a proper *Kaddish.*

SEPTEMBER, 1969

[2.]
Media Response: Medium Fool*

The two of us spent the past week interviewing media executives and reporters about the Justice Department's attempt to subpoena unedited newsmagazine files and television film footage. Most of the bureaucrats we spoke to seemed to us surprisingly ignorant about what goes on in their own organizations, and somewhat naïve about the connection between last week's rather narrow episode and the overall policy of repression the Nixon administration seems to have adopted—the kind of people who thought that "Medium Cool" was just a movie.

For example, Richard Salant, director of CBS Television News, told us the issue of the subpoenas had been "festering in our legal department from last October until very recently when I learned about it." It was a film librarian, he added, who complied with the first subpoena, submitting films to the Justice Department without informing any superiors.

Hal Bruno, *Newsweek*'s news editor, told us that when his magazine received its subpoenas last fall he checked with the editors of *Time* and was told they hadn't received similar papers. "I guess I should have called the legal department," he said later. "It turns out they knew and the editors didn't."

Don Wilson, *Time*'s vice-president for corporate and public affairs, corroborates Bruno's story. "This is a big organization," he said. "No one really zeroed in on the issue. I just learned about it last week although the subpoenas were served three months ago."

Now, while the executives deplore the Justice Department policy, they seem to feel it represents nothing more sinister than an effort by some "lazy" government bureaucrats "to get us to do their work for them," as Salant put it. The government went on a "fishing expedition" for the Panther film because its employees

---

* This piece was written jointly with Paul Cowan.

were unwilling to decide what they wanted and search for it reel
by reel, Salant suggests; it subpoenaed CBS's interoffice memo-
randa relating to the Panther interviews, and a logbook of phone
calls between the revolutionary organization and network employees, because those documents promised to save legwork. In a
subsequent interview Wilson would use almost the same language to explain why the Justice Department wanted *Time*'s
files.

By the end of last week some media executives were claiming
that the Justice Department's agreement to negotiate with lawyers for the press and television before issuing subpoenas represented a victory. "Imagine that," Wilson said as we began our interview. "John Mitchell admitting he was wrong." (Later that
weekend Wilson, an unusually candid and introspective man,
would decide his optimism might be ill founded: "I got suspicious when the attorney general offered to meet with us.")

To us, the Justice Department concession seems like a cosmetic
too. The government will continue to get pretty much all the information it needs to harass and prosecute dissenters, if not
through the media then through informers and wiretaps; the
only change is that the administration's relations with the press
may be a little more gentlemanly. Indeed, the subpoena controversy may even have produced an unexpected benefit for Nixon
and Mitchell. The attorney general's about-face on a narrow but
highly publicized issue might persuade some corporate liberals
and part of the public that the Justice Department is becoming
reasonable at last, and make them less wary of the constant, increasing danger of Agnewism.

As we made our tour through the labyrinthine media bureaucracies we kept discovering new, disturbing aspects of the government's relations with the press which have not yet been reported:

—THE GOVERNMENT has not confined its reconnaissance
of media files to efforts to get information about leftwing groups.
The House Commerce Committee, which has jurisdiction over
television, has subpoenaed a CBS documentary on hunger in
America and some CBS film on Marks, Mississippi. "They don't
seem to believe hunger and poverty really exist," Salant says.
"They seem to think they can prove we staged these things for effect."

The antitrust division of the Justice Department subpoenaed
Fortune magazine last October for tape recordings, interview

notes, early drafts relating to an interview with James Ling, head of the conglomerate Ling-Temco-Vought. The magazine's executives heard about that subpoena at once and refused to honor it ("Our actions were exemplary in this case," says Wilson), arguing that in the forty years *Fortune* has been interviewing businessmen there had been no other noncriminal case in which a government agency subpoenaed raw materials. Thus, Time-Life executives were more sensitive to James Ling's rights than the Weathermen's, but the Justice Department still obtained the material through Ling himself and through another snarl at a lower level of the bureaucracy. "They couldn't use any of it," says Wilson. "It was just another fishing expedition."

—ALTHOUGH the Justice Department insists the current wave of subpoenas in no way represents a change of policies, Salant told us that right after the Democratic Convention there was a dramatic increase in the use of them, which has not yet subsided.

Some people connected with the media argue that the government, besides intimidating the press, wants to increase the difficulty of news-gathering. If stories about radicals—or poverty or big business—mean the press and television must spend money duplicating reams of material, hire lawyers, spend hours of executive time defining policies which must vary from case to case, then eventually they will lose the incentive to hustle after risky news. They will be reluctant to spend time and money muckraking government agencies, as well as investigating radical organizations. And—the argument runs—media which operate from press release to press release are not very difficult to control.

Some reporters and many radicals feel the entire episode was designed to increase tension between the media and the Left, to isolate the Movement so it can be destroyed.

—ALTHOUGH Salant insists CBS gives a subpoena issued by the defense exactly the same status as a subpoena issued by the government, a complicated sort of double standard seems to have been involved in the distribution of television news film and tape at the Chicago Conspiracy trial.

CBS itself has not charged either the defense or prosecution for film or tape. But the U.S. Attorney's office in Chicago still has all the CBS videotape of the convention, according to Salant (who told a *Time* reporter that "we can't get it back"), while the Conspiracy—with a much lower budget—has had to pay about

$1500 to a film processing house to have the CBS material duplicated, according to Linda Minor of the Conspiracy staff.

Representatives of the Conspiracy, who saw all the network material last summer, are certain some of it has vanished. Linda Minor adds, "For example, everytime a nightstick is about to fall on a kid the film seems to end. I talked to a cameraman who told me about a scene he'd shot that has been missing since two days after the convention ended. He's been looking for it ever since. Other cameramen have told me similar stories."

—IF THE MEDIA had accepted the advice of their legal department, they would never have opposed the Justice Department. But at *Newsweek,* where resistance to the subpoena was boldest, those making the decisions have been the reporters whose files were involved, the top-level editors, and the chairman of the board. *Time* and CBS relied much more heavily on their lawyers. But "the legal departments just don't realize they can resist these things," according to Salant.

At *Newsweek* there is discontent among some younger staffers, though they feel the magazine displayed a measure of courage when it refused to divulge its sources (the editors decided to cut half a page out of a file on the Weathermen rather than leave hints that might let a prosecutor identify a source). They think the magazine should have refused to share its information—as well as the names—with the government.

Newsweek has not been gutsy or creative enough to fashion a test case that would bring the Justice Department into court, they add. "Some people here think the executives are trying to avoid the issues, praying they'll vanish," said one staffer who complained of *Newsweek*'s "defeatist attitude," its "fear of losing in court."

—IT SEEMS to us that the naïveté media executives displayed about the workings of their bureaucracies is matched by an inability to consider using their collective power in a fight against government repression, and an innocence about the extent to which their organizations have already been corrupted.

For example, Wilson says it never occurred to him to call executives of *Newsweek,* CBS, and the *Times* to coordinate a campaign against misuse of the subpoena. So far as he knows no other media official had that thought either. Apparently, the men who control the Establishment press that Agnew attacked have not been able to devise a general strategy against him ei-

ther. They are not used to fighting, probably have forgotten how. That is why Agnew could graciously claim his campaign was a success the week before last.

Nor, of course, are the men who control the media alert to the fact that free press in America has been seriously compromised throughout the decade. Collusion between the White House and the Establishment press was a constant fact of life in Kennedy and Johnson years, only then the interlocking corridors were smoothed by common social class and political affiliation: Jack Kennedy had only to phone Scotty Reston to convince the *Times* to kill its story on the Bay of Pigs; according to Gay Talese's book *The Kingdom and the Power,* Punch Sulzberger and the rest of the *Times* senior staff felt that as gentlemen they had to allow CIA director John McCone to see their series on the agency before it was published, to let him make suggestions and even do some editing (it is hard to imagine Sulzberger extending the same courtesy to Eldridge Cleaver or Mark Rudd).

When Kennedy or Johnson sent a delegation abroad, a newsmagazine foreign correspondent was usually on hand to act as statesman and brief the delegates. Liberal Democrats were always at chummy Washington parties with people from *Time* and *Newsweek*—many of them, in fact, half-wished they were working for those publications themselves.

The new, crude element in the situation is the subpoena, which has replaced the gentleman's agreement. It largely results from the fact that the self-made Nixonians who are now in Washington are not able to get what they want through informal arrangements with the working press.

Years of collusion have deadened the moral nerve of many media executives and, still worse, destroyed their reflexes. It took *Ramparts* to reveal the covert subversion of NSA and *Encounter* by the CIA. Many of the Ivy Leagues who control (and, to a great extent, staff) the liberal news-gathering institutions were not able to realize that members of their social class could do such things. And those who did know about the infiltration probably believed it was perfectly moral.

So far, the men who run the Establishment media have done alarmingly little to combat the increasingly obvious fact that CIA and FBI agents are disguising themselves as members of the working press. (It happened last week in Saigon; it has been revealed a number of times during the Conspiracy trial; and any

reporter in New York knows the man who stands next to him covering a demonstration might be a member of the FBI or CIA.)

Some reporters and writers on *Time* and *Newsweek* seem to believe that agents have periodically infiltrated the magazines' foreign desks—and perhaps even their domestic operations. But their corporate superiors appear to be as skeptical about the possibility of such infiltration as, six months ago, they would have been about the increasing danger of federal subpoenas. When it was suggested to Don Wilson (who was Edward R. Murrow's assistant at USIA) he seemed genuinely shocked. "Of course we'd raise motherfucking hell if we found an agent. But I'm almost positive it's never happened."

—ONE OF THE MOST important unresolved issues that has arisen out of the subpoena crisis is: who owns the information that a newsmagazine reporter obtains? Who decides whether a particular file or article or notebook should be turned over to the government? The individual or the corporation?

Wilson, who agrees the issue is ambiguous, seems to feel it will usually be resolved during compassionate consultations between reporters, editors, and lawyers, and people at *Newsweek* echo him. But when we tried to push the matter further, hypothesizing specific cases, the discussions usually trailed to a halt.

A limited part of the answer is clear, and true for everyone in the communications industry. Whatever actually appears belongs to the media—*Rat, The Voice, Time,* or CBS—unless the author has it copyrighted. But newspaper journalism is usually an individual enterprise: a *Voice* or *Times* reporter selects what he will put in print from his own notes: an editor might edit what has been written, might suggest different angles, but he rarely culls new material from the reporter's notebook. And the Earl Caldwell case (where a *Times* reporter had to make an individual decision whether to give his notebooks on the Panthers to the Justice Department) suggests that the raw material of a newsman's story is his own property. (Some press people argue that even that area is shady, but Wilson says that at *Time,* too, the reporters' notebooks are their own property.)

The situation in corporate journalism is different. The information collected by a *Newsweek* or *Time* reporter is included in the "file" he sends to his superiors. The files become, in effect,

the institution's notebooks, and editors in New York select the material they want to use. Legally, the files are the corporation's property. A *Newsweek* reporter who wanted to protect the information as well as the names in the Weatherman file would have had no power to prevent Hal Bruno from giving that part of the document to the Justice Department.

Thus, the more creative or aggressive a corporate reporter, the more dangerous he can become to the people he hopes to interpret. He wins the trust of black militants or student activists; decides to include everything they've told him in his file so he can persuade the New York office to produce a more accurate, open-minded story. But the file he submits in good faith can go directly to an administration whose intent is to prosecute, not explain.

Sometimes, as we talked to reporters and editors on *Time* and *Newsweek*, we thought they might be willing to fight for control over their information. "Maybe we're good Germans," said one. "I don't know what I'll do if I become convinced of that."

But it is hard to imagine a sustained, militant confrontation within a newsmagazine. They are such chatty, clubby institutions —like college newspapers only with profit-sharing plans, expense accounts, air credit cards. As you sit inside offices, chatting with reporters under posters of Chairman Mao or Allen Ginsberg, you are haunted by memories of the easy Ivy League tolerance of the New Frontier. An angry mood would be hard to sustain there; it would seem crude and ungracious in that context.

"Most people here are privately disturbed about the subpoenas, but I don't know whether they'd do much publicly," said the *Time* reporter who was worried about being a good German. It is hard to know whether the *Newsweek* staffers, who are now considering petitions urging that the subpoenas be stopped and that the magazine withhold all information, would fight any harder than people at *Time* if resistance seemed likely to cost them their jobs. "I don't know whether I would have quit if the magazine had caved in to the Justice Department. I certainly don't think most people here would have," said one.

Now, listen to Champ Clark, *Time*'s bureau chief in Chicago. He had been told about the Justice Department's subpoenas a week after he filed his Weatherman story last October. But he never thought to ask his superiors whether they had honored it. They never thought to bring him into the decision-making pro-

cess, though Wilson insists he would be carefully consulted if the
episode were to repeat itself today. But would it matter if he
were? Clark considers the ignorance in which he was kept between late October and mid-January a natural and acceptable
state: "After all, the files belong to management. They have a
right to do anything they want with them."

To us, the most revealing aspect of the entire subpoena episode has been the performance of most media executives, and of
editors like Champ Clark. They are the people who issue constant, Olympian judgments of public figures and political movements, but who allow themselves, as judges, to be protected by
the mask of corporate anonymity. Now that they have been
forced to perform in the open, it is clear that they and their organizations are at least as naïve, disorganized, and—in some
cases—amoral as the men and institutions they criticize so self-
righteously.

Will there be reporters, editors, and executives within the corporate news-gathering institutions who take risks to resist further
collusion with the government? Clearly, many of the most important battles of this decade must be waged inside the vast, faceless
organizations that control so much of this country. As the Nixon
administration becomes more repressive it will naturally try to
force the media to accustom people to an increasingly repressive
political climate. The media will probably keep trying to disguise major concessions behind small, well-publicized stalemates.
Decent people who work inside news-gathering organizations will
be tempted to let their personalities and ideals be subverted by
pressures which force them to mute their opposition to ugly compromises (to talk their objections out with a superior, then accept
a bad situation or discover a clever way to ignore it), lest they be
fired for protesting too loudly.

There must be public fights, and we want to suggest five specific issues around which people working in the media can organize them. (Some of these demands are drawn from a petition
that is being circulated by the Media Mobilization.)

1) A pledge by all news-gatherers to destroy confidential raw
material rather than submit to the state;

2) A campaign for a national confidentiality law that would
prohibit the government from trespassing on the relationship between the press and its sources;

3) An angry, sustained campaign by all media institutions to rid the profession of police and government agents;

4) A guarantee from the management of all media institutions that their staffs be informed of all government requests for information, both formal and informal;

5) A guarantee that management supply legal counsel to all individuals who are subpoenaed.

FEBRUARY, 1970

[3.]

All the News That Fits Editors' Views*

The liberal attitude toward the Chicago Conspiracy verdict became clear last week; its first expressions were in two *New York Times* editorials, and in columns and editorials in the New York *Post* by James Wechsler. The argument, quickly echoed by many liberal politicians, held that the judge, the prosecution, and defendants and their lawyers all were equally to blame, but that the jury had vindicated the American court system with its wise, discriminating verdict.

(A *Times* editorial called the defendants' contempt citations "richly deserved," though too severe, but never let its readers evaluate that opinion by listing the precise citations in its news columns. William Kunstler, for example, was given a year in jail for "embracing Reverend Abernathy in front of the jury.")

The *Times* argued that "by . . . finding five of the seven [defendants] guilty of crossing state lines with an intent to start a riot, the jury has opened the way for a clear test of the constitutionality of the 1968 riot act"—which is very much like saying that a Missouri District Court in 1846, by denying Dred Scott his freedom, opened the way for a clear constitutional test of slavery.

We think the liberal response is both bland and blind.

The *Times* especially has failed to place the trial in its historical perspective—to recall the outrages committed in 1968, which must affect any total apportioning of blame. (Throughout the decade, *Times* editorials about innovative political actions have proved to be shortsighted. For example, in February 1960, two weeks after the first sit-ins, it devoted its fourth editorial, placed just above a eulogy to Lithuanian independence, to a criticism of the "so-called sit-ins." They would hurt the South's economy, the *Times'* editorial said. It advised Negroes to be patient and urged that the entire integration effort be placed in the hands of effec-

* This piece was written jointly with Paul Cowan.

tive moderate biracial committees. The *Times* also opposed the 1963 March on Washington and the early protests and teach-ins against the war in Vietnam.)

The *Times* and *Post* base their editorial judgments on media interpretations of what went on in the courtroom. Neither Wechsler nor any member of the *Times* editorial board bothered to spend a single hour at the trial.

And we have learned that Pulitzer Prize winner J. Anthony Lukas's news stories for the *Times,* the strongest influence on all editorial writers, were heavily edited, and that at least one interpretive piece Lukas submitted (last Thursday) was killed by the *Times'* editors. In any case, no short article could ever substitute for the feeling and specific taste of Judge Hoffman's repressive court.

Finally, we are convinced that the liberal media, and the many new politicians who take their cues from its opinions, are dangerously sanguine about the general condition of liberty and democratic process in America. It is clear to us that the Chicago Conspiracy trial, Fred Hampton's murder, the omnibus crime bill, the Panther 21 trial in New York, the Supreme Court nominations of Haynsworth and Carswell, the Justice Department's firing of procivil-rights lawyers like Gary Greenberg, its removal of U.S. Attorney Robert Morgenthau, John Mitchell's notion of inaugurating preventive detention, the accelerated use of subpoenas and wiretaps, the investigation into the November 15 peace march—all these things present a clear and present danger to law and order.

But a comfortable decade of power has ruined the liberals' reflexes. "Liberalism became the creature of Georgetown, Hyannisport, and Brattle Street," writes Kevin Phillips scornfully in *The Emerging Republican Majority*. As Phillips and his clever colleagues in the Justice Department realize, most of the people who control the *Times* and the *Post,* and most of the readers who identify with their views, no longer know when, or how, to fight.

The Chicago trial did not occur in a historical vacuum. It is vital to recall the series of public events that created it.

There was the 1968 Democratic Convention itself, which was not democratic. McCarthy and Kennedy won seven out of seven contested Presidential primaries, but by the time the convention

started, it was clear that Hubert Humphrey was going to be nominated because of the backroom maneuverings of big city bosses like Daley, Tate, Barr, and Alioto, and a few hawkish union leaders, led by Meany and I. W. Abel.

The demonstrators came to Chicago to protest the Vietnam war, racism, and the closed character of the Democratic Party; many were supporters of Kennedy or McCarthy, not SDSers or Yippies. The protesters had applied for a legal permit to rally in Soldiers' Field and sleep in Grant Park. Their request was turned down by Mayor Daley, and later by a city judge who was Daley's former law partner.

The street violence was initiated, and escalated, by the police —as the Walker Commission Report's subsequent judgment of a "police riot" would confirm.

The defendants were indicted under a dubious conspiracy statute, which most law professors regard as unconstitutional. The indictment included Panther leader Bobby Seale, who had nothing whatever to do with organizing the Chicago protests. Both of us had more to do with it than Seale, who was physically in Chicago only eighteen hours, as a substitute speaker for Eldridge Cleaver. To make things look fair, eight policemen were also indicted, but all have been fully acquitted.

If the Grand Jury had believed the Walker Report, they would have indicted Mayor Daley. Daley said repeatedly during the convention that the demonstrators planned to assassinate the candidates. After the convention the FBI and Attorney General Ramsey Clark agreed there was absolutely no evidence of such a plan. But Daley's statement probably incited police much more than anything Rennie Davis said to incite activists in the park.

All of this is prehistory to the trial itself. And when you think of the trial, it is essential to remember the psychic punishment to which the defendants were exposed in the courtroom day after day—by Judge Hoffman, the prosecution, and the federal marshals.

If we had been defendants, we hope we would have had the courage to act in the same way, as Davis, Hayden, and Dellinger did. They saw Bobby Seale denied his own lawyer, denied the right to defend himself, and then bound and gagged. They watched Ramsey Clark, the former attorney general, who made an original decision not to indict them, told that he could not testify to the jury about that decision—and then heard Judge Hoffman instruct their lawyers that to mention that whole, sorry

episode in front of the jury would be contempt. They watched a series of police agents—the only witnesses the prosecution could produce—lie about them, and then heard the judge outlaw their lawyers' attempts to expose those lies.

Certainly their outrage was far more heroic than the hedging and informing and dissembling and lying that characterized so many of their liberal critics' response to McCarthyism in the 1950s.

The United States may not today be the equivalent of Hitler's Germany, but Judge Hoffman's Chicago courtroom was like many German courtrooms in 1933. But as Jimmy Breslin says: "I'm sure that there were a bunch of liberal lawyers telling the Jews on the way to Auschwitz that if they didn't make any fuss they'd be out in six months for good behavior."

As we talked with *Times* staffers and editors and with the *Post*'s James Wechsler, we realized that many of the two papers' executives had immunized themselves—and their readers—from information that was favorable to the defendants.

Our interviews suggest the *Times* did so more obviously and more consciously than the *Post*. And did so through editorial judgments that surprised many professionals who were familiar with the internal workings of the newspaper.

For when the *Times* first assigned the conspiracy trial story to J. Anthony Lukas, one of its most perceptive journalists (who had been assigned to Chicago so that he could roam the Midwest and write the kind of colorful detailed stories that had won him the Pulitzer Prize), it seemed they were interested in printing rich interpretive articles about the trial. And that impression was heightened by the brilliant article Lukas wrote about Jerry Rubin in *Esquire* last fall, and by a very honest piece he wrote about his reaction to last spring's Harvard strike in *The New York Times Magazine*.

Instead, from the start of the trial, the *Times* harassed Lukas, giving him relatively little space, editing him heavily.

Also, as Lukas told a reporter of *Newsweek*, copy editors modified the language in his stories in a way that was clearly biased against the defense. If he wrote that Judge Hoffman "shouted," the verb would be changed to "said"; but Rubin or Abbie Hoffman or Dave Dellinger always "shouted." That, of course, is exactly the sort of nuance that affects readers most deeply.

"If I'd had as much freedom as Nick Von Hoffman [columnist

for the Washington *Post*] I would have covered the trial very differently," Lukas told the *Newsweek* reporter. Von Hoffman is one of the few journalists for the daily press who along with Pete Hamill and Tom Wicker, displayed a passion for justice in their copy.

Last week, after the jury returned with the verdict, Lukas submitted a 1000-word news analysis which the *Times* failed to publish.

The censoring of Lukas had considerable consequences. For example, Wechsler, chief editorial writer for the *Post,* says his impressions of the trial came mostly from Lukas's stories, after *Post* reporter Jerry Tallmer stopped covering the case in October. Wechsler blames the defendants nearly as much as Judge Hoffman for what went on in the courtroom, characterizing their behavior as "antics" like "jumping up and down in court." Epithets like "fascist pig" seemed to be etched in his mind far more deeply than the lucid protests Dave Dellinger issued so often during the case. But Wechsler says that if he believed that the defendants had responded to injustices in the courtroom more frequently than they took the initiative and "contrived contempt"—the distinction the *Times* seems to have blurred in Lukas's stories—then he might have to reconsider his assessment of the distribution of blame.

After we learned about the fate of Lukas's stories, we tried to talk with the *Times* editorial writers to find out whether they, too, had formed their opinions on the basis of the truncated articles that appeared in their paper.

We were told that no one from the *Times* editorial staff had gone to the trial or consulted with Lukas about the ideas or point of view in the editorials that were published. Nor, so far as we could find out, had John Oakes or Abe Raskin, the two main editorial writers, talked to the defendants or any of their lawyers.

Had they read the articles Tom Hayden has been publishing in the *Guardian*—easily the most lucid accounts of the trial that have appeared anywhere? (Wechsler hadn't.) Had they heard the long, revealing taped interviews with all of the defendants that have been broadcast on WBAI all week? (Wechsler wasn't familiar with them.) Could they even distinguish between the seven defendants—did they see them as abstract symbols or human beings? Did they realize, for example, that Abbie Hoffman, the boldest practitioner of what Wechsler called "contrived con-

tempt," was sentenced to just seven months for contempt of court, while Tom Hayden, whose notion of what he called "revolutionary survival" had caused him to remain relatively silent, was sentenced to fourteen months; and Dave Dellinger, whose ideology tells him that a moral man does not provoke attacks but always responds boldly to provocation, received a two-and-one-half-year sentence?

Had they been disciplined enough or curious enough—or courteous enough—to familiarize themselves with the span of ideas and intentions of the radicals whom they criticized so harshly?

"I can't tell you who wrote those editorials," A. H. Raskin said. "They're the institutional expression of the newspaper." But he did tell us that as a matter of policy the *Times* never consults its reporters about its editorials. "We believe that our editorial writers are responsible men," and that when they write they have "a firm bedrock of information," "all the relevant information."

Raskin had to call a second editorial writer to find out exactly what material had been examined before the paper reached its "institutional opinion." Our next conversation was a very unsatisfying one. The writer, whom Raskin refused to name, had heard one of the defendants speak and had participated in a discussion with him—but Raskin refused to tell us which defendant for fear of implicating the writer. The writer hadn't been to Chicago, according to Raskin, hadn't read the transcript of the trial or Hayden's articles or heard the WBAI tapes—but he had read two long articles about the case (with extracts from Bobby Seale and Allen Ginsberg) in *The New York Review of Books*.

"Would you call that a 'bedrock of information'?" we ask Raskin.

"Yes, and you have to remember that we have one of our best reporters in Chicago. We rely very heavily on Tony Lukas."

Then, we discovered that, unlike the Justice Department, the *Times* editorial writers don't read their reporters' raw files. "I don't know what goes on down there," Raskin said of the news department, when we asked if he knew whether Lukas's articles had been cut.

It was a bad day at bedrock: Raskin and the other anonymous editorial writer had seen only the Lukas material that appeared in the paper.

Our interview with Wechsler suggested how very far he—and,

we assume, Oakes and Raskin—are from understanding the defendants' points of view. In Wechsler's case such ignorance is particularly disturbing since his great strength is usually his ability to convey the outrage of specific injustices to individuals. But there seems to be a line between the reality of people like Dave Hawk, the draft resister and Moratorium leader about whom Wechsler has written some eloquent columns, and Tom Hayden, that Wechsler's imagination can't cross.

He said he thought the defendants displayed a "will to lose" the case—not that they wanted to go to jail individually but that they considered the judicial process so corrupt that they were doomed before the trial began. So their only alternative was disruption. "I disagree with that," Wechsler said.

Well, for the most part, the defendants disagree with that, too. In fact the most important argument within the defense during the trial, came after the prosecution had rested, when most legal observers agreed the government's case was so weak that the defense would win if it rested, too. That was the lawyers' advice, and many of the defendants agreed.

But Tom Hayden insisted the Conspiracy had a political responsibility to show what had happened in Chicago, 1968, and in America during the decade—to show what had created the disillusioned, revolutionary mood that exploded on the streets. It was typical of Hayden. For the past ten years he has displayed faith that there is real decency lying latent in American people, which has caused him to take repeated risks. He has always acted with a humanity that his rhetoric has occasionally belied. In 1961 he was one of the first white activists to join SNCC in the South, and was badly beaten in McComb, Mississippi, for his efforts. After drafting the Port Huron Statement and trying to infuse the white middle-class students who joined SDS with the humanitarian passion of SNCC workers—like Bob Moses—he had known, Hayden founded an ERAP project in black Newark. His main work there was talking to people, helping them plan specific actions—rent strikes or community centers or militant appeals for traffic lights—that would encourage them to see themselves as powerful actors in history. His trips to North Vietnam meant the release of captured U.S. pilots whose freedom the State Department could never had obtained. Then in June of 1968, Hayden stood in St. Patrick's Cathedral weeping over the coffin of Robert Kennedy.

Hayden wanted to proceed with the defense because he had

enough confidence in the courtroom procedures, and in the Americans who had been chosen to serve on the jury, to believe that once the Conspiracy's case had been presented it would create a hung jury. He convinced the other defendants he was right. And it may have been the decision Hayden inspired, to present the dismal story of the '60s, that finally caused four jurors to vote to acquit the defendants until their great weariness, and pressure from an angry judge and some other angry jurors, forced them to agree to a "compromise" verdict that had much more to do with politics than justice.

We told Wechsler all that. But it wasn't enough to make him change his mind. He couldn't even admit Hayden's decision had involved bravery or compassion.

The Chicago five are now in prison for at least five years each. Spiro Agnew has called the jury's decision "an American verdict." The defendants' only chance at freedom would be if the Seventh Circuit Appeals Court grants them bail. The judges on that court will overrule Judge Hoffman and repudiate Mayor Daley only if serious countervailing political pressures are mobilized; this was a political trial, the jury's hotel room compromise was political, and the appeal decision will probably be political.

But this countervailing pressure is simply not happening, partially because the *Times* and *Post* editorials have not alarmed the conscience of the new politics, but instead have reassured it that democracy still works, that the courts are still legitimate, that the defendants and their lawyers behaved just as badly as the judge.

But if the *Times* and *Post* had said the courts are now being systematically used as instruments of government repression, if they said the defendants must be freed immediately on bail, if they connected the trial to the murder of Fred Hampton, preventive detention, and the new repressive crime bill, then maybe the necessary outrage might have been generated. It's an index of that moral decay of liberalism that these libertarian positions are now considered revolutionary.

So most of the liberal politicians, who expect the young to carry them into the White House, have been silent—Mondale, McGovern, Kennedy, McCarthy, Muskie, Harris—they have all gone about their business as usual. The New Democratic Coalition and the Moratorium have also failed to react in any effective way despite pressures and phone calls. Benjamin Rosenthal has

offered to fly to Chicago, but he is only one Congressman from Queens. The only even adequate response from a national political figure has come from Mayor Lindsay, who, while making the ritualistic criticisms of the defendants, did tell the Bar Association last week:

"The blunt, hard fact is that we in this nation appear headed for a new period of repression—more dangerous than at any time in years . . . this new threat of repression imposes on all of us an obligation to stand and be heard. . . .

"All of us, I think, see the recent Chicago trial as a defeat for the integrity of the judicial process. All of us, I think, see in the trial a tawdry parody of our judicial system.

"But it is important to understand the roots of this disaster. When you try political activists under a conspiracy charge—long considered to be the most dubious kind of criminal charge—difficult to define or to limit—and when a trial becomes fundamentally an examination of political acts and beliefs—then guilt or innocence becomes almost irrelevant. The process becomes a matter of political opinion instead of legal judgment, and the sense of a courtroom as an independent, open, and judicious tribunal becomes lost.

"And we lost something else, too. Whatever the ultimate verdicts, who has really won this case? Think of yourself as a young man or woman, entering into political concern. If you had witnessed what happened in Chicago, which of you would believe that our system was open, fair-minded, and humane? Which of you would come away from this trial with a renewed faith in our judicial system?"

With this article, and the one we wrote two weeks ago on the Justice Department's subpoenas of raw files and films, we have attempted to explore normally anonymous processes inside media institutions.

Our conclusion is that liberal media executives have shown a prejudice in favor of familiar authority, have lacked the will to fight against the government's limits on liberty, and have been naïve about what is becoming the characteristic issue of the Nixon Presidency—individual freedom and the new, white-collar McCarthyism.

FEBRUARY, 1970

[4.]
All the News That Fits the Times' Views

"It is more important than ever that the *Times* keep objectivity in its news columns as its number one, bedrock principle."

—Memo by A. M. Rosenthal
to the staff of *The New York Times*.

Archetypal liberal institutions like the NAACP and Yale University have become convinced that the Black Panthers are the victims of an extraordinary amount of repression by the police, the courts, the Justice Department, and the FBI. But the good, gray *New York Times* still doesn't think so.

Over the past year the *Times* has displayed a consistent pattern of prejudice against the Panthers in its supposedly objective news pages, as well as in its supposedly civil libertarian editorial pages. The *Times* has done this through inaccurate reporting, editors killing stories that do not attack the Panthers, editors failing to assign stories that might present the Panthers in a sympathetic or human way, reporters accepting police and D. A. versions of events as the truth.

What follows are just a few concrete examples of the *Times'* bias, gleaned from reading back issues of the paper and interviewing a dozen frustrated reporters.

Two months ago, cultural reporter Israel Shenker interviewed French playwright Jean Genet on assignment for the city desk. Most of Genet's comments were about the repression of the Panthers. Shenker wrote up the interview and submitted it to the city desk. It was never printed.

The first *Times* editorial anyone remembers on the subject of the Panthers was its attack ("elegant slumming") on a fund-raising party for the Panthers' legal defense given by Mrs. Leonard Bernstein. The editorial said that "responsible black leaders"

didn't support the Panthers. The next day Andrew Young of the SCLC and Assemblyman Charles Rangel held a press conference to refute the *Times'* judgment on who spoke for the blacks. The press conference was not fit to print.

Charlaynne Hunter wrote a "New Yorker type" feature story on the Panthers' free breakfast program for hungry children in Harlem. It was mostly description and dialogue. It was published—but under the headline "Panthers Indoctrinate the Young."

John Kifner was assigned to write a Sunday magazine piece after the murder of Fred Hampton and Mark Clark in Chicago. (Kifner had written brilliant copy for the daily paper on the shooting but it was buried in the back.) Kifner interviewed ballistic experts, the coroner, eye-witnesses, and doctors. He wrote a muckraking, factual piece suggesting the police account of the shoot-out was not the whole truth. The magazine did not accept the article, telling him by telegram the story was "Panther propaganda." Last week Kifner's investigative instinct was vindicated when the state of Illinois dropped all criminal charges against the seven other Panthers in the Hampton apartment, and a special federal grand jury report documented the lies in the police version of the shooting. Kifner's rejected piece will soon be published in *Scanlan's* magazine.

The *Times* has published perceptive biographies of white middle-class radicals and hippies like Linda Fitzpatrick, Kathy Boudin, Diane Oughton, and Jane Alpert. But the *Times* has never printed an individual biographical account of any of the lives of the Panthers. Charlotte Curtis, the creative women's page editor, wanted to write a feature story on the wives and girl friends of the Panther 21, but was advised not to by managing editor Rosenthal and assistant managing editor Seymour Topping. Rudy Johnson, a young black reporter, drafted and submitted a feature on Panther Afeni Shakur, but it was never printed. Judy Klemesrud, of the women's page, wrote an exclusive interview with Kathleen Cleaver. It ran in the news section, but was killed after the first edition when Rosenthal objected to it.

When Fred Richardson was indicted with the Panther 21, court reporter Morris Kaplan identified him as a Black Panther, even though Richardson was publicly expelled from the Party a year before, and was believed to be a police agent. Martin Ken-

ner of the Panther Defense Committee wrote to Rosenthal, pointing out the inaccuracy. He never received an answer.

Those *Times* reporters most sensitive to the anti-Panther slant are mystified about the reasons for it. These reporters, loyal to the paper, are quick to point out how much the *Times* has improved in other areas during recent years, with the daily reporting of Joseph Lelyveld and John Kifner, the lively Sunday entertainment section, the cultural criticism of Clive Barnes, Christopher Lehmann-Haupt, and John Leonard, Tom Wicker's column, Miss Curtis's exciting women's page, and even the Panther coverage out of New York City—from Chicago (Kifner) and San Francisco, where Earl Caldwell is based. So no one is even thinking about a corporate conspiracy against favorable Panther coverage.

Several reporters, rather, tend to blame managing editor Rosenthal personally for the problem. One of them told me, "The problem is not our publisher, who is very decent on this question. The problem is Abe Rosenthal. And it's not a question of professional standards, it's not a matter of personal journalism versus objective journalism, because the closest we've ever come to personal journalism here was Rosenthal's own piece in 1968 attacking the Columbia students. The problem is Abe's private attitude toward the young, the poor, and the black."

Another writer, who is black, had a somewhat different analysis of the issue. "It's ignorance and incompetence as much as racism," he said. "The guys on the desk don't know what Panthers are like, they don't know what black people are like. They don't work with the younger black writers enough, they don't give us any help or direction. But when you point something specific out to them that they've done wrong, they feel very guilty."

Another *Times* dissident said, "The trouble here is that all our top editors are upper-class white Manhattan males who don't know what the fuck is happening in America. . . . And there is no available counterpressure on them to make them behave any better. . . . It kills me to admit it, but Don Flynn of the *Daily News* has consistently written better copy on the Panthers than anyone on the *Times'* local news staff." This reporter, like all the others interviewed, emphasized his substantial disagreement with the politics of the Panthers.

Another reporter, one of the national stars of the paper told me, "I think our failure is focused on the city desk in New York. Arthur Gelb [the city editor] is just chickenshit on anything controversial. And he just does what he thinks Rosenthal wants him to do . . .

"The last time I was in New York the morale of the city staff was zero because Gelb had killed so many good stories. Just look at the coverage of the Panther trial—our Sunday Week-in-Review piece is always better than any of the daily stories. That's because of Gelb. Again, just look at our stories out of Los Angeles, or Chicago, or the Bay area about the Panthers, and then compare them to the coverage we get in New York City, and you can tell what Gelb does to us."

But Martin Kenner of the Panther Defense Committee, who recently met with the *Times* editorial board, had a more historical and institutional view of the Panther Problem at the *Times*. Said Kenner, "The *Times* proves its liberalism by attacking the Left because it's a German-Jewish paper published in New York City. The San Francisco *Chronicle* proves its liberalism in California by attacking Reagan and Yorty. The *Times* is just too hung up on being respectable because of the old German-Jewish thing. The *Chronicle* is at least secure psychologically."

FEBRUARY, 1970

[5.]
Journalism: Old, New, and Corporate

To give the news impartially, without fear or favor, re-
gardless of any party, sect, or interest involved.
—Credo of *The New York Times,*
first published on August 19, 1896

You walk into the room with your pencil in your hand,
You see somebody naked and you say, who is that man?
You try so hard, but you don't understand what you
say when you get home
Because something is happening here, but you don't
know what it is, do you, Mister Jones?
—Bob Dylan, "Ballad of a Thin Man"

When I am asked what is my gripe against the respectable
gray pillars of American journalism, I explain it isn't, at bottom,
any of the polite criticisms. It's not just that the journalism
schools have become impersonal factories that mass-produce what
Pete Hamill of the New York *Post* calls "clerks of fact." It isn't
just that there is monopoly ownership in too many cities by publishers who care little about professionalism, and everything
about profits. It isn't just that the newspaper unions have become conservative, dominated by nonwriting commercial employees, and perpetuate a seniority system that protects the lazy and
punishes the imaginative. It isn't just that advertisers have a subtle say about what goes into a newspaper.

My root criticism of the old journalism is simply that it is
blind to an important part of reality, that it just doesn't print all
of the truth. It has a built-in value system that influences every
editorial, every decision on hiring, what syndicated columnist to
buy, what stories to cover, what copy to spike, what reporter to
promote.

Spiro Agnew was right, although for the wrong reasons. A few individuals *do* control the mass media in America. Only most of them are Republicans and Conservatives.

For example, in 1968, 60 percent of the nation's daily papers editorially endorsed Richard Nixon, and only 15 percent endorsed Hubert Humphrey. According to a survey compiled by the perceptive press gadfly Ben Bagdikian, 85 percent of the syndicated columns published across the country can be generally classified as conservative.

The Vice-President, in his famous Des Moines and Montgomery speeches, did not choose to mention the power of conservative media complexes like the Chicago *Tribune,* which owns two Chicago papers, a Chicago FM radio station, a Chicago VHF franchise, WPIX in New York, and The New York *Daily News.* He did not mention the giant publishing empires of Hearst and Annenberg (Triangle Publications, Inc.) or that Mr. Annenberg had recently been appointed by the President to be Ambassador to England. He also did not mention that Nixon had recently appointed Robert Wells to the FCC, and that Mr. Wells owns seven newspapers and four television stations in the Midwest. (One of Wells's first decisions as an FCC member, according to the *Wall Street Journal,* was a vote against "even holding a hearing on the TV license renewal of a Cheyenne, Wyo., broadcaster who owns that city's only TV station, only full-time AM radio station, only community antenna TV franchise, one of two FM stations, and whose associates control Cheyenne's only newspapers.")

The knee-jerk liberals and the panicked network moguls responded to Agnew's jeremiad against the media by screaming "government censorship."

But the disturbing reality is that the press censors itself, through superficiality, through bias, through incompetence, and through a desire to be the "responsible" fourth branch of government.

A few examples of this self-censorship. Geoff Cowan and Judith Colburn exposed Operation Pheonix in *The Village Voice* in November of 1969. Operation Pheonix is a top-secret CIA and Army intelligence program to train counterinsurgency teams to torture and assassinate the NLF's civilian cadre. George Wilson, the Washington *Post's* Pentagon reporter, was on to the story, and wanted to pick it up. But at a special meeting of the *Post's*

senior editors it was decided not to publish the damaging story.

The story of the My Lai massacre was first uncovered by Seymour Hersh and his tiny Dispatch News Service. Yet, when he offered the story initially to both *Life* and *Look*, it was rejected. And it was only after the respected dailies in Europe began to front-page the story, that the television networks finally picked up on it.

And then there is the story Gay Talese shares with us in his book *The Kingdom and the Power*, of how the *Times* editors invited former CIA director John McCone to visit the *Times* building in 1966 to read a series of articles on the Agency before it was published. According to Talese, McCone suggested some changes "where the facts might imperil national security." Can anyone imagine the *Times* inviting Tom Hayden up for a look at a series on SDS before it was printed?

So the men and women who control the technological giants of the mass media are not neutral, unbiased computers. They have a mind-set. They have definite life styles and political values, which are concealed under a rhetoric of objectivity. But those values are organically institutionalized by the *Times*, by AP, by CBS (remember the Smothers Brothers?), into their corporate bureaucracies. Among these unspoken, but organic, values are belief in welfare capitalism, God, the West, Puritanism, the Law, the family, property, the two-party system, and perhaps most crucially, in the notion that violence is only defensible when employed by the state. I can't think of any White House correspondent, or network television analyst, who doesn't share these values. And at the same time, who doesn't insist he is totally objective.

And it is these assumptions—or prejudices—that prevent publishers and editors from understanding, or even being open to, any new reality that might be an alternative to those assumptions. Potential alternatives are buried deep inside the black liberation movement, the white New Left, the counterculture of rock music, long hair, underground newspapers and drugs, as well as in the nonwhite revolutionary movements of the Third World. And it is these threatening and unfamiliar social movements that the mass media most systematically misrepresent. And it is their sympathizers who are excluded from positions of real power within the medial hierarchies.

Why is it that of the dozens of nationally syndicated daily

columnists, with the possible exception of Tom Wicker, not one represents a radical point of view? Why is it that Jimmy Breslin, when his column was offered for syndication, was bought by only five daily papers in the whole country? And Murray Kempton by just one? While the dull, predictable, Muzak prose of Max Lerner and Marquis Childs is printed in more than one hundred papers. Why is it that Andrew Kopkind or I. F. Stone or Serymour Hersh are never invited to join the panel on "Meet the Press?"

Insurgent movements are also distorted because they tend to get covered only in terms of immediate confrontations and personalities, rather than in the context of issues, ideas or historical backgrounds. How many of the news stories written during the 1968 Democratic Convention, for example, took the trouble to mention that the street demonstrators had applied for legal permits to march and assemble in a peaceful rally, and had been denied these elemental rights by the Chicago court system? How many wire service dispatches on the rebellion at Columbia University in April 1968 spread the myth on a conspiracy hatched months before by SDS cadres? Many more, I think, than bothered to report the lengthy history on the Columbia campus of student agitation, through legitimate channels, against the university's real estate expansionism, and its relationship with the military-industrial-security complex.

A textbook case of the differences between the old journalism and the new, might be found in rereading the back issues of *The New York Times* and the underground and campus press during the student movement at Columbia in April and May of 1968. The *Times,* prizing objectivity, underplayed the police violence, misstated facts, ignored the substantive issues in dispute, slanted news stories in favor of the administration, and editorialized emotionally against the students.

Some examples. The *Times* editorial in its April 29 issue said: "The faculty, trustees and administration of Columbia have closed ranks against capitulation to the rule-or-ruin tactics of a reckless minority of students. . . . It was apparent from the start that the youthful junta which has substituted dictatorship by temper tantrum for undergraduate democracy neither cared about, nor received, the support from the majority of students."

But the fact-finding Cox Commission Report, released six months later, and based on 1790 pages of testimony, concluded

that: "By its final days, the revolt enjoyed both wide and deep support among the students and junior faculty. . . . The grievances of the rebels were felt equally by a still larger number, probably a *majority* of the students." (Italics added)

On April 26 the *Times* chose to describe the Institute for Defense Analysis, which was central to the whole controversy, in this benign fashion: "The institute specializes in finding the answers to many of mankind's most pressing problems."

The Cox Report, which was drafted by a commission headed by the former U.S. Assistant Solicitor General, described the IDA as being "established by the Department of Defense and the Joint Chiefs of Staff in 1955 in order to obtain organized university research and counsel upon such matters as weapons systems and the conditions of warfare."

The police bust took place at Columbia at 2:30 A.M. on the night of April 29. More than one hundred forty students were injured and ninety-two hospitalized as a result of the police violence. The Cox Report would later judge that "the police engaged in acts of individual and group brutality for which a layman can see no justification."

The next morning the *Times* reported only "several scuffles," in its news lead on the raid that resulted in six hundred twenty-eight arrests. The following day, after twenty-four hours to reflect, interview victims, and look at the extensive newsreel footage of the wild, stick-swinging bust, the *Times* managed to write an entire editorial without once mentioning the extraordinary police violence. And in the lead news story by Sylvan Fox, "charges" of police brutality were not even mentioned until the twenty-third paragraph. The *Times* story did not mention at all the obvious fact that the police violence had united the students and faculty against the Trustees, as it had done on many other campuses.

One of those hsopitalized by the police was *Times* reporter Robert Thomas, who required twelve stitches in his scalp. But the *Times'* editors didn't think of him when they needed a sidebar story on police brutality. Instead they asked Martin Arnold, who wrote: "To an experienced antiwar or civil rights demonstrator, yesterday morning's police action on the Columbia campus, was for the most part, relatively gentle."

The next day the following sign was tacked to the door of the office of the Columbia student paper:

"The Columbia *Daily Spectator* hereby announces open hostility toward the cretins who form the bulk of the working national press. Your insensitive misrepresentations will receive no aid from this office."

In contrast *Rat* and *Ramparts* published the documents the students "liberated" from Grayson Kirk's office, including an exchange of letters that indicated that *Times* editor A. M. Rosenthal was once used by Columbia University to plant a favorable story in the *Times*. The *Voice* printed stories by Richard Goldstein and myself based on conversations with the students inside the five liberated buildings. The *Times* did have one reporter (John Kifner) inside the Math building at the moment of the police raid, but wouldn't let him write a description of that event. Kifner was told instead to write a follow-up on "student vandalism inside the liberated buildings." And when the troubles were all over, the student *Spectator* published a content analysis by sophomore Michael Stern, carefully documenting the "continual and flagrant disregard for both professional ethics and the facts," by the *Times, Post,* and *News*.

Two final points on the *Times'* coverage of Columbia. The one *Times* reporter whose sympathies were with the students, Steven Roberts, ended up publishing his views not in the *Times,* but in *The Village Voice* ("The University that Refused to Learn," *Voice* May 9). And the *Columbia Journalism Review,* in its summer 1968 issue editorialized that the *Times,* in its news columns, "appeared not only to be trying to tell people what they ought to know about Columbia, but what they ought to think."

The corollary to the mass media's presumption against insurgency, is its bias in the direction of authority. This is not an imperialist conspiracy, as the more paranoid factions of SDS believe. It is just that the editors of *Time,* Eric Sevareid, Walter Cronkite, and James Reston all happen to share many values, friends, fears, and class interests with Richard Nixon's WASP cabinet. So in the *Times,* Tom Hayden generally alleges something, but John Mitchell always announces something. The organs of the old journalism automatically print the press releases and White Papers of the government without any note of scepticism. The presumption of truth is always with the President, or

the university dean, or the local police chief. The burden of proof is always put on the inarticulate poor, who can never afford, like GM or S. I. Hayakawa, to hire a press agent.

But the recent historical evidence suggests that the government—any government—lies as a matter of casual policy. President Eisenhower lied about Gary Power's U-2 flight over the Soviet Union. John Kennedy lied about America's role in the Bay of Pigs landing. Lyndon Johnson lied to the country at each new step of the Vietnam escalation. And Richard Nixon lied to us last November 3, during his nationally televised address to the nation, when while giving wholly distorted history of the Vietnam War, he tried to deny that it was originally a civil war in the south. He also lied to us when he first denied that the CIA was involved in Laos.

The truth, and even the hard news, usually rests beneath the public surface of any event or social conflict. Yet, reporters rarely question what they are told by any politician with a title. But no traditional publication has on its staff a muckraker of the distinction of I. F. Stone, or Sy Hersh or James Ridgeway. Ralph Nader, the consumer's tribune, has shown us just how many scandals and skeletons are waiting to be exposed inside the coils of the federal bureaucracy. But no national columnist, or network reporter, is doing that necessary work.

In the last few years a new kind of journalism has grown up in the space abdicated by the old, just as a new radicalism, and a new cinema, and a new music has grown up beyond the frozen frontiers of the older forms. This new journalism exists, and is flourishing, because it meets real needs. Fashion followers, undercover narcs, and sexual deviates cannot constitute all of *The Village Voice's* 160,000 readers, or *Rolling Stone's* 200,000 or *New York's* 250,000.

Daily newspapers cannot possibly compete with the immediacy and authenticity of color television news. The only way print can compete is to provide something television can't. And that is advocacy, complex detail, personal feeling. Linear weeklies that have been generally closed to the new journalists, like *The New Yorker* and *The New Leader* have failed to gain in readership during a period when *The Village Voice, Rolling Stone* and *New York Magazine* have grown enormously. And the mortality rate

among daily newspapers during the 1960s probably had as much to do with their inability to adjust to television, as with the selfishness of the craft unions.

Before I attempt any definition of this new journalism, let me make four qualifying points to prevent any possible misunderstanding. I am not suggesting here that the new journalism is a substitute or replacement for the more orthodox variety. Although I am an advocate of the newer writers and publications, I understand that they cannot realistically become anything more than a corrective, or example, or gadfly to media corporations as powerful as Time-Life, or the Newsweek-Washington Post Corporation. Second, the new journalism is still in its infancy, and it remains quite a mixed bag. Some of it is brilliant and important, but some of it is also indulgent, repetitive, and paranoid. For example, I would probably rather read the Oakland telephone book than the *East Village Other*. And obviously, some of the underground press is indifferent to good writing and guilty of mindless propaganda.

Third, I am not here making the argument that Norman Podhoretz and Seymour Krim have made elsewhere that articles and journalism have become a new, superior literature replacing the novel. Jimmy Breslin and Pete Hamill are journalists, not city room Balzacs. Their special gift is to write quickly and perceptively about real people and real experiences. As long as Roth, Pynchon, and Heller are writing novels, that form does not need any obituary writers.

And last, just as there are some very bad new journalists, there are some excellent traditional daily reporters whose work I continually admire and respect. Among them are Anthony Lukas of the *Times*, Joseph Lelyveld of the *Times*, Richard Harwood of the Washington *Post*, Nick Kotz of the Des Moines *Register and Tribune*, John Kifner of the *Times*, and Robert Maynard of the Washington *Post*.

One dimension of the new journalism are those individual writers, some of whom publish in quite conventional publications, like *Esquire* and *Life*, whose choice of language, structure, and subject break new ground. They have successfully appropriated the forms and techniques of the short story to enrich and expand the more immediate genre of journalism. They have exploded the old, impersonal, objective journalism school formulas,

to get closer to the human core of reality, to tell more of how it really is after the press agents and ghost-writers go home, to be more than "clerks of fact."

They use symbols, imagery, and imaginative language and structure. They set a mood, and experiment with character development, and try wild stabs of intuitive insight. They have a point of view and they are personally involved in whatever they are writing about.

And most distinctively, the new journalism challenges the central myth of objectivity. The new journalist does not call the anonymous source or the official expert for a quote. He does not try to speak for an institution, only for his own conscience. He does not take into account "the national interest," but only what he sees and thinks. As Andrew Kopkind put it in his *New York Review of Books* essay on James Reston, "Objectivity is the rationalization for moral disengagement, the classic cop-out from choice-making."

The participatory journalist does for his profession exactly what new, activist historians like Howard Zinn and Staughton Lynd do for theirs.

What is also distinctive about the new journalists is that they are working reporters. They go out, and see, and react to real, living events and people. And they examine these spontaneous reactions honestly in print. The very best ones—Breslin, Hamill, Wolfe, Mailer—keep getting better because they keep getting stretched by their own confrontations with raw experience.

The point to keep in mind about Breslin is how his own explosion of talent has kept forcing him to expand his journalistic form. He started off writing 900-word sports columns for the old *Journal American,* and later Runyonesque copy for the *Herald Tribune.* Then he began to write politically unorthodox 2,000- and 3,000-word pieces for *New York Magazine.* After a while, he found even that space inhibiting his imagination, so he wrote his comic, episodic, short novel on the Mafia, "The Gang that Couldn't Shoot Straight." And now Breslin is trying to write a long, serious novel.

But while Breslin was exploding his form and exposing himself to new, raw experiences—Vietnam, Watts, Selma, Oceanhill-Brownsville, the Chicago convention violence—most old journalists remained trapped inside a system that insulated them from

consciousness-changing situations. *Newsweek* editors wrote about distant events they never smelled and touched by reading impersonal files and clippings. And then published their authoritative, "objective" stories with no names attached, stories written to fit a preexisting formula. The editors of *The New York Times* wrote sober editorials expressing an "institutional point of view," about events they never witnessed, from the Chicago Conspiracy trial, to the Black Panther fund raising party given by Mrs. Leonard Bernstein, and without ever consulting the *Times* reporters who did cover them in person.

At a shop like *Newsweek,* which is probably the most permissive and politically liberal incarnation of Luce-style group journalism, senior editors still have the power to arbitrarily change or invert the point of view expressed by the reporter who actually covered the event. In the June 1970 issue of *Scanlan's* magazine, for example, Kate Coleman, an ex *Newsweek* researcher, described how her copy on the 1968 Columbia University uprising was mutilated beyond recognition:

> During the Columbia strike, I was on campus every day and almost every night. The only building that was taken that I did not get into was the hall occupied by the black students. No reporters from the overground press were being admitted into the student-occupied offices of President Kirk in Lowe Library. I managed to gain entry to the office by slipping past police onto the second story ledge on the opposite side from Kirk's offices and then inching my way along the ledge to circumnavigate all of Lowe Library, until I gained entry through the window of the offices. . . .
>
> I duly wrote up my lengthy reports at the end of the week and gave them to the education editor, Peter Janssen, who had also spent a lot of time up on the scene. He had also witnessed the late-night arrests and clubbings of the students. He wrote a cover story that was accurate as well as sympathetic, based on my files, his own reporting, and that of another reporter. Originally, the story had three paragraphs devoted to the beatings of the demonstrators and their injuries. I left early Friday night, exhausted from the whole effort. But the story had not yet been edited, and my leaving was a

sorry mistake. On Monday I read a cover story that was filled with vicious inaccuracies, many of them facts taken from my own files but twisted past recognition.

In the past, *Newsweek* education stories on demonstrations had not been unsympathetic: both Janssen and former education writer Joe Russin were understanding of student attempts to reshape the university system. Both writers were radicalized by the job that put them in frequent contact with student activists and their thinking. Why then was the Columbia cover story as rabid as the New York *Daily News?* The likely answer lies in the fact that Ed Diamond was on vacation. And whatever infighting he may have been into, as an editor he was infinitely preferable to his substitute, Dwight Martin, who still told stale racist jokes and seemed never to have left the era of World War II. He edited Peter's manuscript with a rightist meat cleaver, while downstairs, Kermit Larsner was busy on the phone talking to an old crony who fed him lies about students pissing all over Kirk's office. Taking his friend's word for gospel, he dutifully inserted the tasty tidbit into the story.

When I confronted Elliott with the charge that the magazine had simply lied, he listened carefully as I enunciated each point in the story that was false, and then urged me to put it into a memo. And that was it.

Among the catholic group of writers I would place under the new journalism umbrella are: Tom Wolfe (who has no politics), Jimmy Breslin, Jeremy Larner, Gay Talese, Richard Goldstein, Pete Hamill, Gloria Steinem, Larry Merchant, Sally Kempton, Ron Rosenbaum, Griel Marcus, Gail Sheehy, Michael Lydon, Mike Royko, Norman Mailer, Marshall Frady, Paul Cowan, David Halberstam, Nicholas Von Hoffman, Joe McGiniss and Pete Axthelm. And those over-40 pioneers, Al Aronowitz, Murray Kempton, Jimmy Cannon and W. C. Heinz. (Look up Heinz' piece on Rocky Graziano in *Sport Magazine* in 1947.)

Whether it is Breslin writing about the white working class of horse players, cops, priests, and bartenders, or Michael Lydon writing about the music, groupies, and life style of The Grateful Dead, or Jeremy Larner writing about Eugene McCarthy's cam-

paign from the point of view of his speechwriter, it is reportage about experiences that are an integrated part of the writer's biography. This is the exact opposite of the anonymous group journalism of the newsmagazines. It is journalism so personal that it becomes almost memoir; writing that is too immediate to be called literature; reportage that is too honest to be called propaganda.

The second dimension of the new journalism—and much more ambiguous—are those publications that are actually new and original. These seem to be divided into three generations. The older, and now established ones whose roots go back into the wasteland of the 1950's: *I. F. Stone's Weekly, The Texas Observer,* and *The Village Voice.* The second generation emerged out of the flowering of the drug subculture in the mid-1960's, like *EVO,* the *Oracle, Inner Space* and *Grass Roots.* And third, the current generation of underground and antiestablishment papers like *Rat, Old Mole, Rolling Stone, Hard Times,* the *Ann Arbor Argus,* Atlanta's *Great Speckled Bird,* and *The Chicago Journalism Review.*

Although reflections of their region and staffs, these current publications share a few distinctive characteristics. One is that they are dominated by the sensibilities of their young writers, rather than by the decisions of desk-bound committees of editors. Second, they benefit from liberated language, and experimental layout, and quick publication and impact. Third, they view themselves more as communities based on energy than as institutions dependent on profits. And last, they are all committed to some variety of social change.

Also, these underground papers keep springing up and flourishing despite severe police and right-wing harassment in the more uptight sections of the country.

There were four examples of this just during the first two weeks of August 1969. In New Orleans, police busted the *Nola Express* three times in one week, for pornography, corrupting minors and peddling merchandise on the streets without a permit. The paper had to put up $2,500 in bail.

In Houston, vigilantes hurled a bomb into the offices of the *Space City News,* causing minor damage.

In Ann Arbor, John Sinclair, one of the founders of the *Argus* (and the White Panthers, and the former manager of the MC5

band) was sentenced to ten years in prison for possession of two joints of marijuana.

And in Atlanta, street vendors of the *Great Speckled Bird* were picked up and harassed by police.

In the last month I have read through the back issues of about thirty-five underground papers (there are over one hundred fifty) and have been astonished to notice that in the six or seven that are really first rate, there are frequently stories and subjects ignored by the old journalism, and fresh angles on other stories that have received saturation coverage in the mass media. Women's lib and ecology, for example, received sensitive coverage in the underground press before they became media fads, and continue to do so now.

Rat, for example, printed excerpts from the film script of "Che" before it was released, and incorporated them into a tough-minded analysis of Hollywood commercialization and exploitation of the "youth market." *Hard Times* has consistently printed the most original material on the G.I. Organizing movement and on conditions in military stockades. *El Gritto del Norte* publishes the most extensive and reliable coverage of the growing militancy of the Chicano movement in the Southwest. *Old Mole* was the first paper in the country to print the documents "liberated" from Administration files at Harvard, documents that revealed how a university Dean had tried to circumvent the vote of the faculty against ROTC on campus. *Ramparts* broke the scandal of the CIA-NSA covert relationship.

Reading these underground papers is like visiting another country, which remains invisible to the well-paid, middle-aged white, male editors of the *Times.*

Participation and advocacy remain the touchstones of the new insurgent journalism. The evidence now seems overwhelming that the closer a serious writer gets to his material, the more understanding he gets, the more he is there to record those decisive moments of spontaneity and authenticity. He gets inside the context and sees scenes and details that distance and neutrality deny to the more conventional reporters. He does not have to write about impersonal public rituals like ghost-written speeches, well-rehearsed concerts, and staged and managed press conferences.

He is there to see and react to the human reflexes exposed late at night that illuminate a man's character.

The advocacy journalist breaks down the artificial barrier between work and leisure; between private and public knowledge. He can do this because he is writing, by choice, about subjects that excite his imagination, rather than fulfilling an assignment made by the city desk, and that needs to be approved and edited by the copy desk. He is a free man, relying on his instincts, intelligence, and discipline, liberated from all the middlemen who try to mediate between the writer and reality.

There is now a considerable body of literature based on direct personal involvement. Norman Mailer's seminal "Armies of the Night" is just the most praised example. There is also Sally Belfrage's book "Freedom Summer," based on her experiences as a civil-rights worker in Mississippi during the watershed summer of 1964, a volume that contains truthful (but not neutral) reportage from inside the heart of the movement. There is Tom Wolfe's "Electric Kool Aid Acid Test," written with intelligence from inside the drug subculture of Ken Kesey and the Merry Pranksters. And there is Hunter Thompson's powerful book on the Hell's Angels, also written out of the emotions of personal encounter.

Participation and advocacy, yoked to integrity, were also the literary and personal values that inspired James Agee as he worked on "Let us now Praise Famous Men," Orwell as he fought and wrote from the trenches of the Spanish Civil War, and Albert Camus as he wrote for *Combat* as a member of the French Resistance.

America is now in great danger from a new, white-collar McCarthyism centered in the Justice Department. Historic constitutional guarantees are now menaced by conspiracy indictments, subpoenas, wire-taps, preventive detention, mail checks, repressive no-knock legislation, and pre-dawn police raids.

And so we are in special need of writers, who like Agee, Orwell and Camus, are committed in their bones, to not just describing the world, but changing it for the better.

OCTOBER, 1969

[SIX]
ON OTHER WRITERS: REVIEWS

Sometimes I think I'm actually a cultural conservative, or at least a traditionalist. I've spent many wonderful hours reading Orwell and Hart Crane, and Nathanael West, and James Agee. And I can't help but suspect that the new counterculture is very thin, that yogis and yippies are more likely the symptoms of a decaying culture than portents of any new vanguard. I do not see much craft or professionalism among the new prophets, whether it is Andy Warhol, or Jerry Rubin, or Dr. Timothy Leary. They do not strike me as long-distance runners. And the two authentic innovators of the new culture—Thomas Pynchon and Bob Dylan—have already found their own way home.

Some of my traditionalism, I think, comes through in this section. My respect is for a sensibility as rich as Stephen Spender's, for Irving Howe's rigorous independence from fashion, despite our political differences; and my misgivings about Abbie Hoffman's confusions about Theatre and politics. I wonder what Marx or Malcolm X would say to someone who wanted to make a revolution just for the hell of it.

The pieces on Professors Boorstin and Goldman, Scammon and Wattenberg, and Theodore H. White illustrate a basic idea of the collection. All four are official intellectuals of the Center and, as antennae for the Establishment, they are inadequate because they simply can't see what is going on right in front of them. I suggest the reason for this is that for all their claims to objectivity, their testimony always favors the state. But error does not harm their reputations, since their biases are so popular. We still reward them and call them experts, just as we have rewarded the men most responsible for war in Vietnam. Bundy is now the head of the Ford Foundation. McNamara is now in charge of the World Bank. Westmoreland is now one of the Joint Chiefs of Staff. Humphrey has been elected back to the Senate. I am looking forward to reading White's book on the 1972 campaign.

[1.]
Steady Work

Steady Work: Essays in the Politics of Democratic Radicalism, 1953–1966; by Irving Howe. *Harcourt Brace, and World. 364 pages. $6.95.*

In his introduction to this important collection Irving Howe confesses, "I want this book to be read by younger radicals. . . . I want them to read this book so they will understand, for example, . . . why it is that, after costly and painful debates with ourselves, we have come to believe in the primacy of the democratic values for any political reconstruction."

My first reaction to *Steady Work* was to make me want to write Howe a highly personal letter. But then I decided a public review, however mixed my feelings about the book, was a better approach because it might motivate some people on the New Left to read the book, and because it could help crystallize— through fraternal debate—my differences with Howe and his ideological associates.

What strikes me most sharply about this book is how much Howe and I share—the same radical democratic values, as well as a curiosity concerning the linkage between culture and politics. Yet, despite this, there are passing moments in this book when I detest the image Howe-the-individual projects—his cold, superrational, intellectualized style, his ego-involved overemphasis on anti-Stalinism, his insensitivity to the personal feelings of his political enemies.

There are twenty-six pieces in this anthology of essays, reviews, and journalism written between 1953 and 1966. Some of the writing should make any professional jealous. As Yeats once suggested about other writers, Howe occasionally reaches poetry when he argues with himself, instead of with others. This is con-

spicuously true when he considers, for example, the relevance of socialism and the real value of the 1930s experience.

A few words about the best pieces. The under-thirty radicals may be surprised to read Howe's 1954 essay on Adlai Stevenson, the most perceptive short piece on that tragic Hamlet I have ever seen. It is an acerbic assault on the liberal intellectuals for lusting after the flawed Stevenson, a man who was not even a liberal. Howe understands they loved him because, like they, he hated the sweat and smell of politics. He seemed above it all, with his elegant intellectualizing. Howe concludes the piece by reaffirming his own socialism—not an easy gesture in the pit of the 1950s —and urges Schlesinger and Reuther to "invigorate their liberalism" and "stand in behalf of their own tradition."

There are also deeply felt pieces on the brilliant and obscure Trotskyist novelist Victor Serge, and a review of Whittaker Chambers's confessional *Cold Friday*. And there is Howe's almost classic statement, "Images of Socialism." In this essay Howe argues in his characteristic, closely reasoned, epigrammatic style for his pragmatic approach to democratic socialism and against romanticism and authoritarianism. He ends the internal debate with the paragraph:

> Some time ago one could understandably make of socialism a consoling daydream. Now when we live in the shadow of defeat, to retain, to will the image of socialism is a constant struggle for definition, almost an act of pain that makes creation possible.

At his best, Howe in these essays approaches the heroic, arguing for democracy in an authoritarian decade, for dissent against the swelling tide toward conformity, for radicalism against the easy flirtation with liberalism, against McCarthyism when his lesser colleagues, like Sidney Hook and Irving Kristol, were trying to make a separate peace with that obscene movement.

Yet, still, I feel deeply alienated from Howe at other times in this book. I can only speculate at the reasons. One is that Howe comes out of the overwhelming Jewish and rationalistic radicalism of the 1930s. An extraordinary thing about the New Left is how "goyish" it is. The brightest of its leaders are not Jewish: Mario Savio, Tom Hayden, Bob (Moses) Parris, Carl Oglesby, Julian Bond, Stokely Carmichael, and Staughton Lynd. Nor are

many of the thinkers and writers the young New Leftists most admire Jewish: Frantz Fanon, Camus, Sartre, Celine, Thoreau, Tom Paine, and Norman O. Brown. Paul Goodman is an exception. The radicalism of the 1930s was dominated by the Talmudic mentality of the Jews—Marx, Trotsky, Freud. They analysed forces and prophesied the inevitable. My generation draws closer to the absurd, the irrational, the transcendental—to the novels of Terry Southern and Ken Kesey, to the cop-out catharsis of Tim Leary, to the black humor of Bob Dylan and Lenny Bruce, to the mad agony of Malcolm X and Stokely Carmichael. Howe, a professor, a scholar, a believer in empirical logic, cannot comprehend the irrationality of the new generation, spawned by Watts, Dallas, and LSD.

Seven of Howe's pieces deal in major part with anticommunism. There is his scatter-shot blast at the New Left, two defenses of Pasternak, a masterful refutation of Isaac Deutscher, a piece called "Communism Now," a personal and, I feel, too harsh criticism of C. Wright Mills, and his justly famous polemic "Authoritarians of the Left."

I consider myself to be anticommunist, yet I found the closed-mindedness and emotional intensity of Howe's anticommunism irritating. Energies that should have attacked the CIA, the draft, the imperialism of the West, the military-industrial complex were diverted to reiterating the cause of anticommunism. Where we—and perhaps our generations—differ is that I think America's domestic anticommunism has become a curse upon the rest of humanity, and it is now the duty of the noncommunist Left to attack it with all its minuscule energy. If the United States were not so paranoid about communists, the government would not have been so easily able to escalate the war in Vietnam or invade the Dominican Republic on the flimsy pretext of the presence of fifty-eight communists in a popular movement.

In the 1930s Howe was right, and even heroic, in being the staunch anticommunist he then was. The prevailing tone of the Left and the intellectual communities ran counter to his beliefs. He suffered for his views then, and it has left him with a scar that has never healed. But I think the world has changed. The international communist movement is no longer monolithic, but polycentric. Russia has become a stable, bureaucratic society. The American Communist Party is old, broken, and impotent.

The anticommunism of the 1930s does not help my generation understand the new social systems evolving in Poland and Yugoslavia, and even in Cuba.

Besides the question of anticommunism and the speculative one of Jewishness, there is the obvious one of generation. Howe is forty-five and I am twenty-eight. His sharpest memories are of the 1930s, mine are of the shame I felt at the Bay of Pigs and the commonplace brutality toward the Negro in the South. These things have made me bitter toward America. I don't think Howe is bitter toward America today because he remembers the Depression. The Depression was worse, only I and my generation were not there.

Also, Howe does not travel; he is an intellectual, not a journalist. That means he is smarter than I am, but he lacks concrete experience. He has not visited SDS or SNCC projects, or spent any time on MacDougal Street. He writes brilliantly in the abstract, but lacks a feeling of community with the new movements because they are strangers to him. I wonder—and I would have started my private letter with this—if Howe has ever sat alone for an afternoon and listened, really listened, to the lyrics of Bob Dylan. For example, "I've got nothin', Ma, to live up to," or "It is not he, she, them or it that you belong to." He does not write about it in his book, but I would guess that Howe has minimal sympathy with or interest in the long-haired mobs that clog MacDougal Street on weekends.

But, finally, I must end with a sympathetic coda. Howe is brilliant, honest with himself, and has much to teach my generation of dissenters. Just as Howe would stretch his soul by listening to Dylan, everyone in the Movement could stretch his mind by reading this book.

JANUARY, 1967

[2.]
The Tragedy of Eric Goldman

The Tragedy of Lyndon Johnson; by Eric F. Goldman. *Knopf.*
531 pages. $8.95.

This volume appropriately arrived in my mail on the morning
of Richard Nixon's soporific Inaugural sermon. I was primed to
embrace the book since I was in a rage over the sentimental vale-
dictories attending President Johnson's farewell from power. Pop
historians, *The New York Times,* Teddy Kennedy—everyone
seemed to be playing the game. Exaggerating Johnson's achievements. Ignoring his catastrophes. Suggesting his historical reputation will grow as time passes. He was being compared to Lincoln
and Jackson, when Caligula seemed a more apt analogy to me.

It was beginning to appear as if 750,000 dead Vietnamese, 2,-
000,000 homeless Vietnamese refugees and 31,000 dead Americans
were imagined. James Reston wrote in the *Times,* "Vietnam
drove him out of office, but his policy there will probably be
seen in the long run as a gallant if unsuccessful effort to punish
wickedness and military aggression."

It was as if the Dominican intervention, the crack-up of the
Democratic Party into antiwar and Wallace factions, the estrangement of the high school and college generations, the violent seasons of assassination and riot had never been part of the Johnson
years. Or else, as if they had been easily cleansed away in the
parting shower of sentimentality. So it was in this receptive mood
that I began to read Professor Goldman's thick memoir of his
years as Lyndon Johnson's ambassador to the intellectuals.

Yet, at the end of the journey, this book is offensive. All the
juicy tidbits documenting Johnson's monumental character flaws
are there, but inadvertently Goldman also exposes himself; the
executioner ends up chopping off his own foot.

Professor Goldman is a prize-winning historian, and yet he can trace the bloody roots of Vietnam only as far as Lyndon Johnson's personality, to his failure to communicate, to his Texas provincialism. Goldman writes as if the Vietnam war were unrelated to historical forces, to the liberal anticommunism of the New Frontier and New Deal eras. He writes as if it were unrelated to America's messianic globalism, to recently fashionable theories of counterinsurgency and nation-building, to the warrior caste in the State Department.

The book also raises serious ethical questions. Professor Goldman never pauses to explain why he remained on Johnson's White House staff until September of 1966, nineteen months, and many lives, after the bombings of North Vietnam began, seventeen months after the Dominican intervention, and long after he knew exactly how petty and paranoid the President could be. Didn't he feel any responsibility to the intellectual community to tell us then the details he tells us now? Why did he not quit earlier, when the lonely academic critics of the war needed all the defections, evidence, and support they could get? Why did he stay on to huckster the myth that LBJ was seriously concerned about art and culture?

If I read Goldman's murky prose correctly, his first months of work for Johnson were intentionally kept a secret, while he still taught at Princeton and conducted his public affairs program on NBC-TV. Was that ethical? How many other such covert arrangements were there between government, universities, and the mass media?

The book also suffers from its tone, which tends to be whining, self-inflated, and pseudoconfessional. It calls to mind—of all things—Richard Nixon's memoir, *My Six Crises*. Again and again conversations and confrontations are reconstructed in which Goldman gets off the best lines, always asserts his position with clarity, always seems the more sympathetic figure. It may have happened that way, but I doubt it.

First, a few examples of the Nixonesque tone: "I felt proud. As for the little band who had worked with me, I was busting with pride in them. We had insisted upon quality and integrity . . ." And: "Standing there, I suddenly realized that there were tears in my eyes. This is the silliest thing yet, I told myself; I really must be tired." (This at the conclusion of the White House Festival

for the Arts in June of 1965.) And: "As I walked down Pennsylvania Avenue, a jumble of emotions took over. I was hurt, angry, happy, depressed, and relieved. I was proud of what my office had stood for, and what we had been able to accomplish."

Probably the most interesting and revealing chapter in the book is the one about the 1965 Arts Festival. Here Goldman adopts the oldest political ploy of them all—depicting himself as the beleaguered centrist spokesman for reason; caught between those two equally extreme and evil protagonists, Lyndon Johnson *and Dwight Macdonald!*

The festival was Goldman's idea and his first major project as a member of Johnson's staff, but the Vietnam war intruded when poet Robert Lowell publicly declined his invitation in protest. This aroused the President's paranoia about Eastern intellectuals and frayed the Goldman-LBJ relationship. By the time the festival arrived, world conflicts seemed to hinge on this peripheral event.

Goldman desperately wanted it to be a triumph, in order to improve Johnson's relations with the intellectuals, and his relations with Johnson, but several antiwar writers, taking their cue from Lowell, used the festival to promote their views. Goldman, whose loyalty was to the government, and not to his fellow intellectuals, is vicious and petty in his treatment of Macdonald and Saul Maloff, the two most militant guests.

In his defensive forward, Goldman promises that he has "excluded all personal material which in my judgment does not directly bear on an attempt to increase the reader's understanding of Lyndon Johnson the President, his Administration, and their relationship to the public." Yet, Goldman chooses to describe Macdonald this way at his Festival: "Macdonald remained to show his contempt in all possible ways. During the dinner, he sneered at the exhibits and attacked the President personally in a voice that carried across tables and made other guests squirm. His furious activity left his sports coat wilted, his shirt damp, his face dripping perspiration, his shirt and undershirt pulled out with round pink belly showing, and he made no attempt to repair himself in the break provided before dinner."

Goldman concludes this chapter with this fine, Nixonesque judgment: "I had seen a President reacting with arrogant knownothingism, and influential figures in the cultural world reacting

with an equally arrogant know-it-allness. Lyndon Johnson was obviously a special case, and so were the Macdonalds and Maloffs."

In his glowing review of this book in the *Saturday Review*, Quincy Howe quotes this very passage as proof of the author's good, impartial judgment, but the passage strikes me as self-serving and wrong. Macdonald and Maloff were right to have been "tummeling" against the war in June of 1965. They should be honored as prophets, instead of being maligned. Or does Goldman really believe that "bad manners" at the White House is a sin equal to dropping napalm on children in Vietnam?

This book seems destined to be a bestseller. The *Times* gave it a front page review, *Harper's* published a prepublication chapter. It will satisfy the liberals because it is anti-Johnson, and it has enough gossip to titillate the culture vultures.

But there is a profound moral question to be extracted from this book that I'm afraid most readers will overlook. That is the relationship of intellectuals to power. Intellectuals should be loyal first to ideas, values, and truth, and not to any political party or personality. Otherwise, they end up as commissars or flacks. This is true of communist and capitalist countries, of André Malraux and of Richard Goodwin. Governments must ration truth, and intellectuals must seek it, and the two roles are mutually exclusive. Intellectuals have always suffered whenever they have tried to bend political power to their own purposes. The politicians always have the leverage. In the end, the will to prove kills the will to illuminate.

Intellectuals who should be acting as the antennae of the species end up trying to convince their colleagues that Lyndon Johnson really cares about the arts, even as Lyndon Johnson is picking new bombing targets in Vietnam. That is why this book should really have been called *The Tragedy of Eric Goldman*.

MARCH, 1969

[3.]
The Year of the Young Rebels

The Year of the Young Rebels; by Stephen Spender. *Random House. 200 pages. $4.95.*

For some mysterious reason, perhaps psychological, perhaps literary, two women—Susan Sontag and Mary McCarthy—have written the two most honest and moving books I have read about North Vietnam. Similarly, the most evocative and perceptive prose I have read about the new student radicalism, oddly enough, has come from cultural and literary figures, rather than from political or educational ones. I have in mind Norman Mailer's *The Armies of the Night,* essays by Richard Poirier and Martin Duberman published in the *Atlantic* magazine, and this gentle, wise book by the poet and critic, Stephen Spender.

The reason, I suspect, is that Spender and the other writers can see the personalities, confrontations, and dreams of the young Left in larger than just its surface political dimension. Spender, for example, understands the cultural root of student alienation, that they are trying to change values and consciousness rather than lay down a program and seize state power. He understands they are trying to make *revolutionaries,* rather than make a *revolution,* that they are trying to create a "parallel world," in opposition to consumer cultures in which things manipulate individuals.

Spender also brilliantly sees the symbolic, stylistic, psychic, and mythic layers of their politics. He calls one chapter "The Columbia Happenings," grasping the important role spontaneous anarchic energy plays in the movement. He perceives how much of the movement is based on gesture, myth, and style, as well as the movement's close and subtle relationship with the ideas of sexual liberation, popular and underground culture, and the theater of

the absurd. He knows the new political significance of the epi-grams and poetry chalked on the walls of the Sorbonne. He re-minds us that the phrase, "Up against the wall———," is literary, and comes from the poet LeRoi Jones. He comments on the sig-nificance of liberated sex, obscenity, and the underground press as a kind of cultural politics.

Spender understands that the student occupations of Columbia and the Sorbonne were, since there is no "revolutionary situa-tion" in the West, "a revolution rehearsal, like a war game." He can see this so clearly because he knews some things the students, with whom he so sympathizes, do not yet know. He knows they are probably doomed to failure. And he knows they will soon grow old.

The Year of the Young Rebels is divided into seven chapters. The first four are first-person, journalistic impressions of Spend-er's pilgrimages to Columbia, Paris, Prague, and West Berlin, at the time of the student insurrections last year. The final three chapters are more speculative and analytical. They explore the common threads of student movements, West and East, and they thoughtfully rebut some of the older critics of the students, par-ticularly George Kennan and Zbigniew Brzezinski.

The chapter on Columbia is lucid and fair-minded, without pretending to expertise or a false solidarity with the activists. Spender is especially astute in his observations about the black students, concluding:

> Their behavior was maturer (perhaps because they ac-cepted the advice of older people) and less neurotic than that of the improvising white students. . . . The white students, as I have said, had a problem of identity which they resolved first by being students, secondly, more emphatically by being rebellious students. The black students, opposite here as in other respects, had a problem of losing their identity through segregation. Their identity is, of course, immensely real, in some ways the most real thing in America. . . . So if the neu-rosis of the white students is the fear that they have no identity, the passionate search to find one, that of the blacks is the fear that they will lose theirs, and beyond this the fear of actual extinction.

In his chapter on the Sorbonne, Spender emphasizes the special romantic and surrealist quality of the French students. He quotes the slogan "Imagination is Revolution," as an explanation of why the students rejected "the great trade unions, political parties, official communism." He frequently quotes with approval Daniel Cohn-Bendit, who seems to remind Spender of the anarchists he saw fighting in Spain thirty years ago.

The Czech students, however, are the ones who won the author's heart without cavil or reservation, since they are the most heroic, most tolerant, and the most rooted in reality. Their movement was not a rehearsal or a game, but a now tragic matter of life and death. They were not fighting the materialism of a consumer culture, or the impersonal manipulations of a "formal democracy," but for the elemental freedoms the students at Columbia and the Sorbonne took for granted—free speech, free assembly, no censorship.

Spender approves of most that is really new and distinctive about this internationalist generation of rebels: their passion for community, authenticity, and participation; their rejection of all existing models, parties, and dogmas of the Old Left, especially the Soviet Union; their efforts to strike alliances with the young workers; their lack of selfishness, and their perseverance despite the absence of revolutionary situations. But he has one crucial, and I think justified, criticism to make. He warns the young rebels repeatedly not to destroy the university, not to see it as a simple and vulnerable microcosm of the larger society. He writes:

> Students who attempt to revolutionize society by first destroying the university are like an army which begins a war by wrecking its own base. . . . Thus the militant students should accept the university as their base. . . . without the university there would be no students. The position of the students, even as agitators, depends on there being a university. . . . To say, "I won't have a university until society has a revolution," is as though Karl Marx were to say, "I won't go to the reading room of the British Museum until it has a revolution."

Stephen Spender has, of course, led a remarkable personal and public career. He belonged briefly to the British Communist Party during the 1930s. (His essay in the collection *The God*

That Failed convinced me personally, more than anything else written on the subject, of the futility of communist dogma, of the illegitimacy of the communist notion of the end justifying the means.) Later he was duped by the CIA, while he was coeditor of *Encounter*. He has survived these two potentially embittering experiences still a gentle radical, still a fine poet with a modernist sensibility, still a good man living in a bad time.

MAY, 1969

[4·]
T. H. White: Groupie of the Power Elite

The Making of the President, 1968; by Theodore H. White. *Atheneum. 459 pages. $10.00.*

Theodore H. White is the first groupie of the Power Elite. White loves, yes, *loves*—in a romantic and adolescent fashion—all the existing political institutions of this country. He loves the Presidency, the Congress, the polling organizations, the convention system, the press, even the donkey-symbolized Democratic Party. Thus he can write:

> . . . this venerable party whose achievements in America have made captive the imagination of free nations everywhere, whose triumphs in arms have redrawn the boundaries of Europe and Asia, whose diplomacy has imposed new constitutions on nations illiterate. . . . Yet no good history has ever been written of this majestic institution.

White has unlimited sympathy for any politician in power, but quick suspicion for the powerless, for the insurgent, for all those whose favors and access he probably won't need for the writing of *The Making of the President: 1972.*

The author's social friends staff all Administrations in Washington and manage the two major political parties. He gets to be their Boswell because he has treated them all graciously and generously in his two previous campaign chronicles. Since his maverick days as a China-watcher in the 1940s, he has learned to see the world through the eyes of its executioners rather than its victims. He shares their root values and assumptions: America, for all its faults, is the best of all nations, and getting better all the time; the two-party system, for all its faults, is the best of all pos-

sible systems; the Vietnam war was an honorable if mismanaged cause.

White gets special entré to the candidates and their entourages precisely because he remains a star-struck fan who rarely neglects to flatter the whole cast. Even the worst cretins and crooks of the political subculture manage to escape any stabs of irreverence or exposure.

Thus White describes Creighton Abrams as a "singularly able General." Governor Hughes of New Jersey is "a great gentleman." Mayor Richard Daley has "served his city well." Nelson Rockefeller is "the troubadour and bugleman of new politics." Former Pennsylvania Governor William Scranton was "the most thoughtful man in any American statehouse." Of Lyndon Johnson he writes, "Few men have done more good in their time." Abe Fortas and Dean Acheson are "elder statesmen, wise in war and diplomacy."

But the blacks who rioted in Watts in 1965 are "barbarians." And the Mobilization to End the War in Vietnam "sought confrontation; bloodshed would serve their purpose."

What makes this all so galling is that it is disguised and packaged as objective reporting, as instant, official history. White has a considerable reputation, based largely on his genuinely ground-breaking work on the 1960 campaign. But unfortunately, the current volume will define and enshrine 1968 as history for millions of curious best sellers, *Life* series, and TV specials.

As Harold Rosenberg once wrote, "What is remarkable about the manufacture of myths in the twentieth century is that it takes place under the noses of the living witnesses of the actual events, and, in fact, cannot dispense with their collaboration."

Because White is so involved with personalities and campaign techniques, it is hard to discern the substance of his politics by re-reading his 1960 and 1964 books. In 1960 he is clearly appalled by anticlerical bigotry; in 1964 he seems sympathetic to the integrationist civil rights organizations. One must learn, however, from recalled casual conversations, and fresh interviews with campaign aides, that White has been a moderate hawk on Vietnam and a panicked hard-liner against student activists.

For the cleanest insights into what Theodore H. White actually believes, one must go back and reread the three-part series of articles he published in *Life* magazine in June of 1967 on "the

new priesthood" of "action-intellectuals." As leading examples of this clergy, which Noam Chomsky more accurately baptized as the "new mandarins," White singled out Walt Rostow, Daniel Moynihan, Charles Hitch, and McGeorge Bundy. White wrote in his breathless, exaggerated prose:

> Their ideas are the drivewheels of the Great Society: shaping our defenses, guiding our foreign policy. . . . For such intellectuals, now is a Golden Age, and America is the place. Never have ideas been sought more hungrily. . . . From White House to city hall, scholars stalk the corridors of power. . . . Over the past ten years, theories incubated by such action-intellectuals have reshaped the basing and strike patterns that deploy SAC's bombers around the globe. . . . [have] lifted national income by 50 percent in the past seven years, made us rich.

White then goes on to lavish praise on the RAND Corporation, whose "triumphs are legend within the government: its perception in 1953 of how the ICBM could be fashioned long before official Washington believed it feasible; its spectacular analysis of intercontinental bombing strategy . . ."

The "new elite of American scholars," White concludes, "have become participants, and government is their instrument of expression."

White seems to get stoned on proximity to power. He is a patriot who loves the glamour of government. He yearns to know secrets you and I are not permitted to know. He has endless faith in experts. He is accustomed to getting preferential treatment from important politicians. He is more interested in techniques than values. He is, in brief, a textbook example of an elitist, and that is the key to understanding *The Making of the President: 1968.*

I read this book in a rage from start to finish. It was the first of White's books I could measure against some personal experiences of my own with the same events and personalities. And I can report that the author's middle-aged prejudices against dissenting students, blacks, and intellectuals runs through this book like a spastic's tic. White's bias reveals itself in the pettiest, smallest ways. Aretha Franklin, he comments, sang "The Star-Span-

gled Banner" at the Democratic convention "in a syncopated rock version that sounded more like a yodel than the national anthem." Those people who urged Robert Kennedy to run for President late in 1967 are identified as "self-seekers," but no explanation is given for such a description.

The book also suffers from White's chronic inability to take seriously the younger people in politics. Whenever White needs a source, he obviously goes to men his own age, men he met in the 1950s—Finch, Larry O'Brien, Jim Rowe. Thus he fails totally to grasp the impact of the newer generation of politicians on the events of 1968. The McCarthy campaign, for example, is explained primarily from the point of view of Blair Clark; McCarthy's two under-thirty speechwriters, Jeremy Larner and Paul Gorman, are never even mentioned in the book. Peter Edelman, who worked for Robert Kennedy for four years in the Senate, and who nourished his growth so much, is mentioned only once in passing. Julian Bond is not referred to once in the entire book. And neither is Harold Hughes, the former governor, and now senator, from Iowa, who deserved most of the credit for the rules reforms voted by reformers at the Chicago convention. Harry Truman, however, does rate nine mentions in this history of 1968.

But I wish here to focus on just two chapters in the book. White devotes a full chapter—in sequence right after Kennedy's assassination—to the issue of law and order in America. He blames the young, the intellectuals, and the blacks for the climate of domestic violence. He hardly mentions the Vietnam war. He spends more time attacking the *New York Review of Books* for its Molotov-cocktail cover than attacking white racism. He rebukes the Kerner Report for its "confused analysis." He writes, "The black violence of 1968 began early—with two killed and forty injured in a riot in Orangeburg, South Carolina, on February 8."

What happened in Orangeburg was that South Carolina state troopers shot to death three black college students in the back, and hospitalized forty others, wounding many in the soles of their feet as they ran away. The black students were unarmed. They were nonviolently picketing a segregated bowling alley. To call that incident an example of black violence is like calling Hiroshima an example of oriental violence.

White reaches the apex of his cranky fury at the young in his chapter on the Democratic Convention in Chicago. White's conclusion at the end of the chapter is, "I find it hard to criticize, morally or technically, the strategy and disposition of the Chicago police. . . ." He devotes long narrative passages to describing the language and violence of the "mobs" in the street. He reports that on Monday night of convention week there was "a riot of Yippies against police in Northern Chicago."

What I saw, and what the Walker Report saw, and what the national press saw, was a riot by out-of-control police against young people who were peacefully assembled in a public park. White hardly mentions the salient fact that the demonstrators had requested legal permits to march, rally, and sleep in the parks, and that the city of Chicago rejected those requests, which seem to be guaranteed in the First Amendment.

But it is not hard to understand how White got the street action in Chicago so cockeyed. He wasn't there. The best reporters in the country—I. F. Stone, Richard Harwood, Jimmy Breslin, Mike Royko—were all present in Grant and Lincoln parks. But White, the voyeur of decision-making and nose-picking by the great, was busy in the Hilton Hotel with Humphrey and McCarthy when the midnight police sweeps through the parks took place.

White's description of the violence on Wednesday is too lengthy to quote here. Suffice it to report that he spreads further Mayor Daley's never-substantiated charge that there was a "plot" by the movement to assassinate the candidates. He repeatedly refers to the students as a "mob." He chooses to identify the National Guard as "one of the most useful institutions in American life." And he testifies, "I walked quite unimpeded and unchallenged by the swarming police across the street to the Blackstone Hotel." As if that bit of information makes all the police violence a myth invented by "the mob."

I met Teddy White while covering the Kennedy campaign, and he is a warm and likable man. He has won a Pulitzer Prize, and he has written much that is valuable during a long career. And he is certainly entitled to his growing conservative views.

My complaint here is simply this: White has not told us the truth about difficult events we need very badly to face and un-

derstand if we are not to repeat them. And he has acquitted and flattered those "statesmen" and "action-intellectuals" most responsible for the slaughter in Vietnam and the violence in Chicago. And he has slandered the ordinary, voiceless victims of that violence.

JUNE, 1969

[5.]
The Decline of Radicalism

The Decline of Radicalism; by Daniel J. Boorstin. *Random House. $4.95.*

There is a growing library of literature by respected academic liberals who seem to celebrate their intellectual menopause by joining the war on puberty and attacking the New Left.

There has been a recent blitz of antiyouth articles by Diana Trilling in *Commentary,* by Nathan Glazer in *The Atlantic,* and by Sidney Hook in *Encounter.* And full-length books by George Kennan (*Democracy and the Student Left*), Jacques Barzun (*The American University*), and Lewis Feuer (*The Conflict of Generations*). And now this volume by professor and historian Daniel Boorstin. That Professor Boorstin should contribute to this trend —from which I exempt such writers as Irving Howe and Robert Brustein, who have perceptively criticized the New Left from within a radical stance of their own—is a depressing development, because he has always struck me as an original and trenchant interpreter of the image-making role of the mass media, and of the American colonial experience.

The first two thirds of this collection of previously published pieces and speeches is a dull but informative series of lectures about the loss of and the search for community. It is only in the last third of the book that Professor Boorstin indulges generational grudge, and in a feverish voice totally out of harmony with the cool, erudite tone of the rest of the anthology. And since the author takes his title from this section, I suppose it is appropriate that my review focus on his two essays that belabor the student activists.

In the chapter titled "Dissent, Dissension, and the News," Boorstin seem to make two basic points, that the students have

no real reason to engage in direct political protest, except publicity and ego gratification, and that the mass media have exaggerated the numbers and impact of the activists.

"Dissenters are concerned with identity," he writes. "Professional dissenters do not and cannot seek to assimilate their program or ideals into American culture. . . . They are not interested in the freedom of anybody else."

In the title essay, the author goes even further in trying to discredit the motives of student radicals. "The most vocal and most violent disrupters of American society today," he writes, "are not radicals at all but a new species of barbarian . . . rude, wild, and uncivilized. . . . Contrary to popular belief and contrary to the legends which they would like to spread about themselves, they are not troubled by an excessive concern for others. . . . Theirs is the egoism, the personal chauvinism of the isolationist self. Their 'Direct Action' slogan means nothing but, 'Myself, Right or Wrong.' . . . Each little victory for Student Power or Black Power—or any other kind of Power—is a victory for the New Barbarism."

Such observations by an intellectual I have admired and quoted makes the mind boggle. First on motivation. The student rebellion is rooted in what Marxists like to call "objective conditions." It is the war, the draft, institutionalized racism, the power of the military, and other felt political issues that generate protests. At a deeper level, it is estrangement from straight cultural styles, job options, and the irrelevance of secondary and college education that radicalizes the young. The scholarly studies of Kenneth Keniston at Yale and Richard Flacks at the University of Chicago have shown that the student radicals are the brightest, most mature, and most sensitive members of their generation. And the Cox Commission, which studied the roots of the student insurgency at Columbia, concluded that: "The present generation of young people in our universities is the best informed, the most intelligent, and the most idealistic this country has ever known."

Even moderates and conservatives who disagree with the politics of the young rebels should at least be able to see they are not primarily neurotic or out only for novelty and kicks like the panty-raiders and goldfish gulpers of other generations. The current and recent student generations have risked—and some have lost—their very lives to register black voters in the rural South.

As a matter of conscience, they have gone to jail, and into exile, rather than participate in a war they feel is immoral and purposeless. They have taken head-splitting beatings from police because of their beliefs and in Berkeley, they have been shot at and gassed from helicopters. They are the children of the middle class, and they have, *by conscious choice,* rejected the well-paying jobs in government, and in the professions that their education and heredity qualified them for. They have done this because they yearn for less materialistic definitions of success, and more liberated life styles. Contrary to the professor's cynical psychological interpretation, they are probably the most *selfless* generation ever of American radicals, because they are not motivated by narrow self-interest, but by empathy with Vietnamese peasants and black welfare mothers they have never met, and in whose name they have risked life, family ties, and careers.

Professor Boorstin also argues they are not real radicals (hence, "new barbarians") because they lack a sense of community. But I think it is precisely a desire for a sense of community that characterizes the best of the young radicals. The struggle for People's Park in Berkeley was an effort to create something for a whole community. So was the assembly at Bethel last month. Political support for "community control" in the ghettos is another example. So is the notion of "participatory democracy," whereby everyone has a voice in the now remote and impersonal decisions that affect his life. So are the hippie experiments in tribal living. And so is the new student interest in ecology—the preservation of the natural environment—a symptom of their essential communitarian vision.

The author even mocks the notion of direct action by students. He writes: "Direct action is to politics what the Frug or the Jerk is to the dance." Which, I guess, makes Martin Luther King the Chubby Checkers of nonviolence.

It is quite easy to criticize certain elements of the youth rebellion. SDS has become isolated in a fantasy world of vulgarized Marxist rhetoric, karate classes, and rumbles with white gangs. The Crazies and Motherfuckers have a penchant for tactics so absurdly counterproductive that one might reasonably suspect they are really CIA double agents. The Progressive Labor movement is composed of authoritarian Gletkins straight out of Arthur Koestler's *Darkness at Noon.*

But most high school and college radicals are not members of SDS or PL. (SDS claims only 7,000 members, and the January 1969 issue of *Fortune* estimated there are three million college students sympathetic to the goals of the New Left.) Most student activists are living an ad hoc "No" to the Leviathan by resisting the war, organizing the poor and the powerless, and starting underground newspapers, rock bands, and communes. They may fail, or make mistakes, but they are working and daring.

But what personal risks do the older social critics like Professor Boorstin take? What do they actually DO to stop the war, or build new institutions, or help free the university from the influence of the Pentagon, the CIA, the FBI, and the McClellan Committee's snoopers? What is their *program, their analysis?* We have a right to expect something more imaginative from the tenured generation of university liberals than sideline psychoanalysis.

Will you, Professor Boorstin, be addressing an antiwar rally on October 15? Will you send a modest contribution to Reverend Jesse Jackson? Will you leave your library long enough to write about black lung in West Virginia or lead poisoning in Bedford-Stuyvesant?

Or will you keep on sitting at your typewriter complaining about "the decline of radicalism?"

OCTOBER, 1969

[6.]

Revolution for the Hell of It

Revolution for the Hell of It; by Free (Abbie Hoffman). *Dial Press. 231 pages. Cloth, $4.95; paper, $1.95.*

Abbie Hoffman is a charming combination of Ernie Kovacs, Artaud, and Prince Kropotkin. He is a put-on artist, an acid-head (over seventy trips), a mass-media guerrilla, and now he has anthologized his hallucinations into a book.

Well, sort of a book, since two of the author's many gurus are Andy Warhol and Marshall McLuhan. What Abbie has done is put between formless covers some LSD fantasies: diarylike accounts of the March on the Pentagon and the Battle of Daleyland; pictures of him and his famous friends; clippings; random quotations from gurus like George Sorel, Lewis Carroll, and Martin Buber; a letter to Stokely Carmichael; and a self-interview à la Mailer.

The spirit of the book is foreshadowed in the two epigraphs Abbie invokes at the start of the opening chapter. One is from the international revolutionary Che Guevara, and the other is from a television commercial for a cleansing powder. Abbie, you must understand, is a pure Marxist-Lennonist—Harpo Marx and John Lennon.

The author was once a charter member of the New Left. He worked in the 1962 peace campaign for the Senate of H. Stuart Hughes, and he paid his dues with SNCC in Mississippi and Georgia. But now Abbie is a founder and leader of the Yippies, and he mocks SDS and *Ramparts* no less than he mocks Harvard and *The New York Times*. He writes:

> I was once in the New Left, but I outgrew it. . . .
> The Left masturbates continuously, because it is essentially rooted in an academic tradition. . . . Those pa-

pers that claim to be accurate, i.e., *The New York Times, The Village Voice, Ramparts, The Nation, Commentary,* that whole academic word scene is a total bore. In the end they probably distort things more than *The Daily News.*

Abbie now prefers theater to politics. "Drama is anything you can get away with," he writes. "Stokely yelling, 'Hell no, we won't go,' that was drama, not explanation. The point is nobody gives a [bleep] anymore about troop strength, escalation, crying over napalm."

Between the pratfalls, put-ons, and fraternal hotfoots for the New Left, Abbie seems to intend this volume as a serious manifesto for the growing counterculture of mind drugs, rock bands, sexual freedom, mixed media communes, Free Stores, astrology, colorful costumes, and casual nudity.

If I understand Abbie correctly, there are three essential planks in the Yippie platform. One is street theater, satire, confrontations, put-ons, and the general freakiness he calls "monkey warfare." Its purpose is to get on television to communicate an alternative life style to the global village of the young. Abbie considers youth as a distinct social class, a new, surrogate proletariat.

Second, Abbie stands for mind-expanding drugs, sex, freedom, games, anything that is pleasurable. This is his "politics of ecstasy."

And last, he is in favor of panhandling, stealing, hustling, anything that displays contempt for the "property fetish." Abbie is for free everything (especially toilets) and advocates the abolition of money.

This does not seem to be quite the platform to win the legendary minds and hearts of the American people. I'm not even sure that it would win the minds and hearts of a majority of teenyboppers. I fear, in fact, that it is a recipe for private amusement and public catastrophe. It does not speak at all to the needs of the propertyless—the whites of Appalachia, or Indians on reservations in South Dakota, or Mexican and Filipino farm workers in California, or Negro parents trying to win community control in Ocean Hill-Brownsville. It does not recognize the fact that forty million other Americans do not have the mobility, or leisure, or economic security to drop out. And they probably wish

they had the dollar bills Abbie burned symbolically at the Stock Exchange to pay the rent with.

Injustice in America is congealed in institutions. Building counterinstitutions is fine. But only dull, exhausting politics will transform those gigantic institutions that have power over our lives. Street theater, acid trips, and disruption of liberal rallies won't do it. Even slipping some LSD into Richard Nixon's coffee will not diminish the power of the military-industrial-labor complex, or abolish the draft, or humanize the welfare bureaucracy. Henry Luce took LSD, and *Time* still did not become the *East Village Other*.

What social change there has been in the last eight years has come through radical, parapolitical movements of millions of ordinary people. First in the civil-rights movement. Then in the antiwar movement. And most recently in the "dump Johnson" movement. Student participation was won at Columbia through dogged political activism. And it is *politically* that welfare mothers, agricultural workers, and draft resisters are organizing. And with varied life styles.

There is also a second point on which Abbie and I are in substantive disagreement. While we both favor *radical actions,* I remain in sympathy with *liberal values.* Reason. Democracy. Tolerance. Truth. I find them superior to distortion, violence, chaos and mindless action.

Abbie writes that "action is the only reality; not only reality, but morality as well. . . . Confusion is mightier than the sword. . . . By allowing all: loving, cheating, anger, violence, stealing, trading, you become situation oriented, and as such become more effective."

That would be a wonderful platform for the Chicago Police Department, the Mississippi Highway Patrol, and George Wallace. It is an invitation for them to "do their thing" in the streets, and that is to play the game on the right-wing's home field. This is not a revolutionary country, or a revolutionary period. To act as though it is, and ignore the consequences, is dangerous. And the victims will not be the white, middle-class Yippies. The police—even in Chicago—still just club and Mace Yippies. But they kill blacks. In Orangeburg. In Oakland. In Washington, D.C.

At bottom, I think the Yippies badly confuse cultural and political values. They would profit, I think, by reading a penetrating

1962 essay by William Phillips (collected in *A Sense of the Present*). In it Phillips advocated "purity in politics and impurity in literature. Politically, this meant a stand for morality in politics. In literature, it means a radicalism rooted in tradition and open to experiment, and an awareness that the imagination could not be contained within any orthodoxy."

The Symbolists, Dadaists, and Impressionists have advanced the cause of modernity in poetry and painting, but they had little relevance to the Russian or Chinese revolutions. So while I agree that Bob Dylan and the Living Theater are major cultural pioneers, I do not regard them as particularly useful guides to the new politics.

Politics is more than theater. The Pentagon is more than just a prop. Style is not content. Running a pig for President is not as valuable as electing Harold Hughes to the Senate.

The Absurd has provided the motif for great novelists, from Kafka to Pynchon. But it will not help redistribute the economic and political power of this country. Drugs have also contributed to important art, from Blake and Rimbaud to Allen Ginsberg and Ken Kesey. But what do drugs have to do with community control of the schools and police in the ghettos? Satire has given us the Marx Brothers and the Mothers of Invention. But it will not free us from Mayor Daley and Spiro Agnew.

Revolution for the Hell of It is clever, fun, and should be read. Perhaps its pages should even be smoked. But if one is still serious about redeeming the American Dream, then he should read some of those linear, over-thirty squares, like I. F. Stone, Norman Mailer, and Howard Zinn.

DECEMBER, 1968

[7.]
Eldridge Cleaver

Eldridge Cleaver; Post-Prison Writings and Speeches; edited by
Robert Scheer. *Random House. 211 pages. $5.95.*

It is my strong suspicion that history will not be kind to most of
the men who have sought to lead the black movement in America during this volcanic decade. I think that when future historians measure them against the high quality of the abolitionist, or
early labor leaders, most modern black leaders will seem fatally
flawed by timidity, opportunism, venality, and egomania. But
with four incorruptible exceptions: Martin Luther King, Malcolm X, Robert Parris Moses of SNCC, and Eldridge Cleaver.

Cleaver's first book, *Soul on Ice,* was a seminal work in the tormented odyssey of the black psyche in America. Its ideas were
complex and original. It was written (leisurely, in jail) in an in-
candescent prosody of prophecy. And its publication filled a void
left by the assassination of Malcolm X.

This modest volume is not a sequel to *Soul on Ice.* It is not literature, but propaganda in a clenched-fist tradition of Tom
Paine and William Lloyd Garrison. It consists of manifestos and
speeches scrawled in the trenches and published quickly to fill an
immediate political need.

Judged by the narrow norm of book reviewing, this collection
is not special. But this book should not be read as a typical journalistic collection. It should be read as a new installment of Eldridge Cleaver's existential autobiography, as raw testimony of
how America's racism has converted a powerful young (thirty-
three) writer into a fugitive/exile because of his ideas.

After *Soul on Ice* became a best seller, Cleaver could have
played the game the cozy way like other black writers. Say radical things on television, or to affluent, uptight liberals, and then
pocket big money from publishing corporations, and travel com-

fortably in the literary dinner party orbit. But Cleaver could not live that contradiction. He had to carry his passion into action, to live at the bottom of the ghetto with the brothers. Cleaver became a leader of the Black Panther Party. Although on parole, he spoke at rallies against the war in Vietnam, and challenged Ronald Reagen to a duel. He was wounded in a shoot-out with Oakland police, in which seventeen-year-old Bobby Hutton was shot in the back and killed, with his hands held above his head. Like Lenny Bruce and Che Guevara, Cleaver chose to internalize his values as an example, and that is why his photograph is now in every post office in the land.

The flaws of this book are all out front. The writing lacks the polish and fire of *Soul on Ice;* here Cleaver uses "pig" as an adjective, "racist" as a pronoun and "motherfucker" almost as a conjunction. Also, the book is padded with two affidavits, and uncharacteristically flabby essays on "The Decline of the Muslims" and "The Land Question and Black Liberation."

But this volume does perform two valuable and necessary functions. It gives evidence that Cleaver is *not* antiwhite. And it provides the more plausible Panther version of the now mythicized shoot-out in Oakland that killed Bobby Hutton.

As a result of the distortions of the television networks and the weekly newsmagazines, white America regards Eldridge Cleaver as a racist. But of all the black revolutionaries around, Cleaver is actually the one with the healthiest, most constructive attitude toward whites and white culture. He quotes Bob Dylan. He recommends blacks read Nat Hentoff. He repeatedly calls for political alliances with sympathetic whites, and even suggests that his long-range vision is one of integration rather than separatism. Cleaver is a revolutionary who happens to be black. In a speech given at Stanford University on October 1, 1968, and reprinted here, Cleaver says:

> For all these hundreds of years, black people have had the thrust of their hearts against racism, because racism has been what has been murdering them. So black people oppose racism. The Black Panther Party opposes it, and we would hope that everyone can oppose it whether it's black or white. Because it will do us no good . . . We say, power to the people, all people should have the power to control their own destiny . . .

Cleaver verbalizes his antiracist views even more directly in his *Playboy* interview with Nat Hentoff, which is also included in this collection. At one point he tells Hentoff,

> . . . we think there is a hard core of whites, particularly young whites, who are very alarmed at the course this country is taking. . . . They are turning into a revolutionary force, and that's why the Black Panthers can enter into coalitions with them as equal partners. . . . You see, whites in America really love this country. Especially young white idealists . . . We work with these young people all the time, and we've had nothing but encouraging experiences with them. These young white people aren't hung up battling to maintain the status quo like some of the older people who think they'll become extinct if the system changes. They're adventurous: they're willing to experiment with new forms; they're willing to confront life . . .

Later on, Hentoff asks Cleaver, "In which direction would you like to see America go—toward separation or integration?" And Cleaver responds:

> Keeping in mind that we're talking about the very long view, it seems to me that we're living in a world that has become virtually a neighborhood. If the world is not going to destroy itself, the concept of people going their totally separate ways is really something that can't continue indefinitely. When you start speaking in ultimate terms, I don't see any way in which the world can be administered for the best interests of mankind without having a form of world government that would be responsive and responsible to all the people of the world . . .

Cleaver's affidavit about the shooting in Oakland seems to me much more believable than the official police account of the event. The bizarre incident, which took place two days after the murder of Dr. King, begins with Cleaver stopping to urinate in the street, and reaches a climax with the Oakland police ordering Bobby Hutton, choking on tear gas, to run toward a squad car, and then shooting him in the back. After the killing, Cleaver describes his treatment in the police station:

"Where are you wounded?" he asked me.

I pointed out my wound to him. The Pig of Pigs looked down at my wound [Cleaver's leg], raised his foot and stomped on the wound.

"Get him out of here," he told the other pigs, and they took me away.

I cannot agree with some of Cleaver's central ideas. I think he places too much stress on violence, sometimes substituting it for analysis and strategy, and sometimes unable to resolve his own ambivalence about its use (Cleaver helped avert violence after Dr. King's assassination). And I do not endorse all of the ten basic points in the Panther platform, especially the demand that all black prisoners be immediately released from all jails.

But this is part of the uncomfortable test Eldridge Cleaver puts us to. Are white insurgents and intellectuals prepared to defend ideas they disagree with, when those ideas are being politically repressed here in America? As Robert Scheer puts it at the end of his excellent introduction:

> The intellectual and liberal community in America, which is normally agitated by violations of the rights of Soviet artists, has displayed monumental indifference to the most harassed and promising of its own young writers. The host of organizations, PEN, the Congress of Cultural Freedom, International Rescue Committee, and other "free world" crusaders normally charged with the protection of liberty against totalitarian regimes, seem constitutionally incapable of finding analogous problems in this country. *Newsweek* magazine was terribly agitated about the imprisonment of Soviet writer Daniel, but found Cleaver's plight a source of amusement—"soul on the lam"—and at last report the *Saturday Review* had not yet been heard from, nor had Norman Podhoretz.

In many of his speeches, Cleaver tells his audiences that black and white are irrelevant, that what counts is "whether you're part of the problem, or whether you're part of the solution."

This book, in Cleaver's absence, poses that question still.*

NOVEMBER, 1968

* It seems clear that both Cleaver and the Black Panther Party have become more estranged from reality and more dogmatic over the last two and a half years.

[8.]
Myopia of the Inside Dopesters

The Real Majority; by Richard Scammon and Ben Wattenberg.
Coward-McCann. 333 pages. $7.95.

The Great Hype Machine is being cranked up once again. In the
recent past this McLuhanite monster has sought to persuade us
of the virtues of the Edsel, black capitalism, *Myra Breckinridge,*
the "new Nixon," and the midi-skirt. Now it is being put to the
service of a political theory in the form of a book called *The
Real Majority* (Coward-McCann). Like most clients of this myth-
making apparatus, it is new, slick, attractively packaged, well
publicized and distributed—and bereft of authenticity or value.
   The Real Majority has been plugged on Dick Cavett's television talk show. John Roche, LBJ's former house intellectual,
wrote in his new syndicated column, *"The Real Majority* is the
most incisive and controversial analysis of American politics to
come along in the last decade." The book was also praised by
hawkish Howard K. Smith of ABC-TV, who said: "If I were a politician running for office this year, the first thing I would do,
ahead of all else, is study the book, *The Real Majority."* It has
been boosted in *Newsweek,* not in the form of a book review but
as a news story in the National Affairs section of the weekly that
"separates fact from opinion." According to *Newsweek,* the book
provides "a fascinating guide to who the majority voter really is,"
and the authors "demolish a good deal of wishful liberal thinking. . . ." *The Real Majority* has been promoted by syndicated
columnists Roland Evans and Robert Novak, who wrote: "Advance copies have been pondered by key party figures for the
past month. Seldom has one book had so instant an impact on
political affairs."
   The better-known author of this centrist tract is Richard Scam-

mon, former director of the U.S. Bureau of the Census, now head of the Electronics Research Center in Washington, and a public opinion "consultant" for *Newsweek*. His partner is Ben Wattenberg, a former speech writer for Lyndon Johnson, and now for Hubert Humphrey.

The Scammon-Wattenberg thesis is simple: the average voter "is a forty-seven-year-old housewife from the outskirts of Dayton, Ohio, whose husband is a machinist." Which is to say, the mass of American voters today are "unpoor, unblack, unyoung," and hold "middle-of-the-road" political views. The new, great "social issue" in America, these inside dopesters say, is an increasing opposition to black militancy, student unrest, crime, drugs, the breakdown of the traditional morality.

The authors are knowledgeable; their book is impressive with tables, facts, maps, graphs, statistics, and provides a twenty-five-page appendix of data. The authors write a simple, direct, neutral prose that seems almost scientific in its confident tone. But in the end, they propose a strategy that correlates 100 percent with their bias—the Johnson-Humphrey faction of the Democratic Party. They advise candidates to slide to the right on the social issue—that complex constellation of questions relating to authority and order—while supporting the traditional New Deal programs, and fuzzing on Vietnam, since it is no longer politically important.

Unfortunately when the Scammon-Wattenberg theory is put into practice by impressionable "liberal Democrats," it becomes something cheap and illiberal. It becomes Joseph Tydings of Maryland sponsoring the preventive detention bill in the Senate. It becomes Hubert Humphrey (Wattenberg's employer) repudiating his former support for gun-control legislation, saying he was unreasonably influenced by the emotionalism of the King and Kennedy murders. It becomes Adlai Stevenson naming Chicago Eight prosecutor Tom Foran as co-chairman of his Senate campaign in Illinois, the same Tom Foran who relieved his feelings in public with the notorious "freaking fag revolution" speech at the end of the trial.

Of course blowing up buildings and killing lone cops from ambush is inhuman and demented. But what ambitious politicians are doing this season under the influence of this book is sick in its own right. Scammon and Wattenberg are not just morally wrong, they are wrong even on their own technocratic terms.

The moral point first. *The Real Majority* glorifies technique to the exclusion of substance. Its counsel—and the last chapter is written like a textbook—is geared to devising the best tactics, to putting the best face on a position, to finding the most pragmatic way to phrase something. At such carpentry the authors are truly clever, in the gimmicky way that Theodore Sorensen or Herbert Klein is clever. This, for example, is how they suggest that a candidate talk about student radicalism:

> Do *not* say: "Well, I don't agree with Students for a Democratic Society when they invade a college president's office, but I can understand their deep sense of frustration."
>
> *Do* say: "When students break laws they will be treated as lawbreakers." (Italics in original.)

Nowhere in its 305 pages of text does the book offer any ideas as to how we might actually solve social problems. The whole thrust is on how to get the vote of that machinist in Dayton, not how to improve his unhappy life. The whole unspoken assumption is the infinite projection into the future of the *status quo,* the idea that poverty, racism, militarism and male supremacy are normal permanent conditions to be manipulated, not erased.

But all this is relatively easy moralizing from the Left. Where the book really falls is in its comprehension of the actual forces shaping contemporary politics. For all its data, for all its pose of scholarly objectivity, *The Real Majority* badly underestimates some of the deepest trends running through the American body politic.

No single theory or concept can possibly explain the mood of the American voter in 1970. In this volcanic epoch, most people are too irrational and in too great conflict to be sociologized into voting blocs or categories. Millions of white workingmen switched their allegiance from Robert Kennedy to George Wallace during the 1968 campaign. Others, more upper class and suburban, switched to Richard Nixon when Eugene McCarthy was not nominated in Chicago. Many citizens vote on an intuition about personality; others are rigidly loyal to a party. Unfortunately, only a minority of the electorate is issue-oriented.

A given individual probably dislikes the war in Vietnam and college students about equally; he will suffer from contradictory

impulses in the polling booth. Scammon and Wattenberg are sophisticated enough to understand this, and they do bury some necessary qualifications and modifiers in dependent clauses. But by stressing repeatedly that a firm stand against the militancy of the young, the poor, and the black is required to win elections, they oversimplify human nature. [*See* "The Perils of Quantification," *The Nation,* September 21, 1970, and "The Politics of Prejudice," *The Nation,* September 28, 1970.]

Kevin Phillips was guilty of a similar error in *The Emerging Republican Majority,* which also enjoyed a brief season on the Hype Machine. Only Phillips used Catholic ethnicity and "sunbelt" geography as the anchors of his single theory. Now, the recent defeats of Harrold Carswell, Orval Faubus, and George Mahoney suggest doubts about the viability of the "Southern strategy."

Scammon and Wattenberg enormously underrate the importance of Vietnam, probably because their own political allies, Humphrey and LBJ, have no comfortable way of dealing with a disaster for which history will hold them responsible. Recent primary elections have reaffirmed the capacity of forthright antiwar candidates to attract volunteers, money, and enthusiasm on this still deeply felt issue. Rev. Joseph Duffey won the three-way Senate primary in Connecticut in August largely because of his long-standing commitment against the war. Two weeks after James Reston had penned a *New York Times* column about how conservative Denver has become, the antiwar insurgent, Craig Barnes, upset veteran Republican Byron Rogers in the Democratic primary in that city. In Massachusetts, Father Robert Drinan, an outspoken dove, unseated seventy-two-year-old Philip Philbin, the vice chairman of the Armed Services Committee, and an unreconstructed hawk. In Manhattan's polyglot 19th Congressional District, Mrs. Bella Abzug, running on a platform of immediate withdrawal from Vietnam, upset ten-year Republican Leonard Farbstein, who had an adequate voting record, but showed no passion against the war. And in Maryland's 4th Congressional District, sixty-eight-year-old George Fallon, chairman of the House Public Works Committee, was upset by a thirty-seven-year-old peace candidate, Paul Sarbanes. And what's most important about these races is that the winners all drew substantial backing from blue-collar voters.

Scammon and Wattenberg do not take into account the ability

of neo-Populists to neutralize the backlash by appealing to low- and middle-income whites on the ground of economic self-interest. In 1968 I watched Robert Kennedy win the Indiana and Nebraska primaries. These are not liberal or peace states. He prevailed by standing up in the town squares of South Bend and Omaha, with his hair flopping into his eyes, and shouting about the war, tax reform, bureaucracy and local control, and new economic priorities. The steelworkers and waitresses and small farmers forgot their racism and voted for Kennedy.

Peter Flaherty fashioned a similiar coalition of students, blacks and working-class whites to become the Mayor of Pittsburgh last year. In June, Richard Ottinger invoked the old Populist passions, attacking the corporate polluters, the machine Democrats, and monopolies like Con Edison and the Telephone Company, to win the New York Senate primary. An analysis of Ottinger's votes showed that he carried many workingmen's neighborhoods in Brooklyn and Queens.

And in Connecticut, Duffey won the votes of the "unpoor, unyoung, and unblack" by marching on union picket lines, talking about how his father was a West Virginia coal miner, attacking the war in Southeast Asia, and by pushing Walter Reuther's plan, which would require the management of defense plants to set aside 25 percent of their profits for preparation and research into economic reconversion once the war is over.

As affluent moderates, Scammon and Wattenberg forget how hard it is for a city family to live on $10,000 a year. That family may not like blacks or hippies, but it might vote for a candidate who talks about issues like tax reform, industrial safety, consumer protection, factory layoffs and inflation, free health care, pollution, and higher Social Security benefits—all programs that benefit white workers as much as black workers.

Candidates who follow the advice offered in *The Real Majority* do not automatically prosper. In New York's 1969 Democratic primary for mayor Republican James Scheuer waged a model campaign according to the Scammon-Wattenberg formula. After establishing a solid liberal record in the House, Scheuer veered sharply to the right at the start of his campaign for mayor. He published a book on the subject of crime called *To Walk the Streets Safely*. He went to synagogues to attack Lindsay's softness toward black anti-Semitism and to demand that the Mayor fire

several of his top black appointees. He demanded more police. He spent more money than most of his opponents. And he ran dead last, even trailing Norman Mailer.

The strategy did not work for Representative Scheuer because it was contrived, artificial. It made him go against the grain of his own instincts. And the voters could smell the fraud. For the same reason, this approach did not work for Hubert Humphrey in 1968. It was not organic to his politics; it was a position grafted on to cater to a perceived mood. It has been my observation that unless a politician knows who he is, he will sink under his own programmed oratory. Ambitious politicians would do better to forget *The Real Majority* and follow the counsel of Shakespeare: "To thine own self be true."

In their dialectic of change, Scammon and Wattenberg almost totally ignore nonelectoral movements. But the history of the last decade shows, I think, that movements, not candidates, make history and alter consciousness. It was the civil rights movement, from Rosa Parks to the police dogs in Birmingham, that forged a new national consensus in favor of public accommodations and voting rights. A movement—ordinary people in motion—forced John Kennedy to introduce civil rights legislation in June of 1963. The antiwar movement, which began outside both major parties, finally turned the nation around on Vietnam, and drove Lyndon Johnson into sulky exile. And today the women's liberation movement is making the politicians wake up and pass legislation like abortion reform and the equal pay amendment.

The most conspicuous weakness, perhaps, of Scammon and Wattenberg is their inability to understand the transcendent importance of television. One doesn't have to agree with all of Marshall McLuhan's puns and probes to understand that he is onto something big. Television *is* a surrogate reality for millions of people, and the result is that television is absorbing and centralizing the authority that was once dispersed among the shop steward, the district leader, the minister, and the print publisher. Television is making irrelevant the political middleman or interpreter. Every voter can now see the candidates in his own living room and make a judgment, perhaps frivolous or irrational, about how he will vote. The historic effect of this has been to break down the political party structure, and to project personality above party—a Lindsay or a Kennedy.

The most telling variable in the campaigns this year has not been the law and order issue but the use of television. Those candidates who have had the most money to put the best commercials on the air have won.

Arlen J. Large recognized this when he wrote in *The Wall Street Journal* on June 23:

> All during the '60s, candidates and their clever helpers sharpened the skills of using television to win elections. Paid ads and biographical films were credited with decisive impact in several upset wins: Milton Schapp in the 1966 Democratic Primary for Governor of Pennsylvania; Nelson Rockefeller's 1966 reelection as Governor of New York; Mike Gravel's 1968 dumping of Senator Ernest Gruening in Alaska.
>
> This year, televised ads again have shown their power, in the come-from-behind Senate Democratic primary victories of Lloyd Bentsen over Senator Ralph Yarborough in Texas, and of Howard Metzenbaum over John Glenn in Ohio.

And on the day his article appeared, the clearest triumph yet of television was demonstrated in New York, where Ottinger won the Senate primary largely with his "Ottinger Delivers" blitz of TV commercials.

I have no countertheory with which to supplant *The Real Majority* or *The Emerging Republican Majority*. Nevertheless, what I say is that Scammon and Phillips are wrong, that they are victims of their own prejudices, and are blind to the decisive importance of TV, the economy, Vietnam, and the irrational element in human behavior.

OCTOBER, 1970

[SEVEN]
DOWN AND OUT IN QUEENS COUNTY

These two pieces are about poor white people who live in the borough of Queens. President Nixon says they have no problems and calls them the silent majority. They are not silent. The President is deaf.

[1.]
Crushing of Corona by a Plastic Glacier

I spent last Sunday in Corona, Queens, on 102nd Street, in the condemned home of Mary Moramarco and her friends. She is one of the sixty-nine small homeowners in Corona whose homes the Board of Estimate voted unanimously to tear down in order to build a high school and athletic field.

Corona (crown in Italian) is one of the few authentic communities left in this unheavenly city. The families the city wants to evict—about five hundred people—have lived there all their lives. Three generations ago their families all lived in the same part of Italy. Most of their homes were built by hand, by their fathers, or by their grandfathers. They all worship at the same church. Their parents and their married children still live in the neighborhood. These Italian families live a life style as rich and as precious as the freaks in the East Village, or the Puerto Ricans in the Barrio. And they do not want to leave their turf.

"There was a city dump here," said Ralph Dellacona, "when the Italians first came here in 1900. We took the worst land, and we built homes with our bare hands. Because I want to live with my friends and keep my home, they call me a Mafia."

"I'm afraid they're going to board up my house whenever I go outside," said Lillian Marasseri. "Last week six men came to my house and told me I didn't own it any more. They told me it belongs to the city now. I went to City Hall to complain. I waited three hours on my feet to see this Mike Dontzin. They didn't ever offer us a chair. We kept standing up for three hours. Then they told us it's too late, it's been decided already, that we lost, that we shouldn't give them any more sob stories about our homes."

Mary Moramarco started to talk. She stood in her nice, clean kitchen holding up her dead father's medals. "My father lost his hand and won a purple heart defending this house," she was say-

ing. "No money can pay for the happiness we've had in this house. The Real Estate Department is offering people $8000 for their homes. If I leave here, I go on welfare. I can't afford to pay rent.

"I know how to make a molatov. Maybe I can't say it right, but I can make it. I've tried it already in my bathtub, with sand. We'll get the kids from Stony Brook with the beards, and they'll help us defend our homes. I told the first surveyor for the city who came on our block to make the hole he was digging a little bigger, and I'll put him in it. We hit him a few times and he ran away.

"I went to the Board of Estimate meeting last week. They all sat up there picking their noses and voting us into the street. I told that Garelik"—she pronounced it "garlic"—"when he runs for mayor, we will follow him wherever he goes with a sign and a stick. Even if it is just two of us, we'll follow him to his grave."

Sunday night Pete Hamill and I talked to Mayor Lindsay, Deputy Mayor Richard Aurelio, and Lindsay's aide Sid Davidoff. They all tried to explain the enormously complex history of the Corona conflict, a history involving the Jewish community in Forest Hills, the Board of Education, eight alternate sites, the Board of Estimate, the Queens political establishment, the City Planning Commission, and builder Samuel Lefrak, whose project is adjacent to the sixty-nine homes. In essence, the Lindsay people said that every layer of the bureaucracy had approved the original decision, and that it would now take too much effort to reverse it, even if it was a mistake.

But the fact is the original decision to condemn the homes *was* a mistake. Also, it was probably part of a real estate deal, since as early as June of 1967 newspaper ads taken for rentals in Lefrak City promised "a new high school adjacent to property."

Every public official has approved the demolition of the homes —Lindsay, Garelik, Beame, Sidney Leviss, on down to Councilmen Arthur Katzman and Edward Sadowsky. But the original decision was as bad as the original decision to go into Vietnam. And now the bloated bureaucracy says the decision can't be reversed, citing the original unanimity, the way LBJ would cite the ninety votes in favor of the Gulf of Tonkin resolution.

Also as in Vietnam, the bureaucracy has all the experts and all the facts, and makes its decisions about people from paper maps. Lindsay says the homeowners made "a poor presentation of their

case," and "the Board of Education had all the facts on their side," as if working people with seventh-grade educations had the time and resources to match all the politicians, all the bureaucrats, and Sam Lefrak and his connections.

People like Mary Moramarco vote for the Buckleys and the Agnews because liberal experts from Manhattan evict her from her father's home and destroy a small, genuine community. You don't have to go to Harvard to know that Corona is a community, and Lefrak City is a depersonalized maze for those who run the rat race.

It doesn't matter that the Italian homeowners voted for Procaccino, or that they once threw eggs at Lindsay, or that they oppose public housing in their area. Queens Borough President Sidney Leviss calls himself a liberal, and he is always vetoing public housing projects for middle-class sections. We can't just favor community control for Ocean Hill-Brownsville.

The issue in Corona is the preservation of a special community, its protection from the glacier of plastic moving across the country. Instead of destroying the homes on 102nd Street, Lindsay should declare them a landmark, a shrine to dying folkways, and appropriate funds to keep them as they are.

The issue is also whether Lindsay means what he says, whether his deeds will match his rhetoric.

Mary Moramarco's daughter Maria has been busy doing research in the struggle to save the sixty-nine homes. She is a senior majoring in sociology at Queens College. Before I left her home, she gave me a copy of John Lindsay's "state of the city" address, dated January 11, 1969. In it, Lindsay said:

"I can report progress to you in this field. . . . We have stopped bulldozing neighborhoods into oblivion, displacing people, ignoring what neighborhoods want for their future. We have concentrated on preserving communities, preserving diversity in the city. . . . This has taken time. It means listening to people. It means hearing disputes. It means changing plans already made. But it must be done if this government is to be the servant, and not the master of the people."

NOVEMBER, 1970

One week later the city offered to return the property of thirty-one families and to move the houses of the other twenty-eight to a new site, one block away, thus maintaining the integrity of the neighborhood.

[2.]
Housing: The City's Impersonal Failure

Let us now praise famous women.

Toni Hoffman, a small, shy woman in her mid-thirties, lives in a housing project in Queens. She was born in Germany, is barely literate, has no family, and is on welfare. She lives with her five daughters, all between the ages of one and six. Two of the children suffer from lead poisoning, and one has possible brain damage. Her husband has vanished, and the father of the youngest child is married to someone else. She lives with the five children in a dreary four-and-a-half-room apartment. There are no bars on the closed windows. The stairway stinks of urine, and there has been a wave of muggings in the project.

Toni Hoffman is lonely, depressed, and she can see no escape from her hopeless life. There is nothing singular about her condition. There is no exotic story to tell, no special case to explain, no single mistake to rectify. Just the dull details of a single brutalized human being.

Toni Hoffman is like a majority of the dispossessed people in America—invisible, undramatic, and white. She is an example of the ordinariness of this city's murderous, impersonal failure.

Toni Hoffman lives in the Queensbridge housing project on 21st Street in Long Island City, rows of low, ugly, prematurely decaying houses that begin under the shadow of an el. The project is 90 percent black, and Mrs. Hoffmann is afraid to leave her small, badly lighted apartment. So she sits there all day, day after day, watching her old 10-inch television screen, waiting for the welfare check to come.

Mrs. Hoffman doesn't want to live in this alien, violent project. She wants to live on Beach 91st Street in the Rockaways, where she lived until she was evicted three months ago.

She was evicted by her landlord, the same landlord who let the house run down so badly that her children got lead poisoning

twice from eating the falling chips of paint. She was evicted because the city's welfare bureaucracy wouldn't help her pay the rent, or find another apartment in the same neighborhood, and the city's court system is built to favor landlords, and the city doesn't know how to build new housing.

"I liked where we lived in Rockaway," Mrs. Hoffman says. "I had friends I could talk to. There was a day care center for the children. Here I feel like I am in jail. I'm afraid to go out."

Mrs. Hoffman made an application to get into public housing in Rockaway more than two years ago, "but they told me there was more needy people than me."

She now has two liberal, middle-class friends, Ron and Jill Woronov, who are like a surrogate family and are trying to help her. Jill was a teacher in the day care center in Rockaway, and Ron works for the community development project Robert Kennedy started in Bed-Stuy.

"It's a horror what the city has done to this woman," Ron says. "Welfare wouldn't help her. The Housing Authority made her move to a strange new neighborhood when they could have gotten her an apartment in Rockaway. Toni is now living with her five kids in a four-and-a-half-room apartment in public housing. That's against the law. The Housing Authority told me she couldn't get into public housing in Rockaway because she didn't live in the Urban Renewal area. I know people who got in. But they told Toni there was no room. They've wrecked her life. She had a health facility for the kids in Rockaway. My wife was in the day care center and loved the children. The city made her move because the bureaucracy couldn't deal with her as an individual. The city has hurt Toni a dozen different ways. Welfare refused to pay her rent last month, so she was evicted with the landlord literally screaming at her. Toni gave the welfare people the names of two movers, one for $88 and the other for $125. They picked the more expensive one. There must have been a payoff involved. The courts and the city let the landlord evict her, even though the landlord had never even repaired her apartment, as the law says it must, after the children got lead poisoning.

"But making her leave Rockaway, that was the thing. Toni's neighbors wrote a letter to Lindsay saying it was a crime to make Toni move out of her old neighborhood. They never got an answer from Lindsay."

Toni Hoffman now spends her awful days in fear. Fear that welfare will stop her checks when this story appears. Fear she or her children will be raped or mugged in the project. Fear that "they" will take her children away. Fear her children will contract lead poisoning again. Fear the city will evict her from public housing and force her to live in a motel and go to the welfare office each day for her check. Fear that she will get more obscene and perverse phone calls from a welfare bureaucrat who has been tormenting her.

The person responsible for providing shelter for people like Mrs. Hoffman is Albert Walsh, the administrator of the city's vast housing bureaucracy—HDA.

Everyone except Walsh seems to recognize that New York City is now in the crunch of a housing shortage so catastrophic that only a total application of will can prevent the crisis from becoming insoluble for a generation.

According to the Regional Plan Association, the city must construct 48,000 dwelling units each year from now until the year 2000 just to provide a decent apartment for every family. But according to figures released by New York State, New York City *suffered a net loss of 34,000 housing units during 1969.* This means that abandonment and demolitions are twice the rate of new housing actually being built. And according to Charles Urstadt, the state's commissioner for Housing and Community Renewal, authorizations for building new housing in New York City for this year are running 72 percent below last year's unsatisfactory rate. The state-wide average is a decline of 42 percent in new housing.

But Albert Walsh wrote an article in the real estate section of the Sunday *Times* two weeks ago claiming: "During the last five years New York has led the way in reorganizing its housing programs to preserve existing housing, build new housing, and rehabilitate sound but outmoded housing."

Walsh went on to deny there was a crisis over housing needs, and concluded by writing: "We have the potential, right now, to do the best job of housing our citizens that has ever been done, in any great city in the world."

Intrigued by such Panglossian rhetoric, I spent a few days looking into exactly what sort of job Albert Walsh was doing.

I began with the city's lead poisoning program, which I know something about. The city's new mass testing program has discovered 1800 previously undiagnosed cases of lead poisoning in ghetto children. But of these 1800 cases, the city has been able to repair the apartments in only 265 cases. The Emergency Repair Program is part of Walsh's super-agency. It is a failure. And because it is a failure, many of these children are being repoisoned, since they are released from the hospital back into the same rotting apartments they first ate the peeling paint in.

Then I looked into the squatters' movement, since they are the most dramatic example of the failure of the city to provide decent shelter for poor people. Last week, for the first time, the city twice arrested squatters who were living in city-owned buildings. This repressive precedent was set by Walsh, after consultation with Mayor Lindsay's staff.

Next I interviewed several deputies and employees of Walsh in the HDA bureaucracy. One of them told me: "There is no will here to build housing. And the bureaucracy is incompetent. The city isn't applying for one-fiftieth of the federal funds available for rehabilitation of existing housing. It's hard work, and Walsh doesn't do it. Four or five million dollars a year is being wasted this way. Every year upstate cities like Utica, Syracuse, and Buffalo get the money we could be getting if we were more alert. It's an annual thing. Every year those cities know the money will be waiting for them because our bureaucracy doesn't function to meet the needs of people."

But you don't need statistics or quotes to prove that housing is New York City's biggest problem. Just walk around Tiffany Street in the South Bronx, or Myrtle Avenue in Bed-Stuy, and you can see it is a horror. There are whole streets in Rockaway and on the Lower East Side that look like Hiroshima after the bomb. They have been leveled by the city, their inhabitants relocated. And then they just sit, year after year, with no new housing being built, while slum children play among the rats and broken bottles in these rotting lots.

It is not Walsh's fault alone. The economic recession is nation-wide. The cost of building new housing is spiraling rapidly. Mortgages and interest rates are also rising. Little federal money is available. The buck-passing and lack of accountability in the bureaucracy is immense. The racist construction unions are im-

possible. Walsh's predecessor, Jay Nathan, was even more incompetent than he is. The city has never had an adequate program of rehabilitating structurally sound buildings. And Mayor Lindsay has never given the housing crisis the attention it deserves, preferring to focus on more easily improved and dramatic problems.

Nevertheless, Albert Walsh is a villain. He is a $41,000-a-year Republican bureaucrat, a former aide to Nelson Rockefeller whom Lindsay first hired in 1967 to run the Housing Authority. As a bureaucrat, as a housing professional, Walsh communicates no sense of outrage to the public about the housing shortage. He makes no effort to mobilize a constituency for better housing, the way Jerome Kretchmer does for the environment, or Thomas Hoving did for parks.

Several of Walsh's colleagues in City Hall do not'disguise the fact they would like to see him fired. One of the Mayor's assistants told me that Walsh—whose responsibility, remember, is *New York City's housing*—actually lives with his family in Yonkers, while maintaining a rent-controlled apartment on East 20th Street to technically comply with the law. I checked this out and it was true. Walsh is listed with Yonkers information, while his neighbors on East 20th Street don't know what he looks like.

Another super-agency administrator said, "Walsh is just no good. I've seen him lie to the Mayor, I've seen him lie to Aurelio (Deputy Mayor), and he's lied to me. He lied to the Urban Coalition, and that's why they have demanded he be removed. How can Lindsay run this town when his own appointees don't tell him the truth?"

So Mrs. Hoffman languishes week after week in Queens, waiting for her welfare check, afraid to leave her tiny apartment, living out her private fate.

And Albert Walsh writes articles explaining away the damage to so many lives, while he commutes to Yonkers, and now quietly maneuvers for a top level job in the Nixon administration, where the Peter Principle reigns unchallenged.

As a distant utopian dream, perhaps the city might be able to build more housing in 1971 than it tears down.

As a small, symbolic first step, perhaps the city could give Mrs.

Hoffman and her five small children the apartment Walsh maintains on East 20th Street.

DECEMBER, 1970

Two weeks later the city's Housing Authority agreed to give Mrs. Hoffman a five-room apartment in a housing project in Rockaway that contained a day care center for her children.

[EIGHT]
JAILS: THE ULTIMATE GHETTO

Prisoners are the most powerless people in the society. They have zero power to affect their environment. They have no rights. Their victimization is kept invisible behind thick walls. They inhabit the ultimate ghetto.

These pieces are about inmates in New York's jails, all but one of them about New York City's detention jails, jails where a majority are awaiting trial, too poor to make bail, presumed innocent by our legal system.

Crime in the streets, law and order and similar catch phrases have dominated our politics the last few years. There has been fear, and hysteria, and so we have increased our police forces and given them mace and tanks, and they have made many more arrests.

But we have not reduced the crime rate, we have not made the streets safe. Part of the reason is that we have ignored our jails. New York City allocates only .02 percent of its $843 million criminal justice budget to rehabilitation.

If we as a nation are at all serious about the problem of crime, the place to start dealing with it is where the identifiable criminals are—in the jails. Ramsey Clark has justly called our prisons "factories of crime." As long as we treat lawbreakers like garbage to be dumped far enough away so there is no smell, as long as we use jails for punishment instead of rehabilitation, then the crime rate will continue to soar and none of us will feel safe.

[1.]
The Law Is an Outlaw

"We have no mouth and we must scream."
—An anonymous inmate shouting out of a broken
window in the Tombs last August

It was about 7:45 A.M. on Monday, October 5. Mayor Lindsay and his press secretary Tom Morgan were inside meeting with the inmates of the Long Island City Men's House of Detention after they had ended their revolt peacefully. Released hostages were telling reporters on the sidewalk outside that the inmates had protected them, had saved their lives, and that the basic demands of the rebels—lower bail, speedier trials, less overcrowding—were just.

It was 7:45 A.M. when correction officers—mostly white—began to beat prisoners—mostly black—who had been promised no reprisals by the warden. The correction officers began to systematically club the prisoners in the courtyard of the eighty-six-year-old brick jail with ax handles, baseball bats, and riot sticks. They beat them so savagely that a photographer from the *Daily News* vomited at the sight of the flowing blood and cracking bones.

Michael McCardell is a reporter for the *Daily News*. He witnessed the beatings from the ninth-floor window of a factory-warehouse that looked down on the courtyard. This is how he described what he saw the next morning in the *Daily News:*

> It was a gruesome scene.
> About 250 prisoners were sitting on the grass. Behind them, 30 Correction Department guards were lined up, all of them holding weapons—ax handles, baseball bats, and night sticks.
> One inmate was dragged out a doorway onto a load-

ing platform and five guards attacked him with their clubs. They battered his head and blood flowed over his face and body. He was kicked off the platform and several other guards pounded him again with their clubs.

His limp form then was lifted off the ground and thrown into a bus as another prisoner was hauled out and belted across the back with a club. Then more clubs rained down on him until he was motionless and bloodsoaked. He too was thrown into the bus.

Another man was pushed out, his hands above his head. A bat caught him in the stomach and he doubled over. More clubs came down on his spine. Eight guards were slugging away at one time.

A fourth prisoner emerged but the guards seemed to let go of him. He began running but the guards caught him and one put a knee into his groin. He toppled over and more guards kicked him over and over.

Six more prisoners got the same treatment. . . .

A police official who would not give his name was asked about the beatings. "We don't know," he replied. "That's Correction Department domain. We're only here if they need us."

It was 7:45 A.M. then and Lindsay had been in the prison since 6:20. From behind police barricades one could see the prisoner-occupied east wing of the sixth floor.

Victor Martinez, a leader of the insurrection, leaned out and shouted through a megaphone: "Prisoners are being beaten. They are being killed. The mayor is lying."

Lindsay left at 8:20 A.M. Asked about the beatings, he said, "I have been told there were *injuries* on both sides."

When Tom Morgan left the jail that morning after seventy-two sleepless hours, reporters told him about the beatings. He just couldn't believe it. Later he saw the dark, grainy films on television and was sickened by them. Another Lindsay aide, Barry Gottehrer, who had helped negotiate the settlement with the inmates, was so heartbroken by the brutality that he had to leave town on a vacation to get his emotions back intact. After

Mayor Lindsay learned about the beatings, he directed Corrections Commissioner George McGrath to submit a "full and speedy" report on the incident. He also asked Corporation Counsel J. Lee Rankin to look into the matter.

Three weeks after the beatings, Queens District Attorney Thomas Mackell anticipated the inverted justice at Kent State by announcing the indictment of eight inmates, seven of them black, two of them Panthers. He exonerated all the guards, despite the substantial film and photographic evidence. The inmates were indicted on such charges as kidnapping, attempted larceny, and conspiracy.

That was two months ago. Time passes and people forget. All journalists have been barred from monitoring the city's jails by Commissioner McGrath. New outrages in Vietnam and Spain compete for our attention. The appropriate speeches and editorials urging six-point or ten-point court and penal reforms were churned out, duly noted, and filed away. Once again there was no communication between the outside world and the municipal Cancer Wards. The inmates continued to suffer worse food, worse health care, and less space than the animals caged in the Central Park zoo. But until the next riot it would not be news anymore.

This week I telephoned the office of Commissioner McGrath to see if he had yet submitted his "full and speedy" report to the Mayor.

"What report?" asked the Commissioner's press secretary, Al Castro.

"The one about correction officers beating up inmates with ax handles two months ago" I answered.

"What are you, some wise guy? No one got hit with any ax handles. I don't know when that report will be finished." *

I repeated this conversation to William Vanden Heuvel, the recently appointed chairman of the New York City Board of Correction, and asked him to ascertain the status of McGrath's report.

The next day Vanden Heuvel told me he had been informed by McGrath that the "full and speedy" report was not yet even half finished, and might not be completed until February.

---

* Three months later the report was finally finished. It named eighteen guards as guilty of using excessive force on inmates. Commissioner McGrath, however, refused to suspend the eighteen guards.

Kew Gardens is another jail in Queens. There too, last October, prisoners rioted, surrendered on the promise of no reprisals, and were beaten. Only these beatings were administered in secret behind the stone walls, days after the trouble was over. The brutality was so total, so systematic it can fairly be described as torture.

But four young lawyers for the Legal Aid Society—William Hellerstein, Barbara Shapiro, William Nelson, and Joel Berger —have now collected sworn affidavits from the victims. These statements read like they were smuggled out of Brazil, or Greece, or Stalin's labor camps. But they came from New York City and have now been submitted to the Eastern District Court in a class action law suit in behalf of the 800 inmates against Mayor Lindsay, Commissioner McGrath, Kew Gardens Warden John Kennedy, and Deputy Warden Albert Ossakow.

The suit was argued last week before Justice Orin Judd. The lawyer who represented the Correction Department (Irwin Herzog) is the same lawyer who is investigating the Correction Department's conduct at the Long Island City Jail for the Corporation Counsel, J. Lee Rankin.

Somehow neither the affidavits nor the case have been noticed by the daily press. I will quote at some length from several of these simple, dignified accounts, all from citizens who assert they did not participate in the revolt and did not resist when it was over. Several of these inmates were indicted by Queens District Attorney Mackell on sodomy, bribery, and other felony charges right after they began to talk to Legal Aid Society lawyers about their plight.

From Jonathan Williams:

The officers were shooting more gas onto the floor at this time [October 3]. Inmates were hollering, "We give up." I heard people screaming things like this: "Don't hit me no more," "We give up," "Oh my God, my head.". . .

Then the C.O.s [correction officers] came onto Upper D where I was lying in a corner. . . . As I went downstairs, as ordered, the officers were hitting me and all the other prisoners with nightsticks and ax handles. As I came off the steps an officer drew his club back to him me on the head. I put my arm up to protect my

head and the blow hit my right arm, breaking it. . . .

I saw people bleeding profusely from the head. I saw one man with a bloody towel around his head trying to get up to get a fresh towel. . . . The C.O.s then ordered us to chant, "Power to the C.O.s." If you didn't say it, you would get beaten. One Spanish boy from the Upper D gallery who couldn't understand a word of English got beaten because he did not say, "Power to the C.O.s."

Around 8 or 9 A.M. Sunday morning [October 4], we were put into cells, three or four to a cell. . . . Happy Gray, who was put on Upper C side, where a man died of head wounds. [Correction officers claimed the inmate died of an "overdose of darvon."]

After a cast was put on my arm I was in the custody of a C.O. named P. Baily, handcuffed to him. This was early Tuesday morning, October 6, and I had had nothing to eat since the sandwich early Sunday morning.

We were taken from the bullpen to the third floor "bing" [solitary] on Tuesday afternoon. . . . I was in the cell for about an hour when the beatings began again. I heard about a dozen beatings. One man was hit with a stick across the knees and fell down opposite my cell. The C.O.s beat him until his head opened up.

This continued through Tuesday night. On Thursday or Friday [October 8 or 9] I saw many inmates, naked, being beaten in the dayroom. . . . I have been kept in the bing all this time. I am locked in my cell 24 hours a day. I have gotten no mail from my wife, and I am unable to write to my two children. I know that my wife has written to me. . . . In over three weeks I have been allowed only one shower. All my clothes and other possessions were taken from me, including my mail and my pictures of my family.

About 18 days after I was put in the bing, deputy warden Schaeffer came around and gave everyone an envelope and one sheet of paper. He said we could write to our families and tell them everything was all right with us. I wrote my wife telling her my arm was broken and asking her to send a lawyer to see me. No lawyer has come, and I am sure the letter was not mailed.

Donald Leroland's affidavit:

Late Saturday night or early Sunday morning warden Kennedy spoke over the public address system, telling everyone to lock in their cells and turn their lights on as a signal of surrender. He said that if this were done there would be no reprisals. I locked in and turned my light on. . . .

During the next few days many men were brought down from the floors above, beaten with sticks and clubs. . . .

Friday, October 9, 20 or 30 C.O.s came onto my gallery and ordered everyone to strip naked. We were then marched, hands over heads, into the dayroom. . . . In the dayroom I was lined up with about 40–45 other inmates in three rows, facing a wall. Deputy warden Ossakow ordered us to turn around and face him, saying, "I want to see if any of my friends are here."

Officer McCoy then said, "Everybody line up, pricks to asses. Everyone who gets a hard-on can walk" [meaning anyone who got an erection would not be beaten].

McCoy then started beating everyone in the back row with a club on their buttocks and legs. . . . The physical beating was not as painful as the humiliation.

Ralph Valvano's affidavit:

From what I heard there was no resistance by the prisoners on the fourth floor, that no resistance was possible. The guards came in and brutally beat the prisoners. I heard the screaming and the next day the injured were taken to the third floor. In all about 40 prisoners were beaten. . . . A man named Rabbi is still in Kings County Hospital with a broken leg. Someone named Shorty, a black man, was killed. Although the guards said he died of an overdose, he was seen in a sheet with his head wide open, and the sheet with large red stains, by at least two men: Raymond Minori and Happy Gray. . . .

From Sunday, October 4, to Friday, October 9, the entire prison population was subjected to beatings. I heard many screams and saw with my own eyes three men, naked, being beaten with sticks down the stairs, in

three separate incidents. . . . The official in charge of these beatings was Captain Hall.

On Monday, October 5, I was put in the bing, or segregation. No reason was given. I was locked in 24 hours a day, with no mattress, no visiting rights, and I can neither send nor receive mail. For the first 10 days I was without blankets. My cell is 3 LC 9. . . .

On October 18 one of the prisoners, Richard Tucker, swallowed glass in order to get out of the prison. He was badly beaten, taken to Kings County Hospital, and beaten again when he returned.

I have been threatened with an indictment for leading the riot by Captain Hall. Deputy Warden Ossakow told me, "Valvano, I'm going to get you without even laying a hand on you."

Richard Flowers's affidavit:

I don't know what happened to Sonny Sheara. Another correction officer came by shortly after this beating and said to me, "It's a damn shame the warden ordered these beatings." This particular correction officer did not take part in the beating and he was put on 12-hour turnkey duty as punishment. . . .

The evening of October 5, Monday, we were herded into the dayroom, naked. A correction officer ordered us to stand closer: "I want your dick in the man's ass in front of you," he said. "Anyone whose dick gets hard, you walk without a beating." I can identify the correction officer who made this order, but I do not know his name. Captain Hall was present.

There are a dozen more statements like this, describing wounds not treated, warnings not to talk to Legal Aid Society lawyers, the confiscation of inmates' letters, pictures, and lawbooks, reprisals against guards horrified by the cruelty, days in the bing without toilet paper or blankets or solid food, and sadistic beatings committed in front of Deputy Warden Ossakow.

On November 12, Ralph Valvano dictated a supplemental statement to a Legal Aid lawyer. It concluded:

"I am frightened of losing my life. I find the constant intimidation and abuse almost unbearable. I wish to state here that I

have no intention of harming myself—if I come to harm it will be because the guards have harmed me."

A few facts to meditate on. Almost all the inmates of the Kew Gardens jail, of the Tombs, and of the Long Island City jail have *not* been convicted of a crime. According to the Constitution, they are innocent until proven guilty, by a jury. These institutions are detention facilities, not punishment prisons. The men are detained there usually because they could not raise the $500 or $1,000 bail on the single phone call they are allowed. Most of them have been in these dungeons for six and twelve months *waiting for their trials to begin*, 25 percent on bail of $500 or less. Under any name, this is preventive detention. They rot in these Cancer Wards because they are poor, and because some criminal court judges are political hacks who work only five hours a day. Most of these judges are opposed to the penal reform supported by Chief Justice Burger and Mayor Lindsay, and already adopted by the State of California, the reform that places a sixty-day legal limit on the time between arrest and trial.

Even before the first prison riots last August, the conditions in these detention facilities were subhuman. The Tombs last summer was 900 prisoners above its 930 capacity. The Kew Gardens detention center, with a capacity of 520, held more than 1,000 inmates. During the riots, the bodies of giant dead rats were hurled through the broken shards of glass in the Tombs down onto the sidewalk. The city's entire corrections system has only two exterminators on its payroll. And there are eleven part-time psychiatrists for the approximately 10,000 prisoners.

Today, after all the promises and publicity, nothing has changed. Vague speeches about future court, bail, and penal reforms do not affect daily life in the dungeons. The bing cell, as infamous as the tiger cages of South Vietnam, are still used in all the city's detention facilities without comment by the press. Three inmates have committed suicide just within the last few weeks. Commissioner McGrath has rejected Father Laurence Gibney's (the chaplain at the Tombs) modest requests that the inmates be permitted more than one phone call to raise bail, that they be given more than one uniform for their entire stay in jail, that there be more law books in the prison library so they might help prepare their own defense, and that reporters be given permission to visit and monitor the jails. (In 1968, the Vera Insti-

tute of Justice and the Mayor's Criminal Justice Coordinating Council conducted a study that showed that a prisoner with direct access to a telephone was twice as likely to make bail, and suggested that such access would ease the crisis of overcrowding.)

"We have no mouth and we must scream," the anonymous voice screamed last summer. But there is no one now behind the walls to hear the mouthless voices.

It is always difficult to isolate accountability in a case like this, where there is a closed cycle of error. Who is to blame? Is it the individual guards? The warden? Commissioner McGrath? D.A. Mackell? The nameless, impersonal thing called "the system"?

Why has Commissioner McGrath covered up these beatings? Why hasn't McGrath submitted his report to the Mayor? Why hasn't Lindsay fired McGrath, whose four-year tenure in office has been characterized by riots, brutality, and suicides? How did Corporation Counsel Rankin permit the same lawyer who is investigating the Correction Department behavior at the Long Island City jail represent the Correction Department in the court hearing on the Kew Gardens jail?

What can be done now? Can Governor Rockefeller convene a special grand jury to indict the guilty guards and wardens? Can the City Council hold its own public hearing and subpoena the perpetrators of violence? Why has Investigations Commissioner Ruskin been silent about the whole affair?

Perhaps the answer is that legal authority in New York has become as corrupt as in the film "Z." Once a long time ago in Mississippi, Bob Moses, the old SNCC organizer, asked me, after Goodman, Chaney, and Schwerner had been murdered by the local sheriff, "What do you do when the law is an outlaw?"

More and more that is a question that haunts me. It was the National Guard who killed the four students at Kent State. It was the Chicago police who murdered Fred Hampton. Here in two jails, it was the guards and the wardens who broke the law, and so far no one seems interested in remedying this parody of law and order.

The law is an outlaw. And all the mouthless voices are screaming behind the thick walls for justice.

DECEMBER, 1970

The Law Is an Outlaw: More on Korrections

Last week I described the brutal and systematic beatings inmates of the city's detention jails are subjected to, and recounted how various municipal agencies have covered up this scandal. This week I will report several new episodes of intimidation and repression, and review the recent conduct of Corrections Commissioner George McGrath.

First, Federal District Judge Orin Judd, in a twelve-page decision, has issued a temporary restraining order prohibiting any further violence or threats against inmates of the Kew Gardens jail by guards or wardens. Judge Judd also invited William Vanden Heuvel, the new chairman of the Board of Corrections, to enter the case and "arrange for observers" to monitor the jail. He also mandated Warden Albert Ossakow to "permit representatives of the Legal Aid Society free access to inmates who request to see them in connection with this case."

William Nelson, the young lawyer for the Legal Aid Society who collected most of the original affidavits, then mailed copies of Judge Judd's decision to seven inmates of the Kew Gardens jail. However, Ossakow intercepted the letters and refused to give them to the prisoners. After a meeting last Thursday in Commissioner McGrath's office, it was agreed to permit two of the inmates—Jonathan Williams and Ralph Valvano—whose names appear on the court suit to receive the judge's ruling. But the department refused to let the other five inmates see the ruling. So as of now, most of the inmates of the Kew Gardens jail do not know they have won a partial court victory, do not know their full rights, and think they still have no legal protection against random beatings by correction officers. Also, inmates now know that Warden Ossakow has the power to intercept and stop any letter he does not want them to see—even a judge's decision directly affecting them.

Twenty-one-year-old Alfred Earl Warren was one of the heroes of the October riot in the Tombs. He was a correction officer trainee who was taken hostage. But he was released by the inmates, unharmed, to deliver their list of grievances to Mayor Lindsay. After he gave the message to the Mayor, Warren voluntarily returned to the prison—according to the October 5 *Daily News*—"to see what he could do to help quell the disturbance."

On November 23, Commissioner McGrath fired Warren, who is black, militant, and admitted he related well with the inmates. Last week Warren filed suit in Federal Court to enjoin Commissioner McGrath from firing him. Warren told *The New York Times* that the other guards were angry at him "because I got along with the inmates, I treated them like human beings." He was the only black man among the trainees at the Tombs.

During the week I also spoke to Michael Dontzin, Mayor Lindsay's staff assistant responsible for the jails. He admitted that the same assistant corporation counsel (Irwin Herzog) who is supposed to be investigating the Correction Department's conduct in the Long Island City jail was in court, defending the department's conduct in the Kew Gardens jail. "There is nothing wrong with this," he said.

When I asked Dontzin what he was doing about the brutality in the jails, he replied: "I can't do anything until Commissioner McGrath submits his report to the Mayor." The report was requested ten weeks ago.

In the October 29 issue of *The Voice*, David Gelber asked Dontzin why an independent investigation of the jail brutality was not being conducted. At that time Dontzin also replied he was waiting for the McGrath report, adding: "We have no reason to believe George McGrath will submit anything less than a completely honest report."

George McGrath earns $35,000 a year. He has been Corrections Commissioner for more than four years. During the last six months he has not been a very good commissioner.

On May 23 of this year Congressman Edward Koch conducted a public hearing on the prisons. McGrath spoke at this crowded meeting, asserting at one point that the city now provided mattresses for every prisoner in the Tombs.

Suddenly, a man jumped up from the front row and shouted:

"What are you talking about? I just got out of that place on Wednesday, and I spent two days sleeping on a concrete floor!"

McGrath called the man a liar and swore every prisoner in the Tombs had a mattress. Representative Koch then offered to accompany both the Commissioner and the ex-inmate to the Tombs to establish the truth of the matter. McGrath declined, saying, "This is all a publicity stunt."

Five days later McGrath admitted to Koch that indeed hundreds of prisoners in the Tombs were still sleeping on the cold, rat-infested floors—without mattresses.

At the same public hearing McGrath stated that the city's jails "are wide open to all of the responsible people who want access to any of those places."

"That's a lie," a voice in the audience shouted.

New York Times reporter David Burnham, who along with Donald Singleton of the *Daily News* has done the best writing on the city's jails, interceded to point out to the Commissioner his own rule against journalists visiting the jails.

McGrath then remembered his own prohibitive policy, explaining, "It is an administrative impossibility to permit every newspaperman in the city to talk to any prisoner."

McGrath went on to say that civilian monitoring of the jails was not necessary "because inmates can write to any lawyer or public official."

"The one time I did get into the Tombs," shot back Burnham, "many prisoners asked me to send them paper."

On August 26, Dr. Violet Stephenson, the Correction Department's director of psychiatry, quit her post after holding it for only three months. In her letter of resignation, she said McGrath ran the department "along military and bureaucratic lines" and was "phobic about any program that represents change."

Dr. Stephenson said the Correction Department, under McGrath, "does not believe in psychiatric help for inmates." She said she tried to set up a psychiatric evaluation unit at the Rikers Island prison, but was overruled by McGrath. Such a unit could have speeded up the chances for bail for many inmates.

Dr. Stephenson also submitted a private report to McGrath citing the "disgracefully inadequate" facilities at the Tombs one month before the August rebellion. She said McGrath "ignored" her report.

When asked on ABC-TV's "Eyewitness News Conference" about Dr. Stephenson's resignation, McGrath said: "People keep looking at prisons as a place for rehabilitating criminals. They forget that prisons have as their aim keeping these types of people under control."

Commissioner McGrath apparently forgot that most of the inmates of the Tombs are not criminals. They are poor people awaiting trail because they can't make bail, usually bail of less than $1,000.

The second round of jail revolts broke out on October 1. On that day Commissioner McGrath was in Philadelphia on a $100-a-day consultant's job, advising that city on how to avoid trouble in its jails.

According to Burnham, who broke this story, McGrath spent eight days last summer advising Philadelphia on how to handle its prison problems.

In his *Times* article Burnham quoted Section 1100 of the City Charter, which reads: "Every head of an administration, department, or related office, except Councilmen, who receives a salary from the city, shall give his whole time to his duties and shall not engage in any other occupation, profession, or employment."

Several readers have written and called me, asking what concretely might be done now to correct the conditions in the jails.

The first thing, I think, would be for the Mayor to dismiss Commissioner McGrath. It is my conviction that McGrath has covered up these beatings and has made no effort to suspend or punish the guilty guards in any way. McGrath has also lied to the Mayor about the most basic facts of the conditions in the jails. For example, he has told the Mayor that the press is banned from monitoring the jails in all the other states. This is not so. Many states, including Pennsylvania and California, permit reputable journalists into the jails. Sources at City Hall tell me that the only reason Mayor Lindsay did not fire McGrath long ago is that McGrath does not ask for a bigger budget to run his department, and that he is well connected with the correction officers' union.

Second, if justice is really to be done in this case, the guards and warden should be indicted, not the inmates. Right now, the D.A.s and police agencies spend an immense amount of time and

effort infiltrating the crazies, the yippies, and the Panthers. Why haven't a couple of undercover black detectives been placed in the city's detention facilities to gather evidence of brutality against guards? Also, why doesn't Attorney General Lefkowitz or U.S. Attorney Edward Neaher convene a grand jury to investigate the long history of violence and questionable suicides in the city's jails?

And last, what is needed is for the light of publicity to shine into these dark dungeons. It seems amazing to me that the only paper to follow up my story last week was the *Washington Post* (see Karl Meyer's page three story in the December 21 edition) and not one of the New York City dailies.

But in the end, only a combination of all three approaches can begin to bring justice to the thousands of men and women rotting in these jails, vulnerable to sadists only because they are too poor to raise $500 bail.

DECEMBER, 1970

[3.]
A Tale of Two Jails

I suspect that all the crimes committed by all the jailed criminals do not equal in social damage that of the crimes committed against them.
—Dr. Karl Menninger, The Crime of Punishment

A tale of two jails, one federal, the other municipal, one the responsibility of Attorney General John Mitchell, the other the responsibility of Mayor John Lindsay.

On January 5, two days after a small riot, Congressman Edward Koch and I spent three hours inspecting the Federal House of Detention, at 427 West Street near Eleventh Street. It is old, overcrowded, and understaffed. But it is, on balance, one of the less dehumanizing jails in the country. Inmates voluntarily told us that the new warden, Louis Gengler, was "humane," "honest," and "liberal." One even said he'd sent the warden a Christmas card.

Warden Gengler permitted Koch and myself to go into the cells alone to talk to inmates without any guards present. One inmate told me, "I've been in the Tombs, in Brooklyn, in Newark, and this is paradise."

Inmates told us there was no brutality, that they get clean underwear three times a week, that the food was "okay," and that they have a gym to work out in. One of them said: "The warden comes around twice a day and asks us for our complaints. He tries to do what he can for us." Other inmates told us there were lawbooks in the library and that common-law wives and friends were allowed to visit them on holidays. The inmates were permitted to leave their cells and walk around the cellblock during the day.

At one point Koch asked a famous alleged Mafioso if he had any grievances about the jail, and the man answered, "Just that

we don't have girls and weekend passes. . . . This is a very decent joint." When I asked another group of about twelve inmates playing cards in one cell if they had any complaints, the only one offered was the absence of kosher food. Again, this conversation was conducted with no guards within hearing distance.

The visit persuaded me that despite antiquated physical facilities and not enough funds, and despite slow courts and unfair bail, a relatively humane administration was still possible within the rotting shell of the existing criminal justice system.

When Koch returned to his office he drafted a letter to Norman Carlson, director of the Bureau of Prisons. In it Koch wrote: "Over the past two years I have visited four prisons in New York City and elsewhere, and I must tell you that no other wardens in any other prison that I visited had the same laudatory comments made about them as did Warden Gengler. . . . In my opinion he is doing an excellent job in spite of the handicaps."

It was not easy getting a view inside a New York City jail. My first request to visit a detention facility, made six weeks ago, was rejected by Commissioner McGrath. A tour scheduled for January 13 with Congressman Koch was canceled at the last minute. John Parsons of CBS-TV was promised an "open door" tour of the Tombs last week, but was not permitted to talk to inmates, or see the isolation cell (bing). A tour of Kew Gardens for about forty-five print and television reporters last week also excluded any direct contact with inmates. I insisted that any legitimate tour must include access to inmates, as did my visit to the Federal House of Detention.

Finally, on Monday of this week, Representative Koch, Representative Joseph Adabbo of Queens, and I were given a two-hour tour of the Kew Gardens jail by Commissioner McGrath. This is the newest of the city's six detention jails and was completed in 1962. On the outside it looks impressive with its clean new bricks and modern design.

Inside, the human part of it, is another story. The prison holds 530 inmates. They are locked in their cells twenty-one hours a day. For three hours they are permitted to congregate in the narrow corridors outside their cells. They have no recreation facilities whatever, no radios, no checker games even. They have no methadone withdrawal treatment for narcotics addicts, and about 60 percent of all the inmates are addicts. About half of the jail

population is awaiting trial; most have been waiting for more than four months. The warden of this jail is Albert Ossakow, who was named in several affidavits filed in federal court as personally witnessing the brutal beating of inmates after the October riot, and not objecting. One part-time psychiatrist, on duty nine hours a week, services all the 530 inmates.

We first visited a tier of cells on the fifth floor. About fifteen inmates were sitting in the four-foot-wide corridor, as part of their "recreation time" outside their six-by-eight cells. Congressman Koch asked them if they had any complaints.

One man, about forty-five, said in broken English that he had been wearing the same underwear and the same pants ever since he was arrested six months ago. He said he had no family to bring him clean clothes. "I've asked the guards to get me clean underwear," he said, "but they don't listen."

Warden Ossakow, who looks and sounds like the comedian Phil Foster, said, "Maybe his English isn't understandable." When I asked how many of the guards speak Spanish, he said, "Two, and one is the cashier in the commissary."

We next spoke to a narcotics addict in his cell. "I came in here sick as a dog," he began. "I'm a junkie. I stayed awake for twenty-five days. I didn't eat for fourteen days. I asked the guard to let me see a doctor, but they wouldn't let me. I belong in a hospital. I need methadone. I kicked heroin here alone. I was in agony. The guard told me there was no doctor available. They only gave me tranquilizers."

Koch, who was instrumental in obtaining a twenty-bed methadone withdrawal program at the Tombs jail, repeated the man's story to Commissioner McGrath, who said, "I can't believe it."

At the end of the tour we went down to the medical office to look up the inmate's record. It consisted of a blue card with information filled in.

"You see, he's lying," McGrath said.

Koch, examining the record closely, said, "He's not lying, Commissioner. Look here." Koch then showed the Commissioner that the story the inmate had told us of being arrested in Brooklyn and then being transferred to Queens was substantiated. The blue card described the prisoner as a "four bundles a day" heroin addict, but "not in withdrawal." It showed no record of medical treatment, except for tranquilizers, since he was admitted to the jail. (There

was one part of the card that neither Koch nor McGrath could decipher.)

"This man belongs in a hospital!" Koch exclaimed.

The combined presence of the Commissioner and the warden could offer no response.

The next inmate we talked to also was an addict. He said he had been in his cell for the last four days and had no soap, no razor, and no towel.

"All he has to do is just ask for a towel," said Ossakow. Koch asked the guard (black) if the prisoner had in fact requested a towel.

"Yes, he did," said the guard, "and I told the A officer about it." However, the A officer (white) claimed he had received no such request for a towel. The inmate said, "If I can't get a towel with the Commissioner standing right here, what chance do I have when he's not around?"

Later, when Koch suggested to the warden that the second guard was lying, Ossakow replied, "Let's just say he was fearful of making a mistake."

Similar Catch-23 absurdities were apparent at other points of the visit. One inmate complained that he had not been permitted to receive visits from his common-law wife. The warden said the inmate had to "fill out a slip" for that privilege. Then the inmate explained that he was told there were no more of those particular slips available to be filled out.

When Koch asked why prisoners in the bing cell were not allowed mattresses, he was told that was to prevent suicides. When Koch asked why drug addicts were not placed in a dormitory, rather than the six-by-eight cells, he was told that "suicides were more likely in dormitories." ("Nonsense," Koch said later.)

At the end of the tour I remarked to mayoral aide Michael Dontzin that it all seemed crazy to me, particularly that the most modern of all the city's jails was without dormitories or hospital facilities. Dontzin said: "Of course this is all crazy. Kew Gardens is a maximum security prison, and half the people in it have never been convicted. An idiot designed this jail. In 1962 Wagner was the mayor."

When the tour was completed I asked Koch to compare the physically deteriorated federal jail with the brand-new city jail.

"Of course the federal jail is much better," Koch replied. "It's totally different there because the warden is a good human

being. There is a different attitude here in Kew Gardens. Basic indignities are committed against inmates here. There is a bad attitude here, and it is compounded because they want to hide things here. But Kew Gardens represents the normal corrections mentality. Gengler is the exception."

There's almost nothing more I can say about this city's jails. (Kew Gardens, remember, is the best.) Everyone who cares now knows these are zoos where 6,000 men and women, waiting for trials, are rotting because they are too poor to make bail, and where they are subject to the most brutalizing conditions imaginable. Cold turkey, dirty clothes, no towels, no recreation, locked in their cells twenty-one hours a day. Ten years ago *New York Times* editorials called the city's detention jails "dehumanizing" and "barbaric." But nothing has changed. It is as if the riots never happened.

There comes a time when even a writer—perhaps especially a writer—feels that words are worthless. The situation with the jails is now comparable to Germany in 1943 in the sense that there can be no more good New Yorkers; no one can pretend any longer that he is ignorant of what is happening behind the walls.

We all know it is a horror and a scandal. We know men have been stripped naked and beaten; we have seen the photographs of inmates having limbs smashed by baseball bats and ax handles. We know there have been seventeen suicides during the last twenty-four months. We know inmates have been beaten and persecuted after all the official promises of no reprisals.

We don't need any more studies or articles or committees. We know all there is to know. No more words of shame, no more words of regret, no more words of anger. Only action.

JANUARY, 1971

[4.]
Behind Prison Walls: The Auburn Horrors

Approximately eighty inmates of the state prison at Auburn, New York, have been locked in solitary confinement since a revolt there on November 4, 1970. All of them are black and Puerto Rican, although most of the prison population of 1,700 participated in the protest. Many of them have been denied representation by legal counsel and many have been denied a formal hearing.

In solitary, the inmates have been deprived of recreation, mail, toilet paper, clothes, towels, books, magazines, and eligibility for parole. Some have been beaten by guards. In December they staged a nonviolent protest that was crushed and never reported. Six of them have been indicted by a Cayuga County grand jury on assault charges. All have been locked into their small, unsanitary cells with nothing to do for twenty-four hours a day, for the last fourteen weeks.*

And all the inmates had been promised "no reprisals" after they had released, unharmed, the fifty hostages they took during the November 4 riot.

It has taken a long time for this story to emerge from behind the thick walls of the old Auburn prison. Auburn is isolated, a small town in mid-state away from any large city. The press is not allowed into state-run jails to interview inmates. Letters written by prisoners to their families and to public officials have been censored and sporadically intercepted. And, of course, there have been no press releases, or press conferences, to announce that Nelson Rockefeller sanctions conditions as barbaric as those in Greece or Brazil.

Nevertheless, word has slowly gotten out from behind the secrecy of the walls because about fifty prisoners have written let-

* As of May, 1971, seventy-two Auburn inmates were still locked in solitary.

ters to the Fortune Society, an organization of former inmates that seeks to promote prison reform and help rehabilitate ex-convicts.

I spent all of Friday afternoon reading these letters, all written out in longhand on lined prison paper, sometimes in barely literate scrawls, sometimes desperate and articulate. I would like to quote from several of these letters.

From Donald Crawford (61749):

> I am an indigent inmate of Auburn prison contesting my fundamental rights which are being severly deprived by the administration of Auburn.
>
> On November 4, 1970, a rebellion occurred by the inmate population to give voice to grievances which was not allowed expression. As a result, a group of inmates was selected to be formally charged with and for the results of the disturbance, in which a majority of the prison population took part.
>
> On November 27, 1970, I was taken from my cell by three officers and placed in a special punishment area of the prison for unknown reasons. On November 29, 1970, I received, as well as others, a piece of paper from Harry Fritz, Warden.
>
> On December 20, 1970, I, as well as others, protested for our grievances to be heard, and was tear gassed, Maced, beaten, put into strip cells, left with no clothes, and with the windows left open all night. . . . [This protest was never announced to the press.]
>
> Our letters are being held up, we are locked in our cells twenty-four hours a day, no clean set of clothes, no recreation, no church, etc.
>
> On January 15, 1971, I received formal charges and was still being told that I am not in title to counsel at proceedings in which I am subjected to lose good time and more time in my cell, not in title to ministers at proceedings, or evidence of formal charges. The notary refuses to come up and notarize my legal work unless I submit them first. . . . Please inform me of receipt of this letter because they are being held up.

From Leroy Barnes, Jr. (62453), after detailing how the riot ended with the release of all the hostages, and the promise of no reprisals:

Subsequent actions by prison administrators have been violent and unremitting. There can be no exaggeration of the profound and insufferable vengeance being exacted. Over one hundred black inmates are being held in punitive segregation. Personal property such as Afro hair combs and black political writings have been confiscated. No mail to families informing them of the factual events or situations are allowed out, and visits are illegally censored by which a guard warns you not to mention what occurred, and a guard sits beside your visitors listening to every word. Letters seeking legal assistance have been intercepted, although we have been informed of possible indictments. Black inmates were tear gassed, Maced, and badly beaten in their cells on December 20, 1970. [Again, this is a reference to the rebellion that was never revealed to the media.]

In light of recent federal court decisions, one by Constance Baker Motley in the Sostre vs. Rockefeller case, we are being treated in an unconstitutional way. . . . We have written to many people but we have no way of knowing if they received the letters. . . . Please visit me.

From James Dunn (61726):

I have been confined to a cell under twenty-four hours daily lock-up since October 26, 1970. On November 26, eight officers appeared and forcefully transferred me to a segregated punishment area. I was placed in a filthy cell under twenty-four hours daily lock-up and deprived of my sacred rights to being a man. . . . I wrote request slips daily to Superintendent Harry Fritz but never received any reply whatsoever. The authorities here are not only punishing me excessively without even informing me of why I was being illegally detained. But they are holding me incommunicado. My mail to attorneys, private organizations, and my friend, all requesting legal help, was prevented—and still is—from leaving this prison.

On December 20, 1970, thirty-eight of us assembled peacefully on a locked-in gallery to acquire an audience with any higher official who could hear and redress the

multiplying grievances we were suffering daily. Tear gas and Mace were fired at us in over-abundance, and numerous guards all well-armed with tree trunks, etc., stormed us and placed us all in strip cells.

On January 26, 1971, over thirty guards all armed with baseball bats, tree trunks, forcefully transferred me to ultra-punitive segregation—the roof. This is where I am presently appealing to you from. I may be murdered at any moment and your assistance is needed immediately.

From Ronald Jones (61346), after also describing the unreported December 20 protest:

> On January 25, 1971, I and the inmates peacefully refused to eat until we saw a captain or a lieutenant to find out why we were being kept in our cell twenty-four hours a day without recreation; why our food is being brought to us on a garbage truck, with hair and vermin; why we have to submit to rectal examinations; why we are not issued clothing when our other set was taken away during a shake-down. . . . I think you should know what the response to this was.
>
> The water in the sink and toilet bowl was shut off about 9 A.M. I couldn't wash up and couldn't flush the toilet after usage. The windows was opened up on us all day and all night. They stopped all visits, interviews, medical attention, etc. . . . later a guard said to me shut up you black sonofabitch because I am ready to put the hose on you. Then the windows was open up on us all night during a snow storm and I didn't have any clothes.

The Fortune Society also had a copy of a letter the mother of Ronald Jones wrote to Governor Rockefeller. This is what she said:

> I am writing to you on behalf of my son, Ronald Jones (61346) who is at present in Auburn Prison. Ronald made parole at the end of October when he went before the Board. At that time, he was given an open date to come home on November 19. He was allowed to write his wife and tell her to bring his clothing on her visit.

When she arrived at Auburn on November 15, after traveling for eight hours by bus to get there and paying $28 for a round trip ticket which she cannot afford, she was not allowed to visit with him but for only forty-five minutes, and was personally told by the Warden that Ronald was being held for investigation to determine if he was involved in the riot that took place there on November 4. I can understand that because rioting is a very serious thing. I don't approve of them and I believe anyone that commits these crimes should be punished. But at the same time, my son told his wife and has written letters to me telling me that he did not participate in that riot in any way knowing that he was to be released the following week.

I am not a lawyer and unfortunately I cannot afford one even though this is my son that I am trying to help. I ask you would it seem logical that a person knowing he is being released from prison in a few days would get mixed up in something serious? I also would like to bring to your attention that his record speaks for itself, since he has been in prison he has never been in any trouble stayed away from the troublemakers and has never been known to be militant in his life. He has witnesses at the prison black and white who are willing to state that Ronald did not take part in that riot. I called the prison and spoke to the warden and he will not tell me what Ronald is suppose to have done. He wouldn't tell his wife either and that seems very strange when my son was visited by his wife she said he looked very frighten. I know my son does not have any suicidal tendencies and really believe that since they can't tell me what he has done it's probably a fact that they know he hasn't done anything, and are trying to find out if he knows who really took part in this riot. You know as well as I do, that if he does that he would be hurt by some of those inmates, I am financially unable to visit him to talk to him, his letters to me is a constant repeat of his innocence (but I can detect that he is afraid).

I am appealing to you and Commissioner McGinnis to please see that my son is given a fair hearing because at present I am in fear of something happening to him

in there that is not just. I would also like to bring to your attention that since Ronald has been in prison he has taken advantage of every course made available to him including his High School Equivalency Diploma and a Dale Carnegie Award. He has a very good wife who has tried very hard to raise their daughter who is four years old now, and Ronald has been confined since his daughter was one year old.

I believe he has tried to correct the wrong he has done in the past and I am appealing to you to give him a chance to take his place back in society to live a decent and honest life.

Several civil liberties lawyers recently entered the case of the "Auburn 80," as the inmates choose to identify themselves. Stanley Bass of the NAACP Legal Defense Fund, Herman Schwartz of the New York Civil Liberties Union, and Mrs. Elizabeth Friedlander of Waverly, New York, have secured an order from the federal district court in Utica directing the warden of the Auburn jail to show cause why he should not be held in violation of the Federal Civil Rights Act. A hearing will be held on this motion on February 22.

Also, Bass has filed a class action lawsuit, in the Northern District Court, in behalf of all the inmates held in solitary, arguing that the rules and regulations of the Auburn jail have denied due process under the law to the prisoners.

On Saturday I spoke to Bass. He singled out two problems particular to the Auburn prison.

"First," he said, "is that Auburn is so isolated, so out of the way, that the injustices done there have no visibility. The mass media have mostly ignored this situation at Auburn. And on top of that, the state is even worse than the city in permitting reporters into jails to see what is actually going on inside.

"Second is the problem of racism. The original demonstration at Auburn on November 4 began as part of Black Solidarity Day. There were demands directly connected to the identity of black prisoners. And now the authorities are trying to make these eighty guys the scapegoats for the whole prison. The Warden doesn't permit any expressions of black identity. Everyone is dehumanized into a thing. And on top of that, you have a situation in a small, upstate town like Auburn, where almost all the

guards are white, and a majority of the prisoners are black. . . . The whole philosophy there is not rehabilitation but revenge. That's the attitude."

That's where the situation now rests. A court hearing scheduled next week, another class action suit slowly moving through another crowded court, and little notice in the media otherwise. State Correction Commissioner Russell Oswald has so far been silent on the horrors at Auburn.

Meanwhile, eighty men rot in their cells with nothing to do, with no hope, except writing letters to the Fortune Society they can't even be sure get delivered.

FEBRUARY, 1971

[5.]
"It Was Just a Regular Suicide"

"It was just a regular suicide."

That's what Al Castro, press representative for the city's Correction Department, said to *New York Times* rewrite man Robert Tomasson Saturday night after twenty-year-old Robert Cruz had hanged himself with his own shirt in his cell at the Rikers Island prison.

But it wasn't "just a regular suicide." Cruz was the fourth inmate to kill himself in a city jail since the start of the year, and the sixth suicide in the last four months—the highest suicide rate among prisoners in any city in the country.

Moreover, news of Cruz's death, which took place at 8:55 P.M. on Friday, was withheld by the Correction Department for more than twenty-four hours. *The New York Times* found out about it when Brooklyn police reporter Ed Ringer noticed it listed on a detective's report.

William Vanden Heuvel, chairman of the citizen watchdog agency over the jails, was never informed of the death by prison officials; he found out about it when rewrite man Tomasson called him at 11:30 P.M. on Saturday.

"I am outraged that news of this death was withheld from me and from the public," Vanden Heuvel said on Sunday. "I have asked Commissioner McGrath to notify me immediately of any fatality in a city jail. He has promised on many occasions to do that. I have that commitment in writing from all the wardens. Yet I have not been called after any of the four suicides this year."

Castro, McGrath's PR man, also told the *Times* on Saturday night that "there were no extenuating circumstances" surrounding Cruz's death, and that Cruz "was not suicidal." Vanden Heuvel, however, found out on Sunday that a psychiatrist's report on Cruz, written eight hours before he hanged himself, said

the inmate was "in a traumatic state as a result of a homosexual approach." Also, Cruz had slashed his wrists the same afternoon he died. Yet Castro told Tomasson the prisoner was not suicidal. On top of all this, Cruz was also a fifteen-bag-a-day heroin addict.

On Sunday afternoon Vanden Heuvel was at the Rikers Island jail (McGrath didn't even bother to visit the jail) collecting information about Cruz's death when he was informed—by the *Times* again—of yet another death of a prison inmate over the weekend. Richard James was found dead Sunday in the prison psychiatric ward at Bellevue of an overdose of heroin. Vanden Heuvel said it was "incredible" how a prisoner could get access to heroin which is "locked up behind four sets of locked doors, bars, and gates."

Bernard Weinstein, executive director of the hospital, said: "Security controls for the prison wards in the hospital are the direct responsibility of the Correction Department. I think they should make a complete investigation of this."

On Sunday night, after spending eight hours at Bellevue, Vanden Heuvel said: "I feel sick. It's like going to the Pentagon and getting the daily body count."

Commissioner McGrath was not at work on Monday. He was in Philadelphia—where he also was last October 1, the day the riot in the Tombs started—advising that city how to solve its jail problems.

FEBRUARY, 1971

[6.]
Beaten in Bellevue: An Inmate's Affidavit

There has been another episode of brutality by prison guards against an inmate in a New York City correction facility.

According to sworn statements signed by six witnesses—three prisoners and three medical personnel—on January 19 correction officers in the Bellevue medical prison ward savagely beat a forty-one-year-old black inmate named James Ainsley.

Ainsley had been in jail four months awaiting trial because he could not raise $25 cash alternative or a $1,000 bond. He was beaten while recuperating from two kidney operations, the second of which took place less than a month before the beating.

And after Ainsley was beaten, one correction officer then charged Ainsley with assault, a charge which virtually ruined the inmate's chances to make bail.

Ainsley, however, has never been arraigned on the assault charge. This is a violation of court procedures and according to lawyers could invalidate the most recent charge.

Affidavits sworn by the three noninmate eyewitnesses to the beating were sent to Correction Commissioner George McGrath, Manhattan D.A. Frank Hogan, and U.S. Attorney Whitney Seymour two weeks ago. But so far nothing has happened.

The correction officer who beat Ainsley most cruelly, and then charged the victim with assault, has been on sick leave since the incident on January 19. The reason for his sick leave is that both his hands are fractured.

I found out about this beating three weeks ago, through sources in the Tombs, where Ainsley is now incarcerated. Two weeks ago, on a live television interview shown on NBC, I asked Board of Correction chairman William Vanden Heuvel about "an incident of brutality" in Bellevue. Vanden Heuvel said there was a reported episode of custodial violence and that he was "looking into it."

I then waited two weeks, hoping that some daily reporter would follow up the news lead, or that Commissioner McGrath would respond to the evidence forwarded to him by Vanden Heuvel.

In the interim I received from Ainsley a copy of his affidavit on the beating. Since I am now convinced that as in all the other episodes of guard violence—Kew Gardens, the beating of Lavon Moore, etc.—Commissioner McGrath has no intention of disciplining his own department, I will quote Ainsley's statement in full. I also quote it because it has been my hope in writing this series of articles on the jails to present the prison reality as much as possible from the point of view of inmates, through affidavits, through letters, rather than from my own vantage point.

James Ainsley's affidavit:

> I am forty-one years old, and was arrested on September 18, 1970, on charges of sale of a dangerous drug and possession of a weapon.
>
> On September 20, 1970, I was admitted to Bellevue Hospital for treatment of a kidney ailment and hypertension and was incarcerated there as an inmate patient until February 18, 1971. During my hospitalization at Bellevue, surgery was performed on each of my kidneys.
>
> Throughout my incarceration on the ward, and particularly on January 19, 1971, the correction officer in charge of opening the inside gate to the ward has tended to make doctors and nurses wait to be admitted to the ward.
>
> On January 19, 1971, I was housed on the I-1 male prison ward. At approximately 11:20 A.M., the officer on the gate (whose name I did not then know but later learned to be Joseph) was talking to an inmate at the gate, when Mr. Coger, a male nurse, came to the gate. While Mr. Coger waited, Officer Joseph continued speaking with the inmate. The telephone inside the nurses' station began ringing, and Mr. Coger said, "Somebody please answer the phone." After it had rung approximately eight times, I stepped into the booth and picked up the phone, as Officer Joseph said, "Uh uh uh uh." I did not speak into the telephone, but stepped outside the booth and handed it to Mr. Coger, who had just been admitted to the ward.

Officer Joseph said to me, "Don't you know that patients can't answer the phone?" I replied, "I didn't know that." Then Officer Joseph threatened me; he told me what he was going to do to me and that he was going to hurt me. I replied that he was going to do nothing to me. Officer Joseph told Correction Officer Motley, who was stationed inside the gate on the ward, that I had gone in to answer the phone. Officer Motley then asked me if I did not know that I was not permitted to answer the phone. I said that I did not, and explained that the nurse had asked me to answer it. Officer Motley then threatened me. I walked away to my bed and told Officer Motley that he was not going to do anything; that he was just threatening me.

Officer Joseph, who was still outside the gate in the hallway, said if I said so and so, he would do such and such. I told him he was not going to do anything.

Officer Joseph said, "Oh, yeah? Come on out here." I walked to the gate, and Officer Joseph opened it. He said, "Come out here." I said, "This is as far as I am allowed to go," and told him that I was not supposed to go past the line of the gate unless I had the permission of a correction officer.

At this point, Officer Motley came up behind me, grabbed me, turned me around toward my right, and punched me in my face. Simultaneously as I was being turned, Officer Joseph kicked me in the groin. I hit back and opened a small cut on Officer Motley's head. Other inmates separated us. One told me to go away, and I did. Officer Motley was following me with a blackjack. [It's against department regulations for a guard to have a blackjack in his possession.—J.N.]

At this point, Captain Malinsky was letting other officers into the outer gate. I went and sat on my bed. As other officers came on the ward, Officer Motley arrived at my bed. As one officer put a handcuff on my left hand, Officer Motley hit me in the mouth. Another officer grabbed my right arm and put it behind my back; Officer Motley hit me and knocked out a lower front tooth. Officer Joseph also hit me, using handcuffs as brass knuckles.

Four officers (including Officers Joseph and Motley)

took me from my bed on the ward to the utility room off the hallway; I was still handcuffed. They started to pummel me. I was hit across the shoulders with what felt like a blackjack. I was also hit on the back of the head, on the front of the head, on the face, and in the kidneys. In addition, I was kicked. Officer Joseph took dead aim and hit me on the eye. This continued for at least ten minutes, during which time I was hit about one hundred times. During this time, I said nothing and did not yell out. Then apparently, the Deputy Warden came on the ward.

The four officers who were in the utility room with me were Officers Motley and Joseph, a fat white officer, and a tall white officer, who had tried to stop the others previously. This last officer had put the handcuffs on me on the ward; I am not sure he hit me at all. The tall white officer said, "That's enough, the Dep's here," and tried to open the door. Officer Motley closed it and hit me again. . . .

The Deputy Warden asked me some questions and tried to get me to say that I had attacked the officer.

The following day, I fainted in the shower. For three days after the events described above, I urinated blood. I told this to a doctor (whose name I did not know), but did not tell a nurse.

Last week I also spoke to one of the three civilian witnesses whose affidavits were forwarded to McGrath and Hogan two weeks ago. This witness is an employee of Bellevue Hospital and asked me not to print his name "because I'm scared, I'm afraid of reprisals by the correction officers."

"I saw Mr. Ainsley get the hell beat out of him," the witness said. "Mr. Ainsley was a quiet man, a nice guy who sang a lot—down home blues mostly. He had a good voice. Anyway, I saw him taken off the ward and pushed into the utility room by the correction officers. I saw one of the guards hit Mr. Ainsley on the neck with his hand. The door of the room kept opening and closing while the beating went on. When it opened again the next thing I saw was Mr. Ainsley down on the floor. I saw the same officer kicking him on the kidney area, the same place where Mr. Ainsley was operated on twice. The whole time Mr. Ainsley never said a word. He just took it."

The witness added: "I'm afraid nothing will come of all this. Me and two other people have signed statements about what we saw. I've just seen too many prisoners come through here who were beaten up. I've seen guys from the Tombs and Rikers Island come through this hospital with closed eyes, and swollen lips, and everything. They all say they were beaten up by guards. They all say it, and nothing ever happens."

There is only one realistic way to halt the violence done by guards to inmates behind the secrecy of the walls. Commissioner McGrath must make it clear that force will not be tolerated. He must set examples as deterrents against future beatings. But so far he has not. So far he has done nothing about disciplining his own department. Today the Correction Department has no administrative apparatus, no personnel to even look into violence in the jails. The establishment of such an independent investigative staff, within the Correction Department, was one of the fifty-one points of reform suggested by William Vanden Heuvel in *The Voice* last month.

Up to now, whenever violence has been committed by correction officers, McGrath has responded by passing the buck. He has never investigated or disciplined the dozen guards accused by fifteen inmates of systematic brutality at the Kew Gardens jail. McGrath's excuse is that a court case is pending. In the case of the death of Lavon Moore, McGrath passed the buck to Manhattan D.A. Hogan, and then to U.S. Attorney Seymour, who in turn passed it to the FBI.

None of these outside agencies—especially the FBI—has ever displayed any evidence of being seriously concerned with the rights of inmates. Their purpose is to cover up the beatings, to whitewash the violence, to stall the search for truth until the media lose interest.

George McGrath is bureaucratically skilled in the high art of fuzzing accountability. It is one of the reasons he has endured in his job for five years. But it is McGrath's responsibility to stop his employees from brutalizing inmates. And it is John Lindsay's responsibility to make sure his commissioners maintain the most minimal levels of civilized conduct.

MARCH, 1971

The Consultant Hustle: $10,000,000 Caper

Consultants are people who borrow your watch and tell
you what time it is, and then walk off with the watch.
— Robert Townsend, *Up the Organization*

ITEM: New York City is broke. Five hundred city employees, mostly secretaries without political connections, have been dismissed. A "job freeze" is in operation prohibiting the hiring of new city employees. The Mayor has warned of "payless paydays" in the future. There is a projected budget deficit of $300 million. The education budget for 1971–72 will probably be $300 million less than for last year.

ITEM: Over the last three years the Lindsay administration has spent *over $10 million for management consultant contracts,* as compared to $40,000 for such contracts during the last year of the Wagner administration. The bulk of this money has gone to the New York City Rand Institute, whose directors include City Budget Director Edward Hamilton and Deputy Mayor Timothy Costello. This seems a clear conflict of interest by Hamilton, who also approves all of Rand's contracts with the city, which are kept secret.

ITEM: This sudden growth in consultant contracts has come under sharp attack from a variety of sources, from Comptroller Abe Beame, to *The New York Times,* to reform Democrats on the City Council like Edward Sadowsky, who chaired a special subcommittee that looked into the consultant contracts. Sadowsky's public hearings revealed that the consultant contracts were negotiated in secret, without competitive bidding, without approval by the Board of Estimate, and without the reports ever being released to the public or the press.

I have spent the last two weeks doing my own investigation of the role played by private consulting corporations in the govern-

ing of the city. I have obtained and read confidential Rand reports. I have interviewed present and past city commissioners. I have talked to politicians, journalists, and many middle-level employees of the city government.

This article represents an interim report about the consultants. Some of the consultant work in fire, sanitation, and other technical areas has clearly been of value. But this piece will focus on Education, Housing, Welfare, and especially Correction, and on the general mentality of consultants and their advocates in the city administration.

During the fiscal year 1969–70 the Correction Department had a $150,000 contract with the Rand Institute. For fiscal 1970–71 the contract was increased to $250,000. Currently Rand and Correction are quietly negotiating for a new *$300,000 contract for 1971–72.* (This is in addition to the separate $137,000 consulting contract given to Learning System, Inc., which I wrote about two weeks ago.)

None of the documents Rand has produced for its first $400,-000 have led to any specific improvements of conditions in the jails. All of them have been kept secret by the city. They were not even placed on file in the municipal reference library as required by law.

But those few insiders who did read them were shocked by their lack of merit. Councilman Sadowsky, who chaired the special subcommittee, told me, "The Rand reports on the jails were totally irrelevant and worthless."

I read several of them and agree with the councilman. None dealt directly with the real problems of the jails—overcrowding, narcotics, addiction, custodial violence, incompetent health care, inadequate training of guards, unfair bail, and absence of rehabilitation programs like job training or education classes. Most concerned themselves with bureaucratic efficiency. Not one proposed a new idea or a new policy. None examined the fundamental conceptual problem with the jails—the fact they are run on the basis of punishment rather than rehabilitation. (New York City spends less than 1 percent of its criminal justice budget on rehabilitation.)

One Rand study evaluated the use of an electronic surveillance system for parolees. Another was a demographic inmate profile. A third was an efficiency study of the "vehicle schedule and

transportation of inmates to and from court appearances." The last study was on "new methods of supervisory control, electronic surveillance, and computer technology to increase security in correctional institutions."

Rand studies are written in a jargon that has been called the Higher Incoherence. What follows is a taste of a confidential report on the pros and cons of "an automated parolee locater system":

> Experience drawn from present tests of car locater systems, current installation of computerized monitoring systems for the security industry, and the present Housing Authority Police usage of walkie-talkies throughout New York City, support the technological feasibility of a parolee locater system. . . .
>
> Recent accomplishments in microminiaturized electronics, in efficient communication spectrum management, in automatic computer monitoring of thousands of supervised control points. . . .

After reading these unimplemented reports, after running up against the secrecy that shrouds Rand's whole relationship with the city, I decided to find out what monitoring system exists at City Hall to check on Rand's work, and learn how their contracts could keep increasing each year while the city was going broke and jail conditions were deteriorating.

It turned out *no one at City Hall had actually read Rand's prison reports.* Deputy Mayor Richard Aurelio had not read a single prison study and did not know how many there were. The Mayor's press secretary, Tom Morgan, had *never read any Rand study on any subject.* And Michael Dontzin, the City Hall staff assistant directly in charge of Correction, had neither read nor evaluated Rand's work.

No one who is skeptical of Rand's approach gets to read their reports. The only people who read the Rand studies were in Correction and in the Bureau of the Budget, the bureaucrats who negotiated the contracts. There is no independent monitoring system now in operation, as proposed by Councilman Sadowsky in his report released last year. And no one I spoke to, from Aurelio to Sadowsky, even knew that a new $300,000 Rand contract was being inserted in next year's budget. (A representative of Rand confirmed this to me.)

Meanwhile, inmates of the Tombs, presumed innocent and

awaiting trial, too poor to make bail, go without clean under-wear, soap, hot food, decent medical care, and have no recreation facilities, because Commissioner McGrath says he has no money in the budget for such luxuries.

There is a second half to this interim communiqué on consul-tants. It is based on all the information I could assemble on con-sultant reports in the areas of Correction, Welfare, Education, and Housing. It is admittedly impressionistic and tentative, ad-mittedly written out of my own bias toward redistribution of wealth, community control, and decentralization as political solu-tions.

Part of the reason for this impressionistic method is the impen-etrable secrecy the city imposes on Rand's work, and the fact that I can't quote people who work for the city directly, can't quote them on specifics because they are afraid they will be fired if they are quoted by name on the inner workings of the Lindsay admin-istration.

Much of the $10 million the city has paid to private consulting corporations since 1968 I believe has been wasted. Most of these expensive studies have not led to new programs that affect peo-ple, that affect the actual delivery of services, that affect a con-crete reality beyond the corridors of power.

Virtually all the Rand reports I have read are about managing the bureaucracy better, planning the budget, establishing priori-ties within agencies, how to get "more bang for the buck."

The basic problem here is a *mentality*, the technocratic mindset. It is a whole gestalt I am trying to write about, not any single study, or any single consulting corporation (Rand is among the best).

One problem is that the consultants themselves tend not to be issue oriented, or even people oriented. Their stated objective is to "rationalize the bureaucracy," to make it more "cost effective." Their work is for and about bureaucrats, and that is its appeal. It has a built-in disinterest in social injustice or poverty, and a built-in bias toward electronics and the future.

Consultants almost never see or touch or feel the average citi-zens who are affected by their abstract studies. They do not spend time in classrooms talking to children. (McKinsey has done most of the consulting on education.) They do not talk to squatters or people living in welfare hotels. They only see the way the bureaucracy functions, the commissioners, the agency

staffs. They are an elite working for another elite. People are irrelevant to their equations of efficiency.

The reports are distorted by the fact consultants tend not to understand how the whole city works. They do not understand, or take.into account, the civil service, or municipal unions and their internal politics, or the rivalries among political factions within the city. *Consultants try to construct a rational system for an irrational environment.* But they don't know how ordinary people live in Inwood, or Red Hook, or Corona. They understand systems analysis, computers, flow charts, and data banks, but they don't know who Jack Biegle is, or what it's like to live on Myrtle Avenue in Bed-Stuy, or who the chairman of the City Council's Finance Committee is.

Moreover, the consultants themselves represent an unnaturally narrow range of skills, social classes, and methodologies. A majority of consultants come out of Ivy League colleges or graduate schools; many are systems analysts, economists, and accountants. The team working on Correction includes a cost accountant and an electronics expert. The team is led by Clarence Tang, who seems unusually committed and sensitive. But even if it were led by an ex-con, a Spanish-speaking journalist, and a black detective, the studies would be worthless as long as George McGrath remains Commissioner, as long as Albert Ossakow remains warden at Kew Gardens, as long as the doctors in most jails remain seventy-five-year-old incompetents.

Another example of Rand's remoteness from the nitty-gritty is that some of their staff who worked on city projects actually spent more than half their time working for the national Rand Corporation in Santa Monica, California. They sat in their glass offices, watching the Pacific Ocean roll in, and wrote reports on how to solve the narcotics problem in Manhattan. Also, part of the immense bill the city pays Rand includes all those plane tickets for consultants who live in California, and are working on city studies only part time. ("Oh, those expense vouchers, they were a lot of money," Sadowsky said.)

So I believe the use of high-priced consultants (David Hertz of McKinsey was paid $700 a day by the city) has gotten out of hand. And the fault for this is not the consultant corporations', but the city government's, the Bureau of the Budget's.

The Lindsay administration, despite ample criticism and warn-

ings, never established an adequate internal control or monitoring system on the awarding of consultant contracts, or the evaluating of consultant reports. What began as a useful remedy for specific, semiscientific problems, silently and secretly grew into a giant boondoggle, into a white collar form of patronage for old Ivy League classmates. (At least under Mayor Wagner the patronage went to the working class through the clubhouse system.)

And the responsibility for this must rest with the Mayor and the Bureau of the Budget, the city agency most committed to technocratic expertise, the city agency with the power to make the consultant craze a policy, and the city agency whose director is also a director of the Rand Institute.

The Budget Bureau is an elitist enclave within the city government. Of the forty-five program planners on its staff, forty are graduates of Ivy League schools. Of the seventy-five top employees, one is black and none is Puerto Rican. And virtually all the summer interns hired by the Budget Bureau since 1968 have been recruited exclusively at Ivy League graduate schools. When one Budget staffer suggested that at least some interns be recruited at the City University, the idea was scoffed at and rejected.

And then there is the Mayor's culpability. This is how one former top Budget employee explained Lindsay's seduction by the consultants: "The Mayor was just snowed, taken in. It was in 1968, and he wanted to find a way not to deal with the lower-class civil service. And everyone was telling him he was a lousy administrator. And all these bright, Ivy League guys from Rand and McKinsey came to him and said they knew how to rationalize city government. Lindsay really believed they were *supermen*. Their use of statistics and charts just dazzled Lindsay. The statistics made Lindsay feel that somehow the city was controllable with expertise. So the Mayor was converted without really understanding what it was all about. He was convinced that Rand had a skill that was really a *science*. I remember I once wrote a speech for Lindsay, and he made me use the phrase 'new budget science' three times in the speech. And I'm convinced he didn't know what those words actually meant. Lindsay meant well. He just believed these people were supermen."

There is another problem with the consultant boondoggle. The very nature of the consultant process—*secret studies for gov-*

ernmental elites based on the primary value of cost efficiency—
stands in direct opposition to the emerging movement toward
decentralized decision-making, direct citizen participation, community control, and neighborhood government.

The use of consultants, writing secret studies in highly technical jargon, makes governmental decisions even more centralized,
at an even higher level of the bureaucracy. It sets policies and
priorities at a level of government ordinary citizens can neither
influence nor see. Community groups cannot see or rebut these
studies, and they are too poor to hire their own experts. The use
of consultants and experts increases the sense of powerlessness
among working people, and it makes the most basic decisions of
government the exclusive and secret property of technocrats. It
makes the poor even more powerless, and in this sense the entire
process is antidemocratic. It precludes input from below while issues are still being defined.

If the bloody decade of the 1960s offers any lessons for its sur-
vivors, surely one of the clearest is not to trust the judgment of
an elite coterie of experts. It is computer-oriented experts like
Robert McNamara, McGeorge Bundy, and Walt Rostow whom
history will hold most responsible for America's deepening involvement in Vietnam between 1961 and 1965. When Robert
McNamara became Secretary of Defense in 1961 he introduced
Planning Programming Budgeting Systems (PPBS) into the Pentagon. He recruited a generation of mathematical whiz kids to
compute the cost benefits of efficient bombing, of efficient transportation of weapons systems, and of kill ratios for Vietnam. The
smartest men in the government—Yarmolinsky, Enthoven,
Hitch, Gilpatric, and Henry Rowen—came to work for him.
(Enthoven and Hitch were hired away from Rand, while Rowen
is now the president of Rand.)

But they failed miserably because *they asked the wrong questions.* They asked the questions about the most efficient details
and techniques of war, but they never asked *should we be in
Vietnam in the first place?* They never asked *why;* they only
asked *how.* Only means, not ends, interest them. They fed into
their computers only the things that were quantifiable—numbers
of men, numbers of missions, numbers of bombs, numbers of

corpses. But they couldn't measure the courage or the character of the Viet Cong. They couldn't measure the courage and character of Diem and Ky. They failed because they tried to use system analysis to solve a *political problem,* to stop a revolution.

And in Vietnam it was the working reporters who knew better than the famous experts, better than the million-dollar computers, what the reality of the situation was. David Halberstam and Malcolm Browne were there in 1962 and they saw and wrote what was happening. (JFK, remember, tried to muscle the *Times* into removing Halberstam from Vietnam.) At the time McNamara would say of the dovish reporters, "They have a prejudiced data bank." When a White House staff member voiced his own skepticism about the war, about the pacification program, McNamara snapped at him: "Where are your facts? Give me something I can put into a computer!" (quoted by Halberstam in the February 1971 issue of *Harper's*).

The poverty program was the other great social experiment of the 1960s that the technocrats had a decisive role in shaping. And OEO was where the consultant hustle was perfected.

Much of the money the poverty program spent ended up not in the hands of the poor, but in the hands of consultants. As of June 1970, according to Representative Edith Green, OEO had paid more than *$600 million* for studies by consultants. Many of the grants had it written into the contracts that consultants be used for study and evaluation. And most of this money went to consulting companies set up by former OEO bureaucrats. Sixteen corporations that had a total of thirty-five former OEO employees on their staffs received more than $11 million of these consultant fees.

Robert Levine was an executive of the Rand Corporation in Santa Monica. Then he was hired by OEO in the agency's office of research, plans, and evaluations. While he worked for OEO he gave Rand consulting contracts worth $600,000. Then he went back to Rand.

Leo Kramer was associate director of the office of selection and training for VISTA. He quit in 1966 and set up his own consulting corporation. He has since received $2 million worth of antipoverty contracts, most of them from VISTA.

I could go on and on. I have acquaintances I could name who have gotten rich as $150 per diem consultants who know nothing

about curing poverty, who have the social commitment of an ant, and who brag about their racket, their lush weeks in Puerto Rico, their easy access to university and foundation patronage.

So the Lindsay people should have learned from the experiences of Vietnam and OEO that experts were not always right, that overpaid consultants might not be worth their investment, that some of them were power-seeking hustlers, that Rand's performances did not square with its reputation. The Lindsay people should have learned this better than anyone else because so many of them were part of those failures. Former Budget Director Fred Hayes, former City Hall aide Peter Goldmark, and current Deputy Budget Director David Grossman all worked for OEO at the start. Edward Hamilton, the current Budget Director, originally worked in the Pentagon under Robert McNamara. Later he was hired away by Lyndon Johnson as a member of the National Security Council staff during the period of Vietnam escalation. Johnson was so impressed by Hamilton's brilliance that he tried to appoint him director of the AID program, which is a CIA cover in Laos, and in parts of Latin America according to its own former director, Dr. John Hannah. Congressional leaders, however, opposed the idea because they objected to Hamilton's youth—he was twenty-seven at the time.

The Lindsay people should have known that these high-priced experts were not objective and "value free," as they claimed; that they were committed to existing institutions, existing programs, and conventional solutions.

They should have known that new management types never asked the root questions, never thought about first principles or philosophical assumptions. Just as they never asked, Is Vietnam moral? Only What is the kill ratio per weapons system? So they made the same mistake here. The Rand electronics experts walked through the Tombs, saw the agony, heard the screams, and then wrote a nice study of how to transport inmates from A to B more efficiently.

The Lindsay people should have known that formal education, that graduate school credentials, that Robert McNamara's name on a resumé, that none of these status symbols was an index to justice, or truth, or imagination.

They should have known that even the best of these techno-

cratic minds—Henry Rowen, Herman Kahn, Henry Kissinger, Bundy, Charles Hitch, Robert McNamara—even the best were not authentic intellectuals who generated original ideas. Even the very best were, at bottom, only entrepreneurs, brilliant operators skilled at getting grants, influencing rising politicians, and running rich, establishment institutions like the Ford Foundation and the Rand Corporation.

They are Chomsky's "new mandarins" who use a counterfeit knowledge to gain power. And their black art is not a "new budget science" practiced by "supermen." It is more like the old patronage hustle practiced by crackpot clerks.

APRIL, 1971

[NINE]
SOME PEOPLE I LIKED

These last pieces really require no introduction. They are about five men who have tried in different ways to make this a better land. There are certainly others, like Leonard Weinglass or Cesar Chavez that would have been included if I had ever gotten around to writing the pieces about them that I intended to. And I could easily have added the pieces on Bob Moses and Muhammed Ali to this chapter.

I suppose it is a comment on the times that I only discovered five such individuals over five years of writing, that most of the pieces in this collection on individuals are skeptical or critical. But this has been a time when the best get shot, and the worst become President.

I can think of very few personal qualities that link the five men in this section. If Nader and Clark are uncommonly shy for public men, Mailer more than compensates. If Mailer and Rosenthal are New York Jews, then Kennedy was always more Boston than Camelot. And Clark was raised in Dallas. The only common thread is that I met them, and their character and commitment touched me.

[1.]
Courage in Congress: Case of a Quiet Man

The House of Representatives is a notoriously unrepresentative institution. It is more conservative, more Southern, more male, more rural, more Protestant, and older than the nation it is supposed to represent.

Fifteen of the twenty chairmen of standing committees of the House come from small towns or rural areas. Although the median age of today's American is twenty-eight, the median age in Congress is over fifty. Among the committeemen it is over sixty-five. Seventeen of the committee chairmen are Protestant, and eleven of the twenty come from the Old Confederacy, although the South contains less than one fifth of the country's population.

Every two years, five to ten young, liberal pilgrims journey to Washington as freshmen Congressmen to confront the institution, which has its special mores and special temptations. In almost every case it is the individual who bends to the institution, trimming his ideals in order to advance and win his colleagues' approval.

In the early 1960s, Frank Thompson of New Jersey and Morris Udall of Arizona carried the banner of liberal insurgency. They were archetypal of the New Frontiersmen—tough-minded, energetic, and overflowing with the rhetoric of reform. But by 1965 they had become the skilled infighters who aborted the congressional challenge of the Mississippi Freedom Democrats, and this year they chose the tree on which to string up Adam Clayton Powell.

In 1965, the Bronx sent two intelligent, well-known reformers to Congress, Jonathan Bingham and James Scheuer. They had won dramatic primary struggles against the Buckley organization, and they ignited hopes with their liberal campaign speeches. But like so many preceding generations of honest liberals, Scheuer and Bingham have learned to adjust.

Last spring, Bingham gratuitously criticized Martin Luther King, while the civil rights leader was under attack for his Vietnam dissent. Last month he spoke in favor of a bill that makes flag-burning a federal crime, even though House patriarch Emanuel Celler called the bill a violation of civil liberties and the Constitution. His colleague James Scheuer has earned the nickname of "parasite" for his habit of lifting bills introduced by liberal Senators, putting his name on them in the House, and quickly sending out press releases. After gaining a few lines of cold type, he tends to forget the bills.

Scheuer and Bingham are surely on the road to influence in the House. They get choice assignments. The leadership pays attention to their pet projects. They are consulted, and have a direct line into the White House. They have risen to the level of junior executives in the Democratic Study Group, which was once an insurgent spur. It has lately ossified into an arm of the Administration—a whip system for rounding up votes.

Despite all the pressures and opportunities, there remains in the House a small, persistent band of dissenters. There are twelve of them organized into a loose faction. They meet regularly, have hired a researcher and a speech writer. They are the real outsiders. These men have rejected the late Speaker Sam Rayburn's "go along to get along" dictum, and they have made a conscious decision to reconfront the institution; they vote against appropriations for Vietnam, criticize the President in public, open up to debate closed questions, like anticommunism and the draft. They have chosen the long, uncertain outside track that leads to Wayne Morse and the late Congressman Vito Marantonio, rather than the surer inside track that leads to Hubert Humphrey and John Roche.

Perhaps the unlikeliest of the House heretics is balding, forty-four-year-old Benjamin Rosenthal, a political mutation out of the sterile Queens county Democratic machine. Since Queens politicians receive minimal publicity in the daily press, and Rosenthal lacks any talent for self-dramatization, his obscure revolt goes largely unrecorded. A columnist for a New York daily recently confessed he wasn't even sure who Rosenthal was.

Rosenthal was one of the eleven Congressmen to vote against LBJ's latest Vietnam appropriation request; one of sixteen to vote against the flag-burning bill; one of a handful to speak up

publicly in defense of Adam Powell. And two weeks ago, addressing an antiwar rally in Manhattan Center, Rosenthal assailed
"our compulsive, often hysterical, anticommunism." He suggested:

We must recognize the possibility that communism, however
odious and destructive an ideology, often turns out to be the real
outlet for the kind of postcolonial liberation and development
we profess to support."

To be a nonconformist within a bureaucratic structure is never
without discomfort, whether a college fraternity, the army, or the
House of Representatives. And Rosenthal has paid for his indi-
vidualism in a dozen small ways. When he was in line for the
chairmanship of the Democratic Study Group's foreign affairs
steering committee, he was passed over in favor of Bingham—
even though he is and Bingham is not on the Foreign Affairs
Committee of the House. And once on a plane, carrying all of
New York's twenty-two Congressmen, the President went out of
his way to ridicule Rosenthal in front of his friends and colleagues.

Yet, Rosenthal's rebellion is not of the proportions of a Prome-
theus, a Sisyphus, or even a Fulbright. It is closer to the commonplace integrity of a Bernard Malamud hero.

Rosenthal is not an intellectual, even by the measure of his
profession, nor is he goaded by transcendent visions of a new society. He is, in fact, a rather ordinary fellow, very much in the
Jewish mold, shy, tense, and a poor public speaker. But he is not
awed by power. He has no burning ambitions, and he is against
the Vietnam war. He is like Morris Bober in *The Assistant*, a
man who follows his own ethical imperatives, while everyone else
is cheating and compromising.

Last week Rosenthal sat in his Washington office and tried to
explain how he became one of the most radical men in Congress.

Though obviously uncomfortable with introspection, he tried
to analyze his journey from clubhouse lawyer to thorn in Rusk's
side.

"I got my politics in a prosaic way. I joined my local Democratic club in 1949 to help my career as a lawyer. I didn't consider myself anything politically, liberal or conservative, in those
days."

Through the 1950s Rosenthal rose inside the rotting Queens

organization the normal, safe way. By 1962 he was rewarded with the Congressional nomination when Lester Holtzman was elevated to the bench.

"I tried to get the nomination for kicks," Rosenthal said. "I wasn't driven or anything. A lot of guys wanted it—Sy Thaler, Moe Weinstein—but I got it because I had the fewest enemies."

During his first term in Congress he conformed to the institution's ethos. He was quiet, courteous, and worked hard. In 1965 his docility was recognized with a seat on the coveted Foreign Affairs Committee, after he had been stuck on such committees as veterans's affairs and agriculture.

Soon Rosenthal began to develop doubts about our Vietnam policy, but he beat them down and voted for the supplemental arms appropriation in 1965. This year he led the fight against the war request, probably the most radical action a Congressman could have taken.

The difference between 1965 and 1967 was Rosenthal's personal brand of commonsense. He hadn't read Frantz Fanon, or Tom Hayden, or *Le Monde,* but he just decided for himself that the war was pointless and that he wouldn't be bribed or bullied into silence. He had neither an ambition which would be held hostage nor a vanity which invites seduction. Gradually his dissent on Vietnam led him to dissent in other areas.

On his role as a Congressman, he says: "I couldn't care less what McNamara and Rusk think about me. I try to lead. I try to stretch the definition of legitimacy. When I spoke at Queens College, I went to talk to some students who were fasting against the war. My doing that gave them legitimacy. I'm not inhibited by the conventional definitions of politics."

"I really don't know. It's a question of how far I can stretch legitimacy. I can help legitimate the Mississippi Freedom Democratic Party or antiwar fasters, but some things can illegitimate me. It's always a close question."

Rosenthal remains the invisible rebel. There is no great drama to his role, no cathartic release. Although more daring, his image pales beside those of Robert Kennedy and John Lindsay. There are no cheering crowds to give him psychic reinforcement, no sense of history-making. His lot is the daily drudgery and frustration of an isolated Congressman trying to stop a war. Nothing more. But, nothing less, either.

MAY, 1967

[2.]
On the Steps of a Zeitgeist

A beginning in the form of a parody:

Mailer has always been Newfield's favorite writer. He dropped a half-dozen references to Mailer into his book on the New Left. He had gone to the same broken-down high school in Brooklyn as Mailer. Whenever he was bogged down writing a piece, he would use a little trick: he would stop, and read Mailer for an hour, and presto, the images would start flowing again, and his head would be filled with music.

Newfield's friends—writers and first-generation SDS types—were also aficionados of Mailer. Two years ago, Newfield, Paul Cowan of *The Voice*, Jacob Brackman of *The New Yorker*, and Paul Gorman, who is now writing speeches for Eugene McCarthy, went as a noisy claque to the 92nd Street Y to root for Mailer in his debate with those Establishment highbrows, Howe and Podhoretz. Newfield and his friends talked about Mailer all the time, and told each other how much Mailer was an influence on their writing and thinking, particularly in Mailer's fusion of personal, literary, and political radicalism (Cowan and Brackman had both written long, appreciative pieces on Mailer for the *Crimson* while they were still at Harvard).

But Newfield and Mailer did not enjoy much of a relationship. Once Mailer published a letter in *The Voice* rebuking Newfield for certain references to Mailer in a piece he did on the fighter, Joe Shaw. Newfield bled. On another occasion, Mailer wouldn't let Newfield interview him on Channel 13. Newfield brooded.

But recently things were looking up. First of all, Newfield was no longer intimidated by Mailer. Second, Newfield once told Mailer he should listen to Bob Dylan because Dylan was an authentic poet. Mailer laughed, but a few months later admitted to Newfield that he was right about Dylan. Mailer also gave Newfield a mention in his nonfiction history of the Pentagon demonstration.

Newfield ached to review that book, but didn't feel confident enough. Then he went to see Mailer's debate-happening three weeks ago with Herbert Marcuse and Arthur Schlesinger. Marcuse is supposed to be "the philosopher of the New Left," and Schlesinger a philosopher for Bobby Kennedy. But Newfield identified with Mailer that night, as usual. When he saw all the New Left kids cheering Marcuse's antidemocratic rationalizations, while ignoring Mailer's shafts of warm wit and cold wisdom, he decided he must do something to rectify the New Left's romantic crush on Marcuse.

Newfield, for a while now, had been bugged with the New Left's faddish tinsel heroes. Debray. Mao. Marcuse. Leary.

And how could they not dig Mailer? Mailer, who preached revolution before there was a movement. Mailer, who was calling LBJ a monster while the slide rule liberals were still writing speeches for him. Mailer, who was into Negroes, pot, Cuba, violence, existentialism, bureaucratic depersonalization, and hipsters while the New Left was still a twinkle in C. Wright Mills's eye.

So Newfield, bored with writing about Kennedy, and too angry at the Columbia trustees and Lindsay's cops to be coherent, marched off to redeem Mailer's reputation with the New Left.

Last Friday was to be an archetypal Day in the Life of Norman Mailer, novelist, counterpuncher, filmmaker, mayoral candidate, stud, essayist, egomaniac, and successor to Whitman and Henry James as American Zeitgeist.

At 4:30 P.M., Mailer the Artist was finishing up the editing of his second home movie, *Beyond the Law*, at the Leacock-Pennebaker studio on West 45th Street. Mailer the Artist is quite intense and enthusiastic about his filmmaking.

"I've put six months of my life into this film," he said, which is longer than it took him to write his book on the Pentagon march.

Beyond the Law is described in that book as "a study of detectives and suspects in a police precinct," and it stars Mailer, his friend and actor Buzz Farbar, stockbroker Tom Quinn, welterweight contender Joe Shaw, former light-heavyweight champion Jose Torres, and Pete Hamill's younger brother, Brian. Mailer thinks it is not impossible that he had "divined and/or blundered into the making of the best American movie about police he had ever seen."

"I really wanted to call it *Fallen Angels,*" Mailer the Artist said, "because everyone in it looks like an angel."

At 5 P.M. Mailer the Drinker entered a small characterless bar across the street from the film studio. Present were Jose Torres on crutches, with his brother and trainer, Pete Hamill and his brother, Farbar, and Tom Hayden, the revolutionary. Hayden began to discuss revolution with Mailer.

"I'm for Kennedy," said Mailer the Drinker, "because I'm not so sure I want a revolution. Some of those kids are awfully dumb." Hayden the Revolutionary said a vote for George Wallace would further his objective more than a vote for RFK.

But quickly, Mailer and Hayden found two pieces of common turf. Hayden was there because, like the rest of the world, he wanted a small piece of Norman Mailer. He wanted Mailer to help out a movement project geared toward reaching soldiers bound for Vietnam. He wanted Mailer to speak to GIs at a coffeehouse in Columbia, South Carolina. Mailer easily agreed.

But Mailer also discovered he wanted something from Hayden. He wanted to go to Cuba and spend a week with Fidel Castro.

"I want a guarantee," he said, "man to man, that I can see Fidel. Or else, fuck him. I'm not taking any chances of going there and then not seeing him. My time is valuable too."

Hayden said he thought it could be arranged.

At 6:30 P.M., Mailer the Rebel arrived at Dwight Macdonald's apartment on East 87th Street for a fund-raising party for the Columbia University student strikers. They wanted a piece of Mailer too.

Mark Rudd was there with three comrades. The guests included George Plimpton, Art D'Lugoff, Bob Silvers, Frances Fitz-Gerald, plus Mailer's eclectic entourage, which still included Torres, who is rather skeptical about the whole New Left.

While Mailer the Rebel drank bourbons, an SDS kid named Steve made a plea for an immediate $3400 as a down payment for a co-op loft on Wooster Street into which the SDS regional office could move. He explained how SDS had been mysteriously evicted from three offices in the last year. He also explained how SDS sent out a fund-raising letter by Macdonald last week, and had not received any mail since, even letters mailed to themselves as a test. Mailer, the metaphysician of conspiracies, listened. He ended up giving SDS $100 in cash, plus a loan of $900 against

the receipts of a benefit showing of his first film, *Wild 90.* "I can do this because I'm in debt," he explained.

Then Rudd, who faces six years in jail for his activities at Columbia, began to speak. Mailer the Rebel looked into his open, unfinished face.

Rudd said that the fires at Columbia last week were set by police provocateurs dressed as plainclothesmen after the students had left the buildings. Rudd also said that "plainclothesmen began the anticop slogans that started the violence on the sundial. They falsified evidence too."

Mailer the Rebel, nursing his fifth bourbon, interrupted to say, "I'm sure you're telling me the truth in general. About particulars, I don't know. I want the facts. What walls did you paint? What walls did the police paint? You've got to put the police on the defensive. I know that cops create evidence. They've done it to me. All cops are psychopathic liars. Your fight is to show that the people who run the country are full of shit. You've got to come up with the hard evidence of what the cops did. . . . If you win, then America will be a little different place."

Rudd then said something about needing money to pay for lawyers' fees.

Mailer the Rebel, punching his left palm with his right fist, interrupted, leaning forward in his six-button vest.

"Most lawyers are corrupt and filled with guilt. That's the liberal middle-class game, lawyers and fund-raising parties and more bureaucracy. Why don't you kids defend yourselves? If you're cool, and telling the truth, you're better off without lawyers. Let totalitarian America judge each one of your faces."

"We're too ugly," Rudd said, and Mailer mentally gave him that round.

"We need lawyers," Rudd continued, "also to allay the fears of the mothers."

"You have the mothers come to court, too, if you've got the balls," barked Mailer the Rebel, in his Mafia–W. C. Fields voice.

Before he left Macdonald's, Mailer had to remind Steve of SDS that he had not yet written out his promised check. The SDS kid, who had liberated university buildings, said he didn't want to seem presumptuous by pestering Mailer.

As he left, Mailer the Rebel said, "I don't agree with SDS. I gave them the money because they are an active principle. They are taking chances, and they just might be right. I have some

sympathies with them, but not intimate agreement. I'm not a Left hard-on. I'm a Left conservative."

Mailer the Celebrity, in a playful, puckish mood, was a few minutes early for the taping of the Merv Griffin television show. So, wearing his pancake makeup, he went off to Smith's proletarian bar on Eighth Avenue, for another drink.

Did he believe what Rudd said about the police?

"One chance out of a hundred some crazy SDS kid set the fires. But one hundred chances out of one hundred some cop did it. I know cops."

Suddenly, a tall, hip Negro faggot approached Mailer, recognized him, and said he had gone to Choate.

Mailer the Celebrity looked at the man, who had a long knife scar on his face, thinking perhaps of Shago Martin or Sonny Liston, and offered to bet him $100 that he did not go to Choate.

They traded a few verbal jabs, Mailer, in his own judgment, having "to work for my draw," and then split for the television studio.

A little tight, Mailer walked out to face an audience that looked like it was bussed over from the Crimmins murder trial. Empty, pinched faces. They were mindless television fanatics, and Mailer was quite aware that the last time he had been on Griffin's show, he criticized the Vietnam war and was booed by the yahoo audience. But Mailer was up for this one; just before walking out, he had been throwing loving overhand rights that stopped just short of Pete Hamill's smiling face. "Not hitting you, Pete, takes something out of my character," he barked.

"Norman Mailer is one of the leading spectator sports in America," Griffin said, and Mailer swaggered out of the wings, hunching up his shoulders like Carmen Basillio coming to Ray Robinson.

They shook hands and Mailer the Celebrity announced, "My hands are cold because I've been holding drinks for the last two hours."

A current of panic shot through Griffin's all-American face, fearing that Mailer was wild drunk.

"How has the mood of the country changed since you were here last?" Griffin asked, sounding like a Sunday robot-panelist.

"The instances of faggotry have gone up in the country," Mailer said.

"That means more smoking, folks," quipped Griffin.

Griffin then asked Mailer about the Presidential election.

"If Humphrey runs against Rockefeller, I will take the year off and go to Coney Island. . . . Humphrey may slip through because he is a whale who moves like a snake on the way to the hog trough."

Mailer then tossed off passing references to the film *Marty* and Machiavelli, which the yahoo audience did not seem to understand.

"Is this the idiot row?" Mailer barked.

"What is your image of yourself?" Griffin asked.

"An activist."

Suddenly, stand-up comic Morey Amsterdam, a walking file of one-liners, said, "I've come here to learn something, and I'm still waiting."

The audience, finding its spokesman at last, cheered wildly.

Mailer, quite sober by now, then revealed his secret weapon—self-depreciation. "Morey," he said, "once again you've inherited the problem of a landslide."

At 9:30 Mailer the Counterpuncher arrived at Madison Square Garden to see the light heavyweight championship fight between Dick Tiger and Bob Foster. Walking through the smoke-haloed ringside toward his seat, the former welterweight contender, Billy Graham, warmly embraced Mailer, as if he were actually an old fighter. Indeed, Mailer is not built unlike Jake LaMotta, who was standing next to Graham.

Mailer the Counterpuncher wanted Tiger to win, even though Tiger had twice defeated his buddy, Torres. But like any detached professional critic, Mailer was properly impressed by Foster's crunching left hook, which dropped Tiger for the count in the fourth round.

Later, after midnight, Mailer the Zeitgeist traveled up to Columbia and climbed over a fifteen-foot fence to talk to a twenty-year-old named Mark Rudd.

MAY, 1968

[3.]
Nader's Raiders:
The Lone Ranger Gets a Posse

His address is kept secret, yet people somehow find out and wait on the sidewalk to present some problem they've encountered, to provide some clue for him to follow up. In Winsted, Connecticut, where he grew up, more than a dozen letters and almost a dozen long-distance calls reach his parents each week, seeking his help. In Washington, where he lives and works, his mail heaps up in large piles, much of it addressed simply: Ralph Nader, Washington, D.C.

A few seasons back Ralph Nader was the solitary, slightly eccentric crusader for auto safety, a single-issue, individualistic reformer, bereft of staff or money. But now the loner has spawned a movement. Now the Lone Ranger has a posse. He has diversified his sense of outrage into a dozen new areas, from justice for American Indians, to ecology, to reform of the United Mineworkers union. He has set up an activist institute in Washington with a full-time staff and some foundation funds. And he has become a folk hero in the nation's law schools, which provided him with most of the 102 young people (out of 2000 volunteers) who spent the summer burrowing into the soft underbelly of the federal bureaucracy, looking for scandals and skeletons.

The influence of Naderism, that belief in individuals challenging institutions, continues to grow. Consumer groups are organizing across the country to fight for causes, like purity in meat and parity in drug prices, that he forcefully brought to public attention. Adam Walinsky, Robert Kennedy's former speechwriter and a close friend of Nader's, has assembled fifteen of his own Raiders to work in New York. Joe Tom Easley, one of the summer volunteers, plans a similar group for Texas. And all this grass-roots energy has helped to forge an effective bloc of consumer-oriented United States Senators, including Abraham Ribicoff, Warren Magnuson, William Proxmire, Walter Mondale, and

Gaylord Nelson. Nader works with all of them, feeding them data and information, testifying before their subcommittees and suggesting new issues for them to look into. Naderism is becoming an important social force.

The location of Ralph Nader's $107-a-month office is a closely guarded secret. He doesn't have a phone in the file-and-periodical-cluttered, $80-a-month furnished room he lives in. He works roughly eighteen hours a day, cruising the city to meet with his network of subterranean contacts in the press, Congress and corporations, making long-distance calls on the pay phone in the hall of his boardinghouse, drafting articles, speeches, letters, and congressional testimony, and reading dry congressional subcommittee reports and complex legal and scientific journals.

Nader meets friends and interviewers not at home or at work but in places like the lobby of the Dupont Plaza Hotel in Washington. He allows no one to accompany him on his mysterious rounds of Washington where he, among other things, gets copies of secret reports from people in corporations and government agencies, reports which will document old crusades and lead to fresh ones. "Too much of what I do has to remain confidential and secret," he says. "I must have my privacy."

He has totally integrated his concepts of work and leisure. And he has systematically conditioned his body to function on four hours' sleep a night. "I happen to like what I do very much," he explains. "My desire for privacy is a function of my need for time. I actually find the act of staying up till dawn researching a confidential memorandum pleasurable. It's just that I would rather work twenty hours a day on something that gives me real satisfaction than three hours a day on an alienating job that bores me. So I don't have to go to a discotheque at night to relax."

As Nader talks, there are quick, nervous thrusts of his long, bony hands. This is his only distinguishing gesture. The voice is soft and unaccented, his manner is moderate, almost bland. His dress is conventional, his ties are particularly dull. He is not bombastic but, rather, he blends, and this personal style is part of his attraction to the young who work with him. He makes many other people uncomfortable, though, because they can't understand his motives. A Senator once asked him, "Why do you do

this?" and Nader replied, "You wouldn't ask me that if I was representing the A.S.P.C.A., would you?"

His adversaries suspect that baser human drives like money, ego, and power are his real fuel. They speculate that he has a secret Swiss bank account, that he harbors secret political ambitions, that he has been bought off by the bicycle industry.

His friends ridicule the rumors and point out that he draws no steady salary and lives mainly on money from college lectures he gives (about twenty a year ranging from no fee to a maximum of $1,000) and articles he writes, mostly for *The New Republic* at $125 each. He did earn about $60,000 from his book, *Unsafe at Any Speed,* but has spent almost all of that over the past three and a half years financing new investigations. "Ralph is just an old-fashioned moralist," says his confidant and publisher, Richard Grossman. "He's in the Brandeis tradition. He's just very outraged by the breakdown of ethics in business and government. He *is* what he *seems.* All the rest is mythology invented by the press. He's not lonely. He's not crazy. He is not humorless."

A Congressman who has worked closely with Nader suggests that his secret weapon is his "lack of ego. Ralph just isn't desperate to grab all the credit every time he has a scoop. He'd rather call Morton Mintz at the Washington *Post,* or Warren Magnuson over in the Senate, and let them release it, then call a press conference himself. He just has no ulterior motives. He doesn't have an ideology to sell. He won't even tell me if he's a Democrat or Republican."

And another friend, offering that Nader has no car, only four suits, and eats many of his evening meals alone, explains Nader's life style this way: "Look, if you really believe that cars are unsafe, meat and fish are unhealthy, television gives off harmful rays, that jets are dangerous and that air is polluted, you're apt to live a little bit like a nun."

"I don't like to think of myself as an idealist," Nader said recently. "If you define an idealist as someone who recedes from the real world because he wants his own world to be pure, then I'm not an idealist. I think of myself as being very practical because I want to be effective. One of the reasons I do what I do is that I feel very strongly the inadequacies of the traditional reformers. They don't do their homework. They get all involved

with status, egotism, and the rituals of publicity. Even the great
old muckrakers like Upton Sinclair and Lincoln Steffens only
did 20 percent of the job. They stopped with exposure. They
didn't follow through by politically mobilizing a concerned constituency."

Nader has also been labeled an "Ombudsman," a "lobbyist," a
"muckraker." But the title he likes best is "people's lawyer."

"The function of a lawyer," he said with his flair for aphor-
isms, "is to be a good investigator, analytic and careful. And to
be savvy about the uses of power. I am a lawyer. Most lawyers
are too hung up on clients. The most important thing a lawyer
can do is become an advocate of powerless citizens. I am in favor
of lawyers without clients. Lawyers should represent systems of
justice. I want to create a new dimension to the legal profession.
What we have now is a democracy without citizens. No one is on
the public's side. All the lawyers are on the corporations' side.
And the bureaucrats in the Administration don't think the government belongs to the people.

"For example, the industries, corporations and lobbyists manipulate the federal commissions and agencies. The Interstate
Commerce Commission has always been a tool of the railroads,
the bus lines and the trucking industry. The Department of Interior has been easily influenced by the oil and gas industries. The
Department of Agriculture has been an instrument of the tobacco industry. No one represents the public interest. Lawyers
are never where the needs are greatest. I hope a new generation
of lawyers will begin to change that."

So, when Nader began to expand his investigations in the summer of 1968, he imported seven volunteers, including four law
students and two law school graduates, to help him. They came
to Washington to look into the Federal Trade Commission, and
in early January of 1969 Nader personally delivered the students'
185-page report to Washington's media meccas. The report described one $22,000-a-year bureaucrat asleep in his office, docu-
mented other examples of political cronyism and corporate favor-
itism, and three months later President Nixon requested an FTC
investigation by the American Bar Association.

Next Nader helped establish the new tax-exempt, nonprofit
Center for Study of Responsive Law in an old town house off
Dupont Circle. The Center, funded by the Carnegie and other
foundations, has a consultant staff of four young lawyers and a

political scientist, and works on consumer issues. Nader is the unsalaried chairman of the board of trustees.

And in the summer of 1969, his button-down guerrilla band of 102 college and graduate students roamed over Washington. The student volunteers received subsistence salaries (about $50 a week from foundation sources) for their exhausting season of interviewing uptight agency deskmen, pacifying suspicious undersecretaries and studying dusty archives. The agency employees panicked, threw temper tantrums at Nader, refused to open up files to the students, and in general behaved as if they had something to hide.

Most of the Raiders were law students, but a few were studying medicine, engineering, and even anthropology. Twenty-one of them were women. Broken down into teams of between seven and fourteen, they focused on the Departments of Agriculture, Interior, and HEW; the Interstate Commerce Commission (ICC); and on Covington and Burling, one of the capital's most politically connected private law firms. These targets were picked, rather than, say, the Pentagon or the State Department, because they are the agencies most directly related to consumer issues. Covington and Burling was added to the list because of its considerable work in behalf of corporations in consumer areas.

The Raiders seemed to be the sort of students who in 1961 would have volunteered for the Peace Corps or in 1964 have gone to Mississippi to register black voters or in 1968 would have worked for Eugene McCarthy or Robert Kennedy. They are not New Left types, and are quick to criticize the SDS revolutionaries for being too ineffectual, too theoretical, and too irrational. Like their leader, the Raiders tend to be personally and culturally conventional. They don't wear unusually long hair or seem to be rock music fanatics. Most seem to have the liberal, law student's mind-set: hardworking, activist, linear; seekers still of a way to wed morality to legality without violence.

Two of the most impressive were Jim Fallows, a Harvard undergraduate, and Julian Houston, a second-year law student at Boston University. Fallows is the president of the *Harvard Crimson* and spent the previous summer doing civil rights work in the Alabama black belt. Houston, who is black, was a first-generation activist with SNCC and the Northern Student Movement in the early '60s. Explaining his leap from organizing the underclass to exploring the power structure, he said, "Working with Nader I

feel I'm attacking the same problems SNCC was, only at a different access point. With SNCC we tried to organize the people who worked on Senator Eastland's plantation. Here I'm working with the team looking into the Department of Agriculture. That department has influence over small farmers, black people, and poor people every day."

The agriculture team was most concerned with investigating the department's food stamp program, with finding out the status of racial integration in the department's rural extension service, and in determining what influence the tobacco growers and certain senior Congressmen like Jamie Whitten of Mississippi [chairman of the House Appropriations Subcommittee that approves the Agriculture Department's budget] have over the department. Fallows, who worked on the investigation along with Houston, said the Raiders had not received much cooperation. "One division director removed two manuals from the department's public library as soon as we asked to see them. They wouldn't let us examine their files, which we feel should be open to citizens under the Public Information Act. We discovered a lot of employees are actually afraid of losing their jobs if they talk to us. The bureaucracy has turned people into serfs who live in fear. We're trying to penetrate a whole way of life when we dig into this department."

Back at school now, each team of Raiders is drafting a heavily documented report on its findings, and these will be published as a book. Any royalties from the book will be used as the royalties from *Unsafe at Any Speed* were—to subsidize further investigations. And the book will include dozens of episodes gleaned from trips like the one Fallows and Houston made one hot, muggy afternoon to a man in the Agriculture Department's civil rights office. The pair had interviewed the same man the day before, and Houston talked about him while driving across the sultry city. "This guy is a relic," Houston said. "He's a Negro who acts like he's never heard of *de facto* segregation. It's our job to evaluate what kind of job he does for poor people and black people in the South. He has some responsibility for the rural extension service, which should be teaching people how to grow better crops. But that service is *de facto* segregated, and he doesn't do anything about it."

At the Department of Agriculture building, the Raiders had to

explain their purpose and fill out a form to gain entry to the parking lot. Inside the dirty, gray building, the halls were poorly lighted and not air-conditioned. On each side there were dozens of small, Kafkaesque cubicles.

The employee was very nervous. He stammered, his hands trembled a little, and he kept looking down at the floor. "I could get fired," he said, "if I say the wrong thing to these boys."

For a half hour the two Raiders questioned him like zealous district attorneys. From his answers, it appeared that the department was not trying to integrate the extension service, and that white county workers in the South do not help many blacks. Finally, he looked Houston in the eye and said:

"Look, my grantfather was a slave. Now I'm here. I know everything is not perfect. I know things have to change. But not so fast. *You* can keep pushing, but *I* have to go slower. I have to worry about a wife and children. My grandfather was a slave, you understand what that means, don't you?"

Leaving the office, Houston said quietly, "That really moved me, but damn it, the guy is not doing his job because the bureaucracy has him living in terror of being fired or demoted."

The team of Raiders investigating the Food and Drug Administration (FDA) came upon similar fears. One morning in August two Raiders—Jim Turner, a recent graduate of Ohio State Law School, and Peter Gold, a second-year student at NYU Law—interviewed Kenneth Kirk, the No. 3 man in the FDA, for ninety minutes. Their goal was to find out just why in 1966 the FDA had ruled that cola drinks did not have to list caffeine as an ingredient in their bottle labels.

In the course of the prodding but low-keyed interview, the administrator repeatedly asked Gold how and where he had obtained specific memos or files because he, Kirk, had been looking for them himself. He also said he was totally unaware of meetings that Gold casually referred to.

Although Kirk said he was ignorant of the exact details of how the caffeine decision was made, he did reveal that just before the decision was announced, he received two telephone calls. One was from Senator Richard Russell of Georgia, the home state of one large cola company. Another large soft drink producer that would have been affected by the ruling is located in Texas and

the second call was from a member of Lyndon Johnson's White House staff. Both callers "expressed concern about the progress of the issue."

Later, someone said, "Kirk asked to look at the copies of the memos we had, just to try to find out who leaked them. But he gave the ball game away when he told us Russell and Johnson's guy had called up."

At their law schools now, Nader's summer Raiders are beginning to launch student campaigns to reform law school curriculums so that they include and create courses relevant to advocacy law. Most of the Raiders have decided to carve out careers in "public interest law," and Ralph Nader, out of a Winsted, Connecticut, family of moderate means, out of Princeton University, and out of Harvard Law School, hopes to set up a "public interest law firm."

The *Harvard Law Record* commented in a recent editorial that the university "should recognize that Ralph Nader may be the most outstanding man ever to receive a degree from this institution." Norman Dorsen, NYU law professor and noted civil liberties advocate, says, "Nader is one of several important forces —along with Earl Warren he is the most personal—that have helped to liberate law students from rigid commercial attitudes." Bob Walters, investigative reporter for the Washington *Star,* says, "I've seen Nader speak at law schools and the guy is treated as a real saint in those places. They respond to him like they do to Tom Hayden or Eldridge Cleaver at other campuses."

In the long run, Ralph Nader's greatest impact may not be on the corporations, or on the federal bureaucracy, but on the next generation of lawyers and law students that he has inspired by his aggressive yet modest example. Ralph Nader may be generating the legal profession's first cult of nonpersonality.

OCTOBER, 1969

[4.]
Does the Country Deserve
Ramsey Clark in '72?

At first, when this magazine called me up with the assignment, I wasn't very enthusiastic about writing a piece on Ramsey Clark. He seemed to me like an undefined figure in the middle distance. And besides, my head was in another place.

I had made a promise to myself a few months before to write more about specific injustices and insurgent movements. I didn't want to write about personalities anymore, especially liberal political personalities. I wanted more time to myself, to read and think. I wanted time to become an activist again.

The invasion of Cambodia, the murder of innocent college students at Kent State and Jackson State, the slaughter of babies and old women at My Lai, the rampage of the hardhats against the kids at City Hall, Agnew's name-calling and Nixon's anal malice had all combined to push me into the depressed rage that Pete Hamill called the fever zone.

I drove to Washington for the early May peace protest, ready in my own mind to get arrested. I went back to Washington with a group organized by Congressman Richard Ottinger to lobby for passage of the McGovern-Hatfield Amendment to End the War, and I ended up screaming "liar" and "killer" at two stiff bureaucrats from the State Department. I felt that this was a time for something more direct, something more serious, than magazine profiles.

But meanwhile, out of curiosity, not yet consciously working on the assignment, I began to ask my friends active in liberal politics what they happened to think about this guy Ramsey Clark.

These were the insiders, the activists who will be there in New Hampshire in 1972, and they all liked Ramsey Clark very much.

"He's terrific," David Mixner, one of the founders of the Vietnam Moratorium, told me. "He really seems like a principled

guy who will stand up and take a risk for things he believes in."

Marion Wright Edelman, the poor people's tribune in Washington, said, "Ramsey is a beautiful man." Marion's husband, Peter Edelman, who was Robert Kennedy's legislative assistant, said "Ramsey is my first choice for President in 1972. He's tough and he has integrity. He's a real Southern Populist."

Assemblyman Albert Blumenthal, the number two Democrat in Albany, said, "Clark strikes me as a smart Ed Muskie. He seems genuinely committed to peace and civil liberties."

Roger Wilkins, who worked under Clark in the Justice Department and shares a Greenwich Village apartment with him when he's in New York, said simply, "Ramsey Clark is the best liberal hope in the country. He's the best guy I know."

Principled? Tough? Committed? A Southern Populist?

I guess there must be more to Ramsey Clark than I'd thought. Could this Texan, this ex-Marine, this son of a conservative attorney general and a strict-constructionist Justice of the Supreme Court, this member of Lyndon Johnson's cabinet, become a new white hope, a wise Southern voice for freedom, the same way Senator Fulbright has been an oddly accented voice for peace?

Before I called him up, I decided to research Clark's record as attorney general, and to find out just what he has been doing since he moved part-time to Manhattan and joined the Paul, Weiss, Goldberg, etc., law firm last July.

Although for the conspiracy indictment of the Reverend Coffin and Dr. Spock (more on that later), Clark's record on issues turned out to be good otherwise. (Some people said he was a weak administrator.) He was the first AG to oppose capital punishment while in office. He opposed preventive detention. He testified against wiretapping. ("Public safety will not be found in wiretapping . . . Nothing so mocks privacy as the wiretap and electronic surveillance. They are incompatible with a free society.") In a speech in North Carolina, he criticized Mayor Daley's "shoot to kill" order to the Chicago police. ("A reverence for life is the sure way of reducing violent death. There are few acts more likely to cause guerrilla warfare in our cities and division and hatred among our people than to encourage police to shoot looters. . . . How many dead twelve-year-old boys will it take for us to learn this simple lesson?")

He obtained a legal permit for the demonstrators at that doomed shantytown of the poor called Resurrection City. He re-

fused to indict the organizers of the demonstrations at the 1968 Democratic Convention, and despite pressure from the White House and Mayor Daley, he recommended that nine Chicago policemen be indicted. When three black college students were killed by state highway patrolmen at Orangeburg, South Carolina, in February of 1968, and a local white grand jury refused to indict any of them. Clark entered the case and pressed federal prosecution of the nine policemen for murder. (They were acquitted.) He angered J. Edgar Hoover by vetoing bugs and wiretaps on Martin Luther King; and he angered important Congressmen by pushing for strong gun-control legislation.

Since he joined Paul, Weiss, he has attempted to testify for the defense at the Chicago Conspiracy trial. ("It would have been easier for me not to do that. It created problems. Representatives of the current Justice Department made their disapproval clear. But I felt an obligation to testify.") He has joined the citizen's commission that is investigating the police attacks on the Black Panthers, and has really worked at it. He became honorary chairman of the Committee To Save Our Constitution, which is trying to force a Supreme Court test of the constitutionality of the war in Indochina. He has spoken, written, and testified before the Senate Judiciary Committee in behalf of lowering the voting age to eighteen. He is currently representing the Alaskan native population—Aleutian Islanders, Eskimos, and Indians—in their land claims against the federal government. He has given fund-raising parties and campaigned for antiwar candidates like the Reverend Andrew Young in Georgia, Adam Walinsky in New York, and the Reverend Joe Duffey in Connecticut. He has taught a course in law at Howard University called Law as an Effective Instrument of Social Change.

Panthers? Eskimos? Howard University?

I called *New York* and said I was starting to work.

Ramsey Clark is by temperament a modest and tasteful man. (He declined, for example, to pose for a picture in front of the Justice Department building.) Although he grew up in the raunchy rodeo of Texas politics with LBJ, Sam Rayburn, and his father, Tom Clark, he doesn't seem to be a political animal at all. He seems more like a professor or a country preacher. Or a strong-silent sheriff like Gary Cooper. He doesn't seem to have the politician's primitive ego lust for power, or the politician's need for

self-promotion, or even the politician's preoccupation with the appearance of things.

When Clark was attorney general of the United States (March 1967 to January 1969), he used to drive his own beat-up 1949 Oldsmobile to work rather than use the official limousine and chauffeur he was entitled to. As attorney general he refused to escalate his lawyerlike rhetoric to satisfy the appetite of the media. He would tell his staff that the office of attorney general "should be above politics," so he didn't do much to publicize himself or his programs. For example, when he gave speeches, he rarely had prepared texts for the press; he just improvised. He wouldn't even defend himself against the attacks by Richard Nixon during the 1968 campaign that distorted his record. It was Nixon, remember, who, with his nasty habit of personalizing complex issues by innuendo, promised in his acceptance speech at the 1968 Republican convention: "If we are to restore order and respect for law in this country, there's one place we're going to begin: we're going to have a new Attorney General of the United States of America." Ramsey Clark, Nixon implied, was soft on crime, just as Helen Gahagan Douglas had been soft on communism in 1950.

The line set off the biggest roar of the night and quickly became a dominant motive of the whole Nixon campaign. When I asked Roger Wilkins why Clark didn't hit back harder at Nixon during that campaign period, he replied, "Ramsey was naïve. He thought that because Nixon's attacks were based on distortions of the record, the media would point that out. But I think that experience taught him a lesson. He's much less diffident now. He's much more willing to fight now."

But I think something else had been working on Clark during the last two years, something else goading him to overcome his Gary Cooper stoicism. Ramsey Clark, remember, was Attorney General of the United States. He had the rare opportunity to see close up the whole apparatus of repression: twenty-six separate federal agencies capable of investigative work, ranging from the FBI to the IRS to the Secret Service to the Postal Service. And 30,000 full-time government federal investigative agents. He got the memos from J. Edgar Hoover requesting permission to bug the Panthers and Martin Luther King and Tom Hayden. He knew about the computer data banks on private citizens and about the latest technologies in electronic surveillance. He knew

about the CIA's microfilm files and the SACB (Subversive Activities Control Board) snoopers. But Clark had resisted these dark forces and built a fine staff and continued a lot of constructive programs started by Robert Kennedy and Nicholas Katzenbach: programs for prison reform and to rehabilitate juvenile delinquents, programs to protect the rights of defendants in the Office of Criminal Justice, programs to enforce existing civil rights laws, professionalize the police, and use the Community Relations Service to mediate racial disputes.

Now Ramsey Clark is out of power, and he is watching a new attorney general, a former municipal bonds lawyer who was Richard Nixon's campaign manager and who thought up the campaign attacks against him for being soft on crime. He is watching this new and very political attorney general fire liberal lawyers from the Civil Rights Division, support men like Harrold Carswell and Clement Haynsworth for the Supreme Court, and abort plans for school desegregation. He is watching this new attorney general, who believes in, and executed, the very real Southern Strategy, hire as his top deputies Barry Goldwater's former campaign manager (Richard Kleindienst) and a conservative Texas politician who was recommended by Senator John Tower (Will Wilson). And now Ramsey Clark fears that his successors are beginning to tune up the long-dormant machinery of McCarthyism.

Mitchell and his crew have been in power for eighteen months and the hard evidence of repression piles up: the conspiracy indictment and trial of the Chicago Eight, after Clark concluded there was no evidence to justify any prosecution. ("The indictment of Bobby Seale was a scandal.") the subpoenas of media files and notebooks. New, repressive legislation legalizing pretrial detention and giving the police power to enter private homes without knocking first. The whole panoply of bugs, wiretaps, dossiers and police agents. The sudden 5 A.M. police raids on the homes of Black Panthers, like the one in Chicago that killed Fred Hampton and Mark Clark. These are the tactics and mood of 1953. And Ramsey Clark, private citizen, watches it all grow out of the big office on the fifth floor of the Justice Department that he once occupied.

So now, instead of making a lot of money by representing big corporate clients, instead of getting some lucrative consulting hustle, Ramsey Clark is committed, and he travels all around the

country making speeches with his slow Texas twang in defense of such unpopular things as the Bill of Rights and American college students.

One afternoon late last month I flew to Washington and interviewed Clark for several hours in the Paul, Weiss, Goldberg law offices on K Street. In his shirt sleeves, playing nervously with a black-and-red grape-strike button, Clark answered my first question—about what his childhood was like.

"I grew up in Texas. I was born in Dallas. I remember my family used to call me 'the little judge,' although I can't remember why. . . . I remember a fellow named Bill McGraw gave me my first bicycle. He was the Attorney General of Texas and a great Populist. He had quite an effect on me. Then he ran for governor and lost . . .

"My family moved to Washington when I was nine years old. I went to a whole lot of different schools here. Then my father was sworn in as attorney general on July 1, 1945, by President Truman. I was seventeen then, and I had just joined the Marines. I had quit high school to go into the Marines. . . ."

"Why the Marines?" I asked.

"Why did seventeen-year-old kids in Watts join in the riot? It seemed like where the action was. It seemed like a great moral crusade. I didn't want to go to West Point because I had a prejudice against being an officer."

After leaving the Marines, Clark picked up three degrees in four years—a B.A. in history at the University of Texas and an M.A. and law degree at the University of Chicago, all between February of 1947 and December of 1950.

"I didn't even go to the 1948 Democratic Convention. I had met Truman and Wallace and liked them both. But I wasn't really political then."

Changing the subject, I asked Clark how much of a threat he saw to liberty today. Could he, for example, envisage a military take-over in this country in the next few years?

He leaned back in his chair, paused for a long time, and began to answer very deliberately.

"Oh, I suppose there are some people in the government who have those instincts. There are some very frightened and authoritarian people over there who could react to circumstances that way if the kids went wild. It could happen here.

"But I don't think those fellows in Justice now are very com-

petent, or efficient. They just rush around from one fire to the next. They have no plan or vision about the whole thing. Klein- dienst, Wilson, Mitchell, all of them put together, couldn't have an intelligent five-minute conversation about the latest develop- ments in electronic bugging devices. They're not really smart enough to do anything dangerous. . . . Kleindienst is just a guy who likes to win. It doesn't matter much to him what he wins, just so long as he wins. . . . The more serious problem is that all those fellows are so political. They're not professional. They're very ambitious, and there is that Southern Strategy, which does affect things like desegregation and judicial nominations."

I pressed him for details of where the impetus for repression comes—who, how, when?

"Oh, the bureau [FBI] likes to do a lot of bugging [putting a listening device into a room, as opposed to a tap only on the tele- phone]. The bureau sent me a memo just two days before Dr. King was assassinated asking permission to bug his home and of- fice in connection with the Poor People's Campaign . . . the bu- reau wanted me to bug the fellows planning the demonstrations at the 1968 Democratic Convention, but I said no. . . . I remem- ber in August of 1967, when Spiro Agnew was governor of Mary- land, he said that he had evidence that the same people started the riots in Newark and Detroit. So I called him up, and he didn't have any evidence. . . . It was the same with Mayor Daley. He said that people were coming to Chicago in 1968 to assassi- nate the candidates. There was no evidence of that. It was just rumors in police circles, stuff from informants. But a lot of police informants are mentally unbalanced people. The rumor mill among law enforcement agencies is immense. . . . A lot of this surveillance gets silly; at one point there were agents from six dif- ferent agencies following Rap Brown. His mother used to invite them all in for breakfast when they were waiting outside."

Did Clark think there was a systematic plan in the Justice De- partment to eliminate Black Panthers?

"The way it really works is very complicated. It's not so simple as a directive to get the Panthers. It's a mood, a tone, a license. The Justice Department sets a tone toward dissent, toward the Panthers. They circulate profiles of the leaders to the local po- lice. There's a police raid in one city, and then another city gets the idea by example. . . . In Seattle, it was the Treasury Depart- ment, not the Justice Department, that asked the mayor to raid

the Panther headquarters . . . The real root of the problem is the no-knock law that lets the police come in so easily. The best thing the law can do is provide moral leadership. The law can't act immorally. But in fact the law acts immorally constantly. The no-knock law is immoral. That's the problem."

The only blot on Clark's record as attorney general, in my view, is his prosecution of Dr. Spock, the Reverend Coffin and three others on charges of conspiracy to evade the draft laws. I had called Yale's William Sloane Coffin in New Haven the night before I interviewed Clark to seek his opinion about the man who tried to put him in jail.

To my great surprise, Coffin sounded no less enthusiastic about his prosecutor than my friends Mixner and Edelman.

"I get a strong feeling of integrity, of intelligence, and of moral fervor about Ramsey Clark," Mr. Coffin said. "He seems to be for all the right things. I've forgiven him for our case. I think he's done a lot of good work, even before he indicted us. I admire him. Compared to the number of kids resisting the draft, there haven't been that many indictments. He didn't pressure the local U.S. Attorneys to prosecute resisters. He could have gone after the kids, but instead he went after us. That was fair."

That conversation fresh in my mind, I asked Clark if he "regretted" his indictment of Spock, Coffin, and the others,

"I do regret the conspiracy aspect of that case," Clark replied. "I regret the conspiracy aspect of all cases I was involved in because our whole body of conspiracy laws is unjust and unfair. . . . But Spock and Coffin wanted to test the law, so we had to face up to it. . . . I feel that we crippled and hurt a good many young people with our draft prosecutions. Some of the draft resisters were among the best and most sensitive young men in the country. But the law has to proceed with integrity . . . But after the conviction I did urge, through the U.S. Attorney, that there be no jail sentences in the Spock case."

There is beginning to swirl around forty-two year-old Ramsey Clark the intoxicating talk that he might try to run for President in 1972. Two citizens' committees promoting his candidacy have already been started, one in Boston and the other in Raleigh, North Carolina. Clark, somewhat self-consciously, keeps in his desk one blue-and-white RAMSEY CLARK FOR PRESIDENT IN 1972 bumper sticker sent to him by organizers of the Raleigh group.

When I asked a wise lady journalist in Washington what she made of the Clark for President idea, she replied, "It would be

nice if we had a country good enough to elect Ramsey as President. But we don't."

Another, more cynical, Washington writer said, "Are you crazy? Ramsey has no base in any state party in the country. He's never run for office in his life. He's not even political! He has no money and no charisma. And Nixon has smeared him as a coddler of criminals."

But a liberal Democratic Congressman told me, "It's possible. There's a total vacuum at the top of the party now. I think what the country is really looking for is a strong, quiet leader, someone new, someone with integrity. And Ramsey's Texas accent and folksy style should give him some credibility in Middle America."

In April, Clark appeared with his father on *Meet the Press,* and panelist Carl Rowan asked him, "Do you have any Presidential ambitions?"

Clark, in his best Gary Cooper style, answered with a terse "No."

But about a month later, a print journalist asked Clark, "What is your future in national politics?"

This time Clark replied, "As you know, I haven't had a past in national politics. I started out as a lawyer and became a bureaucrat, and now I'm just shuffling around. No one can tell, least of all me, where I'm headed. I *am* concerned. I think there are several sources of real power in this country and, happily, I think political power is one of them."

When I asked Clark about the thought of running for President, he answered:

"Oh, I can't plan anything about that. What I feel is that there have to be some of us who are willing to use up all our power fighting for change. That's where I think I might be of some help. I know I have too many handicaps as a candidate. I'm more liberal than I appear to be. I'm not good at indirection. So many of my positions are not popular. So I just work for change, and see what happens. I think maybe someone who is better than me at indirection, but who believes in the same things, should carry the ball for our side."

On July 1 Ramsey Clark got up with the sun and flew alone and anonymously—tourist class—to Cincinnati for the sixty-first annual convention of the NAACP.

On the plane we talked about Muhammad Ali.

"On the face of it," Clark said, "you could wonder about the equality of his treatment. I certainly feel, quite strongly, that he should not be prohibited from fighting. I think there has been some discrimination in his case. I signed a thing for *Esquire* magazine that he should be allowed to fight again, but they didn't print it. I didn't get around to posing for some silly cover picture they were doing, so I guess they didn't publish what I said."

I noticed that Clark didn't have any mimeographed, or even written, text of his speech, and so I asked him why he makes a point of not catering to the media on such occasions.

"I'd just rather talk to the folks in the hall, I guess, than do up anything fancy for the media. I just think the people who are there are the important ones. . . . Folks have always told me I don't pay enough attention to the media. When I was attorney general I almost never watched the news shows on television. I guess that was one of the mistakes I made, but I'd rather be doing something than just sittin' and watchin' that darn tube."

"Where's your advance text?" was the first thing Warren Marr, the NAACP's press aide, asked Clark when he arrived at the new, air-conditioned convention hall. A few seconds later, the reporters from the New York *Post* and the AP asked Clark for a copy of his speech. He explained he didn't have one, and they looked at him as if he hadn't worn any socks.

Clark was one of the few white liberals I've seen address a black audience who didn't try to affect the repetitive cadences and amen rhythms of a Baptist preacher. He just stood up there, tall and thin (he's six-three), and said what he believed, without notes.

"The real question of our time is whether institutions and human attitudes can change fast enough, whether we can purge racism from our character fast enough . . . black and white, brown and yellow, must live together with dignity, respect and love here in America.

"The young have a lot to teach us. Of all the divisions in America, the one that concerns me most is the one between young and old. The young are our hope. We must listen to them. . . .

"Our first priority must be peace. I remember when Dr. King said peace was a civil rights issue, and I thought he was wrong. But now I know Dr. King was right; peace is essential to a reverence for human life.

"The race problem in America is essentially economic. We need a guaranteed annual income for all our people. I get so sad when I think about the Eskimos who live on the tundra in Alaska. Their average life expectancy is 33.4 years—can you believe it?—and it is declining. Eighty percent of the welfare in Alaska goes to the 20 percent of the population that is native. . . .

"Turbulence is life force, it is opportunity. Let's love turbulence and use it for change."

At the end there were a few shouts of "Wonderful" and "Clark in '72," and a lot of polite applause from the middle-aged, middle-class audience. It was a good, straightforward speech. He had attacked the war and defended Martin Luther King, who had been critized by Roy Wilkins for joining the antiwar movement. He had talked about the suffering of the Eskimos to the satisfied black bourgeoisie. He had said the root of the race problem was economic. He had defended the young.

He didn't do any of the easy things, like attack John Mitchell or Richard Nixon, or tell the NAACP how great it is.

The next morning *The New York Times* gave Clark's speech two inches of type at the end of a longer story about the chairman of the NAACP's board, Bishop Stephen Spottswood, saying the Nixon Administration was "anti-Negro." The New York *Post* ran two stories from the convention, and neither one even mentioned Clark's remarks.

Compared to the people one normally meets cruising the corridors of power, Ramsey Clark is just an exceptionally decent human being. He would be exceptional among shoe salesmen or concert violinists. Among politicians he is a Saint Francis.

Over the seasons I have met, and reported on, and gotten to know, many upwardly mobile politicians and the hungry sharks who swim in their wake. They are, generally speaking, a wormy lot. Most of them are more turned on by money and status than by suffering or war. Most of them are expert at deceit and evasion in order to cover up their real beliefs. Most of them are terrified of losing an election because they are otherwise unemployable, so they let the latest public opinion poll be the puppeteer of their conscience. Most of them don't even know who they are, and have no interior life. A lot of them are plain corrupt and without any idea of what is actually happening in the country. There is something unfortunately endemic to the environment of politics that rewards the worst aspects of human nature. It is

only after you have spent an enormous amount of time around political people—at fund-raising dinners, at conventions, in motels, in campaign headquarters, on the stump—that you can appreciate the special virtues of a Ramsey Clark.

He tells the truth. He is neither for sale nor an egomaniac. His motives are what they seem. He has the courage to take unpopular positions and stick to them. And he really cares about life's casualties and victims because he has the novelist's capacity to imagine the nature of their daily lives.

The President thing now hovers over Clark like a thin vapor. He has some friends like Roger Wilkins and Peter Edelman who think it is a possible dream. In the last days I've talked to law professors and OEO employees and delegates to the NAACP convention who all said they would quit their jobs to work for him. I just don't know if he could raise the money and manipulate the media and create the national constituency. Perhaps my lady journalist friend is right, and Ramsey Clark is too good for this wounded dinosaur of a country. Maybe his own notion that he should use up his power in good causes makes sense.

I can end this piece only on the same personal note that I began it. I don't believe in magical leaders any more. Heroes end up invading Cuba, or getting murdered in hotels.

In ten years as an activist and writer I have found only three human beings whose vision and character moved me to say, yes, you see clearer and farther than I do, and I trust you, and yes, I will follow you. I felt that way about Bob Moses of SNCC, and Tom Hayden ever since I first met him in 1962, and Robert Kennedy the last year of his life. Now I only can believe in movements, ideas, and exemplary actions.

All that said, Ramsey Clark is something special. I believe that character is more important than politics, and men with Clark's character almost never reach his level of political authority.

Maybe the President thing is unrealistic. Maybe Ramsey Clark's fate is to play the role of Ed Murrow or Eleanor Roosevelt to the new McCarthys. Maybe his destiny is to be our Gary Cooper, a good Texas lawman quietly preparing for his High Noon with the Big Bad Bully John Mitchell, to protect the young, the poor, and the black. And maybe such a tall sheriff for justice is what this country needs, even more than it needs another liberal politician running for President.

JULY, 1970

[5.]
The Stone's at the Bottom of the Hill

LOS ANGELES—It was a little before midnight, a half hour before he was to be assassinated as he reached out to grasp the workingman's hand of a $75-a-week Mexican busboy in the bowels of the Ambassador Hotel.

Robert Kennedy was holding a victory cigar in his swollen and stubby fingers, and squatting on the floor of room 511. His famous political and intellectual supporters were in the room with him. The awful little pornographers of power were there too. And so were the special people, the victims and rebels Robert Kennedy identified with. Doris Huerta of the grape strike was there, and Charles Evers, and John Lewis, who once led SNCC, and Budd Schulberg, who runs a writers' workshop in Watts. And Pete Hamill and Jimmy Breslin, two gut journalists who never went to college, but who Kennedy sensed knew more about America than the erudite pundits.

In this last hour, Kennedy seemed the most zestful and most inwardly serene I had seen him since Lyndon Johnson withdrew from the race. When that had happened Kennedy became troubled and confused. He had lost his enemy and his issue—the war and he acted like a lost soul, even as he won in Indiana. He seemed, suddenly, not to know who he was.

Defeat in Oregon, and physical exhaustion in California, had gutted his spirit even more. On Sunday he seemed somber and withdrawn as he looked blankly out of the window of his 727 Electra campaign jet. Normally Kennedy would gossip and joke with me on a campaign trip. But on Sunday all he said was that he hoped Al Lowenstein, who was supporting McCarthy, would win his congressional primary fight on Long Island. Then he turned his worn-out face to the breathtaking landscape of California.

On Monday he was drained, and his speeches flat, and he got

sick to his stomach in the middle of his final campaign speech in San Diego. The press whispered about a premonition of defeat.

But now, just before midnight, he seemed to be discovering his natural rhythm again, finally to feel liberated from gloom, fatalism, and yes, guilt over not running earlier, and somehow betraying the young he so wanted to lead.

He had won Humphrey's native state of South Dakota and in California. The Indians and the Mexicans and the Negroes ("my people") had given him his margin of triumph. The turnout of voters in supposedly fragmented, apathetic Watts was higher than in educated, affluent Beverly Hills. Key supporters and aides of Eugene McCarthy had told Richard Goodwin earlier in the night they might now come over to Kennedy's campaign. He had come back from defeat, and won on his own. Robert Kennedy, who was always more Boston than Camelot, once again found the two things he always needed: a cause—the dispossessed—and a clear enemy.

"I am going to chase Hubert Humphrey's ass all over America," he said. "I'm going to chase his ass into every precinct. Wherever he goes, I'm going to go."

Then he went downstairs carrying his notes for a speech that would attack war and violence.

I spent the death watch in Kennedy's hotel room, watching television, and answering the grieving and bereft phone calls from as far away as London. About twenty people spent the night there, spread out among five or six rooms on the fifth floor. Occasionally a sob or shriek came out of one of the rooms. We drank all the liquor there was, but nobody got drunk.

At about 4 A.M. Adam Walinsky called from the Hospital of the Good Samaritan to mumble that the outlook was bleak. Then a tape of a speech Kennedy gave at Berkeley attacking poverty and racism flashed on, and I finally broke down. As I wept, two crew-cut employees of the Los Angeles telephone company came into the room, and mechanically began to remove the special telephones that had been installed for the evening, direct lines to the ballroom, and phones used to call South Dakota and Washington. They acted as if nothing was happening, just casually pulling the wires out of the wall, and coiling them around the phones.

In another room in the suite John Lewis, who had campaigned among the hostile, middle-class Jews in California, sat on the arm of a chair, tears in his eyes, and mumbling to himself, "Why, why, why?" John Barlow Martin, his gaunt, Modigliani-like face the color of chalk, said to no one in particular, "Bomb America. Make the Coca-Cola someplace else."

Again and again the television played the drama. Kennedy's last speech, the ballsy challenge to Humphrey, the attack on the war, the jibe at Yorty, and the last awkward victory sign with his two fingers. The moan that broke across the ballroom like a wave. Men and women weeping, praying, pounding the floor.

Blair Clark, McCarthy's campaign manager, and columnist Mary McGrory, who loved Bobby almost as much as she loved Gene, came, offered condolences, fought to hold back tears, and left, reeling like sleepwalkers.

At 5:30 A.M. I went downstairs to help pick up Ed Guthman at the hospital. Outside the Ambassador Hotel sat Charles Evers, Medgar's brother. "God, they kill our friends and they kill our leaders," he said. Outside the hospital the press and a few hippies prayed.

Guthman's face said everything. Jimmy Breslin and George Plimpton left the hospital at the same time, and their faces also said that Kennedy's brain was already dead, and only his street-fighter's heart kept him technically alive.

Wednesday morning I wandered around the ugly hotel. Scavengers were stealing mementoes—campaign hats, banners, posters —from the ballroom.

Now he rests next to his brother, and feelings of rage mingle with a few random personal memories of a soulful man the world thought was ruthless.

Rage at the professional Bobby haters. Not just Joe Resnick or Drew Pearson, but all those Reform Democrats and liberal columnists who made hating Bobby so respectable, and even fashionable.

Rage at politicians who now urge passage of the crime bill with its gun-control clause as a "memorial" to Kennedy, even though Kennedy, in life, opposed that legislation because of its provisions for wiretapping and denial of rights to defendants.

Rage at a man like Sam Yorty, who had the Los Angeles police give a traffic ticket to the entire Kennedy motorcade last

week, who began red-baiting before Kennedy's heart stopped beating, and who had crashed the funeral, and refused to leave even after being asked by Jack English.

Rage at men like Archbishop Cooke and Eric Hoffer who say America should feel no national guilt, because the assassin was a Jordanian nationalist. Rage at those eulogizers who never mention the violence of Vietnam, Mississippi, or Texas. Rage at men who cannot face the fact that the truest symbol of America is that lonesome plane from Los Angeles that carried the widows of John Kennedy, Robert Kennedy, and Martin Luther King.

But a few memories linger too.

Kennedy quietly reading the Old Testament as a private gesture of irreverence all through the three-hour funeral mass for Cardinal Spellman. Kennedy sitting in his Manhattan apartment and reading me a poem from Emerson. Kennedy visiting a migrant worker camp near Buffalo, and walking right past the manager who held a gun, and into a rotting trailer that was a home for ten migrants. Kennedy pausing while campaigning in Brooklyn in front of a small girl with glasses and suddenly saying, "My little girl wears glasses too. And I love her very much." Kennedy visiting a hospital for retarded children in Westchester last January, and impulsively taking sixteen patients for a ride to buy ice cream, while doctors and aides panicked.

If I had written these things two weeks ago, *The Voice* would have been deluged with letters calling me a whore. Now such anecdotes fill the papers and the networks, and no one doubts them.

When he sent a plane to take Martin Luther King's widow to Memphis, people called it a cheap political gimmick. Two weeks ago I described him being called out of a shower in Indianapolis, and quipping as he groped for the phone, "Make way for the future leader of the Free World." I got a letter saying that proved his arrogance.

Robert Kennedy was not a saint. He was a politician who could talk about law and order in Indiana.

But anyone who rode on his funeral train last Saturday, and looked out at the rows of wounded black faces that lined the poor side of the tracks, knew what might have been. The stone is once again at the bottom of the hill and we are alone.

JUNE, 1968

[6.]
Pushing the Stone up the Hill Again

"Bobby Kennedy's death marked a turning point in our lives—and now this. This means all hope is off. What's the use? I feel frustrated. I feel what can we do? What kind of democracy is this?"—Mimi Bertucci, a friend of one of the four students murdered at Kent State, as quoted by *The New York Times*, May 10, 1970.

It is now two years since that instant of insanity in a chaotic hotel kitchen pantry in Los Angeles robbed us of Robert Kennedy. It is now June 1970, and America is another country.

Almost 15,000 more Americans have died in Indochina in the interim. And everywhere the geography of bullets and blood: Kent State, Jackson, Augusta, My Lai, the Parrot's Beak, James Rector dead in Berkeley, Fred Hampton dead in his bed in Chicago. On Wall Street, hardhats beat up students and then the leader of the construction workers is invited to the White House and honored by the President.

Professor Daniel Moynihan calls for "benign neglect," and a bus filled with black school children is burned in South Carolina. Nixon talks of "bums," Martha Mitchell of crucifying Senator Fulbright, Agnew of separating rotten apples, Kleindienst of "ideological criminals." And all the while, unemployment increases, prices spiral upward, and the stock market tumbles toward 1929.

All this horror has happened since that briefly hopeful day two years ago when Robert Kennedy won both the California and South Dakota primaries, and then went downstairs to thank his happy campaign workers, thinking, for the first time, that he could win the nomination.

In recent days, two small things happened to remind me once again of what we lost, and how much the nation has unraveled

since June 6, 1968. And why it is that Robert Kennedy's assassination, unlike any of the others in that awful litany, is the one that hurts *more,* not less, as time passes.

One of the most vivid memories I have of Robert Kennedy is the second speech he gave during his truncated run for the Presidency. It was two in the afternoon of March 19 at Kansas University, in rural Lawrence, Kansas. K. U. was a quiet college. There had been no big protests, no violent demonstrations, no SDS chapter. The students were provincial and hardworking, pure Middle America, the children of the Silent Majority. They looked as straight as a Junior Chamber of Commerce luncheon. Short hair, ties and jackets, knee-length skirts, no beards, no sandals, no sweet smell of pot hanging in the air. It was a sea of 18,000 wholesome, corn-fed, prairie faces, spilling over the gleaming basketball court of Phog Allen Fieldhouse, as Kennedy nervously began to talk in a flat monotone.

After about ten minutes he started to speak against the war in Vietnam, and the students began to cheer and clap, and Kennedy began to feel their feeling, and be nourished by it, and build on its playback.

"I am concerned," he said, "that at the end of it all, there will only be more Americans killed, more of our treasure spilled out . . . so that they may say, as Tacitus said of Rome: 'They made a desert and called it peace.' "

The impassioned applause, bouncing off the walls and scoreboard and rafters, grew still louder, and Kennedy candidly confessed his own errors in shaping the early Vietnam policy.

"I am willing to bear my share of the responsibility, before history and my fellow citizens. But past error is no excuse for its own perpetuation. . . . If the South Vietnamese troops will not carry the fight for their own cities, we cannot ourselves destroy them. That kind of salvation is not an act we can presume to perform for them. For we must ask ourselves and we must ask our government: Where does such logic end? If it becomes necessary to destroy all of South Vietnam to save it, will we do that too? And if we care so little about South Vietnam that we are willing to see its land destroyed, and its people dead, then why are we there in the first place?"

It was now near the end of the speech. Kennedy's hair was flopping over his perspiring forehead. He was jabbing the air with

his small, clenched fist, thumb extended, pouring all his pent-up passion into the peroration.

"So I come here today to this great university, to ask your help, not for me, but for your country, and for the people of Vietnam. . . . I urge you to learn the harsh facts that lurk behind the mask of official illusion with which we have concealed our true circumstances from even ourselves. Our country is in danger: not just from foreign enemies, but above all, from our own misguided policies, and what they can do to the nation that Thomas Jefferson once said was the last, best hope of man. . . ."

It was over, and the fieldhouse sounded like it was inside Niagara Falls. The sound of screaming filled the arena, and thousands of those Kansas students surged toward Kennedy, engulfing him, pulling off his cufflinks, shouting his name. It took fifteen minutes to get him out of the building, and even then, hundreds of students ran after his car.

That was in March of 1968. Last month I read how the square students at Kansas burned down their administration building, voted to go on strike, and fought with police.

The last time I had seen Joe Kennedy, Bobby's eldest son, was when he unexpectedly walked through the cars of the Kennedy funeral train, big and strong in a blue pinstripe suit, sticking out his sixteen-year-old's hand and saying, "Hiya. I'm Joe Kennedy and I'm glad to see you. Thank you for coming."

And then I saw Bobby's son again last month, now a senior at Milton Academy. It was in the midst of the hot, gentle throng massed at the Ellipse behind the White House to rally against the President's invasion of Cambodia and the renewed bombings of North Vietnam. Joe Kennedy, anonymous in the assembly of 100,000, was naked to the waist, his hair was long, and he was saying to me, "How could Nixon do it? Why doesn't he go and fight himself if he believes in war so much? Why can't the politicians stop him from invading a new country?"

What did we lose with Robert Kennedy?

The answer is: a lot; more and more, it seems as time passes. Kennedy was not a saint like Gandhi or King, and he never got to be a great national leader like Disraeli or Jefferson. He was a practical politician, who accepted as given the Democratic Party, liberal capitalism, and God. And sure, he made mistakes. He

waited until March 1967 to fully join the antiwar opposition. He waited too long before he finally decided to run for President. He was only a transitional figure between the old politics and the new, not the full avatar of the new.

But that was part of his strength, that was why both Tom Hayden and Mayor Daley, two strong men, could stand over his coffin in St. Patrick's Cathedral and cry real tears for what each had lost.

Now, two years removed from that night in Los Angeles, Kennedy seems to me, more clearly than ever, the most humane, the most committed in his gut against poverty, the least phony politician I have ever seen. And the most capable of growth; he was, after all, in one sense, only five years old when he was murdered.

Kennedy was the first national politician to go to the Delta, and Bed-Stuy, and Delano, and to Appalachia, and say, Yes, hunger is a real political issue in this richest nation in the history of mankind, and we better do something about it. He was the first liberal politician to say, Yes, the conservatives are right, ordinary working people do feel powerless and need more control over their lives, more "participatory democracy," and Yes, the New Dealers had become too hung up on centralizing a big bureaucracy choked with experts in Washington. He was the only, and maybe the last, antiracist politician in the country to win the votes of the steelworkers and construction workers and waitresses and cops, who, after his death, would switch their earthy loyalties to George Wallace.

I remember the last night before the 1968 Indiana primary, and Kennedy riding through Gary, that violent steel mill town, riding in an open car with Mayor Dick Hatcher and Tony Zale, the former middleweight champion. And the crowds pouring out of the bars and houses, those strong Polish and Irish and German faces, cheering and shouting for Kennedy, despite what Kennedy stood for, because he was small, tough, Catholic, because he took on the people in power, because they sensed he meant what he said, that he respected them.

And then, later that night, Kennedy would tell me and David Halberstam how much he loved people who worked hard with their hands, how much he preferred the white poor of West Virginia and Gary to the Manhattan intellectuals, "who spend their time worrying about why they haven't been invited to some party."

The next day, Kennedy won Lake County, the way George Wallace won it in 1964.

Kennedy could have, to use a phrase he liked, "made a difference." He would not have solved everything, or made a utopia, but he would have extricated America from Indochina, he would have transferred some power to the dispossessed, he would have given the movement space to breathe. He was, I'm afraid, the last politician of our time who might have rallied together, from among the young, the black, the blue-collar white, and the educated, a new coalition, a new majority on the side of decency. And new majorities are not purchased easily or often in history.

We can, I think, say of Kennedy now, what Guy Dumur said of Albert Camus after his death: "He would have been a force in reserve, a bridge between the past and the future: he would have been one from whom we awaited a response that, when it came, would have been heard by all."

Since my memoir of Robert Kennedy was published in paperback last March, I have received almost one hundred letters, almost all from students, sweet, moderate students, asking for an answer to their frustration and anger.

The other day I received such a letter from Debby Davis, an undergraduate at the University of Missouri. It was dated May 4, the day of the shootings at Kent State. The letter said in part:

> I just can't keep from thinking that maybe Bobby could have found a solution—but thinking about him does nothing but make things seem even more futile.
>
> Where does one go from here? The campaigns don't work—Nixon is as bad as Johnson—worse now. Demonstrations have gotten us nowhere, not nationally or locally. Nixon is definitely tone deaf. We protested near here at Sedalia, Missouri, the Saturday after Earth Day, against the deployment of the ABM. Nobody heard us. Nobody came or cared, except those who already agreed. We are up against a brick wall with the Agnews and Nixons knocking our heads together.
>
> Bobby said we would have to answer to somebody and explain what we did for our fellow human beings. I believe that, and I'm ready to run and work and fight to help, but my sense of direction is hopelessly screwed

up. . . . It really scares me. I feel totally helpless and
empty. . . .

I don't have many answers for Debby, or the others who write
and ask is Teddy Kennedy or John Lindsay a new Bobby, or
why shouldn't they burn down ROTC buildings since there is no
Kennedy left to save the system?

There are millions of Debbys on college campuses, and in high
schools, who see no reflection of their desperation in the world of
adult politics. They are just as likely to vote as sit in, or go on
strike, or throw a rock at a National Guardsman *because all
strategies seem equally hopeless.* They see no politician on television saying what they feel.

This is what I wrote back to Debby:

> *Dear Debby,*
>
> At the close of my book about Bobby, I wrote that
> the best, the most compassionate political leaders were
> all part of memory now, not hope; that things would
> get worse from this point on, not better; that Kennedy
> was "irreplaceable"; and that Sisyphus' stone was at the
> bottom of the hill, and we were alone.
>
> I still believe most of that elegiac ending. There is
> still no figure to replace Bobby within Presidential poli-
> tics although I keep looking, perhaps too hard. Lindsay
> means well for the black and the young, but he lacks
> Bobby's deep populist empathy with white workingmen.
> George McGovern is a good man with an excellent re-
> cord. He began speaking against the war in 1963, when
> JFK was still President. But I just don't know if the
> blacks even know who he is, if he is electable. Muskie
> reminds me of Ed Sullivan: relaxed, pleasant, and to-
> tally hollow and conventional. Harold Hughes seems
> like a possible bridge to the white workers, but I don't
> know him. Humphrey is unthinkable.
>
> So all I can do in this letter is try to share with you a
> few basic ideas I have come to since Los Angeles.
>
> We can't depend on heroes any more. There are none
> inside politics worth following, and if one does emerge,
> there are still too many Sirhans loose in this loony land.
> We can't count on liberal politicians. They will do only
> as much as we make them do.

Movements will have to invent new leaders from the bottom up. So put your energy and faith in grass-roots movements—students, antiwar, blacks, Chicanos, women's lib, those who preach respect for the earth. And trust the power of ideas, and small, young institutions. I would also like to see a new political party, based on peace and populism, organized by 1972.

Our opposition has to be based on humanity, honesty, perhaps goodness is the awkward word I want. We can't justify rich spoiled Harvard kids thrashing a small shopkeeper in Cambridge, and then looting his goods while they imagine they're bad dudes from Watts. We have to realize what a sick ego trip Jerry Rubin is on when he waves a joint and screams "kill your parents" and "free Sirhan." And there is no excuse for the Crazies breaking up meetings of middle-aged liberals they disapprove of, while they haven't the balls to disrupt a meeting of construction workers or Cuban exiles. It is just stupid to use tactics that alienate people who share our goals. And the evidence shows that some of the people who push the most violent strategies turn out to be agents and informers like George Demmerle.

Work to elect a new Congress, but realize that that is only one thread of a much larger dialectic of renewal. There is no one sure, guaranteed strategy to solve the current crisis. Student strikes, nonviolent civil disobedience, rallies, lobbying for the McGovern-Hatfield amendment to end the war, canvassing for good antiwar candidates—all have their merit. Even now, looking back at 1967 and 1968, I don't know what it was that finally toppled LBJ. Was it the March on the Pentagon? Was it the Vietnam Summer project? Or the "Dump Johnson" movement? Or "Stop the Draft Week"? Or McCarthy? Or Kennedy? Or the Tet offensive of the NLF? It was, I supppose, the interplay of all those events with each other, and it is the same sort of ecumenical mix we need now.

Become a radical within your profession, whether it is law, journalism, teaching, or medicine. We must find ways to take our politics with us, out of college and into middle age, without compromising. Rudi Dutschke is

probably right—we will have to make the "long march through the existing institutions" in order to transform them. Understand we're in a struggle to last a lifetime, not just till 1972.

Think about Rosa Parks, and Howard Levy, and Bob Moses, and Cesar Chavez, and Father Berrigan, and Davis Harris—think about the galvanizing power of exemplary action.

In a time of repressive politics and harsh conflict, don't forget the importance of private virtue and good character. Sometimes I think all I have ever tried to say about Robert Kennedy is that he had a better character than anyone else.

Keep stretching your consciousness. Go back and really read C. Wright Mills and Camus and Frantz Fanon. Try and get I. F. Stone, or Tom Hayden, or Norman Mailer, to speak at your campus.

If things get any worse, we will all have to start acting on our rhetoric of resistance, and that means strikes, tax refusal, creating liberated zones, draft resistance, hiding Black Panthers in our homes the way the Dutch hid the Jews.

But first we have to make the personal commitment to action—to push that stone back up the hill once again. You and me, Debby, because there is no Robert Kennedy to make the burden easier.

Peace,
Jack Newfield

JUNE, 1970

Index

Index